RACING
TRENDS REVEALED

FLAT 2008

DAVID MYERS

HIGH STAKES

First published in 2008 by High Stakes Publishing,
21 Great Ormond Street, London WC1N 3JB
www.highstakespublishing.com

A CIP catalogue record for this book is available
from the British Library.

ISBN 978-1-84344-040-6

2 4 6 8 10 9 7 5 3

Typeset by Avocet Typeset, Chilton, Aylesbury, Bucks

Printed and bound in Great Britain by J.H.Haynes & Co Ltd., Sparkford

IN MEMORY
OF THE FOLLOWING RACING FANS

Brian Myers
Les Cade, Lil Cade, Nicky Tsappis

INTRODUCTION

Three things have always intrigued me about the winners of big races.

❏   What credentials make up the winner's profile?

❏   Have past trends of that race pointed to the winner?

❏   Will the winner be worth following after the race?

I applied these questions to over 200 of the biggest Flat races in the calendar and the answers surprised me.

They might surprise you as well.

These answers can be found on each page of this book, which covers a major Flat race during the calendar.

Featured is every race's 12-year roll of honour, along with accompanying analysis that offers an insight into the ideal profile required for that event.

These tables also highlight whether winners were profitable to follow in the future, records that have never been published before.

It is easy to assume the winner of a big race will succeed again in the future, after all, it's a good horse right?
   However, as with other events outside the equine world, all that glitters doesn't necessarily turn out to be gold.

What do winners of the Junior Wimbledon Tennis Championships, Eurovision Song Contest and X-Factor go on to achieve – future stars or red herrings? What about those that go close on the day – are they capable of eclipsing the winner in future? Some reach the ceiling of their ability and fail to progress, while others are improving graduates, destined to go further. The same applies in horseracing.

By using the material in this book, you will be able to cover both angles of every major horse race – how to find the winner, and whether to stick with it after the race.

TRENDS TABLES EXPLAINED

The trends tables in this book list the past 12 winners of an event. From left to right, they firstly reveal what the winner achieved last time out. A horse's last run is of major relevance, as it reveals whether it has been prepared at a gaff track or at a premier venue. Some runners that attempt to step up in grade at a classier track fail to cut the mustard. The type of race is also included, with distinguished race titles shown, otherwise, they are referred to as just Group Three or Handicap, for instance.

The previous run also highlights if it has proven beneficial to be rested before a big race or if a quick reappearance did the trick. I have used weeks and months to demonstrate this, instead of days, with any period just over a month to seven weeks rounded up to two months, and then every calendar month thereafter. A horse appearing on July 31 that last ran on May 15, for instance, will be shown as three months.

The name of the winning horse and trainer are shown in the second column along with the odds or price it started at. Next come the starting stalls position, or draw, against the number of runners.
   The winner's age is then shown with the weight carried in the next column, in stones and pounds, so 8-10 is 8st10lbs.

Halfway along the table comes the winner's performance rating (PR). Similar to a football player's marks out of 10 in a newspaper, the PR is on a scale of 0-100 and takes into account the following factors:
   The time of the race (fast or slow), quality of opposition (exposed plodders or classy improvers) and the nature of the victory (stumbled over the line or quickened clear).

Also built into the PR rating is the overall profile compared to past winners. Is the winner a typical progressive sort – one worth following – or one that was flattered on the day from a good draw on heavy ground.
   For example, an ideal winner of the mythical 'Trends Cup' may be an unexposed three-year-old – four of whom went on to better things. However, several other winners of that race may have been exposed six-year-olds that peaked on the day with beneficial conditions and were therefore unable to follow up. The former category would be awarded a higher PR compared to the latter type that would be downgraded.
   (Information regarding the updated 2008 PR ratings can be found at www.racingtrendsrevealed.com)

To the right of the performance rating in the second-half of the table comes the winner's next four runs with any subsequent victories in bold. As with the winner's 'last run' category in the first column of the table, any distinguished event is given, such as the 2,000 Guineas, but any other lesser-known events are referred to as Group Two etc.

Directly below the table is the median performance rating based over the previous 12 years, which can be used to compare the merit of each individual winner.

WINNER'S PROFILE

This section takes some of the leading clues from the table along with additional background information to form a detailed, but condensed portrait of the winner with no jargon or waffle. The main trends and patterns are highlighted in bold to form an easy, at-a-glance view of what is required to form the ideal profile.

FUTURE POINTERS

Many unexposed answers can be found in this revealing section regarding the winner's subsequent results.

It highlights the races and venues where winners struck again, along with the locations that caught them out – exchange players may find this section helpful.

The placed runners are also dealt with here and a full breakdown of their next three runs can be viewed underneath with any notable achievements included.

FUTURE SUCCESS RATING

At the foot of the page is an easy-to-use five-star guide to the strength of the race that takes into account not just the winner's achievements, but also the placed runners.

For further details regarding the 2008 updates and ratings, go to:

www.racingtrendsrevealed.com

DONCASTER MILE
March 22, Doncaster – (Listed, Class 1, 4yo+) 1m

Last run	Winner/Trainer & SP	Draw/Ran	Age	Wght	PR	Next four runs			
07 Kemp 1m 5th London Hcp *Six months*	**Banknote** A Balding 4/1	5/6	5	9-00	67	**WON 44/10 Group 3 Bade 1m**	2nd Group 3 Dort 1m1f	6th Summer Mile Ascot 1m	5th Group 2 Veli 1m
06 Wood 6f 4th = Grade 2 *Five months*	**Vanderlin** A Balding 8/1	6/7	7	9-05	70	5th Champions Mile Sha 1m	2nd Conds Stks Ches 7f	7th Sussex Good 1m	12th Grade 1 Wood 1m
06 Nad Al 1m 7th = Handicap *Two weeks*	**Kandidate** C Brittain 7/1	5/7	4	8-12	69	**WON 20/1 Rosebery Hcp Kemp 1m2f**	5th Lockinge Newb 1m	6th Queen Anne Ascot 1m	**WON 9/1 Gala Stks Sand 1m2f**
05 Newm 1m1f 1st Darley Stks *Five months*	**Autumn Glory** G Wragg 15/8JF	3/6	5	9-03	74	2nd Prix du Muguet Sain 1m	3rd Group 3 Long 1m2f	**WON 9/1 Silver Trophy Ling 1m**	13th Betfair Cup Good 7f
04 Newm 1m 4th Ben Marshall *Four months*	**Sublimity** Sir M Stoute 7/2	4/10	4	8-12	70	7th Betfred Mile Sand 1m	4th Festival Stks Good 1m2f	11th Diomed Stks Epsom 1m	3rd Listed Newm 1m
03 Capa 1m 13th Group 2 *Four months*	**Dandoun** J Dunlop 11/10F	6/8	5	8-12	76	**WON 39/10 Prix du Muguet Sain 1m**	7th Prix d'Ispahan Long 1m1f	10th Prix du Moulin Long 1m	8th Group 2 Long 1m
02 Deau 1m2f 5th Group 2 *Seven months*	**Dandoun** J Dunlop 11/10F	3/6	4	8-12	73	3rd Earl of Sefton Newm 1m1f	13th Group 2 Capa 1m	*WON 11/10F Doncaster Mile Donc 1m	*WON 39/10 Prix du Muguet Sain 1m
01 Mars 1m2f 2nd Listed Stks *Four months*	**Right Wing** J Dunlop 11/4	4/5	7	9-03	77	**WON 6/1 Earl of Sefton Newm 1m1f**	5th Masai Mile Sand 1m	4th Scottish Classic Ayr 1m2f	**WON 5/1 Darley Stks Newm 1m1f**
00 Newm 1m 6th Falmouth Stks *Eight months*	**Hasty Words** B Hills 5/1	1/8	4	8-07	63	6th Earl of Sefton Newm 1m1f	4th Dahlia Stks Newm 1m1f	11th Queen Anne Ascot 1m	4th Sun Chariot Newm 1m
99 Ascot 7f 1st Festival Hcp *Six months*	**White Heart** M Johnston 9/4	6/6	4	8-12	69	8th Earl of Sefton Newm 1m1f	4th Leicestershire Leic 7f	6th Shergar Cup Good 7f	4th Ballycorus Stks Leop 7f
98 Sand 1m 12th Hong Kong Hcp *Eight months*	**Hornbeam** J Jenkins 8/1	5/8	4	8-12	62	8th Lockinge Newb 1m	7th Royal Hunt Cup Ascot 1m	6th Strensall Stks York 1m1f	3rd Park Stks Donc 1m
97 Pont 1m 1st Maiden *Five months*	**Canyon Creek** J Gosden 7/2	2/6	4	8-12	61	8th Grade 3 Sain 1m	-	-	-
96 Newm 1m 2nd Marshall Stks *Five months*	**First Island** G Wragg 9/2	7/7	4	8-12	70	3rd Earl of Sefton Newm 1m1f	5th Sandown Mile Sand 1m	**WON 11/2 Hambleton Hcp York 1m**	**WON 9/1 Prince of Wales' Ascot 1m2f**

12-year median performance rating of the winner: 69 (out of 100) (2007 & 2006 Lingfield AW)2006 dead-heat *next year

WINNER'S PROFILE Eleven winners took this on their reappearance and only Kandidate came here off the back of a recent run. Vanderlin was just the second seven-year-old winner to score two years ago – in a dead-heat – while the remainder were **four and five-year-olds**, the former age-group accounted for eight winners.
There haven't been many outsiders and nine of the 10 winners returned at **5/1 or shorter**.
Southern trainers have held the edge, **John Dunlop** notched a hat-trick, while the Newmarket raiders fared well.

FUTURE POINTERS Winners of this early-season event have held their own afterwards as several got on the scoresheet soon after, but they did find it difficult to step up in class in this country. Only Autumn Glory in 2005 won a Group Three event on these shores – Dandoun won a Group Two in France in 2002 – while the best winner with a top performance rating (PR), Right Wing in 2001, managed to land the Listed Earl of Sefton Stakes at Newmarket from the five victors to have tried their luck.

Were Doncaster Mile winners profitable to follow on their subsequent three runs?
Yes - 7 wins from 37 runs returned a **profit of +£19.90** to a £1 level stake.

Placed runners subsequent record (three runs):
Runners-up: 3 wins from 33 runs returned a loss of -£20.00 to a £1 level stake.
2005 Hurricane Alan – Sandown Mile, 2004 Gateman – Earl of Sefton,
2000 Swallow Flight – Royal Windsor Stakes, Doubleprint Handicap

Thirds: 1 win from 10 runs returned a loss of -£5.50 to a £1 level stake.

FUTURE SUCCESS RATING: ★ ★ ☆ ☆ ☆

CAMMIDGE TROPHY
March 22, Doncaster – (Listed, Class 1, 3yo+) 6f

Last run	Winner/ Trainer & SP	Draw/ Ran	Age	Wght	PR	Next four runs			
07 Wind 6f 1st Wentworth Stks *Four months*	**Rising Shadow** D Barron 13/2	8/13	6	9-05	67	4th Duke of York York 6f	19th Golden Jubilee Ascot 6f	4th Chipchase Stks Newc 6f	15th July Cup Newm 6f
06 Ling 5f 1st Conds Stks *One week*	**Les Arcs** T Pitt 15/2	1/13	6	9-02	75	2nd Abernant Newm 6f	8th Temple Stks Sand 5f	11th King's Stand Ascot 5f	**WON 33/1 Golden Jubilee Ascot 6f**
05 Wind 6f 3rd Leisure Stks *Eleven months*	**La Cucaracha** B Hills 16/1	2/11	4	8-11	68	9th Duke of York York 6f	**WON 9/2 Ballyogan Stks Leop 6f**	2nd Summer Stks York 6f	**WON 9/2F Heritage Hcp York 6f**
04 Donc 6f 11th Wentworth Stks *Four months*	**Goldeva** R Hollinshead 40/1	16/17	5	8-11	60	5th Duke of York York 6f	11th Chipchase Stks Newc 6f	5th Summer Stks York 6f	4th Queensferry Stks Ches 6f
03 Newm 7f 5th Challenge Stks *Five months*	**Red Carpet** M Bell 7/2F	3/13	5	9-02	70	6th Leicestershire St Leic 7f	5th Duke of York York 6f	3rd Listed Curr 6f	13th Hackwood Stks Newb 6f
02 Pisa 7f 11th Listed Stks *Three months*	**Falcon Hill** M Johnston 11/1	6/10	3	8-06	71	9th Easter Stks Kemp 1m	9th Abernant Newm 6f	8th Pavilion Stks Ascot 6f	6th Group 3 Muni 7f
01 Donc 6f 4th Wentworth Stks *Four months*	**Now Look Here** B McMahon 10/1	10/15	5	9-02	67	10th Abernant Newm 6f	3rd Palace House Newm 5f	7th Duke of York York 6f	21st International Hcp Ascot 7f
00 Donc 6f 19th Wentworth Stks *Four months*	**Andreyev** R Hannon 9/1	4/13	6	9-02	68	10th Showcase Hcp Newb 5f	10th Abernant Newm 6f	5th Conds Stks Newm 6f	8th Leisure Stks Ling 6f
99 Newm 6f 2nd Bentinck Stks *Five months*	**Tedburrow** E Alston 9/2	3/8	7	9-07	73	13th Abernant Newm 6f	9th Palace House Newm 5f	17th King's Stand Ascot 5f	**WON 9/2 City Wall Stks Ches 5f**
98 Ascot 6f 2nd Diadem *Six months*	**Monaassib** E Dunlop 9/4F	2/9	7	9-07	72	4th Abernant Newm 6f	6th Duke of York York 6f	10th July Cup Newm 6f	4th Hackwood Stks Newb 6f
97 Hayd 6f 9th Sprint Cup *Six months*	**Royal Applause** B Hills 6/4F	7/8	4	9-02	69	**WON 3/1F Duke of York York 6f**	**WON 11/2F Cork & Orrery Ascot 6f**	2nd July Cup Newm 6f	**WON 15/8F Sprint Cup Hayd 6f**
96 Donc 6f 5th Holdings Stks *Four months*	**Fire Dome** R Hannon 11/1	7/8	4	9-02	62	5th Leicestershire St Leic 7f	2nd Conds Stks Hayd 7f	**6th Conds Stks Wolv 6f	**6th Handicap Wolv 6f

12-year median performance rating of the winner: **67** (out of 100) *(2007 Newcastle, 2006 Redcar)* **next two years*

WINNER'S PROFILE Only Les Arcs came here with a prep run as the **majority arrived fresh.** Four picked up where they left off having last run in a similar event at Doncaster, the Wentworth Stakes - run at Windsor in 2006. **Five to seven-year-olds** won eight of the last 10 renewals, with just one three-year-old succeeding from nine runners – the other eight were all unplaced.
Trainers **Richard Hannon** and **Barry Hills** have both won it twice.

FUTURE POINTERS There was a lull following the Millennium, but La Cucaracha and Les Arcs helped put the Cammidge Trophy back on the map as a springboard for later success – both scored in Group One events later that term. Avoiding the winner next time out may be the best ploy, however, as only Royal Applause managed to follow up in the Duke of York Stakes, a race that eluded many winners of the Cammidge, along with the Abernant Stakes at Newmarket. In fact, Fylde Flyer was the last winner of this to triumph at HQ in 1992, and placed runners had the better record *(see below)*.

Were Cammidge Trophy winners profitable to follow on their subsequent three runs?
No – 3 wins from 36 runs returned a loss of -£20.00 to a £1 level stake.

Placed runners' subsequent record (three runs):
Runners-up: 5 wins from 36 runs returned a loss of -£1.60 to a £1 level stake.
2005 The Kiddykid – Duke of York

Thirds: 8 wins from 36 runs returned a **profit of +£40.25** to a £1 level stake.
2006 Reverence – Temple Stakes, 2000 Cretan Gift – Abernant Stakes, 1998 Tedburrow – Abernant Stakes

FUTURE SUCCESS RATING: ★ ★ ☆ ☆ ☆

LINCOLN
March 22, Doncaster – (Heritage Handicap, Class 2, 4yo+) 1m

Last run	Winner/ Trainer & SP	Draw/ Ran	Age	Wght	PR	Next four runs			
07 Ling 1m2f 2nd Tote Hcp *Two weeks*	**Very Wise** W Haggas 9/1	16/20	5	8-11	66	6th Hambleton Hcp York 1m	18th Goddard Hcp York 1m	3rd Kilkerran Cup Ayr 1m2f	22nd Cambridgeshire Newm 1m1f
06 Newm 1m 8th Handicap *Five months*	**Blythe Knight** J Quinn 22/1	9/30	6	8-10	65	11th Spring Cup Newb 1m	3rd Conds Stks Newm 1m2f	4th Hambleton Hcp York 1m	29th Royal Hunt Cup Ascot 1m
05 Newm 7f 1st Handicap *Five months*	**Stream Of Gold** Sir M Stoute 5/1F	13/22	4	9-00	73	4th Betfred Mile Sand 1m	4th Diomed Stks Epsom 1m	4th Select Stks Good 1m2f	*3rd Listed Abu 7f
04 Newm 1m 9th Churchill Stks *Four months*	**Babodana** M Tompkins 20/1	23/24	4	9-10	69	6th Betfred Mile Sand 1m	3rd Spring Trophy Hayd 7f	3rd Midsummer Stks Wind 1m	5th Silver Trophy Ascot 1m
03 Newm 1m 1st Showcase Hcp *Four months*	**Pablo** B Hills 5/1	6/24	4	8-11	72	4th Earl of Sefton Newm 1m1f	5th Huxley Stks Ches 1m2f	5th Ben Marshall Newm 1m	*19th Lincoln Donc 1m
02 Ascot 7f 9th International St *Eight months*	**Zucchero** D Arbuthnot 33/1	7/23	6	8-13	61	17th Tote Hcp Sand 1m	23rd Victoria Cup Ascot 7f	12th Royal Hunt Cup Ascot 1m	12th Ladbrokes Hcp Newb 1m
01 Wolv 1m 1st Arena Hcp *Two weeks*	**Nimello** P Cole 9/2F	1/23	5	8-09	73	**WON 9/2F** **Doubleprint Hp** **Kemp 1m**	9th Hambleton Hcp York 1m	13th Silver Salver Hp Newm 7f	3rd Conds Stks Nott 1m
00 Wolv 1m 3rd Lincoln Trial *Two weeks*	**John Ferneley** P Cole 7/1JF	1/24	5	8-10	68	2nd Royal Hunt Cup Ascot 1m	4th W Hill Hcp Good 1m	4th Brad & Bing Hcp York 1m	3rd Champagne Hcp Newm 1m
99 York 1m 6th Rated Hcp *Five months*	**Right Wing** J Dunlop 9/2F	8/24	5	9-05	71	2nd Conds Stks Ascot 1m	5th Hambleton Hcp York 1m	17th Hong Kong Hcp Sand 1m2f	3rd Motability Hcp York 1m2f
98 Newm 1m 12th Rothmans Hcp *Five months*	**Hunters Of Brora** J Bethell 16/1	23/23	8	9-00	64	5th Spring Cup Newb 1m	6th Royal Hunt Cup Ascot 1m	**WON 7/1** **Conds Stks** **Newc 1m**	14th Hong Kong Hcp Sand 1m2f
97 Wolv 1m 4th Lincoln Trial *Two weeks*	**Kuala Lipis** P Cole 11/1	21/24	4	8-06	62	12th Spring Cup Newb 1m	2nd Handicap Ches 1m2f	7th Whitsun Hcp Sand 1m	15th Bessborough Ascot 1m4f
96 Newm 1m 13th Autumn Hcp *Five months*	**Stone Ridge** R Hannon 33/1	6/24	4	8-07	58	16th Spring Cup Newb 1m	5th Handicap Epsom 1m	15th Handicap Epsom 1m2f	15th Royal Hunt Cup Ascot 1m

12-year median performance rating of the winner: **67** (out of 100)   *(2007 Newcastle, 2006 Redcar) *next year*

WINNER'S PROFILE Ten winners **last ran in either a big-field handicap at Newmarket or on the all-weather**, three in handicaps on Lincoln Trial Day at Wolverhampton. The last two renewals took place away from Doncaster, but with it returning this year, those **drawn either very high or low** should be respected, as the central stalls have struggled. **Four to six-year-olds** stand out as the favoured age group, while those who carried **9st and below** came out triumphant on 10 occasions.
Newmarket trainers have scooped four of the last five renewals, but **Paul Cole** has won it three times in the last 12 years, all with horses that were given a prep race at Wolverhampton.

FUTURE POINTERS The first major handicap of the Flat season, but one in which the winner has by far the worst record next time out. Apart from Nimello, who followed up at Kempton a few months later, the nearest any got to the winner's enclosure again in the near future was John Ferneley and Right Wing in 2000 and 1999, respectively. Layers will be keen to get the Lincoln winner next time out, although it could be worth noting the fourth-placed runner from here as a few future winners of decent handicaps filled that spot over the years *(see below)*.

Were Lincoln winners profitable to follow on their subsequent three runs?
No – 2 wins from 36 runs returned a loss of -£22.50 to a £1 level stake.

Placed runners' subsequent record (three runs):
Runners-up: 4 wins from 36 runs returned loss of -£1.50 to a £1 level stake.
2005 New Seeker – Royal Hunt Cup, 1997 Hawksley Hill – Spring Cup

Thirds: 1 win from 35 runs returned a loss of -£30.50 to a £1 level stake.

Fourths: 5 wins from 35 runs returned a **profit of +£7.00** to a £1 level stake.
2006 Zero Tolerance – Hambleton Handicap, 2001 Mastermind – Spring Cup, 1999 Raheen – Hambleton Handicap

FUTURE SUCCESS RATING: ★ ☆ ☆ ☆

EASTER STAKES
March 22, Kempton (AW) – (Listed, Class 1, 3yo Colts & Geldings) 1m

Last run	Winner/ Trainer & SP	Draw/ Ran	Age	Wght	PR	Next four runs			
07 Newb 7f 10th Horris Hill *Five months*	Dubai's Touch M Johnston 7/2	4/7	3	9-01	72	9th Lennox Stks Good 7f	WON 16/1 Thoroughbred St Good 1m	8th Hungerford Stk Newb 7f	10th Group 2 Veli 1m
06 Sand 7f 3rd Solario Stks *Eight months*	Asset R Hannon 6/4JF	3/6	3	8-10	70	9th 2,000 Guineas Newm 1m	2nd Jersey Stks Ascot 7f	*WON 11/4F Abernant Newm 6f	*3rd Golden Jubilee Ascot 6f
05 Ascot 7f 2nd Nursery *Six months*	Rebel Rebel N Callaghan 5/1	6/8	3	8-08	64	4th Feilden Stks Newm 1m1f	2nd 2,000 Guineas Newm 1m	4th Irish 2,000 Guin Curr 1m	3rd Grade 3 Colo 1m2f
04 Ascot 1m 5th Royal Lodge *Seven months*	Privy Seal J Gosden 9/1	3/7	3	8-11	65	2nd Classic Trial Sand 1m2f	2nd Chester Vase Ches 1m4f	3rd Derby Italiano Capa 1m4f	9th Hampton Court Ascot 1m2f
03 York 7f 1st Conds Stks *Six months*	Prince Tum Tum J Dunlop 10/3	4/6	3	8-08	65	10th Hambleton York 1m	6th Criterion Newm 7f	4th Conds Stks Newb 7f	3rd Conds Stks Warw 7f
02 Newm 7f 9th Tattersall Stks *Five months*	Flat Spin J Dunlop 8/1	3/9	3	8-08	65	5th Craven Newm 1m	8th Premio Parioli Capa 1m	2nd Thoroughbred St Good 1m	4th Conds Stks Donc 1m2f
01 (Unraced)	Herodotus C Brittain 25/1	2/9	3	8-08	64	5th Classic Trial Sand 1m2f	8th Predominate Good 1m3f	11th King Edward VII Ascot 1m4f	5th Prix Eugene Adam Deau 1m2f
00 Ascot 1m 3rd Royal Lodge *Seven months*	Kingsclere I Balding 3/1Jf	1/6	3	8-08	68	5th Chester Vase Ches 1m4f	15th Derby Epsom 1m4f	5th Shergar Cup Ascot 1m4f	9th Winter Hill Wind 1m2f
99 Newm 7f 9th Tattersalls Stks *Seven months*	Dehoush A Stewart 10/1	2/11	3	8-08	62	2nd Classic Trial Sand 1m2f	8th King Edward VII Ascot 1m4f	4th Scottish Classic Ayr 1m2f	*WON 5/4F Conds Stks Newb 1m2f
98 Curr 7f 5th Futurity Stks *Eight months*	Krispy Knight J Hills 6/1	2/4	3	8-08	61	6th Premio Parioli Capa 1m	*6th Doncaster Mile Donc 1m	*4th Conds Stks Sali 1m	*7th Handicap Wind 1m
97 Donc 1m 6th Conds Stks *One week*	Pelham R Hannon 6/1	3/7	3	8-08	62	6th Craven Newm 1m	-	-	-
96 Sand 7f 2nd Conds Stks *Nine months*	Regiment R Hannon 9/1	2/10	3	8-08	60	13th 2,000 Guineas Newm 1m	-	-	-

12-year median performance rating of the winner: **65** (out of 100)   *(All-weather since 2006) *next year*

WINNER'S PROFILE Only the 1997 winner, Pelham, came here with a recent run under his belt as 10 others were **off the track for over four months**. Apart from the debutante in 2001, no maiden took this, as 11 winners already **scored at either six or seven furlongs** – nine had **no more than seven career runs**.
From a draw perspective, it is worth noting that neither of the two highest stalls on the tight inside have won, although the race is now run the all-weather so results may change.
One trainer long associated with this event is **Richard Hannon** who used to cream it in the nineties – not so much these days – while **John Dunlop** also had consecutive winners in 2003 and 2002.

FUTURE POINTERS The Easter Stakes used to be a good pointer for the Classics but has unfortunately deteriorated since the days of 1991, when the first three home that year were Corrupt (later won the Great Voltigeur), Selkirk (QEII), and Environment Friend (Dante and Eclipse) – it may be a long while before we are treated to a line-up of that quality again. However, the last two winners were above par and duly scored again, so things may be changing for the better.
The nearest any of the Easter Stakes winners went to landing the 2,000 Guineas was Rebel Rebel (2005) and Lucky Lindy, who finished second in 1992, while from a betting viewpoint, following Kempton runners-up could be the way to go *(see below)*.

Were Easter Stakes winners profitable to follow on their subsequent three runs?
No - 2 wins from 32 runs returned a loss of -£11.25 to a £1 level stake.

Placed runners' subsequent record (three runs):
Runners-up: 7 wins from 30 runs returned a **profit of +£11.42** to a £1 level stake.
2007 Prime Defender – European Free Handicap, Sandy Lane Stakes, 2006 Royal Power – German 2,000 Guineas, 2003 Dutch Gold – Chester Vase, 1996 Centre Stalls – Fortune Stakes

Thirds: 2 wins from 14 runs returned a loss of -£3.50 to a £1 level stake.
2002 Redback – Greenham Stakes

FUTURE SUCCESS RATING: ★★☆☆☆

14

ROSEBERY STAKES
March 29, Kempton (AW) – (Class 2, Heritage Handicap, 4yo+) 1m3f

Last run	Winner/Trainer & SP	Draw/Ran	Age	Wght	PR	Next four runs			
07 Nad 1m2f 16th Handicap Two months	**Luberon** M Johnston 16/1	11/15	4	9-09	72	17th Suburban Hcp Epsom 1m2f	8th Braveheart Stks Hami 1m4f	16th J Smith's Cup York 1m2f	10th Old Newton Cup Hayd 1m4f
06 Ling 1m 1st Doncaster Mile One month	**Kandidate** C Brittain 20/1	15/16	4	9-10	71	5th Lockinge Newb 1m	6th Queen Anne Ascot 1m	**WON 9/1 Gala Stks Sand 1m2f**	6th Glorious Stks Good 1m4f
05 Ling 1m2f 1st Handicap Two months	**Kew Green** P Webber 9/1	11/20	7	8-08	65	**WON 9/2F Suffolk Hcp Newm 1m1f**	15th Rose Bowl Hcp Epsom 1m2f	29th Cambridgeshire Newm 1m1f	**WON 9/1 Churchill Stks Ling 1m2f**
04 Newm 1m2f 5th Severals Stks Six months	**Silence Is Golden** B Meehan 11/1	19/17	5	8-13	62	2nd Dahlia Stks Newm 1m1f	9th Group 2 Sain 1m3f	2nd Gala Stks Sand 1m2f	2nd Nassau Good 1m2f
03 Pont 1m2f 2nd Class Stks Two weeks	**Broadway Score** J Hills 16/1	6/18	5	9-09	65	14th Vodafone Hcp Epsom 1m2f	7th Summer Hcp Sand 1m2f	14th Showcase Hcp Good 1m2f	10th Rated Hcp Ches 1m5f
02 Donc 1m 12th Lincoln Hcp Two weeks	**Imperial Dancer** M Channon 33/1	2/18	4	8-12	69	3rd Gordon Richards Sand 1m2f	**WON 13/2 Festival Stks Good 1m2f**	3rd Brigadier Gerard Sand 1m2f	5th Mercury Stks Leic 1m4f
01 Newb 1m2f 2nd Handicap Six months	**Gentleman Venture** J Akehurst 16/1	11/19	5	8-08	60	3rd Suburban Hcp Epsom 1m2f	6th Vodafone Hcp Epsom 1m4f	*3rd Suburban Hcp Epsom 1m2f	*7th Showcase Hcp Newb 1m4f
00 Kemp 7f 2nd Handicap One month	**Pulau Tioman** M Jarvis 9/1	10/20	4	9-08	72	2nd Doubleprint Hcp Kemp 1m	4th Listed Capa 7f	**WON 4/1 John of Gaunt Hayd 7f**	2nd Silver Trophy Ascot 1m
99 Siro 1m2f 2nd Listed Nine months	**Carry The Flag** P Cole 14/1	4/20	4	9-06	66	**WON 11/2 Shergar Cup Hp Good 1m4f**	4th Handicap Epsom 1m4f	4th Duke Of Edinburgh Ascot 1m4f	2nd Doonside Cup Ayr 1m3f
98 Donc 1m2f 1st Handicap Six months	**American Whisper** P Harris 12/1	7/16	4	8-06	60	**WON 5/1 Rated Hcp Newm 1m2f**	14th Vodafone Hcp Epsom 1m2f	-	-
97 Donc 1m4f 14th November Hcp Four months	**Romios** P Cole 14/1	10/20	5	9-07	62	4th Rated Hcp Newm 1m2f	4th Zetland Gold Cup Redc 1m2f	5th Rated Hcp Epsom 1m4f	4th Ladbroke Hcp Ascot 1m2f
96 Donc 1m2f 2nd Ladies Hcp Three weeks	**Hazard A Guees** D Nicholls 10/1	11/19	6	8-11	59	3rd Handicap Beve 1m2f	3rd Handicap Ripon 1m2f	7th Handicap Epsom 1m2f	9th Silver Salver Hcp York 1m1f

12-year median performance rating of the winner: **65** (out of 100)   *(All-weather since 2006) *next year*

WINNER'S PROFILE This handicap was switched to the all-weather over a furlong further in 2006, but one feature that remained in tact was the large starting price of the winner. An **average SP of 14/1** since 1996 says plenty about this tricky early-season handicap, however, those wishing to hunt down the winner may want to stick with candidates drawn from the **middle to high stalls** on the inside.
Four to five-year-olds have also performed well, while a **victory or second last time out** is a plus.
Along with the Lincoln, trainer **Paul Cole** likes to get one ready for this and won it twice during the late-nineties.

FUTURE POINTERS Winners that stuck to handicap grade next time out did well as Kew Green, Carry The Flag and American Whisper all triumphed at decent odds. However, those that stepped up into Group company came unstuck, though three managed to win later in Listed class, including one of the best winners of this event, Kandidate, in 2006.

Were Rosebery winners profitable to follow on their subsequent three runs?
Yes – 6 wins from 35 runs returned a **profit of £5.50** to a £1 level stake.

Placed runners' subsequent record (three runs):
Runners-up: 2 wins from 33 runs returned a loss of -£22.50 to a £1 level stake.
2000 Espada – Doubleprint Handicap

Thirds: 4 wins from 36 runs returned a **profit of £+24.50** to a £1 level stake.
2006 Young Mick – Duke of Edinburgh Stakes, 2001 Moon Solitaire – Newmarket Rated Handicap, 1999 Monsajem – Vodafone Handicap

Fourths: 5 wins from 33 runs returned a loss of -£5.00 to a £1 level stake.
2004 Blythe Knight – City & Suburban Handicap, 1996 Beauchamp Jade – Newmarket Handicap

FUTURE SUCCESS RATING: ★ ★ ★ ★ ☆

MAGNOLIA STAKES

March 29, Kempton (AW) – (Listed, Class 1, 4yo+) 1m2f

Last run	Winner/ Trainer & SP	Draw/ Ran	Age	Wght	PR	Next four runs			
07 Leic 1m2f 5th Conds Stks Nine months	Imperial Star J Gosden 8/1	5/10	4	8-13	72	9th Earl of Sefton Newm 1m1f	3rd Festival Stks Good 1m2f	2nd Glorious Stks Good 1m4f	3rd August Stks Wind 1m4f
06 Ling 1m2f 6th Churchill Stks Five months	Simple Exchange D Weld 3/1	3/6	5	8-13	67	5th Mooresbridge St Curr 1m2f	6th Listed Leop 1m	3rd Listed Leop 1m6f	6th Group 3 Leop 1m2f
05 Newb 1m3f 4th Dubai Duty Free Six months	Day Flight J Gosden 4/6F	2/4	4	8-11	78	WON 9/4F John Porter Newb 1m4f	WON 85/40 Ormonde Stks Ches 1m5f	2nd Princess Of Wales's Newm 1m4f	WON 3/1JF St Simon Stks Newb 1m4f
04 Nad Al 1m4f 3rd Sheema Classic Three weeks	Scott's View M Johnston 5/1	6/12	5	9-00	74	3rd QEII Cup Sha 1m2f	3rd Grosser Preis Bade 1m3f	7th Coronation Cup Epsom 1m4f	5th Prince of Wales' Ascot 1m2f
03 Ling 1m2f 1st Winter Derby Two months	Parasol D Loder 7/4F	1/7	4	9-00	77	WON 11/8F Huxley Stks Ches 1m2f	2nd Brigadier Gerard Sand 1m2f	6th Hardwicke Ascot 1m4f	2nd Steventon Stks Newb 1m2f
02 Ling 1m2f 6th Churchill Stks Five months	Border Arrow I Balding 2/1F	6/5	7	8-11	74	9th Earl of Sefton Newm 1m1f	2nd Gordon Richards Sand 1m2f	3rd Festival Stks Good 1m2f	3rd Grosser Preis Bade 1m3f
01 Capa 1m2f 2nd Premio Roma Five months	Border Arrow I Balding 7/2	6/9	6	8-11	74	2nd Gordon Richards Sand 1m2f	WON 11/2 Brigadier Gerard Sand 1m2f	8th Prince of Wales Ascot 1m2f	3rd James Seymour Newm 1m2f
00 Donc 1m 3rd Lincoln Hcp One month	Right Wing J Dunlop 7/2F	6/8	6	8-11	72	2nd Festival Stks Good 1m2f	2nd Gallinule Stks Curr 1m2f	WON 8/1 Strensall Stks York 1m1f	3rd Select Stks Good 1m2f
99 Newm 1m 2nd Marshall Stks Six months	Generous Rosi J Dunlop 10/11F	7/8	4	8-11	70	WON 10/3F Gordon Richards Sand 1m2f	2nd Brigadier Gerard Sand 1m2f	8th Prince of Wales Ascot 1m2f	4th Rated Hcp Good 1m4f
98 York 1m4f 5th Great Voltigeur Eight months	Garuda J Dunlop 3/1JF	2/6	4	8-11	67	2nd Gordon Richards Sand 1m2f	2nd Brigadier Gerard Sand 1m2f	5th Premio di Milano Siro 1m4f	4th Princess Of Wales' Newm 1m4f
97 Curr 1m4f 7th Irish Derby Nine months	Dr Massini Sir M Stoute 11/10F	5/5	4	8-11	68	Ref Tatts Gold Cup Curr 1m2f	*8th Lincolnshire Curr 1m	*Ref Stakes List 1m4f	-
96 Newb 1m3f 2nd Conds Stks One year	Lucky Di L Cumani 11/2	2/12	4	8-11	66	2nd Brigadier Gerard Sand 1m2f	9th Prince of Wales Ascot 1m2f	*5th Hurdle Fake 2m	*7th Hurdle Hunt 2m5f

12-year median performance rating of the winner: **72** (out of 100)   *(All-weather since 2006), *next year*

WINNER'S PROFILE Three of the last six winners **arrived here from Lingfield's Polytrack**, having ran in either the Churchill Stakes or Winter Derby over this trip.
Dual winner Border Arrow was the only seven-year-old winner, while **four-year-olds** took half of the renewals, two of them trained by **John Dunlop**, who had a hat-trick of winning favourites from 1998 to 2000.
Fancied runners have also come out on top and last year's 8/1 shot was the biggest for 12 years.

FUTURE POINTERS Last year's renewal attracted a classier field compared to the inaugural running on Polytrack in 2006 and will hopefully continue to attract future Pattern performers. There has been a mixed subsequent record from Magnolia winners, half of them appeared down the road at Sandown in either the Gordon Richards or Brigadier Gerard Stakes – only Border Arrow took the latter race – while five others were runner-up. Two of the best Magnolia winners both took separate successful routes, Day Flight in the John Porter Stakes at Newbury, while up north, Parasol travelled to Chester's three-day festival to scoop the Huxley Stakes.

Were Magnolia winners profitable to follow on their subsequent three runs?
No – 6 wins from 36 runs returned a loss of -£7.46 to a £1 level stake.

Placed runners' subsequent record (three runs):
Runners-up: 2 wins from 31 runs returned a loss of -£26.63 to a £1 level stake.
2003 Nysaean – Group Three Mooresbridge Stakes

Thirds: 4 wins from 18 runs returned a **profit of +£5.00** to a £1 level stake.
2001 Mubtaker – Listed Festival Stakes, 1996 Captain Horatius – Listed Festival Stakes

FUTURE SUCCESS RATING: ★ ★ ☆ ☆ ☆

MASAKA STAKES
April 12, Kempton (AW) – (Listed, Class 1, 3yo) 1m

Last run	Winner/ Trainer & SP	Draw/ Ran	Age	Wght	PR	Next four runs			
07 Nad Al 10th UAE 1,000 Guin Two months	Precocious Star K Burke 8/1	3/9	3	8-12	50	9th Nell Gwyn Stks Newm 7f	10th Sandringham Hp Ascot 7f	5th Group 3 Leop 7f	12th Handicap Newm 7f
06 Nad Al 3rd UAE Oaks One month	Don't Dili Dali S Moore 12/1	3/11	3	8-10	60	4th Feilden Stks Newm 1m1f	12th Irish 1,000 Guin Curr 1m	*8th Handicap Nad Al 1m	*3rd Handicap Nad Al 1m2f
05 Ling 7f 1st Maiden Two months	Vista Bella M Jarvis 7/2	8/10	3	8-08	65	3rd 1,000 Guineas Newm 1m	**5th Listed Nad Al 1m	**10th Listed Nad Al 1m1f	–
04 Newb 7f 2nd Radley Stks Six months	Hathrah J Dunlop 10/11F	4/9	3	8-08	66	3rd 1,000 Guineas Newm 1m		–	–
03 Newm 7f 11th Rockfel Stks Six months	Nasij E Dunlop 2/1F	7/10	3	8-08	59	4th Swettenham Stk Newb 1m2f	6th Sandringham Hp Ascot 1m	4th Falmouth Newm 1m	9th Oak Tree Stks Good 7f
02 Siro 1m 2nd Group 3 Five months	Kootenay J Dunlop 4/1	10/12	3	8-11	63	8th Group 2 Capa 1m	2nd Lupe Good 1m2f	WON 11/4 Princess Elizabeth Epsom 1m	3rd Falmouth Newm 1m
01 Sain 1m 7th Group 3 Five months	Heavenly Whisper M Bell 20/1	5/12	3	8-08	58	3rd Musidora York 1m2f	6th Pretty Polly Curr 1m2f	2nd Falmouth Newm 1m	4th Prix d' Astarte Deau 1m
00 Newb 1m 4th Radley Stks Six months	Lady Upstage B Hills 11/2	2/7	3	8-08	63	2nd Musidora York 1m2f	5th Oaks Epsom 1m4f	WON 9/2 Pretty Polly Curr 1m2f	7th Nassau Good 1m2f
99 Ayr 1m 1st Maiden Six months	Claxon J Dunlop 9/2	1/8	3	8-08	64	WON 7/4F Lupe Stks Good 1m2f	5th Oaks Epsom 1m4f	2nd Listed Newc 1m2f	WON 7/4F Steventon Stks Newb 1m2f
98 Newm 7f 2nd Rockfel Stks Six months	Tadwiga R Hannon 7/2JF	1/8	3	8-08	61	WON 2/5F Conds Stks Kemp 1m	3rd Daffodil Stks Chep 1m2f	5th Conds Stks Ascot 1m	WON 9/2 Matron Stks Curr 1m
97 Donc 1m 1st Maiden Five months	Calypso Grant P Harris 5/2F	2/8	3	8-08	58	7th Fred Darling Newb 7f	9th Musidora York 1m2f	10th Ballymacoll Newb 1m2f	4th Globetrotter Hcp Good 1m2f
96 Long 1m 10th Marcel Boussac Six months	Sea Spray P Chapple-Hyam 4/1	8/13	3	8-08	56	5th Musidora York 1m2f	10th Ribblesdale Ascot 1m4f	8th Listed Long 1m2f	9th Group 3 Saiin 1m3f

12-year median performance rating of the winner: **60** (out of 100) *(All-weather since 2006), *next year*

WINNER'S PROFILE Prior to 2005, all nine winners made their seasonal reappearance here, but as both domestic and international racing during the winter has grown in popularity, the last three winners arrived with an **outing under their belt**.
Other trends have been hard to detect, although as with the Easter Stakes, it may prove wise to **avoid the highest two drawn** runners as well as keeping an eye on trainer **John Dunlop**'s runners.

FUTURE POINTERS Precocious Star was massively below-par last year and therefore it came as no surprise to see her beaten out of sight during her next few assignments, however, it has been worth keeping close tabs on the classy winners of this Listed event. Claxon and Tadwiga were two of the best during the last 12 years and both followed up before adding more prize money later in the season.
In recent years, another of the best scorers, Hathrah, in 2004, was a creditable third in the 1,000 Guineas, as was Vista Bella a year later. Four winners failed in the Musidora Stakes at York's three-day May meeting, while two failed in the Epsom Oaks.

Were Masaka Stakes winners profitable to follow on their subsequent three runs?
No – 4 wins from 34 runs returned a loss of -£21.60 to a £1 level stake.

Placed runners' subsequent record (three runs):
Runners-up: 3 wins from 35 runs returned a loss of -£5.90 to a £1 level stake.
2003 Mauri Moon – Listed Oak Tree Stakes, 2002 Red Liason – Listed Surrey Stakes

Thirds: 2 wins from 34 runs returned a loss of -£28.50 to a £1 level stake.
2004 Halicardia – Listed Lupe Stakes

FUTURE SUCCESS RATING: ★ ★ ★ ★ ★

FEILDEN STAKES
April 16, Newmarket – (Listed, Class 1, 3yo) 1m1f

Last run	Winner/Trainer & SP	Draw/Ran	Age	Wght	PR	Next four runs			
07 Newb 1m 10th / R Post Trophy / *Six months*	**Petara Bay** / T Mills 4/1	1/8	3	8-13	63	7th Classic Trial Sand 1m2f	15th Derby Epsom 1m4f	-	-
06 Salis 1m 5th / Autumn Stks / *Six months*	**Atlantic Waves** / M Johnston 3/1CF	4/8	3	8-13	62	15th Derby Epsom 1m4f	-	-	-
05 Epso 1m 2nd / Conds Stks / *Six months*	**Rocamadour** / M Channon 25/1	4/10	3	8-11	71	WON 7/4 Newmarket Stks Newm 1m2f	3rd Prix Jockey Club Chan 1m3f	4th St James Palace York 1m	3rd Prix Jean Prat Chan 1m
04 Donc 1m 2nd / Conds Stks / *Three weeks*	**Gold History** / M Johnston 10/3	3/7	3	8-11	65	3rd Classic Trial Sand 1m2f	5th King Edward VII Ascot 1m4f	16th Handicap Newb 1m	10th Handicap Godd 1m2f
03 Ascot 1m 5th / Royal Lodge / *Seven months*	**Magistretti** / N Callaghan 9/2	3/6	3	8-11	72	WON 8/1 Dante York 1m2f	9th Derby Epsom 1m4f	2nd Grand Prix de Paris Long 1m2f	2nd Juddmonte Int York 1m2f
02 Ling 1m2f 1st / Maiden / *Four months*	**Playapart** / G Butler 6/1	3/10	3	8-11	65	3rd Dee Stks Ches 1m2f	6th Predominate Good 1m3f	-	-
01 York 7f 4th / Maiden / *Nine months*	**Olden Times** / J Dunlop 11/4F	4/9	3	8-11	69	5th Dante York 1m2f	WON 48/10 Prix Jean Prat Chan 1m1f	3rd St James Palace Ascot 1m	4th Sussex Good 1m
00 Newm 1m 1st / Maiden / *Six months*	**Pawn Broker** / D Elsworth 14/1	8/8	3	8-11	73	2nd Classic Trial Sand 1m2f	2nd Dante York 1m2f	13th Prix Jockey Club Chan 1m4f	3rd September Stks Kemp 1m4f
99 Donc 1m 1st / Maiden / *Seven months*	**Golden Snake** / B Hills 11/2	7/9	3	8-11	72	2nd Dante York 1m2f	WON 6/1 Prix Jean Prat Chan 1m1f	6th Juddmonte Int York 1m2f	10th Champion Stks Newm 1m2f
98 Newm 1m 1st / Maiden / *Six months*	**Border Arrow** / I Balding 11/4	6/6	3	8-11	65	3rd 2,000 Guineas Newm 1m	3rd Dante York 1m2f	3rd Derby Epsom 1m4f	3rd Shergar Cup Good 1m2f
97 Pont 1m 2nd / Tankard Stks / *Six months*	**Fahris** / B Hanbury 7/1	3/7	3	8-11	69	6th Derby Epsom 1m4f	2nd Scottish Classic Ayr 1m2f	3rd Rose of Lancaster Hayd 1m3f	3rd Winter Hill Wind 1m2f
96 Ascot 1m 2nd / Autumn Stks / *Six months*	**Storm Trooper** / H Cecil 2/1F	2/11	3	8-11	66	11th 2,000 Guineas Newm 1m	6th Dante York 1m2f	15th Derby Epsom 1m4f	3rd Gordon Stks Good 1m4f

12-year median performance rating of the winner: **68** (out of 100)

WINNER'S PROFILE Eleven winners already **won a maiden** – 10 between seven furlongs to a mile – before they lined up in this and only Olden Times, in 2001, came here without a victory to his name.
He was also one of the most **lightly raced** with only one previous appearance, although no winner had raced on more than four occasions. Only two ran that year including Gold History in 2004, trained by **Mark Johnston**, who won it two years ago with Atlantic Waves. Although the event has generally attracted a small field, favourites have a moderate record – only three came out on top – so the **search for a touch of value** is recommended.

FUTURE POINTERS Viewed as one of the early Classic trials, this event has produced a couple of smart performers who subsequently went on to score in Group One company, although none were triumphant in any of the British Classics. The Dante was a popular target as five winners attempted to follow up at York, but only Magistretti was successful, before finishing ninth in the Epsom Derby.
However, the 2001 and 1999 winners, Olden Times and Golden Snake, both managed to regain the winning thread in the Group One Jean Prat over in France when it was staged over nine furlongs.

Were Feilden winners profitable to follow on their subsequent three runs?
No – 4 wins from 32 runs returned a loss of -£7.45 to a £1 level stake.

Placed runners' subsequent record (three runs):
Runners-up: 3 wins from 36 runs returned a loss of -£29.00 to a £1 level stake.
2007 Salford Mill – Listed Newmarket Stakes, 1997 Panama City - Group Three Chester Vase

Thirds: 0 wins from 20 runs returned a loss of -£20.00 to a £1 level stake.

FUTURE SUCCESS RATING: ★★ ☆ ☆ ☆

NELL GWYN STAKES
April 16, Newmarket – (Group 3, Class 1, 3yo) 7f

Last run	Winner/ Trainer & SP	Draw/ Ran	Age	Wght	PR	Next four runs			
07 Newm 7f 1st Rockfel Stks *Six months*	**Scarlet Runner** J Dunlop 15/2	9/10	3	8-12	62	7th 1,000 Guineas Newm 1m	6th Coronation Stks Ascot 1m	6th Oak Tree Stks Good 7f	8th Sprint Cup Hayd 6f
06 Newm 7f 1st Rockfel Stks *Six months*	**Speciosa** Mrs P Sly 9/1	8/9	3	9-01	71	WON 10/1 **1,000 Guineas** **Newm 1m**	4th Oaks Epsom 1m4f	9th Coronation Stks Ascot 1m	6th Park Stks York 7f
05 Ling 1m 1st Maiden *Six months*	**Karen's Caper** J Gosden 15/2	2/14	3	8-09	64	4th 1,000 Guineas Newm 1m	2nd Coronation Stks York 1m	4th Falmouth Newm 1m	6th Matron Leop 1m
04 Redc 6f 12th 2yo Trophy *Six months*	**Silca's Gift** M Channon 25/1	2/13	3	8-09	65	8th 1,000 Guineas Newm 1m	5th Kilvington Nott 6f	9th Jersey Ascot 7f	9th Summer Stks York 6f
03 Newm 7f 1st Oh So Sharp *Six months*	**Khulood** J Dunlop 15/8F	5/8	3	8-09	60	19th 1,000 Guineas Newm 1m	9th Golden Jubilee Ascot 6f	2nd Summer Stks York 6f	6th Park Stks Donc 7f
02 Newm 7f 3rd Rockfel Stks *Six months*	**Misterah** M Tregoning 9/2	1/10	3	8-09	62	6th 1,000 Guineas Newm 1m	4th Coronation Stks Ascot 1m	5th Falmouth Newm 1m	–
01 Newm 7f 12th Rockfel Stks *Six months*	**Lil's Jessy** J Noseda 20/1	6/14	3	8-09	65	10th Poule 'Pouliches Long 1m	12th Coronation Stks Ascot 1m	8th Falmouth Newm 1m	8th Sceptre Donc 7f
00 Leic 7f 1st Maiden *Six months*	**Petrushka** Sir M Stoute 7/2F	4/13	3	8-09	74	3rd 1,000 Guineas Newm 1m	4th Oaks Epsom 1m4f	WON 11/2 Irish Oaks Curr 1m4f	WON 9/10F Prix Barriere Long 1m2f
99 Newm 7f 2nd Rockfel Stks *Six months*	**Valentine Waltz** J Gosden 7/2F	3/11	3	8-09	73	3rd 1,000 Guineas Newm 1m	WON 43/10 Poule'Pouliches Long 1m	3rd Coronation Stk Ascot 1m	–
98 Newm 7f 3rd Conds Stks *Six months*	**Cloud Castle** C Brittain 33/1	4/7	3	8-09	68	4th 1,000 Guineas Newm 1m	8th Irish 1,000 Guin Curr 1m	4th Oaks Epsom 1m4f	7th Nassau Good 1m2f
97 Leic 7f 3rd Cond Stks *Seven months*	**Reunion** J Hills 8/1	4/10	3	8-09	67	15th 1,000 Guineas Newm 1m	*2nd Conds Stks Kemp 7f	*7th Queen Anne Ascot 1m	*11th Falmouth Newm 1m
96 Donc 6f 1st Doncaster Stks *Six months*	**Thrilling Day** N Graham 20/1	9/11	3	8-09	69	11th Duke of York York 6f	6th Coronation Stks Ascot 1m	WON 12/1 Oak Tree Stks Good 7f	7th Hungerford Newb 7f

12-year median performance rating of the winner: **67** (out of 100)   *(1999 July Course),* *next year*

WINNER'S PROFILE Every winner made their **seasonal reappearance here**, seven of the them had their last run at Newmarket, five in the Rockfel Stakes, of whom two scored.
A **top-three effort last time** can be a bonus, although it paid to **avoid short-priced favourites**, as Sander Camillo and Cape Columbine proved in defeat over the last three years, going off at 4/7 and 15/8 respectively.
Runners trained by either **John Dunlop** or **John Gosden** are respected, the pair having won it twice each.

FUTURE POINTERS Until two years ago, winners of this 1,000 Guineas trial had a miserable record in the race itself, before Speciosa followed up in the Classic, and in the process gave the Nell Gwyn a much needed boost.
One of the best winners, Valentine Waltz, only went down by half-a-length in the 1,000 Guineas before she went on to win the French equivalent, a race that hasn't been oversubscribed by English winners in recent years.
Those that attempted the Coronation Stakes at Royal Ascot came unstuck, six failed, while a further three flopped in the Epsom Oaks, although Petrushka redeemed herself in the 2000 Irish version – the only winner that surprisingly took up that engagement.

Were Nell Gwyn winners profitable to follow on their subsequent three runs?
No – 4 wins from 36 runs returned a loss of -£0.20 to a £1 level stake.

Placed runners' subsequent record (three runs):
Runners-up: 6 wins from 36 runs returned a loss of -£16.45 to a £1 level stake.
2006 Spinning Queen – Listed Eternal Stakes, 2004 Incheni – Listed Ballymacoll Stakes,
1999 Hawriyah – Listed Conqueror Stakes

Thirds: 0 wins from 29 runs returned a loss of -£29.00 to a £1 level stake.

FUTURE SUCCESS RATING: ★ ★ ★ ★ ☆

EUROPEAN FREE HANDICAP
April 16, Newmarket – (Listed race, Class 1, 3yo) 7f

Last run	Winner/ Trainer & SP	Draw/ Ran	Age	Wght	PR	Next four runs			
07 Kemp 1m 2nd Easter Stks *Three weeks*	**Prime Defender** B Hills 5/2F	3/7	3	9-05	70	20th 2,000 Guineas Newm 1m	**WON 11/8F Sandy Lane Stk** Hayd 6f	2nd Cathedral Stks Sali 6f	13th July Cup Newm 6f
06 Redc 6f 1st 2yo Trophy *Six months*	**Misu Bond** B Smart 5/2F	9/8	3	8-13	64	5th 2,000 Guineas Newm 1m	3rd Ballycorus Leop 7f	*6th Chipchase Stks Newc 6f	4th Conds Stks Ches 7f
05 Sand 7f 1st Conds Stks *Eight months*	**Kamakiri** R Hannon 4/1	4/8	3	8-10	64	10th Poule 'Poulains Long 1m	13th Jersey York 7f	3rd Midsummer Stk Wind 1m	12th Lennox Stks Good 7f
04 Newm 7f 5th Tattersall Stks *Six months*	**Brunel** W Haggas 9/1	4/11	3	8-13	72	**WON EvsF Ger 2,000 Guin** Colo 1m	5th St James Palace Ascot 1m	11th Maurice 'Gheest Deau 7f	6th Celebration Mile Good 1m
03 Newm 7f 15th Dewhurst *Six months*	**Indian Haven** P D'Arcy 9/2	1/6	3	9-01	70	14th 2,000 Guineas Newm 1m	**WON 8/1 Ire 2,000 Guin** Curr 1m	11th St James Palace Ascot 1m	11th Champion Stks Newm 1m2f
02 Newb 7f UR Horris Hill *Six months*	**Twilight Blues** B Meehan 6/1	5/8	3	9-05	67	5th 2,000 Guineas Newm 1m	11th Jersey Ascot 7f	9th July Cup Newm 6f	4th Maurice 'Gheest Deauv 7f
01 Newb 7f 1st Horris Hill *Six months*	**Clearing** J Gosden 7/4F	1/10	3	9-06	68	2nd Poule 'Poulains Long 1m	-	-	-
00 Newb 7f 2nd Horris Hill *Six months*	**Cape Town** R Hannon 10/3	1/8	3	9-02	72	12th 2,000 Guineas Newm 1m	3rd Ire 2,000 Guin Curr 1m	11th St James's Ascot 1m	2nd Hungerford Newb 7f
99 Newm 6f 2nd Middle Park *Six months*	**Bertolini** J Gosden 5/1	6/6	3	9-07	67	9th Poule 'Poulains Long 1m	3rd Jersey Ascot 7f	3rd July Cup Newm 6f	3rd Maurice 'Gheest Deauv 7f
98 Newm 7f 4th Dewhurst *Six months*	**Desert Prince** D Loder 7/1	7/9	3	9-05	74	3rd Poule 'Poulains Long 1m	**WON 8/1 Ire 2,000 Guin** Curr 1m	2nd St James Palace Ascot 1m	**WON 41/10 Prix du Moulin** Long 1m
97 Newm 7f 3rd Horris Hill *Six months*	**Hidden Meadow** I Balding 5/1JF	3/11	3	9-03	70	13th 2,000 Guineas Newm 1m	**WON 6/5F Conds Stks** Epsom 7f	10th Queen Anne Ascot 1m	4th Conds Stks Newb 7f
96 Redc 6f 2nd 2YO Trophy *Six months*	**Cayman Kai** R Hannon 7/2JF	4/8	3	9-07	71	4th Poule 'Poulains Long 1m	5th St James Palace Ascot 1m	8th Sussex Good 1m	*5th Abernant Stks Newm 6f

12-year median performance rating of the winner: **69** (out of 100)   *(1999 July Course), *next year*

WINNER'S PROFILE Every winner between 1997-2004 came via either **Newbury or Newmarket**, although only Bertolini had ever won at HQ, while 11 arrived with plenty of experience and **raced at least three times as a juvenile** – Prime Defender last year broke that tradition with a recent spin beforehand. Two other winners either won or finished runner-up in the valuable Two-Year-Old Trophy at Redcar, and three-times winning trainer **Richard Hannon** was responsible for one of them, while **John Gosden** won it twice, both times with runners from the **first three in the betting**.

FUTURE POINTERS This is often viewed as a trial for the 2,000 Guineas back here the following month, but it has been a while since the winner followed up, an accolade that fell to Mystiko back in 1991.
Eight winners of the Free Handicap failed since, while five flopped in the French version since 1996, but one route that proved effective was the Irish 2,000 Guineas. The interesting angle here was that only three winners ran at The Curragh over the past 12 years, which resulted in two winners and a third – Indian Haven and Desert Prince in 2003 and 1998 respectively. Only Brunel, in 2004, took up an engagement in the German 2,000 Guineas, which proved worthwhile, and in the process became the only Free Handicap scorer that followed up next time out – which may interest layers.

Were European Free Handicap winners profitable to follow on their subsequent three runs?
No – 5 wins from 34 runs returned a loss of -£9.42 to a £1 level stake.

Placed runners' subsequent record (three runs):
Runners-up: 5 wins from 34 runs a loss of -£13.80 to a £1 level stake.
2007 Tobosa – Silver Bowl Handicap, 2006 Jeremy – King Charles II Stakes, Jersey Stakes

Thirds: 2 wins from 25 runs returned a loss of -£11.50 to a £1 level stake.

FUTURE SUCCESS RATING: ★ ★ ☆ ☆ ☆

ABERNANT STAKES
April 17, Newmarket – (Listed, Class 1, 3yo+) 6f

Last run	Winner/ Trainer & SP	Draw/ Ran	Age	Wght	PR	Next four runs			
07 Ascot 7f 2nd Jersey Stks Ten months	Asset R Hannon 11/4F	5/12	4	9-04	80	3rd Golden Jubilee Ascot 6f	6th July Cup Newm 6f	2nd Lennox Stks Good 7f	6th Sprint Cup Hayd 6f
06 Newm 6f 4th Boadicea Stks Six months	Paradisle Isle C Wall 14/1	16/17	5	8-13	71	20th Palace House Newm 5f	WON 6/1 Cecil Frail Stks Hayd 6f	3rd Summer Stks York 6f	8th Queensferry Stks Ches 6f
05 Donc 6f 5th Cammidge Two weeks	Quito D Chapman 14/1	3/10	8	9-08	75	2nd Spring Trophy Hayd 7f	WON 15/2 Hambleton Hcp York 7f	4th Leisure Stks Wind 6f	5th John of Gaunt Hayd 7f
04 Newm 7f 3rd Challenge Stks Six months	Arakan Sir Michael Stoute 5/2F	5/8	4	9-04	79	3rd Duke of York York 6f	2nd Greenlands Stks Curr 6f	12th Queen Anne Ascot 1m	WON 7/4F Criterion Stks Newm 7f
03 Donc 6f 4th Cammidge One month	Needwood Blade B McMahon 11/4	5/7	5	9-08	80	WON 9/4F Palace House Newm 5f	13th Duke of York York 6f	13th Golden Jubilee Ascot 6f	7th July Cup Newm 6f
02 Kemp 6f 1st Conds Stks Three weeks	Reel Buddy R Hannon 5/1	10/9	4	9-03	76	WON 11/8F Spring Trophy Hayd 7f	6th Duke of York York 6f	10th July Cup Newm 6f	3rd Sussex Good 1m
01 Long 5f 9th Abbaye Six months	Primo Valentino P Harris 9/1	19/23	4	9-09	72	20th Cork & Orrery Ascot 6f	17th July Cup Newm 6f	-	-
00 Newb 5f 5th Showcase Hcp One week	Cretan Gift N Littmoden 14/1	1/12	9	9-03	71	4th Leicestershire St Donc 7f	6th Rated Hcp Newm 6f	5th Conds Stks Yarm 6f	7th Cork & Orrery Ascot 6f
99 Newm 6f 1st Bentinck Stks Six months	Bold Edge R Hannon 9/1	9/13	6	9-07	81	14th Duke of York York 6f	WON 16/1 Cork & Orrery Ascot 6f	2nd July Cup Newm 6f	9th King George Good 5f
98 Donc 6f 3rd Cammidge Three weeks	Tedburrow E Alston 10/1	5/10	6	9-02	74	5th Palace House Newm 5f	8th Duke of York York 6f	18th King's Stand Ascot 5f	WON 9/1 City Wall Stks Ches 5f
97 Kemp 6f 1st Conds Stks Three weeks	Monassib E Dunlop 9/4F	3/8	6	9-02	75	WON 6/5F Conds Stks Good 6f	WON N/O Group 3 Bade 6f	4th Cork & Orrery Ascot 6f	WON 61/10 Group 3 Deau 6f
96 Kemp 6f 1st Handicap Two weeks	Passion For Life G Lewis 11/4F	9/13	3	8-05	70	6th Duke of York York 6f	WON N/O Group 3 Bade 6f	6th Group 3 Long 7f	13th Group 3 Hamb 6f

12-year median performance rating of the winner: **75** (out of 100)

WINNER'S PROFILE Nine winners arrived having either raced here last backend, won at Kempton, or blew the cobwebs away in the Cammidge Trophy at Doncaster.
All bar one **already scored over the trip**, while the same number boasted **Newmarket experience** – four C&D winners – and the majority were **officially rated in excess of 100**. Those drawn **middle to high drawn** have been favoured – more so in large fields – while trainer **Richard Hannon** took his tally in this period to three last year.

FUTURE POINTERS This Listed sprint has attracted quality runners who were capable of better and winners were worthy of following – nine of the last 12 scored again on at least one of their next four outings.
One of the best winners, Needwood Blade, took the Group Three Palace House back here, while Bold Edge won the Group Two Cork and Orrery (now Golden Jubilee) at Royal Ascot after he flopped in the Duke of York, a race that caught out five Abernant winners.
Both the 1997 and 1996 victors found Group Three victories over this trip in Baden Baden, while the runners-up from the Abernant added support to the solidity of the race – two July Cup winners emerged – and it may be time to grant this sprint Group status if subsequent results continue.

Were Abernant winners profitable to follow on their subsequent three runs?
Yes – 8 wins from 35 runs returned a **profit of +£7.32** to a £1 level stake.

Placed runners' subsequent record (three runs):
Runners-up: 6 wins from 36 runs returned a **profit of +£27.00** to a £1 level stake.
2007 Assertive – Leisure Stakes, 2006 Les Arcs – Golden Jubilee Stakes, July Cup,
2004 Frizzante – Palace House Stakes, July Cup, 1996 Iktamal – Haydock Sprint Cup,

Thirds: 6 wins from 33 runs returned a loss of -£0.34 to a £1 level stake.
2005 The Kiddykid – Duke of York Stakes

FUTURE SUCCESS RATING: ★ ★ ★ ★ ★

CRAVEN STAKES
April 17, Newmarket – (Group 3, Class 1, 3yo) 1m

Last run	Winner/ Trainer & SP	Draw/ Ran	Age	Wght	PR	Next four runs			
07 Newm 7f 7th Dewhurst *Six months*	**Adagio** Sir M Stoute 5/4F	2/8	3	8-12	75	12th 2,000 Guineas Newm 1m	4th Dante York 1m2f	7th Grade 2 Belm 1m1f	3rd Stakes Aque 1m
06 Newm 7f 2nd Tattersall Stks *Six months*	**Killybegs** B Hills 9/2	8/9	3	8-12	71	11th 2,000 Guineas Newm 1m	4th International Stk Curr 1m	10th Sovereign Stks Sali 1m	2nd Celebration Mile Good 1m
05 Long 7f 5th Prix Lagardere *Six months*	**Democratic Deficit** J Bolger 12/1	4/8	3	8-12	70	6th 2,000 Guineas Newm 1m	3rd 2,000 Irish Guin Curr 1m	**WON 8/13F Ballycorus Stks Leop 7f**	3rd International Stk Curr 1m
04 Newm 7f 3rd Dewhurst *Six months*	**Haafhd** B Hills 10/3	2/5	3	8-09	79	**WON 11/2 2,000 Guineas Newm 1m**	4th St James Palace Ascot 1m	9th Sussex Good 1m	**WON 12/1 Champion Stks Newm 1m2f**
03 Newm 7f 3rd Tattersall Stks *Six months*	**Hurricane Alan** R Hannon 9/1	2/7	3	8-09	69	7th 2,000 Guineas Newm 1m	6th St James Palace Ascot 1m	5th Lennox Stks Good 7f	2nd Thoroughbred St Good 1m
02 Donc 7f 1st Maiden *Eight months*	**King Of Happiness** Sir M Stoute 9/4F	4/6	3	8-09	77	9th 2,000 Guineas Newm 1m	8th St James Palace Ascot 1m	2nd Criterion Newm 7f	*9th Dubai Duty Free Nad Al 1m1f
01 Newm 7f 8th Dewhurst *Six months*	**King's Ironbridge** R Hannon 12/1	1/8	3	8-09	70	10th 2,000 Guineas Newm 1m	6th Lennox Stks Good 7f	4th Sovereign Stks Sali 1m	*3rd Doncaster Mile Donc 1m
00 Newb 7f 1st Horris Hill *Six months*	**Umistim** R Hannon 8/1	1/6	3	8-09	74	6th 2,000 Guineas Newm 1m	5th Heron Stks Kemp 1m	2nd Jersey Stks Ascot 7f	7th Hungerford Stks Newb 7f
99 Sand 7f 2nd Solario Stks *Eight months*	**Compton Admiral** G Butler 13/2	7/7	3	8-09	72	13th 2,000 Guineas Newm 1m	8th Derby Epsom 1m4f	**WON 20/1 Eclipse Sand 1m2f**	5th Juddmonte Int York 1m2f
98 Newm 7f 1st Dewhurst *Six months*	**Xaar** A Fabre 8/11F	6/6	3	8-12	82	4th 2,000 Guineas Newm 1m	2nd Group 2 Deau 1m2f	3rd Irish Champion Leop 1m2f	*3rd Prince of Wales' Ascot 1m2f
97 Newb 7f 1st Horris Hill *Six months*	**Desert Story** Sir M Stoute 5/2F	4/8	3	8-12	77	6th 2,000 Guineas Newm 1m	2nd Dante York 1m2f	2nd Select Stks Good 1m2f	5th Group 2 Long 1m2f
96 Donc 1m 1st R Post Trophy *Six months*	**Beauchamp King** J Dunlop 9/2	2/5	3	9-00	75	5th 2,000 Guineas Newm 1m	3rd 2,000 Irish Guin Curr 1m	3rd St James' Palace Ascot 1m	7th Eclipse Sand 1m2f

12-year median performance rating of the winner: **74** (out of 100)   *next year*

WINNER'S PROFILE All 12 winners **made their reappearance here**, 10 had their **final stop at either Doncaster, Newbury or Newmarket**, and races like the Dewhurst, Tattersall and Horris Hill Stakes have provided key stepping stones. A Group penalty hasn't been too much of a burden, while an **official rating of 110 or above** can be a bonus. Trainers **Richard Hannon**, **Barry Hills** and **Sir Michael Stoute** have shared eight winners.

FUTURE POINTERS A 2,000 Guineas trial in which the winner has traditionally booked his ticket for the Classic a fortnight later, however, rarely has it been a winning one.
Since 1990, only Tirol and Haafhd completed the Newmarket double as the latter stood out as one of the best recent winners with an above-par performance rating (PR), which has left average scorers as ones to swerve.
Haafhd also managed to land the Champion Stakes back here over a mile-and-a-quarter, the same trip over which Compton Admiral later won the Eclipse in 1999.

Were Craven winners profitable to follow on their subsequent three runs?
No – 3 wins from 36 runs returned a loss of -£3.88 to a £1 level stake.

Placed runners' subsequent record (three runs):
Runners-up: 7 wins from 33 runs returned a loss of -£5.90 to a £1 level stake.
2005 Rob Roy – Group Three Joel Stakes, 2000 King's Best – 2,000 Guineas, 1998 Gulland – Chester Vase

Thirds: 2 wins from 15 runs returned a loss of -£8.75 to a £1 level stake.
2001 Nayef – Rose of Lancaster Stakes

FUTURE SUCCESS RATING: ★ ★ ☆ ☆ ☆

EARL OF SEFTON STAKES
April 17, Newmarket – (Group 3, Listed, 4yo+) 1m1f

Last run	Winner/ Trainer & SP	Draw/ Ran	Age	Wght	PR	Next four runs			
07 Long 1m2f 2nd _Seven months_	**Manduro** Group 2 A Fabre 6/4F	5/9	5	8-12	85	**WON 8/13F** Prix d'Ispahan Long 1m1f	**WON 15/8F** Prince of Wales Ascot 1m2f	**WON 4/5F** Jacques 'Marois Deau 1m	**WON 4/11F** Prix Foy Long 1m4f
06 Newm 1m 1st _Six months_	**Notnowcato** Handicap Sir M Stoute 5/2	5/9	4	8-12	80	**WON 5/4F** Brigadier Gerard Sand 1m2f	5th Prince of Wales Ascot 1m2f	2nd Eclipse Sand 1m2f	**WON 8/1** Juddmonte Int York 1m2f
05 Newm 1m2f 4th _Six months_	**Norse Dancer** Champion Stks D Elsworth 10/3F	2/10	5	8-13	77	5th Sandown Mile Sand 1m	5th Tatts Gold Cup Curr 1m3f	6th Prince of Wales York 1m2f	2nd King George VI Ascot 1m4f
04 Donc 1m 2nd _Three weeks_	**Gateman** Doncaster Mile M Johnston 3/1	3/6	7	8-13	75	2nd Sandown Mile Sand 1m	11th Lockinge Newb 1m	3rd Diomed Stks Epsom 1½m	**WON 5/2F** Midsummer Stk Wind 1m
03 Newb 1m 3rd _Eleven months_	**Olden Times** Lockinge J Dunlop 5/2JF	5/7	5	8-10	78	3rd Lockinge Newb 1m	4th Prince of Wales Ascot 1m2f	4th Eclipse Sand 1m2f	13th Arlington Million Arli 1m2f
02 Newm 1m2f 4th _Five months_	**Indian Creek** James Seymour D Elsworth 11/1	10/11	4	8-10	76	6th Tatts Gold Cup Curr 1m3f	2nd Prince of Wales Ascot 1m2f	5th Eclipse Sand 1m2f	4th Juddmonte Int York 1m2f
01 Donc 1m 1st _One month_	**Right Wing** Doncaster Mile J Dunlop 6/1	6/6	7	8-13	75	5th Sandown Mile Sand 1m	4th Scottish Classic Ayr 1m2f	**WON 5/1** Darley Stks Newm 1m1f	6th Ben Marshall Newm 1m
00 Newm 1m1f 1st _Six months_	**Indian Lodge** Darley Stks Mrs A Perrett 10/1	9/11	4	8-10	80	**WON 9/4F** Sandown Mile Sand 1m	3rd Lockinge Newb 1m	7th Queen Anne Ascot 1m	**WON 113/10** Prix du Moulin Long 1m
99 Kemp 1m1f 1st _Two weeks_	**Shiva** Maiden H Cecil 7/1	1/10	4	8-07	74	**WON 10/3** Tatts Gold Cup Curr 1m3f	7th Prince of Wales Ascot 1m2f	2nd Champion Stks Newm 1m2f	*7th Earl of Sefton Newm 1mf
98 Taby 1m4f 10th _Seven months_	**Apprehension** Group 3 D Loder 16/1	1/7	4	8-10	70	5th Gordon Richards Sand 1m2f	7th Conds Stks Newm 1m2f	4th Beeswing Stks Newc 7f	**6th Handicap Nad Al 1m2f
97 Newm 1m 1st _Five months_	**Ali-Royal** Ben Marshall H Cecil 11/4F	6/11	4	8-10	75	3rd Gordon Richards Sand 1m2f	2nd Lockinge Newb 1m	3rd Queen Anne Ascot 1m	**WON 9/4** Conds Stks York 1m
96 Long 1m4f 13th _Six months_	**Luso** Arc de Triomphe C Brittain 14/1	1/9	4	9-04	78	2nd Prix Ganay Long 1m3f	**WON N/O** Group 2 Capa 1m	2nd Premio di Milano Siro 1m4f	6th King George VI Ascot 1m4f

12-year median performance rating of the winner: **77** (out of 100)   _(1999 July Course), *next year **two years_

WINNER'S PROFILE The last 10 winners finished in the **first four last time out**, four arrived via Newmarket, while the majority were **officially rated 110 or higher**.
Notnowcato was only rated 101 and was also the only winner this century not to have **Pattern experience** – five of the last six finished in the top-four of a Group One event.
Trainers **Henry Cecil**, **John Dunlop** and **David Elsworth** have all landed the Earl of Sefton twice.

FUTURE POINTERS An event to be taken seriously as a springboard for better races later in the year, with recent future Group One winners Manduro and Notnowcato adding to it's rich history. Manduro last year achieved what Notnowcato and four other winners were unable to, and win the Prince of Wales's at Royal Ascot. However, Notnowcato did land the Group Two Brigadier Gerard Stakes, while Indian Lodge in 2000 also followed up at Sandown – unlike five others at the Esher venue, and runners-up actually have a better record in the Sandown Mile (_see below_). Another race that proved advisable to swerve was the Lockinge Stakes at Newbury – four failed.

Were Earl of Sefton winners profitable to follow on their subsequent three runs?
No – 8 wins from 36 runs returned a loss of -£12.88 to a £1 level stake.

Placed runners' subsequent record (three runs):
Runners-up: 8 wins from 34 runs returned a loss of -£7.85 to a £1 level stake.
2005 Hurricane Alan – Sandown Mile, 2003 Desert Deer – Sandown Mile, 1998 Almushtarak – Sandown Mile, 1997 Wixim – Sandown Mile

Thirds: 7 wins from 21 runs returned a **profit of +£12.50** to a £1 level stake.
2005 Valixir – Prix d'Ispahan, Queen Anne Stakes, 1996 First Island – Prince of Wales's Stakes

FUTURE SUCCESS RATING: ★ ★ ★ ☆ ☆

JOHN PORTER STAKES
April 19, Newbury – (Group 3, Class 1, 4yo+) 1m4f

Last run	Winner/ Trainer & SP	Draw/ Ran	Age	Wght	PR	Next four runs			
07 Sha 1m1f 5th *Four months*	**Maraahel** Hong Kong Vase Sir M Stoute 9/4F	7/9	6	9-03	80	**WON 4/6F** **Huxley Stks** Ches 1m2f	3rd Coronation Cup Epsom 1m4f	**WON 10/3** **Hardwicke Stks** Ascot 1m4f	3rd King George VI Ascot 1m4f
06 Newb 1m1f 4th *Six months*	**Mubtaker** St Simon Stks M Tregoning 9/1	11/11	9	9-01	77	5th Ormonde Stks Ches 1m5f	6th Henry II Sand 2m	-	-
05 Kemp 1m2f 1st *Three weeks*	**Day Flight** Magnolia Stks J Gosden 9/4F	6/13	4	8-11	78	**WON 85/40** **Ormonde Stks** Ches 1m5f	2nd Princess of Wales Newm 1m4f	**WON 3/1JF** **St Simon Stks** Newb 1m4f	2nd Serlby Stks Donc 1m4f
04 Newb 1m4f 3rd *Six months*	**Dubai Success** St Simon Stks B Hills 10/1	3/17	4	8-11	73	4th Jockey Club Stk Newm 1m4f	8th Coronation Cup Epsom 1m4f	2nd Curragh Cup Curr 1m6f	2nd Geoffrey Freer Newb 1m5f
03 Newb 1m4f 2nd *Six months*	**Warrsan** St Simon Stks C Brittain 5/1	1/9	5	8-12	77	**WON 12/1** **Jockey Club St** Newm 1m4f	2nd Yorkshire Cup York 1m6f	**WON 9/2** **Coronation Cup** Epsom 1m4f	2nd Premio di Milano Siro 1m4f
02 Sha 1m4f 10th *Four months*	**Zindabad** Hong Kong Vase M Johnston 7/2	4/10	6	8-12	80	4th Jockey Club Stk Newm 1m4f	**WON 2/1** **Yorkshire Cup** York 1m6f	3rd Coronation Cup Epsom 1m4f	**WON 2/1** **Hardwicke Stks** Ascot 1m4f
01 Donc 1m4f 1st *One month*	**Lucido** Doncaster Shield J Dunlop 9/4F	1/13	5	8-12	74	6th Hardwicke Stks Ascot 1m4f	6th Princess of Wales' Newm 1m4f	*3rd Listed Muni 1m2f	**6th Listed Stra 1m3f
00 Nad 1m4f 15th *One month*	**Yavana's Pace** Sheema Classic M Johnston 7/1	11/11	8	9-01	71	8th Jockey Club Stk Newm 1m4f	4th Ormonde Stks Ches 1m5f	3rd Group 2 Long 2m	2nd Hardwicke Stks Ascot 1m4f
99 Donc 1m6f 4th *Seven months*	**Sadian** St Leger J Dunlop 5/1	1/11	4	8-11	70	**WON 2/1F** **Ormonde Stks** Ches 1m5f	7th Hardwicke Stks Ascot 1m4f	3rd Geoffrey Freer Newb 1m5f	4th Group 2 Deau 1m5f
98 Sha 1m4f 2nd *Four months*	**Posidonas** Hong Kong Vase P Cole 5/1	1/12	6	8-12	72	6th Coronation Cup Epsom 1m4f	**WON 15/2** **Hardwicke Stks** Ascot 1m4f	3rd Arc Trial Newb 1m3f	14th Arc de Triomphe Long 1m4f
97 Newb 1m4f 4th *Six months*	**Whitewater Affair** St Simon Stks Sir M Stoute 20/1	13/13	4	8-08	71	3rd Yorkshire Cup York 1m6f	3rd Hardwicke Stks Ascot 1m4f	**WON 13/10** **Group 2** Deau 1m6f	2nd Yorkshire Oaks York 1m4f
96 Ascot 1m4f 3rd *Six months*	**Spout** Princess Royal R Charlton 6/1	4/9	4	8-08	70	6th Curragh Cup Curr 1m4f	**WON 13/2** **Lanc'shire Oaks** Hayd 1m4f	3rd Group 2 Deau 1m6f	2nd Sun Chariot Newm 1m2f

12-year median performance rating of the winner: **74** (out of 100)   *(2000 Haydock), *next year *two years*

WINNER'S PROFILE The majority **made their reappearance** here having been off the track at least four months, and seven ran in either the St Simon Stakes over course and distance or the Hong Kong Vase at Sha Tin. Of the three to have already had a recent spin, two were successful. Only Whitewater Affair arrived here without a **distance victory** to her name, becoming also the second successive filly to land this following Spout in 1996.
It paid to stick with the best performers **officially rated 110 and above**, while 11 of the last 12 winners emerged form the **first three in the betting**.
Trainers **John Dunlop, Mark Johnston and Sir Michael Stoute** all landed this twice, although Johnston boasts the best strike-rate having sent out only six runners.

FUTURE POINTERS This Group Three traditionally draws a competitive field that has been a good pointer for some of the upcoming middle-distance Pattern events and victors consistently found the winner's enclosure soon after Newbury. The Ormonde Stakes at Chester was kind to John Porter winners with two following up from four runners – last year's winner Maraahel also scored at Chester in the Huxley Stakes – while two runners-up were also successful in the Ormonde *(see below)*. The Hardwicke Stakes at Royal Ascot is another popular route, with three scoring from six runners, including one of the best winners, Zindabad, who also took the Yorkshire Cup.

Were John Porter winners profitable to follow on their subsequent three runs?
Yes – 11 wins from 35 runs returned a **profit of +19.91** to a £1 level stake.

Placed runners' subsequent record (three runs):
Runners-up: 5 wins from 36 runs returned a loss of -£22.97 to a £1 level stake.
2004 Gamut – Jockey Club Stakes, Grand Prix Saint-Cloud, 2003 Asian Heights – Ormonde Stakes, 2002 St Expedit – Ormonde Stakes

Thirds: 5 wins from 35 runs returned a loss of -£19.19 to a £1 level stake.
2006 Maraahel – Hardwicke.

FUTURE SUCCESS RATING: ★ ★ ★ ★ ☆

FRED DARLING STAKES
April 19, Newbury – (Group 3, Class 1, 3yo Fillies) 7f

Last run	Winner/ Trainer & SP	Draw/ Ran	Age	Wght	PR	Next four runs			
07 Hami 6f 1st Maiden *Ten months*	**Majestic Roi** M Channon 25/1	3/14	3	9-00	60	2nd Group 2 Chan 1m	7th Coronation Stks Ascot 1m	5th Oak Tree Stks Good 7f	4th Sceptre Stks Donc 7f
06 Newm 1m 3rd Meon Valley Mile *Seven months*	**Nasheej** R Hannon 6/4F	6/11	3	9-00	61	3rd 1,000 Guineas Newm 1m	14th Irish 1,000 Guin Curr 1m	3rd Coronation Stks Ascot 1m	5th Falmouth Stks Newm 1m
05 Newm 7f 2nd Rockfel Stks *Six months*	**Penkenna Princess** R Beckett 7/2	9/11	3	9-00	54	16th 1,000 Guineas Newm 1m	2nd Irish 1,000 Guin Curr 1m	5th Falmouth Stks Newm 1m	7th Nassau Stks Good 1m2f
04 Newm 6f 2nd Cheveley Park *Six months*	**Majestic Desert** M Channon 6/4F	6/8	3	9-00	71	9th 1,000 Guineas Newm 1m	7th Irish 1,000 Guin Curr 1m	2nd Coronation Stks Ascot 1m	2nd Brownstown Stks Leop 7f
03 Newm 6f 1st Maiden *Five months*	**Tante Rose** B Hills 6/1	10/12	3	9-00	64	16th 1,000 Guineas Newm 1m	6th Jersey Stks Ascot 7f	8th July Cup Newm 6f	3rd Lennox Stks Good 7f
02 Newm 6f 1st Cheveley Park *Six months*	**Queen's Logic** M Channon 1/3F	4/8	3	9-00	68	-	-	-	-
01 Siro 1m 10th Group 3 *Six months*	**Rolly Polly** H Cecil 6/1	1/10	3	9-00	63	8th Poule 'Pouliches Long 1m	8th Grade 1 Sant 7f	-	-
00 Newb 7f 2nd Listed *Six months*	**Iftiraas** J Dunlop 7/1	9/9	3	9-00	62	5th Poule 'Pouliches Long 1m	6th Coronation Stks Ascot 1m	9th Falmouth Stks Newm 1m	3rd Prix d'Astarte Deau 1m
99 Newm 7f 7th Rockfel Stks *Six months*	**Wince** H Cecil 9/2JF	4/11	3	9-00	72	WON 4/1F 1,000 Guineas Newm 1m	5th Irish 1,000 Guin Curr 1m	-	-
98 Curr 6f 3rd Tatts Stks *Eight months*	**Daunting Lady** R Hannon 9/2	7/7	3	9-00	68	6th 1,000 Guineas Newm 1m	8th Surrey Stks Epsom 7f	7th Coronation Stks Ascot 1m	7th Listed Ovre 7f
97 Long 1m 11th Marcel Boussac *Six months*	**Dance Parade** P Cole 16/1	9/10	3	9-00	71	12th 1,000 Guineas Newm 1m	*6th Group 2 Sha 7f	-	-
96 Ascot 1m 1st Filles' Mile *Seven months*	**Bosra Sham** H Cecil 2/9F	2/9	3	9-00	75	WON 10/11F 1,000 Guineas Newm 1m	2nd Q Elizabeth II Ascot 1m	WON 9/4 Champion Stks Newm 1m2f	*WON 1/5F Brigadier Gerard Sand 1m2f

12-year median performance rating of the winner: 66 (out of 100)   *next year*

WINNER'S PROFILE Every winner made their **reappearance here** and six of the last nine were **last seen at Newmarket**, two came via the Cheveley Park Stakes. Two of the three winners to have finished out of the frame previously both came in events abroad.
Last year's winner – along with Tante Rose in 2003 – bucked the trends as they arrived having never run in a Pattern event and were officially rated below 100, unlike the majority of winners. Majestic Roi was also unfancied at 25/1, but it has traditionally paid to stick with the **first four or five in the betting**.
Trainer **Mick Channon** developed a liking for the event having won it three times in the last six years, while **Henry Cecil** and **Richard Hannon** have provided five between them.

FUTURE POINTERS Frowned upon by some as a reliable 1,000 Guineas Trial, the Fred Darling has struggled in recent years to provide the winner of that Classic as the standard has marginally declined – demonstrated by their performance ratings (PR). However, two quality winners emerged pre-Millennium in Wince and Bosra Sham, who both secured Classic glory. The resurgent **Henry Cecil** trained both and it could prove the best policy to follow his winners from here – instead of the Channon/Hannon winners – especially as the Newmarket handler enjoyed a decent 2007 and may have some ammunition to fire with. It's also worth pointing out that **John Dunlop** had a few above-par winners of the Fred Darling in the nineties that went onto 1,000 Guineas fame in Salsabil and Shadayid.

Were Fred Darling winners profitable to follow on their subsequent three runs?
No – 3 wins from 30 returned a loss of -£19.84 to a £1 level stake.

Placed runners' subsequent record (three runs):
Runners-up: 1 win from 32 runs returned a loss of -£23.00 to a £1 level stake.
2007 Indian Ink – Coronation Stakes

Thirds: 3 wins from 33 runs returned a **profit of +20.10** to a £1 level stake (two winners at 16/1 and 30/1).
2000 Crimplene – Irish 1,000 Guineas, 1996 Sil Sila – Prix de Diane Hermes (French Oaks)

FUTURE SUCCESS RATING: ★ ★ ☆ ☆ ☆

GREENHAM STAKES
April 19, Newbury – (Group 3, Class 1, 3yo Colts & Geldings) 7f

Last run	Winner/ Trainer & SP	Draw/ Ran	Age	Wght	PR	Next four runs			
07 Ascot 6f 2nd Coventry Stks *Ten months*	**Major Cadeaux** R Hannon 10/3	6/6	3	9-00	71	6th 2,000 Guineas Newm 1m	2nd Criterion Stks Newm 7f	5th Maurice 'Gheest Deau 7f	-
06 Newm 7f 4th Dewhurst Stks *Six months*	**Red Clubs** B Hills 6/4F	2/5	3	9-00	76	12th 2,000 Guineas Newm 1m	6th Jersey Stks Ascot 7f	12th July Cup Newm 6f	2nd Phoenix Sprint Curr 6f
05 Curr 7f 1st Loughbrown Stk *Two weeks*	**Indesatchel** D Wachman 11/10F	2/9	3	9-00	75	**WON 4/6F** **Tetrarch Stks Curr 7f**	2nd Poule 'Poulains Long 1m	8th St James Palace York 1m	9th Renaissance Stk Curr 6f
04 Newb 1m 1st Maiden *Six months*	**Salford City** D Elsworth 10/3	11/10	3	9-00	72	6th 2,000 Guineas Newm 1m	5th Derby Epsom 1m4f	9th Eclipse Sand 1m2f	3rd Claimer Holl 1m2f
03 Newm 7f 2nd Tatts Stks *Six months*	**Muqbil** J Dunlop 5/1	3/8	3	9-00	68	12th 2,000 Guineas Newm 1m	2nd Select Stks Good 1m2f	3rd Joel Stks Newm 1m	4th Darley Stks Newm 1m1f
02 Kemp 1m 3rd Easter Stks *Three weeks*	**Redback** R Hannon 5/1	10/10	3	9-00	67	3rd 2,000 Guineas Newm 1m	9th Poule 'Poulains Long 1m	8th Jersey Stks Ascot 7f	2nd Lennox Stks Good 7f
01 Newb 6f 1st Maiden *Six months*	**Munir** B Hills 8/1	7/7	3	9-00	70	6th 2,000 Guineas Newm 1m	7th Jersey Stks Ascot 7f	2nd Lennox Stks Good 7f	4th Celebration Mile Good 1m
00 Long 1m 2nd Grand Criterium *Six months*	**Barathea Guest** G Margarson 13/2	5/7	3	9-00	66	3rd 2,000 Guineas Newm 1m	4th Irish 2,000 Guin Curr 1m	8th Derby Epsom 1m4f	5th Group 1 Muni 1m2f
99 Newm 7f 4th Dewhurst Stks *Six months*	**Enrique** H Cecil 5/4F	5/7	3	9-00	70	2nd 2,000 Guineas Newm 1m	2nd Irish 2,000 Guin Curr 1m	2nd Jersey Stks Ascot 7f	5th Sussex Good 1m
98 Newb 7f 3rd Horris Hill Stks *Six months*	**Victory Note** P Chapple-Hyam 7/1	1/6	3	9-00	73	**WON 25/1** **Poule 'Poulains Long 1m**	4th St James Palace Ascot 1m	10th Sussex Good 1m	8th Challenge Stks Newm 7f
97 Newm 7f 1st Maiden *Eight months*	**Yalaietanee** Sir M Stoute 5/1	3/6	3	9-00	69	4th Poule 'Poulains Long 1m	4th Irish 2,000 Guin Curr 1m	11th Duty Free Cup Newb 7f	**3rd Stakes Nad Al 7f
96 Newm 7f 2nd Dewhurst Stks	**Danehill Dancer** N Callaghan EvensF	8/8	3	9-00	74	6th 2,000 Guineas Newm 1m	9th Poule 'Poulains Long 1m	5th July Cup Newm 6f	3rd Maurice 'Gheest Deau 7f

12-year median performance rating of the winner: **71** (out of 100)   *(2000 Newmarket), ** next two years*

WINNER'S PROFILE A **top-four outing last time** has been vital, eight winners were last seen either here or at Newmarket during the autumn, while nine victors had already experienced Group company as juveniles. Another statistic which helped eliminate a few was that every winner bar one since 1991 boasted **either a course victory or distance win** to their name.
Fancied runners can't be dismissed as every winner came from the **first four in the betting**, while trainers **Barry Hills** and **Richard Hannon** landed the prize twice each from 10 and nine runners respectively.

FUTURE POINTERS As a pointer towards the 2,000 Guineas, the Greenham had little impact over the past 20 seasons. After landing last year's renewal, Major Cadeaux was predictably cut into single-figure odds to triumph at Newmarket before finishing a disappointing sixth, and though three winners went on to be placed since 1996, the Greenham winner is best avoided in the near future.
The one shining light amongst the Greenham Hall of Fame was Peter Chapple-Hyam's Victory Note, who managed to land the French Guineas in 1998. Considering the trainer's other winner of this event, Turtle Island, was a creditable runner-up in France before landing the Irish equivalent in 1994, a note should be made of the 2008 winner should it emerge from this resurgent yard.

Were Greenham winners profitable to follow on their subsequent three runs?
No – 2 wins from 36 runs returned a loss of -£8.33 to a £1 level stake.

Placed runners' subsequent record (three runs):
Runners-up: 7 wins from 36 runs returned a loss of -£10.06 to a £1 level stake.
2004 Fokine – King Charles II, 2003 Zafeen – St James's Palace Stakes, 2000 Distant Music – Park Stakes

Thirds: 4 wins from 15 runs returned a loss of -£1.13 to a £1 level stake.
2005 Galeota – Surrey Stakes, 2004 So Will I – Carnarvon Stakes, 1996 Tagula – Supreme Stakes

FUTURE SUCCESS RATING: ★ ★ ★ ★ ★

SPRING CUP

April 19, Newbury – (Heritage Handicap, Class 2, 4yo+) 1m

Last run	Winner/ Trainer & SP	Draw/ Ran	Age	Wght	PR	Next four runs			
07 Wind 1m2f 8th Tote Hcp *Five months*	**Pinpoint** W Swinburn 8/1	11/23 Straight	5	9-08	70	2nd Suffolk Hcp Newm 1m1f	4th Brigadier Gerard Sand 1m2f	12th Mile Hcp Good 1m	16th Cambridgeshire Newm 1m1f
06 Wolv 1m 4th Lincoln Trial *Two months*	**Forgery** G Butler 12/1	13/25 Straight	4	8-06	63	7th Royal Hunt Cup Ascot 1m	4th John Smith's Cup York 1m2f	-	-
05 Nott 1m 2nd Conds Stks *Five months*	**Fine Silver** P Cole 9/1	22/19 Straight	4	9-06	64	12th Handicap Sand 1m	7th Hambleton Hcp York 1m	11th Vodafone Mile Epsom 1m	13th Wolferton Hcp York 1m2f
04 Donc 1m 17th Lincoln *One month*	**El Coto** B McMahon 20/1	26/27 Straight	4	9-03	65	5th Spring Trophy Hayd 7f	5th Hambleton Hcp York 1m	9th Victoria Cup Ascot 7f	8th John of Gaunt Hayd 7f
03 Leic 7f 1st Handicap *Two weeks*	**Mystic Man** K Ryan 11/1	14/25 Straight	5	8-07	62	4th Victoria Cup Ascot 7f	7th Zetland Gold Cup Redc 1m2f	9th Vodafone Hcp Epsom 1m	*9th Handicap Sout 7f
02 Donc 1m 18th Spring Mile *One month*	**The Judge** P Cole 12/1	20/21 Straight	4	8-06	67	9th Handicap Sand 1m	14th Jubilee Hcp Kemp 1m	*4th Conds Stks Wind 1m	*7th Rated Hcp Sand 1m
01 Donc 1m 4th Lincoln *One month*	**Mastermind** Mrs Ramsden 10/1	6/24 Straight	4	9-11	72	8th Hambleton Hcp York 1m	8th Royal Hunt Cup Ascot 1m	3rd Celebration Stks Curr 1m	
99 Donc 1m 1st Spring Mile *One month*	**Bomb Alaska** G Balding 12/1	14/19 Round	4	8-01	71	3rd Jubilee Hcp Kemp 1m	**WON 3/1F** **Chichester Hcp** **Good 1m**	2nd Ayrshire Hcp Ayr 1m	2nd Cambridgeshire Newmarket 1m1f
98 Hayd 1m3f 5th Handicap *Seven months*	**Yabint El Sultan** B McMahon 12/1	1/15 Round	4	8-12	63	**WON 9/2** **Dahlia Stks** **Newm 1m1f**	4th Middleton York 1m2f	8th Ladbroke Hcp Ascot 1m2f	9th Falmouth Stks Newm 1m
97 Donc 1m 2nd Lincoln *One month*	**Hawksley Hill** Mrs Ramsden 5/1F	17/20 Round	4	9-06	70	14th Royal Hunt Cup Ascot 1m	**WON 10/1** **Hong Kong Hcp** **Sand 1m**	10th W Hill Hcp Good 1m2f	2nd Brad & Bing Hcp York 1m
96 Newb 1m1f 9th Conds Stks *Seven months*	**Royal Philosopher** J Hills 25/1	12/20 Round	4	8-13	65	11th Spring Trophy Haydock 7f	2nd Whitsun Cup Sand 1m	**WON N/O** **Listed** **Evry 1m**	3rd Group 3 Mais 1m

11-year median performance rating of the winner: **67** (out of 100)   *(2000 abandoned), *next year*

WINNER'S PROFILE As to be expected in an early-season cavalry charge there were a few shocks, although nine winners returned at **12/1 or shorter**. Nine winners also either reappeared – three of whom were dropped in trip – or **had raced in the Lincoln or Spring Mile at Doncaster** within the past month. The draw has had an impact since it was switched to the straight course with every winner **drawn in double-figures** since 2002. Although counting for a majority of the runners, **four and five-year-olds** dominated with the former age group responsible for nine winners, while those at the base of the handicap have a poor record.

FUTURE POINTERS Winners of this struggled to get back on the scoresheet, as only one followed up next time out since 1996, which came during a good spell for subsequent winners between 1996 and 1999. Certain races have been particularly unkind to Spring Cup winners, though, including the Royal Hunt Cup at Royal Ascot, Hambleton Handicap at York, Spring Trophy at Haydock and a mile handicap at Sandown the following week. However, placed runners have fared a touch better of late, borne out by last year's hot renewal that produced two subsequent winners *(see below)*.

Were Spring Cup winners profitable to follow on their subsequent three runs?
No – 4 wins from 35 runs returned a loss of -£13.50 to a £1 level stake.

Placed runners' subsequent record (three runs):
Runners-up: 5 wins from 29 runs returned a **profit of +£1.90** to a £1 level stake.
2007 Royal Oath – Royal Hunt Cup, 2001 Pulau Tioman – Group Three Diomed Stakes, 1996 Cool Edge – Listed Spring Trophy

Thirds: 4 wins from 33 runs returned a **profit of +£1.75** to a £1 level stake.
2007 Heaven Sent – Ascot Heritage Handicap, 2002 Norton – Royal Hunt Cup,

Fourths: 2 wins from 30 runs returned a loss of -£21.67 to a £1 level stake.
2004 Alkaadem – Listed Festival Stakes (Goodwood)

FUTURE SUCCESS RATING: ★ ★ ★ ★ ★

GORDON RICHARDS STAKES
April 25, Sandown – (Group 3, Class 1, 4yo+) 1m2f

Last run	Winner/Trainer & SP	Draw/Ran	Age	Wght	PR	Next four runs			
07 Nad Al 9th Sheema Classic *One month*	**Red Rocks** B Meehan 11/4	2/6	4	9-03	76	4th Prince of Wales' Ascot 1m2f	4th Irish Champion Leop 1m2f	3rd Breeders' Cup Monm 1m4f	-
06 Donc 1m4f 2nd Serlby Stks *Five months*	**Day Flight** J Gosden 10/3	3/10	5	9-03	82	2nd Group 2 Bade 1m3f	4th Hardwicke Ascot 1m4f	2nd Aston Park Newb 1m5f	6th Listed Good 1m4f
05 Bous 1m2f 5th Group 3 *Six months*	**Weightless** Mrs A Perrett 14/1	3/8	5	8-10	70	6th Gala Stks Sand 1m2f	5th Winter Hill Wind 1m2f	5th Foundation Good 1m2f	*5th Gordon Richards Sand 1m2f
04 Kemp 1m2f 9th Magnolia Stks *Two weeks*	**Chancellor** J Dunlop 13/2	11/11	6	8-10	76	8th Prix Ganay Long 1m3f	9th Brigadier Gerard Sand 1m2f	12th Eclipse Sand 1m2f	6th Rose of Lancaster Hayd 1m3f
03 Ling 1m2f 4th Winter Trial *Two months*	**Indian Creek** D Elsworth 3/1JF	8/8	5	8-10	77	3rd Brigadier Gerard Sand 1m2f	**WON 14/1 Hardwicke Ascot 1m4f**	5th Juddmonte Int York 1m2f	3rd September Stks Kemp 1m4f
02 Newm 1m2f 11th Champion Stks *Six months*	**Chancellor** B Hills 9/2	1/7	4	8-10	72	4th Tatt's Gold Cup Curr 1m3f	2nd Meld Stks Curr 1m2f	**WON 2/1F Royal Whip Curr 1m2f**	5th Juddmonte York 1m2f
01 Nad Al 1m4f 9th Sheema Classic *One month*	**Island House** G Wragg 9/2	6/5	5	8-10	75	2nd Huxley Stks Ches 1m2f	3rd La Coupe Long 1m2f	3rd Scottish Classic Ayr 1m2f	6th La Coupe Mais 1m2f
00 Newm 1m2f 1st Seymour Stks *Six months*	**Little Rock** Sir M Stoute 5/2F	3/8	4	8-10	72	6th G Prix Chantilly Chan 1m4f	**WON 10/3 Princess of Wales' Newm 1m2f**	3rd Shergar Cup Ascot 1m4f	4th G Prix Deauville Deau 1m5f
99 Kemp 1m2f 1st Magnolia Stks *Three weeks*	**Generous Rosi** J Dunlop 10/3	3/9	4	8-10	73	2nd Brigadier Gerard Sand 1m2f	8th Prince of Wales' Ascot 1m2f	4th Listed Hcp Good 1m4f	5th Foundation Good 1m2f
98 Bade 1m2f 4th Group 3 *Eight months*	**Germano** G Wragg 8/1	5/5	5	8-10	74	3rd Brigadier Gerard Sand 1m2f	2nd Hardwicke Ascot 1m4f	3rd Princess of Wales' Newm 1m4f	6th G Prix Deauville Deau 1m5f
97 Deau 1m2f 1st Group 2 *Eight months*	**Sasuru** G Wragg 13/2	2/7	4	9-01	79	**WON 6/5F Prix D'Ispahan Long 1m1f**	5th Eclipse Sand 1m2f	*5th Prix Biron Deauv 1m2f	*3rd Select Stks Good 1m2f
96 Donc 1m4f 1st Troy Stks *Seven months*	**Singspiel** Sir M Stoute 11/10F	10/11	4	8-10	74	2nd Coronation Cup Epsom 1m4f	2nd Princess of Wales' Newm 1m4f	**WON 11/10F Select Stks Good 1m2f**	**WON 19/10F Canadian Intn'l Wood 1m4f**

12-year median performance rating of the winner: **75** (out of 100)   *next year*

WINNER'S PROFILE Red Rocks broke the trends last year as he became the first winner since Indian Skimmer in 1989 to lift this prize having already scored in Group/Grade One company. It usually helps to avoid such previous winners, especially Group One-winning fillies, and concentrate on those who have **already triumphed in Listed or Group Two/Threes**. The **highest officially rated runners** have come to the fore, while **four and five-year-olds** dominated, despite representing most of the field. One massive stat was that the past 11 winners tasted victory already over this intermediate distance of 10 furlongs.
As for trainers, **Geoff Wragg** has taken this event three times, with **Sir Michael Stoute** and **John Dunlop** both on two winners apiece.

FUTURE POINTERS Winners have a poor strike-rate next time out, as only Sasuru followed up in a Group One over in France in 1997. Four winners failed back here in the Brigadier Gerard Stakes, although winners that headed to Royal Ascot for the Hardwicke Stakes haven't fared too bad – Indian Creek scored in 2003 – while only three winners contested the Princess of Wales's at Newmarket, which produced a winner, runner-up and a third.

Were Gordon Richards winners profitable to follow on their subsequent three runs?
No – 5 wins from 36 runs returned a loss of -£9.37 to a £1 level stake.

Placed runners' subsequent record (three runs):
Runners-up: 5 wins from 36 runs returned a loss of -£8.00 to a £1 level stake.
2005 Hazyview – Group Three Diomed Stakes, 2004 Nysaean – Group Three Mooresbridge Stakes, 2001 Border Arrow – Brigadier Gerard Stakes, 1996 Pilsudski – Brigadier Gerard Stakes

Thirds: 2 wins from 21 runs returned a loss of -£12.75 to a £1 level stake.
1999 Dark Shell – Aston Park Stakes

FUTURE SUCCESS RATING: ★ ★ ☆ ☆ ☆

SANDOWN MILE
April 26, Sandown – (Group 2, Class 1, 4yo+) 1m

Last run	Winner/ Trainer & SP	Draw/ Ran	Age	Wght	PR	Next four runs			
07 Newm 7f 12th **Jeremy** Challenge Stks Sir M Stoute 2/1F *Six months*		1/9	4	9-00	80	5th Lockinge Newb 1m	2nd Queen Anne Ascot 1m	3rd Sussex Good 1m	7th Prix de la Foret Long 7f
06 Newm 1m2f 14th **Rob Roy** Champion Stks Sir M Stoute 6/4F *Six months*		4/8	4	9-00	73	6th Lockinge Newb 1m	3rd Sussex Good 1m	6th Celebration Mile Good 1m	2nd Champion Stks Newm 1m2f
05 Newm 1m1f 2nd **Hurricane Alan** Earl of Sefton R Hannon 5/1 *Two weeks*		4/8	5	9-00	77	3rd Lockinge Newb 1m	10th Queen Anne York 1m	5th Eclipse York 1m2f	-
04 Newm 1m1f 3rd **Hurricane Alan** Earl of Sefton R Hannon 25/1 *Two weeks*		1/10	4	9-00	76	5th Lockinge Newb 1m	10th Queen Anne Ascot 1m	3rd Silver Trophy Ascot 1m	7th Sussex Good 1m
03 Newm 1m1f 2nd **Desert Deer** Earl of Sefton M Johnston 11/10F *Two weeks*		2/9	5	9-00	77	9th Queen Anne Ascot 1m	*14th Lockinge Newb 1m	-	-
02 Donc 1m 6th **Swallow Flight** Doncaster Mile G Wragg 2/1F *Two months*		4/6	6	9-00	74	5th Lockinge Newb 1m	7th Queen Anne Ascot 1m	4th Scottish Classic Ayr 1m2f	-
01 Donc 1m 3rd **Nicobar** Doncaster Mile I Balding 16/1 *Two months*		6/7	4	9-00	78	WON N/O **Group 2** **San Siro 1m**	3rd Diomed Epsom 1m	2nd Celebration Mile Good 1m	2nd Prix de la Foret Long 7f
00 Newm 1m1f 1st **Indian Lodge** Earl of Sefton Mrs A Perrett 9/4F *Two weeks*		7/6	4	9-00	81	3rd Lockinge Newb 1m	7th Queen Anne Ascot 1m	WON 113/10 **Prix du Moulin** **Long 1m**	7th Queen Elizabeth II Ascot 1m
99 Newm 1m1f 6th **Handsome Ridge** Earl of Sefton J Gosden 5/1 *Two weeks*		4/9	5	9-00	76	WON 5/1 **Shergar Cup** **Good 1m2f**	5th Prix d'Ispahan Long 1m1f	5th Prince of Wale's Ascot 1m2f	7th Park Stks Donc 1m
98 Newm 1m1f 2nd **Almushtarak** Earl of Sefton K Mahdi 4/1 *Two weeks*		6/9	5	9-00	77	5th Lockinge Newb 1m	3rd Diomed Epsom 1m	4th Queen Anne Ascot 1m	2nd Sussex Good 1m
97 Newm 1m1f 2nd **Wixim** Earl of Sefton R Charlton 5/1 *Two weeks*		6/8	4	9-00	66	2nd Prix d'Ispahan Long 1m1f	5th Queen Anne Ascot 1m	4th International Stk Curr 1m	3rd Premio di Capua San Siro 1m
96 Newm 1m1f 4th **Gabr** Earl Of Sefton R Armstrong 13/2 *Two weeks*		2/12	6	9-00	76	5th Lockinge Newb 1m	9th Queen Anne Ascot 1m	WON 14/1 **Criterion Stks** **Newm 7f**	-

12-year median performance rating of the winner: **76** (out of 100)   *next year*

WINNER'S PROFILE Every winner raced at either **Newmarket or Doncaster last time**, eight arrived race-fit after taking in the Earl of Sefton a fortnight beforehand.

There were two shocks in the race, but 10 winners emerged from the **first four in the betting**, while **four and five-year-olds dominated**, although they represented the majority of runners – six-year-olds and above record stands at two winners from 20 runners.

Trainers **Sir Michael Stoute** and **Richard Hannon** have shared the last four renewals with two apiece.

FUTURE POINTERS The winner of this event may interest the layers next time out as they have a miserable record overall and only Handsome Ridge in 1999 managed to record another victory on home soil in the Shergar Cup. The Lockinge has proven a graveyard the following month as seven winners sunk – runners-up have a better record *(see below)* – while the Queen Anne has also been unkind, as seven failed at Royal Ascot.

Were winners of the Sandown Mile profitable to follow on their subsequent three runs?
No – 4 wins from 35 runs returned a loss of -£0.70 to a £1 level stake.

Placed runners' subsequent record (three runs):
Runners-up: 6 wins from 33 runs returned a loss of -£11.07 to a £1 level stake.
2004 Gateman – Midsummer Stakes, 2001 Swallow Flight – Windsor Stakes, 2000 Trans Island – Diomed Stakes, 1997 First Island – Lockinge, 1996 Soviet Line – Lockinge

Thirds: 7 wins from 35 runs returned a **profit of +£15.01** to a £1 level stake.
2007 Take A Bow – Brigadier Gerard, 2004 Soviet Song – Ridgewood Pearl, Falmouth, 2003 Reel Buddy – Sussex

FUTURE SUCCESS RATING: ★ ★ ☆ ☆ ☆

CLASSIC TRIAL
April 26, Sandown – (Group 3, Class 1, 3yo) 1m2f

Last run	Winner/ Trainer & SP	Draw/ Ran	Age	Wght	PR	Next four runs			
07 Newb 1m 7th R Post Trophy *Six months*	**Regime** M Bell 11/2	4/8	3	9-00	65	13th Derby Epsom 1m4f	2nd Group 2 Mais 1m2f	5th Prix d'Ornano Deau 1m2f	3rd Group 3 Leop 1m2f
06 Newm 7f 8th Dewhurst Stks *Six months*	**Primary** W Haggas 4/1	4/5	3	9-00	70	5th Chester Vase Chest 1m4f	**WON 11/10F Premio d'Italia San Siro 1m1f**	3rd Secretariat Stks Arling 1m2f	4th Select Stks Good 1m2f
05 Leop 1m2f 1st Maiden *Two weeks*	**Fracas** D Wachman 9/2	5/8	3	8-10	67	**WON 2/1 Derby Trial Leop 1m2f**	4th Derby Epsom 1m4f	7th Irish Derby Curr 1m4f	*2nd Group 1 Colo 1m4f
04 Newb 1m 1st Rated Hcp *One week*	**African Dream** P Chapple-Hyam 7/2	5/5	3	8-10	69	**WON 2/5F Dee Stks Ches 1m2f**	10th Eclipse Sand 1m2f	4th Prix Adam Mais 1m2f	7th Sovereign Stks Sali 1m
03 Ling 1m2f 1st Maiden *Four months*	**Shield** G Butler 4/1	10/9	3	8-10	62	10th Derby Epsom 1m4f	-	-	-
02 Hayd 1m3f 1st Rated Hcp *Two weeks*	**Simeon** M Johnston 6/4	3/4	3	8-11	70	3rd Prix 'Jock Club Chan 1m4f	5th Princess Of Wales's Newm 14f	5th Royal Whip Curr 1m2f	*7th Handicap Nad Al 1m6f
01 Donc 7f 1st Maiden *Five months*	**Chancellor** B Hills 9/2	5/5	3	8-11	71	10th Derby Epsom 1m4f	2nd Prix d'Ornano Deau 1m2f	5th Arc Trial Newb 1m3f	2nd Prix Barriere Long 1m2f
00 Sand 1m 1st Conds Stks *Six months*	**Sakhee** J Dunlop 11/4	6/6	3	8-11	75	**WON 5/2JF Dante York 1m2f**	2nd Derby Epsom 1m4f	4th Eclipse Sand 1m2f	*WON 8/11F Steventon Stks Newb 1m2f
99 Good 1m 3rd Stardom Stks *Seven months*	**Fantastic Light** Sir M Stoute 13/2	2/7	3	8-11	74	4th Derby Trial Ling 1m3f	2nd Prince of Wales's Ascot 1m2f	3rd Eclipse Sand 1m2f	**WON 4/1 Great Voltigeur York 1m4f**
98 Salis 1m 1st Maiden *Six months*	**Courteous** P Cole 11/1	4/4	3	8-10	69	12th Derby Epsom 1m4f	6th King Edward VII Ascot 1m4f	2nd July Trophy Hayd 1m4f	11th Arc Long 1m4f
97 Evry 1m1f 1st Prix Saint Roman *Five months*	**Voyagers Quest** P Chapple-Hyam 11-2	4/6	3	8-12	68	7th Prix 'Jock Club Chan 1m4f	9th Hollywood Derby Holl 1m1f	-	-
96 Ripon 1m1f 1st Maiden *Three weeks*	**Santillana** J Gosden 6/1	3/9	3	8-10	70	*WON 6/1 Conds Stks Newm 1m2f	*4th Premio Roma Capan 1m2f	*4th Earl Of Sefton Newm 1m1f	*7th Conds Stks Newm 1m2f

12-year median performance rating of the winner: **69** (out of 100) *next year*

WINNER'S PROFILE Maidens have rarely won this and Al Tharib became the latest without a win to be beaten here last year, so it therefore helps to stick with those already boasting a **victory under their belts**. Trainer John Gosden won this on four occasions in the 1990s, the last in 1996, but has only had three placed from seven runners since, compared to **Peter Chapple-Hyam**, who has had two winners from as many runners. **Favourites have a poor record**, unlike the next two in the market, while those drawn on the outside of the field in stalls one and two have struggled.

FUTURE POINTERS This Classic Trial is slowly on the downgrade and a long time has passed since the winner went on to take the Epsom Derby – six have flopped on the Downs since 1996 – where Sakhee, one of the best winners here went closest in 2000, while the 1997 runner-up, Benny The Dip, did step up at Epsom *(see below)*. Primary travelled to Italy in 2006, resulting in a Group prize, which almost worked for Simeon in 2002, while those who headed to Royal Ascot, and the Eclipse failed.
The 1999 winner, Fantastic Light, took the Group Two Great Voltigeur at York later that season, and eventually became a six-time Group/Grade One winner further down the line.

Were Classic Trial winners profitable to follow on their subsequent three runs?
No – 5 wins from 33 runs returned a loss of -£16.00 to a £1 level stake.

Placed runners' subsequent record (three runs):
Runners-up: 7 wins from 29 runs returned **profit of +£2.33** to a £1 level stake.
2001 Asian Heights – September Stakes, 1997 Benny The Dip – Dante Stakes, Derby, 1996 Glory Of Dancer – Dante Stakes

Thirds: 2 wins from 11 runs returned a loss of -£2.00 to a £1 level stake.

FUTURE SUCCESS RATING: ★ ★ ☆ ☆ ☆

LEICESTERSHIRE STAKES
April 26, Leicester – (Listed, Class 1, 4yo+) 7f

Last run	Winner/ Trainer & SP	Draw/ Ran	Age	Wght	PR	Next four runs			
07 San Siro 7f Group 3 *Six months*	9th **New Seeker** P Cole 7/4F	2/5	7	9-05	72	5th Royal Windsor Wind 1m2f	10th St John of Gaunt Hayd 7f	14th City of York York 7f	5th Conds Stks Newb 1m1f
06 Warw 7f Conds Stks *Two weeks*	1st **Etlaala** B Hills 6/5F	5/7	4	8-12	77	13th Duke of York York 6f	**WON 4/1 Cathedral Stks Salis 6f**	14th Golden Jubilee Ascot 6f	5th Lennox Stks Good 7f
05 Long 7f Prix Foret *Six months*	3rd **Le Vie Dei Colori** L Cumani 6/4F	5/11	5	8-12	71	6th Lockinge Newb 1m	6th Criterion Newm 7f	6th Sussex Good 1m	5th Celebration Mile Good 1m
04 Tokyo 1m Listed *Five months*	5th **Tout Seul** F Johnson-Houghton 7/2	8/11	4	8-12	65	15th Lockinge Newb 1m	11th John of Gaunt Hayd 7f	6th Minstrel Stks Curr 7f	10th Sovereign Stks Sali 1m
03 Sha Tin 1m Hong Kong Mile *Four months*	10th **Tillerman** Mrs A Perrett 10/3	3/6	7	9-04	76	6th Lockinge Newb 1m	Disq Queen Anne Ascot 1m	**WON 13/8 Silver Trophy Ascot 1m**	13th Lennox Stks Good 7f
02 Newm 7f Challenge Stks *Six months*	3rd **Warningford** J Fanshawe 10/3	5/5	8	8-12	74	9th Lockinge Newb 1m	**WON 10/3 John of Gaunt Hayd 7f**	12th Challenge Stks Newm 7f	8th Wentworth Stks Donc 6f
01 Newm 6f Abernant Stks *Three weeks*	17th **Warningford** J Fanshawe 4/1	6/11	7	8-12	75	2nd Lockinge Newb 1m	3rd Hungerford Newb 7f	4th Prix du Moulin Long 1m	3rd Prix Foret Long 7f
00 Newm 7f Challenge Stks *Six months*	5th **Sugarfoot** N Tinkler 4/1	1/5	6	9-01	72	5th Lockinge Newb 1m	5th Queen Anne Ascot 1m	**WON 7/2F Silver Trophy Ascot 1m**	13th Tote International Ascot 7f
99 Warw 7f Conds Stks *Three weeks*	1st **Warningford** J Fanshawe 9/2	4/7	5	8-12	71	2nd Duke of York York 6f	**WON 3/1 John of Gaunt Hayd 7f**	2nd Prix Maillot Long 7f	2nd Dubai Duty Free Newb 7f
97 Leop 7f Knockaire Stks *Five months*	1st **Wizard King** Sir M Prescott 7/2	6/10	6	9-06	74	2nd Amethyst Stks Leop 1m	3rd Prix Palais Royal Long 7f	**WON 2/1 Ballycorus Stks Leop 7f**	**WON 7/2 Beeswing Stks Newc 7f**
96 Sha Tin 7f Hong Kong Int *Four months*	10th **Young Ern** S Dow 8/11F	1/6	6	9-02	68	3rd Prix Palais Royal Deauv 7f	4th Queen Anne Ascot 1m	7th Maurice 'Gheest Deauv 7f	-

11-year median performance rating of the winner: **72** (out of 100) (*2001 Newmarket, 2000 Doncaster, 1998 abandoned*)

WINNER'S PROFILE Every winner arrived having either **run outside of England last time out**, or if they had run here previously, it was at **Newmarket or Warwick** – two landed a conditions stakes at the latter venue. Age and weights have been mixed as penalties were carried successfully, but there have been few shocks and it definitely paid to **stick with the fancied runners**. That statistic may be reflected in the fact that the last eight winners were **officially rated 109 or higher** and emerged from the top-two rated each year. Trainers south of Leicestershire have done well, as **James Fanshawe** won it three times with Warningford, while it's also worth noting that high drawn horses failed to figure as the race can develop near the stands' side **favouring low to middle numbers**.

FUTURE POINTERS One message has been made clear when contemplating a bet on the Leicestershire Stakes winner next time out, and that is to swerve it, especially in the Group One Lockinge at Newbury, where six consecutive winners bit off more than they could chew. A further three winners also came unstuck in Group events next time out, but three managed to get back on the winning trail when dropped back into Listed grade a run later – two of them in the John of Gaunt at Haydock (now a Group Three). Four winners were turned over at Royal Ascot, three in the Queen Anne, however, one of the best graduates of this event, Wizard King, did raise his game in Group class later that year.

Were Leicestershire winners profitable to follow on their subsequent three runs?
No – 6 wins from 33 runs returned a loss of -£9.54 to a £1 level stake.

Placed runners' subsequent record (three runs):
Runners-up: 5 wins from 32 runs returned a **profit of +£10.75** to a £1 level stake.
2004 Polar Ben – Joel Stakes, 2003 Gateman – Diomed Stakes, 2000 Tumbleweed Ridge – Ballycorus Stakes, 1997 Polar Prince – Diomed Stakes,

Thirds: 4 wins from 12 runs returned a **profit of +£9.75** to a £1 level stake.
2004 Rockets 'N Rollers – Spring Trophy, 2001 Mount Abu – John of Gaunt Stakes, 1997 Ramooz – Criterion Stakes

FUTURE SUCCESS RATING: ★ ★ ★ ☆ ☆

SAGARO STAKES
April 30, Ascot, (Group 3, Class 1, 4yo+) 2m

Last run	Winner/Trainer & SP	Draw/Ran	Age	Wght	PR	Next four runs			
07 York 2m2f 7th Doncaster Cup *Eight months*	**Tungsten Strike** Mrs A Perrett 9/2	4/6	6	9-00	70	5th Henry II Sand 2m	13th Gold Cup Ascot 2m4f	6th Goodwood Cup Good 2m	**WON 9/1** **March Stks** **Good 2m**
06 Newm 2m 1st Jockey Club Cup *Seven months*	**Cover Up** Sir M Stoute 4/1	1/7	9	9-02	69	7th Henry II Sand 2m	2nd Queen Alexandra Ascot 2m6f	10th Goodwood Cup Good 2m	-
05 Newb 1m4f 6th John Porter Stks *Two weeks*	**Alcazar** H Morrison 5/1	5/9	10	8-13	75	4th Yorkshire Cup 1m6f	3rd Henry II Sand 2m	**WON 6/1** **Group 2** **Deau 1m7f**	2nd Prix du Cadran Long 2m4f
04 Mais 2m 2nd Listed *One month*	**Risk Seeker** E Lellouche 11/2	13/13	4	8-12	67	4th Henry II Sand 2m	4th Group 2 Mais 1m7f	*WON N/O **Stakes** **Deau 2m1f**	-
03 Nott 1m6f 1st F Flight Stks *One month*	**Alcazar** H Morrison 7/2	8/7	8	8-13	74	12th Gold Cup Ascot 2m4f	2nd Prix Royal-Oak Long 2m	4th Serlby Stks Donc 1m4f	*WON 11/8F **Further Flight St** **Nott 1m6f**
02 Sain 2m 3rd Listed *Six months*	**Give Notice** J Dunlop 8/1	6/7	5	8-12	80	5th Gold Cup Ascot 2m4f	2nd Goodwood Cup Good 2m	5th Lonsdale Stks York 2m	**WON 62/10** **Prix du Cadran** **Long 2m4f**
01 Font 2m4f 2nd Hurdle *Three months*	**Solo Mio** Mrs A Perrett 20/1	7/11	7	8-12	78	**WON 7/1** **Henry II** **Sand 2m**	4th Goodwood Cup Good 2m	*5th Sagaro Stks Ascot 2m	*4th Henry II Sand 2m
00 Hayd 1m4f 6th John Porter Stks *Two weeks*	**Orchestra Stall** J Dunlop 6/1	1/9	8	8-12	75	**WON 18/10** **Group 3** **Long 2m**	8th Prix Royal-Oak Long 2m	*10th Sagaro Stks Newm 2m	***6th Group 2 Long 2m
99 Newm 2m 2nd Jockey Club Cup *Six months*	**Celeric** J Dunlop 6/1	5/9	7	8-12	74	5th Henry II Sand 2m	4th Gold Cup Ascot 2m4f	6th Goodwood Cup Good 2m	**WON 10/1** **Lonsdale Stks** **York 2m**
98 Long 2m2f 3rd Prix du Cadran *Seven months*	**Persian Punch** D Elsworth 4/1	5/10	5	9-01	79	3rd Yorkshire Cup York 1m6f	**WON 15/8F** **Henry II** **Sand 2m**	6th Gold Cup Ascot 2m4f	**WON 11/4** **Lonsdale Stks** **York 2m**
97 Hayd 2m 3rd Conds Stks *One month*	**Orchestra Stall** J Dunlop 9/1	1/8	5	8-12	73	7th Henry II Sand 2m	**WON 9/2** **Curragh Cup** **Curr 1m6f**	2nd Group 2 Deau 1m7f	**WON 3/1** **Group 3** **Long 2m**
96 Flem 2m 10th Melbourne Cup *Six months*	**Double Trigger** M Johnston 11/8F	2/7	5	9-05	76	WON 5/6F **Henry II** **Sand 2m**	2nd Gold Cup Ascot 2m4f	**WON EvsF** **Doncaster Cup** **Donc 2m2f**	5th Prix du Cadran Long 2m4f

12-year median performance rating of the winner: **74** (out of 100)   *(2006,2005 Lingfield, 2001,1998 Newmarket)*
*next year ***three years

WINNER'S PROFILE Of the five winners to have had a recent spin within the past month, three finished in the top-two, while two others came sixth in the John Porter Stakes.
Those **proven in this type of event** were the ones to concentrate on as 11 **scored in Listed grade at least**, while 10 had already **won over this trip** – the two exceptions proved themselves over 14 and 15-furlongs.
The best horses have ruled with an **official rating of 108 or more** ideal, borne out by the SP's as there have been few shocks – 10 were **between 7/2 and 9/1** - though Double Trigger was the last winning favourite in 1996.
Although without a runner since 2004, trainer **John Dunlop** triumphed four times from 15 runners in this period.

FUTURE POINTERS As a pointer to the upcoming 'Cup' events later in the season the Sagaro has been of limited value, as those who returned for the Royal meeting flopped, while a few years have passed since anything in the mould of Celeric, Persian Punch or Double Trigger appeared at this midweek fixture.
Give Notice was the last winner who went and took a major prize in the 2002 Prix du Cadran – Alcazar went close in 2005 – while those to take the traditional route to the Henry II Stakes have produced mixed results with three victors from eight, of whom, all three recorded above-par PR's here. The Yorkshire and Goodwood Cups have proven more difficult to land, although placed runners have fared well in the former event *(see below)*.

Were Sagaro winners profitable to follow on their subsequent three runs?
No – 8 wins from 36 runs returned a loss of -£5.00 to a £1 level stake.

Placed runners' subsequent record (three runs):
Runners-up: 5 wins from 34 runs returned a loss of -£8.00 to a £1 level stake.
2006 Tungsten Strike – Henry II, 2005 Franklins Gardens – Yorkshire Cup, 2000 Persian Punch – Henry II,
1998 Busy Flight – Yorkshire Cup, 1996 Grey Shot – Goodwood Cup

Thirds: 2 wins from 20 runs returned a loss of -£6.50 to a £1 level stake.
2004 Millenary – Yorkshire Cup, Doncaster Cup

FUTURE SUCCESS RATING: ★ ★ ☆ ☆ ☆

DAHLIA STAKES
May 3, Newmarket – (Group 3, Class 1, 4yo+) 1m1f

Last run	Winner/Trainer & SP	Draw/Ran	Age	Wght	PR	Next four runs			
07 Good 1m2f 5th Nassau *Nine months*	**Echelon** Sir M Stoute 8/11F	6/8	5	9-01	76	**WON 7/4F** Princess Elizabeth Epsom 1m	5th Windsor Forest Ascot 1m	6th Pretty Polly Curr 1m2f	**WON 7/1** Celebration Mile Good 1m
06 Kemp 1m 2nd Snowdrop Stks *One month*	**Violet Park** B Meehan 15/2	1/8	5	8-12	65	6th Windsor Forest Ascot 1m			
05 Kemp 1m 1st Snowdrop Stks *Two months*	**Tarfah** G Butler 9/4	3/9	4	8-09	64	5th Windsor Forest York 1m	*9th Princess Elizabeth Epsom 1m	-	-
04 Kemp 1m 1st Snowdrop Stks *One month*	**Beneventa** J Dunlop 7/2	6/8	4	8-09	70	2nd Middleton Stks York 1m2f	8th Windsor Forest Ascot 1m	**WON 7/2** Aphrodite Stks Newm 1m4f	10th Group 2 Deau 1m5f
03 Ling 7f 2nd Conds Stks *One month*	**Aldora** M Ryan 10/3	1/10	4	8-09	56	3rd Middleton Stks York 1m2f	**WON 6/1** Conqueror Stks Good 1m	**WON 3/1** Princess Elizabeth Epsom 1m	**7th Snowdrop Stks Kemp 1m
02 Long 1m2f 10th Prix de l'Opera *Seven months*	**Tarfshi** M Jarvis 10/1	4/6	4	8-12	71	4th Brigadier Gerard Sand 1m	**WON 7/2** Pretty Polly Curr 1m2f	6th Nassau Good 1m2f	7th Flower Bowl Belm 1m1f
01 Leop 7f 4th Listed *Six months*	**Cayman Sunset** E Dunlop 8/1	7/7	4	8-09	65	4th Middleton Stks York 1m2f	6th Group 3 Sain 1m3f	4th Diomed Epsom 1m	7th Falmouth Newm 1m
00 Kemp 1m2f 6th Magnolia Stks *Two weeks*	**Cape Grace** R Hannon 11/2	4/6	4	8-09	65	5th Group 3 Sain 1m3f	8th Pretty Polly Curr 1m2f	5th Steventon Stks Newb 1m2f	2nd Daffodil Stks Chep 1m2f
99 Epsom 1m2f 4th Suburban Hcp *Two years*	**Putuna** I Balding 4/1	5/8	4	8-12	63	6th Hoppings Stks Newc 1m2f	3rd Class Stks Ascot 1m2f	4th Motability Hcp York 1m2f	3rd Virginia Hcp Newc 1m2f
98 Newb 1m 1st Spring Cup *Two months*	**Yabint El Sultan** B McMahon 9/2	6/8	4	8-09	60	4th Middleton Stks York 1m2f	8th Ladbroke Hcp Ascot 1m2f	9th Falmouth Stks Newm 1m	15th W Hill Mile Good 1m
97 Newm 1m2f 4th J Seymour Stks *Six months*	**Balalaika** L Cumani 10/11F	5/7	4	8-09	61	4th Conqueror Stks Good 1m	6th Prince of Wales' Ascot 1m2f	3rd Strensall Stks York 1m1f	4th Prix de l'Opera Long 1m1f

11-year median performance rating of the winner: **65** (out of 100)   *next year*

WINNER'S PROFILE Clues haven't been easily identified, especially as the race has gone through a changing process since it became a Group Three in 2004.
Since then, three of the four winners arrived having **already won in either Listed or Group class**, while the Snowdrop Stakes at Kempton has proven an informative stepping stone and supplied three winners. Echelon became only the second winning favourite 12 months ago and though shocks were a rarity in the race, it paid to **shop around for value**. Although **four and five-year-olds** took every renewal, they represented the majority of runners each year apart from the occasional six-year-old who appeared.

FUTURE POINTERS The quality of the Dahlia Stakes has improved steadily since the Millennium, as winners became more productive following Newmarket and the upgrade from Listed to Group Three status has been a contributory factor. Last year's renewal was the best yet, as both the winner, Echelon, and runner-up, Topatoo, both went on to land Group Threes next time out. In fact, Echelon emerged as the first winner to have followed up since 1997, six of the 10 who failed tripped up in either the Listed Middleton Stakes at York or the Group Two Windsor Forest Stakes at Royal Ascot.

Were Dahlia winners profitable to follow on their subsequent three runs?
No – 5 wins from 30 runs returned a loss of -£7.25 to a £1 level stake.

Placed runners' subsequent record (three runs):
Runners-up: 2 wins from 29 runs returned a loss of -£22.00 to a £1 level stake.
2007 Topatoo – Middleton Stakes

Thirds: 0 win from 16 runs returned a loss of -£16.00 to a £1 level stake.

FUTURE SUCCESS RATING: ★ ★ ★ ★ ★

2,000 GUINEAS
May 3 Newmarket – (Group 1, Class 1, 3yo Colts & Fillies) 1m

Last run	Winner/ Trainer & SP	Draw/ Ran	Age	Wght	PR	Next four runs			
07 York 7f 3rd Champage Stks Eight months	Cockney Rebel G Huffer 25/1	15/24	3	9-00	85	WON 6/4F Irish 2,000 Guin Curr 1m	5th St James Palace Ascot 1m		
06 Curr 1m 1st National Stks Eight months	George Washington A O'Brien 6/4F	6/14	3	9-00	88	2nd Irish 2,000 Guin Curr 1m	3rd Celebration Mile Good 1m	WON 13/8F Queen Eliz II Ascot 1m	6th Breeders' Cup Chur 1m2f
05 Leop 7f 1st Kilavullan Stks Six months	Footstepsinthesand A O'Brien 13/2	17/19	3	9-00	81	-	-	-	-
04 Newm 1m 1st Craven Stks Three weeks	Haafhd B Hills 11/2	4/14	3	9-00	85	4th St James Palace Ascot 1m	9th Sussex Good 1m	WON 12/1 Champion Stks Newm 1m2f	-
03 Leop 1m 1st 2,000 Guin Trial Three weeks	Refuse To Bend D Weld 9/2	18/20	3	9-00	80	13th Derby Epsom 1m4f	WON 8/11F Desmond Stks Leop 1m	11th Prix du Moulin Long 1m	11th Breeders' Cup Sant 1m
02 Newm 7f 1st Dewhurst Stks Seven months	Rock Of Gibraltar A O'Brien 9/1	22/22	3	9-00	86	WON 4/7F Irish 2,000 Guin Curr 1m	WON 4/5F St James Pal'c Ascot 1m	WON 8/13F Sussex Good 1m	WON 3/5JF Prix du Moulin Long 1m
01 Chep 7f 1st Maiden Eight months	Golan Sir M Stoute 11/1	19/18	3	9-00	80	2nd Derby Epsom 1m4f	3rd Irish Derby Curr 1m4f	WON 13/10F Prix Niel Long 1m4f	4th Arc de Triomphe Long 1m4f
00 Newm 1m 2nd Craven Stks Three weeks	King's Best Sir M Stoute 13/2	12/27	3	9-00	87	PU Irish Derby Curr 1m4f	-	-	-
99 Sali 6f 1st Conds Stks Eight months	Island Sands S Bin Suroor 10/1	3/16	3	9-00	82	5th Irish 2,000 Guin Curr 1m	*2nd Prix Quincey Deau 1m	**2nd Group 3 Sain 1m	**3rd Masai Mile Sand 1m
98 Curr 1m 1st National Stks Eight months	King Of Kings A O'Brien 7/2	17/18	3	9-00	81	15th Derby Epsom 1m4f	-	-	-
97 Ches 1m 1st Conds Stks Eight months	Entrepreneur Sir M Stoute 11/2	4/16	3	9-00	84	4th Derby Epsom 1m4f	7th Queen Eliz II Ascot 1m	-	-
96 Good 7f 1st Maiden Ten months	Mark Of Esteem S Bin Suroor 8/1	2/13	3	9-00	85	8th St James Palace Ascot 1m	WON 11/4F Celebration Mile Good 1m	WON 10/3 Queen Eliz II Ascot 1m	7th Breeders' Cup Wood 1m

12-year median performance rating of the winner: **84** (out of 100) *(1999 July Course), *next year **two years*

WINNER'S PROFILE **Ten winners won last time out,** although only Haafhd, King's Best and Refuse To Bend raced during the current season – the former pair in the Craven – while Cockney Rebel was placed in the Champagne Stakes at York, as were Haafhd and Rock Of Gibraltar. Be wary of following the trial winners of the Greenham Stakes and European Free Handicap.
Trainers **Aidan O'Brien and Sir Michael Stoute** have won seven of the last 12 renewals, George Washington being the only favourite, although it pays to stick with the **first six in the betting**. In large fields of **18 runners or more, middle to high numbers** have accounted for all seven winners.

FUTURE POINTERS Recent winners have been worth following, as two took the Irish Guineas, while three scored during the autumn – George Washington won the Queen Elizabeth II Stakes, as did Mark Of Esteem back in 1996. Rock Of Gibraltar went on a Group One rampage following Newmarket, his only undoing that season came in the Breeders' Cup, an event that foiled three others. Another banana skin was the Epsom Derby, where four failed, and you have to go back to 1989 when Nashwan last completed the double.

Were 2,000 Guineas winners profitable to follow on their subsequent three runs?
Yes – 10 wins from 27 runs returned a **profit of +£8.20** to a £1 level stake.

Placed runners' subsequent record (three runs):
Runners-up: 7 wins from 33 runs returned a **profit of +£2.13** to a £1 level stake.
2006 Sir Percy – Derby, 2003 Zafeen – St James's Palace Stakes, 2002 Hawk Wing – Eclipse, 2000 Giant's Causeway – St James's Palace Stakes, Eclipse

Thirds: 5 wins from 36 runs returned a loss of -£7.77 to a £1 level stake.
2004 Azamour – St James's Palace Stakes, Irish Champion Stakes, 1996 Bijou D'Inde – St James's Palace Stakes

FUTURE SUCCESS RATING: ★ ★ ★ ☆ ☆

HERITAGE HANDICAP
May 3, Newmarket – (Class 2, 3yo+) 6f

Last run	Winner/ Trainer & SP	Draw/ Ran	Age	Wght	PR	Next four runs			
07 Ling 7f 5th Handicap *Seven months*	**Beaver Patrol** E Johnson Houghton 20/1	23/29	5	8-10	65	5th Victoria Cup Ascot 7f	6th Vodafone Sprint Epsom 6f	11th Wokingham Ascot 6f	5th Heritage Hcp Wind 6f
06 Ling 6f 1st Handicap *Two months*	**Mutamared** K Ryan 12/1	14/26	6	8-11	67	9th Dash Hcp Epsom 5f	25th Wokingham Ascot 6f	2nd Stewards' Cup Good 6f	**WON 5/2F** **Sports Hcp** **Kemp 6f**
05 Newb 6f 1st Rated Hcp *Nine months*	**Indian Trail** D Elsworth 10/1	29/30	5	8-06	65	6th Portland Hcp Donc 5½f	8th Handicap Hayd 6f	*6th Conds Stks Kemp 6f	*9th Handicap Newm 7f
04 Newc 7f 3rd Betfred Hcp *One month*	**Moayed** N Littmoden 25/1	20/30	5	8-13	59	10th Scottish Sprint Muss 5f	4th Handicap Sand 7f	14th Handicap Newm 7f	**WON 8/1** **Ladbrokes Hcp** **Ling 6f**
03 Ascot 6f 1st Tote Hcp *Two months*	**Fire Up The Band** D Nicholls 4/1F	19/30	4	9-10	70	2nd Stewards' Cup Good 6f	11th Great St Wilfrid Ripo 6f	2nd Scarbrough Stks Donc 5f	3rd Ayr Gold Cup Ayr 6f
02 Kemp 7f 7th Showcase Hcp *One month*	**Marsad** J Akehurst 11/2F	23/30	8	9-11	61	3rd Handicap Good 6f	18th Wokingham Ascot 6f	14th Ladbrokes Hcp Good 6f	8th Ayr Gold Cup Ayr 6f
01 Kemp 7f 2nd Handicap *Three weeks*	**Marsad** J Akehurst 20/1	12/29	7	9-05	59	2nd Handicap Good 6f	23rd Wokingham Ascot 6f	2nd Showcase Hcp Newb 6f	8th Stewards' Cup Good 6f
00 Newb 5f 4th Showcase Hcp *One month*	**Sartorial** P Makin 25/1	22/28	4	10-00	70	8th Stewards' Cup Good 6f	7th Rated Hcp Sand 5f	17th Rated Hcp Ascot 5f	*3rd Rated Hcp York 6f
99 Ayr 6f 11th Ayr Gold Cup *Eight months*	**Perryston View** P Calver 20/1	4/17	7	9-10	64	26th Wokingham Ascot 6f	12th Stewards' Cup Good 6f	4th Great St Wilfrid Ripo 6f	11th Portland Hcp Donc 5½
98 Newm 7f 5th Rated Hcp *Three weeks*	**Sheltering Sky** J Dunlop 10/1	28/29	4	9-06	72	2nd Rated Hcp York 6f	5th Wokingham Ascot 6f	14th Rated Hcp York 7f	10th Bentinck Stks Newm 6f
97 Newc 5f 11th Handicap *Seven months*	**Perryston View** P Calver 11/1	5/29	5	8-11	63	20th Wokingham Ascot 6f	10th Rated Hcp Ripo 6f	8th Eagle Lane Hcp York 6f	**WON 11/1** **Ayr Silver Cup** **Ayr 6f**
96 Newb 5f 8th Rated Hcp *Three weeks*	**Jayanpee** I Balding 14/1	10/24	5	9-11	71	**WON 11/2** **Rated Hcp** **York 6f**	9th Dash Hcp Epsom 5f	10th Wokingham Ascot 6f	**WON 16/1** **Hackwood Stks** **Newb 6f**

12-year median performance rating of the winner: **66** (out of 100) *(1999 July Course), *next year*

WINNER'S PROFILE A recent run used to be a must, but that trend has been reversed of late, however, runners with a solid placed outing within the last two months are respected. Those saddled with **8st 10lb or more** came out on top, although since it was open to horses officially rated above 95 three years ago, no horse triumphed above that rating, and 16 failed to defy a mark greater than 100 since 2005. A **double-figure stall** was favoured, as only Perryston View won from a single-figure draw – once on the July Course – while three-year-olds are best avoided.

FUTURE POINTERS An early-season pointer for some of the more valuable sprint handicaps to come, but one in which the winner has failed to shine afterwards, apart from Jayanpee, who followed up at York 12 years ago. Eight winners failed in the Wokingham at Royal Ascot, while five flopped in the Stewards' Cup at Glorious Goodwood. The Ayr Gold Cup also evaded winners later in the year, although Perryston View took the Silver Cup. Had this been written a year earlier, I would've advised steering clear of the placed horses from here in the Wokingham and Stewards' Cup as 20 failed – 10 in each race – since 1996. However, Dark Missile improved on her fourth here last year to take the Wokingham, but long-term, placed runners should be treated carefully in such races.

Were Heritage Handicap winners profitable to follow on their subsequent three runs?
No – 1 win from 36 runs returned a loss of -£29.50 to a £1 level stake.

Placed runners' subsequent record (three runs):
Runners-up: 5 wins from 36 runs returned a loss of -£4.67 to a £1 level stake.
2005 Baltic King – Listed Leisure Stakes, 2003 Perfect Touch – Irish Group Three,
1998 Hill Magic – Showcase Handicap (Lingfield)

Thirds: 5 wins from 36 runs returned a loss of -£13.78 to a £1 level stake.

Fourths: 5 wins from 35 runs returned a **profit of +£4.25** to a £1 level stake.
2007 Dark Missile – Wokingham

FUTURE SUCCESS RATING: ★ ★ ☆ ☆ ☆

JOCKEY CLUB STAKES
May 4, Newmarket – (Group 2, Class 1, 4yo+) 1m4f

Last run	Winner/Trainer & SP	Draw/Ran	Age	Wght	PR	Next four runs			
07 Long 1m4f 6th Arc de Triomphe *Seven months*	**Sixties Icon** J Noseda 5/2	2/5	4	9-03	86	7th Coronation Cup Epsom 1m4f	10th Princess of Wales' Newm 1m4f	-	-
06 Belm 1m4f 1st Breeders' Cup *Seven months*	**Shirocco** A Fabre 10/11F	6/7	5	9-03	88	**WON 8/11F Coronation Cup Epsom 1m4f**	**WON 13/8 Prix Foy Long 1m4f**	7th Arc de Triomphe Long 1m4f	-
05 Kemp 1m4f 2nd September Stks *Eight months*	**Alkaased** L Cumani 2/1F	2/5	5	8-09	84	2nd Coronation Cup Epsom 1m4f	**WON 6/1 G Prix 'St-Cloud Sain 1m4f**	2nd Prix Foy Long 1m4f	5th Champion Stks Newm 1m2f
04 Newb 1m4f 2nd John Porter Stks *Three weeks*	**Gamut** Sir M Stoute 7/4F	7/7	5	8-09	79	**WON 7/2CF G Prix 'St-Cloud Sain 1m4f**	4th King George VI Ascot 1m4f	5th Grosser 'Baden Bade 1m4f	*2nd Jockey Club Newm 1m4f
03 Newb 1m4f 1st John Porter Stks *Three weeks*	**Warrsan** C Brittain 12/1	2/6	5	8-09	83	2nd Yorkshire Cup York 1m6f	**WON 9/2 Coronation Cup Epsom 1m4f**	2nd Premio di Milano Siro 1m4f	6th King George VI Ascot 1m4f
02 Nad Al 1m4f 4th Sheema Classic *Two months*	**Marienbard** S Bin Suroor 9/1	7/9	5	8-09	82	4th Coronation Cup Epsom 1m4f	**WON 17/10 Group 1 Duss 1m4f**	**WON 28/10 Grosser 'Baden Bade 1m4f**	**WON 158/10 Arc 'Triomphe Long 1m4f**
01 Donc 1m6f 1st St Leger *Eight months*	**Millenary** J Dunlop 11/4	1/7	4	9-00	80	3rd Coronation Cup Epsom 1m4f	5th King George VI Ascot 1m4f	2nd Geoffrey Freer Newb 1m5f	2nd Irish St Leger Curr 1m6f
00 Epsom 1m4f 2nd September Stks *Eight months*	**Blueprint** Sir M Stoute 9/2	3/11	5	8-09	75	3rd Hardwicke Stks Ascot 1m4f	6th Grade 1 Holl 1m2f	*3rd Grade 1 Sant 1m6f	-
99 Siro 1m4f 1st Pr Jockey Club *Seven months*	**Silver Patriarch** J Dunlop 9/2JF	7/11	5	9-00	79	4th Coronation Cup Eprom 1m4f	4th King George VI Ascot 1m4f	**WON 7/2 Geoffrey Freer Newb 1m5f**	3rd Irish St Leger Curr 1m6f
98 Wood 1m4f 3rd Canadian Int *Seven months*	**Romanov** P Chapple-Hyam 5/1	5/8	4		74	2nd G Prix 'St-Cloud Sain 1m4f	5th King George VI Ascot 1m4f	-	-
97 Ascot 1m4f 1st Princess Royal *Seven months*	**Time Allowed** Sir M Stoute 13/2	3/10	4	8-06	73	-			
96 Newm 1m2f 2nd Champion Stks	**Riyadian** P Cole 10/11F	2/9	4	8-09	72	*WON 1/4F Conds Stks Hami 1m1f	*3rd G Prix 'St-Cloud Sain 1m4f	**3rd Gordon Richards Sand 1m2f	**5th Ormonde Stks Ches 1m5f

12-year median performance rating of the winner: **80** (out of 100)   *(1999 July Course), *next year **two years*

WINNER'S PROFILE Stick with distance specialists as **11 winners had already scored over a mile-and-a-half**, while those to have **finished in the first two last time** are respected.
Age-wise, **four and five-year-olds have ruled**, with the older horses record standing at 0 from almost 20 runners. Favourites have a fair record in this event as **outsiders are rare**, however, it proved wise to avoid backing those with a Group Two penalty, as **horses with a Group One penalty** performed better, including Sixties Icon last year. Trainer **Sir Michael Stoute** sent out three winners from around a dozen runners.

FUTURE POINTERS The standard of the winner has improved significantly in recent years, making them very much ones to follow since 2002. Shirocco was the best winner in 2006, en route to lifting the Coronation Cup at Epsom, a feat repeated by Warrsan in 2003. Alkaased failed in the 2005 Coronation Cup, however, but soon got back to winning ways in the Grand Prix de Saint-Cloud, a race also won by Gamut the previous year. One race where winners haven't fared so well, though, was the King George VI at Ascot, with four defeats.

Were Jockey Club winners profitable to follow on their subsequent three runs?
Yes – 9 wins from 31 runs returned a **profit of +£2.59** to a £1 level stake.

Placed runners' subsequent record (three runs):
Runners-up: 7 wins from 31 runs returned a **profit of +£4.30** to a £1 level stake.
2005 Gamut – Princess of Wales's Stakes, 2005 Systematic – Ormonde Stakes, 2003 Millenary – Princess of Wales's Stakes, 2001 Sandmason – Hardwicke Stakes, 1998 Silver Patriarch – Coronation Cup

Thirds: 5 winners from 20 runs returned a **profit of +£2.40** to a £1 level stake.
1996 Sacrament – September Stakes

FUTURE SUCCESS RATING: ★ ★ ★ ★ ☆

1,000 GUINEAS
May 4, Newmarket – (Group 1, Class 1, 3yo Fillies) 1m

Last run	Winner/ Trainer & SP	Draw/ Ran	Age	Wght	PR	Next four runs			
07 Newm 7f 1st Rockfel Stks Seven months	Finsceal Beo J Bolger 5/4F	8/21	3	9-00	83	2nd Poule 'Pouliches Long 1m	WON 9/10F Irish 1,000 Guin Curr 1m	8th Coronation Stks Ascot 1m	6th Irish Champion Leop 1m2f
06 Newm 7f 1st Nell Gwyn Stks Three weeks	Speciosa Mrs P Sly 10/1	3/13	3	9-00	73	4th Oaks Epsom 1m4f	9th Coronation Stks Ascot 1m	6th Park Stks York 7f	*2nd Earl of Sefton Newm 1m1f
05 Leop 1m 1st 1,000 Guin Trial Three weeks	Virginia Waters A O'Brien 12/1	1/20	3	9-00	76	8th Irish 1,000 Guin Curr 1m	4th Oaks Epsom 1m4f	6th Coronation Stks York 1m	6th Nassau Good 1m2f
04 Newm 6f 1st Cherry Hinton Ten months	Attraction M Johnston 11/2	8/16	3	9-00	79	WON 2/1F Irish 1,000 Guin Curr 1m	WON 6/4F Coronation Stk Ascot 1m	2nd Falmouth Newm 1m	10th Jacques 'Marois Deau 1m
03 Newm 6f 2nd Cheveley Park Seven months	Russian Rhythm Sir M Stoute 12/1	2/19	3	9-00	81	WON 4/7F Coronation Stk Ascot 1m	WON 4/5F Nassau Good 1m2f	2nd Queen Eliz II Ascot 1m	5th Champion Stks Newm 1m2f
02 Siro 1m 1st Premio Dormello Seven months	Kazzia S Bin Suroor 14/1	12/17	3	9-00	74	WON 10/3F Oaks Epsom 1m4f	4th Yorkshire Oaks York 1m4f	WON 61/20 Flower Bowl Belm 1m1f	6th Breeders' Cup Arli 1m2f
01 Newm 7f 6th Rockfel Stks Seven months	Ameerat M Jarvis 11/1	10/15	3	9-00	70	5th Coronation Stks Ascot 1m	8th Sussex Good 1m	7th Sun Chariot Newm 1m	-
00 Newb 7f 4th Fred Darling One month	Lahan J Gosden 14/1	10/18	3	9-00	72	-	-	-	-
99 Newb 7f 1st Fred Darling Three weeks	Wince H Cecil 4/1F	19/22	3	9-00	76	5th Irish 1,000 Guin Curr 1m	-	-	-
98 Newm 6f 4th Cheveley Park Eight months	Cape Verdi S Bin Suroor 10/3JF	7/16	3	9-00	80	9th Derby Epsom 1m4f	*3rd Falmouth Newm 1m	*8th Nassau Good 1m2f	-
97 Newb 7f 4th Fred Darling Three weeks	Sleepytime H Cecil 5/1	3/15	3	9-00	77	3rd Coronation Stks Ascot 1m	*7th Earl of Sefton Newm 1m2f	-	-
96 Newb 7f 1st Fred Darling Three weeks	Bosra Sham H Cecil 5/1	11/13	3	9-00	78	2nd Queen Eliz II Ascot 1m	WON 9/4 Champion Stks Newm 1m2f	*WON 1/5F Brig' Gerard Sand 1m2f	*WON 4/11F Prince of Wales Ascot 1m2f

12-year median performance rating of the winner:　　**77** (out of 100)　　　*(1999 July Course), *next year*

WINNER'S PROFILE Ten winners had their **last outing at either Newbury or Newmarket**, four emerged from the Fred Darling, and two from the Rockfel. Winners of the Cheveley Park, Fillies' Mile and Moyglare are best avoided in this Classic.
One statistic to have stood out was that all **12 winners had already either won or finished second in a Group race**, while it paid not to look beyond the **first six in the betting**.
Trainer **Henry Cecil took this three times** since 1996 and could be due another after last year's resurgence.

FUTURE POINTERS Of the four fillies to have attempted the Irish equivalent, both the above par winners, Finsceal Beo and Attraction, managed the feat. Russian Rhythm was also one of the top rated winners, and she, along with Attraction found glory in the Coronation Stakes at Royal Ascot.
Not many stepped up in trip for the Epsom Oaks, three in fact, and just Kazzia succeeded, though Cape Verdi may have figured had she not bitten off more than she could chew against the colts in the Derby.

Were 1,000 Guineas winners profitable to follow on their subsequent three runs?
No – 9 wins from 30 runs returned a loss of -£6.40 to a £1 level stake.

Placed runners' subsequent record (three runs):
Runners-up: 7 wins from 31 runs returned a **profit of +£11.20** to a £1 level stake.
2006 Confidential Lady – Group One Prix de Diane Hermes (Oaks), 2005 Maids Causeway – Coronation Stakes, 2003 Six Perfections – Jacques le Marois, 1998 Shahtoush – Oaks, 1996 Matiya – Irish 1,000 Guineas

Thirds: 8 wins from 30 runs returned a loss of -£3.54 to a £1 level stake.
2007 Simply Perfect – Falmouth, 2000 Petrushka – Irish Oaks, Yorkshire Oaks, 1999 Valentine Waltz – Poule d'Essai des Pouliches (1,000 Guineas), 1998 Exclusive – Coronation Stakes

FUTURE SUCCESS RATING: ★ ★ ★ ☆ ☆

PALACE HOUSE STAKES
May 4, Newmarket – (Group 3, Class 1, 3yo+) 5f

Last run	Winner/ Trainer & SP	Draw/ Ran	Age	Wght	PR	Next four runs			
07 Thir 6f 1st M Foster Stks *Three weeks*	**Tax Free** D Nicholls 11/8F	4/10	5	8-13	76	**WON 7/2** **Listed Sprint** Naas 5f	11th King's Stand Ascot 5f	2nd Listed Curr 5f	3rd King George Good 5f
06 Naas 5f 2nd Listed *Three weeks*	**Dandy Man** C Collins 25/1	16/22	3	8-04	77	4th King's Stand Ascot 5f	**WON 5/4F** **Listed** Curr 5f	12th Nunthorpe York 5f	3rd World Trophy Newb 5f
05 Long 5f 5th Abbaye *Six months*	**Avonbridge** R Charlton 11/2	1/9	5	9-05	77	3rd Chan 5f	2nd July Cup Newm 6f	7th Nunthorpe York 5f	3rd Diadem Newm 6f
04 Newm 6f 2nd Abernant *Three weeks*	**Frizzante** J Fanshawe 13/8F	1/13	5	8-09	75	3rd King's Stand Ascot 5f	**WON 14/1** **July Cup** **Newm 6f**	10th Maurice 'Gheest Deau 7f	17th Sprint Cup Hayd 6f
03 Newm 6f 1st Abernant *Three weeks*	**Needwood Blade** B McMahon 9/4F	9/10	5	8-12	72	13th Duke of York York 6f	13th Golden Jubilee Ascot 6f	7th July Cup Newm 6f	9th Hackwood Stks Newb 6f
02 Newb 5f 1st Rated Hcp *Three weeks*	**Kyllachy** H Candy 2/1F	3/12	4	8-12	76	**WON 9/2** **Temple Stks** **Sand 5f**	3rd King's Stand Ascot 5f	**WON 3/1F** **Nunthorpe** **York 5f**	-
01 Newm 6f 3rd Bentinck *Seven months*	**Rushcutter Bay** P Gilligan 20/1	9/18	8	8-12	70	7th Achilles Stks Kemp 5f	17th King's Stand Ascot 5f	14th King George Good 5f	14th Abbaye Long 5f
00 Thir 6f 1st M Foster Stks *Three weeks*	**Pipalong** T Easterby 9/1	4/21	4	8-09	69	2nd Duke of York York 6f	**WON 10/11F** **Cecil Frail** **Hayd 6f**	12th Cork & Orrery Ascot 6f	3rd July Cup Newm 6f
99 Newb 5f 10th World Trophy *Ten months*	**Rambling Bear** M Blanshard 16/1	11/13	6	8-12	66	4th Achilles Stks Kemp 5f	5th King's Stand Ascot 5f	8th King George Good 5f	Fell Nunthorpe York 5f
98 Newm 5f 1st Marshal Stks *Three weeks*	**Yorkies Boy** B McMahon 15/2	8/13	3	8-03	65	8th City Wall Stks Ches 5f	16th Nunthorpe York 5f	11th July Cup Hayd 6f	11th World Trophy Newb 5f
97 Hayd 5f 6th Marshal Stks *Two months*	**Deep Finesse** M Jarvis 14/1	2/12	3	8-06	67	11th King's Stand Ascot 5f	8th Group 3 Deau 6f	6th King George Good 5f	16th World Trophy Newb 5f
96 Newm 6f 5th Abernant *Three weeks*	**Cool Jazz** C Brittain 16/1	1/11	5	9-01	70	9th Temple Stks Sand 5f	12th Cork & Orrery Ascot 6f	9th July Cup Newm 6f	4th King George Good 5f

12-year median performance rating of the winner: **72** (out of 100)   *(1999 July Course)*

WINNER'S PROFILE Nine winners **already ran that season**, five in the Abernant Stakes here or the Michael Foster Stakes at Thirsk. **Proven success in Pattern company** was vital to 11 winners, as was a **victory over the minimum trip** – only Needwood Blade and Cool Jazz failed on that note.
The ages have been spread around, although **three-year-olds** have the best strike-rate despite the fact five-year-olds scored on more occasions. Dandy Man became the fourth **winning favourite** in six years after a lean run for the market leaders.

FUTURE POINTERS This Group Three sprint has provided a springboard for a couple of future Group One winners later on in the year, although the majority failed to move successfully up to that level and settled instead for Listed victories. The two that did manage to cut the mustard at the top were Frizzante and Kyllachy, who went on to take the July Cup and Nunthorpe in 2004 and 2002, respectively.
However, it is worth noting that both failed to win at Royal Ascot, a venue that has been unkind to Palace House winners, as a further eight disappointed at the Berkshire track, including Tax Free last year.
Overall, the performance ratings suggest that the standard has increased since the Millennium and winners returned a profit in the near future.

Were Palace House winners profitable to follow on their subsequent three runs?
No – 6 wins from 36 runs returned a loss of -£2.85 to a £1 level stake. However, a **profit of +£15.25** was returned on their next two outings since 2002.

Placed runners' subsequent record (three runs):
Runners-up: 6 wins from 33 runs returned a loss of -£11.34 to a £1 level stake.
2004 Avonbridge – Group Two Prix du Gros-Chene, 2001 Cassandra Go –Temple Stakes, King's Stand Stakes

Thirds: 1 win from 35 runs returned a loss of -£30.00 to a £1 level stake.

FUTURE SUCCESS RATING: ★ ★ ☆ ☆ ☆

PRETTY POLLY STAKES
May 4, Newmarket – (Listed, Class 1, 3yo) 1m2f

Last run	Winner/ Trainer & SP	Draw/ Ran	Age	Wght	PR	Next four runs			
07 Ling 7f 1st Maiden *Seven months*	**Dalvina** E Dunlop 5/2JF	8/7	3	8-12	64	11th Oaks Epsom 1m4f	3rd Ribblesdale Ascot 1m4f	5th Yorkshire Oaks York 1m4f	3rd Blandford Stks Curr 1m2f
06 Leic 1m 2nd Maiden *Eight months*	**Riyalma** Sir M Stoute 7/2	6/6	3	8-12	67	10th Oaks Epsom 1m4f	-	-	-
05 Newm 1m 1st Maiden *Three weeks*	**Fashionable** B Hills 11/10F	5/7	3	8-10	63	9th Ribblesdale York 1m4f	7th Upavon Stks Sali 1m2f	-	-
04 Newm 1m 3rd Listed Fillies *Six months*	**Ouija Board** E Dunlop 2/1F	4/9	3	8-08	75	**WON 7/2** **Oaks** **Epsom 1m4f**	**WON 4/7F** **Irish Oaks** **Curr 1m4f**	3rd Arc de Triomphe Long 1m4f	**WON 10/11F** **Breeders' Cup** **Lone 1m3f**
03 Newm 7f 2nd Maiden *Nine months*	**Hi Dubai** S Bin Suroor 2/1F	1/8	3	8-08	66	2nd Prix Saint-Alary Long 1m2f	5th Oaks Epsom 1m4f	4th Nassau Good 1m2f	3rd Grade 1 Wood 1m2f
02 Ascot 1m 3rd Fillies' Mile *Eight months*	**Esloob** M Tregoning 10/11F	3/4	3	8-08	63	13th Oaks Epsom 1m4f	**WON 2/1F** **Hoppings Stks** **Newc 1m2f**	6th Aphrodite Stks Newm 1m4f	-
01 Yarm 1m 1st Maiden *Eight months*	**Mot Juste** E Dunlop 8/1	1/11	3	8-08	67	4th Oaks Epsom 1m4f	2nd Irish Oaks Curr 1m4f	8th Yorkshire Oaks York 1m4f	4th Prix Barriere Long 1m4f
00 (Unraced)	**Melikah** S Bin Suroor 5/4F	3/8	3	8-08	62	3rd Oaks Epsom 1m4f	2nd Irish Oaks Curr 1m4f	5th Prix Barriere Long 1m4f	-
99 Kemp 1m 2nd Masaka Stks *One month*	**Alabaq** J Dunlop 5/1	3/9	3	8-08	66	3rd Ribblesdale Ascot 1m4f	6th Nassau Good 1m2f	2nd Winter Hill Wind 1m2f	4th Select Stks Good 1m2f
98 Ascot 1m 5th Fillies' Mile *Eight months*	**Midnight Line** H Cecil 5/2F	9/11	3	9-01	72	2nd Musidora York 1m2f	3rd Oaks Epsom 1m4f	3rd Nassau Good 1m2f	*2nd Grade 1 Holl 1m1f
97 Newb 7f 5th Conds Stks *Seven months*	**Siyadah** S Bin Suroor 10/3F	1/9	3	8-08	68	11th Oaks Epsom 1m4f	7th Ribblesdale Ascot 1m4f	-	-
96 Sand 1m 1st Maiden *Nine months*	**Pricket** S Bin Suroor 4/1	6/7	3	8-08	66	2nd Oaks Epsom 1m4f	-	-	-

12-year median performance rating of the winner: **67** (out of 100)   *next year*

WINNER'S PROFILE The majority **made their reappearance** here – two raced in the Group One Fillies' Mile at Ascot last backend – while the two with a recent run finished first and second. Eleven winners had **no more than four career runs** – nine a maximum of two – and it was only the penalty carrier, Midnight Line who had raced more, including a Group Three victory earned in 1997.
The market spoke volumes as **fancied runners held the call**, with trainer **Saeed Bin Suroor** was responsible for several fancied winners and **Ed Dunlop** a further three – two favourites.

FUTURE POINTERS This may be a recognised Oaks trial, but it only once provided the Classic winner in the shape of the brilliant Ouija Board in 2004, who was also the best recent winner with an inflated performance rating (PR) on the day of her victory. Apart from that globetrotter, the rest struggled to pick up another race as only Esloob took another Listed event in the near future.
As a future guide, average winners of the Pretty Polly should be swerved – or layed – rather than backed as last year's winner, Dalvina, was a timely reminder after flopping in the Oaks.

Were Pretty Polly winners profitable to follow on their subsequent three runs?
No – 3 wins from 30 runs returned a loss of -£20.92 to a £1 level stake.

Placed runners' subsequent record (three runs):
Runners-up: 4 wins from 31 runs returned a loss of -£1.00 to a £1 level stake.
2003 Hold To Ransom – Group Three Musidora Stakes, 2001 Tarshi – Listed Hoppings Stakes, 1999 Ela Athena – Listed Daffodil Stakes, 1998 Leggera – Group Two (France)

Thirds: 3 wins from 19 runs returned a loss of -£5.50 to a £1 level stake.
2004 Rave Reviews – Listed Swettenham Stud Fillies' Trial, 2001 Time Away – Group Three Musidora Stakes

FUTURE SUCCESS RATING: ★ ★ ☆ ☆ ☆

CHESHIRE OAKS
May 7, Chester – (Listed, Class 1, 3yo Fillies) 1m3f 79yds

Last run	Winner/Trainer & SP	Draw/Ran	Age	Wght	PR	Next four runs			
07 Newb 1m2f 1st Conds Stks *Three weeks*	**Light Shift** H Cecil 11/8F	4/11	3	8-12	67	**WON 13/2 Oaks Epsom 1m4f**	2nd Irish Oaks Curr 1m4f	3rd Nassau Stks Good 1m2f	6th Prix de l'Opera Long 1m2f
06 Folk 1m2f 1st Maiden *One month*	**Time On** J Dunlop 2/1F	1/12	3	8-12	61	6th Oaks Epsom 1m4f	**WON 11/4 Group 2 Saint 1m4f**	7th Prix De Pomone Deauv 1m5f	7th Prix Barriere Long 1m4f
05 Newb 1m2f 2nd Maiden *Three weeks*	**Alumni** B Hills 15/8F	4/6	3	8-09	58	6th Prix De Nonette Deauv 1m2f	9th Princess Royal Newm 1m4f	7th Severals Stks Newm 1m2f	-
04 Wind 1m 2nd Maiden *Three weeks*	**Hidden Hope** G Wragg 14/1	1/9	3	8-09	63	5th Ribblesdale Ascot 1m4f	4th Lancashire Oaks Hayd 1m4f	2nd Prix De Pomone Deauv 1m5f	3rd Princess Royal Ascot 1m4f
03 Beve 1m 1st Maiden *Two weeks*	**Hammiya** M Tregoning 9/1	6/9	3	8-09	61	11th Oaks Epsom 1m4f	11th Lancashire Oaks Hayd 1m4f	5th Strensall Stks York 1m1f	-
02 Donc 1m 3rd May Hill Stks *Eight months*	**Shadow Dancing** M Tregoning 9/4JF	4/5	3	8-09	55	3rd Oaks Epsom 1m4f	2nd Ribblesdale Ascot 1m4f	3rd Lancashire Oaks Hayd 1m4f	2nd Prix De Pomone Deauv 1m5f
01 Newb 1m2f 5th Maiden *Three weeks*	**Rockerlong** G Wragg 7/2F	3/7	3	8-09	56	5th Ribblesdale Ascot 1m4f	3rd Aphrodite Stks Newm 1m4f	3rd Yorkshire Oaks York 1m4f	8th Park Hill Stks Donc 1m6f
00 Kemp 1m 4th Masaka Stks *Three weeks*	**Solaia** P Cole 10/1	1/5	3	8-09	62	7th Oaks Epsom 1m4f	2nd Lancashire Oaks Hayd 1m4f	4th Prix De Psyche Deau 1m2f	4th Park Hill Stks Donc 1m6f
99 Long 1m 9th Marcel Boussac *Seven months*	**Valentine Girl** B Hills 5/1	7/9	3	8-12	55	7th Ribblesdale Ascot 1m4f	4th Aphrodite Stks Newm 1m4f	3rd Upavon Stks Sali 1m2f	3rd Park Hill Stks Donc 1m6f
98 Donc 7f 2nd Maiden *Six months*	**High And Low** B Hills 4/1	6/8	3	8-09	57	7th Oaks Epsom 1m4f	2nd Yorkshire Oaks York 1m4f	St Leger Donc 1m6f	-
97 Pont 1m2f 1st Maiden *Three weeks*	**Kyle Rhea** H Cecil 9/4F	1/5	3	8-09	60	6th Group 3 Chant 1m4f	-	-	-
96 Curr 1m 1st EBF Fillies race *One month*	**Tout A Coup** G Cusack 8/1	6/8	3	8-09	61	**WON 11/10F Listed Stks Gowr 1m4f**	6th Irish Oaks Curr 1m4f	5th Listed Stks Leop 1m6f	***WON 9/4F Stakes race List 1m4f**

12-year median performance rating of the winner: **60** (out of 100) *next year*

WINNER'S PROFILE There aren't many patterns to help identify the ideal profile of a Cheshire Oaks winner, although one starting point was that the last five winners came to Chester off the back of a **recent solid run**.
Don't be put off by a filly with no win to her name as five maidens got off the mark here, while **outsiders have rarely figured**, with only two double-figure priced winners.
Trainers to keep onside include **Henry Cecil**, **Barry Hills**, **Marcus Tregoning** and **Geoff Wragg**, but be wary of Sir Michael Stoute's runners as last year's well beaten Lost In Wonder became his ninth loser in 12 years.
The draw also played its part, more so in big fields, as the highest drawn stalls on the outside struggled.

FUTURE POINTERS An Oaks trial that has fluctuated in quality over the years and produced more below par winners than future superstars. However, last year's scorer Light Shift, was well above average and put an end to the drought for Cheshire Oaks winners in the Epsom Oaks by beating Peeping Fawn. Last year's result may now encourage some of the better fillies to experience the sharp bends around here before Epsom.
It wasn't just the Epsom Oaks that evaded winners of this race, but also the Group Two Lancashire and Group One Yorkshire equivalents, as six failed to win either of them.

Were Cheshire Oaks winners profitable to follow on their subsequent three runs?
No – 3 wins from 34 runs returned a loss of -£20.65 to a £1 level stake.

Placed runners' subsequent record (three runs):
Runners-up: 2 wins from 31 runs returned a loss of -£1.93 to a £1 level stake.
2006 Mont Etoile - Ribblesdale Stakes, 2004 Menhoubah – Oaks d'Italia

Thirds: 3 wins from 17 runs returned a loss of -£9.87 to a £1 level stake.
2007 Fashion Statement - Oaks d'Italia

FUTURE SUCCESS RATING: ★ ☆ ☆ ☆ ☆

CHESTER CUP
May 7, Chester – (Heritage Handicap, Class 2, 4yo+) 2m2f 147yds

Last run	Winner/ Trainer & SP	Draw/ Ran	Age	Wght	PR	Next four runs			
07 York 1m6f 5th Mallard Hcp *Eight months*	**Greenwich Meantime** R Fahey 14/1	16/17	7	9-02	70	19th Northumberland Newc 2m	11th Goodwood Cup Good 2m	7th Shergar Cup Ascot 2m	9th Old Borough Cup Hayd 1m6f
06 Aint 2m1f 16th Listed Hcp *Two months*	**Admiral** T Pitt 28/1	1/17	5	8-01	60	6th Handicap Ascot 2m	28th Ascot Stks Hcp Ascot 2m4f	*15th Chester Cup Ches 2m2f	-
05 Newm 2m 7th Jockey Club Cup *Seven months*	**Anak Pekan** M Jarvis 16/1	15/17	5	9-06	69	6th Prix Vigier Long 2m	6th Esher Stks Sand 2m	-	-
04 Kemp 2m 1st Queen's Prize *One month*	**Anak Pekan** M Jarvis 2/1F	4/17	4	8-02	70	3rd Northumberland Newc 2m	*WON 16/1 Chester Cup Ches 2m2f	*6th Prix Vigier Long 2m	*6th Esher Stks Sand 2m
03 Newm 2m2f 5th Cesarewitch *Seven months*	**Hugs Dancer** J Given 9/1	2/16	6	8-11	64	8th Henry II Sand 2m	8th Northumberland Newc 2m	WON 11/2 Silver Listed Hcp York 1m6f	22nd Ebor York 1m6f
02 Newb 2m 5th Handicap *Three weeks*	**Fantasy Hill** J Dunlop 8/1	7/18	6	8-09	62	9th Northumberland Newc 2m	4th Silver List Hcp York 1m6f	3rd Rated Hcp Ches 2m2f	-
01 Newb 1m4f 7th John Porter *Three weeks*	**Rainbow High** B Hills 9/2	5/17	6	9-13	74	11th Henry II Sand 2m	7th Gold Cup Ascot 2m4f	3rd Goodwood Cup Good 2m	6th Lonsdale Stks York 2m
00 Kemp 2m 3rd Queen's Prize *Three weeks*	**Bangalore** Mrs A Perrett 16/1	4/18	4	7-10	62	7th Ascot Stks Hcp Ascot 2m2f	WON 10/3 Festival Hcp Newb 2m	**2nd Handicap Salis 1m6f	**WON 7/2F Handicap Kemp 2m
99 Newb 2m 1st Handicap *Three weeks*	**Rainbow High** B Hills 4/1F	13/16	4	9-00	72	2nd Henry II Sand 2m	10th Gold Cup Ascot 2m4f	3rd Lonsdale Stks York 2m	2nd Doncaster Cup Donc 2m2f
98 Donc 1m7f 2nd Handicap *Seven months*	**Silence In Court** A Bailey 13/2	9/18	7	9-00	59	4th Gold Cup Ascot 2m4f	-	-	-
97 Newb 2m 2nd Handicap *Three weeks*	**Top Cees** Mrs J Ramsden 11/2	6/12	7	8-11	62	5th Northumberland Newc 2m	5th Casinos Hcp Good 1m6f	6th Ebor York 1m6f	WON 9/2JF Whisky Hcp Ayr 1m5f
96 Donc 2m1f 1st Handicap *Six months*	**Merit** P Cole 11/2	12/18	4	7-10	67	6th Ascot Stks Hcp Ascot 2m4f	*5th Limited Stks York 1m4f	*13th Cesarewitch Newm 2m2f	*6th Handicap Donc 2m1f

12-year median performance rating of the winner: **66** (out of 100)   *next year **two years*

WINNER'S PROFILE Both speed and stamina are required by the winner, suiting specialists of the track, and it is no surprise to see two dual winners in Rainbow High and Anak Pekan – both carried the biggest weights in the last 12 years on their second victory. Barring those specialists, the majority carried around **9st or below**, while **four to seven-year-olds** dominated. Eight winners were drawn low, although it is possible to win form a high stall, and of more importance is the capability of the jockey in such a rough race. Every winner raced at a Grade One venue last time out and it is worth noting those from the **Queen's Prize at Kempton** and the **two mile handicap at Newbury**.

FUTURE POINTERS Chester Cup winners have a disastrous record next time out as none followed up. Three failed in the Group Two Henry II Stakes at Sandown, while six were subsequently beaten at Royal Ascot, three in the Ascot Stakes Handicap and three in the Group One Gold Cup. The Northumberland Plate has also proven an unsuccessful route, as five winners sunk up at Newcastle – only Anak Pekan made the frame in 2004.
Following the third and fourth placed runners from here may prove a wiser move, especially those to have performed well from an awkward wide draw. Greenwich Meantime ran a cracker from stall 11 in 2006, before winning at Ayr next time and eventually came back to land this race last year. Two fourths also ran well here before scoring at Royal Ascot *(see below)*.

Were Chester Cup winners profitable to follow on their subsequent three runs?
No – 3 wins from 33 runs returned a loss of -£5.17 to a £1 stake.

Placed runners' subsequent record (three runs):
Runners-up: 2 wins from 33 runs returned a loss of -£29.43 to a £1 level stake

Thirds: 7 wins from 36 runs returned a **profit of +£2.75** to a £1 level stake.

Fourths: 4 wins from 33 runs returned a **profit of +£9.00** to a £1 level stake.
2002 Riyadh – Ascot Stakes Handicap, 2001 Cover Up – Ascot Stakes Handicap

FUTURE SUCCESS RATING: ★ ★ ☆ ☆ ☆

CHESTER VASE
May 8, Chester – (Group 3, Class 1, 3yo) 1m4f 66yds

Last run	Winner/ Trainer & SP	Draw/ Ran	Age	Wght	PR	Next four runs			
07 Long 1m3f 1st Prix Noailles *Two months*	**Soldier Of Fortune** A O'Brien 4/9F	1/4	3	9-02	75	5th Derby Epsom 1m4f	**WON 5/1** **Irish Derby** Curr 1m4f	**WON 9/4** **Prix Niel** Long 1m4f	5th Arc de Triomphe Long 1m4f
06 Newm 1m2f 1st Newmarket Hcp *Three weeks*	**Papal Bull** Sir M Stoute 6/4F	1/5	3	8-12	69	10th Derby Epsom 1m4f	**WON 5/4F** **King Edward VII** Ascot 1m4f	8th Great Voltigeur York 1m4f	5th Prix Barriere Long 1m4f
05 Sand 1m2f 3rd Classic Trial *Two weeks*	**Hattan** C Brittain 11/2	2/8	3	8-10	64	6th Derby Epsom 1m4f	5th Princess of Wales Newm 1m4f	2nd Winter Hill Wind 1m2f	6th St Leger Donc 1m6f
04 Sand 1m2f 2nd Betfred Hcp *Two weeks*	**Red Lancer** R Price 9/1	5/6	3	8-10	63	3rd Predominate Good 1m3f	6th Queen's Vase Ascot 2m	14th Northumberland Newc 2m	6th July Trophy Hayd 1m4f
03 Kemp 1m 2nd Easter Stakes *Three weeks*	**Dutch Gold** C Brittain 13/2	2/4	3	8-10	67	6th Derby Epsom 1m4f	11th Eclipse Sand 1m2f	7th Great Voltigeur York 1m4f	6th G Prix Deauville Deau 1m5f
02 Newm 1m1f 7th Feilden Stks *Three weeks*	**Fight Your Corner** M Johnston 9/2	1/8	3	8-10	69	5th Derby Epsom 1m4f	*5th Dubai Gold Stks Nad Al	*2nd Ashton Park Newb 1m5f	*11th Gold Cup Ascot 2m4f
01 Donc 1m2f 2nd Maiden *Two months*	**Mr Combustible** B Hills 12/1	1/7	3	8-10	71	4th Derby Epsom 1m4f	6th Irish Derby Curr 1m4f	**WON 9/4** **Geoffrey Freer** Newb 1m5f	3rd St Leger Donc 1m6f
00 Newb 1m3f 1st Maiden *One month*	**Millenary** J Dunlop 8/1	4/8	3	8-10	69	8th Prix Jockey Club Chan 1m4f	**WON 9/1** **Gordon Stks** Good 1m4f	**WON 11/4F** **St Leger** Donc 1m6f	*WON 11/4 Jockey Club Newm 1m4f
99 Newb 1m3f 2nd Maiden *Three weeks*	**Peshtigo** B Hills 14/1	2/8	3	8-10	65	5th King Edward VII Ascot 1m4f	5th Group 2 Hopp 1m4f	4th September Stks Epsom 1m4f	-
98 Newm 1m 2nd Craven Stks *Three weeks*	**Gulland** G Wragg 1/2F	1/5	3	8-10	70	11th Derby Epsom 1m4f	10th Park Stks Donc 1m	13th Listed race Newm 1m	-
97 Newm 1m1f 1st Feilden Stks *Three weeks*	**Panama City** P Chapple-Hyam 6/5F	1/5	3	8-10	66	3rd Derby Italiano Capa 1m4f	4th King Edward VII Ascot 1m4f	2nd Geoffrey Freer Newb 1m5f	6th St Leger Donc 1m6f
96 Newb 1m3f 1st Conds Stks *Three weeks*	**High Baroque** P Chapple-Hyam 11/4	3/6	3	8-10	63	9th Prix Jockey Club Chan 1m4f	8th Group 2 Deau 1m5f	-	-

12-year median performance rating of the winner: **68** (out of 100)   *next year*

WINNER'S PROFILE Not many trends to work with, but every winner arrived fit having raced at a Grade One venue within the past two months and 11 of them were able to boast a top-three finish.
Despite the small field sizes, stalls one to three have accounted for 10 winners, while trainers **Clive Brittain**, **Barry Hills**, and **Peter Chapple-Hyam** all recorded doubles. The latter's entries could be interesting in the near future now he has found himself back in the big-time.

FUTURE POINTERS Another of the traditional Derby trials but one that hasn't produced the Classic winner since runner-up Quest For Fame back in 1990. However, the race received a needed boost last year when Soldier Of Fortune became the first winner to defy a Group penalty here, before he went on to land the Irish Derby following a creditable fifth at Epsom. The less exposed Curragh route could also be one worth monitoring with Chester Vase winners as only Mr Combustible tried the same when sixth in 2001.
Papal Bull also contributed towards a revival of this race two years ago when he subsequently took the King Edward VII Stakes at Royal Ascot, a race that foiled two others, while Millenary won his first Group race here in 2000 before a successful career, which included the St Leger later that year.

Were Chester Vase winners profitable to follow on their subsequent three runs?
No – 6 wins from 35 runs returned a loss of -£6.50 to a £1 level stake.

Placed runners' subsequent record (three runs):
Runners-up: 2 wins from 29 runs returned a loss of -£10.00 to a £1 level stake.
1996 St Mawes – Group Three Gordon Stakes

Thirds: 0 win from 12 runs returned a loss of -£12.00 to a £1 level stake.

FUTURE SUCCESS RATING: ★ ★ ☆ ☆ ☆

ORMONDE STAKES
May 9, Chester – (Group 3, Class 1, 4yo+) 1m5f 89yds

Last run	Winner/Trainer & SP	Draw/Ran	Age	Wght	PR	Next four runs			
07 York 1m6f 4th / St Leger / Eight months	Ask / Sir M Stoute 5/2	4/6	4	9-00	82	WON 11/4 Cumb'ld Lodge Ascot 1m4f	2nd Canadian Int Wood 1m4f	-	-
06 Newb 1m4f 5th / John Porter / Three weeks	The Whistling Teal / G Wragg 7/2	5/5	10	9-00	73	6th Prix de Nieuil Long 1m6f	3rd Lonsdale Cup York 2m	3rd Irish St Leger Curr 1m6f	4th St Simon Stks Newb 1m4f
05 Newb 1m4f 1st / John Porter / Three weeks	Day Flight / J Gosden 85/40	1/8	4	9-00	80	2nd Princess Of Wales Newm 1m4f	WON 3/1JF St Simon Stks Newb 1m4f	2nd Listed race Donc 1m4f	*WON 10/3 G Richards Stks Sand 1m2f
04 Newm 1m4f 2nd / Jockey Club / One week	Systematic / M Johnston 5/2F	7/9	5	8-11	72	11th Coronation Cup Epsom 1m4f	5th Hardwicke Ascot 1m4f	6th Princess of Wales Newm 1m4f	-
03 Newb 1m4f 2nd / John Porter / One month	Asian Heights / G Wragg EvensF	6/7	5	9-00	79	*7th St Simon Stks Newb 1m4f	**13th John Porter Newb 1m4f	**10th Listed race Newm 1m4f	***3rd Conds Stks Newm 1m4f
02 Newb 1m4f 2nd / John Porter / Three weeks	St Expedit / G Wragg 11/8F	1/6	5	8-11	75	2nd G Prix Chantilly Chan 1m4f	*3rd Jebel Hatta Nad A 1m1f	*10th Dubai Duty Free Nad Al 1m1f	*13th Gold Cup Nad Al 2m
01 Newb 1m4f 4th / John Porter / Three weeks	St Expedit / G Wragg 5/2JF	5/5	4	8-11	76	2nd G Prix Chantilly Chan 1m4f	7th Princess of Wales Newm 1m4f	*2nd John Porter Newb 1m4f	*WON 11/8F Ormonde Ches 1m5f
00 Ascot 1m4f 8th / King George VI / Ten months	Daliapour / Sir M Stoute 11/8F	1/9	4	8-11	79	WON 11/8F Coronation Cup Epsom 1m4f	3rd King George VI Ascot 1m4f	4th Grosser 'Baden Baden 1m4f	3rd Canadian Int Wood 1m4f
99 Newb 1m4f 1st / John Porter / Three weeks	Sadian / J Dunlop 2/1F	5/7	4	9-00	70	7th Hardwicke Ascot 1m4f	3rd Geoffrey Freer Newb 1m5f	4th G Prix Deauville Deau 1m5f	-
98 Long 1m7f 8th / Prix Royal-Oak / Seven months	Stretarez / Miss V Williams 25/1	5/6	5	9-02	69	10th Gold Cup Ascot 2m4f	*Fell Aintree Hdle Aint 2m4f	-	-
97 Ascot 1m4f 4th / Cumberland / Eight months	Royal Court / P Chapple-Hyam 9/4F	2/7	4	8-11	74	5th Group 2 Chan 1m4f	4th Hardwicke Ascot 1m4f	4th Group 1 Duss 1m4f	-
96 Leop 1m4f 2nd / April Stks / Three weeks	Oscar Schindler / K Prendergast 11/4	2/7	4	8-11	78	WON 7/4F Hardwicke Ascot 1m4f	4th King George VI Ascot 1m4f	WON 4/1 Irish St Leger Curr 1m6f	3rd Arc de Triomphe Long 1m4f

12-year median performance rating of the winner: **76 (out of 100)** *next year **two years ***three years*

WINNER'S PROFILE Six of the last nine winners arrived having **last ran in the Group Three John Porter Stakes** at Newbury, with those who finished in the first two worthy of respect.
It has also paid to stick with the obvious in the Ormonde, as every winner this century was one of the **top- two officially rated** in that year's renewal, while 11 winners since 1996 emerged from the **first two in the betting**. From an age perspective, **four and five-year-olds** held sway with trainers **Geoff Wragg** and **Sir Michael Stoute** responsible for five of them. Six-year-olds and above have a dismal record with just one winner from almost 30 runners and only veteran, The Whistling Teal, bucked that trend two years ago before a fifth last year.

FUTURE POINTERS There have been numerous subsequent routes taken by Ormonde winners that have ranged from Ascot, Epsom, Newbury, Newmarket and France. Only two were sent to the Group One Coronation Cup at Epsom where one of the best winners, Daliapour, justified favouritism on the Downs in 2000, while four others headed to the Hardwicke Stakes at the Royal meeting where only Oscar Schindler succeeded in 1996, before winning the Irish St Leger later in the year.
Those who went abroad have a moderate record as four lost in France next time out, and from a punting perspective, if the Ormonde winner turns out to be below par, it could prove wiser monitoring the runners-up from Chester *(see below)*.

Were Ormonde winners profitable to follow on their subsequent three runs?
No – 5 wins from 34 runs returned a loss of -£16.13 to a £1 level stake.

Placed runners' subsequent record (three runs):
Runners-up: 8 wins from 36 runs returned a loss of -£6.03 to a £1 level stake.
2007 Scorpion – Coronation Cup, 2005 Shabernak – Esher Stakes, 2004 The Whistling Teal – Aston Park Stakes, 2003 Compton Bolter – Listed Braveheart Handicap

Thirds: 0 wins from 6 runs returned a loss of -£6.00 to a £1 level stake.

FUTURE SUCCESS RATING: ★★ ☆ ☆ ☆

DEE STAKES
May 9, Chester – (Group 3, Class 1, 3yo) 1m2f 75yds

Last run	Winner/ Trainer & SP	Draw/ Ran	Age	Wght	PR	Next four runs			
07 Leop 1m 7th 2000 Guin Trial *Two months*	Admiralofthefleet A O'Brien 7/2	5/6	3	8-12	73	10th Derby Epsom 1m4f	5th Eclipse Sand 1m2f	4th Grade 1 Arli 1m2f	-
06 Donc 7f 2nd Conds Stks *Eight months*	Art Deco C Egerton 8/1	6/9	3	8-12	68	4th Prix Jockey Club Chan 1m2f	5th Grand Prix Paris Long 1m4f	*6th Gordon Richards Sand 1m2f	-
05 Leop 7f 1st Maiden *Seven months*	Gypsy King A O'Brien 2/1F	4/9	3	8-08	71	5th Derby Epsom 1m4f	UR Irish Derby Curr 1m4f	-	-
04 Sand 1m2f 1st Classic Trial *Two weeks*	African Dream P Chapple-Hyam 2/5F	2/3	3	8-11	64	10th Eclipse Sand 1m2f	4th Prix Adam Mais 1m2f	7th Sovereign Stks Salis 1m	*8th Winter Derby Ling 1m2f
03 Donc 7f 1st Maiden *Seven months*	Kris Kin Sir M Stoute 20/1	3/4	3	8-08	75	WON 6/1 Derby Epsom 1m4f	3rd King George VI Ascot 1m4f	3rd Prix Enghien Long 1m4f	11th Arc de Triomphe Long 1m4f
02 Thir 1m 2nd Classic Trial *Three weeks*	Sohaib B Hills 9/2	2/5	3	8-08	64	2nd Scottish Classic Ayr 1m2f	3rd Select Stks Good 1m2f	3rd Joel Stks Newm 1m	-
01 Kemp 1m2f 1st Class Stks *One month*	Dr Greenfield G Butler 11/4	2/9	3	8-08	63	9th Belmont Stks Belm 1m4f	-	-	-
00 Newm 7f 9th Conds Stks *One month*	Trillion Delight M Bell 25/1	5/8	3	8-08	67	7th Predominate Good 1m2f	5th Listed Stks Ascot 1m2f	6th Scottish Classic Ayr 1m2f	3rd Listed Stks Good 1m
99 Newb 1m2f 2nd Conds Stks *Three weeks*	Oath H Cecil 2/1F	3/7	3	8-08	76	WON 13/2 Derby Epsom 1m4f	7th King George VI Ascot 1m4f	-	-
98 Thir 1m 1st Classic Trial *Three weeks*	Prolix B Hills 5/2	3/4	3	8-08	70	5th Prix Jockey Club Chan 1m4f	5th Grand Prix Paris Long 1m2f	3rd Great Voltigeur York 1m4f	3rd Conds Stks Donc 1m2f
97 Nott 1m 2nd Conds Stks *One month*	Crystal Hearted H Candy 9/2	4/3	3	8-08	69	12th Derby Epsom 1m4f	WON 8/1 Scott' Classic Ayr 1m2f	2nd Prix Ornano Deau 1m2f	WON N/O Frankfurt Trophy Fran 1m2f
96 Newm 1m2f 1st Spark Hcp *Three weeks*	Prize Giving G Wragg 9/4F	2/7	3	8-08	65	2nd Predominate Good 1m4f	5th King Edward VII Ascot 1m4f	4th Prix Adam Sain 1m2f	4th Select Stks Good 1m2f

12-year median performance rating of the winner: **69** (out of 100)   *next year*

WINNER'S PROFILE Solid form last time has pointed the way, while those with a **Group victory already** to their name have an excellent record. Only Admiralofthefleet last year, and African Dream in 2004, arrived with a Group penalty and both succeeded.
Maidens rarely win this Group Three event, the last came 17 years ago, and 10 winners were **successful as juveniles**, including Sohaib, who was one of the many successful **Newmarket raiders** trained by dual-winner Barry Hills. Although a relatively small field has traditionally gone to post, it's been worth steering clear of those drawn very wide, as the following favourites were all stuffed: Playapart (stall 5 of 5 in 2002), Grandera (8 of 9 in 2001), and Seven Points (7 of 8 in 2000).

FUTURE POINTERS Although the last two winners of this to have run in the Derby both flopped – trained by Aidan O'Brien – this event should be viewed positively as a pointer towards the Epsom Classic having produced Kris Kin and Oath during the last nine years. As always, the performance ratings (PR) help sort the above par winners from the red-herrings, and both Kris Kin and Oath were two of the best winners in the last 12 years, unlike the sub-standard scorers, who disappeared off the radar following Chester.

Were Dee Stakes winners profitable to follow on their subsequent three runs?
No – 3 wins from 32 runs returned a loss of -£8.50 to a £1 level stake.

Placed runners' subsequent record (three runs):
Runners-up: 4 wins from 22 runs returned a loss of -£3.87 to a £1 level stake.
2005 I'm Spartacus – Group Three Gallinule Stakes

Thirds: 1 win from 12 runs returned a loss of -£9.25 to a £1 level stake.

FUTURE SUCCESS RATING: ★ ★ ☆ ☆ ☆

VICTORIA CUP

May 10, Ascot (Heritage Handicap, Class 2, 4yo+) 7f

Last run	Winner/ Trainer & SP	Draw/ Ran	Age	Wght	PR	Next four runs			
07 Sout 7f 1st Tote Hcp *Three weeks*	Wise Dennis A Jarvis 14/1	14/28	5	8-12	64	2nd Hambleton Hcp York 1m	4th Buckingham Hcp Ascot 7f	16th International Hcp Ascot 7f	6th Tote Hcp Ascot 7f
06 Newm 7f 10th Curragh Hcp *Two months*	Partners In Jazz D Barron 8/1	12/20	5	9-01	66	*4th Tote Hcp Sout 7f	*4th Victoria Cup Ascot 7f	*8th Handicap Sand 7f	*19th International Hcp Ascot 7f
05 Kemp 6f 1st Handicap *Two months*	Iffraaj M Jarvis 11/4F	5/18	4	8-07	74	WON 9/4F Wokingham York 6f	14th July Cup Newm 6f	WON 7/1 Park Hill Donc 7f	7th Prix Barriere Long 7f
04 York 1m 3rd Hambleton Hcp *Two weeks*	Mine J Bethell 5/1F	16/20	6	9-07	70	WON 16/1 Royal Hunt Cup Ascot 1m	5th Heritage Hcp Sand 1m	7th Listed Stks Newm 1m	2nd York Stks York 7f
03 Newm 7f 7th Rated Hcp *Two months*	Camp Commander C Brittain 16/1	10/28	4	8-10	64	3rd Hambleton Hcp York 1m	2nd Royal Hunt Cup Ascot 1m	12th Bunbury Cup Newm 7f	10th International Hcp Ascot 7f
02 Kemp 1m2f 15th Rosebery Hcp *One month*	Scotty's Future D Nicholls 33/1	16/28	4	8-11	60	18th Royal Hunt Cup Ascot 1m	6th Buckingham Hcp Ascot 7f	8th Bunbury Hcp Newm 7f	11th International Hcp Ascot 7f
00 Newm 7f 4th Spark Hcp *Seven months*	Bold King J Hills 25/1	22/21	5	8-09	62	13th Hambleton Hcp York 1m	3rd Rated Hcp Newb 7f	17th International Hp Ascot 7f	14th Handicap Ches 1m
99 Leic 7f 2nd Kibworth Hcp *Three weeks*	Great News I Balding 10/1	2/18	4	7-12	59	3rd Echo Hcp Good 7f	10th Journal Hcp Newc 7f	WON 9/2 Rated Hcp Wind 1m	3rd Ayrshire Hcp Ayr 1m
97 Newm 7f 2nd Rated Hcp *Two weeks*	Tregaron R Akehurst 9/1	11/25	6	8-13	68	28th Royal Hunt Cup Ascot 1m	2nd Rated Hcp Ling 1m	8th City of York York 7f	5th Festival Hcp Ascot 7f
96 Newc 1m 1st Maiden *Two months*	Yeast W Haggas 8/1	15/24	4	8-13	67	2nd Limited Stks Ling 1m	WON 8/1F Royal Hunt Cup Ascot 1m	10th Hong Kong Hcp Sand 1m2f	WON 7/2F Crocker Hcp Ascot 1m

12-year median performance rating of the winner: **65** (out of 100) (*2005 Lingfield, 2001 &1998 abandoned*), **next year*

WINNER'S PROFILE Bold King bucked the trends as he took this on his seasonal debut, but the remainder had **already run that season** and six winners arrived via Kempton or Newmarket.
Large weights have rarely been carried, as only Mine shouldered 9st 7lb in 2004 and it paid to stick with those around **9st or below**. Veterans have struggled, giving way to progressive individuals **aged four to six**, while three of the four biggest priced winners came when the ground rode soft, including Wise Dennis at 14/1 last year.
From a draw perspective, those who came down the centre from the **middle to high stalls** have held an edge – the 2005 renewal took place at Lingfield – so ante-post stakes are best held back until the 48-hour stage.

FUTURE POINTERS Often viewed as a stepping stone for some of the more prestigious handicaps at Royal Ascot, two recent winners advertised that theory and followed up at the big meeting. It is important to note, however, that both those winners – Iffraaj in 2005, and Mine in 2004 – were also the classiest to graduate from here during the last 12 years. Yeast, in 1996, also came back to the Berkshire venue to make all in the Royal Hunt Cup and it has been that route which has proven most successful, as the three who ran in the Hambleton Handicap at York soon after, all lost, including Wise Dennis last year.

Were Victoria Cup winners profitable to follow on their subsequent three runs?
Yes – 5 wins from 30 runs resulted in a **profit of +£15.75** to a £1 level stake.

Placed runners' subsequent record (three runs):
Runners-up: 3 wins from 30 runs returned a loss of -£14.00 to a £1 level stake.

Thirds: 5 wins from 30 runs returned a **profit of +£14.00** to a £1 level stake.
2006 Fullandby – Ayr Heritage Handicap, 2000 Caribbean Monarch – Royal Hunt Cup, Showcase H'cp (Sandown)

Fourth: 5 wins from 30 runs returned a **profit of +£38.12** to a £1 level stake.
2006 Pinpoint – John Smith's Handicap (Newbury), 2005 Court Masterpiece – Listed event (Goodwood),
2002 Sea Star – Hambleton Handicap, 1996 Emerging Market – Wokingham

FUTURE SUCCESS RATING: ★★★★☆

SPRING TROPHY
May 10, Haydock - (Listed, Class 1, 3yo+) 7f

Last run	Winner/Trainer & SP	Draw/Ran	Age	Wght	PR	Next four runs			
07 Nad Al 2nd / Listed Sprint / *Two months*	**Munaddam** E Dunlop 11/2	6/9	5	9-07	70	8th Criterion Stks Newm 7f	7th Sussex Good 1m	-	-
06 Belm 1m 5th / Breeders' Cup / *Seven months*	**Majors Cast** J Noseda 2/7F	2/3	5	9-07	72	2nd Lockinge Newb 1m	-	-	-
05 Thir 6f 7th / Conds Stks / *Three weeks*	**Welsh Emperor** T Tate 7/2	4/5	6	9-03	70	3rd Duke of York York 6f	6th John of Gaunt Hayd 7f	8th Listed Race Ches 6f	**WON 16/1 Bentinck Stks Newm 6f**
04 Leic 7f 3rd / Leicestershire Stks / *One week*	**Rockets 'N Rollers** R Hannon 9/1	2/9	4	9-03	63	4th Royal Windsor Wind 1m	5th Prix Palais-Royale Long 7f	4th Ballycorus Stks Leop 7f	8th City of York York 7f
03 Ling 7f 3rd / Cond Stks / *One month*	**Patsy's Double** M Blanshard 9/1	2/7	5	9-03	65	6th Royal Windsor Wind 1m	2nd John of Gaunt Hayd 7f	11th Criterion Stks Newm 7f	4th Conds Stks Ches 7f
02 Newm 6f 1st / Abernant Stks / *Three weeks*	**Reel Buddy** R Hannon 11/8F	7/7	4	9-07	73	6th Duke of York York 6f	10th July Cup Newm 6f	3rd Sussex Good 1m	**WON 7/2 Hungerford Newb 7f**
01 Cork 7f 7th / Concorde Stks / *Seven months*	**Late Night Out** W Jarvis 4/1	4/5	6	9-07	72	2nd Emirates Mile Baden 1m	3rd John of Gaunt Hayd 7f	**WON 7/4 Listed Race Good 1m**	2nd Jaguar Meile Colon 1m
00 Newm 7f 14th / Rated Hcp / *Three weeks*	**Arctic Char** B Meehan 9/1	3/5	4	8-12	63	6th John of Gaunt Hayd 7f	6th Lennox Stks Good 7f	-	-
99 Warw 7f 3rd / Cond Stks / *One month*	**Late Night Out** W Jarvis 5/1	1/10	4	8-11	70	4th John of Gaunt Hayd 7f	4th Chipchase Stks Newc 6f	7th Conds Stks Newb 7f	13th International Hcp Ascot 7f
98 Curr 1m 8th / Desmond Stks / *Nine months*	**Beauchamp King** G Butler 16/1	3/11	5	9-05	65	9th Lockinge Newb 1m	8th Diomed Stks Epsom 1m1f	4th Conds Stks York 1m	13th Rated Hcp Ascot 1m2f
97 Donc 1m 3rd / Conds Stks / *Two months*	**Craigievar** J Fanshawe 9/4F	6/5	3	8-08	61	4th Group 3 Long 7f	8th Group 3 Long 7f	8th Rated Hcp Good 7f	*12th Rated Hcp Newm 7f
96 Newb 1m 2nd / Spring Cup / *Three weeks*	**Cool Edge** M Tompkins 4/1JF	3/12	5	8-10	60	4th Whitsun Cup Sand 1m	**WON 6/1 Rated Hcp Newb 7f**	3rd Rated Hcp Good 7f	2nd Group 3 Tipp 7f

12-year median performance rating of the winner: **67** (out of 100) *(1996-99 handicap), *next year*

WINNER'S PROFILE A cocktail of courses were used prior to Haydock, although the majority **already raced that season** and were also proven in Pattern company having **at least been placed in a Listed event**, so improving handicappers are best avoided. Distance-winning form hasn't been vital, though a **horse with speed** was required as most winners were up with the pace.
Not many three-year-olds turned up and their only triumph was when it was run as a handicap, while **four to six-year olds** have dominated.

FUTURE POINTERS The Spring Trophy hasn't exactly been a reliable pointer for the remainder of the season as every winner since 1996 tripped up at the first hurdle next time out, although Major's Cast was a creditable runner-up in the Lockinge. The only horse that went on to better things in the same season was the best winner of this event, Reel Buddy, who took the Group Three Hungerford at Newbury.
Several races were unkind to winners post-Haydock, including the John of Gaunt back here – five were beaten – along with the Duke of York and the Royal Windsor Stakes.

Were Spring Trophy winners profitable to follow on their subsequent three runs?
No – 2 wins from 32 runs returned a loss of -£22.25 to a £1 level stake.

Placed runners' subsequent record (three runs):
Runners-up: 6 wins from 33 runs returned a **profit of +£10.00** to a £1 level stake.
2005 Quito – Listed Hambleton Handicap, 2004 Polar Ben – Joel Stakes,
1998 Ramooz – Listed Hambleton Handicap - 1997 Ramooz – Criterion Stakes, Minstrel Stakes

Thirds: 0 win from 12 runs returned a loss of -£12.00 to a £1 level stake.

FUTURE SUCCESS RATING: ★ ★ ☆ ☆ ☆

CHARTWELL FILLIES' STAKES
May 10, Lingfield – (Group 3, Class 1, 4yo+) 7f

Last run	Winner/ Trainer & SP	Draw/ Ran	Age	Wght	PR	Next four runs			
07 York 7f 2nd Sceptre Stks *Eight months*	Wake Up Maggie C Wall 15/8	6/8	4	9-03	67	4th Group 3 Leop 7f	**WON 11/1** **Oak Tree Stks** **Good 7f**	4th Hungerford Stks Newb 7f	3rd Park Stks Donc 7f
06 Newm 7f 1st October Stks *Eight months*	Echelon Sir M Stoute 8/15F	7/8	4	9-03	69	**WON 15/8F** **Princess Elizabeth** **Epsom 1m**	2nd Windsor Forest Ascot 1m	5th Nassau Stks Good 1m2f	*WON 8/11F Dahlia Stks Newm 1m1f
05 Newb 7f 3rd Duty Free Cup *Eight months*	Lucky Spin R Hannon 7/2JF	1/10	4	9-03	65	8th Windsor Forest York 1m	**WON 8/1** **Summer Stks** **York 6f**	3rd Oak Tree Stks Good 7f	4th Maurice 'Gheest Deau 7f
04 Newb 7f 1st Maiden *Three weeks*	Illustrious Miss D Loder 4/1	11/11	3	8-05	63	3rd Irish 2,000 Guin Curr 1m	5th Falmouth Stks Newm 1m	-	-
03 Newm 1m 9th 1000 Guineas *One week*	Presto Vento R Hannon 7/2	1/7	3	8-05	60	5th Cecil Frail Stks Hayd 6f	11th Jersey Stks Ascot 7f	12th Oak Tree Stks Good 7f	5th Shergar Cup Ascot 6f
02 Deau 1m 6th Prix d'Astarte *Nine months*	Tempting Fate S Bin Suroor 4/6F	7/8	4	9-03	61	2nd Prix Palais-Royal Long 7f	-	-	-
01 Newm 7f 2nd Euro Free Hcp *One month*	Palace Affair G Balding 5/2F	11/13	3	8-05	65	5th Showcase Hcp Good 7f	11th Jersey Stks Ascot 7f	**WON 11/2** **Summer Stks** **York 6f**	10th Oak Tree Stks Good 7f
00 Thir 6f 2nd Conds Stks *One month*	Hot Tin Roof T Easterby 13/2	8/13	4	9-03	64	**WON 9/2** **Kilvington Stks** **Nott 6f**	2nd Listed Race Ling 6f	2nd John of Gaunt Hayd 6f	6th Criterion Stks Newm 7f
99 Newb 7f 1st Maiden *One month*	Presumed P Makin 7/4F	2/11	3	8-05	58	7th Coronation Stks Ascot 1m	4th Falmouth Newm 1m	3rd Prix d'Astarte Deau 1m	4th Sceptre Stks Donc 7f
98 Newm 7f 6th Nell Gwyn *One month*	Nanoushka R Hannon 4/1	3/9	3	8-05	66	9th Coronation Stks Ascot 1m	**WON 9/1** **Summer Stks** **York 6f**	3rd Flying Fillies Pont 6f	4th Prix de Meautry Deau 6f
97 Newm 1m2f 6th Pretty Polly *One week*	Supercal D Elsworth 6/1	4/7	3	8-05	59	8th Conqueror Stks Good 1m	7th Jersey Ascot 7f	9th Criterion Newm 7f	2nd Hong Kong Hcp Sand 1m
96 Nad Al 6f 3rd Listed Sprint *Two months*	Isla Del Rey S Bin Suroor 15/8F	6/6	4	9-03	61	6th Cork & Orrery Ascot 6f	14th Oak Tree Stks Good 7f	-	-

12-year median performance rating of the winner: **63** (out of 100)   *next year*

WINNER'S PROFILE Not much to work with but eight winners **arrived via either Newbury or Newmarket**, while those with an **official rating in excess of 100** performed well.
Three and four-year-olds – despite covering most of the field each year – at **6/1 or shorter** have won every renewal since 1996, and trainer **Richard Hannon** was responsible for three of them.

FUTURE POINTERS Since this fillies' event was upgraded to Group Three status in 2004, the quality of the winners naturally improved as two of the last three won decent races on their next two runs. Echelon duly followed up in the Group Three Princess Elizabeth at Epsom in 2006, while a year earlier, Lucky Spin dropped back in trip to lift the Group Three Summer Stakes at York, a race that two other winners from here – Palace Affair in 2001 and Nanoushka in 1998 – both also triumphed in. However, Chartwell winners have found the Royal fixture to be a graveyard, as eight winners were outclassed.

Were Chartwell Stakes winners profitable to follow on their subsequent three runs?
Yes – 6 wins from 32 runs returned a **profit of +£13.87** to a £1 level stake.

Placed runners' subsequent record (three runs):
Runners-up: 5 wins from 34 runs returned a loss of -£16.85 to a £1 level stake.
2005 Nufoos – Listed Eternal Stakes, 2004 Gonfilia – Listed Conqueror Stakes, Princess Elizabeth Stakes,
2002 Marika – Cecil Frail Stakes, 1996 Carranita – Summer Stakes

Thirds: 3 wins from 22 runs returned a loss of -£8.16 to a £1 level stake
2004 Golden Nun – Listed Kilvington Stakes, Group Three Ballyogan Stakes,

FUTURE SUCCESS RATING: ★★★☆☆

DERBY TRIAL
May 10, Lingfield – (Group 3, Class 1, 3yo) 1m 3f 106yds

Last run	Winner/ Trainer & SP	Draw/ Ran	Age	Wght	PR	Next four runs			
07 Newb 1m 2nd Cond Stks *Eight months*	**Aqaleem** M Tregoning 12/1	6/7	3	8-12	75	3rd Derby Epsom 1m4f	2nd Gordon Stks Good 1m4f	-	-
06 Long 1m3f 4th Prix Noailles *One month*	**Linda's Lad** A Fabre 15/8F	2/5	3	9-03	71	9th Derby Epsom 1m4f	3rd Prix Eugene Adam Mais 1m2f	*5th Jockey Club Newm 1m4f	
05 Newb 1m3f 2nd Maiden *Three weeks*	**Kong** J Dunlop 9/2	1/6	3	8-10	66	13th Derby Epsom 1m4f	4th Great Voltigeur York 1m4f	4th St Leger Donc 1m6f	4th Cumberland Lodge Newm 1m4f
04 Newm 1m4f 1st Maiden *One month*	**Percussionist** J Gosden 11/4	1/4	3	8-07	73	4th Derby Epsom 1m4f	10th Irish Derby Curr 1m4f	2nd Doonside Cup Ayr 1m3	3rd Prix de Menton Long 1m7f
03 Epsom 1m2f 1st Blue Riband Trial *Three weeks*	**Franklins Gardens** M Tompkins 5/1	2/6	3	8-07	69	14th Derby Epsom 1m4f	*4th Gordon Richards Sand 1m2f	*4th Rose of Lancaster Hayd 1m3f	*7th Grand Prix Barriere Deau 1m5f
02 Pont 1m 1st Silver Tankard *Six months*	**Bandari** M Johnston 11/4	6/6	3	8-07	73	8th Derby Epsom 1m4f	**WON 15/8 Gordon Stks Good 1m4f**	**WON 4/5F Great Voltigeur York 1m4f**	3rd St Leger Donc 1m6f
01 Newm 1m4f 1st Maiden *One month*	**Perfect Sunday** B Hills 11/8F	5/8	3	8-07	69	6th Derby Epsom 1m4f	2nd Grand Prix St-Cloud Sain 1m4f	7th Gordon Stks Good 1m4f	2nd September Stks Kemp 1m4f
00 Kemp 1m2f 1st Class Stks *Three weeks*	**Saddler's Quest** G Butler 10/3F	8/8	3	8-07	69	*9th John Porter Newb 1m4f	*9th Sagaro Stks Newm 2m	*8th Conds Stks Hayd 1m6f	*4th St Simon Stks Newm 1m4f
99 Newb 1m2f 1st Conds Stks *Three weeks*	**Lucido** J Dunlop 3/1	4/5	3	8-07	70	15th Derby Epsom 1m4f	10th Godolphin Stks Newm 1m4f	3rd Prix de Paris Long 1m4f	*5th Jockey Club Newm 1m4f
98 Pont 1m2f 1st Limited Stks *Three weeks*	**High-Rise** L Cumani 15/8	2/6	3	8-07	72	**WON 20/1 Derby Epsom 1m4f**	2nd King George VI Ascot 1m4f	7th Arc de Triomphe Long 1m4f	*8th Dubai World Cup Nad Al 1m2f
97 Sand 1m2f 3rd Classic Trial *Two weeks*	**Silver Patriarch** J Dunlop 5/4F	4/5	3	8-07	74	2nd Derby Epsom 1m4f	5th Irish Derby Curr 1m4f	2nd Great Voltigeur York 1m4f	**WON 5/4F St Leger Donc 1m6f**
96 Newb 1m3f 3rd Cond Stks *Three weeks*	**Mystic Knight** R Charlton 4/1	2/6	3	8-07	64	6th Derby Epsom 1m4f	-	-	-

12-year median performance rating of the winner: **70** (out of 100)   **next year*

WINNER'S PROFILE Aqaleem shook the trends last year as he became only the second horse since 1996 to arrive at Lingfield without a recent run – most **raced within the past month**. He was also only the second maiden winner for nearly 30 years, which went against the grain as 10 of the last 12 winners had **scored on one of their previous two outings**. The third trend Aqaleem defied was that he emerged from outside of the first three in the betting – no doubt due to his untraditional profile – but it usually pays to stick to those priced at **5/1 or shorter** in the market. One trainer to keep tabs on is **John Dunlop**, as he boasts a 100% record since 1996, with three winners from as many runners.

FUTURE POINTERS This Derby Trial has been criticised in recent years for not being a solid pointer to Epsom, despite the fact High-Rise went on to Classic glory in 1998, but as with all races and trials, the quality winners have been the ones to follow. For example, the 2005, 2003, 2001, 2000 and 1996 renewals were below average – based on the winner's performance rating (PR) – and were best swerved at Epsom, but some of the above average winners such as Silver Patriarch, High-Rise, Percussionist and Aqaleem held their own in the Classic. Bandari was also a classy winner here at Lingfield, and despite the blip in the Derby, he redeemed himself by scooping two Group races.

Were Derby Trial winners profitable to follow on their subsequent three runs?
No – 3 wins from 33 runs returned a loss of -£7.32 to a £1 level stake.

Placed runners' subsequent record (three runs):
Runners-up: 4 wins from 33 runs returned a **profit of +£5.44** to a £1 level stake.
2007 Hearthstead Maison – Heritage Handicap (Newmarket)

Thirds: 1 win from 6 runs returned a loss of -£4.81 to a £1 level stake.

FUTURE SUCCESS RATING: ★ ★ ☆ ☆ ☆

OAKS TRIAL

May 10, Lingfield – (Listed, Class 1, 3yo Fillies) 1m3f 106yds

Last run	Winner/Trainer & SP	Draw/Ran	Age	Wght	PR	Next four runs			
07 Nott 1m 1st Maiden *Eight months*	**Kayah** R Beckett 20/1	6/7	3	8-12	51	9th Oaks Epsom 1m4f	6th Park Hill Stks Donc 1m7f	9th Princess Royal Ascot 1m4f	-
06 Newm 1m 4th Listed Race *Seven months*	**Sindirana** Sir M Stoute 7/4JF	5/10	3	8-10	60	11th Ribblesdale Ascot 1m4f	5th Aphrodite Stks Newm 1m4f	6th Chalice Stks Newb 1m4f	-
05 Donc 1m 4th May Hill *Eight months*	**Cassydora** J Dunlop 7/4	6/6	3	8-10	63	7th Oaks Epsom 1m4f	2nd Nassau Good 1m2f	3rd Group 3 Deau 1m2f	11th Taylor Stks Wood 1m2f
04 Curr 7f 9th Fillies Race *Eight months*	**Baraka** A O'Brien 9/4	5/5	3	8-08	65	9th Blandford Stks Curr 1m2f	-	-	-
03 Wind 1m2f 1st Maiden *Two months*	**Santa Sophia** J Dunlop 11/1	4/8	3	8-08	61	7th Oaks Epsom 1m4f	5th Lancashire Oaks Hayd 1m4f	14th Severals Stks Newm 1m2f	-
02 Newc 1m 1st Maiden *Two months*	**Birdie** M Bell 16/1	2/7	3	8-08	54	9th Group 3 Chan 1m4f	5th Lancashire Oaks Hayd 1m4f	6th Daffodil Stks Chep 1m2f	6th Listed Race Siro 1m
01 Sand 1m2f 1st Maiden *Three weeks*	**Double Crossed** H Cecil 11/4	3/3	3	8-08	56	6th Serlby Stks Donc 1m4f	-	-	-
00 Sali 1m4f 1st Maiden *One week*	**Film Script** R Charlton 7/1	7/7	3	8-08	63	3rd King George Hcp Ascot 1m4f	6th Lancaster Stks Hayd 1m4f	**WON 11/4** **Daffodil Stks** **Chep 1m2f**	3rd Chalice Stks Newb 1m4f
99 Newm 1m4f 1st Maiden *One month*	**Ramruma** H Cecil 8/15F	1/7	3	8-08	66	**WON 3/1** **Oaks** **Epsom 1m4f**	**WON 4/9F** **Irish Oaks** **Curr 1m4f**	**WON 5/6F** **Yorkshire Oaks** **York 1m4f**	St Leger Donc 1m6f
98 Newm 7f 4th Listed Race *Seven months*	**Bristol Channel** B Hills 9/4F	3/6	3	8-08	60	2nd Galtres Stks York 1m4f	**WON 9/4** **Harvest Stks** **Ascot 1m4f**	3rd Princess Royal Ascot 1m4f	3rd Long Island Hcp Aque 1m4f
97 Newm 1m2f 4th Pretty Polly *One week*	**Crown Of Light** Sir M Stoute 11/2	4/5	3	8-08	59	3rd Oaks Epsom 1m4f	3rd Ribblesdale Ascot 1m4f	3rd Yorkshire Oaks York 1m4f	6th Park Hill Donc 1m6f
96 Leic 1m 1st Maiden *Seven months*	**Lady Carla** H Cecil 4/11F	2/4	3	8-08	62	**WON 10/3** **Oaks** **Epsom 1m4f**	4th Irish Oaks Curr 1m4f	*9th Hardwicke Ascot 1m4f	*7th Princess Of Wales' Newm 1m4f

12-year median performance rating of the winner: **60** (out of 100)   **next year*

WINNER'S PROFILE Not too many patterns help recognize the ideal profile of an Oaks Trial winner, although maidens were rare and only Aidan O'Brien's Baraka broke her duck here. Seven winners **won their maidens last time out**, while 11 of the 12 winners had **no more than three career runs**.
With trends thin on the ground, it may prove wise to follow trainer **Henry Cecil**'s runners, as he sent out three winners and two runners-up from five runners, including Brisk Breeze last year, while two others to keep onside include dual winners **John Dunlop** and **Sir Michael Stoute**.

FUTURE POINTERS Unlike the Derby Trial here, the Oaks equivalent has been a more useful springboard to Epsom, as two winners followed up in the Classic. Although last year's winner, Kayah, flopped miserably at Epsom, she was amongst a moderate bunch of recent winners here, unlike the classy Ramruma and Lady Carla, who both achieved above par performance ratings (PR). Baraka was also a quality winner but may have been injured subsequently, as she never reappeared until September, while another of the best winners, Film Script, managed to pick up another Listed race. Apart from Ramruma, four winners failed in other versions of an Oaks.

Were Oaks Trial winners profitable to follow on their subsequent three runs?
No – 6 wins from 32 runs returned a loss of -£13.40 to a £1 level stake.

Placed runners' subsequent record (three runs):
Runners-up: 3 wins from 26 runs returned a loss of -£21.50 to a £1 level stake.

Thirds: 2 wins from 6 runs returned a loss of -£2.50 to a £1 level stake.

FUTURE SUCCESS RATING: ★ ★ ☆ ☆ ☆

DERRINSTOWN DERBY TRIAL
May 11, Leopardstown – (Group 2, Class 1, 3yo) 1m2f

Last run	Winner/ Trainer & SP	Draw/ Ran	Age	Wght	PR	Next four runs			
07 Leop 7f 1st EBF Maiden *Seven months*	**Archipenko** A O'Brien 8/1	1/5	3	9-01	70	17th Derby Epsom 1m4f	7th Eclipse Sand 1m2f	5th Sussex Good 1m	5th Prix du Moulin Long 1m
06 Donc 1m 6th R Post Trophy *Seven months*	**Dylan Thomas** A O'Brien 11/2	1/8	3	9-01	74	3rd Derby Epsom 1m4f	**WON 9/2F** **Irish Derby** Curr 1m4f	4th Juddmonte Int York 1m2f	**WON 13/8F** **Irish Champion** Leop 1m2f
05 Sand 1m2f 1st Classic Trial *Three weeks*	**Fracas** D Wachman 2/1	3/5	3	9-00	69	4th Derby Epsom 1m4f	7th Irish Derby Curr 1m4f	2nd KolnBonn Colon 1m4f	8th Preis von Baden Baden 1m4f
04 Curr 1m 1st Maiden *Eight months*	**Yeats** A O'Brien 1/5F	5/4	3	9-00	72	*2nd Mooresbridge Curr 1m2f	*WON 5/1 Coronation Cup Epsom 1m4f	*9th G Prix St-Cloud Sain 1m4f	*4th Irish St Leger Curr 1m6f
03 Leop 1m2f 2nd Ballysax Stks *One month*	**Alamshar** J Oxx 8/15F	1/6	3	9-00	70	3rd Derby Epsom 1m4f	**WON 4/1** **Irish Derby** Curr 1m4f	**WON 13/2** King George VI Ascot 1m4f	4th Irish Champion Leop 1m2f
02 Leop 1m2f 1st Ballysax Stks *One month*	**High Chaparral** A O'Brien 1/5F	5/5	3	9-04	74	**WON 7/2** **Derby** Epsom 1m4f	**WON 1/3F** **Irish Derby** Curr 1m4f	3rd Arc De Triomphe Long 1m4f	**WON 9/10F** Breeders' Cup Arling 1m4f
01 Leop 1m2f 1st Ballysax Stks *One month*	**Galileo** A O'Brien 8/15F	5/5	3	8-11	73	**WON 11/4JF** **Derby** Epsom 1m4f	**WON 4/11F** **Irish Derby** Curr 1m4f	**WON 1/2F** King George VI Ascot 1m4f	2nd Irish Champion Leop 1m2f
00 Leop 1m2f 2nd Ballysax Stks *One month*	**Sinndar** J Oxx 7/4JF	3/4	3	9-04	75	**WON 7/1** **Derby** Epsom 1m4f	**WON 11/10F** **Irish Derby** Curr 1m4f	WON 3/10JF Prix Niel Long 1m4f	WON 6/4 Arc De Triomphe Long 1m4f
99 Leop 1m2f 3rd Ballysax Stks *Three weeks*	**Port Bayou** D Weld 10/1	5/5	3	8-11	66	8th Irish Derby Curr 1m4f	5th Prix D'Ornano Deau 1m2f	-	-
98 Leop 1m2f 2nd Ballysax Stks *Three weeks*	**Risk Material** A O'Brien EvensF	4/9	3	8-11	67	**WON 6/4** **Listed Stks** Curr 1m2f	3rd Gallinule Stks Curr 1m2f	7th Irish Derby Curr 1m4f	8th King George VI Ascot 1m4f
97 Leop 7f 1st EBF Maiden *Seven months*	**Ashley Park** Charles O'Brien 8/1	5/7	3	8-11	70	6th Royal Whip Stks Curr 1m2f	***WON 11/4** *Nov Hdle* *Sand 2m*	**4th Champion Hdle Chel 2m	**2nd Xmas Hdle Kemp 2m
96 Curr 1m 1st Maiden *Two months*	**Truth Or Dare** C Lerner 11/4F	1/7	3	8-11	64	6th Group 2 Curr 1m4f	12th Irish Derby Curr 1m4f	*3rd Stakes Sain 1m3f	*9th Group 3 Sain 1m2f

12-year median performance rating of the winner: **70** (out of 100)   *Italic = jumps, *next year **two years*

WINNER'S PROFILE Every winner either **raced here last time, at The Curragh, or in a British Group event**, and 11 made the first three. Seven of the last eight winners **previously won at least two-thirds of their races**, while two defied a Group One penalty, including High Chaparral in 2002. **Aidan O'Brien** is obviously the trainer to follow with six winners, though his last two were unexpected in the market, while John Oxx sent out two.

FUTURE POINTERS The Derrinstown Derby trial is simply one of the best future pointers in this book as three consecutive winners went on to lift the big one at Epsom since the Millennium, and as a result was deservedly upgraded to Group Two status in 2002. Those three winners were among the best from this trial, and achieved top performance ratings (PR) on the day. Yeats was also a classy winner who took the Coronation Cup before Gold Cup glory at Royal Ascot further down the line, while Alamshar (2003) took the Irish Derby – as did Dylan Thomas in 2006 – before he triumphed in the King George VI at Ascot.
At the rate this Derby Trial is progressing, it may soon be renamed the Irish Derby itself, as five of the last eight returned to triumph on the big day, and it goes without saying, that quality winners from here should be followed.

Were Derby Trial winners profitable to follow on their subsequent three runs?
Yes – 14 wins from 35 runs returned a **profit of +£19.09** to a £1 level stake.

Placed runners' subsequent record (three runs):
Runners-up: 3 wins from 29 runs returned a loss of -£22.09 to a £1 level stake.
2001 Exaltation – Irish Group Three, 1998 Takarin – Irish Group Three

Thirds: 3 wins from 6 runs returned a **profit of +£13.00** to a £1 level stake.
2006 Youmzain – Bahrain Stakes, Great Voltigeur

FUTURE SUCCESS RATING: ★ ★ ★ ★ ★

DUKE OF YORK STAKES
May 14, York – (Group 2, Class 1, 3yo+) 6f

Last run	Winner/ Trainer & SP	Draw/ Ran	Age	Wght	PR	Next four runs			
07 Long 5f 5th Abbaye *Seven months*	**Amadeus Wolf** K Ryan 3/1F	4/17	4	9-02	77	11th Golden Jubilee Ascot 6f	12th July Cup Newm 6f	7th Nunthorpe York 5f	12th Sprint Cup Hayd 6f
06 Curr 7f 5th Gladness Stks *Two months*	**Steenberg** M Tompkins 25/1	2/16	7	9-02	74	7th Nunthorpe York 5f	11th Sprint Cup Hayd 6f	9th Diadem Ascot 6f	5th Guisborough Redc 7f
05 Newm 6f 3rd Abernant Stks *One month*	**The Kiddykid** P Evans 14/1	9/11	5	9-02	73	6th Greenlands Stks Curr 6f	13th Golden Jubilee York 6f	14th Sprint Cup Hayd 6f	5th Dubai Duty Free Newb 7f
04 Curr 7f 1st Gladness Stks *Two months*	**Monsieur Bond** B Smart 4/1F	5/15	4	9-02	80	12th Golden Jubilee Ascot 6f	6th July Cup Newm 6f	9th Maurice 'Gheest Deau 7f	5th Sprint Cup Hayd 6f
03 Leic 7f 4th Leicestershire *Three weeks*	**Twilight Blues** B Meehan 25/1	3/15	4	9-02	75	8th Golden Jubilee Ascot 6f	10th July Cup Newm 6f	7th Sprint Cup Hayd 6f	10th Challenge Stks Newm 7f
02 Newm 6f 4th Abernant Stks *One month*	**Invincible Spirit** J Dunlop 3/1F	6/12	5	9-05	81	5th Temple Stks Sand 5f	6th Golden Jubilee Ascot 6f	**WON 25/1 Sprint Cup Hayd 6f**	-
01 Newm 5f 13th Palace House *Two weeks*	**Pipalong** T Easterby 14/1	8/14	5	9-06	80	8th Cork & Orrery Ascot 6f	13th July Cup Newm 6f	7th Nunthorpe York 5f	7th Sprint Cup Hayd 6f
00 Nad Al 6th Dubai Listed *Two months*	**Lend A Hand** S Bin Suroor 10/3	5/10	5	9-05	83	3rd Cork & Orrery Ascot 6f	5th July Cup Newm 6f	2nd Maurice 'Gheest Deau 7f	-
99 Ascot 6f 1st Gardner Listed *Three weeks*	**Sampower Star** R Hannon 13/2	8/14	3	8-05	73	4th Temple Stks Sand 5f	8th July Cup Newm 6f	7th Maurice 'Gheest Deau 7f	2nd Prix de Meautry Deau 6f
98 Newm 6f 2nd Bentinck Stks *Seven months*	**Bollin Joanne** T Easterby 11/2	3/10	5	8-11	72	16th King's Stand Stk Ascot 6f	15th July Cup Newm 6f	13th Nunthorpe York 5f	4th Scarbrough Stk Donc 5f
97 Donc 6f 1st Cammidge Trop *Two months*	**Royal Applause** B Hills 3/1F	1/10	4	9-00	84	**WON 11/2F Cork & Orrery Ascot 6f**	2nd July Cup Newm 6f	**WON 15/8F Sprint Cup Hayd 6f**	3rd Abbaye Long 5f
96 Newm 6f 2nd Rated Hcp *Two months*	**Venture Capitalist** D Nicholls 11/1	9/12	7	9-00	73	8th John of Gaunt Hayd 7f	7th Cork & Orrery Ascot 6f	2nd Chipchase Stks Newc 6f	2nd Sprint Stks Sand 5f

12-year median performance rating of the winner: **77** (out of 100)

WINNER'S PROFILE Four of the last six winners arrived at York having **last run in either the Abernant or Gladness Stakes** and the majority had a sharpener for this despite last year's winner. Class has very much prevailed in this sprint, as all **12 winners had an official rating of at least 105**.
On what is usually tacky ground at this time of year, 10 winners were **drawn low to middle** – stalls one to six provided seven winners. **Four to five-year-olds** have the best strike-rate and local trainer **Tim Easterby** was responsible for two of them.

FUTURE POINTERS Not a great event from which to follow the winner in upcoming sprints as only the 1997 winner, Royal Applause managed to win next time out in the Cork and Orrery at Royal Ascot (now the Golden Jubilee). In fact, that race hasn't been kind to Duke of York winners, as nine lost down at the Royal fixture, although last year's third, Soldier's Tale, managed to score there.
Royal Applause also managed to win the Sprint Cup at Haydock during the autumn – as did Invincible Spirit in 2002 – but just missed out in the July Cup at Newmarket, a race that halted a further seven Duke of York scorers.

Were Duke of York winners profitable to follow on their subsequent three runs?
No – 3 wins from 36 runs returned a loss of -£0.63 to a £1 level stake.

Placed runners' subsequent record (three runs):
Runners-up: 7 wins from 35 runs returned a loss of -£10.99 to a £1 level stake.
2006 Quito – John of Gaunt Stakes, 2000 Pipalong – Cecil Frail Stakes, 1999 Warningford – Cecil Frail Stakes, 1998 Elnadim – July Cup

Thirds: 6 wins from 33 runs returned a **profit of +£12.85** to a £1 level stake.
2007 Soldier's Tale – Golden Jubilee, 2005 Welsh Emperor – Bentinck Stakes, 2004 Arakan – Criterion Stakes, 2000 Bold Edge – Maurice de Gheest

FUTURE SUCCESS RATING: ★ ★ ★ ★ ★

MUSIDORA STAKES

May 14, York – (Group 3, Class 1, 3yo Fillies) 1m2f 88yds

Last run	Winner/ Trainer & SP	Draw/ Ran	Age	Wght	PR	Next four runs			
07 Saint 1m2f 1st Criterium *Six months*	**Passage Of Time** H Cecil 5/6F	4/5	3	9-01	72	8th Oaks Epsom 1m4f	3rd Prix Vermeille Long 1m4f	3rd Breeders' Cup Monm 1m3f	-
06 Newm 7f 7th Rockfel Stks *Seven months*	**Short Skirt** Sir M Stoute 7/2	4/6	3	8-12	73	3rd Oaks Epsom 1m4f	2nd Yorkshire Oaks York 1m4f	6th Group 2 Long 1m5f	**WON 13/2** St Simon Stks Newb 1m4f
05 Good 1m 2nd Conqueror Stks *Two weeks*	**Secret History** M Johnston 4/1	2/6	3	8-10	67	3rd Princess Elizabeth Epsom 1½m	5th Ribblesdale York 1m4f	10th Nassau Good 1m2f	8th Group 3 Brem 1m3f
04 Ascot 1m 3rd Meon Valley *Eight months*	**Punctilious** S Bin Suroor 8/11F	4/6	3	8-08	71	3rd Oaks Epsom 1m4f	**WON 9/2** Ribblesdale Ascot 1m4f	2nd Irish Oaks Curr 1m4f	4th Yorkshire Oaks York 1m4f
03 Newb 7f 9th Fred Darling *One month*	**Cassis** J Noseda 16/1	1/8	3	8-08	63	5th Prix Hermes Chan 1m3f	4th Coronation Stks Ascot 1m	6th Nassau Good 1m2f	4th Grade 1 Del 1m1f
02 Newb 1m2f 1st Maiden *One month*	**Islington** Sir M Stoute 5/6F	3/5	3	8-08	75	8th Oaks Epsom 1m4f	**WON 10/3** Nassau Good 1m2f	**WON 2/1** Yorkshire Oaks York 1m4f	5th Arc de Triomphe Long 1m4f
01 Newm 1m2f 3rd Pretty Polly *Two weeks*	**Time Away** J Dunlop 7/2	6/11	3	8-08	65	3rd Prix Hermes Chan 1m3f	6th Irish Oaks Curr 1m4f	3rd Nassau Good 1m2f	7th Juddmonte Int York 1m4f
00 Wind 1m 1st Maiden *Seven months*	**Kalypso Katie** J Noseda 10/3	9/9	3	8-08	67	2nd Oaks Epsom 1m4f	5th Irish Oaks Curr 1m4f	*WON 2/5F Stakes Holl 1m1f	*5th Grade 1 Holl 1m1f
99 Newm 7f 6th Maiden *Seven months*	**Zahrat Dubai** S Bin Suroor 6/5F	3/6	3	8-08	71	3rd Oaks Epsom 1m4f	**WON 5/1** Nassau Good 1m2f	4th Yorkshire Oaks York 1m4f	5th Prix de l'Opera Long 1m2f
98 Newb 7f 1st Washington Singer *Nine months*	**Bahr** S Bin Suroor 6/4	1/4	3	8-08	70	2nd Oaks Epsom 1m4f	**WON 13/8F** Ribblesdale Ascot 1m4f	3rd Irish Oaks Curr 1m4f	3rd Prix Vermeille Long 1m4f
97 Newm 1m 6th 1,000 Guineas *Two weeks*	**Reams Of Verse** H Cecil 11/10F	9/10	3	8-11	74	**WON 5/6F** Oaks Epsom 1m4f	4th Yorkshire Oaks York 1m4f	3rd Sun Chariot Newm 1m2f	-
96 Newm 1m2f 3rd Pretty Polly *Two weeks*	**Magnificent Style** H Cecil 5/2	3/5	3	8-08	65	6th Ribblesdale Ascot 1m4f	-	-	-

12-year median performance rating of the winner: **69** (out of 100)   *next year

WINNER'S PROFILE Eleven winners raced at a **Grade One venue last time** – eight arrived via Newbury or Newmarket – while nine **already experienced Pattern company**.
Only one maiden was successful here and those punters that stuck to the **first two in the betting** were rewarded, however, the most helpful clue to finding the winner has concerned the trainers. Ten winners were spread amongst Henry Cecil (3), Jeremy Noseda (2), Sir Michael Stoute (2), and Saeed Bin Suroor (2), although one trainer to avoid was Barry Hills who remains winless from 8 runners.

FUTURE POINTERS This Oaks trial has only provided two winners of the Epsom Classic since 1996, with the 2006 runner-up, Alexandrova putting an end to the dry spell after Reams Of Verse's triumph in 1997.
Although seven winners tripped up in the Epsom Classic, including Passage Of Time last year, several got back on the winning trail later that year, with Islington and Zahrat Dubai in the Group One Nassau at Goodwood, while two others, Punctillious and Bahr, tasted success at Royal Ascot in the Ribblesdale Stakes.

Were Musidora winners profitable to follow on their subsequent three runs?
No – 6 wins from 34 runs returned a loss of -£10.31 to a £1 level stake.

Placed runners' subsequent record (three runs):
Runners-up: 6 wins from 31 runs returned a **profit of +£13.52** to a £1 level stake.
2006 Alexandrova – Oaks, Irish Oaks, Yorkshire Oaks, 2000 Lady Upstage – Pretty Polly Stakes, 1996 Sil Sila – Prix de Diane Hermes (French Oaks)

Thirds: 1 win from 12 runs returned a loss of -£10.87 to a £1 level stake.

FUTURE SUCCESS RATING: ★ ★ ★ ★ ★

DANTE STAKES
May 15, York – (Group 2, Class 1, 3yo) 1m2f 88yds

Last run	Winner/ Trainer & SP	Draw/ Ran	Age	Wght	PR	Next four runs			
07 Newb 1m 1st R Post Trophy *Seven months*	**Authorized** P Chapple-Hyam 10/11F	3/6	3	9-00	82	WON 5/4F Derby Epsom 1m4f	2nd Eclipse Sand 1m2f	WON 6/4F Juddmonte Int York 1m2f	10th Arc de Triomphe Long 1m4f
06 Long 1m2f 7th Prix La Force *One month*	**Septimus** A O'Brien 13/8F	4/6	3	9-00	77	12th Derby Epsom 1m4f	*WON 4/1 **Mooresbridge Stks** Curr 1m2f	*2nd Coronation Cup Epsom 1m4f	*WON 6/5F **Lonsdale Cup** York 2m
05 Donc 1m 1st R Post Trophy *Seven months*	**Motivator** M Bell EvensF	1/6	3	8-11	80	WON 3/1F Derby Epsom 1m4f	2nd Eclipse Sand 1m2f	2nd Irish Champion Leop 1m2f	5th Arc de Triomphe Long 1m4f
04 Good 1m 1st Maiden *Eight months*	**North Light** Sir M Stoute 6/1	1/10	3	8-11	82	WON 7/2JF Derby Epsom 1m4f	2nd Irish Derby Curr 1m4f	5th Arc de Triomphe Long 1m4f	*2nd Brigadier Gerard Sand 1m2f
03 Newm 1m1f 1st Feilden Stks *One month*	**Magistretti** N Callaghan 8/1	4/10	3	8-11	70	9th Derby Epsom 1m4f	2nd G Prix' Paris Long 1m2f	2nd Juddmonte Int York 1m2f	*6th Coronation Cup Epsom 1m4f
02 Newm 1m2f 2nd Newmarket Stks *Two weeks*	**Moon Ballad** S Bin Suroor 13/2	7/9	3	8-11	74	3rd Derby Epsom 1m4f	WON 4/6F **Select Stks** Good 1m2f	2nd Champion Stks Newm 1m2f	*WON N/O **Maktoum Chall** Nad Al 1m1f
01 Donc 1m 1st R Post Trophy *Seven months*	**Dilshaan** Sir M Stoute 9/4F	3/6	3	8-11	74	7th Derby Epsom 1m4f	-		
00 Sand 1m2f 1st Classic Trial *Three weeks*	**Sakhee** J Dunlop 5/2JF	3/5	3	8-11	80	2nd Derby Epsom 1m4f	2nd Eclipse Sand 1m2f	*WON 8/11F **Steventon Stks** Newb 1m2f	*WON 7/4F **Juddmonte Int** York 1m2f
99 Newb 1m3f 1st Maiden *One month*	**Salford Express** D Elsworth 12/1	2/8	3	8-11	72	14th Derby Epsom 1m4f	5th Prix Eugene Mais 1m2f	10th Juddmonte Int York 1m2f	4th Dubai Arc Trial Newb 1m3f
98 Donc 1m 1st R Post Trophy *Seven months*	**Saratoga Springs** A O'Brien 4/1	6/6	3	8-11	74	4th Prix' Jock Club Chan 1m4f	10th Derby Epsom 1m4f	6th Irish Derby Curr 1m4f	*11th Dubai Classic Nad Al 1m4f
97 Sand 1m2f 2nd Classic Trial *Three weeks*	**Benny The Dip** J Gosden 10/3F	4/9	3	8-11	76	WON 10/3F Derby Epsom 1m4f	2nd Eclipse Sand 1m2f	3rd Juddmonte Int York 1m2f	6th Champion Stks Newm 1m2f
96 Sand 1m2f 2nd Classic Trial *Three weeks*	**Glory Of Dancer** P Kelleway 3/1	2/7	3	8-11	75	4th Derby Epsom 1m4f	2nd G Prix' Paris Long 1m2f	4th Rose' Lancaster Hayd 1m3f	4th Arlington Million Arli 1m2f

12-year median performance rating of the winner: **76** (out of 100)   *next year*

WINNER'S PROFILE Eleven winners arrived having **won or finished second last time out**, seven via the Racing Post Trophy or the Sandown Classic Trial. In fact, of the six Racing Post Trophy winners that raced here, four won, and the only two beaten were from Godolphin.
Shocks were a rare occurrence, as most winners emerged from the **first four in the market**, while trainer **Sir Michael Stoute** sent out two winners from eight runners.

FUTURE POINTERS The Dante has been on fire in recent times and now earns bragging rights as the leading three-year-old Derby trial – for now – having supplied three of the last four winners of the Epsom classic. However, it has also taken plenty of knocks over the years with seven winners failing at Epsom, but overall, quality winners of this event that earned above par performance ratings (PR) were worthy of following, and even Septimus added further Group success a year later, including victory in the Lonsdale Cup.
Last year's winner, Authorized, became the joint top-ranked achiever during the last 12 years and duly went on land the Derby in style.

Were Dante winners profitable to follow on their subsequent three runs?
No – 6 wins from 34 runs returned a loss of -£8.04 to a £1 level stake.

Placed runners' subsequent record (three runs):
Runners-up: 6 wins from 34 runs returned a loss of -£15.23 to a £1 level stake.
2004 Rule Of Law – Great Voltigeur, 1999 Golden Snake – Group One Jean Prat, 1996 Dushyantor – Great Voltigeur

Thirds: 2 wins from 15 runs returned a loss of -£9.45 to a £1 level stake.
2002 Balakheri – King Edward VII Stakes

FUTURE SUCCESS RATING: ★ ★ ★ ★ ☆

HAMBLETON STAKES
May 15, York – (Listed Handicap, Class 1, 4yo+) 1m

Last run	Winner/ Trainer & SP	Draw/ Ran	Age	Wght	PR	Next four runs			
07 Ches 1m2f 3rd	**Blythe Knight** J Quinn 9/1 *Two weeks*	4/12	7	8-09	70	**WON 4/1** **Diomed Stks** Eprom 1m	7th Celebration Mile Good 1m	4th Doonside Cup Ayr 1m2f	3rd Grouo 2 Long 1m
06 Sain 1m 10th	**Zero Tolerance** D Barron 9/2 *Three weeks*	8/13	6	9-01	70	5th Diomed Stks Eprom 1m	16th Premier Hcp Curr 1m	10th Addleshaw Hcp York 1m	**WON 15/8** **Superior Stks** Haydock 1m
05 Hayd 7f 2nd	**Quito** D Chapman 15/2 *One week*	6/12	8	9-07	74	4th Leisure Stks Wind 6f	5th John of Gaunt Hayd 7f	9th Golden Jubilee York 6f	2nd Chipchase Stks Newc 6f
04 Donc 1m 1st	**Autumn Glory** G Wragg 9/2F *Two months*	12/17	4	8-07	76	28th Royal Hunt Cup Ascot 1m	16th International Hcp Ascot 7f	6th Sovereign Stks Sali 1m	**WON 14/1** **Group 3** Deau 1m
03 Newm 1m1f 11th	**Funfair** Sir M Stoute 10/3F *Seven months*	11/11	4	8-07	71	8th Royal Hunt Cup Ascot 1m	2nd Scoop6 Hcp Sand 1m	11th International Hcp Ascot 7f	*2nd Porcelanosa Deau 1m
02 Ascot 7f 4th	**Sea Star** H Cecil 6/4F *Two weeks*	1/10	4	8-11	65	5th Royal Hunt Cup Ascot 1m	6th Silver Trophy Ascot 1m	12th Group 3 Sain 1m	*2nd Stakes Long 7f
01 Newm 1m2f 6th	**Soviet Flash** E Dunlop 12/1 *Seven months*	10/13	4	9-00	68	3rd Diomed Stks Eprom 1m	16th Royal Hunt Cup Ascot 1m	17th W Hill Hcp Good 1m	*3rd Magnolia Stks Kemp 1m2f
00 Kemp 1m 18th	**Mayaro Bay** R Hannon 14/1 *One month*	7/13	4	8-11	66	6th Conqueror Stks Good 1m	14th Royal Hunt Cup Ascot 1m	3rd Mail Hcp Newb 1m	22nd W Hill Hcp Good 1m
99 Ascot 1m 3rd	**Sugarfoot** N Tinkler 11/2 *Two weeks*	6/10	5	9-04	69	6th Royal Hunt Cup Ascot 1m	3rd Silver Trophy Ascot 1m	9th International Hcp Ascot 7f	**WON 9/2F** **Brad&Bing Hcp** York 1m
98 Hayd 7f 2nd	**Ramooz** B Hanbury 11/4F *Two weeks*	7/9	5	9-07	75	4th Diomed Stks Eprom 1m	2nd Criterion Stks Newm 7f	4th Group 3 Curr 1m	3rd International Hcp Ascot 7f
97 Sand 1m 7th	**Centre Stalls** F Johnson Houghton 10/1 *Three weeks*	8/14	4	9-07	73	3rd Brigadier Gerard Sand 1m2f	2nd Queen Anne Ascot 1m	3rd Dubai Duty Free Newb 7f	9th QE II Ascot 1m
96 Sand 1m 5th	**First Island** G Wragg 11/2 *Three weeks*	8/13	4	9-07	72	**WON 9/1** **Prince of Wales'** Ascot 1m2f	**WON 5/1** Sussex Good 1m	2nd Juddmonte Int York 1m2f	3rd QE II Ascot 1m

12-year median performance rating of the winner:	**71** (out of 100)	*next year*

WINNER'S PROFILE Ten winners **already raced that season** – six came via either Ascot, Haydock or Sandown – while the two that reappeared both raced at Newmarket in the autumn. Wise Dennis narrowly failed to follow up his Ascot Victoria Cup win here last year, a feat managed by a couple of winners prior to 1996, though Sea Star was fourth in that race in 2002. Eight of the last nine winners were **officially rated between 94 and 104**, while four-year-olds put a good run together until three years ago, trainer **Geoff Wragg** responsible for two of them.

FUTURE POINTERS A smashing early season handicap that has attracted those bordering on Pattern class, however, winners haven't exactly sparkled post-York, and Blythe Knight last year became the first winner since First Island in 1996 to follow up. Several progressive winners looked to have a future in Group events, but not many made the transaction at that level. Bar First Island, those that marched on to Royal Ascot were stuffed – six flopped in the Royal Hunt Cup.
The four stars awarded at the foot of the page were rewarded more for the performances of the placed horses, some of whom had yet to blow their handicap marks and did very well in the bigger handicaps to come.

Were Hambleton winners profitable to follow on their subsequent three runs?
No – 3 wins from 36 runs returned a loss of -£20.00 to a £1 level stake.

Placed runners' subsequent record (three runs):
Runners-up: 8 wins from 33 runs returned a **profit of +£4.33** to a £1 level stake.
2002 With Reason – John of Gaunt, Hungerford Stakes, 2001 Tough Speed – Bradford & Bingley Handicap, Park Stakes, 2002 Caribbean Monarch – Royal Hunt Cup

Thirds: 11 wins from 36 runs returned a **profit of +£33.87** to a £1 level stake.
2006 Dabbers Ridge – International Handicap, 2004 Mine – Victoria Cup, Royal Hunt Cup, 2002 Vintage Premium – Epsom Derby Handicap, 1997 Insatiable – Whitsun Cup

Fourths: 1 win from 3 runs returned a **profit of +£3.00** to a £1 level stake.

FUTURE SUCCESS RATING: ★ ★ ★ ★ ☆

MIDDLETON STAKES
May 16, York – (Group 3, Class 1, 4yo+) 1m2f 88yds

Last run	Winner/Trainer & SP	Draw/Ran	Age	Wght	PR	Next four runs			
07 Newm 1m1f 2nd Dahlia Stks *Two weeks*	**Topatoo** M Tompkins 7/2	2/7	5	8-12	67	4th Gala Stks Sand 1m2f	8th Winter Hill Stks Wind 1m2f	-	-
06 Donc 1m2f 1st Listed Fillies *Six months*	**Strawberry Dale** J Bethell 8/1	4/6	4	8-12	70	5th Group 2 Deau 1m2f	9th Blandford Stks Curr 1m2f	-	-
05 Curr 1m2f 3rd Blandford Stks *Eight months*	**All Too Beautiful** A O'Brien 1/2F	2/5	4	8-09	66	-	-	-	-
04 Nad Al 1m1f 4th Dubai Duty Free *Two months*	**Crimson Place** S Bin Suroor 6/4F	4/6	5	8-09	71	6th Windsor Forest Ascot 1m	**WON 99/10** Grade 1 Arli 1m2f	-	-
03 Newm 1m2f 2nd Severals Stks *Seven months*	**Zee Zee Top** Sir M Stoute 11/10F	1/6	4	8-09	73	3rd Pretty Polly Curr 1m2f	3rd Nassau Good 1m2f	6th Yorkshire Oaks York 1m4f	**WON 14/1** Prix de l'Opera Long 1m2f
02 Ascot 1m4f 6th Princess Royal *Seven months*	**Jalousie** C Wall 8/1	2/9	4	8-09	62	4th Lancashire Oaks Hayd 1m4f	7th Aphrodite Stks Newm 1m4f	2nd Listed Long 1m2f	5th Harvest Stks Ascot 1m4f
01 Newm 1m1f 4th Dahlia Stks *Two weeks*	**Moselle** W Haggas 5/1	1/8	4	8-09	64	9th Group 3 Sain 1m3f	10th Duke of Edinburgh Ascot 1m4f	5th Lancashire Oaks Hayd 1m4f	11th Glorious Listed Good 1m4f
00 Newm 1m2f 9th Rated Hcp *Two weeks*	**Lafite** J Hills 20/1	3/8	4	8-09	60	11th Handicap Epsom 1m2f	-	-	-
99 Newm 1m2f 1st Severals Stks *Seven months*	**Lady In Waiting** P Cole 13/8	5/6	4	8-12	69	2nd Pretty Polly Curr 1m2f	2nd Nassau Good 1m2f	11th Yorkshire Oaks York 1m4f	**WON 5/1** Sun Chariot Newm 1m2f
98 Newm 1m2f 7th Handicap *Two weeks*	**Arriving** J Hills 33/1	1/7	4	8-09	62	5th Group 3 Hamb 1m3f	2nd Daffodil Stks Chep 1m2f	8th Nassau Good 1m2f	3rd Group 3 Siro 1m3f
97 Ascot 1m4f 4th Princess Royal *Seven months*	**Papering** L Cumani 8/11F	1/5	4	8-12	60	2nd Group 2 Siro 1m4f	3rd Nassau Good 1m2f	5th Yorkshire Oaks York 1m4f	**WON N/O** Group 3 Siro 1m3f
96 Newm 7f 5th Maiden *Seven months*	**Bathilde** Sir M Stoute 6/1	3/6	3	8-09	66	5th Ribblesdale Ascot 1m4f	3rd Daffodil Stks Chep 1m2f	4th Galtres Stks York 1m4f	4th Conds Stks Kemp 1m4f

12-year median performance rating of the winner: **66** (out of 100) *(3yo only prior to 1997)*

WINNER'S PROFILE **Newmarket provided the last stop** for seven winners – two contested the Dahlia Stakes and two via the Severals Stakes the previous season – while two winners came via the Princess Royal at Ascot. Nine of the last 11 already **scored over at least this distance**, while last year's winner was only the second triumph for five-year-olds over the **four-year-olds** since it switched from a three-year-olds only contest in 1997. Despite the small fields, there were a few shocks and the market informs us to **search for value**, while **Newmarket trainers** have a great record – Sir Michael Stoute took it twice.

FUTURE POINTERS This fillies event hasn't provided much of a guide for the remainder of the season as winners failed to progress – exchange layers take note – although some recent runners-up fared well *(see below)*. To be fair, two winners of the Middleton Stakes managed to score again at the highest level abroad in 2004 and 2003, however, those that headed to Royal Ascot, the Pretty Polly in Ireland and the Nassau at Glorious Goodwood, all failed.

Were Middleton Stakes winners profitable to follow on their subsequent three runs?
No – 1 win from 28 runs returned a loss of -£17.10 to a £1 level stake.

Placed runners' subsequent record (three runs):
Runners-up: 7 wins from 34 runs returned a loss of -£7.00 to a £1 level stake.
2007 Anna Pavlova – Doonside Cup, Prix de Royallieu, 2005 La Persiana – Listed Upavon Stakes, 2004 Beneventa – Listed Aphrodite Stakes, 2003 Chorist – Group Three Daffodil Stakes

Thirds: 0 win from 9 runs returned a loss of -£9.00 to a £1 level stake.

FUTURE SUCCESS RATING: ★ ★ ☆ ☆ ☆

YORKSHIRE CUP
May 16, York (Group 2, Class 1, 4yo+) 1m6f

Last run	Winner/ Trainer & SP	Draw/ Ran	Age	Wght	PR	Next four runs			
07 Newb 1m4f 4th *One month*	**Sergeant Cecil** John Porter R Millman 10/3F	5/10	8	9-03	85	14th Gold Cup Ascot 2m4f	6th King George VI Ascot 1m4f	5th Lonsdale Cup York 2m	-
06 Hayd 2m 3rd *Nov Hdle* *Four months*	**Percussionist** J Howard Johnson 9/1	4/7	5	8-12	76	7th Irish St Leger Curr 1m6f	**WON 5/2** *Beg Chase* Weth 2m	2nd Nov Chase Ayr 2m	2nd Nov Chase Kels 2m
05 Ling 2m 2nd *Sagaro Stks* *Three weeks*	**Franklins Gardens** M Tompkins 13/2	7/9	5	8-10	74	6th Gold Cup York 2m4f	8th Irish St Leger Curr 1m6f	24th Melbourne Cup Flem 2m	*2nd Lonsdale Cup York 1m
04 Ascot 2m 3rd *Sagaro Stks* *Three weeks*	**Millenary** J Dunlop 9/2	1/10	7	8-13	82	3rd Lonsdale Cup York 2m	**WON 7/1** Doncaster Cup Donc 2m2f	**WON 7/2JF** Jockey Club Newm 1m4f	*9th Yorkshire Cup York 1m6f
03 Nad Al 1m6f 1st *Handicap* *Three months*	**Mamool** S Bin Suroor 11/2	2/8	4	8-09	79	5th Gold Cup Ascot 2m4f	3rd Geoffrey Freer Newb 1m5f	**WON 54/10** Grosser 'Baden Baden 1m4f	**WON 2/5F** Preis 'Europa Colon 1m4f
02 Newm 1m4f 4th *Jockey Club St* *Two weeks*	**Zindabad** M Johnston 2/1F	5/7	6	8-09	79	3rd Coronation Cup Epsom 1m4f	**WON 4/1** Hardwicke Ascot 1m4f	3rd King George VI Ascot 1m4f	5th Canadian Int Wood 1m4f
01 Newb 1m4f 2nd *St Simon Stks* *Seven months*	**Marienbard** S Bin Suroor 5/1	2/8	4	8-09	76	5th Gold Cup Ascot 2m4f	2nd G Prix Deauville Deau 1m5f	3rd Irish St Leger Curr 1m6f	7th Melbourne Cup Flem 2m
00 Curr 1m6f 1st *Irish St Leger* *Eight months*	**Kayf Tara** S Bin Suroor 15/8F	7/8	6	9-00	85	**WON 11/8F** **Gold Cup** Ascot 2m4f	-	-	-
99 Good 1m4f 3rd *Shergar Cup* *One month*	**Churlish Charm** R Hannon 25/1	1/9	4	8-09	75	11th Gold Cup Ascot 2m4f	*7th Jockey Club Newm 1m4f	*3rd Yorkshire Cup York 1m6f	*2nd Henry II Sand 2m
98 Newm 2m 2nd *Sagaro Stks* *Two weeks*	**Busy Flight** B Hills 2/1F	6/6	5	8-09	73	2nd Doncaster Cup Donc 2m2f	5th Jockey Club Newm 2m	-	-
97 Newm 1m4f 4th *Jockey Club St* *Two weeks*	**Celeric** D Morley 7/2	2/9	5	8-09	78	2nd Henry II Sand 2m	**WON 11/2** **Gold Cup** Ascot 2m4f	5th Princess of Wales Newm 1m4f	4th Lonsdale Stks York 2m
96 Donc 1m6f 1st *St Leger* *Eight months*	**Classic Cliche** S bin Suroor 2/1	5/5	4	9-00	83	**WON 3/1** **Gold Cup** Ascot 2m4f	2nd King George VI Ascot 1m4f	15th Arc de Triomphe Long 1m4f	*9th Yorkshire Cup York 1m6f

12-year median performance rating of the winner: **79** (out of 100)   *italic=jumps, *next year*

WINNER'S PROFILE The majority of winners **arrived fit** – five came via the **Sagaro or Jockey Club Stakes** – while the three not to have run for over six months were all Godolphin inmates. Every winner finished either **first or second during their last three runs,** so any with a form-line of unplaced efforts can be scratched.
Sergeant Cecil became the third horse in this period to carry a Group One penalty when justifying favouritsm, while there were few surprises on the Knavesmire, as 10 winners returned at **13/2 or shorter** – only Churlish Charm went off at a double-figure price. Although field sizes weren't large, those drawn wide in the highest stalls failed to make a big impact.

FUTURE POINTERS This early-season pointer for the staying prizes ahead has often drawn a mix of quality middle-distance performers, along with the real stamina merchants, that has proved a worthy guide and supplied plenty of future winners. Nine winners of this marched onto Royal Ascot where an impressive tally of four triumphed, three in the Gold Cup and one in the Hardwicke, while those that travelled across Europe fared well.
Further down the line, only two ran in the Doncaster Cup in September, which returned a tidy record of one winner and a runner-up.

Were Yorkshire Cup winners profitable to follow on their subsequent three runs?
Yes – 8 wins from 33 runs returned a **profit of +7.27** to a £1 level stake.

Placed runners' subsequent record (three runs):
Runners-up: 6 wins from 36 runs returned a loss of -£7.61 to a £1 level stake.
2003 Warrsan – Coronation Cup, 2002 Boreas – Lonsdale Cup, 1997 Mons – Godolphin Stakes, 1996 Strategic Choice – Group One Gran Premio Di Milano.

Thirds: 3 wins from 21 runs returned a loss of -£10.80 to a £1 level stake.
2003 Arctic Owl – Henry II Stakes,

FUTURE SUCCESS RATING: ★★★☆☆

ASTON PARK STAKES
May 17, Newbury – (Listed, Class 1, 4yo+) 1m5f 61yds

Last run	Winner/ Trainer & SP	Draw/ Ran	Age	Wght	PR	Next four runs			
07 Ches 1m5f 4th Ormonde Stks Two weeks	**Peppertree Lane** M Johnston 9/2	1/5	4	8-12	77	3rd Listed Castle Stk Pont 1m4f	**WON EvsF Curragh Cup Curr 1m6f**	6th Ballycullen Stks Curr 1m6f	5th German St Leger Dort 1m6f
06 Flem 2m 19th Melbourne Cup Six months	**Distinction** Sir M Stoute 3/1	5/6	7	9-07	79	3rd Gold Cup Ascot 2m4f	-	-	-
05 Curr 1m2f 3rd Mooresbridge Two weeks	**Wolfe Tone** A O'Brien 7/1	4/9	4	8-12	72	4th Henry II Sand 2m	4th Gold Cup Ascot 2m4f	-	-
04 Ches 1m5f 2nd Ormonde Stks Two weeks	**The Whistling Teal** G Wragg 5/4F	2/8	8	8-12	73	5th Curragh Cup Curr 1m6f	4th St Simon Newb 1m4f	4th Glorious Stks Good 1m4f	3rd September Stks Newm 1m4f
03 Donc 1m4f 4th Troy Stks Eight months	**Gamut** Sir M Stoute 6/4F	10/10	4	8-12	72	3rd Princess of Wales' Newm 1m4f	**WON 5/4F Conds Stks Wind 1m4f**	2nd Irish St Leger Curr 1m6f	3rd Serlby Stks Donc 1m4f
02 Newm 1m4f 7th Jockey Club Stks Three weeks	**High Pitched** H Cecil 4/1	3/6	4	9-04	80	4th Hardwicke Ascot 1m4f	2nd Geoffrey Freer Newb 1m5f	-	-
01 Ripo 1m4f 1st Conds Stks Three weeks	**Water Jump** J Dunlop 2/1	1/5	4	8-12	79	**WON 6/4F Berkshire Stks Wind 1m4f**	*3rd John Porter Newb 1m4f	*6th Ormonde Stks Ches 1m5f	***6th Novice Hurdle Wind 2m
00 Kran 1m2f 13th International Cup Three months	**Sea Wave** S Bin Suroor 7/4F	3/8	5	8-12	73	5th Princess of Wales' Newm 1m4f	-	-	-
99 Sand 1m2f 3rd Gordon Richards One month	**Dark Shell** Sir M Stoute 11/4	7/6	4	8-12	77	3rd Group 1 Duss 1m4f	**2nd Maiden Hdle Winc 2m	**WON 4/7F Maiden Hdle Hunt 2m1f	**10th Novice Hdle Aint 2m1f
98 Newb 1m4f 2nd Conds Stks Nine months	**Yorkshire** P Cole 8/1	2/8	4	8-12	71	7th Group 2 Chan 1m4f	2nd Queen Alexandra Ascot 2m6f	6th Goodwood Cup Good 2m	5th Ebor York 1m6f
97 Newm 1m4f 7th Jockey Club Stks Three weeks	**Persian Punch** D Elsworth 4/1	6/6	4	9-01	80	**WON 3/1 Henry II Sand 2m**	12th Gold Cup Ascot 2m4f	5th Goodwood Cup Good 2m	5th Group 2 Deau 1m7f
96 Ches 1m5f 2nd Ormonde Stks Two weeks	**Election Day** Sir M Stoute 5/2	6/8	4	8-12	77	8th Hardwicke Ascot 1m4f	4th Serlby Stks Donc 1m4f	*5th John Porter Newb 1m4f	*3rd Sagaro Stks Ascot 2m

12-year median performance rating of the winner: **76** (out of 100) *next year **two years*

WINNER'S PROFILE Five winners arrived fit from either the Jockey Club Stakes at Newmarket or the Ormonde at Chester. There weren't many shocks, and it helps not to complicate things by keeping it simple, as 10 winners had **already experienced Group company** – three defied a Listed/Group penalty – while the **first three in the betting** pointed the way to the winner almost every time.

It has also proven a shrewd move in keeping with the **four-year-olds**, as they won nine renewals, with three-times winning trainer **Sir Michael Stoute** responsible for two of them.

FUTURE POINTERS The winners haven't exactly covered themselves in glory subsequently – placed runners did well *(see below)* – though Persian Punch won the Henry II at Sandown next time out and Peppertree Lane boosted the race last year in landing the Curragh Cup.

Two further winners found success again at Windsor, however, the majority flopped in major summer festivals at Royal Ascot, Newmarket (July meeting) and Glorious Goodwood.

Were Aston Park winners profitable to follow on their subsequent three runs?
No – 5 wins from 30 runs returned a loss of -£17.68 to a £1 level stake.

Placed runners' subsequent record (three runs):
Runners-up: 8 wins from 33 runs returned a **profit of +£8.25** to a £1 level stake.
2001 Sandmason – Hardwicke Stakes, 1997 Further Flight – Chester Listed event

Thirds: 3 wins from 12 runs returned a **profit of +£15.50** to a £1 level stake.
2000 Zaajer – Chester Listed event, 1996 Posidonas – Prince of Wales's Stakes

FUTURE SUCCESS RATING: ★ ★ ★ ☆ ☆

LOCKINGE STAKES
May 17, Newbury – (Group 1, Class 1, 4yo+) 1m

Last run	Winner/ Trainer & SP	Draw/ Ran	Age	Wght	PR	Next four runs			
07 Newm 1m 5th Sun Chariot *Eight months*	**Red Evie** M Bell 8/1	7/8	4	8-11	80	7th Queen Anne Ascot 1m	7th Falmouth Newm 1m	**WON 5/1 Hungerford Stks Newb 7f**	2nd Matron Stks Leop 1m
06 Newm 7f 4th Challenge Stks *Seven months*	**Peeress** S M Stoute 4/1	10/9	5	8-11	79	4th Queen Anne Ascot 1m	4th Falmouth Newm 1m	3rd Jacques 'Marois Deau 1m	2nd Matron Stks Leop 1m
05 Sha 1m2f 7th Hong Kong Cup *Six months*	**Rakti** M Jarvis 7/4F	5/8	6	9-00	85	2nd Queen Anne York 1m	4th Queen Elizabeth II Newm 1m	6th Champion Stks Newm 1m1f	11th Hong Kong Mile Sha 1m
04 Newm 1m2f 5th Champion Stks *Seven months*	**Russian Rhythm** Sir M Stoute 3/1F	3/15	4	8-11	80	-	-	-	-
03 Arlin 1m2f 7th Breeders' Cup *Seven months*	**Hawk Wing** A O'Brien 2/1F	4/6	4	9-00	90	6th Queen Anne Ascot 1m	-	-	-
02 Sain 1m 1st Prix du Muguet *Three weeks*	**Keltos** C Laffron-Parais 9/1	7/10	4	9-00	86	**WON N/O Prix Carteret Mais 7f	**2nd Listed Race Nant 1m	**2nd Listed Race Vicy 1m	**2nd Prix Quincey Deau 1m
01 Ascot 1m 4th QEII Stks *Eight months*	**Medicean** S M Stoute 3/1	5/7	4	9-00	84	**WON 11/2 Queen Anne Ascot 1m	**WON 7/2 Eclipse York 1m2f	3rd Juddmonte Int York 1m2f	
00 Long 1m 4th Prix du Moulin *Eight months*	**Aljabr** S Bin Suroor 8/13F	1/7	4	9-00	80	4th Queen Anne Ascot 1m	5th Sussex Stks Good 1m	-	-
99 Chur 1m 5th Breeders' Cup *Six months*	**Fly To The Stars** S Bin Suroor 9/1	6/6	5	9-00	86	7th Queen Anne Ascot 1m	8th Prix du Moulin Long 1m	*7th Dubai Duty Free Nad Al 1m1f	*5th Diomed Epsom 1m
98 Nad Al 2nd Maktoum Chall *Three months*	**Cape Cross** S Bin Suroor 20/1	8/10	4	9-00	80	5th Queen Anne Ascot 1m	3rd Jacques 'Marois Deau 1m	Queen Elizabeth II Ascot 1m	Breeders' Cup Chur 1m
97 Sand 1m 2nd Sandown Mile *Three weeks*	**First Island** G Wragg 11/4	1/10	5	9-00	83	-	-	-	-
96 Sand 1m 2nd Sandown Mile *One month*	**Soviet Line** Sir M Stoute 13/2	1/7	6	9-00	78	5th Queen Anne Ascot 1m	7th Queen Elizabeth II Ascot 1m	9th Group 2 Long 1m	*WON N/O Mile Sarat 1m

12-year median performance rating of the winner: **83** (out of 100)   *next year **two years*

WINNER'S PROFILE The first Group One event of the season for older horses and one that has produced few shocks over the years, which allowed those at **9/1 or shorter** to come out on top.
Six-year-old winners were also rare – Peeress struggled to defend her crown last year – and it paid to stick with **four and five-year-olds**. Those with a **Group One victory already** have a good record, while **fillies have performed well** of late, Red Evie was the third winner in the last four years to take advantage of a 3lb allowance. There wasn't an ideal prep race for the Lockinge and the majority reappeared here, although **two runners-up of the Sandown Mile were successful**. However, a word of caution regarding the winners of the Sandown Mile in this, as over 15 flopped here since 1986, including Jeremy last year.

FUTURE POINTERS First Island and Russian Rhythm never raced again following Newbury, but nine winners took the traditional route to Royal Ascot for the Group One Queen Anne Stakes. However, only Medicean, in 2001 was good enough to complete the Berkshire double and the Royal meeting has proven a real graveyard for Lockinge winners. Ramonti last year joined Charnwood Forest (1996) in becoming the second runner-up from here to have gone one further in the Queen Anne Stakes.

Were Lockinge winners profitable to follow on their subsequent three runs?
No – 4 wins from 27 runs returned a loss of -£9.00 to a £1 level stake.

Placed runners' subsequent record (three runs):
Runners-up: 6 wins from 33 runs returned a loss of -£6.60 to a £1 level stake.
2007 Ramonti – Queen Anne Stakes, Sussex, 2000 Trans Island – Diomed Stakes, 1997 Ali-Royal – Sussex, 1996 Charnwood Forest – Queen Anne Stakes

Thirds: 1 win from 18 runs returned a loss of -£10.50 to a level stake.
2006 Court Masterpiece – Sussex, 2000 Indian Lodge – Prix du Moulin

FUTURE SUCCESS RATING: ★ ★ ☆ ☆ ☆

LONDON GOLD CUP
May 17, Newbury – (Heritage Handicap, Class 2, 3yo) 1m2f

Last run	Winner/ Trainer & SP	Draw/ Ran	Age	Wght	PR	Next four runs			
07 Sand 1m 3rd Esher Cup *One month*	**Zaham** M Johnston 4/1	6/13	3	8-11	60	**WON 7/2** **Vodafone Hcp** Epsom 1m2f	**WON 7/2F** **Hampton Court** Ascot 1m2f	3rd Rose of Lancaster Hayd 1m3f	2nd Select Stks Good 1m2f
06 Redc 1m2f 1st Handicap *Three weeks*	**Pearly King** Sir M Stoute 9/2	1/15	3	9-02	61	7th K George V Hcp Ascot 1m4f	3rd Ladbrokes Hcp Good 1m2f	2nd Totesport Hcp Beve 1m2f	6th J Smith's Hcp Newb 1m2f
05 Leic 1m4f 3rd Everards Hcp *Three weeks*	**I'm So Lucky** M Johnston 4/1	6/9	3	9-00	58	6th 888 Hcp Hayd 1m4f	4th K George V Hcp Ascot 1m4f	**WON 9/2** **Handicap** **Sand 1m2f**	6th J Smith's Cup York 1m2f
04 Ling 1m2f 1st Maiden *Six months*	**Pukka** L Cumani 11/1	8/10	3	8-07	57	9th Derby Epsom 1m4f	2nd July Trophy Hayd 1m4f	5th Great Voltigeur York 1m4f	*4th Braveheart Stks Hami 1m4f
03 Bath 1m2f 6th Class Stks *Two weeks*	**Prince Nureyev** R Millman 20/1	5/13	3	9-06	55	20th Derby Epsom 1m4f	2nd Class Stks Ascot 1m4f	4th Class Stks Ascot 1m2f	4th Class Stks Sali 1m6f
02 Newm 1m2f 4th Swaffham Hcp *One month*	**Shagraan** J Dunlop 5/1CF	6/13	3	9-04	54	4th K George V Hcp Ascot 1m4f	-	-	-
01 Thir 1m4f 1st Maiden *Two weeks*	**Villa Carlotta** J Dunlop 9/4	3/3	3	9-01	56	3rd Rated Hcp Hayd 1m4f	2nd Handicap Hayd 1m4f	2nd Showcase Stks Hayd 1m4f	2nd Several Stks Newm 1m4f
00 Pont 1m4f 1st Handicap *Three weeks*	**Cephalonia** J Dunlop 9/2	8/8	3	9-02	59	6th Rated Hcp Hayd 1m4f	**WON 8/1** **Bahrain Trophy** **Newm 1m7f**	7th Park Hill Stks Donc 1m7f	11th Harvest Stks Ascot 1m4f
99 York 1m6f 1st Conds Stks *One week*	**Turtle Valley** S Dow 9/4F	4/9	3	8-04	54	**WON 10/3** **Rated Hcp** **Sali 1m6f**	8th Queen's Vase Ascot 2m	7th Group 3 Chan 1m5f	5ht Listed Deau 1m7f
98 Bath 1m2f 3rd Maiden *Three weeks*	**Jaazim** Sir M Stoute 9/2	3/7	3	9-05	56	9th K George V Hcp Ascot 1m4f	5th Old Newton Hcp Hayd 1m4f	2nd Knavesmire Hcp York 1m4f	3rd Joy UK Hcp Donc 1m4f
97 Nott 1m2f 2nd Limited Stks *Two weeks*	**Cyrian** P Cole 14/1	2/10	3	8-07	55	10th Old Newton Cup Hayd 1m4f	8th Tote Gold Trophy Good 1m4f	6th Melrose Hcp York 1m6f	*3rd Great Met Hcp Epsom 1m4f
96 Newm 1m4f 3rd Conds Stks *Two weeks*	**Samraan** J Dunlop 4/1	9/9	3	9-05	54	**WON 14/1** **K George V Hcp** **Ascot 1m4f**	4th July Trophy Hayd 1m4f	6th Gordon Stks Good 1m4f	4th Geoffrey Freer Newb 1m5f

12-year median performance rating of the winner: **57** (out of 100) *next year*

WINNER'S PROFILE A solid effort prior to Newbury was vital as 10 winners finished in the **first three last time out** and the majority proved their fitness with a **run during the past month**.
Those drawn low to middle came out on top in bigger fields, while the classier sorts in the **top-half of the handicap** held the edge with an **official rating of 85 or more**. The classy trainers also shined with **John Dunlop** (4), **Mark Johnston** (2) and **Sir Michael Stoute** (2) responsible for two-thirds of the renewals.

FUTURE POINTERS A quality handicap that has seen a mixed bag of results from winners post-Newbury with both the first and last winners in the period analysed winning at Royal Ascot – Zaham in the 2007 Hampton Court and Samraan in the 1996 King George V Handicap. There may have been more subsequent scorers had victors of this handicap not been thrown in the deep end next time, as the likes of Pukka and Prince Nureyev tackled the Derby, though Cephalonia raised her game to take the Listed Bahrain Trophy.

Were London Gold Cup winners profitable to follow on their subsequent three runs?
Yes – 6 wins from 34 runs returned a **profit of +£8.83** to a £1 level stake.

Placed runners' subsequent record (three runs):
Runners-up: 4 wins from 33 runs returned a loss of -£23.41 to a £1 level stake.
2004 Maraahel – Group Three Gordon Stakes

Thirds: 4 wins from 28 runs returned a loss of -£0.17 to a £1 level stake.
2004 Frank Sonata – Listed July Trophy, 1999 Moutahddee – Hong Kong Handicap

FUTURE SUCCESS RATING: ★ ★ ★ ☆ ☆

SANDY LANE STAKES
May 24, Haydock – (Listed, Class 1, 3yo) 6f

Last run	Winner/Trainer & SP	Draw/Ran	Age	Wght	PR	Next four runs			
07 Newm 1m 20th 2,000 Guineas *Three weeks*	**Prime Defender** B Hills 11/8F	6/8	3	9-03	71	2nd Cathedral Stks Salis 6f	13th July Cup Newm 6f	5th King George Good 5f	3rd Group 3 Curr 6f
06 York 7f 2nd VC Hcp *Two weeks*	**Skhilling Spirit** D Barron 3/1F	6/8	3	8-11	63	8th NGK Hcp Newm 6f	12th Ayr Gold Cup Ayr 6f	2nd Tote Hcp Newm 7f	10th Coral Sprint York 6f
05 Donc 7f 3rd Conds Stks *Eight months*	**Camacho** H Cecil 8/1	1/7	3	8-11	70	2nd Jersey Stakes York 7f	10th July Cup Newm 6f	7th Bentinck Stks Newm 6f	-
04 Ches 5f 1st Handicap *Three weeks*	**Moss Vale** B Hills 5/2	9/9	3	8-11	76	**WON 4/9F** **Cathedral Stks** **Salis 6f**	20th July Cup Newm 6f	9th Nunthorpe York 5f	2nd Renaissance Stk Curr 6f
03 Nott 6f 1st Class Stks *One week*	**The Kiddykid** P D Evans 7/1	8/10	3	9-07	67	5th W Hill Trophy York 6f	3rd Showcase Hcp Newm 6f	6th Queensferry Stk Ches 6f	5th Shergar Cup Ascot 6f
02 Newb 7f 4th Horris Hill *Seven months*	**Whitbarrow** R Millman 4/1	3/6	3	9-07	68	6th Cathedral Stks Salis 6f	6th King George Good 5f	3rd Shergar Cup Ascot 6f	17th Nunthorpe York 5f
01 Newm 1m 11th 2,000 Guineas *Three weeks*	**Firebolt** M Tompkins 7/1	17/17	3	9-02	74	**WON 6/4F** **Chipchase Stks** **Newc 6f**	8th July Cup Newm 6f	6th Shergar Cup Ascot 6f	*WON 53/10 HK Sprint Cup Sha 5f
00 Newm 1m 10th 2,000 Guineas *Three weeks*	**Lincoln Dancer** M Jarvis 7/1	1/12	3	9-07	73	2nd July Cup Newm 6f	7th Sprint Cup Hayd 6f	9th Diadem Ascot 6f	2nd Prix Couvert Long 5f
99 Ling 6f 2nd Showcase Hcp *Three weeks*	**Cubism** J Hills 9/1	4/15	3	8-12	65	6th Chipchase Stks Newc 6f	6th Group 3 Deau 6f	23rd International Hcp Ascot 7f	6th Hopeful Stks Newm 6f
98 Ches 5f 10th Handicap *Three weeks*	**Eastern Purple** R Fahey 14/1	8/11	3	8-09	70	21st W Hill Trophy York 6f	7th Porcelanosa Sand 5f	5th Rated Hcp Newb 6f	3rd Stewards' Cup Good 6f
97 Newb 6f 1st Conds Stks *Two weeks*	**Tomba** B Meehan 4/1	2/7	3	9-07	73	4th Conds Stks Epsom 7f	**WON 5/4F** **Chipchase Stks** **Newc 6f**	2nd Listed Muni 7f	**WON N/O** **Group 3** **Hopp 7f**
96 Sali 6f 1st Rated Hcp *Three weeks*	**Farhana** W Jarvis EvensF	1/5	3	9-01	64	2nd Phoenix Stks Leop 6f	*WON N/O Listed Mais	*2nd Duke of York York 6f	*7th Temple Stks Sand 5f

12-year median performance rating of the winner: **70** (out of 100)   *(Listed handicap prior to 2004), *next year*

WINNER'S PROFILE The ideal profile isn't easy to identify as this event experienced a facelift in recent years, although 10 winners arrived at Haydock having **raced within the last three weeks**, four won a sprint and three came via an unplaced effort in the 2,000 Guineas.
Prime Defender defied a penalty for trainer **Barry Hills** last year, who has won it twice since 2004.

FUTURE POINTERS The jury is still out regarding the strength of this event as a springboard for further success since becoming a non-handicap in 2004. Since then, two runners-up from here subsequently won *(see below)*, and Moss Vale went on to win another Listed prize after succeeding here, so a positive view should be held.
Camacho also went very close in the 2005 Jersey Stakes, while Prime Defender was unfortunate to bump into Sakhee's Secret next time out last year.
Prior to 2004, two winners took the Chipchase Stakes at Newcastle on Northumberland Plate day.

Were Sandy Lane winners profitable to follow on their subsequent three runs?
No – 4 wins from 36 runs returned a loss of -£28.80 to a £1 level stake.

Placed runners' subsequent record (three runs):
Runners-up: 5 wins from 36 runs returned a loss of -£11.95 to a £1 level stake.
2007 Hoh Mike – Scurry Stakes, Champagne Sprint, 2005 Nufoos – Listed Eternal Stakes,
2004 Boogie Street Listed – Achilles Stakes, 2001 Palanzo – Coral Sprint Handicap

Thirds: 2 wins from 23 runs returned a loss of -£3.00 to a £1 level stake.
2001 Orientor – William Hill Trophy

FUTURE SUCCESS RATING: ★ ★ ★ ☆ ☆

SILVER BOWL
May 24, Haydock – (Heritage Handicap, Class 2, 3yo) 1m

Last run	Winner/ Trainer & SP	Draw/ Ran	Age	Wght	PR	Next four runs			
07 Newm 1m 14th 2,000 Guineas *Three weeks*	**Tobosa** W Jarvis 10/3F	4/13	3	9-07	70	5th Prix Jean Prat Chan 1m	3rd Thoroughbred St Good 1m	**WON 2/5F Conds Stks Donc 1m**	4th Joel Stks Newm 1m
06 York 1m 2nd VC Handicap *Eight months*	**Anna Pavlova** R Fahey 4/1	6/7	3	9-05	71	6th Ballymacoll Stks Newb 1m2f	**Galtres Stks York 1m4f**	2nd Park Hill York 1m6f	**WON 15/8F Harvest Stks Ascot 1m4f**
05 Newm 7f 9th Dewhurst *Seven months*	**Home Affairs** Sir M Stoute 7/2	3/16	3	8-06	67	3rd Jersey Stks York 7f	4th Prix Jean Prat Chan 1m	7th Sovereign Stks Sali 1m	6th Joel Stks Newm 1m
04 Good 1m1f 1st Heritage Hcp *One week*	**Gatwick** M Channon 11/2	17/18	3	8-13	65	10th Derby Epsom 1m4f	6th Hampton Court Ascot 1m2f	8th Ladbrokes Hcp Good 1m2f	5th Prix d'Ornano Deau 1m2f
03 Beve 7f 3rd Showcase Hcp *One month*	**Jazz Messenger** G Butler 6/1	12/12	3	7-12	64	**WON 5/1JF Vodafone Hcp Epsom 1m2f**	8th John Smiths Cup York 1m2f	17th Cambridgeshire Newm 1m1f	6th Conds Stks Nott 1m
02 Sand 1m 1st Showcase Hcp *One month*	**Common World** G Butler 7/4F	10/12	3	8-13	60	3rd Hampton Court Ascot 1m2f	2nd Goffs Int Curr 1m	7th Irish Champion Leop 1m2f	2nd Conds Stks Newb 1m1f
01 Leic 7f 1st Maiden *Three weeks*	**Olympic Express** J Fanshawe 11/2	9/18	3	8-08	69	2nd Britannia Stks Ascot 1m	***WON 66/10 H Kong Mile Sha 1m**	***WON 27/10F H Kong Derby Sha 1m2f**	*8th QEII Cup Sha 1m2f
00 Good 1m1f 4th Showcase Hcp *One week*	**Atlantic Rhapsody** M Johnston 11/1	12/16	3	8-03	61	2nd Vodafone Hcp Epsom 7f	5th Britannia Hcp Ascot 1m	6th Tote Hcp Sand 1m2f	11th Showcase Hcp Newm 1m2f
99 Thir 1m 2nd Conds Stks *Two weeks*	**Date** E Dunlop 12/1	16/17	3	8-13	65	-	-	-	-
98 Hami 1m 1st Maiden *Three weeks*	**French Connection** J Berry 12/1	7/10	3	7-12	60	2nd Handicap Newc 1m2f	4th Food Broker Hcp Newm 1m	5th Handicap Ches 1m2f	17th Ladbrokes Hcp Donc 1m2f
97 Hami 1m 1st Maiden *Three weeks*	**Alezal** W Jarvis 5/2F	6/6	3	9-01	62	20th Britannia Hcp Ascot 1m	2nd Conds Stks Donc 1m2f	**WON 4/1 Rated Hcp Ascot 1m2f**	*3rd Earl of Sefton Newm 1m1f
96 York 1m 2nd Handicap *Two weeks*	**Winter Romance** E Dunlop 9/4F	8/10	3	9-00	65	13th Britannia Hcp Ascot 1m	14th Hong Kong Hcp Sand 1m2f	6th John Smiths Cup York 1m2f	3rd Listed Evry 1m1f

12-year median performance rating of the winner: **65** (out of 100)   **next year*

WINNER'S PROFILE A **recent solid run** was an important component and the only two that finished outside the first four last time out both faced Group One company. **Lightly raced types** are also favoured with three to six runs the ideal profile, while it paid not to look beyond the **first six in the betting**.
Southern trainers have raided the pot here numerous times and three to note are double-winners **Gerard Butler**, **Ed Dunlop**, and **William Jarvis**.

FUTURE POINTERS A valuable handicap that has regularly attracted progressive types on the up and the last two renewals have been well above par, producing a couple of the best winners for over a decade – the 2006 runner-up was also a useful tool *(see below)*.
However, the road ahead for Silver Bowl winners can be a tough one as they rise into Pattern company, and apart from Olypmic Express, who went to the top over in Hong Kong later in 2002, only Anna Pavlova managed to score in Listed company. Two others found success as they stuck to handicaps, which seems the best route, although four slipped up in the Britannia at Royal Ascot.

Were Silver Bowl winners profitable to follow on their subsequent three runs?
No – 5 wins from 33 runs returned a loss of -£5.70 to a £1 level stake.

Placed runners' subsequent record (three runs):
Runners-up: 7 wins from 36 runs returned a **profit of +£26.65** to a £1 level stake.
2006 Sir Gerard – Britannia Stakes, 2004 Makfool – Vodafone Handicap, 1997 Future Perfect – Globetrotter Handicap

Thirds: 3 wins from 28 runs returned a loss of -£17.80 to a £1 level stake.
2003 Enforcer – Vodafone Handicap

Fourths: 5 wins from 15 runs returned a **profit of +£4.30** to a £1 level stake.
2000 Papabile – Two Ascot Listed events

FUTURE SUCCESS RATING: ★★★ ☆ ☆

CORAL SPRINT

May 24, Newmarket – (Heritage Handicap, Class 2, 3yo) 6f

Last run	Winner/Trainer & SP	Draw/Ran	Age	Wght	PR	Next four runs			
07 Hayd 6f 2nd *Betfred Hcp* *Two weeks*	**Genki** R Charlton 13/2	9/14	3	8-06	55	2nd Handicap Pont 6f	**WON 6/4F** **Shergar Cup** **Ascot 6f**	2nd Handicap Newb 6f	**WON 7/2F** **Handicap** **Ascot 6f**
06 Hayd 6f 1st *Betfred Hcp* *Three weeks*	**Borehan** M Jarvis 5/1	8/10	3	8-12	60	18th W Hill Trophy York 6f	-	-	-
05 Sali 6f 1st *Betfair Hcp* *Three weeks*	**Resplendent Glory** T Mills 3/1F	7/12	3	9-01	65	**WON 10/3F** **Scurry Stks** **Sand 5f**	**WON 2/1F** **Champagne Sprint** **Sand 5f**	*11th Temple Stks Sand 5f	*17th King's Stand Ascot 5f
04 Brig 6f 1st *Maiden* *Two weeks*	**Buy On The Red** W Muir 10/1	2/18	3	8-01	50	7th Class Stks Kemp 6f	2nd Handicap Sand 5f	12th Rated Hcp Good 5f	12th Handicap Ches 6f
03 Newm 6f 2nd *Showcase Hcp* *Two months*	**Dazzling Bay** T Easterby 16/1	13/16	3	8-02	61	**WON 4/1F** **W Hill Trophy** **York 6f**	**WON 1/4F** **Trophy Hcp** **Ripo 6f**	9th Rated Hcp Newm 6f	2nd Rated Hcp Newm 6f
02 Kemp 6f 21st *Handicap* *Two months*	**Just James** J Noseda 20/1	19/20	3	8-07	62	4th W Hill Trophy York 6f	**WON 20/1** **Jersey Stks** **Ascot 7f**	6th Chipchase Stks Newc 6f	4th International Hcp L
01 Hayd 6f 2nd *Rated Hcp* *One week*	**Palanzo** P Harris 8/1	16/21	3	9-04	60	2nd Conds Stks Yarm 6f	2nd Conds Stks Hayd 6f	19th Stewards' Cup Good 6f	4th Ascot 6f Shergar Cup
00 Ascot 6f 7th *Conds Stks* *Three weeks*	**Hunting Lion** M Channon 50/1	16/30	3	9-07	58	3rd Jersey Stks Ascot 7f	*15th Abernant Newm 6f	*2nd Rated Hcp Newm 6f	-
99 Ascot 6f 3rd *Pavilion Stks* *Three weeks*	**Mitcham** T Mills 9/2	6/12	3	9-07	64	5th Dash Hcp Epsom 5f	**WON 20/1** **King's Stand** **Ascot 5f**	13th July Cup Newm 6f	4th World Trophy Newb 5f
98 Ches 6f 4th *Roodeye Hcp* *One month*	**Magic Rainbow** M Bell 20/1	12/19	3	8-02	55	22nd W Hill Trophy York 6f	4th Rated Hcp Newm 6f	10th Handicap Newm 5f	11th Eagle Lane Hcp York 6f
97 Ling 6f 1st *Maiden* *Two weeks*	**Blue Goblin** L Cumani 11/10F	10/12	3	8-13	62	2nd Cork & Orrery Ascot 6f	8th July Cup Newm 6f	9th Hopeful Stks Newm 6f	-
96 Newb 6f 2nd *Conds Stks* *Two weeks*	**Atraf** D Morley 8/1	4/13	3	9-07	67	**WON 12/1** **Cork & Orrery** **Ascot 6f**	9th Beeswing Stks Newc 7f	2nd Hopeful Stks Newm 6f	8th Group 3 Mais 6f

12-year median performance rating of the winner: **60** (out of 100) *(1999 July Course),* *next year*

WINNER'S PROFILE **In-form sprinters** that arrived with a solid recent run are respected – nine were in the first three last time out – while 11 winners **scored over this distance**. In fact, every winner raced over this trip last time out, so be wary of any who faced five furlongs, as stamina is needed here. Three recent winners also used **Haydock as a prep** before here, while those drawn in the **middle to high numbers** have held an edge, especially in large fields. **Only two favourites have won** as there have been a few shocks with several at double-figure odds, while it paid to concentrate on the boys as fillies have a shocking record – their last victory came in 1993.

FUTURE POINTERS Four winners of this classy sprint handicap headed for the William Hill Trophy at York next time, where only Dazzling Bay won, a feat previously matched by Cadeaux Genereux in 1988. Resplendent Glory was an above par winner of this before stamping his ground at Listed level, while another of trainer Terry Mills' winners, Mitcham, went on to take the Group Two King's Stand Stakes, and the Ascot route has proven to be fruitful for Coral Sprint winners. Of the five to have moved up in class at the Royal meeting, three won and two were placed, including Atraf in the 1996 Cork and Orrery, Blue Goblin (runner-up) in the same race a year later, Mitcham (already mentioned), Just James, who scooped the Jersey in 2002, and Hunting Lion (third) also in the Jersey of 2000.

Were Coral Sprint winners profitable to follow on their subsequent three runs?
Yes – 8 wins from 34 runs returned a **profit of +£37.05** to a £1 level stake.

Placed runners' subsequent record (three runs):
Runners-up: 3 wins from 35 runs returned a loss of -£18.00 to a £1 level stake.
2006 Signor Peltro – Sandown Handicap, 1999 Pips Magic – Royal Ascot Handicap

Thirds: 5 wins from 36 runs returned a **profit of +£1.00** to a £1 level stake.
2006 Hogmaneigh – Sandown Handicap, 2003 Crafty Calling – Sandown Handicap, 2001 Orientor – William Hill Trophy, 1998 Night Star – Royal Ascot Handicap

Fourths: 2 wins from 18 runs returned a loss of -£13.09 to a £1 level stake.

FUTURE SUCCESS RATING: ★ ★ ★ ★ ☆

KING CHARLES II STAKES
May 24, Newmarket – (Listed, Class 1, 3yo) 7f

Last run	Winner/ Trainer & SP	Draw/ Ran	Age	Wght	PR	Next four runs			
07 Long 1m 13th Poule' Poulains *Two weeks*	**Tariq** P Chapple-Hyam 7/2	5/6	3	9-00	78	WON 15/2 **Jersey Stks** **Ascot 7f**	WON 7/2 **Lennox Stks** **Good 7f**	5th Prix de la Foret Long 7f	-
06 Newm 7f 2nd Free Handicap *Two months*	**Jeremy** Sir M Stoute 15/8F	3/6	3	8-12	76	WON 9/2 **Jersey Stks** **Ascot 7f**	6th Lennox Stks Good 7f	2nd Hungerford Newb 7f	12th Challenge Stks Newm 7f
05 Kemp 6f 2nd Sirenia Stks *Eight months*	**Council Member** S bin Suroor 8/1	6/7	3	8-12	70	7th Jersey Stks Ascot 7f	5th Thoroughbred St Good 1m	5th Jacques 'Marois Deau 1m	WON 9/1 **Guisborough St** **Redc 7f**
04 Newb 7f 2nd Greenham *Two months*	**Fokine** B Hills 4/1	4/8	3	8-12	67	2nd Jersey Stks Ascot 7f	*9th H Kong Mile Sha 1m	*14th H Kong Derby Sha 1m2f	*5th Sha Tin Vase Sha 6f
03 Newm 7f 3rd Dewhurst *Seven months*	**Trade Fair** R Charlton 5/4F	5/5	3	8-12	73	WON 10/11F **Criterion Stks** **Newm 7f**	6th Sussex Good 1m	WON 1/4F **Dubai Duty Free** **Newb 7f**	5th Challenge Stks Newm 7f
02 Newm 7f 1st Stakes *Three weeks*	**Millennium Dragon** M Jarvis 10/11F	6/7	3	8-12	70	5th Jersey Stks Ascot 7f	5th July Cup Newm 6f	4th Lennox Stks Good 7f	2nd City of York York 7f
01 Newm 7f 1st Maiden *Eight months*	**Malhub** J Gosden 6/1	8/10	3	8-12	71	9th St James Palace Ascot 1m	5th Joel Stks Newm 1m	8th Challenge Stks Newm 7f	*WON 10/11F **Conds Stks** **Yarm 6f**
00 Newm7f 1st Maiden *Two months*	**Shibboleth** H Cecil 2/1F	7/9	3	8-12	71	4th St James Palace Ascot 1m	*WON 6/4F **Conds Stks** **Newm 7f**	*8th Queen Anne Ascot 1m	*WON 11/4 **Criterion Stks** **Newm 7f**
99 Newm 1m 8th 1,000 Guineas *Two weeks*	**Fragrant Oasis** E Dunlop 6/5F	4/5	3	8-07	66	7th Cork & Orrery Ascot 6f	3rd Summer Stks York 6f	3rd Oak Tree Stks Good 7f	2nd Rated Hcp Newm 6f
98 York 6f 2nd Gimcrack *Nine months*	**Bold Fact** H Cecil 11/4JF	5/7	3	9-05	74	9th Jersey Stks Ascot 7f	8th July Cup Newm 6f	WON 6/4F **City of York** **York 7f**	3rd Supreme Stks Good 7f
97 Newm 7f 4th Free Handicap *One month*	**Andreyev** R Hannon 3/1	5/6	3	8-12	67	17th Jersey Stks Ascot 7f	8th Hackwood Stks Newb 6f	*WON 10/3 **Conds Stks** **Kemp 6f**	*10th Duke of York York 6f
96 Thir 1m 3rd Classic Trial *One month*	**Ali-Royal** H Cecil 5/1	3/7	3	8-12	72	5th Jersey Stks Ascot 7f	7th Sussex Good 1m	2nd City of York York 7f	2nd Conds Stks Donc 1m

12-year median performance rating of the winner: **71** (out of 100)   *next year*

WINNER'S PROFILE The last 11 winners raced at a **Grade One venue last time**, seven of them at Newmarket. A **top-three finish** was a positive, while it paid to stick with lightly raced runners with no more than five career runs to date. Outsiders can be ignored, as those in the **first three of the betting** dominated, three of which were trained by **Henry Cecil**, a man whose entries should be monitored closely after a decent 2007.

FUTURE POINTERS The one standout statistic was that 11 winners of the King Charles II Stakes ran at Royal Ascot next time out, where the majority flopped until recently. Following six subsequent losers in the Group Three Jersey Stakes, Jeremy and Tariq both put the record straight and followed up in the last two years, while Fokine was a creditable runner-up in 2004. As with all winners, though, the trick is to keep tabs on the above par scorers by using the performance rating (PR), and both Jeremy and Tariq were above average, as was the 2003 winner Trade Fair, who avoided the Royal meeting for a successful date back here in the Criterion Stakes.
The majority of winners bit off more than they could chew in Group company after this listed event, but some were successful returned to Listed company later on, as both Council Member and Bold Fact proved in 2005 and 1998, respectively, while Millennium Dragon and Ali-Royal also went close back down in grade.

Were King Charles II winners profitable to follow on their subsequent three runs?
No – 6 wins from 36 runs returned a loss of -£5.02 to a £1 level stake.

Placed runners' subsequent record (three runs):
Runners-up: 3 wins from 22 runs returned a **profit of +£9.25** to a £1 level stake.
2003 Membership – Jersey Stakes, 2000 Observatory – Jersey Stakes

Thirds: 0 wins from 6 runs returned a loss of -£6.00 to a £1 level stake.

FUTURE SUCCESS RATING: ★ ★ ★ ☆ ☆

IRISH 2,000 GUINEAS
May 24, Curragh – (Group 1, Class 1, 3yo Colts & Fillies) 1m

Last run	Winner/ Trainer & SP	Draw/ Ran	Age	Wght	PR	Next four runs			
07 Newm 1m 1st 2,000 Guineas *Three weeks*	**Cockney Rebel** G Huffer 6/4F	7/12	3	9-00	80	5th St James Pal' Ascot 1m	-	-	-
06 Newm 1m 4th 2,000 Guineas *Three weeks*	**Araafa** J Noseda 12/1	8/11	3	9-00	83	**WON 2/1F** **St James Pal'** **Ascot 1m**	5th Sussex Good 1m	2nd Q Elizabeth II Ascot 1m	9th Breeders' Cup Chur 1m
05 Newm 1m 5th 2,000 Guineas *Three weeks*	**Dubawi** S Bin Suroor 7/4JF	7/8	3	9-00	85	3rd Derby Epsom 1m4f	**WON 10/3** **Jacques 'Marois** **Deau 1m**	2nd Q Elizabeth II Ascot 1m	-
04 Newm 1m 7th 2,000 Guineas *Three weeks*	**Bachelor Duke** J Toller 12/1	8/8	3	9-00	75	7th St James Pal' Ascot 1m	-	-	-
03 Newm 1m 14th 2,000 Guineas *Three weeks*	**Indian Haven** P D'Arcy 8/1	3/16	3	9-00	76	11th St James Pal' Ascot 1m	11th Champion Stks Newm 1m2f	*5th Betfred Mile Sand 1m	*9th Lockinge Newb 1m
02 Newm 1m 1st 2,000 Guineas *Three weeks*	**Rock Of Gibraltar** A O'Brien 4/7F	4/7	3	9-00	82	**WON 4/5F** **St James Pal'** **Ascot 1m**	**WON 8/13F** **Sussex** **Good 1m**	**WON 3/5JF** **Prix du Moulin** **Long 1m**	2nd Breeders' Cup Arli 1m
01 Long 1m 6th Poule 'Poulains *Two weeks*	**Black Minnaloushe** A O'Brien 20/1	9/12	3	9-00	84	**WON 8/1** **St James Pal'** **Ascot 1m**	5th Eclipse Sand 1m2f	3rd Sussex Good 1m	4th Juddmonte Int York 1m2f
00 Long 1m 1st Poule 'Poulains *Two weeks*	**Bachir** S Bin Suroor 4/1	3/8	3	9-00	75	6th St James Pal' Ascot 1m	5th Celebration Mile Good 1m	-	-
99 Leop 1m 1st 2,000 Guin Trial *Two months*	**Saffron Walden** A O'Brien 12/1	3/10	3	9-00	77	7th Derby Epsom 1m4f	2nd Meld Stks Curr 1m2f	12th Juddmonte Int York 1m2f	*3rd Minstrel Stks Curr 1m
98 Long 1m 3rd Poule 'Poulains *Two weeks*	**Desert Prince** D Loder 8/1	6/7	3	9-00	80	2nd St James Pal' Ascot 1m	**WON 44/10** **Prix du Moulin** **Long 1m**	**WON 10/3F** **Q Elizabeth II** **Ascot 1m**	14th Breeders' Cup Chur 1m
97 Curr 7f 1st Tetrarch Stks *One month*	**Desert King** A O'Brien 3/1	1/12	3	9-00	83	4th St James Pal' Ascot 1m	**WON 11/2** **Irish Derby** **Curr 1m4f**	2nd Juddmonte Int York 1m2f	2nd Irish Champion Leop 1m2f
96 Long 1m 2nd Poule 'Poulains *Two weeks*	**Spinning World** J Pease 7/4F	3/10	3	9-00	76	6th St James Pal' Ascot 1m	**WON 17/10** **Jacques 'Marois** **Deau 1m**	2nd Prix du Moulin Long 1m	2nd Breeders' Cup Wood 1m

12-year median performance rating of the winner: **80** (out of 100)   *next year*

WINNER'S PROFILE No winner during the past 12 years made their reappearance here and 10 **arrived via the English or French Guineas.** The former proved very popular in recent times, but be wary of those that finished in the frame at Newmarket apart from the winners. The two who came a different route were trained by **Aidan O'Brien** and were Pattern winners last time out in Ireland, while all four of O'Brien's victors – from 35 runners – had scored previously at The Curragh. **Saeed Bin Suroor** boasts a very respectable two victories and a second from only three runners, although be careful with Dermot Weld's, as he sent out a dozen losers.

FUTURE POINTERS The most popular route after The Curragh was to Ascot for the St James's Palace Stakes, although only three followed up, two came via Aidan O'Brien, who only sent three winners of this to the Royal meeting. However, the most effective subsequent path has been to France, where only four individual runners resulted in as many winners – two apiece in the Jacques le Marois and Prix du Moulin – and as only one started favourite, it could prove worthwhile keeping an eye out for foreign engagements.
It is also surprising to note that only one winner of this event went on to run in the Irish Derby, which resulted in a success for Desert King in 1997.

Were Irish 2,000 Guineas winners profitable to follow on their subsequent three runs?
Yes – 10 wins from 31 runs returned a **profit of +£9.27** to a £1 level stake.

Placed runners subsequent record (three runs):
Runners-up: 12 wins from 33 runs returned a **profit of +£31.17** to a £1 level stake.
2007 Creachadoir – Joel Stakes, 2006 George Washington – QEII, 2005 Oratorio – Eclipse, 2004 Azamour – St James' Palace, Irish Champion, 2001 Mozart – Jeresy Stakes, July Cup, Nunthorpe, 2000 Giant's Causeway – St James' Palace, Eclipse, Sussex

Thirds: 3 wins from 27 runs returned a loss of -£10.88 to a £1 level stake.
2004 Grey Swallow – Irish Derby

FUTURE SUCCESS RATING: ★ ★ ★ ★ ☆

IRISH 1,000 GUINEAS
May 25, Curragh – (Group 1, Class 1, 3yo Fillies) 1m

Last run	Winner/ Trainer & SP	Draw/ Ran	Age	Wght	PR	Next four runs			
07 Long 1m 2nd Poule 'Pouliches *Two weeks*	**Finsceal Beo** J Bolger 9/10F	8/11	3	9-00	75	8th Coronation Stks Ascot 1m	6th Irish Champion Leop 1m2f	5th Prix de l'Opera Long 1m2f	-
06 Cork 1m1f 1st Maiden *Two months*	**Nightime** D Weld 12/1	15/15	3	9-00	71	15th Coronation Stks Ascot 1m	*8th Tatts Gold Cup Curr 1m3f	-	-
05 Newm 1m 6th 1,000 Guineas *Three weeks*	**Saoire** Ms F Crowley 10/1	19/18	3	9-00	67	8th Pretty Polly Stks Curr 1m2f	6th Irish Oaks Curr 1m4f	5th Matron Stks Leop 1m	-
04 Newm 1m 1st 1,000 Guineas *Three weeks*	**Attraction** M Johnston 2/1F	5/15	3	9-00	76	WON 6/4F Coronation Stks Ascot 1m	2nd Falmouth Stks Newm 1m	10th Jacques 'Marois Deau 1m	2nd Matron Stks Leop 1m
03 Newm 1m 8th 1,000 Guineas *Three weeks*	**Yesterday** A O'Brien 11/2	8/8	3	9-00	72	2nd Oaks Epsom 1m4f	4th Irish Oaks Curr 1m4f	2nd Prix Vermeille Long 1m4f	2nd Prix de l'Opera Long 1m2f
02 Newm 1m 8th 1,000 Guineas *Three weeks*	**Gossamer** L Cumani 4/1F	13/15	3	9-00	73	11th Coronation Stks Ascot 1m	3rd Prix du Moulin Long 1m	5th Breeders' Cup Arli 1m2f	-
01 Curr 7f 3rd Athasi Stks *Three weeks*	**Imagine** A O'Brien 16/1	8/16	3	9-00	75	WON 3/1F Oaks Epsom 1m4f	-	-	-
00 Duss 1m 1st Germ 1,000 Guin *Three weeks*	**Crimplene** C Brittain 16/1	1/13	3	9-00	73	WON 4/1JF Coronation St Ascot 1m	WON 7/4F Nassau Good 1m2f	4th Jacques 'Marois Deau 1m	8th Q Elizabeth II Ascot 1m
99 Newm 1m 6th 1,000 Guineas *Three weeks*	**Hula Angel** B Hills 16/1	2/17	3	9-00	68	8th Coronation Stks Ascot 1m	7th Falmouth Stks Newm 1m	-	-
98 Newm 1m 16th 1,000 Guineas *Three weeks*	**Tarascon** T Stack 12/1	7/13	3	9-00	70	6th Oaks Epsom 1m4f	7th Sussex Good 1m	5th Irish Champion Leop 1m2f	-
97 Leop 7f 1st 1,000 Guin Trial *Two months*	**Classic Park** A O'Brien 20/1	5/10	3	9-00	71	4th Coronation Stks Ascot 1m	5th Sussex Good 1m	5th Prix du Moulin Long 1m	10th Prix de la Foret Long 7f
96 Newm 1m 2nd 1,000 Guineas *Three weeks*	**Matiya** B Hanbury 5/1	10/12	3	9-00	70	3rd Prix 'Diane Hermes Cha 1m3f	10th Sussex Good 1m	10th Prix de l'Opera Long 1m1f	-

12-year median performance rating of the winner: **72** (out of 100)   *next year*

WINNER'S PROFILE Finding clues isn't easy, although nine winners ran in a **European Guineas last time out** – Newmarket provided seven – while all 12 **scored over a minimum of seven furlongs**. Proven at this level of importance, as 11 figured in a Pattern race – 10 made the **top-three of a Group One or Two** – including the five English winners, while every Irish-trained winner previously experienced The Curragh. None of trainer **Aidan O'Brien**'s three winners went off favourite – two at 16/1 and 20/1 – although he had numerous runners and guessing his best performer on the day has proven difficult.

FUTURE POINTERS Mixed fortunes awaited the winner of the Irish 1,000 Guineas although the majority flopped, however, the two best winners, Attraction and Imagine, both did all that was asked next time out in the Coronation Stakes and Oaks respectively. Crimplene also followed up in the Coronation Stakes at Royal Ascot but it has to be noted that more failed – five never even made the top-three – including Finsceal Beo last year. Those that went over to France for further Group glory came unstuck, although two runners-up fared better *(see below)*, and overall, winners of this event must be treated carefully in the near future apart from any above par winners with good performance ratings (PR).

Were Irish 1,000 Guineas winners profitable to follow on their subsequent three runs?
No – 4 wins from 32 runs returned a loss of -£17.75 to a £1 level stake.

Placed runners' subsequent record (three runs):
Runners-up: 5 wins from 35 runs returned a loss of -£10.17 to a £1 level stake.
2004 Alexander Goldrun – Prix de l'Opera, 2003 Six Perfections – Jacques le Marois, Breeders' Cup, 1996 Dance Design – Pretty Polly, Irish Oaks

Thirds: 8 wins from 90 runs returned a loss of -£3.13 to a £1 level stake.
2003 Dimitrova – American Oaks, Flower Bowl Stakes, 1999 Dazzling Park – Matron Stakes

FUTURE SUCCESS RATING: ★ ★ ☆ ☆ ☆

TATTERSALLS GOLD CUP
May 25, Curragh – (Group 1, Class 1, 4yo+) 1m2f 110yds

Last run	Winner/ Trainer & SP	Draw/ Ran	Age	Wght	PR	Next four runs			
07 Sand 1m2f 4th *One month*	**Notnowcato** Gordon Richards Sir M Stoute 7/1	9/9	5	9-00	84	3rd Prince of Wales' Ascot 1m2f	**WON 7/1 Eclipse Sand 1m2f**	3rd Juddmonte Int York 1m2f	6th Champion Stks Newm 1m2f
06 Long 1m4f 1st *Seven months*	**Hurricane Run** A Fabre 1/4F	3/3	4	9-00	90	2nd G Prix St-Cloud Sain 1m4f	**WON 5/6F King George VI Ascot 1m4f**	2nd Prix Foy Long 1m4f	3rd Arc de Triomphe Long 1m4f
05 Long 1m4f 18th Arc de Triomphe *Seven months*	**Grey Swallow** D Weld 13/2	4/6	4	9-00	83	7th King George VI Newb 1m4f	6th Irish Champion Leop 1m2f	4th Canadian Int Wood 1m4f	***WON 3/5F** Grade 2 Holl 1m4f
04 Curr 1m6f 3rd Irish St Leger *Eight months*	**Powerscourt** A O 'Brien 10/3	3/6	4	9-00	80	2nd Prince of Wales' Ascot 1m2f	5th Eclipse Sand 1m2f	2nd Group 1 Muni 1m2f	4th Arlington Million Arli 1m2f
03 Long 1m3f 9th Prix Ganay *One month*	**Black Sam Bellamy** A O'Brien 6/1	1/8	4	9-00	79	3rd Coronation Cup Epsom 1m4f	8th Gold Cup Ascot 2m4f	5th Group 1 Muni 1m2f	2nd Grosser 'Baden Bade 1m4f
02 Curr 1m2f 1st Mooresbridge St *Three weeks*	**Rebelline** K Prendergast 7/1	7/8	4	8-11	75	-	-	-	-
01 Nad Al 1m2f 2nd Sheema Classic *Three months*	**Fantastic Light** S Bin Suroor 5/4F	6/6	5	9-00	89	**WON 10/3 Prince of Wales' Ascot 1m2f**	2nd King George VI Ascot 1m4f	**WON 9/4 Irish Champion Leop 1m2f**	**WON 7/5F Breeders' Cup Belm 1m4f**
00 Toky 1m4f 4th Japan Cup *Six months*	**Montjeu** J Hammond 1/3F	3/5	4	9-00	89	**WON 1/5F G Prix St-Cloud Sain 1m4f**	**WON 1/3F King George VI Ascot 1m4f**	**WON 1/10F Prix Foy Long 1m4f**	4th Arc de Triomphe Long 1m4f
99 Newm 1m1f 1st Earl of Sefton *Two months*	**Shiva** H Cecil 10/3	6/6	4	8-11	86	7th Prince of Wales' Ascot 1m2f	2nd Champion Stks Newm 1m2f	*7th Earl of Sefton Newm 1m2f	***WON 7/2F** Brig' Gerard Sand 1m2f
98 Long 1m 3rd Prix du Moulin *Eight months*	**Daylami** S Bin Suroor 5/4F	4/5	4	9-04	88	3rd Prince of Wales' Ascot 1m2f	**WON 6/4F Eclipse Sand 1m2f**	4th King George VI Ascot 1m4f	**WON 5/4F Man O'War Belm 1m3f**
97 Curr 1m2f 1st Mooresbridge St *One month*	**Dance Design** D Weld 5/2	1/7	4	9-01	81	**WON 4/9F Pretty Polly Stk Curr 1m2f**	2nd Group 1 Muni 1m2f	3rd Grade 1 Arli 1m2f	7th Grade 1 Sant 1m2f
96 Curr 1m2f 1st Mooresbridge St *One month*	**Definite Article** D Weld 15/8F	5/8	4	8-12	80	5th Eclipse Sand 1m2f	4th Grosser 'Baden Bade 1m4f	6th Grade 1 Belm 1m4f	-

12-year median performance rating of the winner: **84** (out of 100)   **next year*

WINNER'S PROFILE Eight winners had their last race at either Longchamp or The Curragh, and the three to have run in the Mooresbridge Stakes here a month beforehand all won that event. Proven **winning form at this level** was important as nine boasted such credentials, while two of the other three had been third in Group Ones but scored in Group Twos – the other took a Group Three. Ten winners **scored between 10 and 12 furlongs**, one of the exceptions was the lightly raced Shiva, who had won over nine furlongs, and was also one of three fillies that shined. Although the field sizes have been relatively small, every winner returned at **7/1 or shorter**, including Grey Swallow, who was trainer **Dermot Weld**'s third winner from 10 runners, while **Saeed Bin Suroor** and **Aidan O'Brien** have bagged a pair each from 10 and nine runners respectively.

FUTURE POINTERS One of the first leading middle-distance events of the season in which the big guns are given the opportunity to shake off any cobwebs for the season ahead, and one that has drawn plenty of stars over the years including the likes of Ile De Chypre, Opera House, Daylami, Montjeu, Fantastic Light and Hurricane Run. The race has had it's share of forgettable winners too, as the sub-standard scorers failed to achieve much subsequently, however, the quality winners have proven worthy of following in the upcoming big events of the summer despite the short-prices. One of the most successful routes was to the Eclipse, and Notnowcato last year became the second from only four to succeed, while there were mixed results in the Prince of Wales's and the King George VI, with two winners from five in the latter event.

Were Gold Cup winners profitable to follow on their subsequent three runs?
No – 9 wins from 33 runs returned a loss of -£8.02 to a £1 level stake.

Placed runners' subsequent record (three runs):
Runners-up: 7 wins from 31 runs returned a loss of -£11.75 to a £1 level stake.
1999 Daylami – Coronation Cup, King George VI, Irish St Leger, 1997 Oscar Schindler – Irish St Leger, 1996 Timarida – German Group One

Thirds: 0 win from 9 runs returned a loss of -£9.00 to a £1 level stake.

FUTURE SUCCESS RATING: ★ ★ ★ ★ ★

ZETLAND GOLD CUP
May 26, Redcar – (Class 2, Heritage Handicap, 3yo+) 1m2f

Last run	Winner/ Trainer & SP	Draw/ Ran	Age	Wght	PR	Next four runs			
07 Beve 1m 1st Handicap One week	**Flipando** D Barron 14/1	4/12	6	9-03	62	2nd Royal Hunt Cup Ascot 1m	11th J Smith's Cup York 1m1f	3rd Handicap Hayd 1m	7th Goddard Hcp York 1m
06 Newm 1m2f 2nd S James Hcp One month	**Chantaco** A Balding 4/1F	16/17	4	9-00	55	7th Rose Bowl Hcp Epsom 1m2f	8th Duke of Edinburgh Ascot 1m4	5th J Smith's Cup York 1m2f	7th Shergar Cup Ascot 1m4f
05 Ches 1m2f 3rd Walker Hcp One month	**Blue Monday** R Charlton 7/2F	3/16	4	9-00	67	4th Duke of Edinburgh Ascot 1m4f	2nd J Smith's Hcp Newb 1m2f	**WON 5/1F** **Cambridgeshire** **Newm 1m1f**	*2nd Cond Stks Ripo 1m2f
04 York 1m 4th Hambleton Hcp Three weeks	**Blue Spinnaker** M Easterby 5/1	1/15	5	9-07	68	10th J Smith's Cup York 1m2f	4th Motablity Hcp York 1m2f	6th Porcelanosa Donc 1m	3rd J Smith's Hcp Newb 1m2f
03 Newm 1m4f 4th Stakes Nine months	**Hazim** Sir M Stoute 10/1	17/17	4	9-11	71	10th Duke of Edinburgh Ascot 1m4f	11th J Smith's Cup York 1m2f	-	-
02 Wind 1m2f 1st Stakes Three weeks	**Flight Sequence** L Herries 5/1	10/10	6	9-04	56	5th Rated Hcp Newm 1m2f	-	-	-
01 Ches 1m2f 2nd Walker Hcp Three weeks	**The Whistling Teal** G Wragg 9/4F	7/13	5	9-01	67	5th Ladbroke Hcp Ascot 1m2f	**WON 7/1** **Motability Hcp** **York 1m2f**	*4th Gordon Richards Sand 1m2f	*2nd Rated Hcp Good 1m4f
00 Wind 1m 6th Windsor Stks Two weeks	**Nobelist** C Brittain 14/1	3/13	5	9-09	62	12th EDS Hcp Eprom 1m2f	12th J Smith's Cup York 1m2f	8th Rated Hcp Ascot 1m2f	8th Motability Hcp York 1m2f
99 Ripo 1m2f 1st Handicap Three weeks	**Colway Ritz** W Storey 5/1	5/8	5	8-05	58	8th Silver Salver Hcp York 1m1f	**WON 9/2F** **Tetley's Hcp** **Redc 1m2f**	3rd Handicap Beve 1m	4th Rated Hcp York 1m4f
98 Newm 1m2f 5th Handicap One month	**Shadoof** W Muir 8/1	3/8	4	8-02	61	**WON 10/1** **Vodafone Hcp** **Epsom 1m2f**	11th H Kong Hcp Sand 1m2f	2nd Rated Hcp Yarm 1m2f	8th Motability Hcp York 1m2f
97 Newm 1m2f 1st Handicap One month	**Champagne Prince** P Harris 6/1	7/12	4	9-02	66	**WON 15/2** **London Hcp** **Epsom 1m2f**	3rd W Hill Hcp Good 1m2f	7th Motability Hcp York 1m2f	11th Courage Hcp York 1m2f
96 Donc 1m2f 1st May Day Hcp Three weeks	**Migwar** L Cumani 3/1F	8/16	3	8-05	65	19th K George V Hcp Ascot 1m4f	9th Courage Hcp Newb 1m2f	*6th Conds Stks Newb 1m2f	*25th Autumn Hcp Newm 1m

12-year median performance rating of the winner: **63** (out of 100)   *next year*

WINNER'S PROFILE The first starting point has been a **solid run last time out**, six ran well at either Chester or Newmarket, while four not to have raced at those venues arrived with a victory under their belt. **Four to six-year-olds** dominated, however, don't write off three-year-olds as only two have run during this period, which resulted in a winner and a runner-up – seven-year-olds and above are winless from 22 attempts. Although those drawn high and wide have won three recent renewals, it certainly helps to be tucked away on the inside from a **low draw**, while those who carried **9st or higher** came out on top during the last eight renewals.

FUTURE POINTERS One of Redcar's highlights of the season and though it has endured a subsequent quiet time in recent years, some top-class handicappers emerged to provide clues to forthcoming handicaps around this trip later in the year. Blue Monday was one of the best winners and subsequently finished runner-up at Newbury, before landing the Cambridgeshire. Two Zetland winners went on to score in a valuable handicap at Epsom on Derby Day next time out – only three tried that route – while six failed at Royal Ascot, three of them in the Duke of Edinburgh over further. Five were unplaced in the John Smith's Cup at York, including Flipando last year.

Were Zetland Gold Cup winners profitable to follow on their subsequent three runs?
Yes – 5 wins from 33 runs returned a **profit of +£6.00** to a £1 level stake.

Placed runners' subsequent record (three runs):
Runners-up: 7 wins from 36 runs returned a loss of -£12.02 to a £1 level stake.
2001 Pantar – Showcase Handicap (Sandown)

Thirds: 7 wins from 34 runs returned a **profit of +£1.75** to a £1 level stake.
2005 Crow Wood – Vodafone Handicap

Fourths: 0 win from 12 runs returned a loss of -£12.00 to a £1 level stake.

FUTURE SUCCESS RATING: ★ ★ ★ ☆ ☆

HILARY NEEDLER TROPHY
May 28, Beverley – (Listed, Class 1, 2yo Fillies) 5f

Last run	Winner/ Trainer & SP	Draw/ Ran	Age	Wght	PR	Next four runs			
07 York 5f 6th Marygate Listed *Two weeks*	Loch Jipp J Wainwright 20/1	1/13	2	8-12	55	9th Albany Stks Ascot 6f	4th Cherry Hinton Newm 6f	4th Princess Margaret Ascot 6f	8th Firth of Clyde Ayr 6f
06 (Unraced)	Roxan K Ryan 3/1F	8/11	2	8-09	53	11th Queen Mary Ascot 5f	2nd Firth of Clyde Ayr 6f	-	-
05 Carl 5f 1st Maiden *Two weeks*	Clare Hills K Burke 16/1	3/12	2	8-08	50	4th Queen Mary York 5f	5th Tower Stks Curr 6f	6th Firth of Clyde Ayr 6f	*8th Handicap Kemp 6f
04 Thir 5f 1st Novice Stks *Three weeks*	Miss Meggy T Easterby 16/1	1/12	2	8-11	60	9th Queen Mary Ascot 5f	6th Cherry Hinton Newm 6f	5th Nursery Beve 5f	6th Nursery Donc 7f
03 Thir 5f 1st Novice Stks *Three weeks*	Attraction M Johnston 11/10F	8/9	2	8-11	66	WON 13/8F Queen Mary Ascot 5f	WON 4/7F Cherry Hinton Newm 6f	*WON 11/2 1,000 Guineas Newm 1m	*WON 2/1 Irish 1,000 Guin Curr 1m
02 Thir 5f 1st Novice Stks *Three weeks*	On The Brink T Easterby 11/8F	12/11	2	8-11	50	12th Queen Mary Ascot 5f	*4th Showcase Hcp Ascot 6f	*6th Field Marshal Hayd 5f	*9th Showcase Hcp Ling 6f
01 Ripo 5f 1st Maiden *One month*	Good Girl T Easterby 9/2	9/10	2	8-08	58	5th Queen Mary Ascot 5f	WON 5/1JF Weatherbys Sprint Newb 5f	4th Lowther Stks York 6f	6th Flying Childers Donc 5f
00 (Unraced)	Freefourracing B Meehan 11/1	6/8	2	8-05	56	WON 2/5F Conds Stks Wind 6f	8th Cherry Hinton Newm 6f	WON 8/1 Prestige Stks Good 7f	WON 11/4 Stakes Keen 6f
99 Pont 5f 7th Novice Stks *Two months*	Tara's Girl J Quinn 16/1	8/9	2	8-08	54	4th Queen Mary Ascot 5f	8th Cherry Hinton Newm 6f	17th Tatts Stks Curr 6f	2nd Harry Rosebery Ayr 5f
98 Beve 5f 1st Maiden *One month*	Flanders T Easterby 4/5F	3/4	2	8-08	59	WON 15/8F Windsor Castle Ascot 5f	WON 6/5F Weatherbys Sprint Newb 5f	3rd Lowther Stks York 6f	2nd Yearling Stks Donc 6f
97 York 5f 4th Novice Stks *One month*	Filey Brigg W Kemp 16/1	3/10	2	8-08	51	15th Queen Mary Ascot 5f	3rd Princess Margaret Ascot 6f	6th Prestige Stks Good 7f	12th Firth of Clyde Ayr 6f
96 York 5f 1st Maiden *One month*	Dance Parade P Cole 2/5F	4/4	2	8-12	58	WON 8/1 Queen Mary Ascot 5f	11th Marcel Boussac Long 1m	*WON 16/1 Fred Darling Newb 7f	*12th 1,000 Guineas Newm 1m

12-year median performance rating of the winner: **56** (out of 100)   *next year*

WINNER'S PROFILE Clues are difficult to find with such lightly raced juveniles, as the majority only ran a **maximum of two races** – two were unraced – and of the 10 experienced winners, all were **prepared at a northern racecourse beforehand**. Three of those came via a novice stakes at Thirsk three weeks earlier, the same number that raced at nearby York. A high draw is usually an advantage here, although three recent winners overcame lower stalls, all of whom were big prices – 11 winners were either favourites with a high draw or a double-figure price! Trainer **Tim Easterby** is one to watch having scored four times from 11 runners.

FUTURE POINTERS Following a successful spell from 1996 to 2000, during which, several winners of this fillies' juvenile event went on to land a couple of Royal Ascot races along with the Prestige Stakes at Goodwood, the Hilary Needler was rightly allocated Listed status in 2001. Since then, though, the number of subsequent winners has disappointingly dried up, but it has produced by far the best winner in its long history in Attraction in 2003. Mark Johnston's wonder-filly won all her next four runs that included the Queen Mary at Royal Ascot next time out – a race that proved too hot for seven other winners apart from Dance Parade in 1996 – before she became a dual 1,000 Guineas winner the following season. Her performance rating (PR) was a firm nod as to what was on the horizon, and it is hoped another smart individual comes along in that mould to boost this event, which has suffered a recent dry spell. Runners-up from Beverley also boast a profitable subsequent record, however, punters that like to follow badly drawn horses would have made a loss from the three qualifiers when a high draw bias was in effect.

Were Hilary Needler winners profitable to follow on their subsequent three runs?
Yes – 10 wins from 35 runs returned a **profit of +£24.36** to a £1 level stake.

Placed runners' subsequent record (three runs):
Runners-up: 7 wins from 27 runs returned a **profit of +£22.64** to a £1 level stake.
2005 Donna Blini – Cherry Hinton, Cheveley Park, 1999 Vita Spericolata – Listed Dragon Trophy

Thirds: 6 wins from 30 runs returned a loss of -£9.87 to a £1 level stake.

FUTURE SUCCESS RATING: ★★★☆☆

HENRY II STAKES
May 29, Sandown – (Group 2, Class 1, 4yo+) 2m 78yds

Last run	Winner/ Trainer & SP	Draw/ Ran	Age	Wght	PR	Next four runs			
07 York 1m6f 5th Yorkshire Cup Two weeks	**Allegretto** Sir M Stoute 12/1	3/7	4	9-00	77	9th Gold Cup Ascot 2m4f	**WON 8/1** **Goodwood Cup** **Good 2m**	2nd Yorkshire Oaks York 1m4f	3rd Doncaster Cup Donc 2m2f
06 Ling 2m 2nd Sagaro Stks One month	**Tungsten Strike** Mrs A Perrett 4/1	4/7	5	9-02	72	8th Gold Cup Ascot 2m4f	3rd Goodwood Cup Good 2m	7th Lonsdale Cup York 2m	7th Doncaster Cup York 2m2f
05 Nad Al 11th Sheema Classic Two weeks	**Fight Your Corner** S Bin Suroor 20/1	8/16	6	9-00	74	7th Gold Cup York 2m4f	-	-	-
04 Good 1m4f 1st Conds Stks Two weeks	**Papineau** S Bin Suroor 9/4	2/9	4	8-12	71	**WON 5/1** **Gold Cup** **Ascot 2m4f**	*5th Yorkshire Cup York 1m6f	*16th Gold Cup York 2m4f	-
03 Long 2m 1st Prix Royal-Oak Seven months	**Mr Dinos** P Cole 6/1	4/10	4	9-03	76	**WON 3/1** **Gold Cup** **Ascot 2m4f**	6th Prix du Cadran Long 2m4f	*4th Yorkshire Cup York 1m6f	*2nd Henry II Sand 2m
02 York 2m 5th Yorkshire Cup Three weeks	**Akbar** M Johnston 16/1	6/11	6	9-00	75	-	-	-	-
01 Newm 2m 1st Sagaro Stks One month	**Solo Mio** Mrs A Perrett 7/1	2/11	7	9-01	74	4th Goodwood Cup Good 2m	*5th Sagaro Stks Ascot 2m	*4th Henry II Sand 2m	*13th Gold Cup Ascot 2m4f
00 York 1m6f 8th Yorkshire Cup Two weeks	**Persian Punch** D Elsworth 11/2	5/7	7	8-12	78	6th Gold Cup Ascot 2m4f	5th Goodwood Cup Good 2m	**WON 32/10** **Group 2** **Deau 2m1f**	3rd Doncaster Cup Donc 2m2f
99 York 1m6f 3rd Yorkshire Cup Three weeks	**Arctic Owl** J Fanshawe 5/1	7/11	5	9-03	77	2nd Princess of Wales' Newm 1m4f	2nd Lonsdale Cup York 2m	2nd Jockey Club Cup Newm 2m	6th Prix Royal-Oak Long 2m
98 York 1m6f 3rd Yorkshire Cup Two weeks	**Persian Punch** D Elsworth 15/8F	9/11	5	9-01	79	6th Gold Cup Ascot 2m4f	**WON 11/4** **Lonsdale Cup** **York 2m**	3rd Melbourne Cup Flem 2m	*4th John Porter Newb 1m4f
97 Newb 1m5f 1st Aston Park Two weeks	**Persian Punch** D Elsworth 3/1	1/7	4	8-10	72	12th Gold Cup Ascot 2m4f	5th Goodwood Cup Good 2m	5th Group 2 Deau 1m7f	2nd Doncaster Cup Donc 2m2f
96 Ascot 2m 1st Sagaro Stks One month	**Double Trigger** M Johnston 5/6F	4/5	5	9-05	81	2nd Gold Cup Ascot 2m4f	**WON EvsF** **Doncaster Cup** **Donc 2m2f**	5th Prix du Cadran Long 2m4f	*8th Sagaro Stks Ascot 2m

12-year median performance rating of the winner: **76** (out of 100)   *next year*

WINNER'S PROFILE Every winner had a **top-three placing in Listed grade at least**, although winning form over two miles hasn't been essential as three of the last four only scored over a mile-and-a-half.

Eight winners had their **prep in either the Yorkshire Cup or Sagaro Stakes**, while **four to six-year-olds** were favoured – eight-year-olds and above have struggled. An official rating of at least 106 can be a bonus, though it pays to look for value as only two favourites obliged.

Trainers **David Elsworth**, **Mark Johnston**, **Amanda Perrett** and **Saeed Bin Suroor** all won this more than once.

FUTURE POINTERS This has been a leading trial for the Gold Cup at Royal Ascot the following month and four winners of that event finished in the first three here, including Sandown winners Papineau and Mr Dinos. That pair were also two of the best to emerge from Sandown, while Double Trigger was also an above par scorer here before a gallant second at Ascot, however, recent Sandown winners have been below average and therefore flopped at Ascot. One race to be wary of backing Henry II winners in is the Goodwood Cup – four sunk – although the three Lonsdale Cup runners at York fared better with a winner and runner-up.

Were Henry II winners profitable to follow on their subsequent three runs?
No – 6 wins from 31 runs returned a loss of -£3.05 to a £1 level stake.

Placed runners' subsequent record (three runs):
Runners-up: 5 wins from 34 runs returned a loss of -£5.63 to a £1 level stake.
2007 Balkan Knight – Esher Stakes, 2005 Lochbuie – Geoffrey Freer Stakes, 1997 Celeric – Ascot Gold Cup

Thirds: 7 wins from 20 runs returned a **profit of +£24.83** to a £1 level stake.
2005 Alcazar – Group One Prix Royal Oak, 2001 Persian Punch – Goodwood Cup, Lonsdale Cup, 1999 Maridpour – Curragh Cup, 1998 Kayf Tara – Ascot Gold Cup

FUTURE SUCCESS RATING: ★ ★ ★ ☆ ☆

NATIONAL STAKES

May 29, Sandown – (Listed, Class 1, 2yo) 5f

Last run	Winner/ Trainer & SP	Draw/ Ran	Age	Wght	PR	Next four runs			
07 Sali 5f 1st Maiden *Two weeks*	**Sweepstake** R Hannon 11/4	8/7	2	8-09	55	19th Queen Mary Ascot 5f	3rd Princess Margaret Ascot 6f	- 	-
06 Newm 5f 1st Maiden *Two months*	**Excellent Art** N Callaghan 8/13F	1/4	2	9-00	62	3rd Railway Stks Curr 6f	3rd Prix Morny Deau 6f	**WON 15/8** **Mill Reef Stks** **Newb 6f**	*4th Poule 'Poulains Long 1m
05 York 5f 4th Marygate Stks *Three weeks*	**Salut D'Amour** J Noseda 11/2	8/11	2	8-10	60	2nd Queen Mary Ascot 5f	2nd Cherry Hinton Newm 6f	6th Meon Fillies' Mile Ascot 1m	*3rd Nell Gwyn Newm 7f
04 Muss 5f 1st Maiden *Two weeks*	**Polly Perkins** N Littmoden 25/1	2/8	2	8-07	56	11th Queen Mary Ascot 5f	8th Empress Stks Newm 6f	**WON 8/1** **Dragon Stks** **Sand 5f**	
03 Wind 5f 2nd Conds Stks *Two weeks*	**Russian Valour** M Johnston 5/1	2/7	2	9-01	63	**WON 4/1** **Norfolk Stks** **Ascot 5f**	*10th Euro Free Hcp Newm 7f	*6th Pavilion Stks Ascot 6f	*7th Conds Stks Leic 5f
02 Sali 5f 1st Conds Stks *One month*	**Presto Vento** R Hannon 7/4F	1/6	2	8-12	55	6th Queen Mary Ascot 5f	7th Cherry Hinton Newm 6f	**WON 6/1** **Weatherbys Sprint** **Newb 5f**	6th Molecomb Stks Good 5f
01 York 6f 5th Novice Stks *Two weeks*	**Shiny** C Brittain 9/1	4/7	2	8-07	53	9th Queen Mary Ascot 5f	5th Cherry Hinton Newm 6f	*9th Masaka Stks Kemp 1m	*3rd Fred Darling Newb 7f
00 Ascot 5f 4th Conds Stks *One month*	**Taras Emperor** J Quinn 6/1	2/6	2	9-01	54	9th Coventry Stks Ascot 6f	5th Molecomb Stks Good 5f	7th Gimcrack Stks York 6f	9th Flying Childers Donc 5f
99 Newb 5f 2nd Conds Stks *Three weeks*	**Rowaasi** M Channon 6/5F	5/7	2	8-07	62	2nd Queen Mary Ascot 5f	4th Lowther Stks York 6f	*9th Lansdown Stks Bath 5f	*10th Chipchase Stks Newc 6f
98 York 5f 2nd Novice Stks *Two weeks*	**Bint Allayl** M Channon 3/1	1/7	2	8-07	63	**WON 2/1F** **Queen Mary** **Ascot 5f**	**WON 15/8F** **Lowther Stks** **York 6f**	- 	-
97 Sali 5f 1st Maiden *Two weeks*	**Pool Music** R Hannon 6/1	5/6	2	9-01	56	5th Norfolk Stks Ascot 5f	3rd July Stks Newm 6f	9th Phoenix Stks Leop 6f	3rd Mill Reef Stks Newb 6f
96 Good 5f 1st Maiden *One week*	**Deadly Dudley** R Hannon 7/4F	7/6	2	9-01	60	3rd Coventry Stks Ascot 6f	8th July Stks Newm 6f	**WON 131/10** **Group 2** **Evry 7f**	*5th Maurice 'Gheest Deau 7f

12-year median performance rating of the winner: **58** (out of 100)   *next year*

WINNER'S PROFILE Excellent Art was the only winner not to have **raced within the past month** – the majority appeared within the past three weeks – while 11 reached the **first four last time out**, including Salut D'Amour, who already raced in a Listed event, unlike the remainder who **raced in Pattern company for the first time here**.

Three maidens got off the mark in this – all were fillies – and it is the **females that lead the colts** by two since 1996, including seven of the last 10 winners.

Trainer **Richard Hannon** took this four times from around a dozen runners – also won it three times from 1992-1994 – while Mick Channon sent out a pair from nine runners.

FUTURE POINTERS One of the first Pattern events of the season for juveniles, but unfortunately not the race it once was, as it has been a while since anything in the mould of Lyric Fantasy (1992) or Marling (1991) graced the Esher venue. However, Excellent Art gave the National Stakes a timely boost last year as he won the Group One St James's Palace Stakes as a three-year-old, after taking the Mill Reef Stakes as a juvenile and was the only winner since 1996 not to have gone to Royal Ascot next time out.

Of the 11 that made the venture into stronger company at Ascot, only two succeeded – both recorded above par performance ratings here (PR) – while those that attempted to get back on the winning trail at Newmarket an outing later also perished.

Bar Bint Allayl, who was the best graduate in the last 12 years, it has proven difficult to profit from winners on their next two outings, and the best option may be to follow those in Listed/Group Three races judged on recent results.

Were National winners profitable to follow on their subsequent three runs?
Yes – 7 wins from 34 runs returned a **profit of +£9.84** to a £1 level stake.

Placed runners' subsequent record (three runs):
Runners-up: 3 wins from 32 runs returned a loss of -£24.50 to a £1 level stake.

Thirds: 0 wins from 6 runs returned a loss of -£6.00 to a £1 level stake.

FUTURE SUCCESS RATING: ★ ★ ★ ☆ ☆

TEMPLE STAKES
May 31, Haydock – (Group 2, Class 1, 3yo+) 5f

Last run	Winner/Trainer & SP	Draw/Ran	Age	Wght	PR	Next four runs			
07 Hayd 5f 1st Rectangle Hcp *One week*	**Sierra Vista** D Barker 5/1	7/8	7	9-01	75	5th Chipchase Stks Newc 6f	8th Champagne Stk Sand 5f	8th Nunthorpe York 5f	11th Sprint Cup Hayd 6f
06 Newm 5f 4th Palace House *One month*	**Reverence** E Alston 9/4F	13/12	5	9-04	80	16th Golden Jubilee Ascot 6f	5th Champagne Stk Sand 5f	**WON 5/1** **Nunthorpe** **York 5f**	**WON 11/4F** **Sprint Cup** **Hayd 6f**
05 Wind 6f 3rd Leisure Stks *Two weeks*	**Celtic Mill** D Barker 16/1	11/13	7	9-04	73	14th King's Stand York 5f	Fell Champagne Stk Sand 5f	3rd Scarbrough Stk Donc 5f	8th World Trophy Newb 5f
04 York 5f 11th Totesport Hcp *Three weeks*	**Night Prospector** J Payne 33/1	9/12	4	9-04	70	10th Champagne Stk Sand 5f	12th Nunthorpe York 5f	8th Scarbrough Stk Donc 5f	*9th Palace House Newm 5f
03 Newm 6f 1st Cheveley Park *Seven months*	**Airwave** H Candy 5/2JF	7/7	3	9-00	79	2nd Golden Jubilee Ascot 6f	3rd July Cup Newm 6f	3rd Sprint Cup Hayd 6f	6th Diadem Stks Ascot 6f
02 Newm 5f 1st Palace House *One month*	**Kyllachy** H Candy 9/2	2/11	4	9-03	85	3rd King's Stand Ascot 5f	**WON 3/1F** **Nunthorpe** **York 5f**	-	-
01 Newm 5f 2nd Palace House *One month*	**Cassandra Go** G Wragg 10/3JF	8/10	5	9-00	79	**WON 8/1** **King's Stand** **Ascot 5f**	2nd July Cup Newm 6f	-	-
00 York 5f 10th Sony Hcp *Two weeks*	**Perryston View** J Glover 8/1	10/9	8	9-03	75	19th King's Stand Ascot 5f	5th Nunthorpe York 5f	5th Sprint Cup Hayd 6f	6th Scarbrough Stk Donc 5f
99 Ling 6f 2nd Leisure Stks *Two weeks*	**Tipsy Creek** B Hanbury 7/1	5/8	5	9-03	76	15th Cork & Orrery Ascot 6f	6th July Cup Newm 6f	6th King George Good 5f	PU Nunthorpe York 5f
98 Beve 5f 1st Conds Stks *Three weeks*	**Bolshoi** J Berry 10/1	2/8	6	9-03	78	**WON 10/1** **King's Stand** **Ascot 5f**	7th July Cup Newm 6f	4th Queensferry Stk Ches 6f	6th Nunthorpe York 5f
97 Donc 6f 9th Wentworth Stks *Six months*	**Croft Pool** J Glover 20/1	9/10	6	9-03	69	9th King's Stand Ascot 5f	7th Group 3 Deau 6f	14th King George Good 5f	11th Nunthorpe York 5f
96 Long 5f 8th Prix de l'Abbaye *Seven months*	**Mind Games** J Berry 7/2F	9/9	4	9-07	80	2nd King's Stand Ascot 5f	7th July Cup Newm 6f	4th Nunthorpe York 5f	6th Sprint Cup Hayd 6f

12-year median performance rating of the winner: **77** (out of 100)   *(2004 Epsom), *next year*

WINNER'S PROFILE The form of the **Palace House Stakes** at Newmarket can be tested here with three winners of the Temple Stakes coming via that race this century, while those that **appeared within the past month** have supplied nine of the last 10 winners. It is hard for the Classic generation to figure so early in the season against their elders and only Airwave triumphed from around 20 three-year-olds – Autumn Pearl was runner-up for the Classic generation in 2004 when staged at Epsom from a beneficial draw. Airwave was also officially rated very high on 117 compared to eight recent winners that came from a band **rated from 100 to 111**.
Two trainers to note are **David Barker** and **Henry Candy** having won four of the last six renewals.

FUTURE POINTERS This sprint was the first Group event Dayjur won in 1990 before subsequent greatness later that year, but it has been a while since anything of that calibre emerged from the Temple Stakes, although Kyllachy and Reverence went on to Group One glory in recent times. Last year's renewal wasn't up to scratch and it was no surprise to see Sierra Vista beaten in two Group Threes subsequently.
The most popular route post-Sandown was to Royal Ascot where two winners from seven followed up in the **King's Stand Stakes** – two were placed – while three were beaten in the Golden Jubilee Stakes. Further down the line, two Temple winners went on to lift the **Nunthorpe** at York after missing out at Ascot, although the July Cup has proven difficult to land as five lost at Newmarket.

Were Temple Stakes winners profitable to follow on their subsequent three runs?
No – 4 wins from 34 runs returned a loss of -£4.00 to a £1 level stake.

Placed runners' subsequent record (three runs):
Runners-up: 2 wins from 34 runs returned a loss of -£24.75 to a £1 level stake
1998 Lochangel – Nunthorpe

Thirds: 2 wins from 34 runs returned a loss of -£22.50 to a £1 level stake
2001 Nuclear Debate – Haydock Sprint Cup, 1998 Elnadim – July Cup

FUTURE SUCCESS RATING: ★★★★★

BRIGADIER GERARD STAKES
June 5, Sandown – (Group 3, Class 1, 4yo+) 1m2f

Last run	Winner/ Trainer & SP	Draw/ Ran	Age	Wght	PR	Next four runs			
07 Wind 1m 2nd Royal Windsor *Three weeks*	**Take A Bow** P Chamings 11/1	5/7	6	9-00	72	3rd York Stks York 1m2f	PU Winter Hill Stks Wind 1m2f	-	-
06 Newm 1m1f 1st Earl of Sefton *Two months*	**Notnowcato** Sir M Stoute 5/4F	1/6	4	9-03	81	5th Prince of Wales Ascot 1m2f	2nd Eclipse Sand 1m2f	**WON 8/1 Juddmonte Int York 1m2f**	8th Champion Stks Newm 1m2f
05 Curr 1m2f 6th Blandford Stks *Eight months*	**New Morning** M Jarvis 12/1	5/5	4	8-07	73	4th Pretty Polly Stks Curr 1m2f	7th Juddmonte Int York 1m2f	-	-
04 Ches 1m2f 1st Huxley Stks *One month*	**Bandari** M Johnston 7/2	3/9	5	8-10	79	**WON 12/1 Prince of Wales' Ascot 1m2f**	7th **Princess of Wales' Newm 1m4f**	King George VI Ascot 1m4f	3rd September Stks Kemp 1m4f
03 Nad Al 1m1f 6th Dubai Duty Free *Two months*	**Sights On Gold** S Bin Suroor 7/1	5/8	5	8-10	75	2nd Scottish Derby Ayr 1m2f	**WON EvsF Conds Stks Epsom 1m2f**	**WON 3/1F Arc Trial Newb 1m3f**	7th Group 2 Long 1m2f
02 Wind 1m4f 2nd Berkshire Stks *Two weeks*	**Potemkin** R Hannon 7/2	4/4	4	8-10	70	5th Hardwicke Stks Ascot 1m4f	5th Steventon Stks Newb 1m2f	3rd Group 3 Bade 1m2f	*5th Earl of Sefton Newm 1m1f
01 Sand 1m2f 2nd Gordon Richards *Two months*	**Border Arrow** I Balding 11/2	5/5	6	8-10	73	8th Prince of Wales' Ascot 1m2f	3rd James Seymour Newm 1m2f	2nd Serlby Stks Donc 1m4f	6th Churchill Stks Ling 1m2f
00 Newm 1m1f 7th Earl of Sefton *Two months*	**Shiva** H Cecil 7/2F	4/8	5	9-00	78	3rd Eclipse Sand 1m2f	7th King George VI Ascot 1m4f	9th Champion Stks Newm 1m2f	-
99 Ches 1m2f 1st Huxley Stks *One month*	**Chester House** H Cecil 9/4	2/6	4	8-10	76	4th Prince of Wales' Ascot 1m2f	4th Eclipse Sand 1m2f	3rd Juddmonte Int York 1m2f	4th Breeders' Cup Gulf 1m2f
98 Newm 1m2f 1st Conds Stks *One month*	**Insatiable** Sir M Stoute 9/2	3/9	5	8-10	79	7th Prince of Wales' Ascot 1m2f	4th Eclipse Sand 1m2f	**WON 5/1 Group 2 Long 1m2f**	2nd Champion Stks Newm 1m2f
97 Newm 1m2f 1st Champion Stks *Seven months*	**Bosra Sham** H Cecil 1/5F	1/6	4	9-00	82	**WON 4/11F Prince of Wales' Ascot 1m2f**	3rd Eclipse Sand 1m2f	4th Juddmonte Int York 1m2f	-
96 Sand 1m2f 2nd Gordon Richards *Two months*	**Pilsudski** Sir M Stoute 11/2	7/11	4	8-10	80	8th Prince of Wales' Ascot 1m2f	**WON 5/2 Royal Whip Stks Curr 1m2f**	**WON N/0 Grosser 'Baden Bade 1m4f**	2nd Arc de Triomphe Long 1m4f

12-year median performance rating of the winner: **77** (out of 100)   *next year*

WINNER'S PROFILE Ten winners arrived having **already raced that season**, eight of whom finished in the **top-two last time out** with two in the Gordon Richards Stakes over the course and distance.

There aren't many clues to be gained from an age perspective, although six horses aged seven and above failed, while nine winners **already scored over this specialist trip** – two exceptions won over nine and 11 furlongs. The Newmarket maestro's, **Henry Cecil** and **Sir Michael Stoute**, both landed the event three times each.

FUTURE POINTERS Considering this race is only a Group Three, it has attracted some monsters of the turf over the years that went on to notable achievements, although the standard of winners varied and last year's victor, Take A Bow, was massively below par.

The favoured path taken by winners post-Sandown was to Royal Ascot, although only Bosra Sham followed up in the Prince of Wales's Stakes, a race that tripped up six others, while one flopped in the Hardwicke Stakes, a race where two placed runners scored *(see below)*. Another event that proved too hard for Brigadier Gerard winners to shine in was the Eclipse back over the course and distance – five failed.

All three of Sir Michael Stoute's winners were worth following with a profit of £10.50 to levels on their next three runs, including Notnowcato and Pilsudski, who lifted Group One honours.

Were Brigadier Gerard winners profitable to follow on their subsequent three runs?
Yes – 8 wins from 34 runs returned a **profit of +£5.86** to a £1 level stake.

Placed runners' subsequent record (three runs):
Runners-up: 1 win from 29 runs returned a loss of -£22.00 to a £1 level stake
1997 Predappio – Hardwicke Stakes

Thirds: 2 wins from 12 runs returned a **profit of +£4.00** to a £1 level stake
2003 Indian Creek – Hardwicke Stakes

FUTURE SUCCESS RATING: ★ ★ ★ ☆ ☆

ROSE BOWL HERITAGE HANDICAP
June 6, Epsom – (Class 2, 4yo+) 1m2f

Last run	Winner/ Trainer & SP	Draw/ Ran	Age	Wght	PR	Next four runs			
07 Epso 1m4f 1st Great Met Hcp Two months	Lake Poet C Brittain 6/1	1/12	4	9-05	63	8th Wolferton Hcp Ascot 1m2f	2nd Heritage Hcp Good 1m2f	8th Ebor York 1m6f	6th Handicap Donc 1m4f
06 Kemp 1m2f 7th RUK Hcp One month	Chancellor E Oertel 40/1	13/17	8	8-03	67	11th Winter Hill Stks Wind 1m2f	19th J Smith's Hcp Newb 1m2f	13th November Hcp Wind 1m4f	6th Nov Hdle Leic 2m
05 Jage 1m1f 5th Listed Three weeks	Eccentric A Reid 8/1	10/17	4	8-02	61	9th Silver Trophy Ling 1m	6th Summer Hcp Good 1m2f	2nd Totesport Hcp Hayd 1m3f	WON 7/1 Winter Hill Stks Wind 1m2f
04 Good 1m4f 4th Conds Stks Three weeks	Persian Lightning J Dunlop 11/2	1/11	5	9-02	70	4th Wolferton Hcp Ascot 1m2f	6th Glorious Hcp Good 1m4f	*5th Conds Stks Newm 1m2f	*WON 15/2 Listed Ling 1m3f
03 Good 1m 1st Class Stks Two weeks	Akshar Sir M Stoute 5/4F	6/14	4	9-00	74	3rd Wolferton Hcp Ascot 1m2f	WON 6/4F Motability Hcp York 1m2f	3rd Strensall Stks York 1m1f	26th Cambridgeshire Newm 1m1f
02 Wind 1m2f 1st Rated Hcp Three weeks	Vintage Premium R Fahey 7/1	10/11	5	9-08	71	6th Wolferton Hcp Ascot 1m2f	WON 20/1 J Smith's Cup York 1m2f	5th Group 3 Ovre 1m1f	2nd Conds Stks Donc 1m2f
01 Wind 1m2f 3rd Rated Hcp One week	Bogus Dreams S Woods 12/1	10/12	4	9-03	64	WON 1/16F Conds Stks Donc 1m2f	2nd Rated Hcp Ascot 1m2f	5th Rated Hcp Good 1m4f	2nd Conds Stks Epsom 1m2f
00 Kemp 1m2f 2nd Handicap Two weeks	Supply And Demand J Gosden 4/1F	14/14	6	8-11	70	-	-	-	-
99 York 1m2f 8th Rated Hcp One month	Monsajem E Dunlop 12/1	10/15	4	9-04	71	20th Hong Kong Hcp Sand 1m2f	WON 5/2 Rated Hcp Newb 1m3f	3rd Rated Hcp Epsom 1m2f	3rd Foundation Stks Good 1m2f
98 Redc 1m2f 1st Zetland G Cup Two weeks	Shadoof W Muir 10/1	3/14	4	8-00	60	11th Hong Kong Hcp Sand 1m2f	2nd Rated Hcp Yarm 1m	8th Motability Hcp York 1m2f	2nd Rated Hcp Epsom 1m2f
97 Redc 1m2f 1st Zetland G Cup Two weeks	Champagne Prince Miss G Kelleway 11/1	7/13	5	8-09	63	3rd W Hill Cup Hcp Good 1m2f	7th Motability Hcp York 1m2f	11th Courage Hcp Newb 1m2f	*6th Hollywood Hcp Holl 1m2f
96 Sand 1m2f 11th Gordon Richards Two months	Ela-Aristokrati L Cumani 16/1	8/16	4	9-10	69	4th Eclipse Sand 1m2f	2nd Rose of Lancaster Hayd 1m3f	3rd September Stks Kemp 1m3f	*2nd John Porter Newb 1m4f

12-year median performance rating of the winner: **67** (out of 100)   *next year*

WINNER'S PROFILE A **recent spin** was important as six winners of late had a prep at either Goodwood, Kempton or Windsor. **Winning form over the trip** has also proven key, as 11 boasted such credentials, 10 of whom had **already scored in this grade**, the same number **officially rated in the 80s or 90s**.
On the age front, **four and five-year-olds** came out best, while favourites have a lousy record.

FUTURE POINTERS Only one winner followed up in the past 12 years, and like some of the Derby winners who also endured a tough race around the Downs, the stuffing may have been knocked out of them as three winners bounced back on their second subsequent start.
One of those was Vintage Premium, who lifted the valuable John Smith's Cup at York, while Akshar also took a nice handicap at York after recovering from a disappointment at Royal Ascot.

Were Rose Bowl winners profitable to follow on their subsequent three runs?
No – 4 winners from 33 runs returned a loss of -£4.93 to a £1 level stake.

Placed runners' subsequent record (three runs):
Runners-up: 2 wins from 31 runs returned a loss of -£9.00 to a £1 level stake.
2004 Desert Quest – Shergar Cup

Thirds: 4 wins from 36 runs returned a loss of -£2.63 to a £1 level stake.
2001 Riberac – William Hill Handicap (Glorious Goodwood)

Fourths: 0 win from 9 runs returned a loss of -£9.00 to a £1 level stake.

FUTURE SUCCESS RATING: ★ ★ ★ ☆ ☆

CORONATION CUP
June 6, Epsom – (Group 1, Class 1, 4yo+) 1m4f

Last run	Winner/ Trainer & SP	Draw/ Ran	Age	Wght	PR	Next four runs			
07 Ches 1m5f 2nd Ormonde *Three weeks*	**Scorpion** A O'Brien 8/1	2/7	5	9-00	80	2nd Hardwicke Stks Ascot 1m4f	5th King George VI Ascot 1m4f	2nd Irish St Leger Curr 1m6f	-
06 Newm 1m4f 1st Jockey Club Stk *One month*	**Shirocco** A Fabre 8/11F	5/6	5	9-00	86	**WON 13/8 Prix Foy Long 1m4f**	7th Arc de Triomphe Long 1m4f	-	-
05 Curr 1m2f 2nd Mooresbridge *One month*	**Yeats** A O'Brien 5/1	9/7	4	9-00	83	9th G Prix St-Cloud Sain 1m4f	4th Irish St Leger Curr 1m6f	6th Canadian Int Wood 1m4f	*****WON 7/1 Gold Cup Ascot 2m4f**
04 Newm 1m4f 3rd Jockey Club Stks *Two months*	**Warrsan** C Brittain 7/1	5/11	6	9-00	80	2nd Eclipse Sand 1m2f	9th King George VI Ascot 1m4f	**Grosser 'Baden Baden 1m4f**	Arc de Triomphe Long 1m4f
03 York 1m6f 2nd Yorkshire Cup *Three weeks*	**Warrsan** C Brittain 9/2	4/9	5	9-00	80	2nd Premio di Milano Siro 1m4f	6th King George VI Ascot 1m4f	3rd Group 1 Pokal Colo 1m4f	3rd Premio Jockey Club Siro 1m4f
02 Nad Al 1m4f 3rd Sheema Classic *Three months*	**Boreal** P Schiergen 4/1	3/6	4	9-00	77	7th King George VI Ascot 1m4f	6th Grosser 'Baden Baden 1m4f	15th Arc de Triomphe Long 1m4f	*16th Sheema Classic Nad Al
01 Nad Al 1m4f 8th Sheema Classic *Three months*	**Mutafaweq** S Bin Suroor 11/2	1/6	5	9-00	79	3rd Hardwicke Ascot 1m4f	8th Group 1 Pokal Colo 1m4f	8th Grade 1 Belm 1m3f	6th Grade 1 Belm 1m4f
00 Ches 1m5f 1st Ormonde *One month*	**Daliapour** Sir M Stoute 11/8F	2/4	4	9-00	80	3rd King George VI Ascot 1m4f	4th Grosser 'Baden Baden 1m4f	3rd Canadian Int Wood 1m4f	**WON 13/10F Hong Kong Vase Sha 1m4f**
99 Curr 1m3f 2nd Tatts Gold Cup *Two weeks*	**Daylami** S Bin Suroor 9/2	3/7	5	9-00	85	**WON 3/1 King George VI Ascot 1m4f**	**WON 6/4 Irish Champion Leop 1m2f**	9th Arc de Triomphe Long 1m4f	**WON 16/10F Breeders' Cup Gulf 1m4f**
98 Newm 1m4f 2nd Jockey Club Stk *Two months*	**Silver Patriarch** J Dunlop 7/2	2/7	4	9-00	78	4th G Prix St-Cloud Sain 1m4f	6th King George VI Ascot 1m4f	2nd Geoffrey Freer Newb 1m5f	2nd Irish St Leger Curr 1m6f
97 Nad Al 1m2f 1st World Cup *Three months*	**Singspiel** Sir M Stoute 5/4F	3/5	5	9-00	84	4th King George VI Ascot 1m4f	**WON 4/1 Juddmonte Int York 1m2f**	-	-
96 Long 1m3f 3rd Prix Ganay *Two months*	**Swain** A Fabre 11/10F	2/4	4	9-00	81	2nd G Prix St-Cloud Sain 1m4f	**WON EvsF Prix Foy Long 1m4f**	4th Arc de Triomphe Long 1m4f	3rd Breeders' Cup Wood 1m4f

12-year median performance rating of the winner: **81** (out of 100)   *next year*

WINNER'S PROFILE Recent good form and fitness have been important, and eight winners arrived via either the World Cup meeting in Nad Al Sheba, the Jockey Club Stakes at Newmarket, or the Ormonde at Chester. Stick with those who finished in the frame in a Group One previously, while **four and five-year-olds** have proven best as six-year-olds and above struck just once from 14 runners, including Maraahel's defeat last year. Outsiders aren't often seen, as every winner returned at **7/1 or shorter**, while trainers to keep onside include **Aidan O'Brien** and **Sir Michael Stoute**.

FUTURE POINTERS Coronation Cup winners have disappointed in the main following Epsom and only Shirocco and Daylami followed up. The latter was also the only winner who took the King George VI at Ascot a month later, a race that foiled seven others, before Breeders' Cup success later in the year. Shirocco scored in the Group Two Prix Foy over in France three months later, as did Swain back in 1996, although the latter was unable to win the Group One Grand Prix de Saint-Cloud in the same country, along with Yeats and Silver Patriarch, who also came up short.

Were Coronation Cup winners profitable to follow on their subsequent three runs?
No – 6 wins from 34 runs returned a loss of -£9.87 to a £1 level stake.

Placed runners' subsequent record (three runs):
Runners-up: 11 wins from 29 runs returned a **profit of +£24.10** to a £1 level stake.
2007 Septimus – Lonsdale Cup, Doncaster Cup, 2006 Ouija Board – Prince of Wales's Stakes, Nassau Stakes, 2005 Alkaased – Grand Prix de Saint-Cloud, 2004 Doyen – Hardwicke Stakes, 1999 Royal Anthem – Juddmonte International, 1998 Swain – King George VI, Irish Champion Stakes, 1997 Dushyantor – Geoffrey Freer Stakes

Thirds: 0 win from 6 runs returned a loss of -£6.00 to a £1 level stake.

FUTURE SUCCESS RATING: ★★★★☆

OAKS STAKES
June 6, Epsom – (Group 1, Class 1, 3yo Fillies) 1m4f 10yds

Last run	Winner/ Trainer & SP	Draw/ Ran	Age	Wght	PR	Next four runs			
07 Ches 1m3f 1st Cheshire Oaks *One month*	**Light Shift** H Cecil 13/2	11/14	3	9-00	83	2nd Irish Oaks Curr 1m4f	3rd Nassau Stks Good 1m2f	2nd Prix de l'Opera Long 1m2f	-
06 York 1m2f 2nd Musidora *Three weeks*	**Alexandrova** A O'Brien 9/4F	5/10	3	9-00	80	**WON 8/15F** Irish Oaks Curr 1m4f	**WON 4/9F** Yorkshire Oaks York 1m4f	3rd Prix de l'Opera Long 1m2f	-
05 Newb 1m2f 1st Swettenham Trial *Three weeks*	**Eswarah** M Jarvis 11/4JF	2/12	3	9-00	75	8th King George VI Newb 1m4f	4th Yorkshire Oaks York 1m4f		
04 Newm 1m2f 1st Pretty Polly *Two months*	**Ouija Board** E Dunlop 7/2	3/7	3	9-00	85	**WON 4/7F** Irish Oaks Curr 1m4f	3rd Arc de Triomphe Long 1m4f	**WON 10/11F** Breeders' Cup Lone 1m3f	*7th Prince of Wales' Ascot 1m4f
03 Newm 1m 6th 1,000 Guineas *Two months*	**Casual Look** A Balding 10/1	7/15	3	9-00	73	3rd Irish Oaks Curr 1m4f	7th Yorkshire Oaks York 1m4f	8th Prix Vermeille Long 1m4f	3rd Grade 1 Keen 1m1f
02 Newm 1m 1st 1,000 Guineas *Two months*	**Kazzia** S Bin Suroor 10/3F	13/14	3	9-00	79	4th Yorkshire Oaks York 1m4f	**WON 61/20** Flower Bowl Belm 1m1f	6th Breeders' Cup Arli 1m2f	-
01 Curr 1m 1st Irish 1,000 Guin *Two weeks*	**Imagine** A O'Brien 3/1F	10/14	3	9-00	76	-	-	-	-
00 Good 1m2f 1st Lupe Stks *Three weeks*	**Love Divine** H Cecil 9/4F	3/16	3	9-00	80	2nd Yorkshire Oaks York 1m4f	4th Prix Vermeille Long 1m4f	4th Champion Stks Newm 1m2f	-
99 Ling 1m3f 1st Oaks Trial *One month*	**Ramruma** H Cecil 3/1	5/10	3	9-00	82	**WON 4/9F** Irish Oaks Curr 1m4f	**WON 5/6F** Yorkshire Oaks York 1m4f	2nd St Leger Donc 1m6½f	*11th Jockey Club Stks Newm 1m4f
98 Curr 1m 10th Irish 1,000 Guin *Two weeks*	**Shahtoush** A O'Brien 12/1	5/8	3	9-00	78	5th Yorkshire Oaks York 1m4f	8th Irish Champion Leop 1m2f		
97 York 1m2f 1st Musidora Stks *One month*	**Reams Of Verse** H Cecil 5/6F	6/12	3	9-00	75	4th Yorkshire Oaks York 1m4f	3rd Sun Chariot Newm 1m2f	-	-
96 Ling 1m3f 1st Oaks Trial *One month*	**Lady Carla** H Cecil 10/30	9/11	3	9-00	80	4th Irish Oaks Curr 1m4f	9th Hardwicke Ascot 1m4f	7th Princess of Wales' Newm 1m4f	-

12-year median performance rating of the winner: **79** (out of 100)   **next year*

WINNER'S PROFILE Nine winners arrived at the top their game having **won last time out** – Kazzia recorded the Classic double following the 1,000 Guineas, while Imagine won the Irish version earlier – and those with **form in either Guineas** are to be respected. There has been an even spread in the trial races, as the **Musidora** provided a couple of winners, while Henry Cecil made good use of the **Lingfield Oaks Trial**, though he chose the **Cheshire Oaks** for last year's winner. The Pretty Polly, however, is a race to be wary of despite producing the winner in 2004, as that was the first time for around 30 years. No winner came from out of the **first six in the betting**, and seven of **Henry Cecil** and **Aidan O'Brien**'s eight winners returned at 13/2 or shorter.

FUTURE POINTERS The Oaks has been a great example of following classy winners with a quality performance rating (PR) as three of best winners doubled up in the Irish equivalent. Two of those, Alexandrova and Ramruma, also took the Yorkshire version at York, a race that evaded six other winners, while Ouija Board went on to Breeders' Cup glory.
At the other end of the scale, the five worst winners of the Oaks never won another race.

Were Oaks winners profitable to follow on their subsequent three runs?
No – 7 wins from 30 runs returned a loss of -£16.24 to a £1 level stake.

Placed runners' subsequent record (three runs):
Runners-up: 7 wins from 30 runs returned a loss of -£11.73 to a £1 level stake.
2007 Peeping Fawn – Pretty Polly Stakes, Irish Oaks, Nassau Stakes, 1999 Noushkey – Lancashire Oaks, 1998 Bahr – Ribblesdale Stakes

Thirds: 2 wins from 31 runs returned a loss of -£17.50 to a £1 level stake.
2006 Short Skirt – St Simon Stakes, 1999 Zahrat Dubai – Nassau Stakes

FUTURE SUCCESS RATING: ★ ★ ★ ☆ ☆

HERITAGE HANDICAP
June 7, Epsom – (Class 2, 3yo) 1m2f

Last run	Winner/Trainer & SP	Draw/Ran	Age	Wght	PR	Next four runs			
07 Newb 1m2f Gold Cup Hcp *Two weeks*	1st **Zaham** M Johnston 7/2	10/14	3	9-02	68	**WON 7/2F** Hampton Court **Ascot 1m2f**	3rd Rose 'Lancaster Hayd 1m3f	2nd Select Stks Good 1m2f	2nd Cumb'lnd Lodge Ascot 1m4f
06 Yarm 1m2f Bet365 Hcp *One month*	1st **Stage Gift** Sir M Stoute 5/2F	8/15	3	9-07	72	7th Great Voltigeur York 1m4f	2nd Strensall Stks York 1m1f	**WON 11/4** **Darley Stks** **Newm 1m1f**	*14th Group 3 Nad Al 1m1f
05 Hayd 1m Silver Bowl Hcp *Two weeks*	3rd **Enforcer** W Muir 5/1	8/11	3	8-05	62	13th Britannia Stks Ascot 1m	9th Heritage Hcp Newm 1m2f	**WON 6/1** **Ladbrokes Hcp** **Good 1m2f**	3rd Heritage Hcp Beve 1m2f
04 York 1m2f Rated Hcp *One month*	3rd **Lord Mayor** Sir M Stoute 11/2	1/18	3	9-05	69	5th Hampton Court Ascot 1m2f	5th July Trophy Hayd 1m4f	6th Prix d'Ornano Deau 1m2f	*7th Earl of Sefton Newm 1m1f
03 Hayd 1m Silver Bowl Hcp *Two weeks*	1st **Jazz Messenger** G Butler 5/1JF	11/17	3	9-04	64	8th J Smith's Cup York 1m2f	17th Cambridgeshire Newm 1m1f	6th Conds Stks Nott m1	*6th Betfred Hcp Sand 1m
02 Ches 1m4f Handicap *One month*	2nd **Lingo** Mrs J Ramsden 7/2	1/10	3	8-10	63	4th Seabeach Hcp Good 1m2f	5th Rated Hcp Newm 1m4f	9th Tote Handicap Donc 1m4f	*14th Lincoln Donc 1m
01 Hayd 1m3f Rated Hcp *Two weeks*	1st **Lailani** E Dunlop 4/1F	1/13	3	9-07	74	**WON 5/1** **Irish Oaks** **Curr 1m4f**	**WON 5/4F** **Nassau** **Good 1m2f**	**WON 49/20** **Flower Bowl** **Belm 1m2f**	8th Breeders' Cup Belm 1m2f
00 Good 1m1f Showcase Hcp *Three weeks*	7th **Forbearing** Sir M Prescott 10/1	1/12	3	8-11	71	**WON EvsF** **Coral Hcp** **Good 1m2f**	**WON 13/8** **Class Stks** **Sali 1m2f**	2nd Bonusprint Hcp Newm 1m2f	2nd Rose 'Lancaster Hayd 1m3f
99 York 1m Rated Hcp *One month*	1st **Tier Worker** T Easterby 5/1	2/15	3	9-00	63	2nd K George V Hcp Ascot 1m4f	****PU Nov Hdle Weth 2m	****14th Nov Hdle Hayd 2m	–
98 Sali 1m4f Conds Stks *One month*	3rd **Dower House** W Jarvis 14/1	11/11	3	9-07	60	3rd Handicap Donc 1m2f	17th J Smith's Cup York 1m2f	*UR Magnolia Stks Kemp 1m2f	*4th Earl of Sefton Newm 1m1f
97 Siro 1m2f Listed *One month*	1st **Jaunty Jack** L Cumani 4/1JF	2/10	3	9-05	70	**WON N/O** **Listed** **Siro 1m2f**	3rd Premio San Siro Siro 1m4f	*4th Stakes Taby 1m2f	*8th Listed Taby 1m2f
96 York 1m Handicap *One month*	3rd **Spirito Libro** C Allen 8/1	12/12	3	7-11	61	4th Handicap Sand 1m1f	3rd Hong Kong Hcp Sand 1m2f	2nd J Smith's Cup York 1m2f	*5th Middleton Stks York 1m2f

12-year median performance rating of the winner: **66** (out of 100)   *next year ****four years*

WINNER'S PROFILE A **good recent effort** was essential as 11 winners arrived with up a **top-three effort within the past month** – two came off the back of a big run in the Silver Bowl Handicap at Haydock – while three advertised their claims at York. A previous victory over this trip wasn't vital as only six boasted such a credential and individuals yet to be unmasked as middle-distance performers are respected.

Those in the **top-half of the handicap** came out best – an **official rating between 86 and 95** ideal – while shocks were rare as eight of the last nine returned at **11/2 or shorter**.

Trainer **Sir Michael Stoute** landed this twice in recent years, while **Sir Mark Prescott**'s rare entries should be noted, as his only two runners finished first and second.

FUTURE POINTERS A handicap that produced some future Pattern performers, proven by last year's winner, Zaham, who gave the event a solid boost in the Listed Hampton Court Stakes at Royal Ascot.

A step up in class may be the best route as only a few took a handicap in the near future, unlike Stage Gift and Jaunty Jack, who like Zaham, gained Listed honours. However, the best winner of this event with a superior performance rating (PR) on the day was Lailani, who went straight to the top following Epsom with Group One victories in the Irish Oaks and Nassau Stakes, before a Grade One in America.

Were Heritage Handicap winners profitable to follow on their subsequent three runs?
No – 9 wins from 36 runs returned a loss of -£3.43 to a £1 level stake.

Placed runners' subsequent record (three runs):
Runners-up: 7 wins from 34 runs returned a loss of -£8.58 to a £1 level stake
2002 Systematic – King George V Handicap, 2001 Foreign Affairs – John Smith's Cup

Thirds: 4 wins from 36 runs returned a loss of -£11.05 to a £1 level stake.

Fourths: 0 wins from 6 runs returned a loss of -£6.00.

FUTURE SUCCESS RATING: ★ ★ ☆ ☆ ☆

DIOMED STAKES
June 7, Epsom – (Group 3, Class 1, 3yo+) 1m 114yds

Last run	Winner/ Trainer & SP	Draw/ Ran	Age	Wght	PR	Next four runs			
07 York 1m 1st Hambleton Hcp Three weeks	Blythe Knight J Quinn 4/1	2/5	7	9-04	70	7th Celebration Mile Good 1m	4th Doonside Cup Ayr 1m2f	3rd Group 2 Long 1m	7th Darley Stks Newm 1m1f
06 Kemp 1m2f 4th Magnolia Stks Two months	Nayyir G Butler 11/2	2/8	8	9-04	75	4th Criterion Stks Newm 7f	4th Lennox Stks Good 7f	13th W Hill Mile Hcp Good 1m	6th Strensall Stks York 1m1f
05 Newm 1m1f 3rd Suffolk Hcp One month	Hazyview N Callaghan 8/1	1/7	4	9-04	77	8th Prince of Wales' York 1m2f	WON 9/4 Midsummer Stk Wind 1m	4th Eclipse Sand 1m2f	5th Desmond Stks Leop 1m
04 Sha 1m 11th Hong Kong Mile Six months	Passing Glance A Balding 20/1	3/11	5	9-09	72	10th Sussex Good 1m	4th Sovereign Stks Sali 1m	5th Celebration Mile Good 1m	-
03 Siro 1m 3rd Group 2 Three weeks	Gateman M Johnston 13/2	9/10	6	9-04	75	4th Queen Anne Ascot 1m	WON 11/10F Superior Mile Hayd 1m	3rd Group 2 Long 1m	5th Group 1 Siro 1m
02 Beve 1m 1st Rated Hcp Three weeks	Nayyir G Butler 5/1JF	6/9	4	9-04	76	4th Queen Anne Ascot 1m	WON 9/2 Lennox Stks Good 1m	3rd Maurice 'Gheest Deau 7f	10th Sprint Cup Hayd 6f
01 Kemp 1m 1st Conds Stks Two months	Pulau Tioman M Jarvis 6/1	6/8	5	9-04	68	7th Listed Curr 1m	4th Winter Hill Stks Wind 1m2f	*7th Diomed Stks Epsom 1½m	*25th Royal Hunt Cup Ascot 1m
00 Newb 1m 2nd Lockinge Three weeks	Trans Island I Balding 5/4F	2/5	5	9-09	74	4th Group 2 Deau 1m	11th Prix de la Foret Long 7f	-	-
99 Good 1m2f 6th Shergar Cup One month	Lear Spear D Elsworth 7/1	4/6	4	9-04	72	WON 20/1 Prince of Wales' Ascot 1m2f	8th Eclipse Sand 1m2f	WON 9/2 Select Stks Good 1m2f	9th Champion Stks Newm 1m2f
98 Nad Al 1m2f 2nd Listed Three months	Intikhab S Bin Suroor 2/1F	3/10	4	9-04	75	WON 9/4F Queen Anne Ascot 1m	*4th Lockinge Newb 1m	-	-
97 Capa 7f 1st Listed Two weeks	Polar Prince M Jarvis 14/1	1/9	4	9-04	67	3rd International Stk Curr 1m	3rd Group 3 Deau 1m	2nd Celebration Mile Good 1m	5th Fortune Stks Epsom 1½m
96 Sand 1m 1st Rated Hcp Two weeks	Blomberg J Fanshawe 6/1	4/8	4	9-04	65	31st Royal Hunt Cup Ascot 1m	4th Desmond Stks Curr 1m	7th Porcelanosa Hp Donc 1m	12th Group 2 Colo 1m

12-year median performance rating of the winner: **72** (out of 100)   *next year*

WINNER'S PROFILE All bar one winner **raced within the past two months**, those to have **made the top-two beforehand** should be respected, while every winner apart from Polar Prince had **already scored over a mile**. Last year's poor turnout saw the victor score from an official rating of 102, but normally a **rating in excess of 106** has been required as progressive handicappers shined in recent years.
The only two to have already recorded a Group victory were trained by Andrew and Ian Balding and both emerged from **low draws** – only one winner was drawn in the highest third – while **four-year-olds and upwards** have held sway with three-year-olds yet to score from 14 runners.

FUTURE POINTERS This Group Three has had it's share of quality winners over the years that went on to triumph in better company, although it does have the odd weak renewal such as last year's, which resulted in a below par performance rating (PR). However, concentrating on only the above par winners has proven worthwhile, as the majority found success near at hand, like the likes of Nayyir in 2002, who subsequently took the Lennox Stakes after disappointing at Royal Ascot. Two of the six that headed to the Royal meeting next time out followed up, although those that travelled to foreign shores or stepped back in trip came unstuck.

Were Diomed winners profitable to follow on their subsequent three runs?
Yes – 6 wins from 34 runs returned a **profit of +£6.60** to a £1 level stake.

Placed runners' subsequent record (three runs):
Runners-up: 7 wins from 32 runs returned a **profit of +£26.47** to a £1 level stake.
2003 Reel Buddy – Sussex, 2002 Highdown – Prix d'Ornano.

Thirds: 2 wins from 17 runs returned a loss of -£10.25 to a £1 level stake.

FUTURE SUCCESS RATING: ★ ★ ★ ☆ ☆

"DASH" STAKES
June 7, Epsom – (Class 2, Heritage Handicap, 3yo+) 5f

Last run	Winner/ Trainer & SP	Draw/ Ran	Age	Wght	PR	Next four runs			
07 York 5f 3rd Totesport Hcp *Three weeks*	**Hogmaneigh** S Williams 7/1	15/18	4	9-04	69	12th Wokingham Ascot 6f	4th Rockingham Hcp Curr 5f	15th Hong Kong Hcp Ascot 5f	7th Scarbrough Stks Donc 5f
06 Ches 5f 5th Betfred Hcp *One month*	**Desert Lord** K Ryan 12/1	17/20	6	8-08	67	2nd City Wall Stks Ches 5f	2nd King George Good 5f	2nd Flying Five Curr 5f	5th Starlit Stks Good 6f
05 Good 7f 5th Conds Stks *Two weeks*	**Fire Up The Band** D Nicholls 14/1	10/20	6	9-09	75	10th Wokingham York 6f	4th Listed Curr 5f	3rd City Wall Stks Ches 5f	**WON 10/1 King George Good 5f**
04 Beve 5f 2nd Conds Stks *Two months*	**Caribbean Coral** J Quinn 20/1	8/20	5	9-05	64	**WON 5/1F Gosforth Cup Newc 5f**	13th Stewards' Cup Good 6f	11th Sprint Stks Beve 5f	3rd Scarbrough Stks Donc 5f
03 Beve 5f 6th Class Stks *One week*	**Atlantic Viking** D Nicholls 9/1	10/11	8	8-07	63	25th Wokingham Ascot 6f	5th Gosforth Cup Newc 5f	14th Hong Kong Hcp Ascot 5f	6th Showcase Hcp Epsom 5f
02 Muss 5f 8th Scottish Sprint *One week*	**Rudi's Pet** D Nicholls 16/1	1/11	8	8-07	68	3rd Handicap York 5f	10th Gosforth Cup Newc 5f	2nd King George Good 5f	9th Nunthorpe York 5f
01 York 5f 14th Handicap *One month*	**Bishops Court** Mrs J Ramsden 9/2JF	12/17	7	9-04	76	7th Listed Curr 5f	4th King George Good 5f	3rd Nunthorpe York 5f	11th World Trophy Newb 5f
00 Colo 5f 1st Listed *One month*	**Astonished** J Hammond 11/4F	3/12	4	9-02	75	4th Porelanosa Sand 5f	**WON 6/4 Listed Deau 5f**	7th Scarbrough Stks Donc 5f	2nd Rous Stks Newm 5f
99 Kemp 5f 3rd Achilles Stks *Three weeks*	**To The Roof** P Harris 5/1	11/11	7	9-01	74	6th Porcelanosa Sand 5f	2nd City Wall Stks Ches 5f	10th King George Good 5f	7th Scarbrough Stks Donc 5f
98 Kemp 5f 4th Achilles Stks *One week*	**Bishops Court** Mrs J Ramsden 9/2F	10/15	4	9-02	72	7th King's Stand Ascot 5f	2nd Pocelanosa Sand 5f	2nd City Wall Stks Ches 5f	5th King George Good 5f
97 Sand 5f 5th Temple Stks *Two weeks*	**Ya Malak** D Nicholls 13/2	10/12	6	9-02	74	10th King's Stand Ascot 5f	**WON 11/2 Sprint Stks Sand 5f**	4th City Wall Stks Ches 5f	11th King George Good 5f
96 Thir 6f 1st Handicap *Three weeks*	**To The Roof** P Harris 6/1CF	14/12	4	8-03	61	6th Wokingham Ascot 5f	9th Sprint Stks Sand 5f	10th Stewards' Cup Good 6f	12th Rated Hcp Ascot 5f

12-year median performance rating of the winner:　　　　**70** (out of 100)

WINNER'S PROFILE Eleven winners **raced within the past month** and all of them filled a **top-three position at some point during the spring**. Six of the last seven winners had their **final outing at a northern venue** and non-southern trainers have a tidy record, with David Nicholls landing it four times.
Winning form over the minimum trip is vital, while those **aged from four to eight** have the best record – three-year-olds are 0 from 26. The draw is important, more so in maximum fields, with those **drawn middle to high** near the stands' rail at an advantage. There have also been two dual winners and those with course and distance form are respected.

FUTURE POINTERS The record of winners next time out has been poor, as only Caribbean Coral followed up, though some recent winners did score in Group class later that year – Desert Lord in the 2006 Abbaye and Fire Up The Band in the 2005 King George. Those that attempted six furlongs were all unplaced, including Hogmaneigh last year, while five winners headed to the Champagne Stakes at Sandown (previously the Porcelanosa and Sandown Park Sprint) between 1996 and 2000, but only Ya Malak triumphed. Five failed in Chester's City Wall Stakes.

Were Dash winners profitable to follow on their subsequent three runs?
No – 3 wins from 36 runs returned a loss of -£21.00 to a £1 level stake.

Placed runners' subsequent record (three runs):
Runners-up: 7 wins from 34 runs returned a **profit of +£9.19** to a £1 level stake.
1998 Repertory – Listed Handicap (Curragh), 1996 Lucky Parkes – City Wall Stakes

Thirds: 3 wins from 35 runs returned a loss of -£4.50 to a £1 level stake.
2005 Corridor Creeper – Hong Kong Handicap

Fourths: 1 win from 15 runs returned even to a £1 level stake.
2001 Repertory – Listed Handicap (Curragh)

FUTURE SUCCESS RATING: ★★ ☆ ☆ ☆

DERBY STAKES
June 7, Epsom – (Group 1, Class 1, 3yo) 1m4f

Last run	Winner/ Trainer & SP	Draw/ Ran	Age	Wght	PR	Next four runs			
07 York 1m2f 1st Dante Stks *Three weeks*	**Authorized** P Chapple-Hyam 5/4F	14/17	3	9-00	88	2nd Eclipse Sand 1m2f	**WON 6/4F** **Juddmonte Int** **York 1m2f**	10th Arc de Triomphe Long 1m4f	-
06 Newm 1m 2nd 2,000 Guineas *One month*	**Sir Percy** M Tregoning 6/1	10/18	3	9-00	81	7th Champion Stks Newm 1m2f	*4th Sheema Classic Nad Al 1m4f	*6th Coronation Cup Epsom 1m4f	*6th Prince of Wales' Ascot 1m2f
05 York 1m2f 1st Dante Stks *One month*	**Motivator** M Bell 3/1F	5/13	3	9-00	87	2nd Eclipse Sand 1m2f	2nd Irish Champion Leop 1m2f	5th Arc de Triomphe Long 1m4f	-
04 York 1m2f 1st Dante Stks *One month*	**North Light** Sir M Stoute 7/2JF	6/14	3	9-00	83	2nd Irish Derby Curr 1m4f	5th Arc de Triomphe Long 1m4f	*2nd Brigarier Gerard Sand 1m2f	-
03 Ches 1m2f 1st Dee Stks *One month*	**Kris Kin** Sir M Stoute 6/1	4/20	3	9-00	82	3rd King George VI Ascot 1m4f	3rd Prix Niel Long 1m4f	11th Arc de Triomphe Long 1m4f	-
02 Leop 1m2f 1st Derrinstown Trial *One month*	**High Chaparral** A O'Brien 7/2	9/12	3	9-00	91	**WON 1/3F** **Irish Derby** **Curr 1m4f**	3rd Arc de Triomphe Long 1m4f	**WON 9/10F** **Breeders' Cup** **Arli 1m4f**	**WON 3/10F** **Royal Whip** **Curr 1m2f**
01 Leop 1m2f 1st Derrinstown Trial *One month*	**Galileo** A O'Brien 11/4JF	10/12	3	9-00	88	**WON 4/11F** **Irish Derby** **Curr 1m4f**	**WON 1/2F** **King George VI** **Ascot 1m4f**	2nd Irish Champion Leop 1m2f	6th Breeders' Cup Belm 1m2f
00 Leop 1m2f 1st Derrinstown Trial *One month*	**Sinndar** J Oxx 7/1	15/15	3	9-00	90	**WON 11/10F** **Irish Derby** **Curr 1m4f**	**WON 3/10JF** **Prix Niel** **Long 1m4f**	**WON 6/4** Arc de Triomphe Long 1m4f	-
99 Ches 1m2f 1st Dee Stks *One month*	**Oath** H Cecil 13/2	1/16	3	9-00	85	7th King George VI Ascot 1m4f	-	-	-
98 Ling 1m3f 1st Derby Trial *One month*	**High-Rise** L Cumani 20/1	14/15	3	9-00	82	2nd King George VI Ascot 1m4f	7th Arc de Triomphe Long 1m4f	*8th Dubai World Cup Nad Al 1m2f	*2nd Arc Trial Newb 1m3f
97 York 1m2f 1st Dante Stks *One month*	**Benny The Dip** J Gosden 11/1	8/13	3	9-00	79	2nd Eclipse Sand 1m2f	3rd Juddmonte Int York 1m2f	6th Champion Stks Newm 1m2f	-
96 Donc 1m 1st Maiden *Seven months*	**Shaamit** W Haggas 12/1	9/20	3	9-00	80	3rd King George VI Ascot 1m4f	4th Irish Champion Leop 1m2f	7th Arc de Triomphe Long 1m4f	-

12-year median performance rating of the winner: **85** (out of 100) *next year

WINNER'S PROFILE It helps not to complicate matters and stick with the obvious in the Derby, as last time out winners that emerged from the **Dante, Derrinstown Derby Trial, and Dee Stakes** have a superb record – provided nine winners – while the 2,000 Guineas and Lingfield Derby Trial have supplied a further two.

Fancied runners also hold sway, as 11 winners came from the **first six in the betting** – 10 were in the first four of the market – while every winner got off the mark as a two-year-old.

FUTURE POINTERS The Derby has received a lot of criticism in recent years, as the last five winners all failed to kick on post-Epsom up until last year when Authorized stopped the rot and took the Juddmonte International two runs later. Prior to 2003, three Irish-trained winners went on to take the Irish equivalent before further glory later in the year, including prestige events such as the Breeders' Cup, King George VI, and Arc de Triomphe. Before that sequence, it was again a gloomy period for the Classic, as the 1999-1996 victors flopped subsequently, and only High-Rise took a lone Listed event two years later.

In a nutshell, it may prove wise to wait for a quality Irish-trained Derby winner, before deciding to support it in the near future, in the meantime another option may be to lay the winner next time out or follow the placed runners.

Were Derby winners profitable to follow on their subsequent three runs?
No – 8 wins from 34 runs returned a loss of -£19.51 to a £1 level stake.

Placed runners' subsequent record (three runs):
Runners-up: 9 wins from 34 runs returned a loss of -£10.71 to a £1 level stake.
2004 Rule Of Law – St Leger, 2002 Hawk Wing – Eclipse, 2001 Golan – Prix Niel,
2000 Sakhee – Juddmonte International, 1997 Silver Patriarch – St Leger, 1996 Dushyantor – Great Voltigeur

Thirds: 11 wins from 34 runs returned a **profit of +£4.48** to a £1 level stake.
2006 Dylan Thomas – Irish Derby, Irish Champion Stakes, 2005 Dubawi – Jacques le Marois,
2003 Alamshar – Irish Derby, King George VI, 2002 Moon Ballad – Select Stakes (later won Dubai World Cup),
2000 Beat Hollow – Grand Prix de Paris (later won Arlington Million)

FUTURE SUCCESS RATING: ★ ★ ★ ☆ ☆

SCOTTISH SPRINT CUP

June 7, Musselburgh – (Heritage Handicap, Class 2, 3yo+) 5f

Last run	Winner/ Trainer & SP	Draw/ Ran	Age	Wght	PR	Next four runs			
07 Thir 5f 8th Handicap _Three weeks_	**Aegean Dancer** B Smart 10/1	8/17	5	8-01	70	10th Coral Hcp Hayd 5f	2nd Handicap Ripo 6f	4th Handicap Leic 5f	2nd Handicap Donc 5f
06 Beve 5f 4th Handicap _One month_	**Handsome Cross** D Nicholls 20/1	12/16	5	7-12	53	2nd Handicap Ches 5f	4th Handicap Ches 5f	2nd Handicap Newm 6f	6th Heritage Hcp Ayr 5f
05 Donc 6f 8th Handicap _One month_	**Bond Boy** B Smart 25/1	3/17	8	8-04	56	3rd Handicap Redc 6f	4th Handicap Beve 5f	6th Gosforth Cup Newc 5f	6th Handicap Hayd 6f
04 Hayd 5f 1st Handicap _One week_	**Raccoon** D Barron 11/4F	1/17	4	8-12	60	16th Dash Hcp Epsom 5f	8th Stewards' Cup Good 6f	7th Handicap Hayd 5f	19th Portland Hcp Donc 5.5f
03 York 5f 1st Tote Hcp _Three weeks_	**Matty Tun** J Balding 9/2F	1/17	4	8-12	65	12th Showcase Hcp Redc 6f	17th Wentworth Stks Donc 6f	*9th Class Stks Beve 5f	*5th Palace House Newm 5f
02 Hayd 5f 1st Handicap _One week_	**Bali Royal** M Bradley 10/1	12/17	4	9-11	69	7th Handicap York 5f	7th Gosforth Cup Newc 5f	3rd Conds Stks Bath 6f	10th Hong Kong Hcp Ascot 5f
01 Thir 5f 3rd Handicap _Two weeks_	**Boanerges** R Guest 7/1	2/17	4	8-10	55	12th Handicap Epsom 6f	5th Handicap Ripon 5f	14th Gosforth Cup Newc 5f	8th Handicap Ascot 5f
00 Thir 6f 13th Handicap _Two weeks_	**Xanadu** Miss L Perratt 14/1	9/14	4	7-11	46	10th Showcase Hcp Hayd 6f	**WON 7/1 Handicap Hayd 5f**	2nd Showcase Hcp Ayr 5f	4th Handicap Pont 5f

8-year median performance rating of the winner: **56** (out of 100)   *next year*

WINNER'S PROFILE This increasingly popular handicap has been included in the book despite still being in its infancy with only eight renewals, as it has been one of the main attractions on a low-key Saturday and was beamed live to punters by Channel 4. However, with it due to fall on Derby Day in 2008, it may now slip under the radar! Battle-hardened sorts that arrived here from a **recent run in a northern sprint handicap** are respected, three emerged from Thirsk and two from Haydock. Age-wise, **four and five-year-olds** accounted for seven winners, while only one winner shouldered more than 9st and those in the **bottom-half of the weights** deserve respect.
The draw has had an effect on the outcome, especially in maximum fields of 17, as no winner was drawn higher than 12 and it can be a real advantage to be berthed in a **low stall** not too far away from the stand's rail, like last year's scorer, Aegean Dancer, who also gave his trainer, **Bryan Smart**, his second victory in three years.

FUTURE POINTERS This competitive handicap must have taken a lot out of some of these sprinters and influenced the winner's immediate future as none followed up – the three winners between 2002 and 2004 arrived on a roll but subsequently flopped miserably. The inaugural winner of this event in 2000, Xanadu, was sensibly given a month to rest, which may have helped him recover in time to land a handicap in July.
The three winners that went for the Gosforth Park Cup at Newcastle in late-June all failed

Were Scottish Sprint winners profitable to follow on their subsequent three runs?
No – 1 win from 24 runs returned a loss of -£16.00 to a £1 level stake.

Placed runners' subsequent record (three runs):
Runners-up: 3 wins from 27 runs (dead-heat in 2003) returned a loss of -£2.75 to a £1 level stake.

Thirds: 0 win from 21 runs returning a loss of -£18.00 to a £1 level stake.

Fourths: 4 wins from 21 runs returned a **profit of +£12.25** to a £1 level stake.

A total of seven wins from around 70 subsequent efforts isn't great, although the fourth-placed runners have been worth watching, especially those that performed well from a disadvantageous high draw.
In 2004, Connect did well to be in the frame from stall 13 before gaining compensation a few runs later, while in 2003, Absent Friends did likewise from stall 11, and then won a month later at 16/1, as did Salviati from stall 17 in 2002, scoring next time at 11/4.

FUTURE SUCCESS RATING: ★ ★ ★ ★

JOHN OF GAUNT STAKES
June 12, Haydock – (Group 3, Class 1, 4yo+) 7f

Last run	Winner/ Trainer & SP	Draw/ Ran	Age	Wght	PR	Next four runs			
07 York 1m 9th Hambleton Hcp *One month*	**Mine** J Bethell 16/1	3/10	9	9-00	69	6th Criterion Stks Newm 7f	12th Bunbury Cup Newm 7f	8th Mile Handicap Good 1m	4th City of York York 7f
06 York 6f 2nd Duke of York *One month*	**Quito** D Chapman 9/2	5/7	9	8-12	73	17th Golden Jubilee Ascot 6f	6th July Cup Newm 6f	10th Lennox Stks Good 7f	**WON 4/1 City of York York 7f**
05 Newm 1m 2nd Ben Marshall *Eight months*	**Sleeping Indian** J Gosden 9/2	6/8	4	9-03	75	5th Sussex Good 1m	**WON 9/4JF Hungerford Newb 7f**	2nd Park Stks Donc 7f	5th Queen Eliz II Newm 1m
04 Good 7f 2nd Conds Stks *Three weeks*	**Suggestive** W Haggas 9/2	5/11	6	8-12	65	4th Group 3 Long 7f	10th Silver Trophy Ascot 1m	2nd Lennox Stks Good 7f	2nd Hungerford Newb 7f
03 York 1m 2nd Hambleton Hcp *One month*	**With Reason** D Loder 10/3	3/7	5	8-12	72	6th International Hcp Ascot 7f	**WON 13/2 Hungerford Newb 7f**	2nd Park Stks Donc 7f	**WON 9/2 Supreme Stks Good 7f**
02 Newb 1m 9th Lockinge *Three weeks*	**Warningford** J Fanshawe 10/3	7/7	8	9-05	74	12th Challenge Stks Newm 7f	8th Wentworth Donc 6f	-	-
01 Newm 7f 3rd Leicestershire *Two months*	**Mount Abu** J Gosden 5/2F	4/10	4	9-05	71	6th July Cup Newm 6f	4th Maurice 'Gheest Deau 7f	2nd Sprint Cup Hayd 6f	6th Diadem Ascot 6f
00 Capa 7f 4th Listed *Two weeks*	**Pulau Tioman** M Jarvis 4/1	5/10	4	8-12	63	2nd Silver Trophy Ascot 1m	18th W Hill Hcp Good 1m	3rd Conds Stks Bath 1m	3rd Conds Stks Newb 1m1f
99 York 6f 2nd Duke of York *One month*	**Warningford** J Fanshawe 3/1	2/6	5	9-05	73	2nd Group 3 Long 7f	2nd Dubai Duty Free Newb 7f	9th Diadem Ascot 6f	6th Challenge Stks Newm 7f
98 York 1m 9th Hambleton Hcp *One month*	**Nigrasine** L Eyre 5/1	2/7	4	8-12	68	4th Rated Hcp York 6f	9th Criterion Newm 7f	4th Stewards' Cup Good 6f	5th Great St Wilfrid Ripon 6f
97 Newb 1m 6th Lockinge *Three weeks*	**Decorated Hero** J Gosden 11/8F	4/4	5	9-03	76	**WON 2/1F Conds Stks Newb 7f**	6th Beeswing Stks Newc 7f	**WON 11/4 Hungerford Newb 7f**	2nd Railway Park Donc 1m
96 Ling 6f 3rd Listed *One week*	**Inzar** P Cole 7/2	8/9	4	9-05	64	2nd Criterion Newm 7f	8th Hackwood Stks Newb 6f	6th Beeswing Stks Newc 7f	6th Prix de la Foret Long 7f

12-year median performance rating of the winner: **70** (out of 100)

WINNER'S PROFILE Eleven winners lined up with a **recent run**, five via York in either the Hambleton or Duke of York, while two arrived having finished down the field in the Lockinge at Newbury.
The betting market has been a solid guide, bar last year's winner – the first to score from a double-figure price – as the remainder were all **5/1 or shorter** which knocked out several each year.
Cream came to the top with the majority all **officially rated at least 107**, including all three of **John Gosden's** winners.

FUTURE POINTERS Only Decorated Hero followed up next time out before going on to score in the Group Three Hungerford Stakes at Newbury, a race that was very kind to John of Gaunt winners as both Sleeping Indian and With Reason also triumphed in 2005 and 2003, respectively. Those that attempted Group company next time out came unstuck – Decorated Hero won a minor event – while those that tried Pattern glory over in France also failed. The placed runners have been profitable to follow and several stepped up to win in Group company *(see below)*.

Were John of Gaunt winners profitable to follow on their subsequent three runs?
No – 4 wins from 35 runs returned a loss of -£17.50 to a £1 level stake.

Placed runners' subsequent record (three runs):
Runners-up: 8 wins from 32 runs returned a **profit of +£30.50** to a £1 level stake.
2006 New Seeker – Listed Guisborough Stakes, 2001 Fath – Group Three Lennox Stakes, 2000 Hot Tin Roof – Listed Summer Stakes, 1999 Tumbleweed Ridge – Group Three Ballycorus Stakes, 1998 Jo Mell – International Handicap

Thirds: 3 wins from 16 runs returned a **profit of +£2.75** to a £1 level stake.
2007 Soldier's Tale – Golden Jubilee Stakes, 2001 Late Night Out – Listed event (Goodwood), 1996 Carranita – Listed Summer Stakes

FUTURE SUCCESS RATING: ★ ★ ★ ★ ★

BALLYMACOLL STUD STAKES
June 12, Newbury – (Listed, Class 1, 3yo Fillies) 1m2f

Last run	Winner/ Trainer & SP	Draw/ Ran	Age	Wght	PR	Next four runs			
07 Eps 1m4f 10th Oaks _Two weeks_	**Darrfonah** C Brittain 11/1	2/8	3	8-12	55	6th Yorkshire Oaks York 1m4f	6th Blandford Stks Curr 1m2f	8th Sun Chariot Stks Newm 1m	-
06 Nott 1m 1st Maiden _Two months_	**Princess Nada** L Cumani 11/2	3/9	3	8-09	62	3rd Lancashire Oaks Hayd 1m4f	2nd Upavon Stks Salis 1m2f	6th Severals Stks Newm 1m2f	6th Gillies Stks Wind 1m2f
05 Newb 1m2f 4th Maiden _Two months_	**Ruby Wine** J Eustace 20/1	5/8	3	8-09	56	4th Lancashire Oaks Hayd 1m4f	5th Chalice Stks Newb 1m4f	*3rd Virginia Hcp Yarm 1m2f	6th Virginia Stks Yarm 1m2f
04 Good 1m 3rd Conqueror Stks _Three weeks_	**Incheni** G Wragg 9/2	7/6	3	8-09	61	4th Daffodil Stks Chep 1m2f	6th Upavon Stks Salis 1m2f	-	-
03 Ascot 1m 6th Meon Fillies Mile _Nine months_	**Approach** Sir M Prescott 5/6F	7/9	3	8-09	60	4th Prix de Malleret Sain 1m4f	7th Gladness Stks Good 1m6f	2nd Grade 2 Keen 1m2f	11th Grade 2 Aque 1m4f
02 Sali 1m2f 1st Maiden _One month_	**Succinct** H Cecil 9/4F	5/7	3	8-09	60	15th Ribblesdale Ascot 1m4f	-	-	-
01 Newb 1m2f 2nd Listed _One month_	**Nafisah** B Hanbury 9/4F	2/6	3	8-09	59	2nd Ribblesdale Ascot 1m4f	2nd Chalice Stks Newb 1m4f	6th Yorkshire Oaks York 1m4f	5th Harvest Stks Ascot 1m4f
00 Ayr 1m 3rd Class Stks _Two weeks_	**Littlepacepaddocks** M Johnston 6/1	1/9	3	8-09	58	4th Irish Oaks Curr 1m4f	2nd Shergar Cup Ascot 1m4f	8th St Leger Donc 1m6f	2nd Princess Royal Newm 1m4f
99 Newb 1m2f 1st Maiden _One month_	**Fairy Godmother** R Charlton 10/11F	1/6	3	8-09	57	*2nd Earl of Sefton Newm 1m1f	*5th Dahlia Stks Newm 1m1f	-	-
98 Good 1m2f 2nd Lupe Stks _One month_	**Putuna** I Balding 13/8F	2/4	3	8-09	56	7th Ribblesdale Ascot 1m4f	5th Daffodil Stks Chep 1m2f	3rd Upavon Stks Salis 1m2f	12th Virginia Hcp Newc 1m2f
97 Redc 7f 1st Conds Stks _Eight months_	**Squeak** J Gosden 13/2	3/10	3	8-09	60	WON 9/2 Lanc'shire Oaks Hayd 1m4f	6th Yorkshire Oaks York 1m4f	2nd Group 2 Long 1m1f	4th Grade 1 Sant 1m2f
96 Sali 1m2f 1st Maiden _One month_	**Sardonic** H Cecil 5/2F	10/10	3	8-09	54	6th Falmouth Newm 1m	6th Nassau Good 1m2f	7th Upavon Stks Sali 1m2f	8th Listed Yarm 1m2f

12-year median performance rating of the winner: **58** (out of 100)   *next year*

WINNER'S PROFILE A host of different tracks supplied the winner of this event, although 10 winners arrived with **a recent run**, including four that **won a maiden last time out** – two at Salisbury.
The profiles of winners prior to Newbury were also mixed, as **six debuted over this trip here**, while three had already won over 10 furlongs, and six of the last eight won from over seven furlongs to a mile.
The last two winners were rated as low as 96 and 83, where as two winners scaled as high as 105. **Newmarket trainers fared well** with **Henry Cecil** having sent out two to victory.

FUTURE POINTERS Certainly not one of the highlights on the Listed calendar, and winners struggled to push on after landing this race. It was also, at times, poorly contested with handicappers throwing their hat into the ring in an attempt to gain 'black type' and boost their paddock value. In fact, it was one of the below par winners, Squeak in 1997, who managed to win the Lancashire Oaks next time out – a race foiled two of the last three winners – before going on to lift two Grade Ones in America later in her career.
Nafisah was one of the best winners in 2001, and she nearly took the Ribblesdale at Royal Ascot, which stumped the 2002 and 1998 victors, while the Upavon Stakes at Salisbury caught out a further three winners later in the year.

Were Ballymacoll Stud winners profitable to follow on their subsequent three runs?
No – 1 win from 32 runs returned a loss of -£26.50 to a £1 level stake.

Placed runners' subsequent record (three runs):
Runners-up: 0 win from 25 runs returned a loss of -£25.00 to a £1 level stake.

Thirds: 2 wins from 18 runs returned a **profit of +£6.40** to a £1 level stake.
2006 High Heel Sneakers – Listed Eden Fillies' Stakes

FUTURE SUCCESS RATING: ★ ★ ★ ★ ★

WILLIAM HILL TROPHY
June 14, York – (Heritage Handicap, Class 2, 3yo) 6f

Last run	Winner/ Trainer & SP	Draw/ Ran	Age	Wght	PR	Next four runs			
06 Wind 5f 1st Handicap One week	Prince Tamino H Morrison 9/1	16/18	3	8-13	70	3rd Tote Hcp Newm 6f	2nd Rous Stks Newm 5f	*12th Dubai Trophy Nad Al 6f	*4th Challenge Hcp Nad Al 7f
05 Newm 6f 1st Totesport Hcp Two months	Tax Free D Nicholls 9/4F	11/20	3	8-09	72	*3rd Palace House Newm 5f	*3rd Group 2 Chan 5f	*15th King's Stand Ascot 5f	*5th Stewards' Cup Good 6f
04 Thir 5f 4th Handicap One month	Two Step Kid J Noseda 14/1	3/20	3	8-09	68	3rd Tote Hcp Newm 6f	4th Heritage Hcp York 6f	4th Stewards' Cup Good 6f	4th Totepool Hcp Good 6f
03 Newm 6f 1st Coral Sprint Hcp Two weeks	Dazzling Bay T Easterby 4/1F	15/19	3	8-02	69	WON 1/4F Handicap Ripon 6f	9th Tote Hcp Newm 6f	2nd Rated Hcp Newm 6f	13th Ayr Gold Cup Ayr 6f
02 Newc 6f 3rd Handicap Two weeks	Artie T Easterby 25/1	1/20	3	7-10	60	15th Tote Hcp Newm 6f	3rd Great St Wilfrid Ripon 6f	11th Portland Hcp Donc 5½f	15th Ayr Gold Cup Ayr 6f
01 Newm 6f 3rd Coral Sprint Hcp Two weeks	Orientor J Goldie 10/1	23/20	3	9-02	64	12th Cork & Orrery Ascot 6f	24th International Hcp Ascot 7f	WON 14/1 Shergar Cup Ascot 6f	5th City of York York 7f
00 Hayd 6f 5th Cecil Frail Stks One week	Cotton House M Channon 25/1	8/23	3	8-13	63	5th Porcelanosa Sand 5f	6th Summer Stks York 6f	*7th Cammidge Trophy Donc 6f	*2nd Listed Long 5f
99 Newc 6f 2nd Handicap Two weeks	Pepperdine D Nicholls 10/1	17/23	3	8-03	68	18th Stewards' Cup Good 6f	10th Ayr Gold Cup Ayr 6f	2nd Coral Trophy York 6f	*3rd Ladbrokes Hcp Newm 6f
98 Thir 5f 13th Handicap One month	Friar Tuck Miss L Perratt 33/1	15/22	3	8-11	63	9th Ayr Gold Cup Ayr 6f	3rd Conds Stks Hamil 6f	9th Rated Hcp Newb 6f	*13th Rated Hcp York 6f
97 Epsom 7f 5th Handicap Two weeks	Return Of Amin J Bethell 11/1	7/19	3	7-07	60	2nd Trophy Hcp Newc 6f	6th Rated Hcp Newm 6f	2nd Rated Hcp York 6f	21st Silver Cup Ayr 6f
96 Newc 6f 2nd Handicap One month	Mallia D Barron 14/1	17/18	3	7-10	66	10th Trophy Hcp Newc 6f	*14th Ladbrokes Hcp Newm 6f	*10th Handicap Thir 6f	*14th Handicap Pont 6f

12-year median performance rating of the winner: **66** (out of 100)   *next year*

WINNER'S PROFILE Those that **arrived bang in-form** are respected, even more so if they came via Newcastle or Newmarket as both venues provided five of the last eight winners – the Coral Sprint at HQ has been a good pointer (Bold Effort was also runner-up there before succeeding here in 1995).
It helped to side with those on the **lighter side of 9st**, while 10 of the last 11 winners were **officially rated 95 or below**. Both **Tim Easterby** and **David Nicholls**' runners should be noted.

FUTURE POINTERS It was a shame last year's renewal was abandoned as the William Hill Trophy has be an informative long-term guide, despite the fact winners struggled for the remainder of their three-year-old season. This may be because they were forced into a higher grade as their handicap mark exploded and found themselves in at the deep end against their elders in races like the Stewards' Cup and Ayr Gold Cup.
Plenty of talented individuals have appeared in the Hall of Fame, but it been a while since a superstar emerged, such as Sheikh Albadou in 1991, who later won the Nunthorpe before Breeders' Cup glory. It may not be a coincidence that both he and Orientor in 2001, were the only winners that defied an official rating of 100 or more – the latter also scored later that season in a valuable event at Ascot before securing two Group Threes later in his career.

Were William Hill Trophy winners profitable to follow on their subsequent three runs?
No – 2 wins from 33 runs returned a loss of -£16.75 to a £1 level stake.

Placed runners' subsequent record (three runs):
Runners-up: 6 wins from 33 runs returned a loss of -£8.30 to a £1 level stake.

Thirds: 4 wins from 33 runs returned a loss of -£1.00 to a £1 level stake.
2005 Salamanca – Newmarket Listed Handicap

Fourths: 4 wins from 33 runs returned a **profit of +£3.50** to a £1 level stake.
2004 Alderney Race – Newmarket sprint handicap (July Meeting), 2002 Just James – Jersey Stakes

FUTURE SUCCESS RATING: ★ ★ ☆ ☆ ☆

COVENTRY STAKES
June 17, Royal Ascot (Group 2, Class 1, 2yo) 6f

Last run	Winner/ Trainer & SP	Draw/ Ran	Age	Wght	PR	Next four runs			
07 Gowr 7f 1st Maiden Two months	Henrythenavigator A O'Brien 11/4F	17/20	2	9-01	69	2nd Phoenix Stks Curr 6f	3rd Futurity Stks Curr 7f	-	-
06 Pont 6f 1st Conds Stks One month	Hellvelyn B Smart 4/1JF	6/21	2	9-01	66	2nd Phoenix Stks Curr 6f	4th Middle Park Stks Newm 6f	*8th July Cup Newm 6f	*WON 4/1 Bullet Sprint Stk Beve 5f
05 Newm 6f 1st Novice Stks Three weeks	Red Clubs B Hills 11/2	2/14	2	8-12	70	7th July Stks Newm 6f	3rd Phoenix Stks Curr 6f	2nd Gimcrack Stks York 6f	2nd Middle Park Stks Newm 6f
04 Newb 6f 1st Maiden One month	Iceman J Gosden 5/1JF	11/13	2	8-12	67	2nd Champagne Stk Donc 7f	3rd Middle Park Stks Newm 6f	4th Dewhurst Stks Newm 7f	*4th Craven Stks Newm 1m
03 Nott 6f 1st Novice Stks One month	Three Valleys R Charlton 7/1	7/13	2	8-12	75	3rd Phoenix Stks Curr 6f	Disq (1st) Middle Park Stks Newm 6f	2nd Dewhurst Stks Newm 7f	*2nd Craven Stks Newm 1m
02 Cork 5f 1st Maiden Three months	Statue Of Liberty A O'Brien 5/2F	8/16	2	8-12	67	*8th St James' Palace Ascot 1m	*2nd Sussex Good 1m	*9th Prix du Moulin Long 1m	*7th Group 2 Long 1m
01 Gowr 7f 1st Maiden Two months	Landseer A O'Brien 20/1	17/20	2	8-12	71	2nd Tatts Sales Newm 7f	2nd Dewhurst Stks Newm 7f	2nd Criterium Int Sain 1m	*3rd Group 3 Long 1m
00 Good 6f 1st Maiden One month	Cd Europe M Channon 8/1	5/12	2	8-12	63	2nd Champagne Stk Donc 7f	4th Grand Criterium Long 1m	8th R Post Trophy Donc 1m	*4th Craven Stks Newm 1m
99 Curr 5f 1st Marble Listed One month	Fasliyev A O'Brien 15/8F	17/18	2	8-12	76	WON 2/7F Phoenix Stks Curr 6f	WON 6/5CF Prix Morny Deau 6f	-	-
98 York 6f 1st Conds Stks Two months	Red Sea P Cole 6/1	19/17	2	8-12	68	7th Prix Morny Deau 6f	2nd Grand Criterium Long 1m	12th Breeders' Cup Chur 1m1f	*12th 2,000 Guineas Newm 1m
97 Curr 5f 7th Marble Listed One month	Harbour Master A O'Brien 16/1	3/15	2	8-12	66	3rd Phoenix Stks Curr 6f	5th Prix Salamandre Long 7f	-	-
96 Leop 6f 1st Maiden Two months	Verglas K Prendergast 9/1	3/15	2	8-12	70	6th Phoenix Stks Curr 6f	*4th National Stks Curr 7f	*2nd Group 3 Curr 7f	*2nd Irish 2,000 Guin Curr 1m

12-year median performance rating of the winner: **69** (out of 100) *(2005 York), *next year*

WINNER'S PROFILE Trends are thin on the ground in the opener at Royal Ascot, but one standout statistic was that 11 winners all **won last time out**, with an array of venues trodden beforehand, **Aidan O'Brien** last year used a seven-furlong maiden at Gowran Park for Henrythenavigator as he did for Landseer, while two others took in the Marble Listed Stakes at the Curragh (named the Isobel Morris Stakes since 2006).
The Irish trainer's full record in the race stands at five winners from 15 runners, two of whom were the biggest outsiders in recent years, but it usually pays to stick with the **first four or five in the betting**.

FUTURE POINTERS The first Group event of the season for juveniles but one in which winners have a miserable immediate future, Henrythenavigator the latest next time out flop at odds-on last year, and only Fasliyev had any sort of two-year-old career post-Coventry in 1999 (Three Valleys was disqualified after winning the Middle Park Stakes in 2003). However, things have improved for winners long-term since 2001, as the likes of Landseer won the French 2,000 Guineas, Three Valleys found Grade Two and Three glory in the States, and Red Clubs belatedly triumphed in the Haydock Sprint Cup last year.

Were Coventry winners profitable to follow on their subsequent three runs?
No – 2 wins from 33 runs returned a loss of -£29.52 to a £1 level stake.

Placed runners' subsequent record (three runs):
Runners-up: 7 wins from 35 runs returned a loss of -£10.69 to a £1 level stake.
2006 Major Cadeaux – Greenham, 2001 Firebreak – Mill Reef Stakes,
1997 Desert Prince – European Free Handicap, 1996 Daylight In Dubai – Railway Stakes

Thirds: 10 wins from 35 runs returned a **profit of +£12.83** to a £1 level stake.
2007 Luck Money – Goffs Million, 2005 Amadeus Wolf – Gimcrack, Middle Park Stakes,
1997 Bold Fact – July Stakes, King Charles II Stakes

FUTURE SUCCESS RATING: ★★ ☆ ☆ ☆

KING'S STAND STAKES
June 17, Royal Ascot – (Group 1, Class 1, 3yo+) 5f

Last run	Winner/Trainer & SP	Draw/Ran	Age	Wght	PR	Next four runs			
07 Caul 6f 1st Group 1 *Four months*	**Miss Andretti** L Freedman 3/1F	19/20	6	9-01	87	15th Golden Jubilee Ascot 6f	**WON 8/11F** **Group 2** Moon 6f	**WON 3/5F** **Group 1** Flem 6f	-
06 Flem 6f 1st Group 1 *Four months*	**Takeover Target** J Janiak 7/1	17/28	7	9-07	85	3rd Golden Jubilee Ascot 6f	7th July Cup Newm 6f	2nd Grade 2 Chuk 6f	**WON 32/10F** **Group 1** Naka 6f
05 Long 5f 1st Group 3 *One month*	**Chineur** M Belzangles 7/1	8/16	4	9-02	79	9th Nunthorpe York 5f	4th Prix de l'Abbaye Long 5f	5th Group 3 Mais 6f	8th H Kong Sprint Sha 5f
04 Chan 5f 4th Group 2 *Two weeks*	**The Tatling** M Bradley 8/1	5/19	7	9-02	77	9th Champagne Stk Sand 5f	3rd King George Good 5f	2nd Nunthorpe York 5f	2nd Group 3 Long 5f
03 Flem 6f 6th Group 1 *Four months*	**Choisir** P Perry 25/1	8/20	4	9-07	89	**WON 13/2** **Golden Jubilee** Ascot 6f	2nd July Cup Newm 6f	-	-
02 Ascot 5f 1st Cornwallis Stks *Eight months*	**Dominica** M Tregoning 16/1	6/15	3	8-07	75	5th Nunthorpe York 5f	*4th King's Stand Ascot 5f	*4th Nunthorpe York 5f	*2nd Listed Hami 5f
01 Sand 5f 1st Temple Stks *One month*	**Cassandra Go** G Wragg 8/1	5/22	5	8-13	80	2nd July Cup Newm 6f	-	-	-
00 Chan 5f 1st Group 2 *Three weeks*	**Nuclear Debate** J Hammond 16/1	22/23	5	9-02	83	**WON 5/2F** **Nunthorpe** **York 5f**	9th H Kong Sprint Sha 5f	*2nd Stakes Nad Al 6f	*4th Group 3 Nad Al 6f
99 Epsom 5f 5th Dash Hcp *Two weeks*	**Mitcham** T Mills 20/1	3/17	3	8-10	77	13th July Cup Newm 6f	4th World Trophy Newb 5f	9th Prix de l'Abbaye Long 5f	*20th Palace House Newm 6f
98 Sand 5f 1st Temple Stks *One month*	**Bolshoi** J Berry 10/1	20/19	6	9-02	75	7th July Cup Newm 6f	4th Queensferry Stk Ches 6f	6th Nunthorpe York 5f	2nd Sprint Cup Hayd 6f
97 Chan 5f 4th Group 3 *Three weeks*	**Don't Worry Me** G Henrot 33/1	4/18	5	8-13	73	7th King George Good 5f	9th Nunthorpe York 5f	**WON N/O** **Group 2** Bade 6f	8th Prix de l'Abbaye Long 5f
96 Folk 5f 1st Conds Stks *Seven months*	**Pivotal** Sir M Prescott 13/2	7/17	3	8-10	81	6th July Cup Newm 6f	**WON 10/3** **Nunthorpe** **York 5f**	-	-

12-year median performance rating of the winner: **80** (out of 100)   (2005 York), *next year*

WINNER'S PROFILE Three of the last five winners were **Australian sprinters** that arrived following a near four-month break and all three winners trod the same path leading to Ascot, having won the Lightning Stakes back home in February.
Eleven winners had already scored over this minimum trip – two in the **Temple Stakes** at Sandown beforehand – while four were prepared in France, three in the **Prix du Gros-Chene** at Chantilly.
Favourites had a woeful record until Miss Andretti landed the spoils last year, while two of the three winning three-year-olds were experiencing Group company for the first time.

FUTURE POINTERS An event in which the presence of Australian sprinters now features heavily and they have contributed to this sprint regaining its Group One status. Although two of them – Takeover Target and Choisir – produced excellent above par performance ratings (PR), they were subsequently unable to land the July Cup, along with four other King's Stand winners; placed runners from here have a better record at Newmarket *(see below)*. However, Choisir did follow up in the Golden Jubilee Stakes later that week at Royal Ascot – Takeover Target and Miss Andretti failed recently – while Nuclear Debate lifted the Nunthorpe next time out, a race also won by Pivotal in 1996.

Were King's Stand winners profitable to follow on their subsequent three runs?
No – 6 wins from 32 runs returned a loss of -£13.35 to a £1 level stake.

Placed runners' subsequent record (three runs):
Runners-up: 5 wins from 35 runs returned a loss of -£6.23 to a £1 level stake.
2006 Benbaun – Flying Five, 2002 Continent – July Cup, 2000 Agnes World – July Cup, 1998 Lochangel – Nunthorpe

Thirds: 6 wins from 33 runs returned a **profit of +£3.44** to a £1 level stake.
2006 Pivotal Point – Champagne Sprint, 2004 Frizzante – July Cup, 2003 Oasis Dream – July Cup, Nunthorpe, 2002 Kyllachy – Nunthorpe

FUTURE SUCCESS RATING: ★ ★ ★ ☆ ☆

ST JAMES'S PALACE STAKES
June 17, Royal Ascot – (Group 1, Class 1, 3yo Colts) 1m

Last run	Winner/Trainer & SP	Draw/Ran	Age	Wght	PR	Next four runs			
07 Long 1m 4th Poule' Poulains *Two months*	Excellent Art A O'Brien 8/1	1/8	3	9-00	86	2nd Sussex Good 1m	2nd Q Elizabeth II Ascot 1m	2nd Breeders' Cup Monm 1m	-
06 Curr 1m 1st Irish 2,000 Guin *One month*	Araafa J Noseda 2/1F	2/11	3	9-00	80	5th Sussex Good 1m	2nd Q Elizabeth II Ascot 1m	9th Breeders' Cup Chur 1m	-
05 Chan 1m3f 1st Prix Jockey Club *Two weeks*	Shamardal S Bin Suroor 7/4F	2/8	3	9-00	85	-	-	-	-
04 Irish 1m 2nd Irish 2,000 Guin *One month*	Azamour J Oxx 9/2	1/11	3	9-00	87	WON 8/1 Irish Champion Leop 1m2f	3rd Champion Stks Newm 1m2f	*4th Tatts Gold Cup Curr 1m3f	*WON 11/8F Prince of Wales York 1m2f
03 Curr 1m 14th Irish 2,000 Guin *One month*	Zafeen M Channon 8/1	5/11	3	9-00	79	4th Sussex Good 1m	-	-	-
02 Curr 1m 1st Irish 2,000 Guin *One month*	Rock Of Gibraltar A O'Brien 4/5F	4/9	3	9-00	89	WON 8/13F Sussex Good 1m	WON 3/5JF Prix du Moulin Long 1m	2nd Breeders' Cup Arli 1m	-
01 Curr 1m 1st Irish 2,000 Guin *One month*	Black Minnaloushe A O'Brien 8/1	1/11	3	9-00	80	5th Eclipse Sand 1m2f	3rd Sussex Good 1m	4th Juddmonte Int York 1m2f	10th Breeders' Cup Belm 1m2f
00 Curr 1m 2nd Irish 2,000 Guin *One month*	Giant's Causeway A O'Brien 7/2F	3/11	3	9-00	88	WON 8/1 Eclipse Sand 1m2f	WON 3/1JF Sussex Good 1m	WON 10/11F Juddmonte Int York 1m2f	WON 8/11F Irish Champion Leop 1m2f
99 Long 1m 1st Poule' Poulains *One month*	Sendawar A Royer-Dupre 2/1F	11/11	3	9-00	86	WON 4/5F Prix du Moulin Long 1m	*WON 4/5F Prix d'Ispahan Long 1m1f	*4th Prince of Wales Ascot 1m2f	*2nd Jacques' Marois Deau 1m
98 Chan 1m1f 3rd Prix Jean Prat *Three weeks*	Dr Fong H Cecil 4/1	4/8	3	9-00	82	WON N/O Prix Adam Masi 1m2f	2nd Q Elizabeth II Ascot 1m	2nd Grade 2 Sant 1m1f	5th Hollywood Derby Holl 1m1f
97 Chan 1m1f 1st Prix Jean Prat *Three weeks*	Starborough D Loder 11/2	5/8	3	9-00	81	2nd Sussex Good 1m	4th Jacques' Marois Deau 1m	*6th QE II Cup Shan 1m2f	*4th Sussex Good 1m
96 Curr 1m 4th Irish 2,000 Guin *One month*	Bijou D'Inde M Johnston 9/1	7/9	3	9-00	82	2nd Eclipse Sand 1m2f	3rd Juddmonte Int York 1m2f	6th Q Elizabeth II Ascot 1m	*4th Stakes Nad Al 1m1f

12-year median performance rating of the winner: **84** (out of 100)   *(2005 York), *next year*

WINNER'S PROFILE Trends and pointers are fairly thin on the ground, but it helps to keep things simple in this event rather than complicate matters and sticking to the following clues should provide a short-list. Every winner **raced in either Ireland or France last time out**, and 11 finished in the **first four of a Guineas** at some stage that season. Punters that stuck with **fancied runners** were rewarded as 11 winners emerged from the first four of the betting, while trainer **Aidan O'Brien** won four renewals.

FUTURE POINTERS An event that has brought together a mix of European Guineas winners, as last year's renewal was represented by the British, Irish and French victors, and winners from here were worthy of following post-Ascot. Although Rock Of Gibraltar followed up in the Sussex at Goodwood, five others failed, including Excellent Art last year, however, races like the Prix du Moulin and Irish Champion have been kinder. A couple of runners-up also found success in the Prix du Moulin, while other Ascot seconds also improved on their placing here in the Sussex *(see below)*.

Were St James's Palace winners profitable to follow on their subsequent three runs?
Yes – 9 wins from 31 runs returned a **profit of +0.71** to a £1 level stake.

Placed runners' subsequent record (three runs):
Runners-up: 9 wins from 35 runs returned a **profit of +£1.79** to a £1 level stake.
2006 Stormy River – Group One Prix Jean Prat, 2001 Noverre – Sussex, 1999 Aljabr – Sussex, 1998 Desert Prince – Prix du Moulin, 1997 Air Express – Queen Elizabeth II, 1996 Ashkalani – Prix du Moulin

Thirds: 7 wins from 36 runs returned a **profit of +0.35** to a £1 level stake.
2005 Oratorio – Eclipse, Irish Champion Stakes, 2000 Medicean – Celebration Mile, 1997 Daylami – Tattersalls Gold Cup,

FUTURE SUCCESS RATING: ★ ★ ★ ★ ☆

QUEEN ANNE STAKES
June 17, Ascot – (Group 1, Class 1, 4yo+) 1m

Last run	Winner/ Trainer & SP	Draw/ Ran	Age	Wght	PR	Next four runs			
07 Newb 1m Lockinge *One month*	2nd **Ramonti** S Bin Suroor 5/1	2/8	5	9-00	85	WON 9/2 **Sussex** Good 1m	2nd Prix du Moulin Long 1m	WON 5/1 **Q Elizabeth II** Ascot 1m	-
06 Curr 7f Gladness Stks *Three months*	6th **Ad Valorem** A O'Brien 13/2	2/7	4	9-00	81	5th Jacques' Marois Deau 1m	3rd Grade 1 Wood 1m	13th Breeders' Cup Chur 1m	-
05 Long 1m1f Prix d'Ispahan *One month*	1st **Valixir** A Fabre 4/1	1/10	4	9-00	85	WON 1/2F **Group 3** Mais 1m	3rd Jacques' Marois Deau 1m	5th Prix du Moulin Long 1m	10th Breeders' Cup Belm 1m
04 Newb 1m Lockinge *One month*	8th **Refuse To Bend** S Bin Suroor 12/1	1/16	4	9-00	85	WON 15/2 **Eclipse** Sand 1m2f	3rd Sussex Good 1m	11th Q Elizabeth II Ascot 1m	5th Champion Stks Newm 1m2f
03 Nott 1m Cond Stks *Two weeks*	1st **Dubai Destination** S Bin Suroor 9/2	10/10	4	9-00	84	5th Jacques' Marois Deau 1m	8th Q Elizabeth II Ascot 1m	-	-
02 Newb 1m Lockinge *One month*	4th **No Excuse Needed** Sir M Stoute 13/2	11/12	4	9-02	80	4th Sussex Good 1m	7th Juddmonte Int York 1m2f	5th Irish Champion Leop 1m2f	-
01 Newb 1m Lockinge *One month*	1st **Medicean** Sir M Stoute 11/2	8/10	4	9-07	88	WON 7/2 **Eclipse** Sand 1m2f	3rd Juddmonte Int York 1m2f	-	-
00 Wind 1m Listed *Two months*	2nd **Kalanisi** Sir M Stoute 11/2	11/11	4	9-02	86	2nd Eclipse Sand 1m2f	2nd Juddmonte Int York 1m2f	WON 5/1 **Champion Stks** Newm 1m2f	WON 46/10 **Breeders' Cup** Chur 1m3f
99 Nad Al 1m Listed *Three months*	3rd **Cape Cross** S Bin Suroor 7/1	2/8	5	9-07	84	WON 5/2 **Celebration Mile** Good 1m	6th Grade 1 Wood 1m	-	-
98 Epsom 1½m Diomed Stks *Two weeks*	1st **Intikhab** S Bin Suroor 9/4F	6/9	4	9-02	89	*4th Lockinge Newb 1m	-	-	-
97 Belm 1m1f Handicap *Eight months*	1st **Allied Forces** S Bin Suroor 10/1	11/11	4	9-05	82	4th Eclipse Sand 1m2f	3rd Sussex Good 1m	6th Arlington Million Arli 1m2f	6th Q Elizabeth II Ascot 1m
96 Newb 1m Lockinge *One month*	2nd **Charnwood Forest** S Bin Suroor 10/11F	6/9	4	9-02	81	2nd Sussex Good 1m	4th Jacques' Marois Deau 1m	4th Q Elizabeth II Ascot 1m	WON 15/8F **Challenge Stks** Ascot 1m

12-year median performance rating of the winner: **84** (out of 100)   *(2005 York), *next year*

WINNER'S PROFILE Those beaten in the **Lockinge** en route to Royal Ascot have an excellent long-term record – only one Newbury winner followed up here since 1996 – while winners of the Sandown Mile should also be swerved. **Four-year-olds** performed very well, unlike the six-year-olds and above whose record stands at 0 from over 20 runners, including the well-fancied Cesare who trailed in fifth last year.
Fillies and mares have also disappointed, while the last favourite to oblige was in 1998.
On the training front one name stands out, as last year's successful handler, **Saeed Bin Suroor**, took this for an impressive seventh time from 17 runners, with **Sir Michael Stoute** chipping in with three winners from 10. In fact, those two trainers dominated last year's finish, which saw Ramonti beating Stoute's Jeremy by a head.

FUTURE POINTERS Awarded Group One status five years ago when restricted to four-year-olds and above, the Queen Anne Stakes has a good recent history for providing winners next time out, with the likes of Refuse To Bend and Medicean landing the Eclipse, the most successful post-route with two winners and a runner-up from just four runners since 1996. Last year's victor, Ramonti, was a rare winner to follow up in the Sussex six weeks later, as it usually pays to follow the placed horses from here in that event *(see below)*.
The Group One events that have been unkind to Queen Anne winners were the Juddmonte International and the Queen Elizabeth II Stakes, prior to last year when Ramonti scored at Ascot.

Were Queen Anne winners profitable to follow on their subsequent three runs?
Yes – 7 wins from 31 runs returned a **profit of +£3.50** to a £1 level stake.

Placed runners' subsequent record (three runs):
Runners-up: 8 wins from 36 runs returned a loss of -£4.36 to a £1 level stake
2005 Court Masterpiece – Sussex, 2004 Soviet Song – Falmouth, Sussex, Matron, 1998 Among Men – Sussex

Thirds: 5 wins from 29 runs returned a loss of -£4.75 to a £1 level stake
2005 Star Craft – Prix du Moulin, QEII, 1997 Ali-Royal – Sussex, 1996 Mistle Cat – Premio Vittorio Di Capua

FUTURE SUCCESS RATING: ★ ★ ★ ☆ ☆

WINDSOR CASTLE STAKES
June 17, Royal Ascot – (Listed, Class 1, 2yo) 5f

Last run	Winner/Trainer & SP	Draw/Ran	Age	Wght	PR	Next four runs			
07 Brig 6f 1st / Novice Stks / Three weeks	Drawnfromthepast J Osborne 9/1	15/20	2	9-03	56	5th Richmond Stks Good 6f	14th St Leger Yearling York 6f	-	-
06 Good 5f 6th / Aubigny Stks / One month	Elhamri S Kirk 20/1	15/18	2	9-03	60	WON 9/1 Weatherbys Sprint Newb 6f	4th Gimcrack Stks York 6f	5th Flying Childers York 5f	5th Cornwallis Stks Ascot 5f
05 Redc 5f 1st / Novice Stks / Three weeks	Titus Alone B Smart 11/4	7/8	2	8-11	58	8th Weatherbys Sprint Newb 6f	7th Gimcrack Stks York 6f	9th Flying Childers Donc 5f	*5th Conds Stks Hami 6f
04 Leic 5f 1st / Maiden / One month	Chateau King Prawn N Littmoden 12/1	7/15	2	8-13	60	7th July Stks Newm 6f	WON 11/1 Flying Childers Donc 5f	9th Middle Park Newm 6f	*9th Group 2 Sha 5f
03 Curr 5f 4th / Listed / One month	Holborn M Channon 5/2F	1/17	2	8-13	60	5th July Stks Newm 6f	4th Sirenia Stks Kemp 6f	4th Mill Reef Stks Newb 6f	2nd Middle Park Newm 6f
02 Nott 6f 2nd / Novice Stks / Two months	Revenue M Bell 14/1	10/14	2	8-11	58	WON 12/1 Richmond Stks Good 6f	4th Gimcrack Stks York 6f	2nd Flying Childers Donc 5f	3rd Cornwallis Stks Ascot 5f
01 Hayd 5f 1st / Maiden / One month	Irony J Osborne 8/1	19/24	2	8-11	55	2nd Molecomb Stks Good 5f	6th Roses Stks York 5f	5th Flying Childers Donc 5f	2nd Mill Reef Stks Newb 6f
00 Hayd 5f 1st / Maiden / Two weeks	Autumnal B Meehan 4/1	4/11	2	8-08	59	2nd Pr'ncss Margaret Ascot 6f	3rd Lowther Stks York 6f	4th Cheveley Park Newm 6f	8th Rockfel Stks Newm 6f
99 Sali 5f 2nd / Novice Stks / Two weeks	Kalindi M Channon 14/1	12/16	2	8-06	54	5th Pr'ncss Margaret Ascot 6f	2nd St Hugh's Stks Newb 5f	10th Flying Childers Donc 5f	10th Cheveley Park Newm 6f
98 Beve 5f 1st / Hilary Needler / Three weeks	Flanders T Easterby 15/8F	14/14	2	8-10	61	WON 6/5F Weatherbys Sprint Newb 6f	3rd Lowther Stks York 6f	2nd St Leger Yearling York 6f	7th Cheveley Park Newm 6f
97 Leic 5f 2nd / Maiden / Three weeks	Asfurah S Bin Suroor 7/1	8/14	2	8-06	60	WON 9/2 Cherry Hinton Newm 6f	2nd Phoenix Stks Leop 6f	4th Listed Newm 6f	-
96 (Unraced)	Dazzle Sir M Stoute 7/2F	11/10	2	8-05	63	WON 2/1F Cherry Hinton Newm 6f	4th Cheveley Park Newm 6f	2nd Rockfel Stks Newm 6f	*3rd 1,000 Guineas Newm 1m

12-year median performance rating of the winner: **59** (out of 100)   *(2005 York) *next year*

WINNER'S PROFILE As you would expect with a summer sprint, the majority lined up fit having **raced within the past month**, while 11 **never saw a racecourse more than twice**. Those with experince **finished at least second**, and only one scored in Pattern company – **maiden and novice performers** proved best.
Although there have been big-priced priced winners, 11 of the 12 emerged from the **first six in the betting**, while middle to high numbers scored 10 times, two of whom were trained by **Jamie Osborne** from as many runners. **Mick Channon** had two from 11 runners, but one to swerve was Richard Hannon with none from 20 runners.

FUTURE POINTERS Often frowned upon as being at the lower end of the Royal Ascot juvenile scale, the Windsor Castle, along with the Queen Mary, have outperformed both the Coventry and Norfolk in terms of immediate subsequent victories, backed up by the superb record from placed horses *(see below)*.
While the majority failed to build any kind of long-term career, two winners of this managed to land the Cherry Hinton next time out, while a further pair took the valuable Weatherbys Super Sprint at Newbury.
In 2002, Revenue succeeded where last year's sub-standard winner, Drawnfromthepast, failed in the Richmond Stakes, while two races less kind to Windsor Castle victors were the Princess Margaret and July Stakes.

Were Windsor Castle winners profitable to follow on their subsequent three runs?
Yes – 6 wins from 35 runs returned a **profit of +£10.70** to a £1 level stake.

Placed runners' subsequent record (three runs):
Runners-up: 12 wins from 36 runs returned a **profit of +£26.65** to a £1 level stake.
2007 Kingsgate Native – Nunthorpe, 2006 Conquest – Gimcrack, 2005 Strike Up The Band – Molecomb, 2004 Tournedos – Molecomb, 1999 Master Fay – Rose Bowl Stakes, 1998 Sarson – Listed Dragon Trophy, 1996 Vax Star – Listed Dragon Trophy
Thirds: 11 wins from 33 runs returned a **profit of +£11.39** to a £1 level stake.
2007 Hatta Fort – Superlative Stakes, 2005 Tabaret – Roses Stakes, 2003 Howick Falls – Roses Stakes, Flying Childers, 2002 Progressing Times – Roses Stakes, 2001 Leggy Lou – Princess Margaret

FUTURE SUCCESS RATING: ★ ★ ★ ★ ☆

JERSEY STAKES

June 18, Royal Ascot – (Group 3, Class 1, 3yo) 7f

Last run	Winner/ Trainer & SP	Draw/ Ran	Age	Wght	PR	Next four runs				
07 Newm 7f 1st King Charles II *One month*	**Tariq** P Chapple-Hyam 15/2	8/15	3	9-01	78	**WON 7/2** **Lennox Stks** Good 7f	5th Prix de la Foret Long 7f	-	-	
06 Newm 7f 1st King Charles II *One month*	**Jeremy** Sir M Stoute 9/2	9/14	3	9-01	74	6th Lennox Stks Good 7f	2nd Hungerford Stks Newb 7f	12th Challenge Stks Newm 7f	***WON 2/1F** **Betfred Mile** Sand 1m	
05 Good 1m 1st Heron Stks *Three weeks*	**Proclamation** J Noseda 7/1	20/21	3	8-10	82	**WON 3/1** **Sussex** Good 1m	11th Sprint Cup Hayd 6f	*3rd Queen Anne Ascot 1m	*5th Q Elizabeth II Ascot 1m	
04 Newm 6f 9th Middle Park *Eight months*	**Kheleyf** S bin Suroor 6/1	1/15	3	8-10	74	14th July Cup Newm 6f	3rd Lennox Stks Good 7f	6th Jacques 'Marois Deau 1m	5th Supreme Stks Good 7f	
03 Newm 7f 2nd King Charles II *Three weeks*	**Membership** C Brittain 20/1	3/14	3	8-10	73	13th July Cup Newm 6f	7th Lennox Stks Good 7f	10th Hungerford Stks Newb 7f	3rd Duty Free Cup Newb 7f	
02 York 6f 4th W Hill Trophy *One week*	**Just James** J Noseda 20/1	2/15	3	8-11	70	6th Chipchase Stks Newc 6f	14th International Hcp Ascot 7f	*2nd Duke of York York 6f	*5th Golden Jubilee Ascot 6f	
01 Curr 1m 2nd Irish 1,000 Guin *One month*	**Mozart** A O'Brien 7/4F	10/18	3	8-11	79	**WON 4/1F** **July Cup** Newm 6f	**WON 4/9F** **Nunthorpe** York 5f	11th Breeders' Cup Belm 6f	-	
00 Newm 7f 2nd King Charles II *Three weeks*	**Observatory** J Gosden 11/2	9/19	3	8-11	77	**WON 11/4** **Lennox Stks** Good 7f	2nd Celebration Mile Good 1m	**WON 14/1** **Q Elizabeth II** **Ascot 1m**	***WON 11/10F** **Prix d'Ispahan** **Long 1m1f**	
99 Sand 1m 4th Doubleprint Hcp *Three weeks*	**Lots Of Magic** R Hannon 33/1	3/12	3	8-11	73	4th Fortune Stks Epsom 7f	10th Challenge Stks Newm 7f	*6th Cammidge Tr'hy Donc 6f	*8th Cork & Orrery Ascot 6f	
98 Leic 7f 1st Conds Stks *One month*	**Diktat** D Loder 3/1F	2/16	3	8-10	78	2nd Beeswing Stks Newc 7f	***WON 11/10F** **Shergar Cup** **Good 7f**	***WON 4/5F** **Criterium Stks** **Newm 7f**	***WON 4/5JF** **Maurice 'Gheest** **Deau 7f**	
97 Kemp 1m 1st Heron Stks *One month*	**Among Men** Sir M Stoute 4/1F	13/20	3	8-13	75	4th Sussex Good 1m	***WON 8/11F** **Celebration Mile** **Good 1m**	*6th Lockinge Newb 1m	*2nd Queen Anne Ascot 1m	
96 Leic 7f 2nd Conds Stks *One month*	**Lucayan Prince** D Loder 50/1	2/16	3	8-10	70	2nd July Cup Newm 6f	5th Sprint Cup Hayd 6f	2nd Diadem Stks Ascot 6f	5th Challenge Stks Newm 7f	

12-year median performance rating of the winner: **75** (out of 100)   *(2005 York), *next year*

WINNER'S PROFILE All bar one **raced within the past month,** four arrived via the **King Charles II Stakes** since the Millennium, while two came from a conditions race at Leicester in the nineties.

Interestingly, the last two winners were successful in the King Charles II, which is a bonus here as Listed winners no longer carry a penalty, however, those with a Group victory under their belt do have to carry extra weight but are best avoided as none succeeded from over 15 attempts.

Every winner finished in the **top-two on either of their last two runs**, while the **males dominated**, Satin Flower the last filly to triumph back in 1991 – over 20 have lost since 1996.

Two trainers that landed this twice in the last 12 years were **Jeremy Noseda** and **Sir Michael Stoute**, although the former has the best strike-rate from just seven runners, including a 14/1 third last year.

FUTURE POINTERS A superb race that has surely outgrown Group Three status having provided a breeding ground for future Group One winners, with the likes of Proclamation, Mozart, Observatory, Diktat and Among Men all going on to land honours at the highest level. Last year's above par winner with a good performance rating (PR), gave the race another shot in the arm by following up in the Lennox Stakes, a race Observatory also took in 2000. Although the classy Mozart was able to cope with a drop in trip to land the July Cup, that tactic has backfired on several Jersey winners and it is best to stick with those over this distance and beyond.

Were Jersey winners profitable to follow on their subsequent three runs?
Yes – 9 wins from 35 runs returned a **profit of £3.31** to a £1 level stake.

Placed runners' subsequent record (three runs):
Runners-up: 3 wins from 32 runs returned a loss of -£23.62 to a £1 level stake.

Thirds: 4 wins from 32 runs returned a loss of -£9.75 to a £1 level stake.
2007 Arabian Gleam – Park Stakes, 1998 Lovers Knot – Falmouth Stakes

FUTURE SUCCESS RATING: ★ ★ ★ ★ ☆

PRINCE OF WALES'S STAKES
June 18, Royal Ascot – (Group 1, Class 1, 4yo+) 1m2f

Last run	Winner/Trainer & SP	Draw/Ran	Age	Wght	PR	Next four runs			
07 Long 1m1f 1st Prix d'Ispahan One month	**Manduro** A Fabre 15/8F	4/6	5	9-00	90	**WON 4/5F** Jacques'Marois Deau 1m	**WON 4/11F** Prix Foy Long 1m4f	-	-
06 Epso 1m4f 2nd Coronation Cup Three weeks	**Ouija Board** E Dunlop 8/1	5/7	5	8-11	86	5th Eclipse Sand 1m2f	**WON EvensF** Nassau Good 1m2f	2nd Irish Champion Leop 1m2f	**WON 6/4F** Breeders' Cup Chur 1m3f
05 Curr 1m3f 4th Tatts Gold Cup One month	**Azamour** J Oxx 11/8F	3/8	4	9-00	87	**WON 5/2F** King George VI Newb 1m4f	5th Irish Champion Leop 1m2f	3rd Breeders' Cup Belm 1m4f	
04 Sha 1m2f 2nd Hong Kong Cup Six months	**Rakti** M Jarvis 3/1	10/10	5	9-00	86	5th Eclipse Sand 1m2f	5th Irish Champion Leop 1m2f	**WON 9/2** Q Elizabeth II Ascot 1m	14th Grade 1 Kyot 1m
03 Nad Al 1m2f 3rd Dubai World Cup Three months	**Nayef** M Tregoning 5/1	6/10	5	9-00	85	2nd Eclipse Sand 1m2f	7th King George VI Ascot 1m4f	3rd Juddmonte Int York 1m2f	8th Champion Stks Newm 1m2f
02 Kran 1m2f 1st International Cup Two months	**Grandera** S Bin Suroor 4/1	3/12	4	9-00	86	5th King George VI Ascot 1m4f	**WON 5/2** Irish Champion Leop 1m2f	3rd Cox Plate Moon 1m2f	7th Hong Kong Cup Sha 1m2f
01 Curr 1m3f 1st Tatts Gold Gup One month	**Fantastic Light** S Bin Suroor 10/3	8/9	5	9-00	90	2nd King George VI Ascot 1m4f	**WON 9/4** Irish Champion Leop 1m2f	**WON 7/5F** Breeders' Cup Belm 1m4f	
00 Nad Al 1m2f 1st Dubai World Cup Three months	**Dubai Millennium** S Bin Suroor 5/4	7/6	4	9-00	92	-	-	-	-
99 Epsom 1½m 1st Diomed Stks Two weeks	**Lear Spear** D Elsworth 20/1	5/8	4	9-03	80	8th Eclipse Sand 1m2f	**WON 9/2** Select Stks Good 1m2f	9th Champion Stks Newm 1m2f	3rd Hong Kong Cup Sha 1m2f
98 Festival Stks One month	**Faithful Son** S Bin Suroor 11/2	7/8	4	9-03	81	2nd Eclipse Sand 1m2f	2nd Juddmonte Int York 1m2f	4th Caulfield Cup Caul 1m4f	7th Melbourne Cup Flem 2m
97 Sand 1m2f 1st Brigadier Gerard Three weeks	**Bosra Sham** H Cecil 4/11F	1/6	4	9-05	87	3rd Eclipse Sand 1m2f	4th Juddmonte Int York 1m2f	-	-
96 York 1m 1st Hambleton Hcp Two months	**First Island** G Wragg 9/1	3/12	4	9-03	85	**WON 5/1** Sussex Good 1m	2nd Juddmonte Int York 1m2f	3rd Q Elizabeth II Ascot 1m	5th Champion Stks Newm 1m2f

12-year median performance rating of the winner: **86** (out of 100)

WINNER'S PROFILE Of the last nine winners, only two were prepared in Britain – both at Epsom – as the other seven **last ran over in Ireland or abroad**. A **top-three effort last time out** was vital, as was **winning form over the trip** with 10 winners already proven, while nine were **victorious at Group One level**.
Four and five-year-olds dominated, but represent most of the field each year – three-year-olds and six-year-olds plus were 0 from 13. The **first four in the betting** have fared well, and **Saeed Bin Suroor** sent out four fancies.

FUTURE POINTERS One of the best events of the week, backed up by the fact that seven winners scored again in the near future, however, since First Island followed up in the Sussex back in 1996, victors built up a losing run next time out – five in the Eclipse – until Azamour took the King George VI at Newbury. Ouija Board was one of the Eclipse losers, but made amends in the Nassau and Breeders' Cup, a feat repeated by Fantastic Light at Belmont in 2001. Fantastic Light also won the Irish Champion beforehand, as did Grandera in 2002, although three failed since, while the Juddmonte International foiled four winners.

Were Prince of Wales's winners profitable to follow on their subsequent three runs?
Yes – 10 wins from 31 runs returned a **profit of +£3.81** to a £1 level stake.

Placed runners' subsequent record (three runs):
Runners-up: 9 wins from 31 runs returned a **profit of +£2.48** to a £1 level stake.
2007 Dylan Thomas – King George VI, Irish Champion Stakes, 2003 Rakti – Champion Stakes, 1999 Fantastic Light – Great Voltigeur,

Thirds: 6 wins from 19 runs returned a loss of -£2.32 to a £1 level stake.
2003 Islington – Yorkshire Oaks, 2002 Banks Hill – Jacques le Marois, 2001 Hightori – Prix Foy, 1998 Daylami – Eclipse, 1996 Tamayaz – Rose of Lancaster

FUTURE SUCCESS RATING: ★★★★☆

ROYAL HUNT CUP
June 18, Royal Ascot – (Heritage Handicap, Class 2, 3yo+) 1m

Last run	Winner/ Trainer & SP	Draw/ Ran	Age	Wght	PR	Next four runs			
07 Newm1m1f 12th Suffolk Hcp Two months	Royal Oath J Gosden 9/1	14/26	4	9-00	76	2nd Summer Mile Ascot 1m	8th Lennox Stks Good 7f	4th Strensall Stks York 1m1f	
06 Redc 1m 12th Lincoln Hcp Three months	Cesare J Fanshawe 14/1	3/30	5	8-08	72	10th Summer Mile Ling 1m	WON 11/10F Conds Stks Warw 7f	5th Duty Free Cup Newb 7f	*WON 2/1F Paradise Stks Ascot 1m
05 Ling 7f 9th Victoria Cup Two months	New Seeker C Cox 11/1	6/22	5	9-00	71	WON 12/1 International Hp Newb 7f	3rd Sovereign Stks Sali 1m	WON 6/4F Duty Free Cup Newb 7f	3rd Supreme Stks Good 7f
04 Ascot 7f 1st Victoria Cup One month	Mine J Bethell 16/1	8/31	6	9-05	70	5th Totescoop6 Hcp Sand 1m	2nd Listed Newm 1m	7th City of York York 7f	5th Porcelanosa Donc 1m
03 Pont 1m 1st Pipalong Stks Two weeks	Macadamia J Fanshawe 8/1	6/32	4	8-13	73	WON 2/1JF Falmouth Stks Newm 1m	5th Nassau Good 1m2f	2nd Sun Chariot Newm 1m	11th Darley Stsks Newm 1m1f
02 Ling 1m 1st Stakes Two months	Norton T Mills 25/1	10/30	5	8-09	63	8th International Hcp Ascot 7f	3rd Shergar Cup Ascot 1m	3rd Motability Hcp York 1m2f	7th Handicap Good 1m1f
01 Donc 7f 1st Handicap One month	Surprise Encounter E Dunlop 8/1	29/30	5	8-09	72	8th Lennox Stks Good 7f	3rd Sovereign Stks Sali 1m	WON 5/4F Sovereign Stks Good 7f	13th Challenge Stks Newm 7f
00 York 1m 2nd Hambleton Hcp Two months	Caribbean Monarch Sir M Stoute 11/2	28/32	5	8-10	75	WON 5/2F Showcase Hcp Sand 1m	12th International Hcp Ascot 7f	8th W Hill Mile Hcp Good 1m	
99 Donc 7f 3rd Handicap Three weeks	Showboat B Hills 14/1	30/32	5	8-09	71	4th Silver Trophy Ascot 1m	2nd Conds Stks Donc 1m	4th International Hcp Ascot 7f	6th Strensall Stks York 1m1f
98 Hayd 7f 2nd Class Stks Two weeks	Refuse To Lose J Eustace 20/1	6/32	4	7-11	63	8th J Smith's Cup York 1m2f	11th W Hill Mile Hcp Good 1m	WON 4/1 Wulfrun Stks Wolv 1m1f	*2nd Wint Derby Trial Ling 1m2f
97 York 1m2f 12th Rated Hcp Two months	Red Robbo R Akehurst 16/1	17/32	4	8-06	64	17th Hong Kong Hcp Sand 1m	12th Brad & Bing Hcp York 1m	8th Rated Hcp Kemp 1m	-
96 Ling 1m 2nd Limited Stks Two months	Yeast W Haggas 8/1F	3/31	4	8-06	68	10th Hong Kong Hcp Sand 1m	WON 7/2F C Bulteel Hcp Ascot 1m	8th Group 3 Bade 1m	WON 11/2 Joel Stks Newm 1m

12-year median performance rating of the winner: **70** (out of 100) *(2005 York), *next year*

WINNER'S PROFILE The majority had **raced within the past two months** and 10 finished in at least the top-two earlier that season – the two exceptions had just the one unplaced run.

A run in either the **Lincoln, Spring Cup, Victoria Cup or the Hambleton** is a bonus, while **four to five-year-olds** have dominated. Those on the **light-side of 9st** are respected, as are **southern-based trainers** – James **Fanshawe** especially one to note with two winners and several placed from only a handful of runners.

FUTURE POINTERS This competitive handicap has produced a good mix of future winners as seven scored again in the near future. As with the Wokingham, the quality of the winners has improved, with Royal Oath, Cesare, New Seeker, Macadamia and Surprise Encounter all performing well in Pattern company.

The third and fourths, whose handicap marks don't suffer like runners-up, also ran creditably after Ascot as several went on to land big handicaps *(see below)*.

Were Royal Hunt Cup winners profitable to follow on their subsequent three runs?
No – 8 wins from 36 runs returned a loss of -£0.15 to a £1 level stake.

Placed runners' subsequent record (three runs):
Runners-up: 3 wins from 32 runs returned a loss of -£21.60 to a £1 level stake.
2006 Stronghold – Supreme Stakes, 1998 Fly To The Stars – French Group Two and Threes,

Thirds: 6 wins from 34 runs returned a **profit of +£3.00** to a £1 level stake.
2000 Persiano – William Hill Mile Handicap, 1996 Crumpton Hill – Bunbury Cup

Fourths: 8 wins from 36 runs returned a **profit of +£30.32** to a £1 level stake.
2006 Hinterland – Heritage Handicap (Sandown), 2003 Pentecost – Shergar Cup,
1998 Sugarfoot – Ascot Handicap, 1996 Donna Viola – Group Two and Three abroad

FUTURE SUCCESS RATING: ★ ★ ★ ★ ☆

QUEEN MARY STAKES
June 18, Royal Ascot – (Group 2, Class 1, 2yo Fillies) 5f

Last run	Winner/ Trainer & SP	Draw/ Ran	Age	Wght	PR	Next four runs			
07 Leop 6f 1st Maiden Two weeks	Elletelle G Lyons 20/1	13/21	2	8-12	65	3rd Cherry Hinton Newm 6f	3rd Phoenix Stks Curr 6f	6th Cheveley Park Newm 6f	-
06 York 5f 1st Marygate Stks Two months	Gilded R Hannon 11/2	12/15	2	8-12	60	3rd Cherry Hinton Newm 6f	6th Weatherbys Spr Newb 5f		
05 Newb 5f 1st Conds Stks Two months	Flashy Wings M Channon 4/1JF	14/17	2	8-10	73	WON 10/11F Lowther Stks York 6f	2nd Watership Sales Newb 7f	3rd Cheveley Park Newm 6f	*11th 1,000 Guineas Newm 1m
04 Naas 6f 1st Swordlestown Stks Two weeks	Damson D Wachman 11/2JF	15/17	2	8-10	71	WON 8/11F Phoenix Stks Curr 6f	3rd Cheveley Park Newm 6f	*9th 1,000 Guineas Newm 1m	*7th Coronation Stks Ascot 1m
03 Beve 5f 1st Hilary Needler Two weeks	Attraction M Johnston 13/8F	7/14	2	8-10	75	WON 4/7F Cherry Hinton Newm 6f	*WON 11/2 1,000 Guineas Newm 1m	*WON 2/1F Irish 1,000 Guin Curr 1m	*WON 6/4F Coronation Stks Ascot 1m
02 Ling 5f 1st Maiden One month	Romantic Liason B Meehan 16/1	9/19	2	8-08	68	3rd Lowther Stks York 6f	*11th King's Stand Ascot 5f	*PU Porcelanosa Stks Sand 5f	-
01 Newb 5f 1st Conds Stks Two months	Queens Logic M Channon 13/2	4/20	2	8-08	70	WON 7/1 Lowther Stks York 6f	WON 10/11F Cheveley Park Newm 6f	*WON 1/3F Fred Darling Newb 7f	-
00 Ches 5f 1st Conds Stks Two months	Romantic Myth T Easterby 4/1F	21/20	2	8-08	64	6th Weatherbys Spr Newb 5f	4th Lowther Stks York 6f	5th Flying Childers Donc 5f	17th Cornwallis Stks Newb 5f
99 Bath 6f 1st Maiden One month	Shining Hour P Chapple-Hyam 20/1	3/13	2	8-08	62	-	-	-	-
98 Sand 5f 1st National Stks One month	Bint Allayl M Channon 2/1F	5/17	2	8-08	74	WON 15/8F Lowther Stks York 6f	-		
97 Sand 5f 3rd National Stks One month	Nadwah P Walwyn 10/1	1/18	2	8-08	63	3rd Lowther Stks York 6f	6th Cheveley Park Newm 6f	*6th Euro Free Hcp Newm 7f	*3rd Somerset Stks Bath 6f
96 Beve 5f 1st Hilary Needler Two weeks	Dance Parade P Cole 8/1	2/13	2	8-08	65	11th Marcel Boussac Long 1m	*WON 16/1 Fred Darling Newb 7f	*12th 1,000 Guineas Newm 1m	**6th Group 2 Sha 7f

12-year median performance rating of the winner: **67** (out of 100)   *(2005 York), *next year **two years*

WINNER'S PROFILE A ferociously difficult event in which trends are thin on the ground, however, a glance to the left of the winner tells us that a **victory last time out is vital**, six winners arrived via the **National Stakes** and **Hilary Needler**, while two of trainer Mick Channon's won a **conditions event at Newbury**.

The **first six in the betting** helped find the winner on 10 occasions, while a **high draw** has been important of late, especially last year, and any earlier clues during the Royal meeting are worth noting.

Mick Channon is very much the man to follow with a record of three winners and two placed from only 10 runners, and a major clue to backing his fillies comes in the betting market. His five fancied runners at 7/1 or shorter finished: 10121, in comparison to those at double-figure prices that finished: 00300. During the last three years, he has saddled only one 40/1 runner and this patient approach could soon pay dividends.

FUTURE POINTERS One of the better juvenile events of the Royal meeting, upgraded to Group Two status in 2004, but not much of a pointer for next year's Classics, as Attraction was the first who went and landed the 1,000 Guineas since the seventies – two have flopped since at HQ in Damson and Flashy Wings.

However, from a punting perspective, winners of the Queen Mary have a crisp post-Ascot record, as five of the last 10 scored next time out – three in the Lowther – and all five earned above par performance ratings (PR) here. The last two winners were both sub-standard and were unsurprisingly turned over in the Cherry Hinton.

Were Queen Mary winners profitable to follow on their subsequent three runs?
Yes – 10 wins from 30 runs returned a **profit of +£15.79** to a £1 level stake.

Placed runners' subsequent record (three runs):
Runners-up: 10 wins from 35 runs returned a **profit of +£4.08** to a £1 level stake.
2005 Salut D'Amour – National Stakes, 2004 Soar – Princess Margaret, Lowther, 2002 Never A Doubt – Prix Robert Papin, 1998 Pipalong – Redcar 2yo Trophy

Thirds: 5 wins from 34 runs returned a loss of -£22.67 to a £1 level stake.
2003 Majestic Desert – Tattersalls Breeders Stakes, Fred Darling

FUTURE SUCCESS RATING: ★ ★ ★ ★ ☆

NORFOLK STAKES
June 19, Royal Ascot – (Group 2, Class 1, 2yo) 5f

Last run	Winner/ Trainer & SP	Draw/ Ran	Age	Wght	PR	Next four runs			
07 Newb 5f 1st Maiden *Two months*	Winker Watson P Chapple-Hyam 2/1F	16/11	2	9-01	70	WON 11/4F July Stks Newm 6f	-	-	-
06 Wind 5f 1st Novice Stks *Three weeks*	Dutch Art P Chapple-Hyam 11/4	3/11	2	9-01	68	WON 4/1 Prix Morny Deau 6f	WON 6/5F Middle Park Stk Newm 6f	*2nd Greenham Newb 7f	*3rd 2,000 Guineas Newm 1m
05 Newc 5f 1st Maiden *Three weeks*	Masta Plasta H Johnson 7/2	10/12	2	8-12	63	8th Molecomb Stks Good 5f	10th Yearling Stks Donc 6f	2nd Rockingham Stk York 6f	*5th Chipchase Stks Newc 6f
04 Wind 5f 1st Conds Stks *One month*	Blue Dakota J Noseda 5/4F	5/9	2	8-12	65	6th Richmond Stks Good 6f	*12th King George Good 5f	**12th Listed Naas	-
03 Sand 5f 1st National Stks *One month*	Russian Valour M Johnston 4/1	7/8	2	8-12	64	*10th Euro Free Hcp Newm 7f	*6th Pavillon Stks Ascot 6f	*7th Conds Stks Leic 5f	*7th Conds Stks Yarm 6f
02 Wind 5f 1st Conds Stks *One month*	Baron's Gift R Hannon 12/1	8/12	2	8-12	66	6th Richmond Stks Good 6f	8th Mill Reef Stks Newb 6f	*2nd Euro Free Hcp Newm 7f	*3rd Pavillon Stks Ascot 6f
01 Fair 6f 1st Maiden *One month*	Johannesburg A O'Brien 11/8F	8/10	2	8-12	70	WON 4/5F Anglesey Stks Curr 6f	WON 2/5F Phoenix Stks Leop 6f	WON 3/5JF Prix Morny Deau 6f	WON 3/10F Middle Park Stk Newm 6f
00 Catt 5f 1st Novice Stks *Two weeks*	Superstar Leo W Haggas 5/1	9/11	2	8-07	67	WON 9/2 Weatherbys Spr Newb 5f	WON 2/1F Phoenix Stks Leop 6f	WON 2/1F Flying Childers Donc 5f	2nd Prix de l'Abbaye Long 5f
99 Newc 5f 1st Maiden *Three weeks*	Warm Heart J Gosden 7/2	11/13	2	8-12	61	2nd Prix Morny Deau 6f	4th Middle Park Stks Newm 6f	-	-
98 Beve 5f 1st B Yardley Stks *Three weeks*	Rosselli J Berry 10/1	1/15	2	8-12	66	3rd Richmond Stks Good 6f	7th Gimcrack Stks York 6f	*9th Nunthorpe York 5f	*14th Sprint Cup Hayd 6f
97 Warw 6f 1st Maiden *Three weeks*	Tippitt Boy K McAuliffe 33/1	2/6	2	8-12	60	5th July Stks Newm 6f	5th Molecomb Stks Good 5f	2nd Flying Childers Donc 5f	8th Cornwallis Stks Ascot 5f
96 Sali 5f 1st Maiden *Two months*	Tipsy Creek B Hanbury 7/2F	11/10	2	8-12	64	6th Molecomb Stks Good 5f	2nd Roses Stks York 5f	*7th World Trophy Newb 5f	*3rd Rous Stks Newm 5f

12-year median performance rating of the winner: **65** (out of 100)   *(2005 York), *next year **two years*

WINNER'S PROFILE Every winner **arrived off the back of a victory** – three of the last six via Windsor – while Johannesburg was the only one in the last 10 years not to have **scored over the minimum trip**.
Fancied runners are reliable as 11 emerged from the **first five in the betting** – six of the last seven winners were first and second favourites. It may only be a coincidence, but low drawn numbers have struggled in recent times, and as the new Ascot favoured high numbers last term, it could pay to note previous results at the 2008 Royal meeting.
Trainer-wise, **Peter Chapple-Hyam** has a cute record with two winners from as many runners – also scored with Turtle Island in 1993 – while **Jeremy Noseda** had a winner and a runner-up from only four runners.
Richard Hannon won it three times going back to Niche in 1992, but his strike-rate is poor, as is Mick Channon's.

FUTURE POINTERS Since granted Group Two status in 2006, trainer Peter Chapple-Hyam has won both renewals with smart individuals, however, as a long-term guide, winners haven't really progressed to achieve much in their Classic year. Both Dutch Art and Johannesburg trod similar paths by landing the Prix Morny and Middle Park Stakes later in the season, with the latter going on to take the prestigious Breeders' Cup Juvenile, while the former managed to be placed in the 2,000 Guineas the following term.
From a punting perspective, above par winners with good PR's have been worth following, as have several of the runners-up *(see below)*.

Were Norfolk winners profitable to follow on their subsequent three runs?
No – 8 wins from 33 runs returned a loss of -£8.75 to a £1 level stake.

Placed runners' subsequent record (three runs):
Runners-up: 9 wins from 36 runs returned a **profit of +£8.04** to a £1 level stake.
2005 Strike Up The Band – Molecomb, 2003 Kheleyf – Jersey Stakes, 2000 Bouncing Bowdler – Roses Stakes, Mill Reef Stakes, 1998 Sheer Viking – Flying Childers, 1996 Raphane – Curragh Stakes

Thirds: 4 wins from 31 returned a loss of -£14.60 to a £1 level stake.
2003 Nevisian Lad – July Stakes

FUTURE SUCCESS RATING: ★ ★ ★ ☆ ☆

RIBBLESDALE STAKES
June 19 – Royal Ascot (Group 2, Class 1, 3yo) 1m4f

Last run	Winner/ Trainer & SP	Draw/ Ran	Age	Wght	PR	Next four runs			
07 Sand 1m2f 1st Handicap Two months	Silkwood M Jarvis 4/1	2/12	3	8-12	72	7th Yorkshire Oaks York 1m4f	-	-	-
06 Ches 1m3f 2nd Cheshire Oaks Two months	Mont Etoile W Haggas 25/1	1/11	3	8-12	69	4th Irish Oaks Curr 1m4f	8th St Leger York 1m6½f	*2nd Pipalong Stks Pont 1m	*5th Lancashire Oaks Newm 1m4f
05 Good 1m2f 2nd Lupe Stks One month	Thakafaat J Dunlop 22/1	3/9	3	8-11	66	7th Irish Oaks Curr 1m4f	11th Park Hill Stks Donc 1m7f	-	-
04 Epso 1m4f 3rd Oaks Two weeks	Punctilious S Bin Suroor 9/2	1/9	3	8-11	73	2nd Irish Oaks Curr 1m4f	4th Yorkshire Oaks York 1m4f	2nd Grade 1 Wood 1m2f	*5th Brigadier Gerard Sand 1m2f
03 Kemp 7f 1st Maiden Nine months	Spanish Sun Sir M Stoute 9/2	6/9	3	8-11	70	6th Irish Oaks Curr 1m4f	-	-	-
02 Naas 1m2f 1st Maiden Three weeks	Irrestible Jewel D Weld 12/1	10/15	3	8-08	71	8th Irish Oaks Curr 1m4f	5th Yorkshire Oaks York 1m4f	WON 7/4F Blandford Stks Curr 1m2f	2nd Prix de l'Opera Long 1m2f
01 Leop 1m4f 1st Maiden Three weeks	Sahara Slew J Oxx 14/1	1/14	3	8-08	65	-	-	-	-
00 Epso 1m4f 16th Oaks Two weeks	Miletrian M Channon 10/1	8/9	3	8-08	67	6th Irish Oaks Curr 1m4f	4th Shergar Cup Ascot 1m4f	4th Yorkshire Oaks York 1m4f	WON 10/1 Park Hill Stks Donc 1m7f
99 Epso 1½m 4th Vodafone Listed Two weeks	Fairy Queen S Bin Suroor 8/1	3/12	3	8-08	71	4th Prix Vermeille Long 1m4f	WON 33/10 Group 2 Long 1m5f	4th Premio Roma Capa 1m2f	-
98 Epso 1m4f 2nd Oaks Two weeks	Bahr S Bin Suroor 13/8F	6/9	3	8-08	67	3rd Irish Oaks Curr 1m4f	5th Prix Vermeille Long 1m4f	3rd Flower Bowl Belm 1m2f	-
97 Epso 1m4f 4th Oaks Two weeks	Yashmak H Cecil 7/2	2/9	3	8-08	74	2nd Irish Oaks Curr 1m4f	WON N/O Flower Bowl Belm 1m2f	-	-
96 Mulh 1m3f 2nd Group 2 One month	Tulipa A Fabre 15/2	10/12	3	8-08	68	8th Prix Vermeille Long 1m4f	*9th Jockey Club Stk Newm 1m4f	*WON N/O Group 2 Siro 1m4f	*2nd Lancashire Oaks Newm 1m4f

12-year median performance rating of the winner: **69** (out of 100)   *next year*

WINNER'S PROFILE Only one filly made her seasonal reappearance here as the majority had been **off the track between two to eight weeks** beforehand. A **top-three outing last time** has been a bonus, with the Epsom Oaks a handy pointer, while two of the three maiden winners beforehand emerged from Ireland.
Winning form was vital, as 11 winners **scored during their previous two runs**, though only Sahara Slew had won over the trip – Silkwood last year became the ninth to have **won between nine and 15 furlongs**.
It paid to **shop for value**, as Bahr in 1998 was the last favourite to oblige, which came via trainer **Saeed Bin Suroor** who had three winners and a runner-up – Teggiano in 2000 – from just eight runners.

FUTURE POINTERS An event that attracts Epsom Oaks runners, but one in which eight winners subsequently flopped in the Irish equivalent – Punctilious and Yashmak went closest.
Overall, Ribblesdale winners have disappointed in this country post-Ascot, four winners found the winner's enclosure again on foreign shores, while Miletrian had to wait until the autumn before stepping down in class to land a Group Three. From a punting viewpoint, it may prove wiser to follow the third-placed runners from the Ribblesdale, as five scored again in the near future this century *(see below)*.

Were Ribblesdale winners profitable to follow on their subsequent three runs?
No – 3 wins from 27 runs returned a loss of - £18.95 to a £1 level stake.

Placed runners' subsequent record (three runs):
Runners-up: 2 wins from 28 runs returned a loss of -£18.33 to a £1 level stake.
1996 Key Changes – Yorkshire Oaks.

Thirds: 9 wins from 36 runs returned a **profit of +£16.00** to a £1 level stake.
2004 Quiff – Yorkshire Oaks, 2003 Mezzo Soprano – Prix Vermeille

FUTURE SUCCESS RATING: ★ ★ ☆ ☆ ☆

GOLD CUP
June 19, Royal Ascot – (Group 1, Class 1, 4yo+) 2m4f

Last run	Winner/Trainer & SP	Draw/Ran	Age	Wght	PR	Next four runs			
07 Leop 1m6f 1st Saval Beg Stks One month	Yeats A O'Brien 8/13F	2/14	6	9-02	82	WON 4/7F Irish St Leger Curr 1m6f	3rd Prix du Cadran Long 2m4f	-	-
06 Wood 1m4f 6th Canadian Int Eight months	Yeats A O'Brien 7/1	8/12	5	9-02	84	WON 10/11F Goodwood Cup Good 2m	2nd Irish St Leger Curr 1m6f	7th Melbourne Cup Flem 2m	*WON 1/3F Vintage Crop Stk Nava 1m5f
05 Long 2m 1st Group 2 One month	Westerner E Lellouche 7/4F	4/17	6	9-02	81	3rd Grosser 'Baden Bade 1m4f	2nd Arc de Triomphe Long 1m4f	5th Hong Kong Vase Sha 1m4f	-
04 Sand 2m 1st Henry II Stks Three weeks	Papineau S Bin Suroor 5/1	4/13	4	9-00	80	*5th Yorkshire Cup York 1m6f	*16th Gold Cup York 2m4f	-	-
03 Sand 2m 1st Henry II Stks One month	Mr Dinos P Cole 3/1	6/12	4	9-00	81	6th Prix du Cadran Long 2m4f	*4th Yorkshire Cup York 1m6f	*2nd Henry II Stks Sand 2m	*6th Gold Cup Ascot 2m4f
02 Sand 2m 8th Henry II Stks Three weeks	Royal Rebel M Johnston 16/1	8/15	6	9-02	75	*5th Sagaro Stks Ascot 2m	**7th Henry II Stks Sand 2m	**4th Gold Cup Ascot 2m4f	**4th Esher Stks Sand 2m
01 Sand 2m 1st Henry II Stks One month	Royal Rebel M Johnston 8/1	10/12	5	9-02	79	6th Goodwood Cup Good 2m	7th Lonsdale Stks York 2m	9th Doncaster Cup Donc 2m2f	4th Prix du Cadran Long 2m4f
00 York 1m6f 1st Yorkshire Cup Two months	Kayf Tara S Bin Suroor 11/8F	6/11	6	9-02	80	-	-	-	-
99 Leop 1m6f 1st Saval Beg Stks One month	Enzeli J Oxx 20/1	16/17	4	9-00	82	4th Irish St Leger Curr 1m6f	*2nd Saval Beg Stks Leop 1m6f	*8th Gold Cup Ascot 2m4f	*WON 15/2 Doncaster Cup Donc 2m2f
98 Sand 2m 3rd Henry II Stks One month	Kayf Tara S Bin Suroor 11/1	17/16	4	9-00	80	5th Goodwood Cup Good 2m	4th Group 2 Deau 1m7f	WON 4/1 Irish St Leger Curr 1m6f	*WON 36/10 Group 2 Long 2m
97 Sand 2m 2nd Henry II Stks One month	Celeric D Morley 11/2	2/13	5	9-02	78	5th Princess of Wales' Newm 1m4f	4th Lonsdale Stks York 2m	2nd Prix du Cadran Long 2m4f	*8th Jockey Club Stks Newm 1m4f
96 York 1m6f 1st Yorkshire Cup Two months	Classic Cliche S Bin Suroor 3/1	7/7	4	9-00	74	2nd King George VI Ascot 1m4f	15th Arc de Triomphe Long 1m4f	*9th Yorkshire Cup York 1m6f	*2nd Gold Cup Ascot 2m4f

12-year median performance rating of the winner: **80** (out of 100) *(2005 York) *next year **two years*

WINNER'S PROFILE The majority raced within the previous two months, Sandown's **Henry II Stakes** provided six winners – two scored there – while two **Yorkshire Cup** winners also followed up here. The two individual Irish winners here both won the Saval Beg Stakes at Leopardstown, including Yeats last year.

A **light campaign** was ideal with a maximum of two runs prior to Ascot, while those to have **already achieved Group Two success** are preferred. Age has been of massive importance as **four to six-year-olds** dominated and it was no surprise to see eight-year-old Sergeant Cecil trail home last in 2007.

Trainer **Saeed Bin Suroor** leads the way with four winners, while **Mark Johnston** and **Aidan O'Brien** have sent out a dual winner each.

FUTURE POINTERS Yeats not only became a dual winner of Royal Ascot's showpiece event last year, but he was also able to follow up post-Ascot for the second time, unlike 10 previous winners who flopped next time out. Aidan O'Brien's star also landed the Irish St Leger last year – as did Kayf Tara in 1998 – which proved to be the best route for Gold Cup winners, while a year earlier, he lifted the Goodwood Cup, a race that eluded two others. In fact, it actually paid to follow the placed runners from the Gold Cup in the Goodwood Cup, runners-up in particular have performed well at the Sussex venue *(see below)*.

Were Gold Cup winners profitable to follow on their subsequent three runs?
No – 3 wins from 31 runs returned a loss of -22.51 to a £1 level stake.

Placed runners' subsequent record (three runs):
Runners-up: 14 wins from 34 runs returned a **profit of +17.31** to a £1 level stake.
2005 Distinction – Goodwood Cup, 2004 Westerner – Prix du Cadran, 2003 Persian Punch – Goodwood Cup,
2002 Vinnie Roe – Irish St Leger, 2001 Persian Punch – Goodwood Cup, Lonsdale Stakes,
1998 Double Trigger – Goodwood Cup, Doncaster Cup, 1996 Double Trigger – Doncaster Cup

Thirds: 5 wins from 28 runs returned a loss of –£14.07 to a £1 level stake.
2004 Darasim – Goodwood Cup, 1999 Kayf Tara – Goodwood Cup, Irish St Leger

FUTURE SUCCESS RATING: ★ ★ ★ ☆ ☆

BRITANNIA STAKES
June 19, Royal Ascot – (Heritage Handicap, Class 2, 3yo) 1m

Last run	Winner/ Trainer & SP	Draw/ Ran	Age	Wght	PR	Next four runs			
07 Wind 1m 3rd Cond Stks *Two months*	Eddie Jock M Bell 33/1	29/30	3	9-07	70	7th Conds Stks Newm 1m	9th Thoroughbred Stk Good 1m	3rd Handicap Donc 1m	-
06 Hayd 1m 2nd Silver Bowl Hcp *One month*	Sir Gerard J Fanshawe 9/2F	2/30	3	8-12	71	4th Totesport Hcp Good 1m	*WON 6/4F Handicap Nad Al 1m	*6th Ya Hala Hcp Nad Al 1m1f	*10th Zabeel Mile Nad Al 1m
05 Ches 1m 2nd Stanleybet Hcp *Two months*	Mostashaar Sir M Stoute 10/3F	1/21	3	9-01	72	4th Listed Ling 1m	4th Listed Good 1m	8th City of York York 7f	2nd Conds Stks Warw 7f
04 Epsom 7f 2nd Vodafone Hcp *Two weeks*	Mandobi A Stewart 8/1	3/27	3	8-12	64	2nd Thoroughbred St Good 1m	3rd Handicap Nad Al 7f	*5th G Desert Hcp Nad Al 1m	*7th San Siro Hcp Nad Al 1m
03 York 7f 3rd W Hill Hcp *Two months*	New Seeker C Cox 16/1	27/29	3	8-08	70	WON 15/2 International Hp Ascot 7f	*2nd Paradise Stks Ascot 1m	*4th B Palace Hcp Ascot 7f	*8th Silver Trophy Ascot 1m
02 Ayr 1m 2nd Class Stks *Three weeks*	Pentecost I Balding 25/1	11/31	3	8-10	68	5th Scoop6 Hcp Sand 1m	13th International Hcp Ascot 7f	18th W Hill Mile Hcp Good 1m	16th Brad & Bing Hcp York 1m
01 Newb 7f 1st Handicap *Two weeks*	Analyser J Gosden 14/1	12/29	3	8-03	67	2nd Ladbroke Hcp Newb 1m	9th W Hill Mile Hcp Good 1m	*2nd University Cup King 1m2f	-
00 Newb 1m 1st Class Stks *Two weeks*	El Gran Papa J Gosden 4/1F	15/32	3	8-04	68	12th Rio Hcp Sand 7f	2nd International Hcp Ascot 7f	10th W Hill Mile Hcp Good 1m	WON 2/1F Conds Stks Donc 1m
99 Leic 7f 3rd Conds Stks *Two weeks*	Pythios H Cecil 10/1JF	1/32	3	9-00	67	*14th Vodafone Hcp Epsom 1½m	*4th Royal Hunt Cup Ascot 1m	*2nd Conds Stks Donc 1m	*15th W Hill Mile Hcp Good 1m
98 Chest 1m 3rd Earl Hcp *Two months*	Plan-B J Gosden 8/1	30/31	3	8-07	68	2nd Handicap Newm 1m	*15th Victoria Cup Ascot 7f	*6th Hambleton Hcp York 1m	*2nd Royal Hunt Cup Ascot 1m
97 Epso 1m2f 4th Vodafone Hcp *Two weeks*	Fly To The Stars M Johnston 20/1	14/28	3	9-03	71	16th Hong Kong Hcp Sand 1m	WON 14/1 Golden Mile Good 1m	2nd Listed Deau 1m	3rd Topkapi Trophy Veli 1m
96 Good 1m1f 1st Maiden *One month*	North Song J Gosden 14/1	23/31	3	8-01	64	2nd Handicap Newm 1m	3rd Rated Hcp Newm 1m	2nd Brad & Bing Hcp York 1m	3rd Handicap Good 1m1f

12-year median performance rating of the winner: **68** (out of 100) *next year*

WINNER'S PROFILE Every winner had a **top-four finish last time** and a recent victory was a bonus, although only two had winning form over a mile. Those on the **light side of 9st** held sway until Eddie Jock shook that trend last year, and in the process became only the second horse to score with an official rating in excess of 100 – **ideal official rating was between 83 and 95.**
Trainer **John Gosden** won it four times since 1996, using Newbury to prepare two of them.

FUTURE POINTERS A dismal future record from winners of this highly competitive handicap, considering they are often branded by pundits as possible Group performers after triumphing here – only three scored again on their next two starts. Even more disappointing was that the majority stuck to handicaps and weren't asked to improve in Pattern company, though four did finish second in decent handicaps, and New Seeker won the International Handicap next time out. Fly To The Stars also won a big handicap in the 1997 Golden Mile at Glorious Goodwood. Overall, Britannia winners and placed runners haven't delivered as much as they promised despite some of the above par winners scoring, but a long-term subsequent level stakes loss from the first four home *(see below)* doesn't encourage a big wager next time out.

Were Britannia winners profitable to follow on their subsequent three runs?
No – 3 wins from 36 runs returned a loss of -£13.00 to a £1 level stake.

Placed runners' subsequent record (three runs):
Runners-up: 7 wins from 30 runs returned a loss of -£4.35 to a £1 level stake.
2001 Olympic Express – Group One Hong Kong Mile, 2000 Sign Of Hope – Group Two abroad

Thirds: 3 wins from 27 runs returned a loss of -£15.59 to a £1 level stake.
2003 Court Masterpiece – Listed Thoroughbred Stakes

Fourths: 3 wins from 33 runs returned a loss of -£17.62 to a £1 level stake.
2006 Smart Enough – York Handicap

FUTURE SUCCESS RATING: ★★☆☆☆

KING GEORGE V STAKES

June 19, Royal Ascot – (Heritage Handicap, Class 2, 3yo) 1m4f

Last run	Winner/Trainer & SP	Draw/Ran	Age	Wght	PR	Next four runs			
07 Hayd 1m4f 3rd / Maiden / *One month*	**Heron Bay** G Wragg 20/1	5/19	3	8-11	63	9th Gordon Stks Good 1m4f	8th Great Voltigeur York 1m4f	14th November Hcp Donc 1m4f	-
06 Sand 1m2f 1st / Betfred Hcp / *Two months*	**Linas Selection** M Johnston 9/2	7/19	3	8-09	70	WON 8/11F Silver Cup Hcp York 1m6f	3rd Gordon Stks Good 1m4f	-	-
05 Ripo 1m1f 1st / Maiden / *Two months*	**Munsef** J Dunlop 14/1	6/14	3	8-07	65	WON 8/1 Godolphin Stks Newm 1m4f	3rd St Simon Stks Newb 1m4f	*2nd John Porter Newb 1m4f	*2nd Jockey Club Stks Newm 1m4f
04 Hayd 1m4f 3rd / Rated Hcp / *Two weeks*	**Admiral** Sir M Stoute 9/1	14/17	3	8-03	61	11th Heritage Hcp Good 1m4f	*5th Nov Hdle Donc 2m1f	*WON 4/5F Maiden Hdle Muss 2m	*12th Triumph Hdle Chel 2m1f
03 Wind 1m4f 2nd / Class Stks / *Three weeks*	**Fantastic Love** M Johnston 10/1	20/20	3	8-11	62	*8th Summer Hcp Good 1m2f	*7th Ebor York 1m6f	*3rd Mallard Hcp Donc 1m7f	*2nd Godolphin Stks Newm 1m4f
02 Epsom 1m2f 2nd / Vodafone Hcp / *Two weeks*	**Systematic** M Johnston 9/1	1/19	3	8-12	66	WON 4/11F Class Stks Newb 1m4f	5th Great Voltigeur York 1m4f	WON 3/1 Troy Stks Donc 1m4f	WON 1/2F Cumberland Lodge Ascot 1m4f
01 Hayd 1m4f 1st / Maiden / *Two months*	**Beekeeper** Sir M Stoute 14/1	5/20	3	9-07	70	4th Great Voltigeur York 1m4f	*9th Henry II Sand 2m	*WON 7/2 Conds Stks Donc 1m2f	*6th Caulfield Cup Caul 1m4f
00 Good 1m1f 2nd / Tote Hcp / *One month*	**Give The Slip** Mrs A Perrett 8/1	5/16	3	9-04	69	4th Gordon Stks Good 1m4f	WON 8/1 Ebor York 1m6f	*WON N/O Group 3 Nad Al 1m4f	*5th Sheema Classic Nad Al 1m4f
99 Hayd 1m3f 2nd / Maiden / *Three weeks*	**Elmutabaki** B Hills 9/1	7/19	3	8-12	68	WON 6/5F Listed Trophy Hayd 1m4f	5th Great Voltigeur York 1m4f	8th St Leger Donc 1m6f	*5th Ormonde Stks Ches 1m5f
98 Good 1m4f 1st / Showcase Hcp / *Three months*	**Double Classic** Sir M Stoute 4/1F	7/17	3	8-12	64	**3rd Handicap Abu 1m4f	***3rd Handicap Nad Al 1m4f	-	-
97 Hayd 1m3f 1st / Maiden / *One month*	**Heritage** J Gosden 15/2	14/20	3	8-06	63	7th Old Newton Cup Hayd 1m4f	7th Rated Hcp York 1m4f	4th Rated Hcp Newm 1m4f	18th November Hcp Donc 1m4f
96 Newb 1m4f 1st / London Cup Hcp / *Two months*	**Samraan** J Dunlop 14/1	17/20	3	9-03	64	4th Listed Trophy Hayd 1m4f	6th Gordon Stks Good 1m4f	4th Geoffrey Freer Newb 1m5f	WON 2/1 Conds Stks Sali 1m6f

12-year median performance rating of the winner: **65** (out of 100) *next year **two years ***three years
(2005 York), italic = jumps

WINNER'S PROFILE Every winner arrived in-form having **finished in the first three last time out**, the majority already won that term, although Heron Bay was a rare maiden to break his duck last year. It proved difficult to shoulder weight, and 11 winners were **officially rated 95 or lower**, while favourites have a poor record – only Double Classic obliged in 1998. He was also trained by **Sir Michael Stoute**, who along with **Mark Johnston**, sent out six between them, while **John Dunlop** had two and it pays to stick with the big yards.

FUTURE POINTERS This handicap brings together a group of improving three-year-olds, and winners on the day have a decent record post-Ascot as four scored next time out – two in Listed grade.
Not many made an immediate impact in Group events, though, as three failed in the Group Three Gordon Stakes, the same number that came unstuck in the Great Voltigeur. However, Give The Slip went on to land another valuable handicap in the 2000 Ebor at York, and those that recorded above par performance ratings here managed to take care of themselves in the correct grade without shooting too high.

Were King George V winners profitable to follow on their subsequent three runs?
Yes – 9 wins from 34 runs returned a **profit of +0.58** to a £1 level stake.

Placed runners' subsequent record (three runs):
Runners-up: 5 wins from 32 runs returned a loss of -£15.93 to a £1 level stake.
2004 Maraahel – Group Three Gordon Stakes

Thirds: 6 wins from 33 runs returned a loss of -£10.67 to a £1 level stake.
2002 Leadership – Motability Handicap, 2000 Film Script – Listed event, 1998 Blueprint – Melrose Handicap

Fourths: 1 win from 30 runs returned a loss of -£24.00 to a £1 level stake.
1997 Memorise – Cambridge Handicap (Newmarket July meeting)

FUTURE SUCCESS RATING: ★ ★ ★ ☆ ☆

KING EDWARD VII STAKES
June 20, Royal Ascot – (Group 2, Class 1, 3yo) 1m4f

Last run	Winner/Trainer & SP	Draw/Ran	Age	Wght	PR	Next four runs			
07 Hami 1m3f 1st Glasgow Stks Two months	Boscobel M Johnston 7/1	3/9	3	8-12	72	4th Irish Derby Curr 1m4f	9th Great Voltigeur York 1m4f	-	-
06 Epso 1m4f 10th Derby Three weeks	Papal Bull Sir M Stoute 5/4F	4/9	3	8-12	75	8th Great Voltigeur York 1m4f	5th Prix Niel Long 1m4f	*4th Jockey Club Stk Newm 1m4f	*5th Brigadier Gerard Sand 1m2f
05 Sain 1m2f 2nd Group 2 Two months	Plea Bargain J Gosden 9/2	4/5	3	8-11	69	4th Grand Prix 'Paris Long 1m4f	-	-	-
04 Chan 1m4f 8th Prix'Jockey Club Two weeks	Five Dynasties A O'Brien 11/4F	7/5	3	8-11	70	8th Irish Derby Curr 1m4f	-	-	-
03 Good 1m3f 1st Predominate One month	High Accolade M Tregoning 5/2F	8/8	3	8-11	69	6th Princess of Wales' Newm 1m4f	2nd Gordon Stks Good 1m4	6th Great Voltigeur York 1m4f	2nd St Leger Donc 1m6f
02 York 1m2f 3rd Dante Stks Two months	Balakheri Sir M Stoute 11/4F	2/7	3	8-10	75	5th Irish Derby Curr 1m4f	6th St Leger Donc 1m6f	*6th Jockey Club Stk Newm 1m4f	*7th Yorkshire Cup York 1m6f
01 Epso 1m4f 5th Derby Two weeks	Storming Home B Hills 9/2	11/12	3	8-08	72	4th King George VI Ascot 1m4f	2nd Great Voltigeur York 1m4f	7th Prix Niel Long 1m4f	*3rd Jockey Club Stk Newm 1m4f
00 Newm 1m2f 2nd Fairway Stks Two weeks	Subtle Power H Cecil 7/4F	5/7	3	8-08	76	5th Great Voltigeur York 1m4f	7th Grade 1 Belm 1m4f	10th Breeders' Cup Chur 1m4f	*WON N/O Grade 1 Gulf 1m3f
99 Donc 1m2f 1st Conds Stks Three months	Mutafaweq S bin Suroor 4/1F	9/10	3	8-08	75	5th Irish Derby Curr 1m4f	4th Great Voltigeur York 1m4f	WON 11/2 St Leger Donc 1m6½f	*3rd Tatts Gold Cup Curr 1m3f
98 Newm 1m2f 1st Fairway Stks Two weeks	Royal Anthem H Cecil 9/4F	1/10	3	8-08	77	3rd King George VI Ascot 1m4f	WON 7/4 Canadian Int Wood 1m4f	7th Breeders' Cup Chur 1m4f	*2nd Coronation Cup Epso 1m4f
97 York 1m2f 4th Dante Stks Two months	Kingfisher Mill Mrs J Cecil 9/4F	2/5	3	8-08	74	8th King George VI Ascot 1m4f	3rd Great Voltigeur York 1m4f	WON 7/2 Cumberland Lodge Ascot 1m4f	*4th Jockey Club Stk Newm 1m4f
96 Newb 1m2f 10th Maiden Two months	Amfortas C Brittain 66/1	6/7	3	8-08	68	13th Irish Derby Curr 1m4f	-	-	-

12-year median performance rating of the winner: **73** (out of 100)   *(2005 York), *next year*

WINNER'S PROFILE The key to finding the winner is siding with a performer yet to have shown their full hand in these conditions, the majority winless over the trip or in Group company.

Those with **winning form over 10 and 11 furlongs** in non-Pattern company did very well – 10 of the last 11 also **won that season** – while three of the last seven winners arrived unplaced from a Derby.

Amfortas took this from out of the blue in 1996 – the last outsider to triumph – and it has proven wiser to follow fancied runners from the **front two in the betting** as favourites actually returned a healthy profit.

Trainers **Henry Cecil** and **Sir Michael Stoute** both tasted victory twice from five and 10 runners respectively.

FUTURE POINTERS It has been 20 years since the winner of the King Edward VII Stakes followed up next time out – that honour fell to Sheriff's Star in the 1988 Great Voltigeur – and Boscobel last year became the latest subsequent flop in the Irish Derby; exchange layers take note. Four more also failed to figure at The Curragh, while three were outclassed in the King George VI, and six missed out in the Great Voltigeur.

A step up in trip helped Mutafaweq find the necessary improvement to secure Group One glory in the 1999 St Leger, a race that hasn't been oversubscribed by King Edward winners, as only two others took up an entry in the final Classic, where they finished runner-up and fifth, while three placed runners from here went on to triumph at Doncaster including Lucarno last year *(see below)*.

Were King Edward VII winners profitable to follow on their subsequent three runs?
3 wins from 29 runs returned a loss of -£15.25 to a £1 level stake.

Placed runners' subsequent record (three runs):
Runners-up: 3 wins from 33 runs returned a loss of £-17.00 to a £1 level stake.
2007 Lucarno – Great Voltigeur, St Leger, 2002 Bollin Eric – St Leger

Thirds: 4 wins from 16 runs returned a **profit of +£1.37** to a £1 level stake.
2007 Yellowstone – Gordon Stakes, 2006 Sixties Icon – Gordon Stakes, St Leger, 1998 Scorned – Arc Trial

FUTURE SUCCESS RATING: ★ ★ ☆ ☆ ☆

CORONATION STAKES
June 20, Royal Ascot – (Group 1, Class 1, 3yo) 1m

Last run	Winner/ Trainer & SP	Draw/ Ran	Age	Wght	PR	Next four runs			
07 Newm 1m 5th 1,000 Guineas Two months	Indian Ink R Hannon 8/1	2/13	3	9-00	81	-	-	-	-
06 Newm 1m 12th 1,000 Guineas Two months	Nannina J Gosden 6/1JF	13/15	3	9-00	77	2nd Falmouth Newm 1m	3rd Nassau Good 1m2f	4th Matron Stks Leop 1m	5th Prix de l'Opera Long 1m2f
05 Curr 1m 5th Irish 1,000 Guin One month	Maids Causeway B Hills 9/2	9/10	3	9-00	76	7th Sun Chariot Newm 1m	-	-	-
04 Curr 1m 1st Irish 1,000 Guin One month	Attraction M Johnston 6/4F	10/11	3	9-00	82	2nd Falmouth Newm 1m	10th Jacques' Marois Deau 1m	2nd Matron Stks Leop 1m	WON 11/4 Sun Chariot Newm 1m
03 Newm 1m 1st 1,000 Guineas Two months	Russian Rhythm Sir M Stoute 4/7F	11/9	3	9-00	86	WON 4/5F Nassau Good 1m2f	2nd Q Elizabeth II Ascot 1m	5th Champion Stks Newm 1m2f	*WON 3/1 Lockinge Newb 1m
02 Long 1m 3rd Poule 'Pouliches Two months	Sophisticat A O'Brien 11/2	3/11	3	9-00	76	6th Matron Stks Leop 1m	-	-	-
01 Chan 1m 1st Prix Sandringham Three weeks	Banks Hill A Fabre 4/1JF	4/13	3	9-00	82	2nd Jacques' Marois Deau 1m	WON 6/1 Breeders' Cup Belm 1m2f	*3rd Prix d'Ispahan Long 1m1f	*3rd Prince of Wales' Ascot 1m2f
00 Curr 1m 1st Irish 1,000 Guin One month	Crimplene C Brittain 4/1JF	6/9	3	9-00	83	WON 7/4F Nassau Good 1m2f	4th Jacques' Marois Deau 1m	8th Q Elizabeth II Ascot 1m	4th Breeders' Cup Chur 1m1f
99 Good 1m 2nd Conqueror Stks One month	Balisada G Wragg 16/1	8/9	3	9-00	77	2nd Falmouth Newm 1m	4th Sussex Good 1m	4th Q Elizabeth II Ascot 1m	-
98 Newm 1m 3rd 1,000 Guineas Two months	Exclusive Sir M Stoute 5/1	10/9	3	9-00	75	6th Juddmonte Int York 1m2f	-	-	-
97 Newm 1m 13th 1,000 Guineas Two months	Rebecca Sharp G Wragg 25/1	3/6	3	9-00	80	6th Falmouth Newm 1m	2nd Group 2 Deau 1m	7th Prix du Moulin Long 1m	2nd Q Elizabeth II Ascot 1m
96 Long 1m 2nd Poule 'Pouliches Two months	Shake The Yoke E Lellouche EvensF	4/7	3	9-00	74	3rd Prix du Moulin Long 1m	2nd Grade 1 Keen 1m1f	-	-

12-year median performance rating of the winner:	79 (out of 100)	*next year

WINNER'S PROFILE Every winner bar Balisada had **run in either the English, Irish or French 1,000 Guineas**, though not many raced in two prior to Ascot unlike Finsceal Beo, who last year failed to emulate Attraction's hat-trick here after landing both English and Irish versions. Winners of the French Guineas are worth swerving, however – eight sunk since 1996 – including Darjina in third last year, and it pays to stick with the placed Longchamp runners, while one German winner from three scored (Crimplene in 2000 prior to her Irish success).
The best fillies came out on top with the last five winners all **officially rated in excess of 111** and 10 winners emerged from the **first four in the betting**, which helps eliminate a few.
Trainers **Sir Michael Stoute** and **Geoff Wragg** are the only two to appear more than once on the recent roll of honour, while Aidan O'Brien's should be treated with caution as he has only struck once in over a dozen attempts.

FUTURE POINTERS An event that has attracted competitive double-figure fields since the Millennium and last year's renewal went a long way to upholding the strength of the race as it drew together the English, French and German 1,000 Guineas title-holders. However, one negative surrounding Coronation winners was that over half failed to score again that season, although amongst that group were a number of below par victors with low performance ratings (PR). The above par winners, though, did shine again in Attraction, Banks Hill, Russian Rhythm and Crimplene, the latter pair followed up in the Nassau Stakes, an event that hasn't been oversubscribed and only Naninna failed to cope with the rise in trip since 1996.
Three Group Ones to have been less kind to Coronation winners were the Falmouth, Matron, and QEII Stakes.

Were Coronation Stakes winners profitable to follow on their subsequent three runs?
No – 3 wins from 26 runs returned a loss of -£14.45 to a £1 level stake.

Placed runners' subsequent record (three runs):
Runners-up: 4 wins from 30 runs returned a loss of -£19.35 to a £1 level stake.
2007 Mi Emma – German Group Two, 1996 Last Second – Nassau Stakes, Sun Chariot Stakes
Thirds: 7 wins from 26 runs returned a **profit of +£4.06 to a £1 level stake**
2007 Darjina – Prix d'Astrate, Prix du Moulin, 2004 Red Bloom – Strensall Stakes, 1998 Winona – Irish Oaks

FUTURE SUCCESS RATING: ★ ★ ★ ★ ★

QUEEN'S VASE
June 20, Royal Ascot – (Group 3, Class 1, 3yo) 2m

Last run	Winner/Trainer & SP	Draw/Ran	Age	Wght	PR	Next four runs			
07 Epso 1m4f 11th Derby *Three weeks*	Mahler A O'Brien 7/1	11/15	3	9-01	62	5th Great Voltigeur York 1m4f	2nd St Leger Donc 1m6½f	3rd Melbourne Cup Flem 2m	-
06 Hayd 1m4f 1st Handicap *Two weeks*	Soapy Danger M Johnston 4/1	10/11	3	9-01	69	**WON 5/1 Princess of Wales' Newm 1m4f**	5th Great Voltigeur York 1m4f	-	-
05 Ling 1m3f 3rd Derby Trial *Two months*	Melrose Avenue M Johnston 4/1	5/10	3	8-11	66	6th Great Voltigeur York 1m4f	8th Glorious Stks Good 1m4f	-	-
04 Newm 1m2f 2nd Fairway Stks *One month*	Duke Of Venice S Bin Suroor 9/2	6/10	3	8-11	65	5th Gordon Stks Good 1m4f	10th Lonsdale Stks York 2m	*16th Henry II Sand 2m	*6th Godolphin Stks Newm 1m4f
03 Ling 1m4f 3rd Derby Trial *Two months*	Shanty Star M Johnston 7/2F	10/12	3	8-11	64	*9th Yorkshire Cup York 1m6f	*PU Henry II Sand 2m	*3rd Godolphin Stks Newm 1m4f	*9th Jockey Club Cup Newm 2m
02 Ling 1m4f 4th Derby Trial *Two months*	Mamool S Bin Suroor 9/1	4/14	3	8-11	70	5th Deutsches Derby Hamb 1m4f	4th St Leger Donc 1m6½f	*WON N/O Handicap Nad Al 1m6f	*WON 11/2 Yorkshire Cup York 1m6f
01 York 1m6f 1st Conds Stks *One month*	And Beyond M Johnston 11/1	16/16	3	8-11	66	7th St Leger Donc 1m6½f	*7th Henry II Sand 2m	*WON N/O Listed Chan 1m7f	*4th Goodwood Cup Good 2m
00 Newm 1m4f 1st Maiden *Three weeks*	Dalampour Sir M Stoute 3/1F	13/13	3	8-11	63	3rd Great Voltigeur York 1m4f	5th St Leger Donc 1m6½f	*3rd John Porter Newb 1m4f	*4th Yorkshire Cup York 1m6f
99 Thir 1m4f 1st Maiden *Two months*	Endorsement H Cecil 5/1	10/11	3	8-06	61	6th Group 2 Deau 1m6f	*10th Gold Cup Ascot 2m4f	*8th Lancashire Oaks Hayd 1m4f	*6th Aphrodite Stks Newm 1m4f
98 Hami 1m4f 1st Maiden *Two months*	Maridpour Sir M Stoute 6/1	5/8	3	8-11	64	17th Northumberland Newc 2m	3rd Lonsdale Stks York 2m	7th Group 3 Long 1m7f	*8th Sagaro Stks Ascot 2m
97 York 1m6f 2nd Conds Stks *Two months*	Windsor Castle P Cole 9/2	12/11	3	8-11	61	**WON 10/1 Northumberland Newc 2m**	3rd Lonsdale Stks York 2m	5th St Leger Donc 1m6½f	*4th Sagaro Stks Newm 2m
96 Leop 1m2f 1st Maiden *One month*	Gordi D Weld 7/1	4/14	3	8-11	60	10th St Leger Donc 1m6½f	6th Irish St Leger Curr 1m6f	*3rd Stakes Leop 1m4f	*4th Curragh Cup Leop 1m6f

12-year median performance rating of the winner: **64** (out of 100) *(2005 York), *next year*

WINNER'S PROFILE A **recent solid run** has proven vital – last year's winner was unplaced in the Derby previously – with the ideal preparation between **three weeks to two months off the track**.
Seven winners arrived having either **won their maiden** or had **run in the Lingfield Derby Trial**. Mahler last year became the tenth horse since 1996 to have **already won that season**, and emerged from the ideal place in the market **between 3/1 and 7/1** – every winner was in the **first six of the betting**.
Despite the distance of the race, those drawn out wide from the low stalls have struggled.
On the training front, the big boys came to the fore, **Mark Johnston**, **Sir Michael Stoute** and **Saeed Bin Suroor** responsible for eight of the last 10 – the former boasts the best record with four winners from 10 runners.

FUTURE POINTERS As a pointer to some of the future staying events, the Queen's Vase has been of limited value, with only Windsor Castle going on to land the Northumberland, although Soapy Danger followed up in the Princess of Wales's back over a mile-and-a-half, while Mamool scooped the Yorkshire Cup the following year. Those that attempted events such as the Great Voltigeur, Lonsdale Cup/Stakes, and St Leger came up short.

Were Queen's Vase winners profitable to follow on their subsequent three runs?
No – 4 wins from 34 runs returned a loss of -£15.00 to a £1 level stake.

Placed runners' subsequent record (three runs):
Runners-up: 5 wins from 33 runs returned a loss of -£23.38 to a £1 level stake.
1997 Three Cheers – Bahrain Trophy

Thirds: 7 wins from 33 runs returned a loss of -£0.49 to a £1 level stake.
1999 Compton Ace – Gordon Stakes, 1998 Capri – Cumberland Lodge, 1996 Persian Punch – Bahrain Trophy

FUTURE SUCCESS RATING: ★★ ☆ ☆ ☆

CHESHAM STAKES
June 21, Royal Ascot – (Listed, Class 1, 2yo) 7f

Last run	Winner/ Trainer & SP	Draw/ Ran	Age	Wght	PR	Next four runs			
07 Newc 6f 1st Maiden *Three weeks*	**Maze** B Smart 11/2	10/12	2	9-03	60	6th Solario Stks Sand 7f	10th Champagne Stk Donc 7f	2nd Rockingham Stks York 6f	7th Doncaster Stks Donc 7f
06 Newb 6f 3rd Maiden *Two months*	**Champain** M Jarvis 7/2	11/11	2	9-03	59	7th Superlative Stks Newm 7f	4th Royal Lodge Ascot 1m	2nd Silver Tankard Pont 1m	*10th Conds Stks Nad Al 7f
05 Newb 6f 1st Maiden *One month*	**Championship Point** M Channon 4/1	10/12	2	9-00	61	2nd Listed Deau 1m	*WON 4/5F Predominate St Good 1m3f	*11th Derby Epsom 1m4f	*9th Great Voltigeur York 1m4f
04 Newb 6f 1st Maiden *Two weeks*	**Whazzat** B Hills 7/1	3/11	2	8-07	57	*6th Superior Mile Hayd 1m	*12th Champion Stks Newm 1m2f	*2nd Fillies' Listed Donc 1m2f	*8th Listed Sain 1m5f
03 Donc 6f 1st Maiden *One month*	**Pearl Of Love** M Johnston 11/10F	4/13	2	9-00	62	WON 5/4F Futurity Stks Curr 7f	3rd National Stks Curr 7f	WON 4/5F Gran Criterium Siro 1m	*7th Jean Prat Chan 1m1f
02 Ayr 6f 1st Novice Stks *Three weeks*	**Helm Bank** M Johnston 25/1	1/12	2	9-00	60	*9th Dante Stks York 1m2f	*11th Silver Bowl Hcp Hayd 1m	*5th Rated Hcp Hayd 1m4f	*2nd Britannia Stks Ascot 1m
01 Newm 6f 1st Maiden *Two months*	**Seba** D Loder 3/1F	1/11	2	8-09	55	9th Moyglare Stud Curr 7f	5th May Hill Stks Donc 1m	*2nd Conds Stks Nad Al 1m	*2nd Mile Stakes Nad Al 1m
00 Ayr 6f 1st Maiden *Three weeks*	**Celtic Silence** M Johnston 15/8F	7/15	2	8-12	58	*4th UAE Derby Nad Al 1m1f	*2nd Dante Stks York 1m2f	**2nd Listed Nad Al 1m2f	**3rd Group 3 Nad Al 1m4f
99 Gowr 7f 1st Maiden *One month*	**Bach** A O'Brien 5/2	5/7	2	8-12	63	*WON 11/10 2,000 Guin Trial Leop 1m	2nd Derby Trial Leop 1m2f	*2nd Jean Prat Chan 1m1f	**2nd Mooresbridge St Curr f
98 Good 6f 2nd Maiden *One month*	**Rhapsodist** J Gosden 6/1	8/10	2	8-12	60	2nd Superlative Stks Newm 7f	7th Vintage Stks Good 7f	3rd Group 3 Chan 1m	*2nd Conds Stks Donc 1m2f
97 Hayd 6f 1st Maiden *Two weeks*	**Central Park** P Cole 7/1	6/12	2	9-00	64	WON 5/4F Vintage Stks Good 7f	7th Dewhurst Stks Newm 7f	*9th 2,000 Guineas Newm 1m	*WON 4/1 Derby Italiano Capa 1m4f
96 (Unraced)	**Shamikh** S Bin Suroor 8/1	4/12	2	8-12	54	*14th 2,000 Guineas Newm 1m	-	-	-

12-year median performance rating of the winner: **59** (out of 100)   *(2005 York) *next year **two years*

WINNER'S PROFILE Clues are hard to pin down, although every winner had a **maximum of just two outings** and it paid to stick with those that arrived following a good run, especially **winners of maidens and novice stakes**. Those yet to have scored triumphed on two occasions but they are best ignored – seven qualifiers lost last year – as are outsiders, 11 emerged from the **first three or four in the betting**.
Trainer Bryan Smart's juveniles have done well at Royal Ascot in recent years, while **Mark Johnston** took this event three times from 10 runners.

FUTURE POINTERS A juvenile event that has provided a decent stepping stone for those with middle-distance blood, although only two winners since 1996 actually went on to score over that sort of trip, while two others delivered at around a mile. No winner scooped a British Classic over the last 20 years and only the 1997 victor, Central Park, scored in that sphere when he took the Italian Derby a year later. However, one Classic winner did emerge from the Chesham in Cape Verdi, who was second to Central Park in a very hot 1997 renewal – resulted in the best performance rating (PR) – before 1,000 Guineas glory at Newmarket in 1998.
It also has to be mentioned that Wilko finished third here in 2004 before Breeders' Cup glory later that campaign, although from a punting angle, it paid to stick with the runners-up from the Chesham *(see below)*.

Were Chesham winners profitable to follow on their subsequent three runs?
No – 5 wins from 34 runs returned a loss of -£23.80 to a £1 level stake.

Placed runners' subsequent record (three runs):
Runners-up: 11 wins from 33 runs returned a **profit of +£2.56** to a £1 level stake.
2000 Baaridd – Listed Ripon Champion 2yo Trophy, 1998 Compton Admiral – Craven, 1997 Cape Verdi – Lowther, 1,000 Guineas, 1996 State Fair – Washington Singer Stakes

Thirds: 3 wins from 31 runs returned a loss of -£25.39 to a £1 level stake.

FUTURE SUCCESS RATING: ★ ★ ☆ ☆ ☆

HARDWICKE STAKES

June 21, Royal Ascot – (Group 2, Class 1, 4yo+) 1m4f

Last run	Winner/ Trainer & SP	Draw/ Ran	Age	Wght	PR	Next four runs			
07 Epso 1m4f 3rd Coronation Cup One month	**Maraahel** Sir M Stoute 10/3	4/7	6	9-00	77	3rd King George VI Ascot 1m4f	5th Irish Champion Leop 1m2f	10th Champion Stks Newm 1m2f	-
06 Ches 1m2f 1st Huxley Stks Two months	**Maraahel** Sir M Stoute 9/2	6/8	5	9-00	79	5th King George VI Ascot 1m4f	2nd Juddmonte Int York 1m2f	6th Champion Stks Newm 1m2f	5th Hong Kong Vase Sha 1m4f
05 Epso 1m4f 5th Coronation Cup One month	**Bandari** M Johnston 10/1	5/6	6	8-09	82	2nd KolnBonn Colo 1m4f	4th September Stks Newm 1m4f	3rd Jockey Club Stk Newm 1m4f	*6th Brigadier Gerard Sand 1m2f
04 Epso 1m4f 2nd Coronation Cup One month	**Doyen** S Bin Suroor 6/5F	7/6	4	8-09	87	**WON 11/10F King George VI Ascot 1m4f**	7th Irish Champion Leop 1m2f	7th Champion Stks Newm 1m2f	*5th Hardwicke York 1m4f
03 Sand 1m2f 3rd Brigadier Gerard One month	**Indian Creek** D Elsworth 14/1	3/9	5	8-09	76	5th Juddmonte Int York 1m2f	3rd September Stks Newm 1m4f	3rd Cumb'land Lodge Ascot 1m4f	3rd Champion Stks Newm 1m2f
02 Epso 1m4f 3rd Coronation Cup One month	**Zindabad** M Johnston 4/1	1/7	6	8-12	81	3rd King George VI Ascot 1m4f	5th Canadian Int Wood 1m4f	*14th Sheema Classic Nad Al 1m4f	*4th Yorkshire Cup York 1m6f
01 Newb 1m5f 2nd Ashton Stks Two months	**Sandmason** H Cecil 12/1	1/7	4	8-09	80	8th Princess of Wales Newm 1m4f	*8th Group 1 Caul 1m1f	*17th Group 1 Rand 1m4f	*23rd Melbourne Cup Flem 2m
00 Toky 1m4f 9th Japan Cup Seven months	**Fruits Of Love** M Johnston 9/2	11/9	5	8-12	83	3rd Grosser 'Baden Bade 1m4f	11th Breeders' Cup Chur 1m4f	12th Japan Cup Toky 1m4f	-
99 Epso 1m4f 6th Coronation Cup One month	**Fruits Of Love** M Johnston 12/1	9/8	4	8-12	85	3rd King George VI Ascot 1m4f	2nd Canadian Int Wood 1m4f	9th Japan Cup Toky 1m4f	***WON 9/2 Hardwicke Ascot 1m4f**
98 Epso 1m4f 6th Coronation Cup Two weeks	**Posidonas** P Cole 15/2	7/7	6	8-09	75	3rd Arc Trial Newb 1m3f	14th Arc de Triomphe Long 1m4f	2nd Prem Jock' Club Siro 1m4f	*11th Jockey Club Stk Newm 1m4f
97 Sand 1m2f 2nd Brigadier Gerard One month	**Predappio** S Bin Suroor 6/1	7/10	4	8-12	81	7th King George VI Ascot 1m4f	3rd Grosser 'Baden Bade 1m4f	5th Arc de Triomphe Long 1m4f	*9th World Cup Nad Al 1m2f
96 Ches 1m5f 1st Ormonde Stks Two months	**Oscar Schindler** K Prendergast 7/4F	8/8	4	8-09	78	4th King George VI Ascot 1m4f	**WON 4/1 Irish St Leger Curr 1m6f**	3rd Arc de Triomphe Long 1m4f	15th Melbourne Cup Flem 2m

12-year median performance rating of the winner: **80** (out of 100)   *next year*

WINNER'S PROFILE Only Fruits Of Love reappeared here when defending his crown in 2000 as the remainder all **saw the racecourse within the past two months** – six of the last 10 came from the **Coronation Cup** at Epsom. All those to have run reached the **top-three prior to Ascot**, and only Sandmason was without a prior **Group victory to his name**. Sandmason, along with Indian Creek, were the only two not to have **won over the trip**, but both represented value and only Doyen justified favouritism four years since 1997.
The better horses have ruled with an **official rating of 115 or more**, including Maraahel – top rated the last twice – who also gave Sir Michael Stoute his second winner. However, Stoute's record beforehand wasn't great with 0 from 12 runners, whereas **Mark Johnston** had four winners from 11, and Saeed Bin Suroor struck twice from 11.

FUTURE POINTERS Traditionally a decent Group Two that has attracted a quality line-up, but one in which winners have made this their high point of the season, as they were subsequently outclassed back in Group One company. The exception since 1996 was Doyen, the best winner of the race in this period, who went on to land the King George VI next time out, a mission that proved beyond six other Hardwicke winners. Only Oscar Schindler managed to secure Group One honours in the near future and along with Doyen, were disappointingly the only two to score again that season, which is a concern for the 2008 winner unless the performance rating (PR) is high.

Were Hardwicke winners profitable to follow on their subsequent three runs?
No – 2 wins from 36 runs returned a loss of -£28.90 to a £1 level stake.

Placed runners' subsequent record (three runs):
Runners-up: 7 wins from 34 runs returned a loss of -£11.08 to a £1 level stake.
2003 Bollin Eric – Lonsdale Stakes, 1999 Royal Anthem – Juddmonte International,
1997 Pilsudski – Eclipse, Irish Champion, 1996 Annus Mirablis – Winter Hill Stakes

Thirds: 2 wins from 17 runs returned a **profit of +£6.30** to a £1 level stake.
1997 Whitewater Affair – Group Two Prix de Pomone, 1996 Posidonas – Princess of Wales's Stakes

FUTURE SUCCESS RATING: ★ ☆ ☆ ☆ ☆

GOLDEN JUBILEE STAKES
June 21, Royal Ascot – (Group 1, Class 1, 3yo+) 6f

Last run	Winner/ Trainer & SP	Draw/ Ran	Age	Wght	PR	Next four runs			
07 Hayd 7f 3rd John of Gaunt Three weeks	Soldier's Tale J Noseda 9/1	11/21	6	9-04	82	-	-	-	-
06 Ascot 5f 11th King's Stand One week	Les Arcs T Pitt 33/1	4/18	6	9-04	84	WON 10/1 July Cup Newm 6f	7th Sprinters Stks Naka 6f	*13th Duke of York York 6f	-
05 York 5f 4th King's Stand One week	Cape Of Good Hope D Oughton 6/1	2/15	7	9-04	78	11th Sprinters Stks Naka 6f	3rd Grade 1 Flem 6f	3rd Grade 2 Flem 6f	5th H Kong Sprint Sha 5f
04 York 6f 13th Duke of York Two months	Fayr Jag T Easterby 12/1	9/14	5	9-04	75	13th July Cup Newm 6f	10th Nunthorpe York 5f	9th Group 2 Bade 6f	16th Sprinters Stks Naka 6f
03 Ascot 5f 1st King's Stand One week	Choisir P Perry 13/2	20/17	4	9-04	84	2nd July Cup Newm 6f	-	-	-
02 Yarm 6f 1st Conds Stks Two weeks	Malhub J Gosden 16/1	12/12	4	9-04	79	7th July Cup Newm 6f	2nd Nunthorpe York 5f	2nd Sprint Cup Hayd 6f	2nd Diadem Stks Ascot 6f
01 Wind 6f 1st Leisure Stks Three weeks	Harmonic Way R Charlton 10/1	1/21	6	9-00	80	11th July Cup Newm 6f	9th Nunthorpe York 5f	8th Sprint Cup Hayd 6f	10th Diadem Stks Ascot 6f
00 Sand 5f 6th Temple Stks One month	Superior Premium R Fahey 20/1	17/16	6	9-00	81	*3rd Abernant Stks Newm 6f	*11th Grade 1 Kran 6f	*6th Cork & Orrery Ascot 6f	*15th July Cup Newm 6f L
99 York 6f 14th Duke of York Two months	Bold Edge R Hannon 16/1	16/19	4	9-00	78	2nd July Cup Newm 6f	9th King George Good 5f	4th Sprint Cup Hayd 6f	WON 12/1 Diadem Stks Ascot 6f
98 Ling 6f 4th Leisure Stks Three weeks	Tomba B Meehan 4/1	13/12	4	9-00	76	12th Maurice 'Gheest Deau 7f	3rd Sprint Cup Hayd 6f	4th Diadem Stks Ascot 6f	WON N/O Group 3 Muni 7f
97 York 6f 1st Duke of York Two months	Royal Applause B Hills 11/2F	16/23	4	9-03	80	2nd July Cup Newm 6f	WON 15/8F Sprint Cup Hayd 6f	3rd Prix de l'Abbaye Long 5f	14th Breeders' Cup Holl 6f
96 Newm 6f 1st Coral Sprint Hcp Three weeks	Atraf D Morley 12/1	2/17	3	8-06	75	9th Beeswing Stks Newc 7f	2nd Hopeful Stks Newm 6f	8th Group 3 Mais 6f	13th Bentinck Stks Newm 6f

12-year median performance rating of the winner: **79** (out of 100) *next year*

WINNER'S PROFILE A **recent run** was a must as those that attempted to score on their reappearance failed – three recent winners arrived having taken in the **King's Stand Stakes** earlier in the week.
Every winner **already had a distance victory** to their name – 10 in Listed or Group company – so any runner missing a 'D' by their name on the racecard should be avoided.
Four-year-olds and above held sway as 40 three-year-olds have struggled since Atraf scored in 1996, while the **males came out on top** – Posada the last filly to score in 1988. There is **value to be found,** favourites have a wretched record, while trainer Saeed Bin Suroor has yet to score from 13 runners.

FUTURE POINTERS Previously known as the Cork and Orrery before the renamed Golden Jubilee title – when it acquired Group One status in 2002 – this event has become one of the leading sprints in the world, regularly forming an international line-up.
However, despite the increase in quality, winners have disappointed post-Ascot, and Les Arcs two years ago became the first horse since Owington in 1994 to follow up in the July Cup. In fact, winners prior to 1996 had a better subsequent record, with the likes of So Factual winning the Nunthorpe (1995), College Chapel taking the Maurice de Gheest (1993), Polish Patriot lifting the July Cup (1991), and Danehill (1989) scoring in the Haydock Sprint Cup.
Since this 'golden- era', only Royal Applause – bar Les Arcs – won major sprint honours again in the same year in the Haydock Sprint Cup, an event that has caught out four Jubilee winners since 1998.

Were Golden Jubilee winners profitable to follow on their subsequent three runs?
No – 2 wins from 31 runs returned a loss of -£17.12 to a £1 level stake.

Placed runners' subsequent record (three runs):
Runners-up: 4 wins from 29 runs returned a loss of -£8.00 to a £1 level stake.
2002 Danehurst – Flying Five, 2000 Sampower Star – Diadem, 1999 Russian Revival – International Handicap

Thirds: 4 wins from 32 runs returned a loss of -£18.83 to a £1 level stake.
2006 Takeover Target – Sprinters Stakes

FUTURE SUCCESS RATING: ★ ★ ★ ★ ★

WOKINGHAM STAKES
June 21, Royal Ascot – (Heritage Handicap, Class 2, 3yo+) 6f

Last run	Winner/ Trainer & SP	Draw/ Ran	Age	Wght	PR	Next four runs			
07 Newm 6f 4th S James Hcp *Two months*	**Dark Missile** A Balding 22/1	27/26	4	8-11	71	9th Summer Stks York 6f	2nd Shergar Cup Ascot 6f	2nd Diadem Ascot 6f	7th Grade 2 Wood 6f
06 Ascot 5f 6th King's Stand *One week*	**Baltic King** H Morrison 10/1	6/28	6	9-10	79	5th Hackwood Stks Newb 6f	14th Maurice' Gheest Deau 7f	**WON 7/2** Listed Bullet St Beve 5f	2nd Diadem Ascot 6f
05 Ling 7f 1st Victoria Cup *Two months*	**Iffraaj** M Jarvis 9/4F	6/17	4	9-06	82	14th July Cup Newm 6f	**WON 7/1** Park Stks Donc 7f	7th Prix Barriere Long 7f	*7th Golden Jubilee Ascot 6f
04 Epsom 6f 3rd Vodafone Hcp *Two weeks*	**Lafi** D Nicholls 6/1F	30/29	5	8-13	71	*6th Stanleybet Hcp Donc 5f	*26th Ladbrokes Hcp Newm 6f	*2nd Champagne Stk Sand 5f	*2nd Hong Kong Hcp Ascot 5f
03 York 6f 1st = Rated Hcp *Two weeks*	**Fayr Jag** T Easterby 10/1	13/29	4	9-06	77	8th Stewards' Cup Good 6f	**WON 11/8** Hopeful Stks Newm 6f	5th Sprint Cup Hayd 6f	**WON 7/2** Ridge' Pearl St Curr 6f
03 Chan 6f 1st = Stakes *Three weeks*	**Ratio** J Hammond 10/1	22/29	5	9-03	74	5th International Hcp Ascot 7f	**WON 9/2** World Trophy Newb 5f	14th Diadem Ascot 6f	*WON 124/10 Listed Deau 5f
02 Good 7f 3rd Handicap *One month*	**Capricho** J Akehurst 20/1	21/28	5	8-11	68	Disq Bunbury Cup Newm 7f	3rd Silver Salver Hp Newm 7f	**WON 7/2JF** Rated Hcp Good 7f	7th Ayr Gold Cup Ayr 6f
01 Newm 6f 3rd Rated Hcp *Newm 6f*	**Nice One Clare** J Payne 7/1F	4/30	5	9-03	73	4th Criterion Stks Newm 7f	2nd International Hcp Ascot 7f	9th Flying Fillies' Stk Pont 6f	**WON 7/2** Sceptre Stks Donc 7f
00 York 6f 2nd Showcase Hcp *Two months*	**Harmonic Way** R Charlton 12/1	28/30	5	9-06	77	6th Chipchase Stks Newc 6f	2nd Hackwood Stks Newb 6f	9th Nunthorpe York 5f	4th Sprint Cup Hayd 6f
99 Donc 7f 2nd Handicap *Three weeks*	**Deep Space** E Dunlop 14/1	3/30	4	8-07	66	10th Bunbury Cup Newm 7f	11th Stewards' Cup Good 6f	**WON 7/2** Conds Stks Nott 6f	2nd Conds Stks Yarm 6f
98 Epsom 6f 1st Vodafone Hcp *Two weeks*	**Selhurstpark Flyer** J Berry 16/1	20/29	7	9-07	69	20th Stewards' Cup Good 6f	6th Hopeful Stks Newm 6f	15th Ayr Gold Cup Ayr 6f	*6th Cammidge Tr'hy Donc 6f
97 Epsom 6f 3rd Vodafone Hcp *Two weeks*	**Selhurstpark Flyer** J Berry 25/1	5/30	6	9-00	65	5th Rated Hcp Ches 6f	28th Stewards' Cup Good 6f	21st Ayr Gold Cup Ayr 6f	*8th Cammidge Tr'hy Donc 6f
96 Newm 6f 6th Rated Hcp *Two months*	**Emerging Market** J Dunlop 33/1	7/29	4	8-13	64	11th Bunbury Cup Newm 7f	16th Stewards' Cup Good 6f	6th Ayr Gold Cup Ayr 6f	9th Rated Hcp Newm 7f

12-year median performance rating of the winner: **72** (out of 100)   *(2005 York, 2003 dead-heat) *next year*

WINNER'S PROFILE A mixed-bag, but those in-form with a **top four finish last time out** are respected – six emerged from Newmarket, Epsom and York – while Victoria Cup, Ayr Gold Cup and Portland runners also fared well. **Four and five-year-olds** make the short-list, but don't write off three-year-olds – the last was Bel Byou in1987 – as two runners-up, Beckermet and Danetime, almost took advantage of the 7lb allowance.

FUTURE POINTERS The first of three major sprint handicaps of the season – along with the Stewards' Cup and Ayr Gold Cup – and one that now produces classy winners. However, scoring here has left a mark as none followed up since Knight Of Mercy in the 1990 Stewards' Cup, whereas numerous Ascot winners flopped since - placed runners have a better record there *(see below)*. Since the Millennium, though, more winners went into Pattern class – only one ran in the Stewards' Cup – showing the rise in quality. The 1997 Wokingham had only five officially rated 100+ runners (lowest weight 8st 4lb) compared to 2007, when over half the field were at least 100 (lowest weight 8st 10lb).

Were Wokingham winners profitable to follow on their subsequent three runs?
No – 6 wins from 36 runs returned a loss of -£6.62 to a £1 level stake, but a profit was shown since the Millennium.

Placed runners' subsequent record (three runs):
Runners-up: 5 wins from 32 runs returned a loss of -£1.13 to a £1 level stake. *2006 Firenze – Boadicea Stakes, 2005 Beckermet – Hackwood Stakes, 1999 Halmahera – Chipchase Stakes, 1997 Danetime – Stewards' Cup*
Thirds: 9 wins from 36 runs returned a **profit of +£10.91** to a £1 level stake.
2007 Balthazaar's Gift – Hackwood Stakes, 2003 The Tatling – Pocelanosa Stakes, 1998 Superior Premium – Stewards' Cup, 1997 Bollin Joanne – Scarbrough Stakes
Fourths: 10 wins from 36 runs returned a profit of **+£50.32** to a £1 level stake.
2006 Borderlescott – Stewards' Cup, 2003 Capricho – Group Three Holsten Trophy, 2002 Crystal Castle – International Handicap, Diadem Stakes, 2001 Indian Spark – Gosforth Park Handicap

FUTURE SUCCESS RATING: ★ ★ ★ ★ ☆

DUKE OF EDINBURGH STAKES
June 21, Royal Ascot – (Heritage Handicap, Class 2, 3yo+) 1m4f

Last run	Winner/Trainer & SP	Draw/Ran	Age	Wght	PR	Next four runs			
07 York 1m2f 12th Timeform Hcp *Two months*	Pevensey J Quinn 8/1	2/14	5	8-10	58	9th J Smith's Cup York 1m2f	19th Ebor York 1m6f	5th Kilkerran Cup Hcp Ayr 1m2f	10th Heritage Hcp Ascot 1m4f
06 Kemp 1m2f 6th Handicap *Three weeks*	Young Mick G Margarson 28/1	4/20	4	8-08	67	6th Old Newton Cup Hayd 1m4f	**WON 10/1** **Heritage Hcp** **Ascot 1m4f**	**WON 9/4F** **Shergar Cup** **Ascot 1m4f**	3rd Ebor York 1m6f
05 Newm 1m2f 1st Handicap *Two months*	Notable Guest Sir M Stoute 4/1	15/16	4	9-08	73	16th J Smith's Cup York 1m2f	**WON 5/1** **Rose'Lancaster** **Hayd 1m3f**	3rd Dubai Arc Trial Newb 1m3f	*2nd Gordon Richards Sand 1m2f
04 Newm 1m4f 1st Class Stks *Two weeks*	Wunderwood Lady Herries 15/2	13/14	5	9-01	67	**WON 7/4F** **Fullerton Tr'hy** **Ascot 1m2f**	3rd Torne Hcp Donc 1m4f	8th Group 3 Bord 1m2f	*4th City & Sub Hcp Epsom 1m2f
03 Redc 1m2f 5th Zetland G Cup *One month*	Waverley H Morrison 14/1	1/20	4	9-00	62	2nd Old Newton Cup Hayd 1m4f	**6th Steventon Stks Newb 1m2f	**9th Ebor York 1m6f	**5th Ladbrokes Hcp Donc 1m2f
02 Newm 1m4f 3rd Class Stks *One month*	Thundering Surf J Jenkins 11/1	12/20	5	9-00	59	**13th P Power Hcp Newb 1m4f	**9th Class Stks Newb 1m4f	-	-
01 Leic 1m2f 1st Class Stks *One week*	Takamaka Bay M Johnston 10/1	9/20	4	9-00	57	8th Old Newton Cup Hayd 1m4f	*6th EDS Hcp Epsom 1m2f	*6th Duke of Edinburgh Ascot 1m4f	*2nd Sunday Hcp Donc 1m2f
00 Gowr 1m4f 1st Listed *Two weeks*	Katiykha J Oxx 10/1	7/20	4	9-09	70	**WON 13/8F** **Listed** **Curr 1m6f**	7th Irish St Leger Curr 1m6f	-	-
99 Newm 1m4f 1st Handicap *Two months*	Blueprint Sir M Stoute 4/1F	7/18	4	9-09	73	**WON 5/4F** **Fred Archer Stk** **Newm 1m4f**	3rd Geoffrey Freer Newb 1m5f	2nd September Stks Epsom 1m4f	*WON 9/2 Jockey Club Stk Newm 1m4f
98 Newm 1m2f 9th Rated Hcp *Two months*	Greek Palace Sir M Stoute 9/1	10/20	4	9-08	72	3rd Hong Kong Hcp Sand 1m2f	4th Listed Hcp Good 1m4f	-	-
97 York 1m4f 5th Handicap *Two months*	Zaralaska L Cumani 8/1	4/19	6	8-13	68	**WON 5/1** **Old Newton Cup** **Hayd 1m4f**	4th W Hill Cup Good 1m2f	*WON 10/11F *Nov Hdle *Ascot 2m1f	2nd Nov Hdle Leic 2m
96 Beve 1m4f 1st Handicap *Two weeks*	Tykeyvor Lady Herries 14/1	14/20	6	8-06	55	*7th Handicap Kemp 1m2f	*2nd Handicap Beve 1m4f	*5th Bessborough Ascot 1m4f	*11th Handicap Sand 1m4f

12-year median performance rating of the winner: **65** (out of 100) *next year **two years*

WINNER'S PROFILE A light campaign has proven best as the majority **raced no more than three times**, while seven were **prepared at either Newmarket or York**. Although two six-year-olds won in 1996/1997, the last 10 renewals fell to **four and five-year-olds** and those **officially rated between 90-100** have done well.
Sticking with the **first five in the betting** has rewarded punters, and **Sir Michael Stoute** was responsible for three fancied winners.

FUTURE POINTERS Formerly known as the Bessborough Handicap until 1999 when it was renamed the Duke of Edinburgh Stakes, this historic handicap continues to flourish and has attracted plenty of competitive fields. Although three winners were faced into lengthy absences soon after scoring here, the majority performed creditably post-Ascot and quality winners should be viewed in a positive light regarding future engagements. Three above par winners were good enough to score in Pattern company, while two took valuable handicaps, including Zaralaska, who scooped the Old Newton Cup in 1997, a race in which Waverley was runner-up in 2003.
Three runners-up gained compensation in Listed events following Ascot, adding further strength to this handicap.

Were Duke of Edinburgh winners profitable to follow on their subsequent three runs?
Yes – 8 wins from 33 runs returned a **profit of +£2.77** to a £1 level stake.

Placed runners' subsequent record (three runs):
Runners-up: 4 wins from 35 runs returned a loss of -£16.00 to a £1 level stake.
2003 Researched – Listed Glorious Handicap, 2001 Akbar – Listed Silver Cup Handicap,
1998 Sabadilla – Listed Glorious Handicap

Thirds: 5 wins from 33 runs returned a loss of -£19.75 to a £1 level stake.

Fourths: 6 wins from 28 runs returned a loss of -£11.23 to a £1 level stake.
2005 Blue Monday – Cambridgehire

FUTURE SUCCESS RATING: ★★★★☆

CHIPCHASE STAKES
June 28, Newcastle – (Group 3, Class 1, 3yo+) 6f

Last run	Winner/ Trainer & SP	Draw/ Ran	Age	Wght	PR	Next four runs			
07 Curr 1m 7th 2,000 Guineas Two months	Confuchias F Ennis 12/1	2/10	3	9-00	71	5th Listed Curr 6f	13th Bentinck Stks Newm 6f	-	-
06 Ascot 6f 15th Golden Jubilee One week	Fayr Jag T Easterby 5/2F	3/7	7	9-02	76	10th July Cup Newm 6f	WON 16/1 Hackwood Stks Newb 6f	5th King George Good 5f	5th Phoenix Sprint Curr 6f
05 York 6f 1st Handicap Two months	Soldier's Tale J Noseda 6/4F	1/12	4	9-02	80	4th July Cup Newm 6f	**3rd Duke Of York York 6f	**3rd John of Gaunt Hayd 7f	**WON 9/1 Golden Jubilee Ascot 6f
04 Capa 6f 5th Group 3 Seven months	Royal Millennium M Channon 8/1	4/11	6	9-02	74	12th Maurice 'Gheest Deau 7f	4th Sprint Cup Hayd 6f	WON 7/2F Renaissance Stk Curr 6f	3rd Prix de l'Abbaye Long 5f
03 Ascot 6f 12th Golden Jubilee One week	Orientor J Goldie 6/1	6/12	5	9-02	69	9th July Cup Newm 6f	7th Phoenix Sprint Curr 6f	5th Nunthorpe Stks York 5f	8th Sprint Cup York 6f
02 York 6f 11th Duke Of York Two months	Tedburrow E Alston 11/1	4/8	10	9-02	73	5th City Wall Stks Ches 5f	11th HK Sprint Hcp Ascot 5f	*5th Abernant Stks Newm 6f	*13th Rated Hcp Newm 6f
01 Hayd 6f 1st Rated Hcp Two months	Firebolt M Tompkins 6/4F	9/12	3	8-09	75	8th July Cup Newm 6f	6th Shergar Cup Ascot 6f	*WON 53/10 Grade 1 Sha 5f	*3rd Group 1 Sha 5f
00 York 6f 8th Duke Of York Two months	Tedburrow E Alston 12/1	6/11	8	9-05	72	3rd City Wall Stks Ches 5f	7th Queensferry Stk Ches 6f	2nd Flying Five Leop 5f	6th Diadem Stks Ascot 6f
99 Ascot 6f 2nd Wokingham Two weeks	Halmahera I Balding 7/4F	4/9	4	9-01	67	2nd Stewards' Cup Good 6f	4th Group 3 Deau 6f	9th Sprint Cup Hayd 6f	6th Diadem Stks Ascot 6f
98 Cork & Orrery Two weeks 3rd	Andreyev R Hannon 3/1	2/8	4	9-05	74	3rd Group 3 Deau 6f	4th Phoenix Sprint Curr 6f	WON 7/2 Group 3 Deau 6f	4th Sprint Cup Hayd 6f
97 Epsom 7f 4th Conds Stks Three weeks	Tomba B Meehan 5/4F	9/5	3	8-12	73	2nd Listed Muni 7f	WON N/O Group 3 Hopp 7f	3rd Sprint Cup Hayd 6f	3rd Prix de la Foret Long 7f
96 Newb 7f 8th Greenham Three months	Sea Dane P Harris 16/1	4/10	3	8-08	64	15th Hackwood Stks Newb 6f	11th Hopeful Stks Newm 6f	9th Rated Hcp York 6f	13th Portland Hcp Donc 5½f

12-year median performance rating of the winner: **72** (out of 100) *next year ** two years*

WINNER'S PROFILE Every winner raced at a **Grade One venue last time** – seven of the last 10 via **Royal Ascot and York** – while the same number lined up with a **distance victory** under their belt.
Geldings have an excellent record, unlike fillies and mares, and it helped to concentrate on the better runners with an **official rating in excess of 109**.
The entire field switched to the far side last year, which has happened previously, leaving high numbers a lot to do, and those **drawn six or lower** have a good record as they triumphed on 10 occasions out of 12.

FUTURE POINTERS A decent Group Three sprint upgraded from Listed status in 2001, and one in which Royal Ascot form has often been tested. However, the Chipchase hasn't traditionally shined as one of the hottest sprints of the season, a fact borne out by the winner's subsequent efforts as the last 12 all met with defeat next time out.
Two winners in the late-nineties managed to secure further Group Three success abroad, while the 2004 and 2001 victors both left these shores in order to reach the winner's enclosure.
Those who attempted Group One glory have been well outclassed, including the 2006 winner, Fayr Jag, who flopped in the July Cup before hitting back at a more suitable level in the Listed Hackwood Stakes, an event the 2002 runner-up also landed (see below).

Were Chipchase winners profitable to follow on their subsequent three runs?
No – 5 winners from 35 runners returned a loss of -£1.70 to a £1 level stake.

Placed runners' subsequent record (three runs):
Runners-up: 3 wins from 36 runs returned a loss of -£11.00 to a £1 level stake.
2004 Somnus – Maurice de Gheest, 2001 Bahamian Pirate – Phoenix Sprint, 1996 Iktamal – Beeswing Stakes

Thirds: 3 wins from 28 runs returned a loss of -£1.75 to a £1 level stake.
2002 Ashdown Express – Hackwood Stakes, 1998 Jo Mell – International Handicap

FUTURE SUCCESS RATING: ★ ☆ ☆ ☆ ☆

NORTHUMBERLAND PLATE
June 28, Newcastle – (Heritage Handicap, Class 2, 3yo+) 2m

Last run	Winner/ Trainer & SP	Draw/ Ran	Age	Wght	PR	Next four runs			
07 Ascot 2m4f 2nd Ascot Stks Hcp Two weeks	**Juniper Girl** M Bell 5/1F	13/20	4	9-02	60	7th Lonsdale Cup York 2m	5th Prix du Cadran Long 2m4f	-	-
06 Hayd 2m 5th Shank Lane Hcp Three weeks	**Toldo** G M Moore 33/1	16/20	4	8-05	58	-	-	-	-
05 Epsom 1m4f 3rd Vodafone Hcp Three weeks	**Sergeant Cecil** R Millman 14/1	7/20	6	8-08	67	3rd Summer Hcp Good 1m6f	**WON 11/1** **Ebor** **York 1m6f**	2nd Donaster Cup Donc 2m2f	**WON 10/1** **Cesarewitch** **Newm 2m2f**
04 Kels 2m7f 10th Hcp Hdle Two months	**Mirjan** L Lungo 33/1	5/19	8	8-03	55	7th Cesarewitch Newm 2m2f	*7th Handicap York 1m4f	*8th Northumberland Newc 2m	*12th Old Borough Cup Hayd 1m6f
03 Worc 2m 1st Hcp Hdle Two months	**Unleash** P Hobbs 10/1	1/20	4	8-11	56	4th Shergar Cup Ascot 2m	4th Ebor York 1m6f	2nd *Hcp Hdle* *Chep 2m1f*	32nd Cesarewitch Newm 2m2f
02 Kemp 2m 1st Handicap One month	**Bangalore** Mrs A Perrett 8/1	9/16	6	9-05	66	4th Lonsdale Stks York 2m	2nd Group 3 Long 2m	10th Prix du Cadran Long 2m4f	*2nd Conds Stks Ripon 1m4f
01 Ascot 2m 7th Queen's Vase Two weeks	**Archduke Ferdinand** P Cole 12/1	17/18	3	8-04	64	20th Ebor York 1m6f	28th Cesarewitch Newm 2m2f	*6th Conds Stks Nott 1m6f	*8th Chester Cup Ches 2m2f
00 York 1m6f 3rd Rated Hcp Three weeks	**Bay Of Islands** D Morris 7/1	4/18	8	8-04	61	3rd Silver Cup Hcp York 1m6f	16th Ebor York 1m6f	3rd Mallard Hcp Donc 1m7f	*8th Handicap Newb 2m
99 Ascot 2m4f 2nd Ascot Stks Hcp Two weeks	**Far Cry** M Pipe 9/2JF	6/20	4	8-10	65	**WON 6/1** **Donaster Cup** **Donc 2m2f**	5th Cesarewitch Newm 2m2f	**WON 4/5F** **Nov Hdle** **Newb 2m1f**	2nd *Bula Hdle* *Chel 2m1f*
98 Ascot 2m4f 8th Ascot Stks Hcp Two weeks	**Cyrian** P Cole 12/1	2/20	4	7-13	67	10th Ebor York 1m6f	4th Tripleprint Hcp Newb 2m	***25th Cesarewitch Newm 2m2f	-
97 Ascot 2m 1st Queen's Vase Two weeks	**Windsor Castle** P Cole 10/1	20/18	3	8-10	62	3rd Lonsdale Stks York 2m	5th St Leger Donc 1m6f	*4th Sagaro Stks Newm 2m	*3rd Group 2 Long 2m
96 York 1m6f 2nd Rated Hcp Three weeks	**Celeric** D Morley 2/1F	7/13	4	9-04	66	**WON EvsF** **Silver Cup Hcp** **York 1m6f**	**WON 9/4F** **Lonsdale Stks** **York 2m**	2nd Donaster Cup Donc 2m2f	**WON 11/4** **Jock' Club Cup** **Newm 2m**

12-year median performance rating of the winner: **62** (out of 100)   *italic = jumps, *next year ***three years*

WINNER'S PROFILE A **recent run was vital** as all 10 winners that arrived via the Flat performed within the past month – nine between two and three weeks – while the two prepared over the sticks raced within the previous two months. Chester Cup winners should be avoided as the last winner of that to succeed here came over 30 years ago, but those who **raced at Royal Ascot** are respected.

Weight has been crucial, and favoured those on the **light side of 9st** – Juniper Girl dipped under that band last year as her claimer took off 5lb – and the two who lumped more than 9st did so on firm ground. While it proved an advantage being **drawn low to middle**, just as important was having **speed to gain a handy pitch**. Three-year-olds rarely appear but should be noted – two won from seven runners. **Dual-purpose trainers** have a decent record, while from only 11 runners, **Paul Cole** scored three times along with two narrow runners-up (in 2004 and 2002).

FUTURE POINTERS Newcastle's showpiece of the Flat season has long been a ferociously competitive affair and winners have produced a mixed bag of results following success here. York racecourse featured heavily in the near future of Northumberland winners, but only one followed up from six attempts, although Sergeant Cecil took the Ebor two runs later, an event that halted four others. Those who attempted the Lonsdale Cup/Stakes also came unstuck, as last year's winner, Juniper Girl, became the third to bid for Group glory there. One of the best winners, though, in Far Cry, did score at that level in the Doncaster Cup, where Sergeant Cecil and Celeric also went close.

Were Northumberland Plate winners profitable to follow on their subsequent three runs?
No – 5 wins from 32 runs returned a loss of -£5.95 to a £1 level stake.

Placed runners' subsequent record (three runs):
Runners-up: 5 wins from 36 runs returned a loss of -£15.90 to a £1 level stake.
2002 Mr Dinos – Prix Royal-Oak
Thirds: 4 wins from 33 runs returned a loss of -£3.65 to a £1 level stake.
2006 Greenwich Meantime – Chester Cup, 1998 Arctic Owl – Jockey Club Cup.
Fourths: 7 wins from 35 runs returned a **profit of +£22.70** to a £1 level stake.
2004 Collier Hill – Group Three Stockholm Cup International, 2002 Hugs Dancer – Ebor

FUTURE SUCCESS RATING: ★ ★ ☆ ☆ ☆

CRITERION STAKES
June 28, Newmarket (July) – (Group 3, Class 1, 3yo+) 7f

Last run	Winner/ Trainer & SP	Draw/ Ran	Age	Wght	PR	Next four runs			
07 Curr 6f 8th Greenlands Stks *Two months*	**Silver Touch** M Channon 10/1	5/10	4	9-00	71	3rd Maurice 'Gheest Deau 7f	5th Hungerford Newb 7f	12th Diadem Ascot 6f	-
06 Hayd 7f 6th John of Gaunt *One month*	**Suggestive** W Haggas 10/1	7/6	8	9-02	70	6th Summer Mile Ling 1m	8th Lennox Stks Good 7f	5th Group 3 Long 7f	2nd Guisborough Stk Redc 7f
05 Newm 7f 1st Handicap *One month*	**Vortex** Miss G Kelleway 16/1	6/8	6	9-02	73	3rd Silver Trophy Ling 1m	14th Lennox Stks Good 7f	7th Hopeful Stks Newm 6f	2nd Listed Taby 1m
04 Ascot 1m 12th Queen Anne *Two weeks*	**Arakan** Sir M Stoute 7/4F	2/8	4	9-02	76	*2nd Paradise Stks Ling 1m	*5th Lockinge Newb 1m	*5th Criterion Stks Newm 7f	*8th July Cup Newm 6f
03 Newm 7f 1st King Charles II *One month*	**Trade Fair** R Charlton 10/11F	9/11	3	8-07	81	6th Sussex Good 1m	**WON 1/4F Duty Free Cup Newb 7f**	5th Challenge Stks Newm 7f	*14th Duke of York York 6f
02 Ascot 1m 12th Queen Anne *Two weeks*	**Atavus** G Margarson 7/1	5/6	5	9-02	72	26th International Hcp Ascot 7f	5th Lennox Stks Good 7f	8th Hungerford Newb 7f	**WON 10/1 Fortune Stks Epsom 7f**
01 Ascot 1m 8th Queen Anne *Two weeks*	**Shibboleth** H Cecil 11/4	4/6	4	9-02	77	5th July Cup Newm 6f	10th Grade 1 Aque 7f	-	-
00 York 6f 4th Duke Of York *Two months*	**Arkadian Hero** L Cumani 10/3F	6/9	5	9-01	78	6th Sussex Good 1m	**WON 5/2 Hungerford Newb 7f**	2nd Grade 1 Wood 1m	14th Breeders' Cup Chur 1m
99 Good 7f 1st Shergar Cup *Two months*	**Diktat** S Bin Suroor 4/5F	5/6	4	9-07	82	**WON 4/5JF Maurice 'Gheest Deau 7f**	**WON 13/8F Sprint Cup Hayd 6f**	5th Prix de la Foret Long 7f	*6th Group 2 Toky 7f
98 Ascot 1m 9th Queen Anne *Two weeks*	**Muchea** M Channon 16/1	3/10	4	9-07	73	5th Group 2 Hopp 1m	8th Sussex Good 1m	3rd Maurice 'Gheest Deau 7f	6th Celebration Mile Good 1m
97 Ascot 1m 7th Royal Hunt Cup *Two weeks*	**Ramooz** B Hanbury 11/4F	1/9	4	9-02	68	**WON 2/1 Minstrel Stks Curr 1m**	4th Beeswing Stks Newc 7f	6th City of York York 7f	2nd Stakes Veli 1m
96 Ascot 1m 9th Queen Anne *Two weeks*	**Gabr** R Armstrong 14/1	6/9	6	9-10	77	-	-	-	-

12-year median performance rating of the winner: **75** (out of 100)   **next year*

WINNER'S PROFILE Every winner **raced at a Grade One venue last time out**, five of whom were soundly beaten in the Queen Anne at Royal Ascot. Only Arkadian Hero failed to have **already won over the distance**, while **four to six-year-olds** proved best – three-year-olds struck just once from 25 runners. The best horses came out on top with an **official rating of 107 or more**, as was the rating of last year's winner, Silver Touch, who gave her trainer **Mick Channon** his second win in the race from only three runners.

FUTURE POINTERS The Criterion has often been a tactical affair resulting in a clouded outcome and winners haven't set the pulse racing post-Newmarket despite a few landing decent races, although there was one standout performance from Diktat in 1999. After recording the best performance rating (PR) this event has witnessed in 12 years, Diktat then secured Group One honours in the Haydock Sprint Cup.

Two races to have proven beyond several Criterion victors were the Lennox and Sussex Stakes, while the six year-old and above winners haven't kicked on subsequently. If there were an ideal profile to follow from here, it would be an above par four or five-year-old.

Were Criterion winners profitable to follow on their subsequent three runs?
5 wins from 32 runs returned a loss of -£19.82 to a £1 level stake.

Placed runners' subsequent record (three runs):
Runners-up: 2 wins from 33 runs returned a loss of -£11.00 to a £1 level stake.
2005 Court Masterpiece – Lennox Stakes, 2003 Just James – Challenge Stakes

Thirds: 3 wins from 24 runs returned a loss of -£14.88 to a £1 level stake.
2004 Trade Fair – Minstrel Stakes, 1996 Bin Rosie – Hungerford

FUTURE SUCCESS RATING: ★ ★ ☆ ☆ ☆

PRETTY POLLY STAKES
June 28, Curragh – (Group 1, Class 1, 3yo+ Fillies & Mares) 1m2f

Last run	Winner/Trainer & SP	Draw/Ran	Age	Wght	PR	Next four runs			
07 Epso 1m4f 2nd Oaks *One month*	**Peeping Fawn** A O'Brien 7/4F	7/9	3	8-11	77	**WON 3/1** Irish Oaks Curr 1m4f	**WON 2/1F** Nassau Stks Good 1m2f	**WON 4/9F** Yorkshire Oaks York 1m4f	-
06 Curr 1m3f 2nd Tatts Gold Cup *Two months*	**Alexander Goldrun** J Bolger 11/8F	1/7	5	9-08	79	2nd Nassau Stks Good 1m2f	3rd Irish Champion Leop 1m2f	3rd Sun Chariot Newm 1m	9th Hong Kong Cup Sha 1m2f
05 Kran 1m2f 3rd International Cup *Two months*	**Alexander Goldrun** J Bolger 9/4F	5/10	4	9-07	78	2nd Falmouth Stks Newm 1m	**WON 13/8F** Nassau Stks Good 1m2f	3rd Irish Champion Leop 1m2f	3rd Prix de l'Opera Long 1m2f
04 Pont 1m 1st Pipalong Stks *Three weeks*	**Chorist** W Haggas 7/4	1/6	5	9-07	74	3rd Nassau Stks Good 1m2f	3rd Group 2 Deau 1m2f	2nd Champion Stks Newm 1m2f	-
03 Epso 1m4f 6th Oaks *One month*	**Hanami** J Toller 5/2	4/8	3	8-09	65	11th Irish Oaks Curr 1m4f	10th Sun Chariot Newm 1m	*3rd Ridgewood Pearl Curr 1m	*6th Pretty Polly Stks Curr 1m2f
02 Sand 1m2f 4th Brigadier Gerard *One month*	**Tarfshi** M Jarvis 7/2	5/7	4	9-05	66	6th Nassau Stks Good 1m2f	*7th Flower Bowl Int Belm 1m1f	-	-
01 Curr 1m 5th Irish 1,000 Guin *Two months*	**Rebelline** K Prendergast 2/1F	2/12	3	8-07	65	7th Irish Oaks Curr 1m4f	3rd Prix de l'Opera Long 1m2f	8th Champion Stks Newm 1m2f	*WON 8/1 Gladness Stks Curr 1m2f
00 Epso 1m4f 5th Oaks *One month*	**Lady Upstage** B Hills 9/2	1/10	3	8-08	63	7th Nassau Stks Good 1m2f	3rd Prix de l'Opera Long 1m2f	2nd Grade 1 Wood 1m2f	-
99 Naas 7f 1st Stakes *One month*	**Polaire** K Prendergast 12/1	5/8	3	8-08	64	6th Irish Oaks Curr 1m4f	6th Meld Stks Leop 1m2f	3rd Royal Whip Stks Curr 1m2f	7th Grade 1 Belm 1m1f
98 Curr 7f 1st Weld Park Stks *Eight months*	**Alborada** Sir M Prescott 7/4F	1/6	3	8-08	70	**WON 4/1** Nassau Stks Good 1m2f	2nd Irish Champion Leop 1m2f	**WON 6/1** Champion Stks Newm 1m2f	*5th Nassau Stks Good 1m2f
97 Curr 1m2f 1st Tatts Gold Cup *Two months*	**Dance Design** D Weld 4/9F	6/6	4	10-00	72	2nd Group 1 Muni 1m2f	3rd Grade 1 Arli 1m2f	7th Grade 1 Sant 1m2f	11th Breeders' Cup Holl 1m4f
96 Ascot 1m 3rd Coronation Stks *Two weeks*	**Dance Design** D Weld EvensF	5/7	3	8-08	71	**WON 9/2** Irish Oaks Curr 1m4f	2nd Irish Champion Leop 1m2f	*WON 4/5F Mooresbridge Curr 1m2f	*WON 5/2 Tatts Gold Cup Curr 1m2f

12-year median performance rating of the winner: **70** (out of 100)   *next year*

WINNER'S PROFILE Only one winner made their reappearance here as the remainder **raced within the past two months**, three of whom were dropped in trip after being held in the English Oaks. Every winner **finished in the top- three of a Pattern event**, 10 of whom scored – seven in a Listed/Group Three – while three older fillies took Group Ones. The market proved correct as 11 winners emerged from the **first two in the betting**, including **Jim Bolger** and **Dermot Weld**'s dual winners, while **Kevin Prendergast** also sent out two.

FUTURE POINTERS The Pretty Polly produced a couple of subsequent Group One winners pre-Millennium before a dry run up until 2004 when the race was upgraded to Group One status, since when two excellent fillies have scored. In fact, Peeping Fawn and Alexander Goldrun were the best winners of this event by some way and both went on to lift the Nassau Stakes at Goodwood, as did Alborada in 1998. Peeping Fawn also took the Irish Oaks along with Dance Design, and above par winners here deserve respect in that Classic – the three well beaten were all sub-standard fillies.
Two events to have proven tricky for Pretty Polly winners, though, were the Irish Champion Stakes and Prix de l'Opera, although Alexander Goldrun did land the latter event after a second here in 2004, as did runner-up, Zee Zee Top, the year before.

Were Pretty Polly winners profitable to follow on their subsequent three runs?
Yes – 11 wins from 35 runs returned **profit of +£3.80** to a £1 level stake.

Placed runners' subsequent record (three runs):
Runners-up: 5 wins from 32 runs returned a loss of -£3.12 to a £1 level stake.
2005 Red Bloom – Blandford Stakes, 2004 Alexander Goldrun – Prix de l'Opera, Hong Kong Cup, 1999 Lady In Waiting – Sun Chariot Stakes

Thirds: 2 wins from 11 runs returned a **profit of +£26.00** to a £1 level stake.
2003 Zee Zee Top – Prix de l'Opera

FUTURE SUCCESS RATING: ★★★ ★ ★

RAILWAY STAKES
June 29, Curragh – (Group 2, Class 1, 2yo) 6f

Last run	Winner/ Trainer & SP	Draw/ Ran	Age	Wght	PR	Next four runs			
07 Leop 6f 2nd Maiden Two weeks	**Lizard Island** A O'Brien 10/3	2/4	2	9-01	61	2nd Vintage Stks Good 7f	4th National Stks Curr 7f	6th Beresford Stks Curr 1m	-
06 Ascot 6f 15th Coventry Stks Two weeks	**Holy Roman Emperor** A O'Brien 4/1	1/9	2	9-01	73	**WON 13/8JF** Phoenix Stks Curr 6f	2nd National Stks Curr 7f	**WON 7/4** Grand Criterium Long 7f	2nd Dewhurst Stks Newm 7f
05 Curr 6f 1st Maiden Two months	**George Washington** A O'Brien 2/5F	5/5	2	9-00	70	**WON 8/13F** Phoenix Stks Curr 6f	**WON 2/11F** National Stks Curr 7f	*WON 6/4F 2,000 Guineas Newm 1m	*2nd Irish 2,000 Guin Curr 1m
04 Leop 6f 1st Maiden Two months	**Democratic Deficit** J Bolger 7/1	6/7	2	9-00	65	2nd Futurity Stks Curr 7f	4th National Stks Curr 7f	5th Prix 'Lagardere Long 7f	*WON 12/1 Craven Stks Newm 1m
03 Gowr 7f 1st Maiden Two months	**Antonius Pius** A O'Brien 4/7F	8/7	2	9-00	63	11th Dewhurst Stks Newm 7f	*4th Group 3 Long 1m	*5th Poule 'Poulains Long 1m	*3rd St James's Palace Ascot 1m
02 Leop 6f 1st Maiden Three weeks	**Hold That Tiger** A O'Brien 5/4	2/4	2	8-10	67	9th Phoenix Stks Curr 6f	**WON 7/2** Grand Criterium Long 7f	3rd Breeders' Cup Arli 1m1f	*17th 2,000 Guineas Newm 1m
01 Ascot 6f 6th Coventry Stks Two weeks	**Rock Of Gibraltar** A O'Brien 1/2F	5/7	2	8-10	72	**WON 11/4** Gimcrack Stks York 6f	2nd Champagne Stks Donc 7f	**WON 4/5F** Grand Criterium Long 7f	**WON 4/6F** Dewhurst Stks Newm 7f
00 Gowr 1f 1st Maiden One month	**Honours List** A O'Brien 1/4F	3/5	2	8-10	64	2nd Prix 'Salamandre Long 7f	3rd Grand Criterium Long 1m	-	-
99 Curr 6f 1st Maiden Two months	**Bernstein** A O'Brien 2/7F	1/4	2	8-13	63	5th National Stks Curr 7f	*26th 2,000 Guineas Newm 1m	*WON 5/1 Shergar Cup Ascot 6f	*11th Nunthorpe Stks York 5f
98 Leop 6f 2nd Listed Stks One month	**Camargo** D Weld 2/1F	2/5	2	8-07	64	12th Moyglare Stud Curr 7f	*7th Grade 1 Del 1m1f	-	-
97 Curr 6f 1st Maiden Two months	**King Of Kings** A O'Brien 2/9F	1/5	2	8-10	69	2nd Anglesey Stks Curr 6f	**WON 2/9F** Listed Stks Curr 7f	**WON 4/9F** National Stks Curr 1m	*WON 7/2 2,000 Guineas Newm 1m
96 Ascot 6f 2nd Coventry Stks Two weeks	**Daylight In Dubai** P Chapple-Hyam 9/10F	2/5	2	8-10	63	8th National Stks Curr 7f	6th R Post Trophy Donc 1m	**10th Group 3 Mais 1m2f	**7th Group 3 Lyon 1m2f

12-year median performance rating of the winner: **66** (out of 100)   *next year **two years*

WINNER'S PROFILE There may be more value in following the winner from here rather than finding it, as six of Aidan O'Brien's winners went off at odds-on, although his last two surprisingly started at decent prices.
Three of his victors won a maiden over this trip at The Curragh, while two scored over a furlong further at Gowran Park, the same number that were unplaced in the Coventry at Royal Ascot.

FUTURE POINTERS Very much a race in which to sit up and take notice with a view to the following year's Classics and one that deserved it's upgrade to Group Two status in 2003, as it produced numerous Group One winners, including three in the 2,000 Guineas since 1996.
Two of the three non-Aidan O'Brien winners were sub-standard as they never achieved a great deal subsequently, while three of O'Brien's below par winners also under-achieved, including Lizard Island last year. However, five of the six quality O'Brien winners were ones to follow. Two won the Phoenix Stakes next time out – a more recent ploy of his – the same number that took the National Stakes, while three triumphed in the prestigious Grand Criterium over in France.
Overall, Aidan O'Brien has used this race for three of his four 2,000 Guineas winners, and while we may not see a repeat of the 2001 renewal in which both the first two home, Rock Of Gibraltar and Hawk Wing, finished first and second at Newmarket, the opportunity may arise to back one for the Guineas here at an ante-post price.

Were Railway Stakes winners profitable to follow on their subsequent three runs?
No – 11 wins from 34 runs returned a loss of -£4.63 to a £1 level stake.

Placed runners' subsequent record (three runs):
Runners-up: 4 wins from 22 runs returned a loss of -£12.59 to a £1 level stake.
2005 Amigoni – Anglesey Stakes, 2001 Hawk Wing – Futurity Stakes, National Stakes, 1998 Namid – Anglesey Stakes

Thirds: 1 win from 3 runs returned a loss of -£0.12 to a £1 level stake.
2006 Excellent Art – Mill Reef Stakes

FUTURE SUCCESS RATING: ★★★★ ☆

IRISH DERBY

June 29, Curragh– (Group 1, Class 1, 3yo Colts & Fillies) 1m4f

Last run	Winner/ Trainer & SP	Draw/ Ran	Age	Wght	PR	Next four runs			
07 Epso 1m4f 5th **Derby** *One month*	**Soldier Of Fortune** A O'Brien 5/1	11/11	3	9-00	87	**WON 9/4** **Prix Niel** **Long 1m4f**	5th Arc de Triomphe Long 1m4f	-	-
06 Epso 1m4f 3rd **Derby** *One month*	**Dylan Thomas** A O'Brien 9/2F	9/13	3	9-00	86	4th Juddmonte Int York 1m2f	**WON 13/8F** **Irish Champion** **Leop 1m2f**	4th Grade 1 Belm 1m2f	***WON 8/15F** **Alleged Listed** **Curr 1m2f**
05 Chan 1m3f 2nd **Prix 'Jockey-Club** *Three weeks*	**Hurricane Run** A Fabre 4/5F	6/9	3	9-00	89	**WON 4/5F** **Prix Niel** **Long 1m4f**	**WON 11/4** Arc de Triomphe Long 1m4f	***WON 1/3F** Tatts Gold Cup Curr 1m3f	*2nd G Prix St-Cloud Sain 1m4f
04 Curr 1m 3rd **Irish 2,000 Guin** *Two months*	**Grey Swallow** D Weld 10/1	6/10	3	9-00	83	4th Irish Champion Leop 1m2f	18th Arc de Triomphe Long 1m4f	-	-
03 Epso 1m4f 3rd **Derby** *One month*	**Alamshar** J Oxx 4/1	2/9	3	9-00	87	**WON 13/2** **King George VI** **Ascot 1m4f**	4th Irish Champion Leop 1m2f	6th Champion Stks Newm 1m2f	-
02 Epso 1m4f 1st **Derby** *One month*	**High Chaparral** A O'Brien 1/3F	4/9	3	9-00	89	3rd Arc de Triomphe Long 1m4f	**WON 9/10F** **Breeders' Cup** **Arli 1m4f**	***WON 9/10F** **Royal Whip Stk** **Curr 1m2f**	***WON 4/1** **Irish Champion** **Leop 1m2f**
01 Epso 1m4f 1st **Derby** *One month*	**Galileo** A O'Brien 4/11F	8/12	3	9-00	88	**WON 1/2F** **King George VI** **Ascot 1m4f**	2nd Irish Champion Leop 1m2f	6th Breeders' Cup Belm 1m2f	-
00 Epso 1m4f 1st **Derby** *One month*	**Sinndar** J Oxx 11/10F	1/11	3	9-00	92	**WON 3/10F** **Prix Niel** **Long 1m4f**	**WON 6/4** Arc de Triomphe Long 1m4f	-	-
99 Chan 1m3f 1st **Prix 'Jockey-Club** *Three weeks*	**Montjeu** J Hammond 13/8F	2/10	3	9-00	95	**WON 1/10F** **Prix Niel** **Long 1m4f**	**WON 6/4CF** Arc de Triomphe Long 1m4f	4th Japan Cup Toky 1m4f	***WON 1/3F** **Tatts Gold Cup** **Curr 1m3f**
98 Chan 1m3f 1st **Prix 'Jockey-Club** *One month*	**Dream Well** P Bary 2/1F	6/10	3	9-00	81	3rd Prix Niel Long 1m4f	8th Arc de Triomphe Long 1m4f	*2nd Prix Ganay Long 1m3f	*3rd Coronation Cup Epso 1m4f
97 Ascot 1m 4th **St James' Palace** *Two weeks*	**Desert King** A O'Brien 11/2	4/10	3	9-00	84	2nd Juddmonte Int York 1m2f	2nd Irish Champion Leop 1m2f		
96 Leop 1m4f 2nd **Beef Stks** *Three weeks*	**Zagreb** D Weld 20/1	12/13	3	9-00	82	13th Arc de Triomphe Long 1m4f	-	-	-

12-year median performance rating of the winner: **87** (out of 100)   *next year*

WINNER'S PROFILE Ignoring the twice-raced Zagreb, who had no experience at this level, the remainder all finished in the **first three of a Group One**, and nine of the last 10 **arrived via the English or French Derby** – majority made the top-three. Every winner scored earlier in the campaign and the market spoke volumes as 11 came from the **first three in the betting**, including all five of **Aidan O'Brien**'s winners from over 40 runners – sent out the first three home last year. **Irish and French-trained** runners have dominated, the last British-trained victor came 14 years ago, although Sir Michael Stoute won this three times in the eighties, but nearly 10 have lost since 1996.

FUTURE POINTERS Bar a few forgettable winners prior to 1999, the Irish Derby boasts an admirable Hall of Fame – one of the best in this book – and winners certainly franked the strength of the event subsequently, which has arguably eclipsed the English version. In fact, the only three Epsom Derby winners to score next time out were all Irish-trained and followed-up here!
Subsequent form doesn't come any stronger than the achievements from Irish Derby winners, as three went on to lift the biggest title in Europe, the Arc de Triomphe – the 2003 runner-up also took that event – while two won the King George VI Stakes at Ascot. Throw in a Breeders' Cup, two Irish Champion Stakes, two Tattersalls Gold Cups and four Prix Niel's – more beyond their next four runs – and the mouth salivates in anticipation of the 2008 winner.

Were Irish Derby winners profitable to follow on their subsequent three runs?
Yes – 13 wins from 30 runs returned a **profit of +£2.95** to a £1 level stake.

Placed runners' subsequent record (three runs):
Runners-up: 8 wins from 23 runs returned a loss of -£1.97 to a £1 level stake.
2005 Scorpion – Grand Prix de Paris, St Leger, 2003 Dalakhani – Prix Niel, Arc de Triomphe, 2001 Morshdi – Grosser Preis von Baden, 1999 Daliapour – Ormonde Stakes, Coronation Cup

Thirds: 8 wins from 32 runs returned a loss of -£10.60 to a £1 level stake.
2007 Eagle Mountain – Royal Whip Stakes, 2002 Ballingarry – Canadian International, 2001 Golan – Prix Niel, 2000 Ciro – Grade One Secretariat Stakes

FUTURE SUCCESS RATING: ★ ★ ★ ★

OLD NEWTON CUP
July 5, Haydock – (Class 2, Heritage Handicap, 3yo+) 1m4f

Last run	Winner/ Trainer & SP	Draw/ Ran	Age	Wght	PR	Next four runs			
07 Good 1m2f 8th Heritage Hcp Two weeks	Dansili Dancer C Cox 15/2	8/11	5	9-03	63	5th Chester Hcp Ches 1m5f	3rd Old Borough Cup Hayd 1m6f	-	-
06 Ascot 1m4f 7th Duke of Edinburgh Two weeks	Consular M Jarvis 16/1	14/16	4	8-08	60	4th Heritage Hcp Ascot 1m4f	12th Ebor York 1m6f	*13th Handicap Nad Al 1m4f	-
05 York 1m4f 9th Handicap Two months	Zeitgeist L Cumani 9/1	3/15	4	8-10	67	5th Ebor York 1m6f	*WON 1/3F Nov Hdle Catt 2m3f	*3rd Nov Hdle Sedg 2m6f	*5th Nov Hdle Catt 2m
04 Newm 1m4f 2nd Class Stks One month	Alkaased L Cumani 7/1	11/15	4	9-01	74	WON 11/4F Glorious Stks Good 1m4f	2nd September Stks Kemp 1m4f	*WON 2/1F Jockey Club St Newm 1m4f	*2nd Coronation Cup Epsom 1m4f
03 Hami 1m5f 1st Tote Hcp Two months	Collier Hill A Swinbank 8/1	16/19	5	8-10	52	6th Rated Hcp York 1m4f	11th Diamond Hcp Ascot 1m4f	3rd Rated Hcp Hami 1m5f	14th Showcase Hcp Ayr 1m5f
02 Carl 1m 13th Carlisle Hcp Two weeks	Sea Bird R Allan 40/1	4/16	4	7-12	53	3rd Rated Hcp Newm 1m2f	4th Rated Hcp Newb 1m3f	3rd Hambleton Cup Thir 1m4f	12th Courage Hcp Newb 1m2f
01 Good 1m4f 1st Handicap Three weeks	Hannibal Lad M Brisbourne 14/1	15/14	5	8-08	61	4th Rated Hcp York 1m4f	6th Glorious Stks Good 1m4f	6th Shergar Cup Ascot 1m4f	14th Ebor York 1m6f
00 Ascot 1m4f 18th Duke of Edinburgh Three weeks	Rada's Daughter I Balding 11/1	8/14	4	8-11	65	7th Chalice Stks Hayd 1m4f	8th Ebor York 1m6f	2nd Park Hill Stks Donc 1m7f	7th Princess Royal Newm 1m4f
99 Hayd 1m3f 1st Showcase Hcp One month	Celestial Welcome Mrs M Reveley 16/1	1/15	4	8-10	59	6th Rated Hcp York 1m4f	6th Handicap Pont 1m4f	12th Handicap Ayr 1m2f	7th Ritz Club Hcp Ascot 1m4f
98 York 1m6f 7th Ebor Trial Hcp One month	Perfect Paradigm J Gosden 14/1	7/8	4	9-02	68	7th Grosvenor Hcp Good 1m6f	2nd Conds Stks Ascot 1m4f	3rd Rated Hcp Ches 1m5f	3rd Rated Hcp Hayd 1m4f
97 Ascot 1m4f 1st Bessborough Hp Three weeks	Zaralaska L Cumani 5/1	13/16	6	9-08	73	4th W Hill Cup Hcp Good 1m2f	*WON 10/11F Nov Hdle Ascot 2m1f	*2nd Nov Hdle Leic 2m	*PU Nov Hdle Kemp 2m
96 Ches 1m4f 2nd Conds Stks One month	Key To My Heart Miss S Hall 9/2	2/8	6	10-00	68	5th Rose of Lancaster Hayd 1m3f	5th Geoffrey Freer Newb 1m5f	WON 6/4F Doonside Cup Ayr 1m3f	2nd Godolphin Stks Newm 1m4f

12-year median performance rating of the winner: **64** (out of 100) *italic=jumps *next year*

WINNER'S PROFILE The majority **ran within the past month**, three came via the Duke of Edinburgh Handicap at the Royal meeting. However, those that went off favourite here from Ascot may be cursed, as Futun last year became the latest to miss out, along with the likes of Thunder Rock, Promotion and Swagger Stick in recent years. Eleven winners proved themselves with **prior victories between 11 and 13 furlongs**, while the last 10 were **four or five-year-olds** – the Classic generation remain winless from 15 runners. The 1996 and 1997 winners were both officially rated in excess of 100, but nine since then have come from a **rating band between 85 and 95**. Trainer **Luca Cumani** has without doubt been the man to follow with three winners from four runners.

FUTURE POINTERS Run a month later last year owing to a waterlogged track, this valuable handicap has attracted competitive fields over the years, but one negative was it's failure to lure many unexposed three-year-olds that should be seen in races like this, which slightly detracts from its quality. This has possibly been reflected in the winner's subsequent record as only Alkaased – the owner of the best performance rating (PR) of the Old Newton Cup since 1996 – managed to follow up next time at Glorious Goodwood, before Pattern success the following year. Another of the best winners, Zaralaska, also trained by Luca Cumani, was sent hurdling, while Zeitgeist, from the same yard, took a similar route. In a nutshell, avoid winners of this race unless they record a performance rating above 70, or hail from the Luca Cumani yard.

Were Old Newton Cup winners profitable to follow on their subsequent three runs?
No – 5 wins from 35 runs returned a loss of -£22.51 to a £1 level stake.

Placed runners' subsequent record (three runs):
Runners-up: 2 wins from 36 runs returned a loss of -£23.50 to a £1 level stake
2000 Alva Glen – March Stakes

Thirds: 3 wins from 34 runs returned a loss of -£11.25 to a £1 level stake.

Fourths: 1 win from 11 runs returned a loss of -£5.50 to a £1 level stake

FUTURE SUCCESS RATING: ★ ★ ★ ★ ★

LANCASHIRE OAKS
July 5, Haydock – (Group 2, Class 1, 3yo+) 1m4f

Last run	Winner/ Trainer & SP	Draw/ Ran	Age	Wght	PR	Next four runs			
07 Catt 1m4f 1st Maiden *Two months*	**Turbo Linn** A Swinbank 6/1	13/12	4	9-05	75	**WON 6/5F** Aphrodite Stks Newm 1m4f	10th Park Hill Stks Donc 1m6f	-	-
06 Chep 1m4f 1st Maiden *One month*	**Allegretto** Sir M Stoute 13/2	6/8	3	8-06	67	3rd Yorkshire Oaks York 1m4f	3rd Park Hill Stks York 1m6f	*5th Yorkshire Cup York 1m6f	*WON 12/1 Henry II Sand 2m
05 Ascot 1m 1st Meon Valley Mile *Ten months*	**Playful Act** J Gosden 11/4	4/8	3	8-05	66	2nd Irish Oaks Curr 1m4f	10th Yorkshire Oaks York 1m4f	Prix de l' Opera Long 1m2f	-
04 Hayd 1m3f 1st Pinnacle Stks *Two months*	**Pongee** L Cumani 9/2	6/8	4	9-03	68	2nd Lily Langtry Good 1m6f	2nd Yorkshire Oaks York 1m4f	-	-
03 Sain 1m3f 1st Listed *Eight months*	**Place Rouge** J Gosden 25/1	8/12	4	9-03	69	7th Nassau Good 1m2f	2nd Blandford Stks Curr 1m2f	7th Group 2 Long 1m5f	4th St Simon Stks Newb 1m4f
02 Epso 1m4f 6th Oaks *One month*	**Mellow Park** J Noseda 13/8F	1/6	3	8-05	72	7th Irish Oaks Curr 1m4f	8th Yorkshire Oaks York 1m4f	-	-
01 Leic 1m4f 3rd Mercury Stks *Three weeks*	**Sacred Song** H Cecil 7/4F	6/8	4	9-06	74	2nd Yorkshire Oaks York 1m4f	-	-	-
00 Curr 1m2f 4th Pretty Polly Stks *One week*	**Ela Athena** M Jarvis 5/1	7/11	4	9-03	68	2nd Nassau Good 1m2f	5th Yorkshire Oaks York 1m4f	2nd Grade 1 Belm 1m3f	3rd Grade 1 Belm 1m4f
99 Epso 1m4f 2nd Oaks *One month*	**Noushkey** M Jarvis 2/1F	1/7	3	8-04	72	8th Yorkshire Oaks York 1m4f	6th St Leger Donc 1m6f	-	-
98 Kemp 1m4f 1st Maiden *One month*	**Catchascatchcan** H Cecil 8/1	3/6	3	8-04	71	**WON EvsF** Aphrodite Stks Newm 1m4f	**WON 2/1F** Yorkshire Oaks York 1m4f	-	-
97 Newb 1m2f 1st Ballymacoll Stud *One month*	**Squeak** J Gosden 9/2	2/8	3	8-04	64	6th Yorkshire Oaks York 1m4f	4th Prix de l' Opera Long 1m1f	4th Grade 1 Sant 1m2f	*3rd Grade 1 Holl 1m1f
96 Curr 1m6f 6th Curragh Cup *One week*	**Spout** R Charlton 13/2	6/10	4	9-06	65	3rd Group 2 Deau 1m4f	2nd Sun Chariot Newm 1m2f	2nd Princess Royal Ascot 1m4f	-

12-year median performance rating of the winner: **69** (out of 100)   *(2007 Newmarket), *next year*

WINNER'S PROFILE Seven winners lined up off the back of a **victory last time**, including the last five, while 11 either **won over at least 10 furlongs or had experience over the trip** – Playful Act, by Sadler's Wells, was the exception. The only three winners not to have made the top-three last time all faced Group rivals.
Only two mares turned up in this period, both soundly beaten in 2003, while those in the **first four of the betting** came out on top – only one outsider triumphed five years ago trained by **John Gosden**, who won this three times from 10 runners. Alan Swinbank last year put a stop to southern trainers' domination, but two Newmarket handlers to monitor are **Michael Jarvis**, with a crisp record of two winners from three runners, and **Henry Cecil**, who not only took it twice from six runners in this period, but also a further three times between 1991-1994.

FUTURE POINTERS Upgraded to Group Two status in 2004, winners have mainly disappointed post-Haydock, although the race received a much-needed boost last year when Turbo Linn emulated Catchascatchcan's feat of following up in the Aphrodite Stakes – the only two winners to have taken up that engagement. Catchascatchcan also took the more competitive Yorkshire Oaks subsequently, a race that proved too much for eight Lancashire victors, while from a punting angle, it proved profitable to follow runners-up from here *(see below)*.

Were Lancashire Oaks winners profitable to follow on their subsequent three runs?
No – 3 wins from 29 runs returned a loss of -£21.75 to a £1 level stake.

Placed runners' subsequent record (three runs):
Runners-up: 7 wins from 31 runs returned a **profit of +1.36** to a £1 level stake.
2004 Sahool – Chalice Stakes, 2001 Ranin – Aphrodite Stakes, 1999 Mistle Song – Park Hill Stakes,
1998 Rambling Rose – Galtres Stakes, 1997 Tulipa – Prix de Royallieu, 1996 Phantom Gold – Geoffrey Freer

Thirds: 1 win from 22 runs returned a loss of -£22.00 to a £1 level stake.

FUTURE SUCCESS RATING: ★★☆☆☆

CHAMPAGNE SPRINT STAKES
July 5, Sandown – (Group 3, Class 1, 3yo+) 5f

Last run	Winner/ Trainer & SP	Draw/ Ran	Age	Wght	PR	Next four runs			
07 Newc 6f 9th Chipchase Stks One week	Hoh Mike M Bell 9/2	8/10	3	8-12	74	6th Nunthorpe York 5f	13th Prix de l'Abbaye Long 5f	-	-
06 Ascot 6f 11th Golden Jubilee Two weeks	Pivotal Point P Makin 5/1	11/12	6	9-03	75	8th July Cup Newm 6f	3rd Phoenix Sprint Curr 6f	*4th Cathedral Stks Sali 6f	*13th King's Stand Ascot 5f
05 Sand 5f 1st Scurry Stks Three weeks	Resplendent Glory T Mills 2/1F	2/8	3	8-12	72	*11th Temple Stks Sand 5f	*17th King's Stand Ascot 5f	-	-
04 Curr 5f 3rd Listed One week	Orientor J Goldie 5/1	3/12	6	9-03	70	5th Nunthorpe York 5f	7th Sprint Cup Hayd 6f	6th Prix de l'Abbaye Long 5f	*8th Cammidge Trophy Donc 6f
03 Newc 5f 6th Gosforth Park Two weeks	The Tatling M Bradley 7/2F	13/13	6	9-03	78	3rd Hackwood Stks Newb 6f	WON 11/4F King George Good 5f	2nd Nunthorpe York 5f	6th Sprint Cup Hayd 6f
02 Sali 6f 1st Cathedral Stks Three weeks	Palace Affair T Balding 7/1	7/8	4	9-02	75	WON 5/4F Summer Stks York 6f	8th Rotary Stks Good 6f	11th Bentinck Stks Newm 6f	-
01 Ascot 6f 5th Cork & Orrery Three weeks	Misraah Sir M Stoute 7/2F	9/10	4	9-03	69	3rd July Cup Newm 6f	4th International Hcp Ascot 7f	5th Hungerford Stks Newb 7f	*5th Duke of York York 6f
00 Ascot 5f 11th King's Stand Three weeks	Watching R Hannon 9/2	7/10	3	9-02	72	4th King George Good 5f	4th Nunthorpe York 5f	5th Flying Five Leop 5f	10th Prix de l'Abbaye Long 5f
99 Ascot 5f 7th King's Stand Three weeks	Cortachy Castle B Meehan 8/1	3/8	4	9-03	70	11th King George Good 5f	3rd Conds Stks Yarm 6f	8th Nunthorpe York 5f	13th World Trophy Newb 5f
98 Newc 6f 5th Chipchase Stks One week	Fire Dome D Nicholls 33/1	5/11	6	9-03	67	14th Stewards' Cup Good 6f	15th Great St Wilfrid Ripon 6f	13th Rated Hcp York 6f	*3rd Conds Stks Hayd 6f
97 Ascot 5f 10th King's Stand Three weeks	Ya Malak D Nicholls 11/2	12/14	6	9-07	76	4th City Wall Stks Ches 5f	11th King George Good 5f	WON 11/1 Nunthorpe York 5f	*8th Palace House Newm 5f
96 Ascot 5f 10th King's Stand Three weeks	Eveningperformance H Candy 7/1	13/12	5	9-02	70	6th King George York 5f	2nd Nunthorpe York 5f	WON 9/10F Flying Five Leop 5f	6th Prix de l'Abbaye Long 5f

12-year median performance rating of the winner: **72** (out of 100) *next year*

WINNER'S PROFILE Every winner was fit having **been on the racecourse within the past three weeks**, six were outclassed at Royal Ascot, while three arrived via Newcastle's Northumberland meeting.
A previous win over the trip hasn't proved vital of late as only four of the last seven had such criteria, however, what has been significant was an **official rating of 104 or higher**. Although the classy sprinters done well, Group One winners that attempted to carry a penalty failed – Reverence the latest to slip up last year at 5/2.
Those at the head of the betting came out on top as 11 winners started at **8/1 or shorter**, including the last two winners who both had a beneficial **middle to high draw**.

FUTURE POINTERS Upgraded to Group Three status in 2004, this sprint has regularly attracted a competitive field of performers just beneath the top echelon, but only one winner went on to land a Group One since 1996. Before the Champagne Sprint matured into a Group event four years ago, the majority of winners attempted a similar level of race in the near future, such as the King George Stakes at Glorious Goodwood, but since 2004, three of the four victors moved unsuccessfully straight into Group One company.
Overall, winners are best avoided unless they stick to a more suitable Group Three/Listed level, and a better option may be to follow the runners-up *(see below)*.

Were Champange Sprint winners profitable to follow on their subsequent three runs?
No – 4 wins from 34 runs returned a loss of -£14.10 to a £1 level stake.

Placed runners' subsequent record (three runs):
Runners-up: 9 wins from 36 runs returned a **profit of +£23.72** to a £1 level stake.
2006 Benbaun – Flying Five, 2004 Ringmoor Down – King George Stakes, Flying Five,
2003 Bali Royal – Listed Flower of Scotland, 2002 Boleyn Castle – Hong Kong Sprint Handicap,
2000 Lord Kintyre – Scarbrough Stakes

Thirds: 4 wins from 35 returned a loss of -£18.25 to a £1 level stake.
2001 Astonished - Scarbrough Stakes

FUTURE SUCCESS RATING: ★ ★ ☆ ☆ ☆

TOTESCOOP6 STAKES
July 5, Sandown – (Heritage Handicap, Class 2, 3yo+) 1m

Last run	Winner/ Trainer & SP	Draw/ Ran	Age	Wght	PR	Next four runs			
07 Sali 1m 1st Handicap *Two weeks*	**Ordnance Row** R Hannon 11/1	12/17	4	9-05	67	2nd Sovereign Stks Sali 1m	5th Winter Hill Stks Wind 1m2f	2nd Foundation Stks Good 1m2f	5th Darley Stks Newm 1m1f
06 Ascot 1m 4th Royal Hunt Cup *Three weeks*	**Hinterland** M Jarvis 7/2F	11/17	4	9-03	72	9th International Hcp Ascot 7f	5th Rose' Lancaster Hayd 1m3f	28th Cambridgeshire Newm 1m1f	*13th Handicap Nad Al 1m
05 Ripo 1m1f 1st Totescoop6 Hcp *Three weeks*	**Ace Of Hearts** C Wall 9/1	4/17	6	8-09	63	7th Ladbrokes Hcp Newb 1m	**WON 7/2F** **Handicap** **Wind 1m**	10th Silver Salver Hp York 1m1f	5th Cambridgeshire Newm 1m1f
04 Ascot 1m 25th Royal Hunt Cup *Three weeks*	**Pentecost** A Balding 20/1	1/15	5	8-10	68	4th Silver Trophy Ascot 1m	9th W Hill Mile Hcp Good 1m	**WON 9/2F** **Shergar Mile** **Ascot 1m**	9th Sovereign Stks Sali 1m
03 York 1m 6th Hambleton Hcp *One month*	**Putra Pekan** M Jarvis 12/1	10/16	5	9-03	72	13th W Hill Mile Hcp Good 1m	7th Park Stks Donc 7f	**WON 9/2** **Conds Stks** **Newb 1m1f**	7th Darley Stks Newm 1m1f
02 Hayd 7f 2nd Class Stks *One month*	**Heretic** J Fanshawe 7/1	1/17	4	9-06	65	6th Desmond Stks Leop 1m	*4th Sandown Mile Sand 1m	*WON 2/1 Conds Stks Donc 1m	*10th W Hill Mile Hcp Good 1m
01 Pont 1m 1st Handicap *Two months*	**Desert Deer** M Johnston 4/1	12/12	3	8-07	69	*WON 11/8F Conds Stks Newm 1m2f	*11th Prince of Wales' Ascot 1m2f	*3rd Strensall Stks York 1m1f	*2nd Park Stks Donc 1m
00 Ascot 1m 1st Royal Hunt Cup *Three weeks*	**Caribbean Monarch** Sir M Stoute 2/5F	8/18	5	9-11	71	12th International Hcp Ascot 7f	8th W Hill Mile Hcp Good 1m	-	-
99 Ascot 1m2f 1st Ladbrokes Hcp *Three weeks*	**Brilliant Red** Mrs L Richards 11/2	10/10	6	9-00	64	3rd Diamond Hcp Ascot 1m2f	7th Courage Hcp Newb 1m2f	9th Cambridgeshire Newm 1m1f	7th Melbourn Hcp Newm 1m
98 Ascot 1m 15th Royal Hunt Cup *Three weeks*	**For Your Eyes Only** T Easterby 15/2	2/13	4	9-04	68	WON 14/1 W Hill Mile Hcp Good 1m	7th Strensall Stks York 1m1f	6th Cambridgeshire Newm 1m1f	*4th Listed Nad Al 1m1f
97 Redc 1m2f 9th Zetland Gold Cup *Two months*	**Clan Ben** H Cecil 10/1	2/10	5	8-12	64	14th Hong Kong Hcp Sand 1m2f	16th W Hill Mile Hcp Good 1m	**WON 7/1** **Conds Stks** **Newb 1m2f**	-
96 Bath 1m 1st Handicap *Two weeks*	**Concer Un** S Williams 6/1JF	1/13	4	8-08	59	12th C Bulteel Hcp Ascot 1m	**WON 16/1** **Brad & Bing Hcp** **York 1m**	**WON 11/2JF** **Rated Hcp** **Ches 7f**	9th Rothmans Hcp Newb 1m

12-year median performance rating of the winner: **67** (out of 100)   **next year*

WINNER'S PROFILE Ten winners arrived having **raced within the past month**, five via Ascot – four of whom ran in the Royal Hunt Cup – and those with a **first or second in their previous two runs** are respected. **Winning form over the distance** was important as all 12 winners qualified on that basis, while the last 11 were **officially rated between 91 to 102**. Desert Deer became the only three-year-old to score in 2001 from 33 runners and it has paid to stick with **four to six-year-olds**, while trainer **Michael Jarvis** won it twice from only six runners.

FUTURE POINTERS A quality handicap that has produced some progressive individuals, and though victors haven't exactly gone on to greater achievements, the majority found their way back to the winner's enclosure. Those to have run in conditions events fared well with four winners from four runners, while two winners in the nineties landed big handicaps, including For Your Eyes Only in the 1998 William Hill Mile, although that event was unkind to four other Sandown winners. Another unsuccessful route that punters should be careful of supporting the winner in was at the Ascot King George meeting, while the Cambridgeshire later in the season foiled several more.

Were winners of this handicap profitable to follow on their subsequent three runs?
Yes – 9 wins from 35 runs returned a **profit of +£32.37** to a £1 level stake.

Placed runners' subsequent record (three runs):
Runners-up: 8 wins from 33 runs returned a **profit of +£6.50** to a £1 level stake.
1999 Lonesome Dude – William Hill Mile Handicap, 1997 Aunty Jane – Sceptre Stakes

Thirds: 3 wins from 34 runs returned a loss of -£27.23 to a £1 level stake.

Fourths: 1 win from 18 runs returned a loss of -£9.75 to a £1 level stake.
2007 Pride Of Nation – Sovereign Stakes

FUTURE SUCCESS RATING: ★ ★ ★ ☆ ☆

ECLIPSE STAKES
July 5, Sandown – (Group 1, Class 1, 3yo+) 1m2f

Last run	Winner/Trainer & SP	Draw/Ran	Age	Wght	PR	Next four runs			
07 Ascot 1m2f 3rd / Prince of Wales' / Three weeks	**Notnowcato** Sir M Stoute 7/1	1/8	5	9-07	84	3rd Juddmonte Int York 1m2f	6th Champion Stks Newm 1m2f	-	-
06 Ascot 1m2f 4th / Prince of Wales' / Three weeks	**David Junior** B Meehan 9/4	2/9	4	9-07	82	13th Breeders' Cup Chur 1m2f	-	-	-
05 York 1m 3rd / St James' Palace / Three weeks	**Oratorio** A O'Brien 12/1	1/7	3	8-10	86	**WON 7/1** Irish Champion Leop 1m2f	5th Champion Stks Newm 1m2f	11th Breeders' Cup Belm 1m2f	-
04 Ascot 1m 1st / Queen Anne / Three weeks	**Refuse To Bend** S Bin Suroor 15/2	9/12	4	9-07	83	11th Sussex Good 1m	3rd Q Elizabeth II Ascot 1m	5th Champion Stks Newm 1m2f	-
03 Ascot 1m2f 5th / Prince of Wales' / Three weeks	**Falbrav** L Cumani 8/1	14/15	5	9-07	89	5th King George Ascot 1m4f	**WON 5/2** Juddmonte Int York 1m2f	2nd Irish Champion Leop 1m2f	**WON 6/4F** Q Elizabeth II Ascot 1m
02 Epso 1m4f 2nd / Derby / One month	**Hawk Wing** A O'Brien 8/15F	6/5	3	8-10	87	2nd Irish Champion Leop 1m2f	2nd Q Elizabeth II Ascot 1m	7th Breeders' Cup Arli 1m2f	*WON 2/1F Lockinge Newb 1m
01 Ascot 1m 1st / Queen Anne / Three weeks	**Medicean** Sir M Stoute 7/2	7/8	4	9-07	79	3rd Juddmonte Int York 1m2f	-	-	-
00 Ascot 1m 1st / St James' Palace / Three weeks	**Giant's Causeway** A O'Brien 8/1	4/8	3	8-10	90	**WON 3/1JF** Sussex Good 1m	**WON 10/11F** Juddmonte Int York 1m2f	**WON 8/11F** Irish Champion Leop 1m2f	2nd Q Elizabeth II Ascot 1m
99 Epso 1m4f 8th / Derby / One month	**Compton Admiral** G Butler 20/1	7/8	3	8-10	87	5th Juddmonte Int York 1m2f	**3rd Conds Stks Newb 1m2f	-	-
98 Ascot 1m2f 3rd / Prince of Wales' / Three weeks	**Daylami** S Bin Suroor 6/4F	5/7	4	9-07	88	4th King George Ascot 1m4f	**WON 5/4F** Grade 1 Belm 1m3f	3rd Champion Stks Newm 1m2f	*5th Dubai World Cup Nad Al 1m2f
97 Ascot 1m4f 2nd / Hardwicke Stks / Three weeks	**Pilsudski** Sir M Stoute 11/2	1/5	5	9-07	89	2nd King George Ascot 1m4f	**WON 5/4F** Irish Champion Leop 1m2f	2nd Arc de Triomphe Long 1m4f	**WON EvsF** Champion Stks Newm 1m2f
96 Long 1m1f 1st / Prix d'Ispahan / Two months	**Halling** S Bin Suroor 10/3	1/7	5	9-07	89	**WON 6/4F** Juddmonte Int York 1m2f	2nd Champion Stks Newm 1m2f	-	-

12-year median performance rating of the winner: **86** (out of 100)   *next year*

WINNER'S PROFILE The last 11 winners **arrived via either the Royal meeting or Espom** – three of the last five were held in the **Prince of Wales's Stakes** – while **Group One winning form** was a must as only the rank outsider, Compton Admiral, failed in that sphere.

The four three-year-old winners all ran in the 2,000 Guineas, while half a dozen six-year-olds and above all lost. Winning form over this trip hasn't been a necessity, although an **official rating of 117 or more** was, and those in the **first four of the betting** proved best.

Trainers **Aidan O'Brien** (three from 15), **Sir Michael Stoute** (three from 12) and **Saeed Bin Suroor** (three from 14) have accounted for nine of the last 12 winners, O'Brien's were all three-year-olds. Stoute also took this three times in the early-nineties, while Suroor's patience in the last four years has resulted in one winner from as many runners.

FUTURE POINTERS Two Derby winners in the last three years have lined up in this clash of the generations following a lull since Benny The Dip's runner-up slot in 1997, with Authorized and Motivator also finishing second – Nashwan last completed the Epsom/Sandown double in1989. Although Derby winners came unstuck in the Eclipse, fellow three-year-olds that won here were worth following, as Oratorio and Giant's Causeway scored next time out at decent odds. Three successful five-year-olds did well subsequently, with Falbrav and Halling both taking the Juddmonte International, however, only Daylami struck a blow for the four-year-olds subsequently.

Were Eclipse winners profitable to follow on their subsequent three runs?
No – 8 wins from 29 runs returned a loss of -£2.87 to a £1 level stake.

Placed runners' subsequent record (three runs):
Runners-up: 6 wins from 30 runs returned a **profit of +£2.93** to a £1 level stake.
2006 Notnowcato – Juddmonte International, 2004 Warrsan – Grosser Preis von Baden, 2000 Kalanisi – Champion Stakes, Breeders' Cup

Thirds: 5 wins from 19 runs returned a loss of -£2.66 to a £1 level stake.
1999 Fantastic Light – Great Voltigeur

FUTURE SUCCESS RATING: ★ ★ ★ ☆ ☆

HERITAGE HANDICAP
July 9, Newmarket (July) – (Class 2, 3yo) 6f

Last run	Winner/Trainer & SP	Draw/Ran	Age	Wght	PR	Next four runs			
07 Ascot 1m 29th / Britannia Stks / *Three weeks*	**Shmookh** / J Dunlop 12/1	10/19	3	8-07	60	3rd / Handicap / Good 7f	6th / Starlit Stks / Good 6f	-	-
06 Kemp 6f 1st / Handicap / *Three weeks*	**Dark Missile** / A Balding 16/1	1/20	3	8-06	64	9th / Oak Tree Stks / Good 7f	**WON 4/1** / **Shergar Cup** / **Ascot 6f**	9th / Flying Fillies / Pont 6f	21st / Ayr Gold Cup / Ayr 6f
05 Donc 7f 1st / Totesport Hcp / *One month*	**Tax Free** / D Nicholls 10/1	4/20	3	8-00	67	**WON 9/4F** / **W Hill Trophy** / **York 6f**	*3rd / Palace House / Newm 5f	*3rd / Group 2 / Chan 5f	*15th / King's Stand Stk / Ascot 5f
04 York 6f 1st / W Hill Trophy / *One month*	**Alderney Race** / R Charlton 13/2	17/19	3	8-07	64	2nd / Shergar Cup / Ascot 6f	**WON 4/1** / **Rated Hcp** / **Newm 6f**	*4th / Conds Stks / Kemp 6f	*4th / Ladbrokes Hcp / Newm 6f
03 Ascot 5f 8th / Balmoral Hcp / *Three weeks*	**Move It** / R Charlton 11/2	2/14	3	8-13	62	**WON 9/2** / **Shergar Cup** / **Ascot 6f**	3rd / Rated Hcp / Newm 6f	-	-
02 Ling 6f 1st / Showcase Hcp / *Two months*	**Feet So Fast** / W Musson 10/3F	5/18	3	9-03	67	**WON 6/4F** / **Shergar Cup** / **Ascot 6f**	7th / Sheikh Trophy / Nad Al 6f	*3rd / Conds Stks / Nad Al 6f	*WON N/O / Listed / Abu 7f
01 Ascot 5f 9th / Palan Hcp / *Three weeks*	**Flying Millie** / R Beckett 16/1	4/12	3	9-00	60	3rd / Showcase Hcp / Yarm 6f	**WON 6/1** / **Shergar Cup** / **Ascot 6f**	17th / Showcase Hcp / Ascot 6f	*9th / Handicap / Good 6f
00 Sand 5f 1st / Handicap / *One week*	**Blue Velvet** / K Ivory 8/1	13/14	3	8-04	58	6th / Bonusprint Hcp / Good 7f	5th / Rated Hcp / Leic 6f	7th / Rated Hcp / York 6f	6th / Class Stks / Hayd 6f
99 Hayd 1m 15th / Silver Bowl Hcp / *Two months*	**Haafiz** / B Hanbury 14/1	10/17	3	9-07	66	**WON 4/5F** / **Conds Stks** / **Yarm 6f**	6th / City of York / York 7f	5th / Rated Hcp / York 6f	14th / Bentinck Stks / Newm 6f
98 Ascot 1m 9th / Britannia Stks / *Three weeks*	**Misbah** / B Hanbury 7/2F	1/15	3	9-02	62	13th / International Hcp / Ascot 7f	6th / Rated Hcp / Good 7f	*2nd / Stakes / Nad Al 7f	-
97 Ascot 6f 2nd / Wokingham / *Three weeks*	**Danetime** / N Callaghan 13/8F	1/10	3	9-07	66	**WON 5/1F** / **Stewards' Cup** / **Good 6f**	2nd / Sprint Cup / Hayd 6f	*3rd / Abernant Stks / Newm 6f	*3rd / Duke of York / York 6f
96 York 6f 3rd / W Hill Trophy / *One month*	**Wildwood Flyer** / R Hannon 7/1	8/9	3	8-08	57	5th / Stewards' Cup / Good 6f	**WON 8/1** / **Ladbroke Hcp** / **Good 6f**	5th / Ayr Gold Cup / Ayr 6f	5th / Bentinck Stks / Newm 6f

12-year median performance rating of the winner: **63** (out of 100) **next year*

WINNER'S PROFILE The final outing provided handy clues, as six of the seven that made the frame did so away from Royal Ascot – the exception was Danetime – while four of the five to arrive unplaced were outclassed or failed to stay a mile at that prestige meeting – Haafiz ran in the ultra-competitive Silver Bowl at Haydock.
Unexposed types **yet to have raced more than 10 times** are favoured, while there was an even spread regarding official ratings and weights. **Roger Charlton** is a trainer to side with having sent out two winners from only a few runners, however, one to be wary of is Mick Channon with several losers.

FUTURE POINTERS One of the hottest sprint handicaps of the season for three-year-olds, and while it doesn't attract the same attention as earlier ante-post events run on a Saturday, such as the Coral Sprint and William Hill Trophy, it provided a springboard for those graduating onto better things and winners have been worth supporting in the near future. Amazingly, five winners of this event all trod the same path post-Newmarket and ran in the Shergar Cup at Ascot, where four won – the other finished runner-up.
As a pointer to the major sprint handicaps, Danetime was a rare three-year-old winner of the Stewards' Cup next time, while Dark Missile and Wildwood Flower both scooped the Wokingham and Ayr Gold Cup as four-year-olds. Last year, Utmost Respect was an unlucky third here before going on to hammer his elders in the Ayr Silver Cup.

Were sprint handicap winners from here profitable to follow on their subsequent three runs?
Yes – 9 wins from 34 runs returned a **profit of +£10.05** to a £1 level stake.

Placed runners' subsequent record (three runs):
Runners-up: 3 wins from 34 runs returned a loss of -£24.00 to a £1 level stake.
1997 Elnadim – Hopeful Stakes, Diadem Stakes
Thirds: 3 wins from 32 runs returned a loss of -£14.25 to a £1 level stake.
2007 Utmost Respect – Ayr Silver Cup
Fourths: 4 wins from 21 runs returned a **profit of +£10.00** to a £1 level stake.
2006 Ripples Maid – Fillies' Listed, 1999 Emma Peel – Falmouth Handicap

FUTURE SUCCESS RATING: ★ ★ ★ ★ ★

CHERRY HINTON STAKES
July 9, Newmarket (July) – (Group 2, Class 1, 2yo Fillies) 6f

Last run	Winner/ Trainer & SP	Draw/ Ran	Age	Wght	PR	Next four runs			
07 Ascot 6f 2nd Albany Stks *Three weeks*	You'resothrilling A O'Brien 6/4F	13/14	2	8-12	66	9th Lowther Stks York 6f	-	-	-
06 Ascot 6f 1st Albany Stks *Three weeks*	Sander Camillo J Noseda 11/8F	4/10	2	8-12	73	*2nd Nell Gwyn Newm 7f	*8th Poule 'Pouliches Long 1m	*18th July Cup Newm 6f	*16th Oak Tree Stks Good 7f
05 Beve 5f 2nd Hilary Needler *Two months*	Donna Blini B Meehan 12/1	2/8	2	8-09	64	WON 12/1 Cheveley Park Newm 6f	*13th 1,000 Guineas Newm 1m	*13th Coronation Stks Ascot 1m	*2nd Summer Stks York 6f
04 Ascot 6f 1st Albany Stks *Three weeks*	Jewel In The Sand R Hannon 2/1F	8/10	2	8-09	62	11th Moyglare Stud Curr 7f	7th Cheveley Park Newm 6f	*3rd Scurry Stks Sand 5f	**5th Lansdown Stks Bath 5f
03 Ascot 5f 1st Queen Mary *Three weeks*	Attraction M Johnston 4/7F	3/8	2	8-12	80	*WON 11/2 1,000 Guineas Newm 1m	*WON 2/1F Irish 1,000 Guin Curr 1m	*WON 6/4F Coronation Stk Ascot 1m	*2nd Falmouth Stks Newm 1m
02 Good 7f 1st Maiden *Two weeks*	Spinola P Harris 7/1	1/9	2	8-09	60	7th Prestige Stks Good 7f	*13th 1,000 Guineas Newm 1m	*10th Group 3 Long 7f	*6th Falmouth Stks Newm 1m
01 Newm 6f 1st Maiden *One month*	Silent Honor D Loder 3/10F	6/7	2	8-09	60	3rd Lowther Stks York 6f	-	-	-
00 Pont 6f 1st Maiden *Three weeks*	Dora Carrington P Harris 12/1	11/9	2	8-09	66	3rd Phoenix Stks Leop 6f	*15th 1,000 Guineas Newm 1m	-	-
99 Ascot 5f 6th Albany Stks *Three weeks*	Torgau G Bravery 12/1	7/12	2	8-09	62	2nd Moyglare Stud Curr 7f	2nd Cheveley Park Newm 6f	*7th 1,000 Guineas Newm 1m	-
98 Newm 6f 1st Empress Stks *Two weeks*	Wannabe Grand J Noseda 11/1	7/10	2	8-09	71	4th Pr'ncss Margaret Ascot 6f	2nd Lowther Stks York 6f	4th Moyglare Stud Curr 7f	WON 3/1F Cheveley Park Newm 6f
97 Ascot 5f 1st Windsor Castle *Three weeks*	Asfurah S Bin Suroor 9/2	6/12	2	8-09	64	2nd Phoenix Stks Leop 6f	*4th Fillies' Listed Newm 6f	-	-
96 Ascot 5f 1st Windsor Castle *Three weeks*	Dazzle Sir M Stoute 2/1F	3/9	2	8-09	70	4th Cheveley Park Newm 6f	2nd Rockfel Stks Newm 7f	*3rd 1,000 Guineas Newm 1m	*9th Irish 1,000 Guin Curr 1m

12-year median performance rating of the winner: **67** (out of 100)   *next year **two years*

WINNER'S PROFILE Clues were hard to find, although 11 winners arrived having **raced within the past month**, seven of whom were seen at **Royal Ascot** where five triumphed.
Winning form has also been amongst the last 12 winners' previous two runs, and three successive maiden winners emerged since 2000. **Favourites** have now won five of the last seven renewals, one of whom was trained by **Jeremy Noseda**, who has sent out two winners from only five runners.

FUTURE POINTERS Talk of the following year's 1,000 Guineas can be in the air following the Cherry Hinton as bookmakers flash their prices around, but only Attraction went on to land that Classic during the last 12 years showing this event to be of limited value regarding long-term significance – Sayyedati the only other to do the double in the last 20 years. Attraction was also head and shoulders above any other winner of this event since 1996 earning a quality performance rating (PR) – recorded the second-fastest time in the last 20 years after Dazzle – and it may be a few years before anything else comes along that is worth taking fancy ante-post odds about.

Were Cherry Hinton winners profitable to follow on their subsequent three runs?
No – 4 wins from 30 runs returned a loss of -£5.00 to a £1 level stake.

Placed runners' subsequent record (three runs):
Runners-up: 6 wins from 31 runs returned a loss of -£11.35 to a £1 level stake.
2000 Enthused – Princess Margaret, Lowther Stakes, 1998 Pipalong – Redcar 2yo Trophy

Thirds: 2 wins from 28 runs returned a loss of -£20.38 to a £1 level stake.
2000 Lady Lahar – Futurity Stakes

FUTURE SUCCESS RATING: ★ ★ ☆ ☆ ☆

FALMOUTH STAKES
July 9, Newmarket (July) – (Group 1, Class 1, 3yo+ Fillies & Mares) 1m

Last run	Winner/ Trainer & SP	Draw/ Ran	Age	Wght	PR	Next four runs			
07 Epsom 1m4f 6th Oaks *Two months*	Simply Perfect J Noseda 6/1	4/7	3	8-10	74	3rd Prix d'Astarte Deau 1m	4th Sun Chariot Newm 1m	PU Breeders' Cup Monm 1m3f	-
06 Ascot 1m 5th Coronation Stks *Three weeks*	Rajeem C Brittain 50/1	4/7	3	8-10	75	-	-	-	-
05 York 1m 3rd Windsor Forest *Three weeks*	Soviet Song J Fanshawe 7/4F	1/7	5	9-01	84	2nd Sussex Good 1m	*4th Lockinge Newb 1m	*WON 11/8F Windsor Forest Ascot 1m	*6th Falmouth Stks Newm 1m
04 Ascot 1m 2nd Queen Anne *Three weeks*	Soviet Song J Fanshawe 11/4	3/7	4	9-01	85	WON 3/1 Sussex Good 1m	WON 8/13F Matron Stks Leop 1m	6th Q Elizabeth II Ascot 1m	*3rd Windsor Forest York 1m
03 Ascot 1m 1st Royal Hunt Cup *Three weeks*	Macadamia J Fanshawe 2/1JF	8/8	4	9-01	71	5th Nassau Good 1m2f	2nd Sun Chariot Newm 1m	11th Darley Stks Newm 1m1f	-
02 Ascot 1m 1st Sandringham Hcp *Three weeks*	Tashawak J Dunlop 5/2F	9/9	3	8-06	73	7th Jacques 'Marois Deau 1m	-	-	-
01 Chan 1m 8th Group 3 *Two months*	Proudwings R Suerland 10/1	2/11	5	9-04	72	Disq (1st) Jacques 'Marois Deau 1m	7th Q Elizabeth II Ascot 1m	WON N/O Stakes Toky 1m	9th Hong Kong Mile Sha 1m
00 Long 1m 3rd Poule'Pouliches *Two months*	Alshakr B Hanbury 9/2	1/10	3	8-06	67	2nd Sun Chariot Newm 1m	13th Champion Stks Newm 1m2f	-	-
99 Chan 1m 1st Group 3 *One month*	Ronda C Laffon-Parias 8/1	7/8	3	8-06	69	3rd Grade 1 Belm 1m1f	6th Grade 1 Keen 1m1f	-	-
98 Ascot 7f 3rd Jersey Stks *Three weeks*	Lovers Knot Sir M Stoute 11/4F	3/13	3	8-06	71	6th Group 2 Deau 1m	3rd Celebration Mile Good 1m	2nd Challenge Stks Newm 7f	5th Group 3 Chur 1m1f
97 Chan 1m3f 4th Prix D Hermes *One month*	Ryafan J Gosden 4/1	3/7	3	8-06	80	WON 9/4F Nassau Good 1m2f	WON N/O Grade 1 Keen 1m1f	WON N/O Grade 1 Sant 1m2f	WON N/O Grade 1 Holl 1m2f
96 Chan 1m 1st Group 3 *Two months*	Sensation Mme C Head 10/11F	7/9	3	8-06	68	9th Jacques 'Marois Deau 1m	7th Grade 1 Keen 1m1f	*8th Grade 2 Siro 1m	*12th Group 2 Long 1m1f

12-year median performance rating of the winner: **74** (out of 100)   *next year*

WINNER'S PROFILE Simply Perfect was last year the first filly for around 25 years to arrive via the Oaks, whereas the remainder came from either the **Royal meeting or France**.
It paid to avoid fillies from the 1,000 Guineas – no winner emerged from there for 17 years – though the last seven did have a **distance victory** to their name. Often run at a slow gallop, it helps to have a runner **blessed with speed or who sits handy**, rather than a hold-up performer needing a fast pace.
Trainer **James Fanshawe** leads the way with three winners from eight runners.

FUTURE POINTERS Since maturing into a Group One four years ago, this event has attracted the best female milers around with Soviet Song gracing the roll of honour twice before further riches, while two recent runners-up also went on to secure major races, underlining the growing strength of the Falmouth.
Another of the best winners, Ryafan, earned an above par performance rating (PR) in 1997, before taking the Nassau Stakes, to go with three Grade Ones in America. However, the majority of Falmouth winners failed to kick on post-Newmarket with the Jacques le Marois in Deauville, and the Sun Chariot Stakes at Newmarket, catching several out, although two placed from here scored in the latter race *(see below)*.

Were Falmouth winners profitable to follow on their subsequent three runs?
No – 7 wins from 29 runs returned a loss of -£14.76 to a £1 level stake.

Placed runners' subsequent record (three runs):
Runners-up: 2 wins from 21 runs returned a loss of -£14.62 to a £1 level stake.
2005 Alexander Goldrun – Nassau, 2004 Attraction – Sun Chariot

Thirds: 5 wins from 17 runs returned a **profit of +£10.57** to a £1 level stake.
2000 Danceabout – Sun Chariot

FUTURE SUCCESS RATING: ★ ★ ☆ ☆ ☆

JULY STAKES

July 10, Newmarket (July) – (Group 2, Class 1, 2yo Colts & Geldings) 6f

Last run	Winner/ Trainer & SP	Draw/ Ran	Age	Wght	PR	Next four runs			
07 Ascot 5f 1st Norfolk Stks One month	**Winker Watson** P Chapple-Hyam 11/4F	1/13	2	9-01	74	-	-	-	-
06 Ascot 5f 5th Norfolk Stks Three weeks	**Strategic Prince** P Cole 16/1	4/9	2	8-12	69	WON 6/1 Vintage Stks Good 7f	3rd Dewhurst Stks Newm 7f	*8th 2,000 Guineas Newm 1m	*16th Derby Epsom 1m4f
05 Leop 6f 1st Maiden Two months	**Ivan Denisovich** A O'Brien 7/2	5/11	2	8-10	67	2nd Prix Morny Deau 6f	4th Middle Park Newm 6f	12th Breeder's Cup Belm 1m	*8th Group 3 Long 1m
04 Sali 6f 2nd Maiden Two weeks	**Captain Hurricane** P Chapple-Hyam 10/1	6/7	2	8-10	68	4th Prix Morny Deau 6f	16th Yearling Sales Donc 6f	*9th Greenham Newb 7f	*14th Golden Jubilee York 6f
03 Ascot 5f 3rd Norfolk Stks Three weeks	**Nevisian Lad** M Bell 4/1	1/8	2	8-10	63	9th Vintage Stks Good 7f	10th Middle Park Newm 6f	**7th Handicap Nad Al 6f	-
02 Newb 6f 1st Conds Stks One month	**Mister Links** R Hannon 2/1F	3/10	2	8-10	64	2nd Gimcrack Stks York 6f	2nd Yearling Sales Donc 6f	10th Prix de l'Abbaye Long 5f	*3rd Greenham Newb 7f
01 Ascot 6f 3rd Coventry Stks One month	**Meshaheer** D Loder 1/3F	1/5	2	8-10	67	3rd Prix Morny Deau 6f	*19th 2,000 Guineas Newm 1m	*3rd Jersey Stks Ascot 7f	*13th July Cup Newm 6f
00 Mais 6f 1st Listed One month	**Noverre** D Loder 5/2F	4/6	2	8-13	71	2nd Prix Morny Deau 6f	WON 7/2 Champagne Stk Donc 7f	2nd Dewhurst Stks Newm 7f	11th Breeder's Cup Chur 1m
99 Chan 6f 1st Listed One month	**City On A Hill** D Loder 11/2	2/7	2	8-13	75	7th Prix Morny Deau 6f	*10th Stakes Nad Al 6f	-	-
98 Ascot 6f 5th Coventry Stks One month	**Bertolini** J Gosden 3/1	1/6	2	8-10	77	2nd Group 2 Mais 6f	4th Gimcrack Stks York 6f	7th Champagne Stk Donc 7f	2nd Middle Park Newm 6f
97 Ascot 6f 3rd Coventry Stks One month	**Bold Fact** H Cecil EvensF	6/8	2	8-10	69	2nd Gimcrack Stks York 6f	*WON 11/4JF King Charles II Newm 7f	*9th Jersey Stks Ascot 7f	*8th July Cup Newm 6f
96 Newc 6f 1st Maiden Two weeks	**Rich Ground** J Bethell 40/1	7/9	2	8-10	62	4th Prix Morny Deau 6f	9th Middle Park Newm 6f	*3rd Euro Free Hcp Newm 7f	*2nd Group 2 Curr 7f

12-year median performance rating of the winner: **68** (out of 100)   *next year **two years

WINNER'S PROFILE Clues are thin on the ground, although 11 winners lined up having **run within the past month** – no winner had **run more than twice** – while six arrived via Royal Ascot, where they all reached the top-five; the Coventry has been best guide long-term. Those coming here from the Windsor Castle Stakes are best avoided, while the Norfolk winner, Winker Watson, last year became the first to follow up a Royal Ascot win in this period and in the process carried a penalty, as did two other winners.
A previous victory over the distance wasn't essential, demonstrated by Captain Hurricane in 2004, who was trainer **Peter Chapple-Hyam**'s first of two winners from only three runners.

FUTURE POINTERS Not even an upgrade to Group Two status in 2003 helped this event provide a significant stepping stone for the future, and only Strategic Prince managed to follow up in Group Two company next time out. Six winners since 1996 met with defeat in the Prix Morny, while three went down in the Gimcrack, and five were beaten in either the Dewhurst or Middle Park.
Only three winners of the July Stakes since 1987 ever scored in Group One company, with First Trump taking the Middle Park in 1993, Tagula landing the Prix Morny in 1995, and Noverre in the Sussex the following year in 2001. During this 20-year period, those to have attempted the 2,000 Guineas finished: 8th, 11th, 19th, 7th, and 4th.

Were July Stakes winners profitable to follow on their subsequent three runs?
No – 3 wins from 32 runs returned a loss of -£16.75 to a £1 level stake.

Placed runners' subsequent record (three runs):
Runners-up: 6 wins from 30 runs returned a loss of -£2.70 to a £1 level stake.
2007 River Proud – Tattersalls Stakes, 2004 Council Member – King Charles II,
2003 Cape Fear – St Leger Yearling Sales, 1999 Mull Of Kintyre – Gimcrack

Thirds: 3 wins from 19 runs returned a loss of -£3.50 to a £1 level stake.
2003 Byron – Mill Reef Stakes

FUTURE SUCCESS RATING: ★ ☆ ☆ ☆ ☆

HERITAGE HANDICAP

July 10, Newmarket (July) – (Class 2, 3yo) 1m2f

Last run	Winner/ Trainer & SP	Draw/ Ran	Age	Wght	PR	Next four runs			
07 Ascot 2m 15th Queen's Vase *Three weeks*	**Hearthstead Maison** M Johnston 25/1	8/19	3	9-07	76	15th Heritage Hcp Good 1m2f	4th Rose of Lancaster Hayd 1m3	7th Great Voltigeur York 1m4f	**WON 9/2** Group 3 Leop 1m2f
06 Pont 1m2f 1st Handicap *One month*	**Formal Decree** A Swinbank 3/1F	6/14	3	8-13	65	4th Totesport Hcp Beve 1m2f	3rd J Smith's Hcp Newb 1m2f	Cambridgeshire Newm 1m1f	*WON 11/4F Handicap Nad Al 1m1f
05 Pont 1m2f 2nd Handicap *Three weeks*	**Danehill Willy** N Callaghan 20/1	5/16	3	8-01	60	WON 11/4 Class Stks Epsom 1m2f	2nd Handicap York 1m2f	13th J Smith's Hcp Newb 1m2f	10th Handicap Newm 1m2f
04 Ascot 1m4f 13th K George V Hcp *Three weeks*	**Woodcracker** M Bell 10/1	9/11	3	9-00	65	*2nd Handicap Newm 1m2f	*17th J Smith's Cup York 1m2f	*16th Heritage Hcp Hayd 1m3f	*14th Motability Hcp York 1m2f
03 Newm 1m 3rd Class Stks *Three weeks*	**Leporello** P Harris 12/1	16/15	3	8-09	68	WON 13/8F Showcase Hcp Hayd 1m3f	WON 5/2 Winter Hill Stks Wind 1m2f	WON 15/8 Select Stks Good 1m2f	*3rd Huxley Stks Ches 1m2f
02 Ascot 1m 5th Britannia Stks *Three weeks*	**Bonecrusher** J Dunlop 7/1	18/21	3	9-06	66	*4th Listed Nad Al 1m2f	*6th Handicap Nad Al 1m2f	*4th Rated Hcp Wind 1m2f	*WON EvsF Conds Stks Newm 1m2f
01 Sout 1m 2nd Maiden *Ten months*	**Alphaeus** Sir M Prescott 5/1	5/9	3	8-00	70	WON EvsF Rated Hcp Newm 1m2f	15th Cambridgeshire Newm 1m1f	-	-
00 Ascot 1m 10th Britannia Stks *Three weeks*	**Moon Solitaire** E Dunlop 12/1	1/13	3	8-11	65	3rd Rated Hcp Hayd 1m3f	3rd Courage Hcp Newb 1m2f	11th Handicap Newm 1m2f	*3rd Rosebery Hcp Kemp 1m2f
99 Good 1m2f 6th Predominate Stk *Two months*	**Zindabad** B Hanbury 12/1	11/13	3	9-06	74	WON 11/4JF Diamond Hcp Ascot 1m2f	WON 7/4F Winter Hill Stks Wind 1m2f	5th Select Stks Good 1m2f	*3rd Mercury Listed Leic 1m4f
98 Yarm 1m 1st Maiden *Two months*	**Hitman** H Cecil 4/1F	5/16	3	9-03	72	3rd Gordon Stks Good 1m4f	6th Great Voltigeur York 1m4f	*PU Nov Hdle Kemp 2m	**4th Bula Hurdle Chel 2m1f
97 Ascot 1m4f 4th K George V Hcp *Three weeks*	**Memorise** H Cecil 5/1F	12/16	3	8-12	68	2nd Tote Gold Tr'py Good 1m4f	2nd Troy Stks Donc 1m4f	2nd Godolphin Stks Newm 1m4f	*3rd Ormonde Stks Ches 1m5f
96 Donc 1m2f 3rd Maiden *Two weeks*	**Freedom Flame** M Johnston 9/1	12/13	3	8-05	59	4th Rated Hcp Wind 1m2f	14th Globetrotter Hcp Good 1m2f	-	-

12-year median performance rating of the winner: **67** (out of 100)   *italic = jumps, *next year ** two years*

WINNER'S PROFILE There aren't many clues leading to the ideal profile as winners had mixed backgrounds – those that stepped up from a mile in the Britannia to ones dropping down from two miles like last year – while horses at the top and bottom of the handicap have scored. However, since 1996 only Alphaeus from the Sir Mark Prescott yard hadn't **run within the past two months**, and five performed at Royal Ascot last time out, including Hearthstead Maison, who was the sixth winner in the last nine years to start at a **double-figure price**. That also gave trainer **Mark Johnston** his second victory, along with **Henry Cecil**, who sent out two winning favourites.
Those **drawn five and above** were favoured, as stalls one to four only made the top-three on three occasions.

FUTURE POINTERS A top-class handicap that has traditionally drawn a host of improving three-year-old handicappers on the up, and the last two renewals raised it's profile further in providing a couple of Cambridgeshire winners with Pipedreamer – fourth here last year – and Formal Decree in 2006.
In fact, winners since 1999 have regularly found their way back to the winner's enclosure, as the likes of Leporello and Zindabad progressed to lift the Listed Winter Hill Stakes at Windsor, while last year's winner, Hearthstead Maison, managed to secure Group Three success in Ireland.
Below par winners aside, this is a handicap to follow the protagonists, as can be seen from the runners-up below.

Were winners of this handicap profitable to follow on their subsequent three runs?
No – 8 wins from 34 runs returned a loss of -£2.76 to a £1 level stake.

Placed runners' subsequent record (three runs):
Runners-up: 8 wins from 32 runs returned a **profit of +£0.55** to a £1 level stake.

Thirds: 3 wins from 30 runs returned a loss of -£14.37 to a £1 level stake.

Fourths: 4 wins from 11 runs returned a **profit of +£15.50** to a £1 level stake.
Pipedreamer – Heritage Handicap (Goodwood), Cambridgeshire

FUTURE SUCCESS RATING: ★ ★ ★ ★ ★

PRINCESS OF WALES'S STAKES
July 10, Newmarket (July) – (Group 2, Class 1, 3yo+) 1m4f

Last run	Winner/Trainer & SP	Draw/Ran	Age	Wght	PR	Next four runs			
07 Sand 1m2f 5th Brigadier Gerard *Two months*	Papal Bull Sir M Stoute 11/1	8/12	4	9-02	84	WON 6/4F Geoffrey Freer Newb 1m5f	3rd Arc Trial Newb 1m3f	-	-
06 Ascot 2m 1st Queen's Vase *Three weeks*	Soapy Danger M Johnston 5/1	1/4	3	8-03	79	5th Great Voltigeur York 1m4f	-	-	-
05 York 1m4f 3rd Hardwicke Stks *Three weeks*	Gamut Sir M Stoute 2/1	4/5	6	9-02	82	9th King George VI Newb 1m4f	5th Geoffrey Freer Newb 1m5f	5th Irish St Leger Curr 1m6f	-
04 Ascot 1m2f 9th Prince of Wales *Three weeks*	Bandari M Johnston 12/1	8/8	5	9-02	80	7th King George VI Ascot 1m4f	3rd September Stks Kemp 1m4f	3rd Cumberland Lodge Ascot 1m4f	9th Premio Jockey Siro 1m4f
03 Sain 1m4f 2nd Group 2 *Two months*	Millenary J Dunlop 5/1	2/6	6	9-02	79	8th King George VI Ascot 1m4f	4th Group 2 Deau 1m5f	2nd Jockey Club Cup Newm 2m	*3th Sagaro Stks Ascot 2m
02 Ascot 1m4f 3rd Hardwicke Stks *Three weeks*	Millenary J Dunlop 5/2F	6/7	5	9-02	77	3rd Group 1 Pokal Colo 1m4f	5th Irish St Leger Curr 1m6f	5th Premio Jockey Siro 1m4f	*2nd Jockey Club Stks Newm 1m4f
01 Chur 1m4f 4th Breeders' Cup *Eight months*	Mutamam A Stewart 11/2	2/9	6	9-02	83	9th King George VI Ascot 1m4f	WON 4/6F September Stk Kemp 1m4f	WON 17/4 Canadian Int Wood 1m4f	11th Breeders' Cup Belm 1m4f
00 Chan 1m4f 6th Group 2 *One month*	Little Rock Sir M Stoute 10/3	4/6	4	9-02	78	3rd Shergar Cup Ascot 1m4f	4th Group 2 Deau 1m5f	5th Irish St Leger Curr 1m6f	*4th Prix Ganay Long 1m2f
99 Donc 1m7f 1st Conds Stks *Eight months*	Craigsteel H Cecil 13/2	6/8	4	9-02	78	2nd Geoffrey Freer Newb 1m5f	7th St Simon Stks Newb 1m4f	*3rd Grade 2 Wood 1m3f	*2nd Grade 2 Wood 1m4f
98 Kemp 1m2f 2nd Gala Stks *One week*	Fruits Of Love M Johnston 7/1	3/7	3	8-03	74	3rd Meld Stks Curr 1m2f	5th Group 2 Deau 1m5f	8th Cumberland Lodge Ascot 1m4f	4th Group 2 Long 1m4f
97 Siro 1m4f 1st Premio 'Milano *One month*	Shantou J Gosden 11/4	7/7	4	9-07	83	5th King George VI Ascot 1m4f	3rd Geoffrey Freer Newb 1m5f	-	-
96 Ascot 1m4f 3rd Hardwicke Stks *Three weeks*	Posidonas P Cole 20/1	6/8	4	9-07	80	2nd Group 1 Duss 1m4f	2nd Geoffrey Freer Newb 1m5f	4th Irish St Leger Curr 1m6f	10th Grade 1 Belm 1m4f

12-year median performance rating of the winner: **80** (out of 100)   *next year*

WINNER'S PROFILE **Winning form in Group company** has proven vital, 11 had such criteria, although those with a Group One victory should be treated with caution as only Shantou from over a dozen runners since 1997 achieved such a feat – Sixties Icon flopped at 7/4 last year.
Five arrived via the Royal meeting – three finished third in the **Hardwicke Stakes** – while an **official rating of 111 or higher** is the level required, and those with a **prior victory at Newmarket** – both courses – have come back to do well at HQ. Fancied runners in the **top-three of the betting** held sway, although only one favourite obliged, while from a training perspective, **Mark Johnston** and **Sir Michael Stoute** led the way with three winners each, but the latter has a better strike-rate from just eight runners.

FUTURE POINTERS Some distinguished names have won this prize over the years including the likes of Shantou, Mutamam and Millenary, but as pointer to the upcoming middle-distance Group events, the Princess of Wales's Stakes hasn't been a great guide. In fact, only last year's winner, Papal Bull and Mutamam found the winner's enclosure again in the near future, the latter bounced back after finding the King George VI too hot, as did five others. Papal Bull managed to land the Geoffrey Freer, a race in which four failed, the same number that came unstuck in the Irish St Leger.
Overall, winners should be swerved post-Newmarket, unlike runners-up, who have a superior record *(see below)*.

Were Princess of Wales's winners profitable to follow on their subsequent three runs?
No – 3 wins from 32 runs returned a loss of -£22.59 to a £1 level stake.

Placed runners' subsequent record (three runs):
Runners-up: 11 wins from 31 runs returned a **profit of +£31.04** to a £1 level stake.
2005 Day Flight – St Simon Stakes, Gordon Richards, 2004 Sulamani – Juddmonte International, Canadian International, 2002 Mubtaker – Geoffrey Freer, 1998 Multicoloured – Geoffrey Freer, 1997 Swain - King George VI, 1996 Singspiel – Canadian International

Thirds: 2 wins from 12 runs returned a loss of -£2.57 to a £1 level stake.

FUTURE SUCCESS RATING: ★ ★ ☆ ☆ ☆

SUPERLATIVE STAKES

July 11, Newmarket (July) – (Group 2, Class 1, 2yo) 7f

Last run	Winner/ Trainer & SP	Draw/ Ran	Age	Wght	PR	Next four runs			
07 Ascot 5f 3rd Windsor Castle *One month*	**Hatta Fort** M Channon 4/1	9/10	2	9-00	63	4th Prix 'Lagardere Long 7f	6th Dewhurst Stks Newm 7f	-	-
06 Newm 7f 1st Maiden *Three weeks*	**Halicarnassus** M Channon 33/1	5/7	2	9-00	68	14th Dewhurst Stks Newm 7f	*3rd Greenham Newb 7f	*17th 2,000 Guineas Newm 1m	**WON 7/2 Cocked Hat Stk Good 1m3f
05 Curr 7f 1st Maiden *Two weeks*	**Horatio Nelson** A O'Brien 9/4F	2/11	2	8-11	69	WON 2/7F Futurity Stks Curr 7f	WON 4/7F Grand Criterium Long 7f	2nd Dewhurst Stks Newm 7f	*8th 2,000 Guineas Newm 1m
04 Good 6f 1st Maiden *Two months*	**Dubawi** S Bin Suroor 15/8F	12/12	2	8-11	68	WON 8/13F National Stks Curr 7f	*WON 7/4JF 2,000 Guineas Newm 1m	*3rd Irish 2,000 Guin Curr 1m	Derby Epsom 1m4f
03 Good 6f 1st Maiden *Two weeks*	**Kings Point** R Hannon 6/1	1/9	2	8-11	63	6th Vintage Stks Good 7f	*5th Shadwell Stks Ling 1m	*10th Greenham Newb 7f	*5th Listed Stks Good 1m
02 Ascot 6f 12th Coventry Stks *One month*	**Surbiton** B Hills 16/1	5/7	2	8-11	67	**WON N/O Stakes Nad Al 1m	**5th Handicap Nad Al 1m1f	**9th Handicap Nad Al 1m2f	**9th Group 3 Nad Al 1m1f
01 Curr 6f 4th Railway Stks *Two weeks*	**Redback** R Hannon 11/2	1/4	2	9-02	64	7th Vintage Stks Good 7f	WON 14/1 Solario Stks Sand 7f	4th Tattersalls Stks Newm 7f	3rd R Post Trophy Donc 1m
00 (Unraced)	**Vacamonte** H Cecil 7/4F	8/8	2	8-11	62	5th Solario Stks Sand 7f	6th Dewhurst Stks Newm 7f	-	-
99 Gowr 7f 1st Maiden *One month*	**Thady Quill** A O'Brien EvensF	1/5	2	8-11	59	3rd Stakes Gulf 1m1f	**2nd Grade 2 Sant 1m	***5th Breeders' Cup Holl 1m	
98 (Unraced)	**Commander Collins** P Chapple-Hyam 4/5F	1/6	2	8-11	70	2nd Champagne Stk Donc 7f	WON 2/1F R Post Trophy Donc 1m	*11th 2,000 Guineas Newm 1m	*4th Group 2 Deau 1m2f
97 Yarm 6f 1st Maiden *Two months*	**Baltic State** H Cecil 8/11F	3/4	2	9-00	61	5th Vintage Stks Good 7f	*3rd Conds Stks Yarm 7f	*4th Conds Stks Newb 7f	*WON 5/2 Conds Stks Newc 7f
96 Pont 6f 3rd Conds Stks *Three weeks*	**Recondite** M Channon 14/1	6/6	2	9-00	62	2nd Futurity Stks Curr 7f	8th Royal Lodge Ascot 1m	*7th Feilden Stks Newm 1m	**4th Stakes Long 7f

12-year median performance rating of the winner: **65** (out of 100) *next year **two years ***three years

WINNER'S PROFILE It's hard to pin down clues that highlight an ideal profile, with debutants, last time out maiden winners and beaten runners from Royal Ascot succeeding.
The market proved reliable on a number of occasions, but on the other hand three outsiders sprung up, including two trained by **Mick Channon**, who has won it three times from nine runners. It could be the trainers, however, that provide the best guide, as Richard Hannon had a pair from five runners, Aidan O'Brien had two from six, while the governor of this event, **Henry Cecil**, boasts superb credentials. Since 1988, the Newmarket handler has a truly remarkable and very rare record, for he has sent out eight winners from as many runners, the last in 2000.
In a nutshell, anything he run, won.

FUTURE POINTERS Although no winner of the Superlative went on to land a British Classic since Dr Devious in 1991 – who took the following year's Derby – it still boasts an impressive Hall of Fame featuring several subsequent Group One winners, including Dubawi, who took the Irish 2,000 Guineas a year later in 2005.
Horatio Nelson and Commander Collins were two other top-class juveniles to have gained Group One honours, contributing in the process to the Superlative's elevation from Listed to Group Two status. Two races, however, to have been less kind to Newmarket winners were the Vintage and Dewhurst Stakes, as six met with defeat.

Were Superlative Stakes winners profitable to follow on their subsequent three runs?
No – 7 wins from 34 runs returned a loss of -£7.79 to a £1 level stake.

Placed runners' subsequent record (three runs):
Runners-up: 3 wins from 20 runs returned a **profit of +£5.50** to a £1 level stake.
2005 Leo – Royal Lodge, 2004 Wilko – Breeders' Cup Juvenile (six runs later), 2002 Magistretti – Feilden Stakes

Thirds: 1 win from 14 runs returned a loss of -£12.83 to a £1 level stake.

FUTURE SUCCESS RATING: ★ ★ ★ ☆ ☆

BUNBURY CUP

July 11, Newmarket (July) – (Class 2, Heritage Handicap, 3yo+) 7f

Last run	Winner/Trainer & SP	Draw/Ran	Age	Wght	PR	Next four runs			
07 Ches 7f 3rd Handicap *One month*	Giganticus B Hills 16/1	3/18	4	8-08	69	4th International Hp Ascot 7f	WON 7/2 Sky Hcp Newm 7f	10th Heritage Hcp Ches 7f	12th Tote Hcp Ascot 7f
06 Ascot 1m 8th Royal Hunt Cup *One month*	Mine J Bethell 10/1	14/19	8	9-10	71	10th International Hp Ascot 7f	2nd Fortune Stks Hayd 7f	12th Totesport Hcp Ascot 7f	*9th Hambleton Hcp York 1m
05 York 1m 11th Royal Hunt Cup *One month*	Mine J Bethell 16/1	6/18	7	9-09	70	10th International Hp Newb 7f	10th Sovereign Stks Sali 1m	12th Porcelanosa Hcp Donc 1m	9th Guisborough Stk Redc 7f
04 Warw 7f 1st Class Stks *Two weeks*	Material Witness W Muir 25/1	6/19	7	9-03	67	2nd Class Stks Good 7f	9th Stewards' Cup Good 6f	4th City of York York 7f	WON 11/2 Rated Hcp Good 7f
03 Ascot 6f 5th Wokingham *Three weeks*	Patavellian R Charlton 4/1F	2/20	5	9-01	74	WON 4/1 Stewards' Cup Good 6f	WON 9/1 Prix 'Abbaye Long 5f	*3rd Group 3 Long 5f	*10th July Cup Newm 6f
02 Newc 7f 3rd Journal Hcp *Two weeks*	Mine J Bethell 5/1F	3/16	4	8-12	64	9th International Hp Ascot 7f	12th Showcase Hcp York 6f	11th Ayr Gold Cup Ayr 6f	18th Tote Hcp Ascot 7f
01 Ascot 1m 4th Royal Hunt Cup *One month*	Atavus G Margarson 10/1	14/19	4	8-12	67	WON 11/1 International Hp Ascot 7f	4th W Hill Mile Hcp Good 1m	WON 33/1 Hungerford Stk Newb 7f	14th Diadem Stks Ascot 6f
00 Newc 7f 3rd Journal Hcp *Two weeks*	Tayseer D Nicholls 9/1	8/19	6	8-09	68	3rd International Hp Ascot 7f	WON 13/2 Stewards' Cup Good 6f	7th City of York York 7f	7th Ayr Gold Cup Ayr 6f
99 Sand 7f 2nd Tote Hcp *One month*	Grangeville I Balding 13/2JF	20/19	4	9-03	67	7th International Hp Ascot 7f	3rd Showcase Hcp Newm 7f	3rd Hopeful Stks Newm 6f	WON 11/1 Ayr Gold Cup Ayr 6f
98 Ascot 7f 13th Jersey Stks *One month*	Ho Leng Miss L Perratt 14/1	20/20	3	9-07	65	12th Ayr Gold Cup Ayr 6f	4th Bentinck Stks Newm 6f	7th Conds Stks Donc 7f	*10th Hambleton Hcp York 1m
97 Ascot 6f 13th Wokingham *Three weeks*	Tumbleweed Ridge B Meehan 20/1	19/20	4	9-06	63	3rd Rated Hcp Yarm 7f	8th Hungerford Stks Newb 7f	13th Rated Hcp Good 7f	4th Rated Hcp Good 7f
96 Ascot 1m 3rd Royal Hunt Cup *One month*	Crumpton Hill N Graham 7/1	3/16	4	8-12	57	3rd N Zealand Hcp Newm 7f	*16th Victoria Cup Ascot 7f	*4th Whitsun Cup Hp Sand 1m	*8th Royal Hunt Cup Ascot 1m

12-year median performance rating of the winner: **67** (out of 100) *next year*

WINNER'S PROFILE Race fitness was important as every winner had **seen a racecourse within the past month**, eight of whom ran at the **Royal meeting**. The last 11 winners **recorded a victory over this seven-furlong** intermediate distance, while the same number were either **winless or had only scored once earlier** in the season – only one was victorious last time out in a classified stakes race.

The draw has been important, and as a rule of thumb, concentrate on those low when the race is on the far side, but go high if it is run on the stands' side.

There aren't many trainer clues, although those with patience may be interested in **Michael Jarvis**'s careful record, as the underrated handler sent out the winner twice at the start of the nineties but has only had two runners since.

FUTURE POINTERS The betting highlight of the Newmarket July meeting is always a competitive event whose standard has increased over the years. Back in 1996, only three horses lined up with an official rating of 100 or more, in comparison to last year when it rose to 10 – over half the field – which has had a positive effect on the winner's subsequent results. If you exclude the triple winner Mine, who was aimed at this race and therefore wasn't expected to go on after, several Bunbury Cup winners since 1999 went on to land major handicaps, including Patavellian, who after scooping the Stewards' Cup raised his game in the Group One Prix de l'Abbaye.

Were Bunbury Cup winners profitable to follow on their subsequent three runs?
Yes – 6 wins from 36 runs returned a **profit of +£37.00** to a £1 level stake.

Placed runners' subsequent record (three runs):
Runners-up: 5 wins from 31 runs returned a **profit of +2.50** to a £1 level stake.
2004 Court Masterpiece – International Handicap, 2000 Persiano – William Hill Mile Handicap

Thirds: 0 win from 35 runs returned a loss of -£35.00 to a £1 level stake.

Fourths: 1 win from 34 runs returned a loss of -£29.50 to a £1 level stake

FUTURE SUCCESS RATING: ★ ★ ★ ☆ ☆

JULY CUP

July 11, Newmarket (July) – (Group 1, Class 1, 3yo+) 6f

Last run	Winner/ Trainer & SP	Draw/ Ran	Age	Wght	PR	Next four runs			
07 Sali 6f 1st Cathedral Stks One month	**Sakhee's Secret** H Morrison 9/2	16/18	3	8-13	85	5th Sprint Cup Hayd 6f	-	-	-
06 Ascot 6f 1st Golden Jubilee Three weeks	**Les Arcs** T Pitt 10/1	15/15	6	9-05	81	7th Sprinters Stks Naka 6f	*13th Duke of York York 6f		
05 York 1m 7th Queen Anne One month	**Pastoral Pursuits** H Morrison 22/1	10/19	4	9-05	82	-	-	-	-
04 Ascot 5f 3rd King's Stand One month	**Frizzante** J Fanshawe 14/1	18/20	5	9-02	80	10th Maurice' Gheest Deau 7f	17th Sprint Cup Hayd 6f	-	-
03 Ascot 5f 3rd King's Stand One month	**Oasis Dream** J Gosden 9/2	11/16	3	8-13	90	**WON 4/9F Nunthorpe York 5f**	2nd Sprint Cup Hayd 6f	10th Breeders' Cup Sant 1m	-
02 Ascot 6f 5th Golden Jubilee Three weeks	**Continent** D Nicholls 12/1	2/15	5	9-05	84	4th Nunthorpe York 5f	6th Sprint Cup Hayd 6f	**WON 4/1JF Prix' Abbaye Long 5f**	14th H Kong Sprint Sha 5f
01 Ascot 7f 1st Jersey Stks One month	**Mozart** A O'Brien 4/1F	19/18	3	8-13	92	**WON 4/9F Nunthorpe York 5f**	11th Breeders' Cup Belm 6f		
00 Ascot 5f 2nd King's Stand One month	**Agnes World** H Mori 4/1F	6/10	5	9-05	82	2nd Sprinters Stks Naka 6f	8th Breeders' Cup Chur 6f	-	-
99 Ascot 7f 4th Jersey Stks One month	**Stravinsky** A O'Brien 8/1	6/17	3	8-13	93	**WON EvsF Nunthorpe York 5f**	6th Breeders' Cup Chur 6f		
98 Sand 5f 3rd Temple Stks Two months	**Elnadim** J Dunlop 3/1F	18/17	4	9-05	85	11th Nunthorpe York 5f	12th Sprint Cup Hayd 6f	3rd Listed Keen 6f	-
97 Ascot 5f 12th King's Stand Three weeks	**Compton Place** J Toller 50/1	1/9	3	8-13	79	14th Nunthorpe York 5f	*6th Temple Stks Sand 5f	*12th Cork & Orrery Ascot 6f	*14th July Cup Newm 6f
96 Deau 5f 1st Group 2 Two months	**Anabaa** Mme C Head 11/4	2/10	4	9-05	86	**WON 1/2F Maurice' Gheest Deau 7f**	2nd Prix' Abbaye Long 5f	-	-

12-year median performance rating of the winner: **85** (out of 100) *next year*

WINNER'S PROFILE Sakhee's Secret last year took an original route to Newmarket, making his debut in Group company here, unlike the past 11 winners, nine of whom came via the **Royal meeting**. A further 11 winners arrived with a **distance victory** to their names, while **three to five-year-olds** came out on top – no three-year-old filly has won for almost 25 years – and only Les Arcs struck for the older horses from over 30 runners.

High numbers were favoured in recent years with five of the last six **drawn in double-figures**, while on the training front, **Aidan O'Brien** and **Hughie Morrison** have two wins each, the latter striking with his only two runners.

FUTURE POINTERS A race that often decides Europe's best sprinter in the end of season classifications, and one that has grown in attracting an international line-up of late, although victors haven't had a prolonged career – only Continent made the racecourse on more than four occasions again.

The most successful route post-Newmarket was to York for the Nunthorpe, three of the last four to take that route succeeded, although it has to be noted all were above par winners of the July Cup.

The four who attempted the Sprint Cup came up short as the ground can be different at Haydock in the autumn, and it may prove wiser to follow placed horses from here in that event *(see below)*. A further four July Cup winners were also beaten in the Breeders' Cup at the end of term, and a better overseas option has been the Prix de l'Abbaye with a winner and runner-up from only two runners.

Were July Cup winners profitable to follow on their subsequent three runs?
No – 5 wins from 25 runs returned a loss of -£13.61 to a £1 level stake.

Placed runners subsequent record (three runs):
Runners-up: 6 wins from 28 runs returned a **profit of +10.53** to a £1 level stake.
2006 Iffraaj – Lennox Stakes, Park Stakes, 2005 Avonbridge – Prix de l'Abbaye, 1999 Bold Edge – Diadem, 1998 Tamarisk – Haydock Sprint Cup, 1997 Royal Applause – Haydock Sprint Cup

Thirds: 3 wins from 34 runs returned a loss of -£16.75 to a £1 level stake.
2007 Red Clubs – Haydock Sprint Cup, 2002 Danehurst – Flying Five, 2000 Pipalong – Haydock Sprint Cup

FUTURE SUCCESS RATING: ★ ★ ★ ☆ ☆

SUMMER STAKES
July 11, York – (Group 3, Class 1, 3yo+ Fillies & Mares) 6f

Last run	Winner/Trainer & SP	Draw/Ran	Age	Wght	PR	Next four runs			
07 Ascot 7f 7th, Jersey Stks, *One month*	**Theann** A O'Brien 5/1	1/10	3	8-10	64	-	-	-	-
06 Ascot 5f 13th, King's Stands, *One month*	**La Chunga** J Noseda 11/4F	5/11	3	8-10	69	11th Maurice 'Gheest Deau 7f	7th Diadem Stks Ascot 6f	-	
05 York 1m 8th, Windsor Forest, *One month*	**Lucky Spin** R Hannon 8/1	9/11	4	9-04	65	3rd Oak Tree Stks Good 7f	4th Maurice 'Gheest Deau 7f	8th Sprint Cup Hayd 6f	6th Diadem Stks Newm 6f
04 Hayd 6f 1st, Cecil Frail Stks, *Two months*	**Tante Rose** R Charlton 11/4F	1/9	4	9-00	72	**WON 10/1 Sprint Cup Hayd 6f**	-	-	-
03 Ascot 6f 6th, Wokingham, *Three weeks*	**Torosay Spring** J Fanshawe 7/2	11/11	5	9-00	61	9th Shergar Cup Ascot 6f	2nd Starlit Stks Good 6f	11th Diadem Stks Ascot 6f	4th Rous Stks Newm 5f
02 Sand 5f 1st, Porcelanosa Stk, *One week*	**Palace Affair** G Balding 5/4F	5/9	4	9-04	65	8th Starlit Stks Good 6f	11th Bentinck Stks Newm 6f	-	-
01 Ascot 7f 11th, Jersey Stks, *One month*	**Palace Affair** G Balding 11/2	11/10	3	8-12	62	10th Oak Tree Stks Good 7f	9th Flying Fillies Stk Pont 6f	*10th Cammidge Tr'py Donc 6f	*2nd Landsdown Stk Bath 5f
00 Newm 7f 6th, Criterion Stks, *Two weeks*	**Hot Tin Roof** T Easterby 11/2	9/9	4	9-04	64	4th Maurice 'Gheest Deau 7f	8th Flying Fillies Stk Pont 6f	*3rd Conds Stks Warw 6f	*11th Duke of York York 6f
99 Newm 1m 18th, 1,000 Guineas, *Three months*	**Imperial Beauty** P Makin 10/3JF	6/7	3	8-08	66	2nd King George Good 5f	8th Sprint Cup Hayd 6f	**WON 6/1 World Trophy Newb 5f**	2nd Prix de l'Abbaye Long 5f
98 Ascot 1m 9th, Coronation Stks, *One month*	**Nanoushka** R Hannon 9/1	1/7	3	8-12	60	3rd Flying Fillies Stk Pont 6f	4th Group 3 Deau 6f	7th Supreme Stks Good 7f	*6th Abernant Stks Newm 6f
97 Newm 6f 1st, Conds Stks, *Three weeks*	**Bint Albaadiya** Sir M Stoute 4/1	1/8	3	8-08	64	4th Duty Free Cup Newb 7f	-	-	-
96 Newc 6f 4th, Chipchase Stks, *Three weeks*	**Carranita** B Palling 5/1	1/8	6	9-04	69	7th Oak Tree Stks Good 7f	**WON 10/3F Hopeful Stks Newm 6f**	11th Diadem Stks Ascot 6f	7th Bentinck Stks Newm 6f

12-year median performance rating of the winner: **65** (out of 100) *next year*

WINNER'S PROFILE Race fitness was vital as 11 winners entered the stalls having **run within the past month**, five of the last seven came via the **Royal meeting**, the same number that boasted a **previous victory over this trip**. Those with an **official rating between 101 to 111** dominated, which was reflected in the market where **fancied runners at 11/2 and shorter** won on 10 occasions – trainer **Richard Hannon** was responsible for the two biggest from nine runners. Progressive **three and four-year-olds** very much held the edge, while those who carried Group penalties have a good record.

FUTURE POINTERS A decent sprint for females which has fallen under the radar somewhat with the July Cup taking the spotlight at Newmarket on the same day, although it has proven disappointing that winners haven't really kicked on post-York, bar Tante Rose in 2004. By far the best winner since 1996, she subsequently took the Group One Haydock Sprint Cup – the only winner who followed up.
The majority took a route that included the Oak Tree Stakes, Flying Fillies' Stakes, and Maurice de Gheest, all of which were unkind to Summer Stakes winners.

Were Summer Stakes winners profitable to follow on their subsequent three runs?
No – 3 wins from 27 runs returned a loss of -£4.67 to a £1 level stake.

Placed runners' subsequent record (three runs):
Runners-up: 9 wins from 34 runs returned a **profit of +£35.88** to a £1 level stake.
2005 La Cucaracha – Nunthorpe, 2000 Cassandra Go – King George, Temple Stakes,
1999 Pipalong – Great St Wilfrid, 1997 Bollin Joanne – Scarbrough Stakes, 1996 Daring Destiny – Phoenix Sprint

Thirds: 4 wins from 26 runs returned a **profit of +£3.50** to a £1 level stake.
2001 Vita Spericolata – Queensferry Stakes

FUTURE SUCCESS RATING: ★ ★ ☆ ☆ ☆

JOHN SMITH'S CUP

July 12, York – (Heritage Handicap, Class 1, 3yo+) 1m2f 88yds

Last run	Winner/Trainer & SP	Draw/Ran	Age	Wght	PR	Next four runs			
07 Ches 1m2f 4th Breitling Hcp *Three months*	**Charlie Tokyo** R Fahey 11/1	4/17	4	8-09	62	6th York Stks York 1m2f	7th Doonside Cup Ayr 1m2f	5th Conds Stks York 1m2f	-
06 Sali 1m2f 2nd Handicap *Three weeks*	**Fairmile** W Swinburn 6/1JF	9/20	4	8-12	60	2nd Totesport Hcp Hayd 1m3f	18th Cambridgeshire Newm 1m1f	*WON 9/4F Handicap Nad Al 1m2f	*3rd Handicap Nad Al 1m2f
05 York 1m2f 2nd Wolferton Hcp *One month*	**Mullins Bay** A O'Brien 4/1F	19/20	4	9-07	76	WON 5/2 Strensall Stks Newm 1m	6th Q Elizabeth II Newm 1m	2nd Darley Stks Newm 1m1f	*2nd Group 2 Capa 1m
04 Ayr 1m2f 1st Handicap *Two months*	**Arcalis** J Howard Johnson 20/1	18/21	4	9-02	72	WON 4/9F Nov Hdle Ayr 2m	WON 1/5F Nov Hdle Newc 2m	4th Christmas Hurdle Kemp 2m	*3rd Nov Hdle Newb 2m1f
03 York 1m2f 3rd Rated Hcp *Two months*	**Far Lane** B Hills 7/1	4/20	4	9-04	75	2nd Rose' Lancaster Hayd 1m3f	3rd Conds Stks Donc 1m2f	3rd Foundation Stks Good 1m2f	5th Cambridgeshire Newm 1m1f
02 Ascot 1m2f 6th Wolferton Hcp *One month*	**Vintage Premium** R Fahey 20/1	9/20	5	9-09	74	5th Group 3 Ovre 1m1f	2nd Conds Stks Donc 1m2f	2nd Doonside Cup Ayr 1m3f	9th Group 2 Long 1m2f
01 Good 1m2f 1st Handicap *One month*	**Foreign Affairs** Sir M Prescott 5/2F	8/19	3	8-06	71	2nd Ebor York 1m6f	10th Arc de Triomphe Long 1m4f	*WON 8/13F Conds Stks Donc 1m2f	*2nd Steventon Stks Newb 1m2f
00 Sand 1m 5th Showcase Hcp *One week*	**Sobriety** F Johnson Houghton 20/1	8/22	3	8-08	73	3rd Gordon Stks Good 1m4f	*9th Group 1 Sha 1m1f	*3rd Stakes Sha 1m1f	*WON N/O Handicap Sha 1m2f
99 Sand 1m2f 10th Hong Kong Hcp *Two weeks*	**Achilles** K Burke 25/1	6/15	4	8-11	65	2nd Showcase Hcp Good 1m2f	2nd Motability Hcp York 1m2f	3rd Doonside Cup Ayr 1m3f	3rd Grade 3 Sant 1m4f
98 Good 1m1f 1st Maiden *Two months*	**Porto Foricos** H Cecil 6/1	7/20	3	8-03	69	9th Sussex Good 1m	7th Winter Hill Stks Wind 1m2f	4th Conds Stks Donc 1m	9th Darley Stks Newm 1m1f
97 York 1m2f 1st Handicap *Nine months*	**Pasternak** Sir M Prescott 13/2	1/21	4	8-03	70	WON 4/1F Cambridgeshire Newm 1m1f	*2nd J Smith's Cup York 1m2f	*2nd Handicap Leop 1m1f	*21st W Hill Mile Hcp Good 1m
96 Sand 1m2f 5th Hong Kong Hcp *Two weeks*	**Wilcuma** P Makin 10/1	2/17	5	9-02	66	2nd Rated Hcp Ascot 1m2f	WON 5/1 Rated Hcp Newb 1m1f	WON N/O Listed Evry 1m2f	*3rd Conds Stks Newm 1m2f

12-year median performance rating of the winner: **69** (out of 100)   *(2007 1m1f), *next year*

WINNER'S PROFILE Six of the last seven winners were **rested for over three weeks** prior to this big prize, one of the few major handicaps that winners from the Royal meeting have swerved – **10 John Smith's victors since 1996 avoided Ascot** – while those to have run well there have disappointed in this.
A light campaign has been a bonus as no winner **competed more than four times**, and a **top-six effort last time out** was common. **Three and four-year-olds** dominated, although not many of the Classic generation made the cut of late – last 11 winning **official ratings were 90 or more**.
A **low to middle draw** can be helpful as both of trainer **Richard Fahey**'s winners proved in recent times.

FUTURE POINTERS One of the most valuable handicaps for middle-distance performers of the season that can fall to a progressive sort, and though several went on to win at a better level, not many matured into the Group horses they looked at the winning line. Only Far Lane managed to triumph in a Group Three event on these shores subsequently – Sobriety won a Group One in Hong Kong – while Mullins Bay and Foreign Affairs both scored in Listed company but struggled above that level. Two more distinguished winners were Arcalis, who found a fruitful career over the sticks, and Pasternak, who landed a monster gamble in the Cambridgeshire. Three placed runners came back to win the Motabliity Handicap over course and distance *(see below)*.

Were John Smith's Cup winners profitable to follow on their subsequent three runs?
No – 8 wins from 36 runs returned a loss of -£13.00 to a £1 level stake.

Placed runners' subsequent record (three runs):
Runners-up: 3 wins from 35 runs returned a loss of -£30.00 to a £1 level stake.

Thirds: 3 wins from 33 runs returned a loss of -£14.77 to a £1 level stake.
2005 Realism – Motability Handicap, 2002 Leadership – Motability Handicap, Berkshire Stakes

Fourths: 5 wins from 30 runs returned evens to a £1 level stake
2007 Greek Well – Motability Handicap, 2002 Beauchamp Pilot – Cambridgeshire

FUTURE SUCCESS RATING: ★ ★ ☆ ☆ ☆

IRISH OAKS
July 13, Curragh – (Group 1, Class 1, 3yo Fillies) 1m4f

Last run	Winner/ Trainer & SP	Draw/ Ran	Age	Wght	PR	Next four runs			
07 Curr 1m2f 1st Pretty Polly Stks *Three weeks*	**Peeping Fawn** A O'Brien 3/1	4/12	3	9-00	85	**WON 2/1F** Nassau Stks Good 1m2f	**WON 4/9F** Yorkshire Oaks York 1m4f	-	
06 Epso 1m4f 1st Oaks *Two months*	**Alexandrova** A O'Brien 8/15F	2/6	3	9-00	83	**WON 4/9F** Yorkshire Oaks York 1m4f	3rd Prix de l'Opera Long 1m2f	-	-
05 Chan 1m4f 1st Group 3 *Two months*	**Shawanda** A De Royer-Dupre 9/2	7/13	3	9-00	80	**WON 4/9F** Prix Vermeille Long 1m4f	6th Arc de Triomphe Long 1m4f	-	-
04 Epso 1m4f 1st Oaks *Two months*	**Ouija Board** E Dunlop 4/7F	4/7	3	9-00	83	3rd Arc de Triomphe Long 1m4f	**WON 10/11F** Breeders' Cup Lone 1m3f	*7th Prince of Wales York 1m2f	*WON 11/8F Princess Royal Newm 1m4f
03 Curr 7f 2nd Athasi Stks *Three months*	**Vintage Tipple** P Mullins 12/1	8/11	3	9-00	74	7th Irish Champion Leop 1m2f	6th Rathbarry Listed Curr 1m4f	-	
02 Curr 1m2f 4th Pretty Polly Stks *Three weeks*	**Margarula** J Bolger 33/1	12/12	3	9-00	75	6th Irish Champion Leop 1m2f	6th Irish St Leger Curr 1m6f	-	
01 Epso 1m4f 1st Vodafone Hcp *Two months*	**Lailani** E Dunlop 5/1	1/12	3	9-00	80	**WON 5/4F** Nassau Stks Good 1m2f	**WON 49/20** Flower Bowl Int Belm 1m2f	8th Breeders' Cup Belm 1m2f	
00 Epso 1m4f 4th Oaks *Two months*	**Petrushka** Sir M Stoute 11/2	10/10	3	9-00	82	**WON 5/4F** Yorkshire Oaks York 1m4f	**WON 9/10F** Prix de l'Opera Long 1m2f	5th Breeders' Cup Chur 1m3f	*5th Coronation Cup Epso 1m4f
99 Epso 1m4f 1st Oaks *Two months*	**Ramruma** H Cecil 4/9F	1/7	3	9-00	78	**WON 5/6F** Yorkshire Oaks York 1m4f	2nd St Leger Donc 1m6f	*11th Jockey Club Stks Newm 1m4f	*3rd Yorkshire Oaks York 1m4f
98 Ascot 1m 3rd Coronation Stks *One month*	**Winona** J Oxx 12/1	6/9	3	9-00	76	9th Prix Vermeille Long 1m4f	8th Grade 1 Sant 1m2f	-	
97 Epso 1m4f 6th Oaks *Two months*	**Ebadiyla** J Oxx 9/2	10/11	3	9-00	78	12th Arc de Triomphe Long 1m4f	**WON N/O** Prix Royal-Oak Long 1m7f	*5th Tatts Gold Cup Curr 1m2f	*3rd Coronation Cup Epso 1m4f
96 Curr 1m2f 1st Pretty Polly Stks *Three weeks*	**Dance Design** D Weld 9/2	1/6	3	9-00	77	2nd Irish Champion Leop 1m2f	*WON 4/5F Mooresbridge St Curr 1m2f	*WON 5/2 Tatts Gold Cup Curr 1m2f	*WON 4/9F Pretty Polly Stk Curr 1m2f

12-year median performance rating of the winner: **79** (out of 100)   **next year*

WINNER'S PROFILE Every Irish Oaks winner **raced within the past two months**, eight **came via the English Oaks or the Pretty Polly**, including two winners of the latter event. Winners of the English Oaks have a good record here, despite Light Shift's second last year, as three of the five previous attempts were successful, while Peeping Fawn became only the second filly since 1996 to have been placed at Epsom before scoring here. **Winners already that season** are preferred – both exceptions were the only ones not to have raced beyond a mile – while the market has been a decent guide as 11 victors returned **12/1 or shorter**.

Trainer **Ed Dunlop**'s raiders command respect, while **John Oxx** struck twice for the home contingent from 15 runners. **Aidan O'Brien** failed to score from over 20 runners prior to 2006, but has now scooped the last two.

FUTURE POINTERS As with the Irish Derby, winners of the Irish Oaks have a much superior subsequent record than the English equivalent. One informative pattern to have developed was the 100% record of Curragh victors in the Nassau Stakes and Yorkshire Oaks, compared to those who flopped in the Irish Champion or Arc.

Aidan O'Brien and Ed Dunlop's future runners could be worth following if achieving top performance ratings (PR) like their previous winners – all four proved to be high-class – while several of those that recorded sub-standard ratings from other yards failed to put together any sort of career.

Were Irish Oaks winners profitable to follow on their subsequent three runs?
No – 13 wins from 30 runs returned a loss of -£2.79 to a £1 level stake, although they scored at an impressive strike-rate during their next two starts at short-prices.

Placed runners' subsequent record (three runs):
Runners-up: 2 wins from 26 runs returned a loss of -£19.50 to a £1 level stake.

Thirds: 1 win from 19 runs returned a loss of -£15.75 to a £1 level stake.

FUTURE SUCCESS RATING: ★ ★ ★ ★ ★

HACKWOOD STAKES
July 19, Newbury – (Group 3, Class 1, 3yo+) 6f

Last run	Winner/Trainer & SP	Draw/Ran	Age	Wght	PR	Next four runs			
07 Newm 6f 17th July Cup Two weeks	Balthazaar's Gift L Cumani 15/2	5/11	4	9-03	78	6th Stewards' Cup Good 6f	2nd Hopeful Stks Newm 6f	3rd Sprint Cup Hayd 6f	14th Diadem Stks Ascot 6f
06 Newm 6f 10th July Cup Two weeks	Fayr Jag T Easterby 16/1	8/7	7	9-07	79	5th King George Stk Good 5f	5th Phoenix Sprint Curr 6f	9th Nunthorpe York 5f	4th Scarbrough Stks York 5f
05 Hayd 6f 4th Conds Stks Two weeks	Beckermet R Fisher 14/1	10/11	3	8-12	75	11th Skybet Dash Hcp York 6f	15th Hayd 6f	3rd Starlit Stks Good 6f	11th World Trophy Newb 5f
04 Sand 7f 2nd Surrey Stks Two months	Pastoral Pursuits H Morrison 15/8F	1/11	3	8-12	74	WON 5/1 Park Stks Donc 7f	5th Prix de la Foret Long 7f	*7th Queen Anne York 1m	*WON 22/1 July Cup Newm 6f
03 Hayd 6f 1st Conds Stks Two weeks	Somnus T Easterby 5/1	8/14	3	8-12	80	4th Shergar Cup Ascot 6f	2nd Hopeful Stks Newm 6f	WON 12/1 Sprint Cup Hayd 6f	7th Prix de l'Abbaye Long 5f
02 Newc 6f 3rd Chipchase Stks Three weeks	Ashdown Express C Wall 8/1	4/8	3	8-12	71	6th Lennox Stks Good 7f	2nd Shergar Cup Ascot 6f	8th Group 3 Deau 7f	*3rd Abernant Stks Newm 6f
01 Ascot 6f 9th Cork & Orrery One month	Invincible Spirit J Dunlop 3/1F	3/8	4	9-03	75	2nd Group 3 Deau 7f	WON 5/2 Gr 3 Boland Stk Curr 6f	*4th Abernant Stks Newm 6f	*WON 3/1F Duke of York York 6f
00 Bade 6f 1st Group 2 Ten months	Auenklang S Bin Suroor 9/2	9/11	3	8-12	77	2nd Shergar Cup Ascot 6f	11th Sprint Cup Hayd 6f	-	-
99 Newm 6f 4th July Cup Two weeks	Arkadian Hero L Cumani 11/8F	10/10	4	9-03	80	WON 1/2F Hopeful Stks Newm 6f	3rd Sprint Cup Hayd 6f	8th Prix de l'Abbaye Long 5f	*4th Abernant Stks Newm 6f
98 Leic 7f 6th Leicestershire St Three months	Grazia Sir M Prescott 5/2	3/8	3	8-07	73	2nd Phoenix Sprint Curr 6f	16th Sprint Cup Hayd 6f	-	-
97 Yarm 6f 1st Conds Stks Two months	Hattab P Walwyn 7/1	5/14	3	8-12	70	5th City of York York 7f	7th Duty Free Cup Newb 7f	**4th Stakes Nad Al 7f	**4th Listed Nad Al 6f
96 Ascot 6f 10th Wokingham One month	Jayanpee I Balding 16/1	8/16	5	9-03	72	9th Stewards' Cup Good 6f	4th Hopeful Stks Newm 6f	WON N/O Listed Taby 6f	8th Diadem Stks Ascot 6f

12-year median performance rating of the winner: **75 (out of 100)** *(2007 Ascot), *next year ** two years*

WINNER'S PROFILE It isn't easy locating clues in a race undergoing a facelift, although four of the five not to have made the first four last time had run in either the July Cup or at Royal Ascot, including the last two winners since when it became a Group Three event.

The last two winners also arrived with Group One and Two victories between them, something only two others had since 1996, while 10 winners boasted a **distance win**. Two of the triumphant three-year-olds had lifted the valuable Redcar Two-Year-Old Trophy as juveniles, and the better performers with an **official rating of 108 or more** came out on top – only Beckermet was rated lower in recent times.

Trainers **Tim Easterby** and **Luca Cumani** sent out two winners each.

FUTURE POINTERS Upgraded from Listed status in 2006, this mid-season sprint has gradually moved up the ladder in terms of quality, providing a couple of subsequent Group One winners amongst it's recent roll of honour, while Reverence took his place in the line-up last year. The winner of the 2007 renewal – re-routed to Ascot owing to the abandonment at Newbury – trod a similar post-route to past winners in the Hopeful Stakes and Haydock Sprint Cup. However, those events haven't been too receptive to Hackwood winners, with only the above par Somnus and Arkadian Hero succeeding, although two Newbury victors since the Millenium scooped a Group Two and Three in 2004 and 2001 respectively.

Were Hackwood winners profitable to follow on their subsequent three runs?
No – 5 wins from 34 runs returned a loss of -£9.00 to a £1 level stake.

Placed runners' subsequent record (three runs):
Runners-up: 4 wins from 36 runs returned a loss of -£24.32 to a £1 level stake.
2007 Al Qasi – Phoenix Sprint, 2001 Mugharreb – Hopeful Stakes

Thirds: 4 wins from 29 runs returned a **profit of +£4.15** to a £1 level stake.
2005 Baron's Pit – Diadem Stakes, 2003 The Tatling – King George Stakes, 2001 Bouncing Bowdler – Fortune Stakes

FUTURE SUCCESS RATING: ★ ★ ★ ☆ ☆

INTERNATIONAL STAKES
July 26, Ascot – (Heritage Handicap, Class 2, 3yo+) 7f

Last run	Winner/Trainer & SP	Draw/Ran	Age	Wght	PR	Next four runs			
07 Newm 7f 1st Handicap *Three weeks*	Third Set R Charlton 9/1	4/27	4	8-02	78	WON 5/2F W Hill Mile Hcp Good 1m	-	-	-
06 Ascot 1m 12th Royal Hunt Cup *Two months*	Dabbers Ridge B Hills 12/1	12/20	4	8-09	70	5th City of York York 7f	3rd Fortune Stks Hayd 7f	*18th Victoria Cup Ascot 7f	*3rd B Palace Hcp Ascot 7f
05 York 1m 1st Royal Hunt Cup *Two months*	New Seeker C Cox 12/1	13/24	5	9-04	77	3rd Sovereign Stks Sali 1m	WON 6/4F Duty Free Cup Newb 7f	3rd Supreme Stks Good 7f	9th Challenge Stks Newm 7f
04 Newm 7f 2nd Bunbury Cup *One month*	Court Masterpiece E Dunlop 7/1	10/21	4	9-02	74	4th Celebration Mile Good 1m	3rd Park Stks Donc 7f	6th Supreme Stks Good 7f	*4th Victoria Cup Ling 7f
03 Ascot 1m 1st Britannia Stks *Two months*	New Seeker C Cox 15/2	3/22	3	7-12	71	*2nd Paradise Stks Ascot 1m	*4th B Palace Hcp Ascot 7f	*8th Silver Trophy Ascot 1m	*6th International Hcp Ascot 7f
02 Ascot 6f 4th Wokingham *Two months*	Crystal Castle J Hammond 14/1	13/28	4	8-00	72	WON 86/10 Group 3 Deau 6f	WON 3/1F Diadem Ascot 6f	*4th Group 3 Nad Al 6f	*7th Group 1 Nad Al 6f
01 Newm 7f 1st Bunbury Cup *Three weeks*	Atavus G Margarson 11/1	9/28	4	8-04	68	4th W Hill Mile Hcp Good 1m	WON 33/1 Hungerford Stk Newb 7f	14th Diadem Ascot 6f	10th Challenge Stks Newm 7f
00 Newm 7f 11th Bunbury Cup *Three weeks*	Tillerman Mrs A Perrett 10/1	2/24	4	8-10	79	6th Hungerford Stk Newb 7f	*4th Cork & Orrery Ascot 6f	*9th July Cup Newm 6f	*3rd International Hcp Ascot 7f
99 Ascot 6f 2nd Cork & Orrery *Two months*	Russian Revival J Gosden 9/1JF	25/27	6	9-07	82	-	-	-	-
98 Newm 7f 16th Bunbury Cup *One month*	Jo Mell T Easterby 14/1	10/25	5	8-04	72	2nd City Of York York 7f	*5th Conds Stks Warw 7f	*7th Spring Trophy Hayd 7f	*7th Hambleton Hcp York 1m

10-year median performance rating of the winner: **74** (out of 100)　　(2005 Newbury), *next year

WINNER'S PROFILE As expected with a summer handicap, the majority **appeared within the past few months**, all having either raced at the **Royal meeting or in the Bunbury Cup**, including three winners of those events, although only Atavus defied a penalty here from over 40 qualifiers that shouldered extra weight.
Four and five-year-olds boast the best record – only one three-year-old succeeded from over 40 runners – while those priced at **14/1 or shorter** ruled as shocks were rare, a surprise considering the field sizes.
A distance victory wasn't essential, nor was a specific weight or official rating, although those drawn in the **low to middle numbers** have triumphed on nine occasions.

FUTURE POINTERS Originally formulated to attract an international field of handicappers, only a dozen or so from outside Britain have appeared amongst almost 300 runners since the inaugural running, which often allows a re-run of earlier handicaps such as the Bunbury Cup and Royal Hunt Cup.
However, a talented improver in Third Set won the tenth anniversary last year, before landing another prestigious handicap at Goodwood the following week, and two fellow four-year-olds also proved worth following. Crystal Castle came back to win the Group Two Diadem Stakes, while Atavus took the Group Three Hungerford Stakes.
Overall, a handicap to be viewed in a positive light, backed up by the strength of the successful runners-up (*see below*).

Were International Stakes winners profitable to follow on their subsequent three runs?
Yes – 5 wins from 25 runs returned a **profit of +£28.60** to a £1 level stake.

Placed runners' subsequent record (three runs):
Runners-up: 5 wins from 27 runs returned a **profit +£6.22** to a £1 level stake.
2005 Goodricke – Haydock Sprint Cup, 2001 Nice One Clare – Sceptre, Diadem Stakes

Thirds: 4 wins from 30 runs returned a loss of -£12.41 to a £1 level stake.
2000 Tayseer – Stewards' Cup, 1998 Ramooz – Group Three Boland Stakes

Fourths: 6 wins from 29 runs returned a loss of -£0.44 to a £1 level stake.
2006 Appalachian Trail – Hopeful Stakes, 2000 Duke Of Modena – Totesport Festival Handicap

FUTURE SUCCESS RATING: ★ ★ ★ ★ ☆

KING GEORGE VI AND QUEEN ELIZABETH STAKES
July 26, Ascot – (Group 1, Class 1, 3yo+) 1m4f

Last run	Winner/ Trainer & SP	Draw/ Ran	Age	Wght	PR	Next four runs			
07 Ascot 1m2f 2nd Prince of Wales' Two months	Dylan Thomas A O'Brien 5/4F	5/7	4	9-07	91	2nd Juddmonte Int York 1m2f	WON 8/15F Irish Champion Leop 1m2f	WON 11/2 Arc de Triomphe Long 1m4f	5th Breeders' Cup Monm 1m4f
06 Sain 1m4f 2nd G Prix St-Cloud Two months	Hurricane Run A Fabre 5/6F	4/6	4	9-07	85	2nd Prix Foy Long 1m4f	3rd Arc de Triomphe Long 1m4f	3rd Champion Stks Newm 1m2f	6th Breeders' Cup Chur 1m4f
05 Ascot 1m2f 1st Prince of Wales' Two months	Azamour J Oxx 5/2F	12/12	4	9-07	89	5th Irish Champion Leop 1m2f	3rd Breeders' Cup Belm 1m4f	-	-
04 Ascot 1m4f 1st Hardwicke Stks Two months	Doyen S Bin Suroor 11/10F	5/11	4	9-07	84	7th Irish Champion Leop 1m2f	7th Champion Stks Newm 1m2f	*5th Hardwicke Stks York 1m4f	*6th King George VI Newb 1m4f
03 Curr 1m4f 1st Irish Derby One month	Alamshar J Oxx 13/2	5/12	3	8-09	90	4th Irish Champion Leop 1m2f	6th Champion Stks Newm 1m2f	-	-
02 Toky 1m4f 6th Japan Cup Eight months	Golan Sir M Stoute 11/2	8/9	4	9-07	86	2nd Juddmonte Int York 1m2f	6th Breeders' Cup Arli 1m4f	7th Japan Cup Naka 1m3f	-
01 Curr 1m4f 1st Irish Derby One month	Galileo A O'Brien	7/12	3	8-09	89	2nd Irish Champion Leop 1m2f	6th Breeders' Cup Belm 1m2f	-	-
00 Sain 1m4f 1st G Prix St-Cloud One month	Montjeu J Hammond 1/3F	5/7	4	9-07	94	WON 1/10F Prix Foy Long 1m4f	4th Arc de Triomphe Long 1m4f	2nd Champion Stks Newm 1m2f	7th Breeders' Cup Chur 1m4f
99 Epsom 1m4f 1st Coronation Cup Two months	Daylami S Bin Suroor 3/1	8/8	5	9-07	92	WON 6/4 Irish Champion Leop 1m2f	9th Arc de Triomphe Long 1m4f	WON 16/10F Breeders' Cup Gulf 1m4f	-
98 Ascot 1m4f 3rd Hardwicke Stks Two months	Swain S Bin Suroor 11/2	5/8	6	9-07	91	WON 6/4F Irish Champion Leop 1m2f	3rd Breeders' Cup Chur 1m2f	-	-
97 Newm 1m4f 2nd Princess of Wales' Three weeks	Swain S Bin Suroor 16/1	5/8	5	9-07	92	3rd Arc Trial Newb 1m3f	7th Arc de Triomphe Long 1m4f	*2nd World Cup Nad Al 1m2f	*2nd Coronation Cup Epsom 1m4f
96 Sand 1m2f 3rd Eclipse Three weeks	Pentire G Wragg 10/3	7/8	4	9-07	95	2nd Prix Foy Long 1m4f	10th Arc de Triomphe Long 1m4f	8th Japan Cup Toky 1m4f	-

12-year median performance rating of the winner: **90** (out of 100)   **next year*

WINNER'S PROFILE Only Golan made his reappearance here as the majority **raced within the past two months** and eight of the last 10 came via Royal Ascot, The Curragh or Saint-Cloud – both winning three-year-olds since 1996 had won the Irish Derby. Proven form at this level was vital as 11 **finished in the top-two of a Group One** over this trip, while 11 years have passed since an outsider won and it pays to follow the **first three or four in the betting**. It may be a coincidence, but those drawn wide in one to three have struggled, favouring **middle to high stalls**. **Saeed Bin Suroor** tops the list with four winners from 24 runners – ignore his outsiders at double-figure prices – while **Aidan O'Brien** last year joined **John Oxx** on two victories.

FUTURE POINTERS An event that used to traditionally match the Derby winner against his elders over a mile-and-a-half, but one that has lost its sparkle in recent times, for not since 2003 has the Epsom winner lined up and only a couple of three-year-olds were seen in that time. This may have led to the poor results of subsequent winners of late, but Dylan Thomas last year gave the King George a needed boost in becoming the first victor since Daylami in 1999 to land the Irish Champion Stakes, before turning up the heat in the Arc de Triomphe.
The Breeders' Cup has been a popular end of season target, but only Daylami succeeded over in the States.

Were King George VI winners profitable to follow on their subsequent three runs?
No – 6 wins from 32 runs returned a loss of -£15.26 to a £1 level stake.

Placed runners' subsequent record (three runs):
Runners-up: 9 wins from 25 runs returned a **profit of +£1.15** to a £1 level stake.
2003 Sulamani – Arlington Million, 2002 Nayef – Juddmonte International, Prince of Wales's, 2001 Fantastic Light – Irish Champion, Breeders' Cup, 2000 Fantastic Light – Man O'War, 1997 Pilsudski – Irish Champion, Champion Stakes

Thirds: 4 wins from 20 runs returned a loss of -£9.90 to a £1 level stake.
2004 Sulamani – Juddmonte International, Canadian International, 2001 Hightori – Prix Foy, 1998 Royal Anthem – Canadian International

FUTURE SUCCESS RATING: ★ ★ ★ ☆ ☆

PRINCESS MARGARET STAKES

July 27, Ascot – (Group 3, Class 1, 2yo Fillies) 6f

Last run	Winner/Trainer & SP	Draw/Ran	Age	Wght	PR	Next four runs			
07 Newm 6f 2nd Maiden One month	Visit Sir M Stoute 10/3JF	5/13	2	8-12	69	2nd Lowther Stks York 6f	8th Cheveley Park Newm 6f	-	-
06 Ascot 6f 3rd Albany Stks Two months	Scarlet Runner J Dunlop 5/1	7/10	2	8-12	66	5th Lowther Stks York 6f	8th Cheveley Park Newm 6f	*WON 15/2 Nell Gwyn Stks Newm 7f	*7th 1,000 Guineas Newm 1m
05 Newb 6f 3rd Rose Bowl Stks One month	Mixed Blessing A Jarvis 25/1	12/12	2	8-09	63	3rd Prestige Stks Good 7f	9th Firth of Clyde Ayr 6f	9th Cheveley Park Newm 6f	-
04 Ascot 5f 2nd Queen Mary Two months	Soar J Fanshawe EvensF	4/6	2	8-09	61	WON 2/1F Lowther Stks York 6f	6th Cheveley Park Newm 6f	*6th Conds Stks Leic 5f	-
03 Ascot 6f 1st Maiden Three weeks	River Belle A Jarvis 4/1JF	3/9	2	8-09	60	5th Moyglare Stud Curr 7f	6th Meon Fillies' Mile Ascot 1m	*3rd Grade 3 Monm 1m1f	*3rd Grade 1 Keen 1m1f
02 Newm 6f 1st Maiden One month	Russian Rhythm Sir M Stoute EvensF	7/6	2	8-09	73	WON 8/13F Lowther Stks York 6f	2nd Cheveley Park Newm 6f	*WON 12/1 1,000 Guineas Newm 1m	*WON 4/7F Coronation Stks Ascot 1m
01 Wind 5f 1st Maiden Two weeks	Leggy Lou J Noseda 6/1	2/8	2	8-09	70	8th Lowther Stks York 6f	-	-	-
00 Newm 6f 2nd Cherry Hinton Three weeks	Enthused S M Stoute 2/1F	3/9	2	8-09	66	WON 9/4 Lowther Stks York 6f	6th Cheveley Park Newm 6f	*5th 1,000 Guineas Newm 1m	*8th Coronation Stks Ascot 1m
99 Pont 6f 1st Maiden Three months	Saintly Speech P Chapple-Hyam 7/2	8/8	2	8-09	63	-	-	-	-
98 Newm 6f 1st Maiden Three weeks	Mythical Girl D Loder 7/4F	1/6	2	8-09	64	6th Lowther Stks York 6f	*WON 5/2F Shergar Cup Good 1m	*17th Irish 1,000 Guin Curr 1m	-
97 Newm 6f 1st Maiden Three weeks	Embassy D Loder 5/2JF	6/6	2	8-09	65	2nd Lowther Stks York 6f	WON 5/2 Cheveley Park Newm 6f	-	-
96 Sand 5f 1st Maiden Two weeks	Seebee I Balding 6/1	3/8	2	8-09	60	3rd Lowther Stks York 6f	3rd Mill Reef Stks Newb 6f	*2nd Fred Darling Newb 7f	*2nd Poule 'Pouliches Long 1m

12-year median performance rating of the winner: **65** (out of 100)   *(2005 Newbury) *next year*

WINNER'S PROFILE A **top-three finish last time** has proven best – seven of the eight who ran in maidens scored – while three of the four without a victory to their name on their most recent outing were held in Listed company at least, and only Saintly Speech had raced in the north.
Fancied runners have dominated the **first three in the betting** taking 11 renewals, including all three of **Sir Michael Stoute**'s winners – from as many runners – while **Alan Jarvis** sent out a pair from four runners.
Be wary of Richard Hannon and Brian Meehan's, whose joint-record stands at 0 from just over 20 runners.

FUTURE POINTERS Although viewed as an early pointer for next year's 1,000 Guineas, the Princess Margaret winner has only once gone on to follow up in that event during the last 20 years, that honour fell to the 2002 Ascot heroine, Russian Rhythm. Trainer Sir Michael Stoute's filly began her road to stardom post-Ascot in the Lowther Stakes next time out, while two more of Stoute's winners also fared well in that event, Enthused winning in 2000, and Visit narrowly failing last year. It proved costly to follow Ascot winners blindly at York, though, as only one other scored from six runners, while six of the seven that headed for the Cheveley Park all came unstuck.
Only one winner attempted the Meon Fillies' Mile back here without success, but interestingly, two recent thirds managed to triumph in that event (see below).

Were Princess Margaret winners profitable to follow on their subsequent three runs?
Yes – 7 wins from 29 runs returned a **profit of +£7.36** to a £1 level stake.

Placed runners' subsequent record (three runs):
Runners-up: 6 wins from 33 runs returned a loss of -£13.64 to a £1 level stake.
2006 Vital Statistics – Dick Poole Listed, 2005 Nidhaal – Dick Poole Listed

Thirds: 4 wins from 21 runs returned a loss of -£2.50 to a £1 level stake.
2006 Simply Perfect – May Hill, Meon Fillies' Mile, 2005 Nannina – Prestige Stakes, Meon Fillies' Mile

FUTURE SUCCESS RATING: ★ ★ ★ ☆ ☆

HONG KONG JOCKEY CLUB STAKES
July 27, Ascot – (Class 2, Heritage Handicap, 3yo+) 5f

Last run	Winner/ Trainer & SP	Draw/ Ran	Age	Wght	PR	Next four runs			
07 Ayr 5f 9th Heritage Hcp Two weeks	Stoneacre Lad P Grayson 66/1	16/24	4	8-07	62	13th Rous Stks Newm 5f	-	-	-
06 Hami 6f 2nd Scott Stew' Cup Three weeks	Machinist D Nicholls 10/1	23/23	6	8-04	61	17th Great St Wilfrid Ripon 6f	2nd Handicap Good 6f	9th Handicap Hayd 6f	*9th Group 3 Nad Al 6f
05 Ches 5f 4th City Wall Stks Three weeks	Corridor Creeper M Bradley 16/1	21/18	8	9-10	72	4th Listed Deau 5f	4th Bullet Sprint Beve 5f	13th World Trophy Newb 5f	5th Conds Stks Beve 5f
04 Wind 6f 8th Leisure Stks Two weeks	Baltic King H Morrison 9/1	21/24	4	9-04	74	3rd Bullet Sprint Beve 5f	6th Scarbrough Stks Donc 5f	WON 7/4F Conds Stks Beve 5f	3rd Rous Stks Newm 5f
03 Catt 5f 1st Handicap Two months	Salviati J M Bradley 7/1	1/14	6	8-02	62	18th Coral Hcp Hayd 5f	12th SunAlliance Hcp York 6f	12th Handicap Hayd 5f	4th Conds Stks Yarm 6f
02 Sand 5f 2nd Porcelanosa Stk One month	Boleyn Castle T Mills 20/1	21/19	5	9-08	75	10th World Trophy Newb 5f	*3rd Achilles Stks Kemp 5f	*19th King's Stand Ascot 5f	*10th Porcelanosa Stk Sand 5f
01 Ascot 5f 10th Gala Hcp Three weeks	Smokin Beau J Cullinan 20/1	8/17	4	8-00	65	14th Stewards' Cup Good 6f	7th Handicap Newb 5f	WON 20/1 Ladbrokes Hcp Good 6f	2nd Rated Hcp Sand 5f
00 Ascot 6f 5th Rated Hcp One week	Magic Rainbow M Bell 8/1	6/19	5	7-10	63	5th Rated Hcp Sand 5f	7th Portland Hcp Donc 5½f	*11th Ladbrokes Hcp Newm 6f	*5th Handicap Kemp 6f
99 Ascot 5f 2nd Ladbrokes Hcp Two weeks	Rudi's Pet D Nicholls 2/1F	6/9	5	9-07	76	WON 6/1F King George St Good 5f	6th H Kong Sprint Sha 5f	*WON 4/1 Ballyogan Stks Leop 5f	*20th King's Stand Ascot 5f
98 York 5f 1st Handicap Two weeks	Blessingindisguise M Easterby 4/1F	1/13	5	9-04	65	20th Eagle Lane Hcp York 6f	10th Portland Hcp Donc 5½f	9th Rated Hcp Ascot 5f	*17th Showcase Hcp Donc 5f
97 Ayr 5f 1st Handicap Two weeks	Blessingindisguise M Easterby 11/2	1/13	4	8-07	57	3rd Coral Hcp Hayd 5f	3rd Eagle Lane Hcp York 6f	UR Scarbrough Stks Donc 5f	8th Ayr Gold Cup Ayr 6f
96 Newm 5f 7th Handicap One week	Bolshoi J Berry 6/1	9/9	4	8-07	59	4th Stewards' Cup Good 6f	4th Great St Wilfrid Ripon 6f	5th Portland Hcp Donc 5½f	8th Ayr Gold Cup Ayr 6f

12-year median performance rating of the winner: **66** (out of 100) *(2005 Newbury), *next year*

WINNER'S PROFILE Those to have had a **recent spin** feature strongly on the winner's list, nine ran within the past three weeks, while 11 boasted a **distance success** – winning form earlier in the season wasn't essential. There were a few notable pointers including a handicap over this trip at Ayr, while an earlier appearance here in the month found several winners, including Magic Rainbow who raced on the first day of this three-day meeting. As an early-closing race, two winners took advantage and carried penalties.
Four to six-year-olds were the ones to stick with as the last three-year-old winner came 17 years ago, and the Classic generation failed to hit the target from over 20 runners since 1996.
Trainers **David Nicholls** and **Milton Bradley** both sent out two winners apiece from numerous runners.

FUTURE POINTERS Traditionally the big betting event on the final day of the King George meeting, this has been a very competitive sprint handicap in recent times but winners have tended to be only of this level without going on to better things in the near future.
The exception was Rudi's Pet who scored in Group Three company next time out, while in the longer-term, Baltic King eventually won the Wokingham here and Bolshoi scored in the Group Two Temple Stakes. Overall, though, winners have proven best swerved, especially in some of the other handicaps like the Stewards' Cup and Portland.

Were Hong Kong Stakes winners profitable to follow on their subsequent three runs?
Yes – 4 wins from 34 runs returned a **profit of +£1.75** to a £1 level stake (owing to a 20/1 winner)

Placed runners' subsequent record (three runs):
Runners-up: 4 wins from 36 runs returned a loss of -£2.50 to a £1 level stake.
2004 Pivotal Point – Stewards' Cup, 2000 Compton Banker – Portland Handicap

Thirds: 2 wins from 36 runs returned a loss of -£20.50 to a £1 level stake.

Fourths: 0 win from 21 runs returned a loss of -£21.00 to a £1 level stake

FUTURE SUCCESS RATING: ★ ☆ ☆ ☆ ☆

PHOENIX STAKES
July 27, Curragh – (Group 1, Class 1, 2yo Colts & Fillies) 6f

Last run	Winner/ Trainer & SP	Draw/ Ran	Age	Wght	PR	Next four runs			
07 Leop 7f 1st *Silver Listed* *One month*	**Saoirse Abu** K Manning 25/1	1/6	2	8-12	75	**WON 13/2** **Moyglare Stud** **Curr 7f**	3rd Meon Fillies' Mile Ascot 1m	-	-
06 Curr 6f 1st *Railway Stks* *Two months*	**Holy Roman Emperor** A O'Brien 13/8JF	4/7	2	9-01	80	2nd National Stks Curr 7f	**WON 7/4** **Prix Lagardere** **Long 7f**	2nd Dewhurst Stks Newm 7f	-
05 Curr 6f 1st *Railway Stks* *Two months*	**George Washington** A O'Brien 8/13F	6/7	2	9-00	83	**WON 2/11F** **National Stks** **Curr 7f**	*WON 6/4F 2,000 Guineas Newm 1m	*2nd Irish 2,000 Guin Curr 1m	*3rd Celebration Mile Good 1m
04 Ascot 5f 1st *Queen Mary* *Two months*	**Damson** D Wachman 8/11F	1/6	2	8-11	72	3rd Cheveley Park Newm 6f	*9th Irish 2,000 Guin Curr 1m	*7th Coronation Stks York 1m	*9th Phoenix Sprint Curr 6f
03 Curr 6f 1st *Anglesey Stks* *One month*	**One Cool Cat** A O'Brien 11/8	2/7	2	9-00	77	**WON 4/6** **National Stks** **Curr 7f**	*13th 2,000 Guineas Newm 1m	*5th International Stk Curr 1m	*WON 3/1F **Phoenix Sprint** **Curr 6f**
02 Curr 6f 2nd *Anglesey Stks* *One month*	**Spartacus** A O'Brien 16/1	5/9	2	9-00	75	7th Grand Criterium Long 7f	**WON 13/10F** **Gran Criterium** **Siro 6f**	*11th G Prix de Paris Long 1m2f	*9th Sussex Good 1m
01 Curr 6f 1st *Anglesey Stks* *One month*	**Johannesburg** A O'Brien 2/5F	7/11	2	9-00	82	**WON 3/5JF** **Prix Morny** **Deau 6f**	**WON 3/10F** **Middle Park** **Newm 6f**	**WON 72/10** **Breeders' Cup** **Belm 1m1f**	*2nd Gladness Stks Curr 7f
00 Ascot 6f 2nd *Maiden* *Three weeks*	**Minardi** A O'Brien 7/2	9/10	2	9-00	80	**WON 5/6F** **Middle Park** **Newm 6f**	*4th 2,000 Guineas Newm 1m	*3rd Irish 2,000 Guin Curr 1m	*8th St James Palace Ascot 1m
99 Ascot 6f 1st *Coventry* *Two months*	**Fasliyev** A O'Brien 2/7F	4/6	2	9-00	75	**WON 6/5CF** **Prix Morny** **Deau 6f**	-	-	-
98 Curr 6f 6th *Maiden* *One month*	**Lavery** A O'Brien 14/1	7/11	2	9-00	70	5th Champagne Stk Donc 7f	*WON 5/1 **Shergar Cup** **Good 6f**	*10th Poule 'Poulains Long 1m	*14th July Cup Newm 6f
97 Curr 6f 3rd *Anglesey Stks* *One month*	**Princely Heir** M Johnston 12/1	8/9	2	9-00	72	*4th Craven Stks Newm 1m	*4th Germ 2,000 Guin Colo 1m	*8th Cork & Orrery Ascot 6f	*3rd Conds Stks Donc 1m
96 Leop 6f 1st *Maiden* *Two months*	**Mantovani** J Bolger 20/1	9/9	2	9-00	71	*****5th Handicap Nad Al 1m	*****4th Handicap Ghan 7f	-	-

12-year median performance rating of the winner: **76** (out of 100) *(2001-1996 Leopardstown)* **next year *****five years*

WINNER'S PROFILE Clues to identify the ideal profile don't leap out, although one starting point was that every winner **raced within the past two months**, 11 of whom finished **in the top-three last time out**. Eight winners already scored over this trip – two others won over the minimum and seven-furlongs – while nine of the last 11 had experience in Group company, the two exceptions were both maidens trained by **Aidan O'Brien** who has dominated since 1998. It hasn't been a case of following the Irish handler's runners blindly, though, as he sent out 25 losers to go with his eight winners, four of whom had run at Royal Ascot – two won – and last year's Coventry winner, Henrythenavigator, got turned over here at odds-on. O'Brien won this with unfancied maidens, Group winners and Royal Ascot flops, so nailing one of his here for a profit has been no easy task.

FUTURE POINTERS This mid-season Group One for juveniles is an event on the up, and has regularly attracted some of the best around including British raiders – four of the last five featured Coventry Stakes winners from Royal Ascot. However, despite George Washington's subsequent 2,000 Guineas victory the following year, Phoenix winners rarely took the Newmarket route – only four since 1990 – nor have they kicked on as three-year-olds, as only three since 1996 won again in their Classic year. This suggests the time to follow these precocious juveniles is soon after The Curragh, and though some prices were short, the strike-rate during their next two outings was high, and last year's winner, Saoirse Abu, followed up in the Moygalre Stakes at 13/2.
Aidan O'Brien's post-race selection for his winners has been accurate, as the only two he sent for the Prix Morny both scored – the same record as the Middle Park – while two of the three chosen for the National Stakes also won.

Were Phoenix winners profitable to follow on their subsequent three runs?
Yes – 12 wins from 32 runs returned a **profit of +£7.02** to a £1 level stake.

Placed runners' subsequent record (three runs):
Runners-up: 6 wins from 31 runs returned a loss of -£11.60 to a £1 level stake.
2004 Oratorio – Futurity Stakes, Group One Prix Jean-Luc Lagardere
Thirds: 0 win from 14 runs returned a loss of -£14.00 to a £1 level stake.

FUTURE SUCCESS RATING: ★ ★ ★ ★

HERITAGE HANDICAP
July 29, Glorious Goodwood – (Class 2, 4yo+) 1m2f

Last run	Winner/ Trainer & SP	Draw/ Ran	Age	Wght	PR	Next four runs			
07 Ascot 1m2f 1st Wolferton Hcp *Two months*	**Championship Point** M Channon 8/1	6/16	4	9-10	74	4th Royal Whip Stks Curr 1m2f	6th Winter Hill Stks Wind 1m2f	11th Doonside Cup Ayr 1m2f	9th Champion Stks Newm 1m2f
06 Epso 1m2f 4th Conds Stks *Three weeks*	**Crosspeace** M Johnston 12/1	9/16	4	9-10	77	**WON 10/3** **Glorious Stks** **Good 1m4f**	8th Group 3 Deau 1m2f	2nd September Stks Kemp 1m4f	2nd Select Stks Good 1m2f
05 Newb 1m2f 1st Handicap *Two weeks*	**Evaluator** T Mills 7/1	7/20	4	8-11	71	12th J Smith's Hcp Newb 1m2f	2nd Cambridgeshire Newm 1m1f	*5th Handicap Nad Al 1m2f	*10th Handicap Nad Al 1m2f
04 York 1m2f 16th J Smith's Cup *Three weeks*	**Coat Of Honour** Sir M Prescott 10/1	11/15	4	8-12	70	2nd Totesport Hcp Hayd 1m3f	*WON 4/5F* *Stakes* *Down 1m5f*	*WON 1/3F* *Maiden Hurdle* *Muss 2m4f*	*WON 8/11F* *Nov Hdle* *Muss 2m*
03 Ayr 1m2f 5th Scottish Derby *Two weeks*	**Imperial Dancer** M Channon 14/1	8/15	5	9-10	72	2nd Royal Whip Stks Curr 1m2f	3rd Prix Foy Long 1m4f	*WON 7/4JF* *Doonside Cup* *Ayr 1m3f*	6th Group 2 Long 1m2f
02 Good 1m1f 5th Handicap *Two months*	**Prairie Wolf** M Bell 13/2	8/11	6	8-08	63	3rd Rated Hcp Newb 1m3f	7th Class Stks Epsom 1m2f	4th Rated Hcp Ascot 1m2f	*16th Rosebery Hcp Kemp 1m2f
01 Ascot 1m4f 4th Doubleprint Hcp *Three weeks*	**Kuster** L Cumani 6/1	1/12	5	8-06	66	11th Ebor York 1m2f	19th Cambridgeshire Newm 1m1f	*4th Rosebery Hcp Kemp 1m2f	*9th Rated Hcp Newm 1m2f
00 York 1m 4th Rated Hcp *Three weeks*	**Sharp Play** M Johnston 11/2	5/11	5	9-09	64	13th W Hill Mile Hcp Good 1m	11th Motability Hcp York 1m2f	6th Courage Hcp Newb 1m2f	*4th Zetland G Cup Redc 1m2f
99 Ascot 1m4f 5th Duke'Edinburgh Hcp *Two months*	**Ormelie** P Chapple-Hyam 6/1	7/8	4	9-00	60	*7th Mail Hcp Newb 1m	*5th Diamond Hcp Ascot 1m2f	*3rd Showcase Hcp Ascot 1m2f	*3rd Rated Hcp Newb 1m3f
98 Wind 1m2f 3rd Rated Hcp *Three weeks*	**Supply And Demand** G L Moore 3/1F	8/17	4	9-00	64	12th Motability Hcp York 1m2f	2nd Conds Stks Epsom 1m2f	11th Cambridgeshire Newm 1m1f	5th Rated Hcp Leic 1m2f
97 Ling 1m2f 1st Limited Stks *Three weeks*	**Danish Rhapsody** Lady Herries 14/1	11/18	4	8-06	59	12th Motability Hcp York 1m2f	2nd Rated Hcp Epsom 1m2f	**WON 10/1** **Schroder Hcp** **Good 1m1f**	**WON 3/1** **Foundation Stk** **Good 1m2f**
96 Kemp 1m2f 1st Handicap *Three weeks*	**Grand Selection** M Bell 12/1	2/13	4	8-03	55	6th Motability Hcp York 1m2f	9th Cecil Frail Hcp Hayd 1m4f	-	-

12-year median performance rating of the winner: **66** (out of 100)   *Italic = jumps, *next year*

WINNER'S PROFILE Fitness played a big part as all winners **raced within the past two months** – nine within the past three weeks – while only one lined up having not **made the top-five last time** and he was the single graduate from the ultra-competitive John Smith's Cup. A previous victory in the campaign wasn't vital, nor was one over the trip, however, one requirement involved a **draw in the high to middle** numbers – stalls one to five best avoided in large fields. **Four and five-year-olds** dominated as those six and above scored just once from over 40 runners. Trainers **Michael Bell**, **Mick Channon** and **Mark Johnston** have all struck twice.

FUTURE POINTERS Traditionally a curtain-raiser to Glorious Goodwood, this competitive handicap has thrown up a couple of decent performers over the years, although the fact it excludes three-year-olds detracts from it's quality somewhat. Three winners managed to handle the step up into Listed company, and two of them, Crosspeace and Danish Rhapsody returned back here to gain black type. Those that attempted further success in better handicaps such as the Motability Handicap and Cambridgeshire when faced with improving three-year-olds, all came unstuck and are best swerved in the future.

Were winners of this Heritage Handicap profitable to follow on their subsequent three runs?
No – 5 wins from 35 runs returned a loss of -£13.79 to a £1 level stake.

Placed runners' subsequent record (three runs):
Runners-up: 5 wins from 36 runs returned a loss of -£7.50 to a £1 level stake.

Thirds: 2 wins from 33 runs returned a loss of -£8.00 to a £1 level stake.

Fourths: 1 win from 15 runs returned a loss of -£13.09 to a £1 level stake

FUTURE SUCCESS RATING: ★ ★ ☆ ☆ ☆

GORDON STAKES
July 29, Glorious Goodwood – (Group 3, Class 1, 3yo) 1m4f

Last run	Winner/ Trainer & SP	Draw/ Ran	Age	Wght	PR	Next four runs			
07 Sand 1m2f 4th *Eclipse* *One month*	**Yellowstone** A O'Brien 5/2JF	1/9	3	9-00	71	2nd Great Voltigeur York 1m4f	6th Man O'War Belm 1m3f	11th Arc de Triomphe Long 1m4f	-
06 Ascot 1m4f 3rd *King Edward VII* *Two months*	**Sixties Icon** J Noseda 7/4F	1/7	3	9-00	81	**WON 11/8F** St Leger York 1m6f	6th Arc de Triomphe Long 1m4f	*WON 5/2 Jockey Club St Newm 1m4f	*7th Coronation Cup Epsom 1m4f
05 Hayd 1m4f 1st *July Trophy* *One month*	**The Geezer** D Elsworth 3/1	3/5	3	8-10	77	2nd Great Voltigeur York 1m4f	2nd St Leger Donc 1m6f	4th Group 2 Long 1m7f	*5th Yorkshire Cup York 1m6f
04 Ascot 1m4f 2nd *K George V Hcp* *Two months*	**Maraahel** Sir M Stoute 9/4	8/8	3	8-10	76	4th St Leger Donc 1m6f	*8th Sheema Classic Nad Al 1m4f	*5th John Porter Newb 1m4f	*WON 10/3F Huxley Stks Ches 1m2f
03 Newb 1m4f 1st *Maiden* *One month*	**Phoenix Reach** A Balding 12/1	8/10	3	8-10	75	3rd St Leger Donc 1m6f	**WON 54/10** Canadian Int'nl Wood 1m4f	*6th Prince of Wales' Ascot 1m2f	*6th G Prix St-Cloud Sain 1m4f
02 Epso 1m4f 8th *Derby* *Two months*	**Bandari** M Johnston 15/8	5/4	3	8-13	82	**WON 4/5F** Great Voltigeur York 1m4f	3rd St Leger Donc 1m6f	*4th Jockey Club Stk Newm 1m4f	*4th Coronation Cup Epsom 1m4f
01 Newm 1m2f 1st *Maiden* *Three weeks*	**Alexius** Sir M Stoute 7/1	5/11	3	8-10	76	-	-	-	-
00 Chan 1m4f 8th *Prix Jockey-Club* *Two weeks*	**Millenary** J Dunlop 9/1	4/10	3	8-13	80	**WON 11/4F** St Leger Donc 1m6f	*WON 11/4F Jockey Club St Newm 1m4f	*3rd Coronation Cup Epsom 1m4f	*5th King George VI Ascot 1m4f
99 Ascot 2m 3rd *Queen's Vase* *Two months*	**Compton Ace** G Butler 12/1	2/6	3	8-10	72	*2nd Conds Stks Newb 1m2f	*3rd Gold Cup Ascot 2m4f		
98 Hayd 1m4f 3rd = *July Trophy* *One month*	**Nedawi** S Bin Suroor 5/1	2/6	3	8-10	75	**WON 5/2F** St Leger Donc 1m6f	*2nd Turf Classic Nad Al 1m4f	*5th Gold Cup Ascot 2m4f	*2nd King George VI Ascot 1m4f
98 Hayd 1m4f 1st = *July Trophy* *One month*	**Rabah** J Dunlop 5/2	3/6	3	8-10	71	2nd Great Voltigeur York 1m4f	2nd Cumb'lnd Lodge Ascot 1m4f	*9th Jockey Club St Newm 1m4f	*8th Hardwicke Stks Ascot 1m4f
97 Donc 1m2f 2nd *Conds Stks* *Three months*	**Stowaway** S Bin Suroor 10/3JF	5/10	3	8-10	76	**WON 6/5F** Great Voltigeur York 1m4f	4th Champion Stks Newm 1m2f	*WON N/O Turf Classic Nad Al 1m4f	
96 Epso 1m4f 17th *Derby* *Two months*	**St Mawes** J Dunlop 12/1	12/12	3	8-10	70	5th St Leger Donc 1m6f	6th Cumberland Lodge Ascot 1m4f	-	-

12-year median performance rating of the winner: **76** (out of 100)   *next year*

WINNER'S PROFILE Every winner raced at a **Grade One venue last time out**, five took in the **Epsom Derby** or **Royal Ascot**, with the King Edward VII a worthy long-term pointer. Five others either won the **July Trophy** at Haydock, or got off the mark in **maidens**. Those not to have appeared in a Group One last time all finished in the top-three. Two winners lumped a Group penalty to victory – Aqaleem almost made it three last year – while those with an **official rating of 107 or more** are respected.

Trainer **John Dunlop** is one to monitor with three victories from seven runners, including a runner-up and a third, while **Saeed Bin Suroor** won it twice from five runners, and **Sir Michael Stoute** twice from 10.

FUTURE POINTERS Although traditionally viewed as a St Leger trial, the Gordon Stakes has also pointed up two winners and three runners-up of the more near-at-hand Great Voltigeur at York. The two Voltigeur runners from here to have appeared in the St Leger were both placed, whereas, of the six Gordon Stakes winners to head straight to the Classic, three triumphed. Two of the three St Leger winners recorded above par PR's here, unlike Phoenix Reach and St Mawes, who were both sub-standard winners of this event and unsurprisingly failed at Doncaster. Two Gordon victors failed in Ascot's Cumberland Lodge, although two placed succeeded (see below).

Were Gordon Stakes winners profitable to follow on their subsequent three runs?
No – 9 wins from 34 runs returned a loss of -£5.72 to a £1 level stake.

Placed runners' subsequent record (three runs):
Runners-up: 3 wins from 25 runs returned a loss of -£15.35 to a £1 level stake.
2003 High Accolade – Cumberland Lodge, 2000 Air Marshall – Great Voltigeur

Thirds: 4 wins from 18 runs returned a loss of -£11.52 to a £1 level stake.
2001 Nayef – Rose of Lancaster, Select Stakes, Cumberland Lodge

FUTURE SUCCESS RATING: ★ ★ ★ ☆ ☆

LENNOX STAKES
July 29, Glorious Goodwood – (Group 2, Class 1, 3yo+) 7f

Last run	Winner/ Trainer & SP	Draw/ Ran	Age	Wght	PR	Next four runs			
07 Ascot 7f 1st Jersey Stks Two months	**Tariq** P Chapple-Hyam 7/2	2/13	3	8-09	76	5th Prix de la Foret Long 7f	-	-	-
06 Newm 6f 2nd July Cup Three weeks	**Iffraaj** S Bin Suroor 6/4F	10/10	5	9-04	85	WON 4/6F Park Stks York 7f	-	-	-
05 Ling 1m 2nd Silver Trophy Three weeks	**Court Masterpiece** E Dunlop 4/1	13/14	5	9-00	79	3rd Celebration Mile Good 1m	3rd Park Stks Donc 7f	WON 8/1 Prix de la Foret Long 7f	5th Hong Kong Mile Sha 1m
04 Ascot 1m 8th St James Palace Two months	**Byron** S Bin Suroor 16/1	5/8	3	8-07	74	9th Jacques' Marois Deau 1m	*2nd Group 3 Long 7f	*6th Golden Jubilee York 6f	*2nd Supreme Stks Good 7f
03 Newc 6f 6th Chipchase Stks One month	**Nayyir** G Butler 6/1	5/13	5	9-04	80	8th Maurice' Gheest Deau 7f	2nd Challenge Stks Newm 7f	*3rd Dubai Duty Free Nad Al 1m1f	*16th July Cup Newm 6f
02 Ascot 1m 4th Queen Anne Two months	**Nayyir** G Butler 9/2	7/9	4	9-04	78	3rd Maurice' Gheest Deau 7f	10th Sprint Cup Hayd 6f	WON 7/1 Challenge Stks Newm 7f	*6th Chipchase Stks Newc 6f
01 Ches 7f 1st Conds Stks Two months	**Fath** M Tregoning 14/1	4/9	4	9-00	73	10th Park Stks Donc 7f	2nd Challenge Stks Newm 7f	*6th John of Gaunt Hayd 7f	-
00 Ascot 7f 1st Jersey Stks Two months	**Observatory** J Gosden 11/4	6/8	3	8-12	83	2nd Celebration Mile Good 1m	WON 14/1 Q Elizabeth II Ascot 1m	*WON 11/10F Prix d'Ispahan Long 1m1f	*4th Prince of Wales' Ascot 1m2f

8-year median performance rating of the winner: **79** (out of 100)   **next year*

WINNER'S PROFILE All eight winners to date **visited the racecourse within the past two months**, six took part in the **Royal meeting**, two of whom won the Jersey Stakes including Tariq last year, who escaped a penalty. However, those that **shouldered a penalty** came out on top four times, while seven winners entered the stalls boasting a **distance victory**, the same number that finished either **first or second on one of their last two starts**. Trainer **Saeed Bin Suroor** has already made a splash with two victories from four runners since it became a Group Two in 2003.

FUTURE POINTERS Although in its infancy, this Group Two has produced some useful winners, with the likes of Court Masterpiece and Observatory moving on to land Group One events later in the season, while the classy Iffraaj took the Group Two Park Stakes next time out before retiring to stud.
Last year's winner, Tariq, was slightly below the median performance rating and was unable to follow up in the Prix de la Foret on Arc day, unlike Court Masterpiece two years prior, while two races to have been unkind to winners post-Goodwood were the Celebration Mile back here and the Maurice de Gheest in Deauville.

Were Lennox Stakes winners profitable to follow on their subsequent three runs?
Yes – 5 wins from 20 runs returned a **profit of +£15.76** to a £1 level stake.

Placed runners' subsequent record (three runs):
Runners-up: 3 wins from 23 runs returned a **profit of +£6.00** to a £1 level stake.
2001 Munir – Challenge Stakes

Thirds: 1 win from 22 runs returned a loss of -£16.50 to a £1 level stake.

FUTURE SUCCESS RATING: ★ ★ ★ ☆ ☆

MOLECOMB STAKES
July 29, Glorious Goodwood – (Group 3, Class 1, 2yo) 5f

Last run	Winner/ Trainer & SP	Draw/ Ran	Age	Wght	PR	Next four runs			
07 Nott 5f 1st Maiden *Two months*	**Fleeting Spirit** J Noseda 8/1	2/16	2	8-11	69	3rd Lowther Stks York 6f	**WON 5/4F** **Flying Childers** **Donc 5f**	2nd Cheveley Park Newm 6f	-
06 Wolv 5f 1st Nov Stks *Two weeks*	**Enticing** W Haggas 3/1F	6/13	2	8-11	72	13th Nunthorpe York 5f	3rd Cornwallis Stks Ascot 5f	*WON 9/4F **Lansdown Stks** **Bath 5f**	*5th King's Stand Stk Ascot 5f
05 York 5f 2nd Windsor Castle *Two months*	**Strike Up The Band** D Nicholls 6/1	15/15	2	9-01	64	*8th Euro Free Hcp Newm 7f	*3rd Pavillon Stks Ling 6f	*3rd Carnarvon Stks Newb 6f	*15th Wokingham Ascot 6f
04 Newb 5f 8th Weatherbys Sprint *Two weeks*	**Tournedos** M Channon 14/1	1/13	2	8-12	63	7th Prix Morny Deau 6f	3rd Group 2 Bade 6f	2nd Flying Childers Donc 5f	5th Levy Stks Curr 6f
03 Ches 5f 1st Conds Stks *Three weeks*	**Majestic Missile** W Haggas 9/4F	5/9	2	8-12	68	6th Gimcrack Stks York 6f	**WON 11/4** **Cornwallis Stks** **Ascot 5f**	*5th King's Stand Stk Ascot 5f	*8th King George Good 5f
02 Newb 5f 2nd Weatherbys Sprint *Two weeks*	**Wunders Dream** J Given 8/1	12/13	2	8-07	66	5th Lowther Stks York 6f	**WON 9/2** **Flying Childers** **Donc 5f**	16th Prix de l' Abbaye Long 5f	*9th Palace House Newm 5f
01 Newb 5f 13th Weatherbys Sprint *Two weeks*	**Whitbarrow** B Millman 10/1	8/14	2	9-01	61	8th Prix Morny Deau 6f	13th Flying Childers Donc 5f	4th Horris Hill Stks Newb 7f	*WON 4/1 **Rated Hcp** **Hayd 6f**
00 Sand 5f 1st Dragon Stks *One month*	**Misty Eyed** Mrs P Dutfield 3/1F	6/9	2	8-10	62	2nd Flying Childers Donc 5f	5th Dubai Duty Free Newb 6f	*10th Temple Stks Sand 5f	*2nd King's Stand Stk Ascot 5f
99 Bath 5f 2nd Novice Stks *Two weeks*	**Misty Miss** D Evans 33/1	3/10	2	8-07	59	**WON 2/5F** **Conds Stks** **Wolv 6f**	11th Flying Childers Donc 5f	3rd Firth Of Clyde St Ayr 6f	*10th Nell Gwyn Newm 7f
98 Newb 5f 3rd Conds Stks *Three weeks*	**Inya Lake** M Channon 20/1	9/9	2	8-07	63	7th Flying Childers Donc 5f	12th Cornwallis Stks Ascot 5f	*WON 5/1 **Field Marshal** **Hayd 5f**	*2nd Lansdown Stk Bath 5f
97 Curr 6f 1st Anglesey Stks *Three weeks*	**Lady Alexander** C Collins 10/3F	2/13	2	8-12	60	7th Moygiare Stud Curr 7f	*2nd Cornwallis Stks Ascot 5f	*6th Greenlands Stks Curr 6f	*6th Ballyogan Stks Leop 6f
96 Ches 5f 2nd Conds Stks *Three months*	**Carmine Lake** P Chapple-Hyam 6/1	2/7	2	8-07	65	4th Lowther Stks York 6f	5th Prix de l' Abbaye Long 5f	*3rd Scarbrough Stks Donc 5f	*WON 168/10 **Prix de l Abbaye** **Long 5f**

12-year median performance rating of the winner: **64** (out of 100)   *next year*

WINNER'S PROFILE A maiden hasn't triumphed here since the mid-eighties, as every winner since 1996 **arrived with a distance victory** on their CV, while those to have run – but not won – in either the Weatherbys Super Sprint or at Royal Ascot are respected; the Norfolk and the Windsor Castle best.
Fillies stood out, outperforming the males with eight wins to four in the last 12 years, while the last two winning favourites were trained by **Willie Haggas**, whose runners are a tip in themselves, having sent out just two runners. Mick Channon has also won it twice, but from nine runners,

FUTURE POINTERS An event that has produced decent sprinters of late and last year's vintage renewal lifted its reputation further. Not only did the winner, Fleeting Spirit, dip below 58 seconds for the first time since Hoh Magic in 1994, but she also took the Group Two Flying Childers at Doncaster, a feat achieved by Wunders Dream in 2002. However, the strength of the 2007 Molecomb was further boosted when the runner-up, Kingsgate Native, sensationally landed the Group One Nunthorpe next time out, before a creditable second in the Abbaye, adding to the runners-up decent record from here *(see below)*. The 2007 third and fourth also went on to Pattern success, with Captain Gerrard repeating Bouncing Bowdler's – the 2000 runner-up - achievement in landing the Roses Stakes at York. Willie Haggas's two winners also turned out to be decent, both triumphing in Pattern company, although one negative was the overall poor record of winners next time out - 11 failed, eight of whom were upped in trip.

Were Molecomb winners profitable to follow on their subsequent three runs?
No – 6 wins from 36 runs returned a loss of -£13.85 to a £1 level stake.

Placed runners' subsequent record (three runs):
Runners-up: 7 wins from 32 runs returned a **profit of +£13.75** to a £1 level stake.
2007 Kingsgate Native – Nunthorpe, 2006 Wi Dud – Flying Childers,
2002 Bouncing Bowdler – Roses Stakes, Mill Reef Stakes, 1998 Amazing Dream – St Hugh's Stakes

Thirds: 3 wins from 33 runs returned a loss of -£25.66 to a £1 level stake.
2007 Captain Gerrard – Roses Stakes, Harry Rosebery Stakes

FUTURE SUCCESS RATING: ★ ★ ★ ☆ ☆

VINTAGE STAKES
July 30, Glorious Goodwood – (Group 2, Class 1, 2yo) 7f

Last run	Winner/ Trainer & SP	Draw/ Ran	Age	Wght	PR	Next four runs			
07 Newm 7f 1st Maiden Three weeks	Rio De La Plata S Bin Suroor 8/13F	3/7	2	9-00	79	2nd National Stks Curr 7f	WON 8/13F Prix 'Lagardere Long 7f	4th Dewhurst Stks Newm 7f	-
06 Newm 6f 1st July Stks Three weeks	Strategic Prince P Cole 6/1	1/10	2	9-03	72	3rd Dewhurst Stks Newm 7f	*8th 2,000 Guineas Newm 1m	*16th Derby Epsom 1m4f	*13th Jersey Stks Ascot 7f
05 Sali 6f 1st Maiden Two months	Sir Percy M Tregoning 4/1	2/7	2	8-11	77	WON 9/2 Dewhurst Stks Newm 7f	*2nd 2,000 Guineas Newm 1m	*WON 6/1 Derby Epsom 1m4f	*7th Champion Stks Newm 1m2f
04 Ayr 6f 1st Maiden Three weeks	Shamardal M Johnston 8/13F	10/10	2	8-11	76	WON 9/2 Dewhurst Stks Newm 7f	*9th UAE Derby Nad Al 1m1f	*WON 4/1F Poule' Poulains Long 1m	WON 4/1 Prix Jock' Club Chan 1m3f
03 Pont 6f 1st Conds Stks One month	Lucky Story M Johnston 6/5F	3/9	2	8-11	73	WON 2/1 Champagne Stk Donc 7f	*2nd Sovereign Stks Sali 1m	*7th Prix du Moulin Long 1m	*2nd Q Elizabeth II Ascot 1m
02 Newb 7f 1st Conds Stks Two weeks	Dublin D Loder 11/1	2/10	2	8-11	65	3rd National Stks Curr 7f	16th Dewhurst Stks Newm 7f	*7th UAE 2,000 Guin Nad Al 1m	*WON N/O Stakes Nad Al 1m
01 Epsom 7f 1st Maiden Two weeks	Naheef D Loder 8/1	11/10	2	8-11	67	2nd National Stks Curr 7f	*14th 2,000 Guineas Newm 1m	*7th Derby Epsom 1m4f	*WON 6/4F Winter Hill Stks Wind 1m2f
00 Sand 7f 1st Maiden One month	No Excuse Needed Sir M Stoute 12/1	3/10	2	8-11	71	5th Royal Lodge Stk Ascot 1m	St James Palace Ascot 1m	*2nd Sussex Good 1m	*WON 8/11F Celebration Mile Good 1m
99 Newm 7f 2nd Maiden One month	Ekraar M Tregoning 7/4	5/5	2	8-11	70	4th Champagne Stk Donc 7f	3rd R Post Trophy Donc 1m	*3rd Craven Stks Newm 1m	*4th Poule' Poulains Long 1m
98 Sand 7f 1st Maiden One month	Aljabr S Bin Suroor 4/6F	2/7	2	8-11	78	WON 6/4F Pr' Salamandre Long 7f	*2nd St James Palace Ascot 1m	*WON 11/10F Sussex Good 1m	*4th Prix du Moulin Long 1m
97 Ascot 7f 1st Chesham Stks Two weeks	Central Park P Cole 5/4F	1/6	2	9-00	73	7th Dewhurst Stks Newm 7f	*9th 2,000 Guineas Newm 1m	*WON 4/1 Derby Italiano Capa 1m4f	*4th King Edward VII Ascot 1m4f
96 Sand 7f 1st Maiden Two months	Putra P Cole 10/3	6/8	2	8-11	71	*15th 2,000 Guineas Newm 1m	-	-	-

12-year median performance rating of the winner: **73** (out of 100)   *next year*

WINNER'S PROFILE **Winning form last time** out has proven vital and those that graduated from Newmarket (July meeting) and Sandown (Eclipse meeting) maidens are much respected as they have been an excellent long-term guide. Every winner entered the stalls having **no more than three races** on the clock, while it paid to stick with the best horses, as 11 emerged from the **first four in the betting**.
Trainers **Paul Cole** and **Saeed Bin Suroor** haven't wasted many entries, boasting records of three from five and two from two, respectively, while Marcus Tregoning and Mark Johnston had two apiece. Two handlers to be wary of, however, were Aidan O'Brien and Richard Hannon, who sent out almost 20 losers between them.

FUTURE POINTERS A juvenile event to be taken more seriously than the Richmond Stakes here later in the week, not only as a pointer for the remainder of the season, but as a springboard for long-term achievement.
Two of the last four winners, Sir Percy and Shamardal, both took Group One honours in the Dewhurst next time out, before going on to land Classics the following year, while Naheef, No Excuse Needed, Ekraar, Central Park and Aljabr were all Group winners as three-year-olds – the latter stood out in the Sussex at Goodwood.
Looking further back, both Dr Devious and Mister Baileys took this in the early nineties before striking in the Derby and 2,000 Guineas respectively, although five Vintage winners since all met with defeat at Newmarket, Sir Percy going closest.

Were Vintage winners profitable to follow on their subsequent three runs?
Yes – 9 wins from 34 runs returned a **profit of +£3.21** to a £1 level stake.

Placed runners' subsequent record (three runs):
Runners-up: 7 wins from 31 returned a loss of -£9.93 to a £1 level stake.
2005 Cool Creek – Mill Reef, 2002 Bourbonnais – Acomb, 1999 Sarafan – Stardom Stakes,
1998 Raise A Grand – Solario Stakes, 1996 Grapeshot – Tattersalls Stakes, Predominate Stakes

Thirds: 3 wins from 18 runs returned a **profit of +£1.93** to a £1 level stake.
2006 Kirklees – Gran Criterium, 1996 Equal Rights – Futurity Stakes

FUTURE SUCCESS RATING: ★ ★ ★ ★ ☆

SUSSEX STAKES
July 30, Glorious Goodwood – (Group 1, Class 1, 3yo+) 1m

Last run	Winner/Trainer & SP	Draw/Ran	Age	Wght	PR	Next four runs			
07 Ascot 1m 1st Queen Anne *Two months*	Ramonti S Bin Suroor 9/2	8/8	5	9-07	87	2nd Prix du Moulin Long 1m	WON 5/1 Q Elizabeth II Ascot 1m	-	-
06 Ascot 1m 2nd Queen Anne *Two months*	Court Masterpiece E Dunlop 15/2	5/7	6	9-07	79	3rd Q Elizabeth II Ascot 1m	7th Grade 1 Kyot 1m	9th Group 2 Hans 9th	*8th Group 2 Nad Al 1m
05 York 7f 1st Jersey Stks *Two months*	Proclamation J Noseda 3/1	7/12	3	8-13	85	11th Sprint Cup Hayd 6f	*3rd Queen Anne Ascot 1m	*5th Q Elizabeth II Ascot 1m	-
04 Newm 1m 1st Falmouth Stks *Two months*	Soviet Song J Fanshawe 3/1	5/11	4	9-04	84	WON 8/13F Matron Stks Leop 1m	6th Q Elizabeth II Ascot 1m	*3rd Windsor Forest York 1m	*WON 7/4F Falmouth Stks Newm 1m
03 Epso 1½m 2nd Diomed Stks *Two months*	Reel Buddy R Hannon 20/1	7/9	5	9-07	76	14th Prix du Moulin Long 1m	-	-	-
02 Ascot 1m 1st St James' Palace *Two months*	Rock Of Gibraltar A O'Brien 8/13F	3/5	3	8-13	89	WON 3/5JF Prix du Moulin Long 1m	2nd Breeders' Cup Arli 1m	-	-
01 Ascot 1m 2nd St James' Palace *Two months*	Noverre S Bin Suroor 9/2	11/10	3	9-00	83	3rd Jacques' Marois Deau 1m	2nd Q Elizabeth II Ascot 1m	7th Breeders' Cup Belm 1m	*2nd Dubai Duty Free Nad Al 1m1f
00 Sand 1m2f 1st Eclipse Stks *One month*	Giant's Causeway A O'Brien 3/1JF	6/10	3	9-00	87	WON 10/11F Juddmonte Int York 1m2f	WON 8/11F Irish Champion Leop 1m2f	2nd Q Elizabeth II Ascot 1m	2nd Breeders' Cup Chur 1m2f
99 Ascot 1m 2nd St James' Palace *Two months*	Aljabr S Bin Suroor 11/10F	6/8	3	8-13	84	4th Prix du Moulin Long 1m	*WON 8/13F Lockinge Newb 1m	*4th Queen Anne Ascot 1m	*5th Sussex Good 1m
98 Yarm 7f 1st Conds Stks *One month*	Among Men Sir M Stoute 4/1	10/10	4	9-07	80	2nd Jacques' Marois Deau 1m	5th Q Elizabeth II Ascot 1m	11th Breeders' Cup Chur 1m	-
97 York 1m 1st Conds Stks *Three weeks*	Ali-Royal H Cecil 13/2	3/9	4	9-07	82	-	-	-	-
96 Ascot 1m2f 1st Prince of Wales' *Two months*	First Island G Wragg 5/1	9/10	4	9-07	83	2nd Juddmonte Int York 1m2f	3rd Q Elizabeth II Ascot 1m	5th Champions Stks Newm 1m2f	WON 9/5F Hong Kong Cup Sha 1m1f

12-year median performance rating of the winner: **83** (out of 100)   *next year*

WINNER'S PROFILE Every winner came here with a **previous run in the last two months**, all of whom **finished in the first two**, six came via **Royal Ascot**, including four three-year-olds.
A **previous victory in Group company** has been key, along with a **placed effort in a Group One event** – those from the **Lockinge in May** are respected – while those in the **first four of the betting** fared well.
Middle to high stalls can be favoured as those drawn wide in stalls one and two struggled.
Trainer **Saeed Bin Suroor** sent out three winners from 15 runners, while Aidan O'Brien had two from 16. Jockeys **Frankie Dettori** and **Mick Kinane** have ridden seven of the last 10 winners between them.

FUTURE POINTERS Winners of the Sussex have a mixed subsequent record although those since the Millennium have equipped themselves well post-Goodwood, Ramonti last year became the fourth in eight years who followed up in Group One company. Ramonti was also the first since Bigstone in 1993 to land the Queen Elizabeth II Stakes at Ascot – seven failed since – and a clue to his potential was highlighted by the performance rating (PR) here, as he was of similar calibre to other above par winners that found future glory such as Soviet Song, Rock Of Gibraltar and Giant's Causeway. One race, however, that not even some of these great stars could win was the Breeders' Cup in America, which proved beyond the last four Sussex winners to have attempted that feat.

Were Sussex winners profitable to follow on their subsequent three runs?
No – 5 wins from 29 runs returned a loss of -£14.56 to a £1 level stake.

Placed runners' subsequent record (three runs):
Runners-up: 4 wins from 34 runs returned a loss of -£24.88 to a £1 level stake.
2005 Soviet Song – Windsor Forest, 2001 No Excuse Needed – Celebration Mile,
1999 Docksider – Hong Kong Mile, 1996 Charnwood Forest – Challenge Stakes

Thirds: 5 wins from 28 runs returned a loss of -£7.90 to a £1 level stake.
2000 Medicean – Celebration Mile

FUTURE SUCCESS RATING: ★ ★ ★ ☆ ☆

HERITAGE HANDICAP
July 30, Glorious Goodwood – (Class 2, 3yo) 1m4f

Last run	Winner/ Trainer & SP	Draw/ Ran	Age	Wght	PR	Next four runs			
07 Epsom 1m2f 8th Vodafone Hcp Two months	Regal Flush Sir M Stoute 14/1	3/16	3	8-11	67	WON 4/1JF Old Bor'gh Cup Hayd 1m6f	4th St Leger Donc 1m6f	-	-
06 Nott 1m6f 1st Handicap Three weeks	Strategic Mount P Cole 6/1	7/15	3	8-06	56	7th Mallard Hcp York 1m6f	*6th Summer Hcp Good 1m6f	*WON 11/8F Shergar Cup Ascot 1m4f	-
05 Newm 1m2f 5th Heritage Hcp Three weeks	Foxhaven P Chamings 20/1	13/13	3	9-03	61	*6th Handicap Sand 1m2f	*2nd Glorious Stks Good 1m4f	*7th Ebor York 1m6f	*WON 3/1 Listed Ches 1m4f
04 Ascot 1m4f 2nd Handicap Three weeks	Cutting Crew P Harris 12/1	14/16	3	8-08	58	-	-	-	-
03 Ripo 1m4f 2nd Handicap One month	No Refuge Sir M Prescott 7/1	1/15	3	8-09	62	2nd Svenskt Derby Jage 1m4f	2nd Rated Hcp Hami 1m5f	*3rd Listed Bade 1m6f	*WON 28/10 Listed Colo 1m7f
02 Wind 1m4f 4th Class Stks One month	Dawn Invasion Mrs A Perrett 12/1	2/16	3	9-07	57	4th Ebor York 1m6f	*10th Glorious Stks Good 1m4f	*4th March Stks Good 1m6f	*WON 16/1 Rated Hcp Newm 1m4f
01 Sali 1m4f 1st Handicap One month	Ovambo P Makin 9/1	8/12	3	8-11	56	2nd Melrose Hcp York 1m6f	*3rd Ormonde Stks Ches 1m5f	*6th Henry II Stks Sand 2m	*2nd Fred Archer Newm 1m4f
00 Newm 1m2f 10th Bonusprint Hcp Three weeks	Blue Gold R Hannon 14/1	10/10	3	9-01	60	2nd Conds Stks Wind 1m4f	3rd Troy Stks Donc 1m4f	*4th Festival Stks Good 1m2f	*6th Mercury Listed Leic 1m4f
99 Good 1m2f 1st Handicap Two months	Mary Stuart Sir M Stoute 9/4F	7/11	3	8-09	62	*5th Yorkshire Oaks York 1m4f	-	-	-
98 York 1m2f 7th J Smith's Cup Three weeks	Muhib Sir M Stoute 10/1	14/15	3	9-01	66	10th Sunday Hcp Ascot 1m4f	*2nd Shergar Cup Good 1m4f	*3rd Mercury Listed Leic 1m4f	*3rd Scottish Classic Ayr 1m2f
97 Newm 1m2f 2nd Cambridge Hcp Three weeks	Maylane A Stewart 13/2	15/14	3	9-04	65	WON 3/1 September Stks Epsom 1m4f	UR Cumb'lnd Lodge Ascot 1m4f	*8th Turf Classic Nad Al 1m4f	*7th Gold Cup Ascot 2m4f
96 Newm 1m2f 6th Cambridge Hcp Three weeks	Frequent L Cumani 9/1	4/12	3	8-09	64	4th March Stks Good 1m6f	4th Premio d'Italia Siro 1m4f	7th Serlby Stks Donc 1m4f	*8th Motability Hcp York 1m2f

12-year median performance rating of the winner: **61** (out of 100) *next year*

WINNER'S PROFILE A recent run rates a bonus as 10 **raced within the past month**, while good form is also relevant, 11 **won earlier in the campaign**, 10 of whom came within their last three runs. Five winners competed in the 10-furlong handicap at the Newmarket July meeting in the last 13 years – a distance victory isn't vital – although those straight from maidens were rare, with preference for hardened handicappers that boasted an **official rating below 100**. Although a few low drawn numbers succeeded, a **middle to high draw** was preferable, while trainer **Sir Michael Stoute** heads the list with four winners from around 14 runners since 1995.

FUTURE POINTERS This quality handicap – formerly the Tote Gold Trophy – had gone through a quiet spell prior to last year when Regal Flush achieved a smart performance (above par PR) for trainer Sir Michael Stoute, who sent out the subsequent globetrotting Pilsudski to land this in 1995. While Regal Flush may not be of that calibre, he was one of the best winners of this for a while and franked the event after he took the competitive Old Borough Cup next time out before a gallant fourth in the St Leger.
Those that headed to York next time out drew a blank, as did those that returned here for Listed events.

Were winners of this heritage handicap profitable to follow on their subsequent three runs?
No – 3 wins from 30 runs returned a loss of -£18.63 to a £1 level stake.

Placed runners' subsequent record (three runs):
Runners-up: 2 wins from 32 runs returned a loss of -£26.67 to a £1 level stake.

Thirds: 6 wins from 32 runs returned a loss of -£7.50 to a £1 level stake.
2005 Tawqeet – Melrose Handicap, 2003 Trust Rule – Knavesmire Handicap, 2000 Alva Glen – March Stakes

Fourths: 3 wins from 9 runs returned a **profit of +£3.75** to a £1 level stake.
2007 Malt Or Mash – November Handicap, 2002 Dune – Old Borough Cup

FUTURE SUCCESS RATING: ★ ★ ☆ ☆ ☆

KING GEORGE STAKES
July 29, Glorious Goodwood – (Group 3, Class 1, 3yo+) 5f

Last run	Winner/ Trainer & SP	Draw/ Ran	Age	Wght	PR	Next four runs			
07 Newm 5f 1st Handicap Three weeks	Moorhouse Lad B Smart 10/1	14/17	4	9-00	72	10th Nunthorpe York 5f	-	-	-
06 Newm 6f 11th July Cup Three weeks	La Cucaracha B Hills 7/2	2/18	5	8-11	76	-	-	-	-
05 Ches 5f 3rd City Wall Stks Three weeks	Fire Up The Band D Nicholls 10/1	13/12	6	9-00	71	13th Nunthorpe York 5f	8th Scarbrough Stks Donc 5f	3rd Prix de l'Abbaye Long 5f	*5th Conds Stks Ling 5f
04 York 6f 4th Summer Stks One month	Ringmoor Dawn D Arbuthnot 10/1	12/13	5	8-11	74	WON 5/2 Flying Five Curr 5f	7th Diadem Stks Ascot 6f	8th Prix de l'Abbaye Long 5f	2nd Boadicea Listed Newm 6f
03 Newb 6f 3rd Hackwood Stks Three weeks	The Tatling J M Bradley 11/4F	2/9	6	9-00	72	2nd Nunthorpe York 5f	6th Sprint Cup Hayd 6f	5th World Trophy Newb 5f	5th Diadem Stks Ascot 6f
02 Curr 5f 2nd Listed Stks Two months	Agnetha D Weld 11/2	14/14	3	8-07	68	4th Flying Five Curr 5f	5th Group 3 Curr 6f	3rd World Trophy Newb 5f	5th Prix de l'Abbaye Long 5f
01 Ascot 5f 11th King's Stand Two months	Dietrich A O'Brien 11/2	12/15	3	8-12	67	7th Prix de l'Abbaye Long 5f	-	-	-
00 York 5f 2nd Summer Stks Three weeks	Cassandra Go G Wragg 11/2	1/13	4	8-10	73	*2nd Palace House Newm 5f	*WON 10/3JF Temple Stks Sand 5f	*WON 8/1 King's Stand Ascot 5f	*2nd July Cup Newm 6f
99 Ascot 5f 1st Rated Hcp One week	Rudi's Pet D Nicholls 6/1F	10/15	5	9-00	75	6th H Kong Sprint Sha 5f	*WON 4/1 Ballyogan Stks Leop 5f	*20th King's Stand Ascot 5f	*3rd King George Good 5f
98 Ascot 5f 14th King's Stand Two months	Land Of Dreams M Johnston 5/1	4/15	3	8-07	71	9th Nunthorpe York 5f	9th Sprint Cup Hayd 6f	10th Prix d le'Abbaye Long 5f	-
97 Newb 6f 5th Hackwood Stks Two weeks	Averti W Muir 11/1	3/15	6	9-00	70	3rd Nunthorpe York 5f	4th Sprint Cup Hayd 6f	3rd Diadem Stks Ascot 6f	5th Prix de l'Abbaye Long 5f
96 Newb 6f 5th Hackwood Stks Two weeks	Rambling Bear M Blanshard 10/1	6/14	3	8-10	65	3rd Hopeful Stks Newm 6f	8th Sprint Cup Hayd 6f	9th Prix d le'Abbaye Long 5f	*6th Abernant Stks Newm 6f

12-year median performance rating of the winner: **71** (out of 100) **next year*

WINNER'S PROFILE The majority of winners had been **active within the last two months** – 10 via either Ascot, Newbury, Newmarket or York – while 11 since 1996 boasted a **distance victory**. Experience at this level can be important as all 12 **raced in Group company** earlier in their career, although only La Cucaracha and Land Of Dreams won in that sphere, whereas five scored in a Listed event. Fillies and mares held their own against the males with six victories apiece, and though four winners started at 10/1, **none were bigger than 11/1**, which eliminated the outsiders in big fields.
Trainer **David Nicholls** has long been associated with his sprinters at this fixture, and is the only handler to figure more than once in the past 12 years with two winners from 13 runners.

FUTURE POINTERS As it suggests on the tin, a Group Three sprint, and one that has traditionally failed to attract the top-notchers around, which is borne out by the winner's subsequent results where they consistently fell short in Group One events such as the Nunthorpe, Haydock Sprint Cup and Prix de l'Abbaye – Moorhouse Lad the latest to flop in the former event last year.
It is no surprise, therefore, to note that only one King George winner managed to triumph later that season in Ringmoor Down, who was sensibly kept to Group Three company.

Were King George winners profitable to follow on their subsequent three runs?
No – 4 wins from 29 runs returned a loss of -£4.47 to a £1 level stake.

Placed runners' subsequent record (three runs):
Runners-up: 6 wins from 34 runs returned a **profit of +£14.50** to a £1 level stake.
2006 Desert Lord – Prix de l'Abbaye, 2005 The Tatling – World Trophy, 2004 The Tatling – World Trophy, 1999 Imperial Beauty – World Trophy

Thirds: 4 wins from 34 runs returned a loss of -£16.75 to a £1 level stake.
1998 Lochangel – Nunthorpe

FUTURE SUCCESS RATING: ★ ★ ☆ ☆ ☆

GOODWOOD CUP

July 31, Glorious Goodwood – (Group 2, Class 1, 3yo+) 2m

Last run	Winner/ Trainer & SP	Draw/ Ran	Age	Wght	PR	Next four runs			
07 Ascot 2m4f 9th Gold Cup *Two months*	**Allegretto** Sir M Stoute 8/1	11/15	4	9-05	78	2nd Yorkshire Oaks York 1m4f	3rd Doncaster Cup Donc 2m2f	**WON 52/10** Prix Royal-Oak Long 2m	-
06 Ascot 2m4f 1st Gold Cup *Two months*	**Yeats** A O'Brien 10/11F	8/15	5	9-10	86	2nd Irish St Leger Curr 1m6f	7th Melbourne Cup Flem 2m	*WON 1/3F Vintage Crop St Nav 1m5f	*WON 1/7F Saval Beg Stk Leop 1m6f
05 York 2m4f 2nd Gold Cup *Two months*	**Distinction** Sir M Stoute 11/4F	2/10	6	9-05	77	2nd Lonsdale Cup York 2m	6th Doncaster Cup Donc 2m2f	19th Melbourne Cup Flem 2m	*WON 3/1 Aston Park Stk Newb 1m5f
04 Ascot 2m4f 3rd Gold Cup *Two months*	**Darasim** M Johnston 11/8F	8/9	6	9-04	72	5th Doncaster Cup Donc 2m2f	6th Prix du Cadran Long 2m4f	*6th Listed Nott 1m6f	*9th Group 3 Bade 2m
03 Sand 2m 1st Esher Stks *One month*	**Persian Punch** D Elsworth 7/2	9/9	10	9-04	81	4th Lonsdale Stks York 2m	**WON 3/1** Doncaster Cup Donc 2m2f	8th Prix du Cadran Long 2m4f	**WON 5/2** Jock' Club Cup Newm 2m
02 Ascot 2m4f 9th Gold Cup *Two months*	**Jardines Lookout** A Jarvis 10/1	3/9	5	9-02	75	6th Lonsdale Stks York 2m	4th Doncaster Cup Donc 2m2f	7th Melbourne Cup Flem 2m	*6th Yorkshire Cup York 1m6f
01 Ascot 2m4f 2nd Gold Cup *Two months*	**Persian Punch** D Elsworth 6/1	1/12	8	9-05	85	**WON 10/3F** Lonsdale Stks York 2m	4th Irish St Leger Curr 1m6f	3rd Melbourne Cup Flem 2m	*2nd Sagaro Stks Ascot 2m
00 Leop 1m6f 2nd Listed *Two weeks*	**Royal Rebel** M Johnston 10/1	2/8	4	9-02	81	**WON 2/1JF** Lonsdale Stks York 2m	3rd Prix du Cadran Long 2m4f	2nd Jockey Club Cup Newm 2m	6th Prix Royal-Oak Long 2m
99 Ascot 2m4f 3rd Gold Cup *Two months*	**Kayf Tara** S Bin Suroor 9/4JF	5/7	5	9-07	84	**WON 4/5F** Group 2 Deau 1m7f	**WON 1/2F** Irish St Leger Curr 1m6f	*WON 15/8F Yorkshire Cup York 1m6f	*WON 11/8F Gold Cup Ascot 2m4f
98 Ascot 2m4f 2nd Gold Cup *Two months*	**Double Trigger** M Johnston 11/2	4/9	7	9-05	81	**WON 9/4JF** Doncaster Cup Donc 2m2f	-	-	-
97 Ascot 2m4f 8th Gold Cup *Two months*	**Double Trigger** M Johnston 16/1	1/10	6	9-00	80	4th Doncaster Cup Donc 2m2f	5th Prix du Cadran Long 2m4f	*6th Sagaro Stks Newm 2m	*8th Henry II Sand 2m
96 Bade 2m 5th Group 3 *Two months*	**Grey Shot** I Balding 3/1	4/7	4	9-00	73	4th Lonsdale Stks York 2m	7th Melbourne Cup Flem 2m	*4th Sagaro Stks Ascot 2m	*2nd Group 2 Long 2m

12-year median performance rating of the winner: **79** (out of 100)   *next year*

WINNER'S PROFILE Ten winners lined up having **run in the Ascot Gold Cup** – Persian Punch ran in the 2003 renewal before Sandown – but only Yeats was successful at the Royal meeting, and joined legendary names Le Moss, Ardross and Double Trigger (1995) who all recorded the Ascot/Goodwood Cup double.
Allegretto last year became the first filly for nearly 50 years to score, while runner-up, Veracity, was almost the first three-year-old to win since it switched to two miles in 1991, and that age-group deserve respect as three have gone close since 1996. A penalty can be overcome, as can the lack of a two-mile victory, but the ability to have figured in a **Group event over at least 15 furlongs** linked 11 winners, while **none raced more than four times** earlier in the year. Quality prevailed and an **official rating of at least 107** was key, while those at the **forefront of the betting** have fared well, especially first and second favourites. Trainer **Mark Johnston** won the prize four times from 16 runners, while Sir Michael Stoute and David Elsworth have two each. Jockey **Mick Kinane** rode four winners.

FUTURE POINTERS The Lonsdale and Doncaster Cup have both featured on the future agenda of Goodwood Cup winners, the record stands at two wins from six runners in each event. Two of the best Goodwood winners that achieved high PR's, namely Persian Punch in 2001 and Royal Rebel, both followed up in the Lonsdale, while Kayf Tara took the Irish St Leger, before Ascot Gold Cup glory a year later. Sub-standard winners were best avoided, as the likes of Distinction, Darasim, Jardines Lookout, and Grey Shot all struggled to win in the near future, while the Prix du Cadran outfoxed three winners, although two placed Goodwood runners did score there *(see below)*.

Were Goodwood Cup winners profitable to follow on their subsequent three runs?
No – 9 wins from 34 runs retuned a loss of -£5.72 to a £1 level stake.

Placed runners' subsequent record (three runs):
Runners-up: 4 wins from 31 runs returned a loss of -£20.35 to a £1 level stake.
2002 Give Notice – Prix du Cadran
Thirds: 6 wins from 25 runs returned a **profit of +£20.95** to a £1 level stake.
2006 Tungsten Strike – Sagaro Stakes, 2005 Millenary – Lonsdale Cup, Doncaster Cup,
2000 San Sebastian - Prix du Cadran, 1998 Celeric – Sagaro Stakes, 1997 Double Eclipse – Lonsdale Stakes

FUTURE SUCCESS RATING: ★★★ ☆ ☆

HERITAGE HANDICAP
July 31, Glorious Goodwood – (Class 2, 3yo) 1m2f

Last run	Winner/Trainer & SP	Draw/Ran	Age	Wght	PR	Next four runs			
07 Newm 1m2f 4th Heritage Hcp *Three weeks*	**Pipedreamer** J Gosden 11/2F	16/17	3	8-04	74	**WON 5/1F** **Cambridgeshire** **Newm 1m2f**	-	-	-
06 Ascot 1m2f 1st Brunswick Hcp *One week*	**Road To Love** M Johnston 11/4F	2/16	3	9-03	72	6th Rose' Lancaster Hayd 1m3f	3rd Conds Stks Epsom 1m2f	3rd Select Stks Good 1m2f	3rd Joel Stks Newm 1m
05 Newm 1m2f 9th Heritage Hcp *One month*	**Enforcer** W Muir 6/1	10/11	3	8-09	64	3rd Heritage Hcp Beve 1m2f	6th Select Stks Good 1m2f	2nd Foundation Stks Good 1m2f	**WON 12/1** **Darley Stks** **Newm 1m1f**
04 Newm 1m2f 2nd Rated Hcp *Two weeks*	**Art Trader** Mrs A Perrett 7/2F	11/16	3	8-10	65	*9th Group 3 Hcp Sha 1m4f	*5th Group 2 Sha 1m4f	**2nd Handicap Sha 1m	**WON N/O** **Group 3** **Sha 1m**
03 Newm 1m2f 2nd Showcase Hcp *One month*	**Tiber** J Gosden 7/2F	16/17	3	8-12	73	*WON N/O** **Handicap** **Sha 1m**	*WON N/O** **H Kong Mile** **Sha 1m**	*2nd H Kong Derby Sha 1m2f	*14th QE II Cup Sha 1m2f
02 Newm 1m2f 1st Rated Hcp *Two weeks*	**Macaw** J Goldie 7/1	9/12	3	8-08	63	4th Group 2 Belm 1m1f	*4th Grade 1 Belm 1m2f	*3rd Grade 2 Belm 1m3f	*2nd Grade 1 Sara 1m4f
01 Newm 1m2f 2nd Showcase Hcp *One month*	**Askham** L Cumani 11/4F	11/11	3	8-10	70	2nd Winter Hill Stks Wind 1m2f	2nd Select Stks Good 1m2f	10th Joel Stks Newm 1m	*5th Earl of Sefton Newm 1m1f
00 Ascot 1m2f 1st Diamond Hcp *One week*	**Happy Diamond** M Johnston 15/2	9/11	3	9-06	71	*WON N/O** **Handicap** **Nad Al 1m2f**	*12th Dubai Duty Free Nad Al 1m1f	**WON N/O** **Handicap** **Nad Al 1m2f**	**3rd Group 3 Kran 1m1f
99 Donc 1m 4th Conds Stks *Three weeks*	**Azouz Pasha** H Cecil 9/1	11/17	3	8-09	67	2nd Conds Stks Wind 1m4f	**WON 6/4F** **Troy Stks** **Donc 1m4f**	*5th Magnolia Stks Kemp 1m2f	*5th Conds Stks Newm 1m2f
98 Good 1m4f 4th Tote Gold Trophy *One week*	**Gypsy Passion** M Johnston 6/1	2/10	3	8-10	60	***3rd Stakes Mala 1m4f	***3rd Stakes Mala 1m4f	-	-
97 Wind 1m2f 2nd Rated Hcp *Three weeks*	**Future Perfect** P Cole 25/1	1/18	3	8-09	62	6th November Hcp Donc 1m4f	*2nd Rated Hcp Newm 1m4f	*4th Rated Hcp York 1m2f	*2nd Vodafone Hcp Epsom 1m2f
96 Newm 1m 1st Handicap *One month*	**Fahim** A Stewart 5/2F	14/14	3	8-13	65	2nd Motability Hcp York 1m2f	3rd Foundation Stks Good 1m2f	*4th Listed Nad Al 1m1f	2nd Handicap Sara 1m4f

12-year median performance rating of the winner: **67** (out of 100)   **next year **two years ***three years*

WINNER'S PROFILE Every winner entered the stalls fit having **been on the racecourse within the past month**, with Newmarket's equivalent event at the July meeting a natural stepping stone having now provided an impressive six winners since 2001. A **top-three effort over this trip** was important, along with a similar placing in handicap class, while those **officially rated from 87 to 98** dominated.
Stalls one and two came up three times but a **middle to high draw** is preferred, especially 10 or above in meaty fields. Trainer **Mark Johnston** won it three times from 15 runners – all reappeared within a week – while **John Gosden** struck twice from eight runners.

FUTURE POINTERS This cracking three-year-old handicap has drawn plenty of progressive middle-distance performers and the quality winners were worth following. Three of the best winners over the past 12 years were all useful tools in Happy Diamond, Tiber and Pipedreamer, and while the first two had to wait until the following season to score on their reappearances, the latter soon followed up in the Cambridgeshire impressively last year. It is possible John Gosden's promising sort may follow in the footsteps of another from the yard, the aforementioned Tiber, who went on to secure Group One honours abroad.
The third-placed runners are worth monitoring as Six Of Diamonds last year won the following month at 3/1.

Were winners of this handicap profitable to follow on their subsequent three runs?
No – 6 wins from 33 runs returned a loss of -£20.50 to a £1 level stake.

Placed runners' subsequent record (three runs):
Runners-up: 5 wins from 33 runs returned a loss of -£11.70 to a £1 level stake.
2004 Fine Silver – Spring Cup, 2001 Masterful – Prix d'Ornano

Thirds: 10 wins from 35 runs returned a **profit of +£0.40** to a £1 level stake.
2000 Water Park – Ashton Park Stakes

Fourths: 2 wins from 16 runs returned a loss of -£10.25 to a £1 level stake.

FUTURE SUCCESS RATING: ★ ★ ★ ☆ ☆

OAK TREE STAKES

August 1, Glorious Goodwood – (Group 3, Class 1, 3yo+ Fillies and Mares) 7f

Last run	Winner/ Trainer & SP	Draw/ Ran	Age	Wght	PR	Next four runs			
07 Leop 7f 4th Brownstown Stk One month	**Wake Up Maggie** C Wall 11/1	18/16	4	9-04	68	4th Hungerford Stks Newb 7f	3rd Park Stks Donc 7f	9th Sun Chariot Newm 1m	-
06 Ascot 1m 1st Sandringham Hp Two months	**Red Evie** M Bell 15/8F	9/9	3	8-09	69	**WON 6/1 Matron Stks Leop 1m**	5th Sun Chariot Newm 1m	*WON 8/1 Lockinge Newb 1m	*7th Queen Anne Ascot 1m
05 York 1m 4th Windsor Forest Two months	**Majestic Desert** M Channon 6/1	10/10	4	8-13	63	3rd Desmond Stks Leop 1m	9th Matron Stks Leop 1m	-	-
04 Newb 6f 5th Hackwood Stks Two weeks	**Phantom Wind** J Gosden 16/1	7/12	3	8-06	65	3rd Matron Stks Leop 1m	Grade 1 Keen 1m1f	-	-
03 Yarm 7f 1st Conds Stks One week	**Tantina** B Hills 9/4F	8/13	3	8-07	69	**WON 13/8F Sceptre Stks Donc 7f**	3rd Supreme Stks Good 7f	-	-
02 Ascot 1m 5th Sandringham Hp Two months	**Desert Alchemy** Mrs A Perrett 4/1	7/7	3	8-06	65	7th Hungerford Stks Newb 7f	2nd October Stks Ascot 7f	-	-
01 Newb 1m2f 4th Ballymacoll Stks Two months	**Mauri Moon** G Wragg 20/1	9/13	3	8-07	64	7th Sceptre Stks Donc 7f	10th Sun Chariot Newm 1m	*WON 3/1 Conds Stks Nott 1m	*3rd Conds Stks Yarm 7f
00 Newm 1m 3rd Falmouth Stks One month	**Danceabout** G Wragg 15/8F	11/11	3	8-07	68	2nd Matron Stks Leop 1m	**WON 9/2 Sun Chariot Newm 1m**	*4th Lockinge Newb 1m	*4th Falmouth Stks Newm 1m
99 Ling 1m 1st Class Stks Three weeks	**Selfish** H Cecil 13/2	6/6	5	9-00	62	2nd Atalanta Stks Sand 1m	2nd Fortune Stks Epsom 1m	5th Sceptre Stks Donc 7f	3rd Conds Stks Donc 7f
98 Newm 1m 4th Falmouth Stks One month	**Beraysim** M Jarvis 15/8F	9/9	3	8-07	70	5th Hungerford Stks Newb 7f	2nd Supreme Stks Good 7f	9th Challenge Stks Newm 7f	-
97 Curr 1m 9th Irish 1,000 Guin Three months	**Dazzle** Sir M Stoute 11/4	7/8	3	8-07	64	6th Hungerford Stks Newb 7f	2nd Sceptre Stks Donc 7f	5th Diadem Stks Ascot 6f	8th Challenge Stks Newm 7f
96 Ascot 1m 6th Coronation Stks Two months	**Thrilling Day** N Graham 12/1	13/11	3	8-13	63	7th Hungerford Stks Newb 7f	3rd Supreme Stks Good 7f	4th Challenge Stks Newm 7f	9th Grade 3 Chur 1m1f

12-year median performance rating of the winner: **66** (out of 100)   *next year*

Eleven winners arrived at Goodwood having **seen the racecourse within the past two months**, the same number that had **run in Listed company at least**.
A previous victory over the distance wasn't essential, nor was a triumph earlier that season, however, of more importance was that three-year-olds escaped a penalty, unlike their elders, two of whom broke the age trend of late. Offical ratings weren't much help with an even spread amongst the 100s and 90s, although the draw has been relevant as every winner emerged from the **middle to high numbers**.
Trainer **Geoff Wragg** sent out two winners and two thirds from just six runners.

Allocated Group Three status in 2004, the Oak Tree Stakes can be viewed as just an average heat for females as it lacked any real distinguished winners amongst its roll of honour – only the 2006 winner, Red Evie, went on to score in Group One company.
The recent trend to understandably pack winners off to the paddocks, although one did manage to score again next time out, when Tantina took the 2003 Sceptre Stakes – a race only four winners entered – Dazzle was a creditable second, while the 1998 runner-up, Ashraakat managed to improve on her placing there *(see below)*. Three winners headed to the Sun Chariot where Danceabout was victorious – runner-up Independence also won at Newmarket – while one event to have been less kind was the Hungerford Stakes where five Oak Tree winners sunk.

Were Oak Tree winners profitable to follow on their subsequent three runs?
No – 5 wins from 32 runs returned a loss -£3.87 to a £1 level stake.

Placed runners' subsequent record (three runs):
Runners-up: 4 wins from 35 runs returned a loss of -£26.14 to a £1 level stake.
2006 Makderah – October Stakes, 1999 Wannabe Grand – Flying Fillies' Stakes, 1998 Ashraakat – Sceptre Stakes

Thirds: 4 wins from 24 runs returned a loss of -£3.00 to a £1 level stake.
2004 Chic – Hungerford, Celebration Mile, 2001 Independence – Matron Stakes, Sun Chariot Stakes

FUTURE SUCCESS RATING: ★ ★ ☆ ☆ ☆

WILLIAM HILL MILE HANDICAP
August 1, Glorious Goodwood – (Heritage Handicap, Class 1, 3yo+) 1m

Last run	Winner/ Trainer & SP	Draw/ Ran	Age	Wght	PR	Next four runs			
07 Ascot 7f 1st International Hcp *One week*	**Third Set** R Charlton 5/2F	20/19	4	8-04	73	-	-	-	-
06 Ling 1m 5th Summer Mile *Three weeks*	**Spectait** Sir M Prescott 9/2	16/17	4	8-09	65	16th Cambridgeshire Newm 1m1f	*WON 4/5F Maiden Hdle Aint 2m1f*	*6th Grade 2 Hdle Chel 2m1f*	-
05 Newm 1m 2nd RBS Hcp *One month*	**Unshakable** B Jones 7/1	16/18	6	8-01	60	4th Racing Hcp Newm 1m	6th Nov Hdle Donc 2m1f	*17th Royal Hunt Cup Ascot 1m	*6th Variety Hcp Sand 7f
04 Nott 1m 2nd Conds Stks *Two months*	**Ancient World** S Bin Suroor 9/2F	20/21	4	9-10	74	8th Sovereign Stks Sali 1m	WON 5/1 Winter Hill Stks Wind 1m2f	WON 6/4F Premio 'Capua Siro 1m	5th H Kong Cup Sha 1m2f
03 Sand 1m 6th Scoop6 Hcp *One month*	**Lady Bear** R Fahey 10/1	22/21	5	8-06	68	6th Rated Hcp York 1m	WON 5/4F Atalanta Stks Sand 1m	4th Cambridgeshire Newm 1m1f	-
02 Newb 1m 2nd Ladbrokes Hcp *Two weeks*	**Smirk** D Elsworth 12/1	21/21	4	9-05	72	5th Darley Stks Newm 1m1f	WON 7/1 Ben Marshall St Newm 1m	*9th Grade 2 Sant 1m	*3rd Doncaster Mile Donc 1m
01 Sand 1m2f 3rd Tote Hcp *One month*	**Riberac** M Johnston 12/1	19/21	5	8-12	70	**WON 15/8F Valiant Listed Ascot 1m**	8th Park Stks Donc 1m	3rd Sun Chariot Newm 1m	4th Severals Stks Newm 1m2f
00 Ascot 7f 5th International Hcp *One week*	**Persiano** J Fanshawe 10/1	18/22	5	8-12	67	14th Brad & Bing Hcp York 1m	*UR Rated Hcp Newm 7f	*16th Doubleprint Hcp Kemp 1m	*2nd Handicap Sali 1m
99 Sand 1m 2nd Kingston Hcp *One month*	**Lonesome Dude** Sir M Stoute 7/1	12/20	4	9-07	71	11th Grade 1 Wood 1m	**3rd Handicap Del 1m1f	-	-
98 Sand 1m 1st Kingston Hcp *One month*	**For Your Eyes Only** T Easterby 14/1	8/22	4	9-06	70	7th Strensall Stks York 1m1f	6th Cambridgeshire Newm 1m1f	*4th Listed Nad Al 1m	*8th Listed Nad Al 1m1f
97 Sand 1m 16th Hong Kong Hcp *Three weeks*	**Fly To The Stars** M Johnston 14/1	19/20	3	9-06	71	2nd Listed Deau 1m	3rd Stakes Veli 1m	*2nd Listed Nad Al 1m	*3rd Stakes Nad Al 1m1f
96 Newm 1m 4th H & K Hcp *One month*	**Moscow Mist** Lady Herries 66/1	16/18	5	7-10	61	10th Rothmans Hcp Redc 1m	15th Mail Hcp Ascot 1m	*6th Tote Hcp Sali 1m	*16th Rothmans Hcp Ches 1m

12-year median performance rating of the winner: **69** (out of 100) *italic = jumps *next year **two years*

WINNER'S PROFILE Eleven winners **raced within the past month**, the same number that finished in the **first six last time**, as Ascot, Newmarket and Sandown provided a final stepping stone for nine victors.
Four to five-year-olds dominated – three-year-olds struck just once from over 40 runners – while those at **14/1 and shorter** came home best. The most significant factor in the winner's profile was a high draw, as 10 were allocated **stall 16 or higher**, including trainer **Mark Johnston**'s winning pair from nearly 20 runners.

FUTURE POINTERS The quality of this event has improved, and though Fly To The Stars was a classy and rare three-year-old winner in 1997 – subsequently won a Group One for Godolphin – winners since 2001 consistently went on to win Pattern races in the same season, as Ancient World emulated Fly To The Stars at the highest level. However, one downside shown by winners was their poor record next time out – only Riberac managed to follow up.

Were Mile winners profitable to follow on their subsequent three runs?
No – 6 wins from 32 runs returned a loss of -£8.57 to a £1 level stake.

Placed runners' subsequent record (three runs):
Runners-up: 3 wins from 35 runs returned a loss of -£18.87 to a £1 level stake.
Thirds: 9 wins from 35 runs returned a **profit of +£32.33** to a £1 level stake.
2006 Prince Of Thebes – Shergar Cup, 2005 Cesare – Royal Hunt Cup, 1999 Indian Lodge – Joel Stakes, 1998 Right Wing – Porcelanosa, Lincoln
Fourths: 5 wins from 36 runs returned a **profit of +£7.98** to a £1 level stake.

Were badly drawn runners worth following?
High numbers dominated this handicap, so any runner to be placed from a disadvantageous single figure draw did well – their handicap marks weren't hiked up too much – and they proved worthy of following. The last 12 renewals produced nine such qualifiers, of whom six gained compensation during their next two runs, including Sir Gerard and Pride Of Pendle, who both scored next time out, while Cesare took the Royal Hunt Cup a year later.

FUTURE SUCCESS RATING: ★★★★☆

RICHMOND STAKES
August 1, Glorious Goodwood – (Group 2, Class 1, 2yo) 6f

Last run	Winner/Trainer & SP	Draw/Ran	Age	Wght	PR	Next four runs			
07 Mais 6f 3rd / Prix R Papin / *Two weeks*	**Strike The Deal** / J Noseda 7/1	7/9	2	9-00	64	9th Champagne Stk Donc 7f	2nd Mill Reef Stks Newb 6f	2nd Middle Park Newm 6f	4th Breeders' Cup Monm 1m
06 Newm 6f 1st / Novice Stks / *One month*	**Hamoody** / P Chapple-Hyam 5/6F	6/7	2	9-00	63	13th Dewhurst Stks Newm 6f	*7th Euro Free Hcp Newm 7f	*21st Golden Jubilee Ascot 6f	-
05 Newb 5f 5th / Weatherbys Sprint / *Two weeks*	**Always Hopeful** / E O'Neill 12/1	6/6	2	8-11	66	3rd Prix Morny Deau 6f	3rd Middle Park Newm 6f	-	-
04 Folk 7f 1st / Maiden / *One month*	**Montgomery's Arch** / P Chapple-Hyam 13/2	5/8	2	8-11	66	4th Prix Larardere Long 7f	3rd Dewhurst Newm 7f	*7th Craven Stks Newm 1m	*12th Poule' Poulains Long 1m
03 Curr 6f 1st / Goffs Challenge / *Two months*	**Carrizo Creek** / B Meehan 5/1	6/7	2	8-11	62	5th Prix Morny Deau 6f	*7th Euro Free Hcp Newm 7f	*7th Hungerford Stks Newb 7f	-
02 Ling 6f 1st / Maiden / *Two weeks*	**Elusive City** / G Butler 9/2	7/9	2	8-11	75	**WON 19/10 Prix Morny Deau 6f**	3rd Middle Park Newm 6f	*5th Greenham Stks Newb 7f	*9th Poule' Poulains Long 1m
01 Newb 6f 4th / Rose Bowl Stks / *Two weeks*	**Mister Cosmi** / M Johnston 7/1	6/8	2	8-11	68	9th Gimcrack Stks York 6f	5th Dubai Duty Free Newb 6f	3rd Gran Criterium Sain 1m	*6th Greenham Stks Newb 7f
00 Newb 6f 1st / Novice Stks / *Two weeks*	**Endless Summer** / J Gosden 2/1F	6/8	2	8-11	71	2nd Prix Morny Deau 6f	2nd Middle Park Newm 6f	**3rd Claimer Holl 6f	**3rd Claimer Holl 6f
99 Chep 6f 1st / Maiden / *One month*	**Bachir** / J Gosden 11/8F	5/7	2	8-11	66	3rd Prix Morny Deau 6f	3rd Prix Salamandre Long 7f	*WON N/O **Stakes** Nad Al 1m	*2nd UAE Derby Nad Al 1m1f
98 Good 6f 2nd / Novice Stks / *Two months*	**Muqtarib** / J Dunlop 9/2	4/4	2	8-11	70	*9th Bentinck Stks Newm 6f	*10th Wentworth Stks Donc 6f	**7th Stakes Nad Al 6f	**5th Listed Nad Al 6f
97 Newm 6f 1st / Novice Stks / *One month*	**Daggers Drawn** / H Cecil 8/13F	5/6	2	8-11	72	**WON 4/6F Champagne Stk Donc 7f**	6th Dewhurst Newm 7f	*5th Craven Stks Newm 1m	*18th 2,000 Guineas Newm 1m
96 Newm 5f 1st / Conds Stks / *Two weeks*	**Easycall** / B Meehan 7/2	2/7	2	8-11	71	4th Gimcrack Stks York 6f	**WON 5/1 Flying Childers Donc 5f**	6th Middle Park Newm 6f	**WON 11/2 Cornwallis Stks Ascot 5f**

12-year median performance rating of the winner: **68** (out of 100)　　　　*next year **two years

WINNER'S PROFILE Strike The Deal last year became the first winner since 1996 to have already run in a Group event, although no winner arrived having **raced more than three times**, six via Newbury or Newmarket. A prior victory over the distance wasn't essential, but a **victory last time out** can be a bonus, along with a **middle to high draw**. Eleven winners returned at **7/1 or shorter**, including trainer **Peter Chapple-Hyam**'s recent pair – from as many runners – while two others to note were **John Gosden**, with two from five, and **Brian Meehan**, with two from eight, however, be wary of Richard Hannon's, who is winless from 15 runners.

FUTURE POINTERS This juvenile event has unfortunately spiralled in recent years and as a pointer for the following year's Classics, it has been of limited value, producing more sprinters than milers.
The drop in standard has been reflected in the poor performance ratings (PR) from some of the recent forgettable winners and the last victor with a respectable rating was Elusive City – later disqualified – who took the Prix Morny next time out.
Taking a longer view, you have to go back to 1993 for the last subsequent Group One winner on British soil with First Trump in the Middle Park, while the 1987 winner, Warning, was successful at that level as a three-year-old. The only winner in the last 20 years to land a Classic was the 1999 winner, Bachir, who took the Irish and French Guineas in 2000, while Mac's Imp won the Group One Phoenix Stakes in 1990 – Polaris Flight scored at the same level in France in 1995.

Were Richmond winners profitable to follow on their subsequent three runs?
No – 4 wins from 35 runs returned a loss of -£23.43 to a £1 level stake.

Placed runners' subsequent record (three runs):
Runners-up: 1 win from 27 runs returned a loss of –£25.43 to a £1 level stake.
2007 Fat Boy – Listed Ripon 2yo Trophy

Thirds: 1 win from 11 runs returned a loss of -£9.20 to a £1 level stake.
2002 Checkit – Group Two Lacroix Trophy (Germany)

FUTURE SUCCESS RATING: ★ ☆ ☆ ☆ ☆

NASSAU STAKES
August 2, Glorious Goodwood – (Group 1, Class 1, 3yo+) 1m2f

Last run	Winner/ Trainer & SP	Draw/ Ran	Age	Wght	PR	Next four runs			
07 Curr 1m4f 1st Irish Oaks *Three weeks*	**Peeping Fawn** A O'Brien 2/1F	8/8	3	8-10	83	**WON 4/9F** Yorkshire Oaks York 1m4f	- 	- 	-
06 Sand 1m2f 5th Eclipse Stks *One month*	**Ouija Board** E Dunlop EvensF	7/7	5	9-05	86	2nd Irish Champion Leop 1m2f	**WON 6/4F** **Breeders' Cup** **Chur 1m3f**	3rd Japan Cup Toky 1m4f	-
05 Newm 1m 2nd Falmouth Stks *One month*	**Alexander Goldrun** J Bolger 13/8F	9/11	4	9-03	77	3rd Irish Champion Leop 1m2f	3rd Prix de l'Opera Long 1m2f	8th Champion Stks Newm 1m2f	8th Hong Kong Cup Sha 1m2f
04 Newm 1m 6th Falmouth Stks *One month*	**Favourable Terms** Sir M Stoute 11/2	2/6	4	9-02	74	*WON 5/6F Sceptre Stks Donc 7f	*8th Sun Chariot Newm 1m	*5th Breeders' Cup Belm 1m2f	-
03 Ascot 1m 1st Coronation Stks *Two weeks*	**Russian Rhythm** Sir M Stoute 4/5F	7/8	3	8-06	83	2nd Q Elizabeth II Ascot 1m	5th Champion Stks Newm 1m2f	*WON 3/1F Lockinge Newb 1m	-
02 Epso 1m4f 8th Oaks *Two months*	**Islington** Sir M Stoute 10/3	6/10	3	8-06	82	**WON 2/1** Yorkshire Oaks York 1m4f	5th Arc de Triomphe Long 1m4f	3rd Breeders' Cup Arli 1m2f	*3rd Prince of Wales' Ascot 1m2f
01 Curr 1m4f 1st Irish Oaks *Three weeks*	**Lailani** E Dunlop 5/4F	5/7	3	8-06	84	**WON 49/20** Flower Bowl Int Belm 1m2f	8th Breeders' Cup Belm 1m2f	- 	-
00 Ascot 1m 1st Coronation Stks *Two months*	**Crimplene** C Brittain 7/4F	3/7	3	8-06	75	4th Jacques' Marois Deau 1m	8th Q Elizabeth II Ascot 1m	4th Breeders' Cup Chur 1m1f	-
99 Epso 1m4f 3rd Oaks *Two months*	**Zahrat Dubai** S Bin Suroor 5/1	3/8	3	8-06	72	4th Yorkshire Oaks York 1m4f	5th Prix de l'Opera Long 1m1f	- 	-
98 Curr 1m2f 1st Pretty Polly *Two months*	**Alborada** Sir M Prescott 4/1	5/9	3	8-09	77	2nd Irish Champion Leop 1m2f	**WON 6/1** **Champion Stks** **Newm 1m2f**	*5th Nassau Good 1m2f	*WON 5/1 Champion Stks Newm 1m2f
97 Newm 1m 1st Falmouth Stks *One month*	**Ryafan** J Gosden 9/4F	5/7	3	8-09	78	**WON N/O** Grade 1 Keen 1m1f	**WON N/O** Grade 1 Sant 1m2f	**WON N/O** Grade 1 Holl 1m2f	-
96 Ascot 1m 2nd Coronation Stks *Two months*	**Last Second** Sir M Prescott 7/4F	1/8	3	8-06	76	**WON 9/4F** Sun Chariot Newm 1m2f	*7th Prix Ganay Long 1m3f	*5th Nassau Good 1m2f	-

12-year median performance rating of the winner: **79** (out of 100)   *next year*

WINNER'S PROFILE **Good recent form**, especially at this level was a key ingredient, every victor visited the **winner's enclosure on either of their last two runs**, the same number that **scored in Group One or Two** company. Eleven had run in the Coronation Stakes, Falmouth, Pretty Polly or an Oaks at some point that season – Peeping Fawn became the second winner of the Irish Oaks to follow up here last year.
Three-year-olds dominated until recently when the event became an attraction for older runners and it has to be noted that five-year-olds don't have a bad record with one winner and two runners-up from just six runners.
A **middle to high draw** can be a bonus, while from a training perspective, **Sir Michael Stoute** sent out three winners from nine runners, while **Sir Mark Prescott** had two from five.

FUTURE POINTERS An event that has continued to attract the best females around over this trip with last year's renewal including the winners of the Epsom and Irish Oaks, along with the 2006 Prix de l'Opera victor, while in 2006, the globetrotting Ouija Board scored here before Breeders' Cup glory, justifying the upgrade to Group One status in 1999. The only three winners not to have won on their next three runs were all sub-standard, achieving below par performance ratings (PR) here, including Alexander Goldrun in 2005, who lost 10 of her next 11 races.
Last year, Peeping Fawn emulated Islington by landing the Yorkshire Oaks next time out, a race that hasn't been oversubscribed by Nassau winners, however, the Irish Champion Stakes caught out three winners.

Were Nassau winners profitable to follow on their subsequent three runs?
No – 11 wins from 32 runs returned a loss of -£2.52 to a £1 level stake.

Placed runners' subsequent record (three runs):
Runners-up: 3 wins from 30 runs returned a loss of -£18.72 to a £1 level stake.
1999 Lady In Waiting – Sun Chariot Stakes

Thirds: 3 wins from 18 runs returned a **profit of +£8.20** to a £1 level stake.
2005 Red Bloom – Blandford Stakes, 2003 Zee Zee Top – Prix de l'Opera, 1996 Annaba – Prix de Royallieu

FUTURE SUCCESS RATING: ★★★★☆

STEWARDS' CUP

August 2, Glorious Goodwood (Class 1, Heritage Handicap, 3yo+) 6f

Last run	Winner/ Trainer & SP	Draw/ Ran	Age	Wght	PR	Next four runs			
07 Ascot 6f 7th Wokingham *Two months*	**Zidane** J Fanshawe 6/1F	11/27	5	9-01	75	4th Diadem Stks Ascot 6f	11th Bentinck Stks Newm 6f	8th Wentworth Stks Donc 6f	-
06 Fair 6f 2nd Listed *Two weeks*	**Borderlescott** R Bastiman 10/1	19/27	4	9-05	71	2nd Ayr Gold Cup Ayr 6f	6th Listed Chan 6f	2nd Bentinck Stks Newm 6f	*2nd Conds Stks Hayd 6f
05 Epsom 6f 1st Vodafone Hcp *Two months*	**Gift Horse** D Nicholls 9/2	19/27	5	9-07	70	17th Sprint Cup Hayd 6f	5th Duke of York York 6f	*13th Golden Jubilee Ascot 6f	*9th July Cup Newm 6f
04 Ascot 5f 2nd H Kong Sprint *One week*	**Pivotal Point** P Makin 7/1CF	1/28	4	8-11	74	WON 3/1 Group 3 Long 5f	5th World Trophy Newb 5f	WON 11/2 Diadem Stks Ascot 6f	13th H Kong Sprint Sha 5f
03 Newm 7f 1st Bunbury Cup *One month*	**Patavellian** R Charlton 4/1	27/29	5	8-11	75	WON 9/1 Abbaye Long 5f	*3rd Group 3 Long 5f	*10th July Cup Newm 6f	*3rd Sprint Cup Hayd 6f
02 York 6f 18th Miller Hcp *Three weeks*	**Bond Boy** B Smart 14/1	29/28	5	8-02	61	9th Showcase Hcp York 6f	21st Ayr Gold Cup Ayr 6f	WON 12/1 Rated Hcp Donc 5f	7th Wentworth Stks Donc 6f
01 Ascot 5f 9th H Kong Sprint *One week*	**Guinea Hunter** T Easterby 33/1	19/30	5	9-00	64	3rd Portland Hcp Donc 5 1/2f	11th Ayr Gold Cup Ayr 6f	6th Rated Hcp Ascot 5f	2nd Tote Cup Ascot 5f
00 Ascot 7f 3rd International Hcp *One week*	**Tayseer** D Nicholls 13/2	28/30	6	8-11	66	7th City of York York 7f	7th Ayr Gold Cup Ayr 6f	2nd Diadem Stks Ascot 6f	5th Stakes Nad Al 6f
99 Newb 6f 2nd Rated Hcp *Three weeks*	**Harmonic Way** R Charlton 12/1	8/30	4	8-06	69	2nd Conds Stks Nott 6f	2nd Rated Hcp York 6f	15th Ayr Gold Cup Ayr 6f	10th Bentinck Stks Newm 6f
98 Hayd 6f 1st Conds Stks *One month*	**Superior Premium** R Fahey 14/1	28/29	4	9-03	64	5th Sprint Cup Hayd 6f	18th Ayr Gold Cup Ayr 6f	*2nd Conds Stks Hayd 6f	*9th Duke of York York 6f
97 Newm 6f 1st Rated Hcp *One month*	**Danetime** N Callaghan 5/1F	5/30	3	8-10	72	2nd Sprint Cup Hayd 6f	*3rd Abernant Stks Newm 6f	*3rd Duke of York York 6f	*5th Group 2 Chan 5f
96 York 5f 1st Handicap *One month*	**Coastal Bluff** T D Barron 10/1JF	29/30	4	8-05	67	WON 3/1F Ayr Gold Cup Ayr 6f	*5th July Cup Newm 6f	*WON 8/11F Conds Stks Newm 5f	*11th Stewards' Cup Good 6f

12-year median performance rating of the winner: **69** (out of 100)   *next year

WINNER'S PROFILE Every winner **raced within the past two months**, the same number that already **scored over this trip**, while eight **ran in the Wokingham** at Royal Ascot – all finished in the top-half of the field.
The market was a good guide as 11 winners were **14/1 or shorter**, while **four and five-year-olds** came out best.
Those on the **light side of 9st 5lb** did well, while **Roger Charlton** and **David Nicholls** struck twice each.
The draw favoured high numbers, but they came down the middle last year so any midweek clues can be vital.

FUTURE POINTERS Lochsong emerged from the sea mist to land this back in 1992 – when it was run on the Tuesday – before going on to land the Ayr Gold Cup, a feat matched by Coastal Bluff in 1996; six failed since. Like Lochsong, the latter also landed Group One honours the following season, while the best winner of this, Patavellian, didn't have to wait that long as he took the Prix de l'Abbaye next time out, before Pivotal Point in 2004 soon won Group honours, highlighting the strength of this sprint – last year's resembled a Group sprint with an incredible 20 runners officially rated 100 or higher.
Despite a few dry subsequent years, overall, it paid to side with progressive four and five-year-old winners.

Were Stewards' Cup winners profitable to follow on their subsequent three runs?
Yes – 6 wins from 36 runs returned a **profit of +£3.22** to a £1 level stake.

Placed runners' subsequent record (three runs):
Runners-up: 2 wins from 36 runs returned a loss of -£25.50 to a £1 level stake. *2002 Halmahera – Portland H'cp*
Thirds: 4 wins from 36 runs returned a **profit of +£10.00** to a £1 level stake. *2006 Firenze – Boadicea Fillies Stakes, Kilvington Stakes, 2003 Colonel Cotton – Rous Stakes, 1997 Dashing Blue – Portland Handicap*
Fourths: 3 wins from 35 runs returned a loss of -£20.00 to a £1 level stake.
2006 Excusez Moi – Great St Wilfrid, 2003 Frizzante – Listed Boadicea Fillies' Stakes
Were badly drawn runners worth following?
Mixed results since 1996, during which time nine qualifiers emerged from a poor draw when a strong bias was present – four gained compensation. In 2003, Frizzante took the Listed Boadicea Stakes, and in 2002, Halmahera won the Portland Handicap, while Night Star (1997) and Wildwood Flower (1996) both took handicaps next time out.

FUTURE SUCCESS RATING: ★ ★ ★ ☆ ☆

ROSE OF LANCASTER STAKES
August 9, Haydock – (Group 3, Class 1, 3yo+) 1m2f 120yds

Last run	Winner/ Trainer & SP	Draw/ Ran	Age	Wght	PR	Next four runs			
07 Good 1m2f 12th Heritage Hcp Two weeks	**Halicarnassus** M Channon 9/1	4/6	3	8-07	74	2nd Strensall Stks York 1m1f	5th Select Stks Good 1m2f	**WON 9/1 Arc Trial Newb 1m3f**	17th Japan Cup Toky 1m4f
06 Newb 1m2f 4th Steventon Stks Three weeks	**Mulaqat** M Tregoning 25/1	5/8	3	8-07	73	5th Winter Hill Stks Wind 1m2f	*11th Group 3 Nad Al 1m1f	*4th Group 3 Nad Al 1m4f	*5th Handicap Nad Al 1m4f
05 York 1m2f 16th J Smith's Cup One month	**Notable Guest** Sir M Stoute 5/1	3/5	4	9-03	75	3rd Arc Trial Newb 1m3f	*2nd Gordon Richards Sand 1m2f	*5th Coronation Stks Epsom 1m4f	*9th Eclipse Sand 1m2f
04 Ascot 1m2f 1st Diamond Hcp Two weeks	**Mister Monet** M Johnston EvensF	6/6	3	8-07	79	**WON 9/2F Prix d'Ornano Deau 1m2f**	PU Champion Stks Newm 1m2f	-	-
03 Newm 1m2f 1st Fairway Stks Three months	**Sabre D'Argent** D Loder 5/1	3/5	3	8-07	78	**WON 15/8F Conds Stks Donc 1m2f**	***5th Grade 3 Gulf 1m4f	***3rd Grade 3 Aque 1m1f	***4th Grade 2 Piml 1m1f
01 Good 1m4f 3rd Gordon Stks Two weeks	**Nayef** M Tregoning 5/4F	4/5	3	8-07	81	**WON 8/13F Select Stks Good 1m2f**	**WON 8/13F Cumb'ld Lodge Ascot 1m4f**	**WON 3/1F Champion Stks Newm 1m2f**	*WON 9/4F Sheema Classic Nad Al 1m4f
00 Newb 1m2f 1st Conds Stks One month	**Ekraar** M Tregoning 7/4F	4/9	3	8-07	80	**WON 10/11F Select Stks Good 1m2f**	*4th Group 3 Nad Al 1m2f	*7th Dubai World Cup Nad Al 1m2f	*3rd Prix d'Ispahan Long 1m1f
99 Sain 1m4f 7th G Prix St-Cloud Two months	**Greek Dance** Sir M Stoute 2/1	2/5	4	9-03	82	2nd Juddmonte Int York 1m2f	6th Arc de Triomphe Long 1m4f	5th Champion Stks Newm 1m2f	*2nd Prix Ganay Long 1m3f
98 Sand 1m2f 1st Conds Stks One month	**Mutamam** A Stewart 8/11F	2/6	3	8-07	78	**WON 11/8F Select Stks Good 1m2f**	4th Champion Stks Newm 1m2f	*8th Turf Classic Nad Al 1m4f	**2nd Conds Stks Newm 1m2f
97 Sain 1m2f 3rd Group 2 One month	**Romanov** P Chapple-Hyam 5/2JF	3/7	3	8-07	76	2nd Cumb'lnd Lodge Ascot 1m4f	3rd Canadian Int Wood 1m4f	*WON 5/1 Jockey Club St Newm 1m4f	*2nd G Prix St-Cloud Sain 1m4f
96 Curr 1m 3rd Group 2 Two months	**Tamayaz** S Bin Suroor 11/2	7/8	4	9-03	77	6th Irish Champion Leop 1m2f	6th Breeders' Cup Wood 1m2f	*2nd Listed Nad Al 1m1f	*WON N/O Dubai Duty Free Nad Al 1m2f

12-year median performance rating of the winner: **71** (out of 100)   *one year **two years ***three years (2002 abandoned)*

WINNER'S PROFILE Winners have taken different paths although they all **raced at Grade One venues last time** out, while the last six all scored in Listed and handicap company earlier in their career – only Ekraar had a Group victory to his name. Non-stayers need not apply, as 10 winners all **scored between 10 and 12 furlongs** – the two exceptions were both third over the former trip – while an **official rating of 105 or more** was vital.
Three-year-olds have a superb wins-to-runs ratio and have outscored the older horses, two of whom were trained by **Sir Michael Stoute**. Trainer **Marcus Tregoning** has followed in the footsteps of his former mentor – the late Major Dick Hern who took this with Free Fact in 1987 – having produced three winners from only five runners.

FUTURE POINTERS Although this middle-distance event suffered a temporary subsequent dry spell between 2005-2006, Halicarnassus got the show back on the road last year in the Arc Trial three runs later, and this event has built a solid reputation since earning Group Three status in 1989.
The Rose of Lancaster has produced winners with a long-term significance in middle-distance races around the world, including some cracking three-year-olds that tasted Group success for the first time here before taking the Select Stakes at Goodwood – an event runner-up, David Junior, also won three years ago *(see below)*.
Overall, an event from which to side with the classy three-year-old winners – four-year-olds have been less productive – while runner-up, David Junior, gave the race further strength in depth three years ago.

Were Rose of Lancaster winners profitable to follow on their subsequent three runs?
Yes – 9 wins from 32 wins returned a **profit of +£1.86** to a £1 level stake.

Placed runners' subsequent record (three runs):
Runners-up: 5 wins from 32 runs returned a **profit of +£12.37** to a £1 level stake.
2005 David Junior – Select Stakes, Champion Stakes, Dubai Duty Free

Thirds: 0 win from 9 runs returned a loss of -£9.00 to a £1 level stake.

FUTURE SUCCESS RATING: ★ ★ ★ ★ ☆

SWEET SOLERA STAKES
August 9, Newmarket – (Group 3, Class 1, 2yo Fillies) 7f

Last run	Winner/ Trainer & SP	Draw/ Ran	Age	Wght	PR	Next four runs			
07 Ascot 6f 1st Maiden *Three weeks*	**Albabilia** C Brittain 7/2	2/7	2	8-12	61	4th Moyglare Stud Curr 7f	22nd Goffs Million Curr 7f	-	-
06 Wind 6f 1st Maiden *Three weeks*	**English Ballet** B Hills 7/2	9/6	2	8-12	62	2nd May Hills Stks York 1m	3rd Meon Fillies Mile Ascot 1m	5th Rockfel Stks Newm 7f	-
05 Sand 7f 2nd Star Listed Stks *Three weeks*	**Nasheej** R Hannon 4/1	6/8	2	8-08	67	**WON 4/1 May Hill Stks Donc 1m**	3rd Meon Fillies Mile Ascot 1m	*WON 6/4F **Fred Darling Newb 7f**	*3rd 1,000 Guineas Newm 1m
04 Sand 7f 2nd Star Listed Stks *Three weeks*	**Maids Causeway** B Hills 5/1	10/11	2	8-08	63	3rd May Hill Stks Donc 1m	2nd Meon Fillies Mile Ascot 1m	WON 3/1 **Rockfel Stks Newm 7f**	*2nd 1,000 Guineas Newm 1m
03 Newb 6f 1st Maiden *One week*	**Bay Tree** B Hills 10/3	4/8	2	8-08	55	9th Marcel Boussac Long 1m	7th Rockfel Stks Newm 7f	*6th Nell Gwyn Stks Newm 7f	*3rd Musidora Stks York 1m2f
02 Kemp 6f 1st Maiden *One month*	**Soviet Song** J Fanshawe 4/1	3/8	2	8-08	70	WON 11/10 **Meon Fillies Mile Ascot 1m**	*4th 1,000 Guineas Newm 1m	*2nd Coronation Stks Ascot 1m	*4th Prix du Moulin Long 1m
01 Kemp 7f 1st Maiden *One month*	**Muklah** B Hills 2/1	3/7	2	8-08	63	*7th Conds Stks Donc 1m	-	-	-
00 Sand 7f 5th Star Listed Stks *Three weeks*	**Peaceful Paradise** J Hills 7/1	5/7	2	8-08	59	3rd Group 3 Deau 7f	*10th 1,000 Guineas Newm 1m	*5th Conqueror Stks Good 1m	*6th Rated Hcp Ascot 1m
99 Ascot 6f 1st Maiden *One month*	**Princess Ellen** P Chapple-Hyam 9/2	11/11	2	8-08	58	9th May Hill Stks Donc 1m	5th Rockfel Stks Newm 7f	*8th Nell Gwyn Stks Newm 7f	*2nd 1,000 Guineas Newm 1m
98 Newm 7f 1st Maiden *One month*	**Kareymah** D Loder 2/1	3/5	2	8-08	57	WON 4/5F **Group 3 Deau 7f**	-	-	-
97 Newm 6f 3rd Nursery *One week*	**Diamond White** G Bravery 25/1	3/8	2	8-08	55	8th Listed Deau 1m	7th Oh So Sharp Stk Newm 7f	*11th Pretty Polly Newm 1m2f	*10th Doubleprint Hcp Sand 1m
96 Newm 7f 6th Maiden *One month*	**Catwalk** W Haggas 20/1	7/10	2	8-08	58	9th Park Hill Stks Donc 1m	4th Autumn Stks Ascot 1m	-	-

12-year median performance rating of the winner: **61** (out of 100)   *next year*

WINNER'S PROFILE The 1996 and 1997 winners were both maidens, but the trends shifted since as the last 10 all lined up having **scored on either of their last two outings**.

One solid pattern to have emerged concerned the three winners since 1998 that never won a maiden last time out, as they all ran in the **Listed Star Stakes at Sandown** – last year's qualifier was a respectable third here at 16/1. A distance victory wasn't essential, although those that went off at **7/1 or shorter** have fared best, despite no winning favourites.

Trainer **Barry Hills** was responsible for the aforementioned third last year at a big price, and an overall record of four victories from only eight runners suggests his entries should be noted.

FUTURE POINTERS The Sweet Solera has been a decent guide for some of the better juvenile events to come later in the season, although it has hardly been a breeding ground for Classic types as no winner for 20 years went on to score in that sphere. However, in recent years, three Solera winners made the top-four in the 1,000 Guineas – two of them since this was upgraded to a Group Three in 2004 – while the standout winner on PR's, Soviet Song, took Group One honours on five occasions throughout her fruitful career.

Were Sweet Solera winners profitable to follow on their subsequent three runs?
No – 5 wins from 30 runs returned a loss of -£14.60 to a £1 level stake.

Placed runners' subsequent record (three runs):
Runners-up: 5 wins from 32 runs returned a loss of -£0.75 to a £1 level stake.
2002 Summitville – May Hill Stakes, 1998 Etizaaz – Atlanta Stakes

Thirds: 2 wins from 19 runs returned a loss of -£12.37 to a £1 level stake.

FUTURE SUCCESS RATING: ★ ★ ☆ ☆ ☆

ROYAL WHIP STAKES
August 10, Curragh – (Group 2, 3yo+) 1m2f

Last run	Winner/ Trainer & SP	Draw/ Ran	Age	Wght	PR	Next four runs			
07 York 1m2f 2nd York Stks Three weeks	**Eagle Mountain** A O'Brien 4/5F	5/5	3	9-03	79	2nd Champion Stks Newm 1m2f	-	-	-
06 Curr 1m 1st International Stk One month	**Mustameet** K Prendergast 3/1	3/4	5	9-09	77	4th Irish Champion Leop 1m2f	14th Hong Kong Mile Sha 1m	*WON 5/4F Gladness Stks Curr 7f	*6th Mooresbridge Stk Curr 1m2f
05 Leop 1m2f 1st Meld Stks Three weeks	**Tropical Lady** J Bolger 5/2	2/5	5	9-03	70	*6th Mooresbridge Stk Curr 1m2f	*4th Pretty Polly Curr 1m2f	*9th EBF Listed Cork 1m4f	-
04 Leop 1m2f 2nd Meld Stks Three weeks	**Solskjaer** A O'Brien 9/4	4/6	4	9-06	71	8th Juddmonte Int York 1m2f	*7th Gladness Stks Curr 7f	*WON 10/1 **Heritage Listed** Leop 1m	*2nd Huxley Stks Ches 1m2f
03 Arli 1m4f 1st Breeders' Cup Ten months	**High Chaparral** A O'Brien 9/10F	4/6	4	9-13	83	WON 4/1 **Irish Champion** Leop 1m2f	3rd Arc de Triomphe Long 1m4f	WON 11/2 **Breeders' Cup** Sant 1m4f	
02 Curr 1m2f 2nd Meld Stks Three weeks	**Chancellor** B Hills 2/1F	1/6	4	9-03	79	5th Juddmonte Int York 1m2f	5th Champion Stks Newm 1m2f	14th Premio Roma Capa 1m2f	*4th Prix Ganay Long 1m3f
01 Good 1m 7th Sussex Three weeks	**Bach** A O'Brien 9/4	4/5	4	9-02	73	3rd Irish Champion Leop 1m2f	4th Q Elizabeth II Ascot 1m	3rd Breeders' Cup Belm 1m	4th Hong Kong Cup Sha 1m2f
00 Curr 1m2f 1st Meld Stks One month	**Takali** J Oxx 13/8F	1/5	3	8-08	72	*2nd Stakes Taif 1m2f	-	-	-
99 Donc 1m2f 1st Conds Stks Two months	**Zomaradah** L Cumani 3/1	9/9	4	9-05	77	2nd Group 3 Siro 1m3f	**WON 3/5F** **Group 2** **Capa 1m2f**	3rd Breeders' Cup Gulf 1m3f	*4th Listed Good 1m2f
98 Curr 1m2f 2nd Meld Stks Three weeks	**Make No Mistake** D Weld 5/1	1/6	3	8-08	73	6th Irish Champion Leop 1m2f	*3rd Tatts Gold Cup Curr 1m3f	*7th Premio di Milano Siro 1m4f	*WON 7/2 **Meld Stks** **Curr 1m2f**
97 Ascot 1m4f 7th Hardwicke Stks Two years	**King Alex** R Charlton 7/2	4/7	4	9-01	72	*4th Gala Stks Kemp 1m2f	*3rd Scottish Classic Ayr 1m2f	*3rd Conds Stks Newb 1m1f	*8th Darley Stks Newm 1m1f
96 Ascot 1m2f 8th Prince of Wales Two months	**Pilsudski** Sir M Stoute 5/2	4/5	4	9-04	80	WON N/O Grosser 'Baden Bade 1m4f	2nd Arc de Triomphe Long 1m4f	**WON N/O** **Breeders' Cup** **Wood 1m4f**	*3rd Prix Ganay Long 1m3f

12-year median performance rating of the winner: **76** (out of 100)   *next year*

WINNER'S PROFILE Nine of the last 10 winners **finished in the top-two last time out**, five in the Meld Stakes which has been a good pointer for this, while those proven at this level were ones to side with as all 12 finished in the **first two of a Pattern event** – eight were Group winners. Proven form over this intermediate distance is also relevant as 11 either **won or finished runner-up over 10 furlongs**.

Three-year-olds used to dominate having won it eight times from 1987 to 1995, but older horses eclipsed the Classic generation in recent times, and preference is just for the four-year-olds. Although field sizes were consistently small, the **first two or three in the betting** spoke, and trainer **Aidan O'Brien**'s four winners – from 12 runners – all emerged from the short end of the market. Although John Oxx's strike-rate has been low in recent times with only one winner and two runners-up from nine runners, he did land this three times in the nineties.

FUTURE POINTERS There have been a number of sub-standard winners of this Group Two event over the past few decades, however, scattered amongst them have been a couple of superstars that went on to better things. Both High Chaparral and Pilsudski followed up in Group One events before a successful raid on the Breeders' Cup, while the latter added further Group/Grade One events around the world. The former won the Irish Champion Stakes next time out, a race that proved too much for three other Royal Whip winners, while Eagle Mountain last year narrowly missed out in the British equivalent at Newmarket, as did Chancellor in 2002. Barry Hills's below par winner was also held in the Juddmonte International next time, along with Solskjaer in 2004, and those to have returned average performance ratings (PR) here were worth avoiding.

Were Royal Whip winners profitable to follow on their subsequent three runs?
No – 7 wins from 32 runs returned a loss of -£3.65 to a £1 level stake.

Are placed runners profitable to follow on their subsequent three runs?
Runners-up: 4 wins from 26 runs returned a loss of -£18.66 to a £1 level stake.

Thirds: 0 win from 3 runs returned a loss of -£3.00 to a £1 level stake.

FUTURE SUCCESS RATING: ★ ★ ☆ ☆ ☆

GEOFFREY FREER STAKES
August 16, Newbury – (Group 3, Class 1, 3yo+) 1m5f 61yds

Last run	Winner/ Trainer & SP	Draw/ Ran	Age	Wght	PR	Next four runs			
07 Newm 1m4f 1st Princess of Wales' Two months	**Papal Bull** Sir M Stoute 6/4F	6/5	4	9-07	75	3rd Arc Trial Newb 1m3f	7th Japan Cup Toky 1m4f	-	-
06 Good 1m4f 3rd Gordon Stks Three weeks	**Admiral's Cruise** B Meehan 8/1	4/5	4	9-03	73	3rd Arc Trial Newb 1m3f	*5th John Porter Newb 1m4f	*2nd Jockey Club Stks Newm 1m4f	*4th Hardwicke Ascot 1m4f
05 Good 2m 4th Goodwood Cup Three weeks	**Lochbuie** G Wragg 12/1	1/5	4	9-03	75	7th Group 2 Deau 1m7f	5th Jockey Club Cup Newm 2m	-	-
04 Long 1m4f 2nd Arc de Triomphe Ten months	**Mubtaker** M Tregoning 3/10F	4/4	7	9-03	81	7th Grosser 'Baden Bade 1m4f	4th Candian Int Wood 1m4f	*3rd Brigadier Gerard Sand 1m4f	*11th King George VI Newb 1m4f
03 Newb 1m2f 1st Steventon Stks One month	**Mubtaker** M Tregoning 4/6F	3/5	6	9-03	83	**WON 8/13F** **September Stks** **Kemp 1m4f**	2nd Arc de Triomphe Long 1m4f	*WON 3/10F *Geoffrey Freer Newb 1m5f	*7th Grosser 'Baden Bade 1m4f
02 Newm 1m4f 2nd Princess of Wales' Two months	**Mubtaker** M Tregoning 11/8F	7/7	5	9-03	82	*WON 2/1F *Steventon Stks Newb 1m2f	*WON 4/6F *Geoffrey Freer Newb 1m5f	*WON 8/13F *September Stk Kemp 1m4f	*2nd Arc de Triomphe Long 1m4f
01 Curr 1m4f 6th Irish Derby Two months	**Mr Combustible** B Hills 9/4	2/5	3	8-06	76	3rd St Leger Donc 1m7f	*5th John Porter Newb 1m4f	-	-
00 Ascot 1m4f 2nd Shergar Cup One week	**Murghem** M Johnston 7/4F	6/6	5	9-03	76	4th Group 3 Taby 1m4f	6th Canadian Int Wood 1m4f	6th Hong Kong Vase Sha 1m4f	*16th Sheema Classic Nad Al 1m4f
99 Ascot 1m4f 4th King George VI Three weeks	**Silver Patriarch** J Dunlop 7/2	1/4	5	9-09	85	3rd Irish St Leger Curr 1m6f	2nd Prem Jock'Club Siro 1m4f	11th Hong Kong Vase Sha 1m4f	-
98 Newm 1m4f 2nd Princess of Wales' Two months	**Multicoloured** Sir M Stoute 10/1	1/6	5	9-03	78	-	-	-	-
97 Newm 1m4f 6th Princess of Wales' Two months	**Dushyantor** H Cecil 9/2	5/4	4	9-06	79	2nd September Stks Epsom 1m4f	*WON 6/4F Grade 3 Gold 1m3f	*3rd Grade 1 Sara 1m2f	*4th Grade 1 Belm 1m4f
96 Duss 1m4f 5th Group 1 Three weeks	**Phantom Gold** Lord Huntingdon 6/1	5/7	4	9-03	73	-	-	-	-

12-year median performance rating of the winner: **78** (out of 100)   *next year*

WINNER'S PROFILE Clues have been hard to come by as the race experienced a change, plus Mubtaker's three wins accounted for a quarter of the victories, which disguises some of the stats, but it is with this horse we start. When Marcus Tregoning's colt landed his third Geoffrey Freer in 2004, he became the only winner not to have run that season, while those to have already appeared finished **at least runner-up along the way**, and those that raced in the Princess of Wales's at Newmarket did well.

There was an even spread amongst weight – penalty carriers scored – age and previous form, although those to have already finished in the frame at this level were favoured, while **four and five-year olds** held the edge.

FUTURE POINTERS Some decent performers have landed this event over the years, although it has been a while since a horse like the 1991 winner, Drum Taps, turned up before graduating into a dual winner of the Ascot Gold Cup. The failure to lure any major stars and lack of competitiveness – reflected in the small field sizes – have both been contributory factors to the race losing its Group Two status in 2006.

Bar the three-times winner, Mubtaker, only Dushyantor got back on the scoresheet during his next four runs as some failed to cut the mustard in Group/Grade One events home and abroad.

Overall, winners of the Geoffrey Freer shape as ones to be wary of in the near future, unless another Mubtaker turns up with an above par performance rating.

Were Geoffrey Freer winners profitable to follow on their subsequent three runs?
No – 6 wins from 27 runs returned a loss of -£15.31 to a £1 level stake.

Are placed runners profitable to follow on their subsequent three runs?
Runners-up: 5 wins from 20 runs returned a loss of -£5.91 to a £1 level stake.
2005 Mubtaker – Cumberland Lodge, 1998 Silver Patriarch – Gran Premio del Jockey-Club, Jockey Club Stakes

Thirds: No qualifiers due to small fields of seven or less.

FUTURE SUCCESS RATING: ★ ☆ ☆ ☆ ☆

HUNGERFORD STAKES
August 16, Newbury – (Group 2, Class 1, 3yo+) 7f

Last run	Winner/ Trainer & SP	Draw/ Ran	Age	Wght	PR	Next four runs			
07 Newm 1m 7th Falmouth Stks *Two months*	**Red Evie** M Bell 5/1	3/10	4	9-04	75	2nd Matron Stks Leop 1m	10th Prix de la Foret Long 7f	-	-
06 York 6f 14th Duke of York *Four months*	**Welsh Emperor** T Tate 13/2	8/7	7	9-03	74	8th Park Stks York 7f	2nd Prix de la Foret Long 7f	10th Challenge Stks Newm 7f	*9th Duke of York York 6f
05 Good 1m 5th Sussex *Three weeks*	**Sleeping Indian** J Gosden 9/4JF	8/9	4	9-00	75	2nd Park Stks Donc 7f	5th Q Elizabeth II Newm 1m	2nd Challenge Stks Newm 7f	*WON 11/8F Dubai Duty Free Newb 7f
04 Good 7f 3rd Oak Tree Stks *Three weeks*	**Chic** Sir M Stoute 9/2	7/13	4	8-11	78	WON 4/1 **Celebration Mile Good 1m**	2nd Sun Chariot Newm 1m	*6th Silver Trophy Good 1m	*12th Sussex Good 1m
03 Ascot 7f 6th International Hcp *Three weeks*	**With Reason** D Loder 13/2	4/11	5	8-13	73	2nd Park Stks Donc 7f	WON 9/2 **Supreme Stks Good 7f**	*13th Lockinge Newb 1m	*WON 11/2 **Superior Mile Hayd 1m**
02 Good 1m 3rd Sussex *Three weeks*	**Reel Buddy** R Hannon 7/2	6/10	4	8-13	73	3rd Celebration Mile Good 1m	16th Challenge Stks Newm 7f	*8th Doncaster Mile Donc 1m	*11th Cammidge Tr'py Donc 6f
01 Good 1m 4th W Hill Mile Hcp *Three weeks*	**Atavus** G Margarson 33/1	6/7	4	8-13	69	14th Diadem Stks Ascot 6f	10th Challenge Stks Newm 7f	*3rd Leicestershire St Leic 7f	*7th Lockinge Newb 1m
00 Good 1m 6th Sussex *Three weeks*	**Arkadian Hero** L Cumani 5/2	5/8	5	9-02	76	2nd Grade 1 Wood 1m	14th Breeders' Cup Chur 1m	*5th Dubai Duty Free Nad Al 1m1f	*6th Lockinge Newb 1m
99 Toky 7f 10th Grade 2 *Three months*	**Lend A Hand** S Bin Suroor 10/11F	5/7	4	9-00	80	2nd Challenge Stks Newm 7f	4th Breeders' Cup Gulf 1m	*6th Listed Nad Al 6f	*WON 10/3 **Duke of York York 6f**
98 Donc 1m 1st Conds Stks *Three weeks*	**Muhtathir** J Gosden 7/4	4/9	3	8-08	77	WON 11/4F **Celebration Mile Good 1m**	7th Q Elizabeth II Ascot 1m	9th Prix de la Foret Long 7f	*2nd Listed Nad Al 1m
97 Newc 7f 6th Beeswing Stks *Three weeks*	**Decorated Hero** J Gosden 11/4	2/10	5	9-00	74	2nd Park Stks Donc 1m	WON 6/4F **Supreme Stks Good 7f**	WON 6/5 **Group 2 Long 1m**	5th Challenge Stks Newm 7f
96 Mais 1m 1st Listed *One month*	**Bin Rosie** D Loder 9/2	8/8	4	9-00	70	2nd Park Stks Donc 1m	3rd Group 2 Long 1m	*3rd Sandown Mile Sand 1m	*8th Lockinge Newb 1m

12-year median performance rating of the winner: **75** (out of 100) *next year*

WINNER'S PROFILE Half of the winners this century arrived via **Glorious Goodwood,** none reached the first two there, although 11 winners **scored at some point earlier in the season**.
It proved vital to have **winning form over the distance**, as every victor since 1996 passed on that score, while **four and five-year-olds** dominated – three-year-olds record is one win from almost 40 runners.
The best horses came to the fore as 11 emerged from the **first three in the betting**, and those with an **official rating of 107 or more** are respected – Red Evie last year fit both those trends, while becoming the second filly in the last four years to strike a blow.
Trainer **John Gosden** has led the way with three victories from only six runners – Stronghold last year finished third.

FUTURE POINTERS Allocated Group Two status in 2006, the Hungerford now shapes like a race on the up, having last year attracted two previous Group One winners for the first time, one of whom managed to shoulder a penalty to victory in Red Evie. There have been mixed subsequent results post-Newbury, although two of the best winners with above par performance ratings (PR) both took the Celebration Mile at Goodwood next time out, a race that wasn't oversubscribed by Hungerford winners.
Two other Newbury scorers got back to winning ways in the Supreme Stakes after they had narrowly missed out in the Park Stakes – an event that halted three others – while three Hungerford victors waited until the following year before visiting the winner's enclosure again.

Were Hungerford winners profitable to follow on their subsequent three runs?
No – 4 wins from 35 runs returned a loss of -£17.05 to a £1 level stake.

Placed runners' subsequent record (three runs):
Runners-up: 7 wins from 33 returned a loss of -£13.19 to a £1 level stake.
2006 Jeremy – Sandown Mile, 1996 Mistle Cat – Group One Premio Vittorio Di Capua

Thirds: 3 wins from 24 runs returned a loss of -£13.72 to a £1 level stake.
2003 Ashdown Express – Bentinck Stakes

FUTURE SUCCESS RATING: ★ ★ ☆ ☆ ☆

GREAT ST WILFRID

August 16, Ripon – (Heritage Handicap, Class 1, 3yo+) 6f

Last run	Winner/Trainer & SP	Draw/Ran	Age	Wght	PR	Next four runs			
07 Good 6f 22nd Stewards' Cup *Two weeks*	**Kostar** C Cox 10/1	22/23	6	9-06	64	-	-	-	-
06 Good 6f 4th Stewards' Cup *Two weeks*	**Excusez Moi** C Brittain 10/1	12/19	4	9-04	67	6th Sprint Cup Hayd 6f	2nd World Trophy Newb 5f	12th Prix de l'Abbaye Long 5f	*9th Handicap Nad Al 6f
05 Newm 6f 5th Handicap *Three weeks*	**Ice Planet** D Nicholls 10/1	23/23	4	8-07	63	15th Ayr Silver Cup Ayr 6f	*4th Handicap Pont 6f	*2nd Stan James Hcp Newm 6f	*5th Handicap York 6f
04 Hayd 6f 1st Coral Hop *One week*	**Smokin Beau** N Littmoden 16/1	11/19	7	9-10	72	**WON 2/1F Rated Hcp Sand 5f**	Conds Stks Ling 5f	*9th Cammidge Tr'py Donc 6f	*2nd Conds Stks Good 5f
03 Yarm 6f 3rd Conds Stks *Two weeks*	**Hidden Dragon** P Blockley 16/1	23/23	4	9-01	64	4th Tote Sprint Hcp Epsom 5f	7th Ayr Gold Cup Ayr 6f	11th Rated Hcp Ascot 5f	9th Rated Hcp Newb 5f
02 Newm 7f 7th Silv' Salver Hcp *One week*	**Deceitful** D Evans 20/1	18/22	4	8-08	60	5th Rated Hcp Ches 7f	3rd Class Stks Hayd 6f	2nd Ladies Hcp Donc 7f	18th Ayr Gold Cup Ayr 6f
01 Newm 6f 1st J Jennings Hcp *Three weeks*	**Antonio Canova** B Jones 7/2F	17/23	5	9-09	63	4th Ayr Gold Cup Ayr 6f	*11th Handicap Good 6f	*27th Wokingham Ascot 6f	*30th Handicap Newm 7f
00 Pont 5f 1st Chaplin's Club Hcp *Two weeks*	**William's Well** M Easterby 14/1	4/22	6	7-13	55	6th Ladbrokes Hcp Good 6f	15th Ayr Silver Cup Ayr 6f	9th Handicap Hayd 5f	13th Handicap York 5f
99 Ches 6f 4th Queensferry Stks *Three weeks*	**Pipalong** T Easterby 16/1	17/23	3	9-07	67	2nd Flying Fillies Stk Pont 6f	11th Sprint Cup Hayd 6f	5th Ayr Gold Cup Ayr 6f	2nd Bentinck Stks Newm 6f
98 Leic 6f 1st Class Stks *One week*	**Cadeaux Cher** B Hills 8/1	2/22	4	8-06	67	16th Eagle Lane Hcp York 6f	14th Rated Hcp York 6f	**WON 20/1 Portland Hcp Donc 51/2f**	28th Ayr Gold Cup Ayr 6f
97 Hayd 6f 4th Coral Hcp *One week*	**Tadeo** M Johnston 12/1	19/21	4	9-08	64	13th Rated Hcp York 6f	7th Portland Hcp Donc 51/2f	24th Ayr Gold Cup Ayr 6f	**WON 5/2JF Conds Stks Nott 5f**
96 York 6f 4th Handicap *Three months*	**Samwar** Miss G Kelleway 15/2	2/17	4	8-06	58	2nd Ladbrokes Hcp Good 6f	2nd Rated Hcp Ascot 5f	15th W Dixon Hcp Ascot 5f	11th Rated Hcp Newb 6f

12-year median performance rating of the winner: **64** (out of 100)   **next year*

WINNER'S PROFILE As you would expect in a summer sprint, the last 11 winners had been **active within the past three weeks**, and Haydock, Newmarket and Goodwood provided a final stop on seven occasions – four ran in the Stewards' Cup a few weeks earlier. Every winner ran in a **sprint worth at least £19k that season**, while 11 were **at least fourth on one of their previous two runs**. The draw was a factor as high stalls dominated, however, on fast ground low numbers can emerge, something not seen for eight years. Favourites did badly, along with trainer David Nicholls' runners, who struck just once from over 40 runners, while on the age front, **four to six-year-olds** were favoured with four-year-olds doing best – three-year-olds have just one victory from over 25 runners.

FUTURE POINTERS The majority of winners were flattered from an advantageous draw and failed to cope with a weight rise in the future – only Smokin Beau, who won from a central draw followed up – and those that head to Ayr, Haydock and York should be swerved. It could prove wiser to follow certain placed runners *(see below)*.

Were Great St Wilfrid winners profitable to follow on their subsequent three runs?
No – 2 wins from 33 runs returned a loss of -£9.00 to a £1 level stake.

Placed runners' subsequent record (three runs):
Runners-up: 3 wins from 36 runs returned a loss of -£15.00 to a £1 level stake.
Thirds: 4 wins from 36 runs returned a **profit of +£27.50** to a £1 level stake.
2001 Abbajabba – Coral Sprint Trophy (20/1), 2000 Bahamian Pirate – Ayr Gold Cup (33/1)
Fourths: 2 wins from 36 runs returned a loss of -£11.00 to a £1 level stake.

Were badly drawn runners worth following?
Horses to have run well from a disadvantageous draw are often hailed as 'ones to follow', and there is evidence to support this in certain cases. In recent years high numbers were favoured, and those to have made the first three from a low draw showed a profit since 1999. Last year, Indian Trail qualified from stall nine (top two were 22 & 20) and won his next two, while in 2001, Abbajabba did the same before taking the Coral Sprint three runs later at 20/1. Those to finish first home from the low numbers but *not in the first three* are not profitable to follow.
In a nutshell, the ones to watch are those in the first three from a low number when high numbers dominate.

FUTURE SUCCESS RATING: ★ ★ ☆ ☆ ☆

LONSDALE CUP
August 19-22, York – (Group 2, Class 1, 3yo+) 2m 88yds

Last run	Winner/ Trainer & SP	Draw/ Ran	Age	Wght	PR	Next four runs			
07 Epso 1m4f 2nd Coronation Cup Three months	Septimus A O'Brien 6/5F	2/9	4	9-01	79	WON 11/10F Doncaster Cup Donc 2m2f	-	-	-
06 Good 2m 4th Goodwood Cup Three weeks	Sergeant Cecil R Millman 11/4F	7/11	7	9-01	80	WON EvsF Doncaster Cup York 2m2f	WON 2/1F Prix du Cadran Long 2m4f	3rd Prix Royal-Oak Long 2m	*4th John Porter Newb 1m4f
05 Good 2m 3rd Goodwood Cup Three weeks	Millenary J Dunlop 12/1	7/8	8	9-04	82	WON 11/4 Doncaster Cup Donc 2m2f	3rd Jockey Club Cup Newm 2m	-	-
04 Good 1m4f 2nd Glorious Stks Three weeks	First Charter Sir M Stoute 7/1	2/10	5	9-01	75	3rd Irish St Leger Curr 1m6f	-	-	-
03 Ascot 1m4f 4th King George VI One month	Bollin Eric T Easterby 7/4F	2/6	4	9-06	76	4th Irish St Leger Curr 1m6f	8th Arc de Triomphe Long 1m4f	-	-
02 Mais 1m6f 5th Group 2 Two months	Boreas L Cumani 13/2	6/7	7	9-01	78	WON 7/2 Doncaster Cup Donc 2m2f	2nd Jockey Club Cup Newm 2m	*5th Jockey Club Stks Newm 1m4f	*5th Henry II Sand 2m
01 Good 2m 1st Goodwood Cup Three weeks	Persian Punch D Elsworth 10/3F	7/10	8	9-06	80	4th Irish St Leger Curr 1m6f	3rd Melbourne Cup Flem 2m	*2nd Sagaro Stks Ascot 2m	*4th Yorkshire Cup York 1m6f
00 Good 2m 1st Goodwood Cup Three weeks	Royal Rebel M Johnston 2/1JF	3/5	4	9-06	79	3rd Prix du Cadran Long 2m4f	2nd Jockey Club Cup Newm 2m	6th Prix Royal-Oak Long 2m	*6th Yorkshire Cup York 1m6f
99 Good 2m 6th Goodwood Cup Three weeks	Celeric J Dunlop 10/1	3/8	7	9-04	75	3rd Doncaster Cup Donc 2m2f	3rd Jockey Club Cup Newm 2m	*3rd Sagaro Stks Ascot 2m	*7th Yorkshire Cup York 1m6f
98 Ascot 2m4f 6th Gold Cup Two months	Persian Punch D Elsworth 11/4	2/5	5	9-04	78	3rd Melbourne Cup Flem 2m	*4th John Porter Newb 1m4f	*7th Jockey Club Stks Newm 1m4f	*5th Yorkshire Cup York 1m6f
97 Good 2m 3rd Goodwood Cup Three weeks	Double Eclipse M Johnston 5/2	4/6	5	9-01	74	2nd Group 3 Long 2m	2nd Jockey Club Cup Newm 2m	5th Prix Royal-Oak Long 2m	*2nd Fred Archer Stks Newm 1m4f
96 York 1m6f 1st Silver Cup Two months	Celeric D Morley 9/4F	7/7	4	9-04	73	2nd Doncaster Cup Donc 2m2f	WON 11/4 Jock' Club Cup Newm 2m	*4th Jockey Club St Newm 1m4f	*WON 7/2 Yorkshire Cup York 1m6f

12-year median performance rating of the winner: **77** (out of 100)   *next year*

WINNER'S PROFILE Although the **Goodwood Cup** has been a sound pointer for this event – half emerged from Sussex – four of the last seven winners of the Lonsdale Cup **debuted over this trip** and were yet to be unmasked as genuine stayers.

Since becoming a Group race 10 years ago, winners lined up with at least a Listed victory to their name. Only a handful of three-year-olds were unsuccessfully tried – just one since it was a Group Two that came last – while Bollin Eric proved that a Group One penalty can be shouldered. The market has proven a solid guide, as 10 winners came from the **first four in the betting** – John Dunlop was responsible for the two outsiders.

Trainer **David Elsworth**'s rare runners deserve respect with two winners and a runner-up from five entries, while **Aidan O'Brien** could be back for more after striking with his only runner to date last year.

FUTURE POINTERS In keeping with the other staying 'Cup' races on the calendar, this event inherited Group Two status in 2004 along with a change in title from the Lonsdale Stakes. It's strange to think it was only a Listed race until 1998, but it's reputation has grown, for not only have recent renewals seen three of the four largest fields, but the last three winners all followed up in the Doncaster Cup – only two others had managed that feat from eight Lonsdale winners since 1990.

Were Lonsdale Cup winners profitable to follow on their subsequent three runs?
No – 6 wins from 30 runs returned a loss of -£10.90 to a £1 level stake. However, four of the last six winners scored next time out for a level **profit of +£6.35.**

Placed runners' subsequent record (three runs):
Runners-up: 5 wins from 36 runs returned a loss of -£22.00 to a £1 level stake.
2005 Distinction – Aston Park Stakes, 1998 Celeric – Sagaro Stakes

Thirds: 5 wins from 14 runs returned a **profit of +£11.00** to a £1 level stake.
2007 Anna Pavlova – Doonside Cup, Group Two Prix de Royallieu,
2004 Millenary – Doncaster Cup, Jockey Club Cup, 1999 Rainbow High – Jockey Club Cup

FUTURE SUCCESS RATING: ★ ★ ★ ★ ☆

GREAT VOLTIGEUR STAKES
August 19-22, York – (Group 2, Class 1, 3yo Colts and Geldings) 1m4f

Last run	Winner/ Trainer & SP	Draw/ Ran	Age	Wght	PR	Next four runs			
07 Newm 1m4f 4th *Two months*	**Lucarno** Princess of Wales J Gosden 7/2	7/9	3	8-12	80	**WON 7/2** St Leger Donc 1m6f	-	-	-
06 Newm 1m5f 1st *Two months*	**Youmzain** Bahrain Trophy M Channon 12/1	3/10	3	8-12	79	2nd Prix Niel Long 1m4f	**WON 4/5F** Preis 'Europa Colo 1m4f	*3rd Sheema Classic Nad Al 1m4f	*3rd Tatts Gold Cup Curr 1m3f
05 Ling 1m3f 1st Maiden *One month*	**Hard Top** Sir M Stoute 6/1	3/6	3	8-09	76	5th St Leger Donc 1m6f	*7th Jockey Club Stk Newm 1m4f	*5th Group 2 Chan 1m4f	*5th Hardwicke Stks Ascot 1m4f
04 Curr 1m4f 4th Irish Derby *Two months*	**Rule Of Law** S Bin Suroor 11/8F	2/7	3	8-09	81	**WON 3/1JF** St Leger Donc 1m6f	-	-	-
03 Leop 1m2f 1st Stakes *Two months*	**Powerscourt** A O'Brien 5/1	7/9	3	8-09	82	3rd Irish St Leger Curr 1m6f	*WON 10/3 Tatts Gold Cup Curr 1m3f	*2nd Prince of Wales' Ascot 1m2f	*5th Eclipse Sand 1m2f
02 Good 1m4f 1st Gordon Stks *Three weeks*	**Bandari** M Johnston 4/5F	5/6	3	8-09	76	3rd St Leger Donc 1m6f	*4th Jockey Club Stk Newm 1m4f	*4th Coronation Cup Epsom 1m4f	*4th Hardwicke Stks Ascot 1m4f
01 Ascot 1m4f 4th K Edward VII *Two months*	**Milan** A O'Brien 6/1	8/9	3	8-09	82	**WON 13/8F** St Leger Donc 1m6f	5th Arc de Triomphe Long 1m4f	2nd Breeders' Cup Belm 1m2f	*PU Mooresbridge Stk Curr 1m2f
00 Good 1m4f 2nd Gordon Stks *Three weeks*	**Air Marshall** Sir M Stoute 7/2	2/5	3	8-09	75	2nd St Leger Donc 1m6f	*7th Jockey Club Stk Newm 1m4f	***4th Mdn Hdle Clon 2m4f	***14th Mdn Hdle Thur 2m
99 Sand 1m2f 3rd Eclipse *Two months*	**Fantastic Light** Sir M Stoute 4/1	6/7	3	8-09	81	**WON 9/4** Arc Trial Newb 1m3f	11th Arc de Triomphe Long 1m4f	*WON N/O Sheema Classic Nad Al 1m4f	*2nd Coronation Cup Epsom 1m4f
98 Leic 1m4f 1st Mercury Listed *Three months*	**Sea Wave** S Bin Suroor 7/2	2/6	3	8-09	77	UR Prix Niel Long 1m4f	9th Arc de Triomphe Long 1m4f	*3rd Hardwicke Stks Ascot 1m4f	*4th Princess of Wales' Newm 1m4f
97 Good 1m4f 1st Gordon Stks *Three weeks*	**Stowaway** S Bin Suroor 6/5F	3/5	3	8-09	76	4th Champion Stks Newm 1m2f	*WON N/O Turf Classic Nad Al 1m4f	-	-
96 Curr 1m4f 4th Irish Derby	**Dushyantor** H Cecil 3/1	2/5	3	8-09	77	2nd St Leger Donc 1m6f	7th Breeders' Cup Wood 1m4f	*2nd Coronation Cup Epsom 1m4f	*6th Hardwicke Stks Ascot 1m4f

12-year median performance rating of the winner: **79** (out of 100) *next year ***three years*

WINNER'S PROFILE The majority were **rested for at least three weeks** prior to York as 10 had either run in a Derby, at Royal Ascot (King Edward VII non-winners best guide) or in the Gordon Stakes at Glorious Goodwood. The most straightforward clue to finding the Great Voltigeur winner was to follow the market, 11 times since 1996 has it favoured those that went off at **6/1 or shorter**, although those that carried a penalty suffered, Boscobel last year trailed in last at 9/2.

It may be a coincidence, but those drawn in the widest stall have yet to score, including the favourite Yellowstone last year from the **Aidan O'Brien** yard, who sent out two winners, while **Sir Michael Stoute** and **Saeed Bin Suroor** have three apiece.

FUTURE POINTERS Named after the winner of the 1850 St Leger, Voltigeur, last year's victor, Lucarno, became the seventh horse in the last 11 renewals to go on and land that Classic, stamping the Great Voltigeur's authority as the leading trial for Doncaster – the four beaten here at York included two runners-up, a third and a fourth. Despite the success of those in St Leger, the three who later attempted the Arc are all well beaten, while of the five to have swerved Doncaster next time out, four scored away from these shores – two in Dubai.

Were Great Voltigeur winners profitable to follow on their subsequent three runs?
No – 8 wins from 31 runs returned a loss of -£8.50 to a £1 level stake.

Placed runners' subsequent record (three runs):
Runners-up: 7 wins from 33 runs returned a loss of -£6.50 to a £1 level stake.
2006 Red Rocks – Breeders' Cup, 2003 Brian Boru – St Leger, 2000 Marienbard – Yorkshire Cup, 1997 Silver Patriarch – St Leger

Thirds: 0 win from 7 runs returned a loss of -£7.00 to a £1 level stake.

FUTURE SUCCESS RATING: ★ ★ ★ ☆

JUDDMONTE INTERNATIONAL STAKES
August 19, York – (Group 1, Class 1, 3yo+) 1m2f

Last run	Winner/ Trainer & SP	Draw/ Ran	Age	Wght	PR	Next four runs			
07 Sand 1m2f 2nd Eclipse *Two months*	**Authorized** P Chapple-Hyam 6/4F	1/7	3	8-11	88	10th Arc de Triomphe Long 1m4f	-	-	-
06 Sand 1m2f 2nd Eclipse *Two months*	**Notnowcato** Sir M Stoute 8/1	5/7	4	9-05	85	8th Champion Stks Newm 1m2f	*4th Gordon Richards Sand 1m2f	*WON 7/1 Tatts Gold Cup Curr 1m3f	*3rd Prince of Wales' Ascot 1m2f
05 Siro 1m4f 1st Premio di Milano *Two months*	**Electrocutionist** V Valiani 9/2	5/7	4	9-05	90	3rd Canadian Int Wood 1m4f	*Group 2 Nad Al 1m2f	*WON 5/4F World Cup Nad Al 1m2f	*2nd Prince of Wales' Ascot 1m2f
04 Ascot 1m4f 3rd K George VI *One month*	**Sulamani** S Bin Suroor 3/1	9/9	5	9-05	89	WON 17/20F Canadian Int Wood 1m4f	-	-	-
03 Ascot 1m4f 5th K George VI *One month*	**Falbrav** L Cumani 5/2	2/8	5	9-05	90	2nd Irish Champion Leop 1m2f	WON 6/4F Q Elizabeth II Ascot 1m	3rd Breeders' Cup Sant 1m4f	3rd Hong Kong Cup Sha 1m2f
02 Ascot 1m4f 2nd K George VI *One month*	**Nayef** M Tregoning 6/4F	5/7	4	9-05	84	3rd World Cup Nad Al 1m2f	*WON 5/1 Prince of Wales' Ascot 1m2f	*2nd Eclipse Sand 1m2f	*7th King George VI Ascot 1m4f
01 Newb 1m2f 1st Steventon Stks *One month*	**Sakhee** S Bin Suroor 7/4F	5/8	4	9-05	94	WON 22/10F Arc 'Triomphe Long 1m4f	2nd Breeders' Cup Belm 1m2f	*WON N/O Conds Stks Nad Al 1m2f	*3rd World Cup Nad Al 1m2f
00 Good 1m 1st Sussex *Three weeks*	**Giant's Causeway** A O'Brien 10/11F	5/6	3	8-11	90	WON 8/11F Irish Champion Leop 1m2f	2nd Q Elizabeth II Ascot 1m	2nd Breeders' Cup Chur 1m2f	-
99 Ascot 1m4f 2nd Hardwicke Stks *Two months*	**Royal Anthem** H Cecil 3/1JF	9/12	4	9-05	94	5th Irish Champion Leop 1m2f	2nd Breeders' Cup Gulf 1m4f	*WON 2/5F Grade 1 Gulf 1m3f	-
98 Chep 1m2f 1st Daffodil Stks *One month*	**One So Wonderful** L Cumani 6/1	5/8	4	9-02	82	4th Irish Champion Leop 1m2f	5th Champion Stks Newm 1m2f	-	-
97 Ascot 1m4f 4th K George VI *One month*	**Singspiel** Sir M Stoute 4/1	2/4	5	9-05	91	-	-	-	-
96 Sand 1m2f 1st Eclipse *Two months*	**Halling** S Bin Suroor 6/4F	1/6	5	9-05	89	2nd Champion Stks Newm 1m2f	-	-	-

12-year median performance rating of the winner: **89** (out of 100)   **next year*

WINNER'S PROFILE Every winner had **seen the racetrack within the past two months** where three came via the Eclipse in which they finished in the first two, while four arrived having failed in the King George VI.
A **prior victory over this intermediate distance** was an absolute must, along with a placed effort at least in Group One company. Fancied runners that started **8/1 or shorter** held sway, while **four and five-year-olds** were favoured despite Authorized's victory last year – the first Derby winner since Troy in 1979.
On the training front, records since 1996 show **Saeed Bin Suroor** out in front with three winners from 10 runners, while **Luca Cumani** has two from just three runners, Sir Michael Stoute two from 13, and Aidan O'Brien one from 16.

FUTURE POINTERS Always a strong event that has traditionally had a say in some of the big autumn Group Ones to come both at home and abroad, and 2007 was no exception, as it brought together the Derby, King George and Eclipse winners. Although the 2007 victor, Authorized, was unable to emulate Sakhee in taking the Arc de Triomphe next time out, the runner-up, Dylan Thomas, did manage to reverse form at Longchamp to join Bago, who was also placed here in 2004 *(see below)*.
Juddmonte International winners have very much been ones to stick with this century, an impressive list of subsequent triumphs at the highest level spread throughout every year – bar Authorized – including the Tattersalls Gold Cup, Dubai World Cup, Canadian International, Queen Elizabeth II, Prince of Wales's, Arc de Triomphe and Irish Champion Stakes.

Were Juddmonte International winners profitable to follow on their subsequent three runs?
Yes – 10 wins from 26 runs returned a **profit of +£4.12** to a £1 level stake.

Placed runners' subsequent record (three runs):
Runners-up: 7 wins from 32 runs returned a loss of -£4.48 to a £1 level stake.
2000 Kalanisi – Champion Stakes, Breeders' Cup, 1996 First Island – Hong Kong Cup

Thirds: 3 wins from 10 runs returned a **profit of +£4.01** to a £1 level stake.
2004 Bago – Arc de Triomphe, Prix Ganay

FUTURE SUCCESS RATING: ★ ★ ★ ★ ☆

ACOMB STAKES
August 19-22, York – (Group 3, Class 1, 2yo) 7f

Last run	Winner/ Trainer & SP	Draw/ Ran	Age	Wght	PR	Next four runs			
07 Sali 7f 1st Maiden Two months	**Fast Company** B Meehan 11/4	9/7	2	9-00	66	2nd Dewhurst Stks Newm 7f	-	-	-
06 Ripo 6f 1st Novice Stks Three months	**Big Timer** I Semple 5/4F	5/7	2	9-00	59	10th Grade 1 Belm 1m	*9th Listed Spring Cup Ling 7f	-	-
05 Catt 6f 1st Maiden One month	**Palace Episode** K Ryan 16/1	6/8	2	8-13	68	3rd Royal Lodge Newm 1m	5th Dewhurst Stks Newm 7f	WON 20/1 R Post Trophy Donc 1m	*6th Dante Stks York 1m2f
04 York 7f 1st Maiden Two months	**Elliots World** M Johnston 5/2	5/7	2	8-13	61	6th Champagne Stks Donc 7f	4th Royal Lodge Ascot 1m	7th R Post Trophy Donc 1m	*2nd Blue Riband Trial Epsom 1m2f
03 York 7f 1st Maiden Two months	**Rule Of Law** D Loder 15/8F	6/7	2	8-13	66	3rd Royal Lodge Ascot 1m	*2nd Dante Stks York 1m2f	*2nd Derby Epsom 1m4f	*4th Irish Derby Curr 1m4f
02 Good 7f 2nd Vintage Stks Three weeks	**Bourbonnais** M Johnston 5/6F	5/6	2	8-13	62	*3rd UAE 2,000 Guin Nad Al 1m	*5th UAE Derby Nad Al 1m2f	*8th Poule 'Poulains Long 1m	-
01 Ascot 7f 3rd Maiden One month	**Comfy** Sir M Stoute 7/2	7/9	2	8-10		5th Dewhurst Stks Newm 7f	**WON 4/1 Conds Stks Leic 7f	**7th Eclipse Sand 1m2f	**3rd Conds Stks Kemp 1m1f
00 Galw 7f 1st Maiden One month	**Hemingway** A O'Brien 8/13F	1/5	2	9-01	65	-	-	-	-
99 Newm 7f 1st Maiden Two weeks	**King's Best** Sir M Stoute 4/7F	2/5	2	8-13	72	5th Dewhurst Stks Newm 7f	*2nd Craven Stks Newm 1m	*WON 13/2 2,000 Guineas Newm 1m	*PU Irish Derby Curr 1m4f
98 Donc 7f 1st Maiden Three weeks	**Auction House** B Hills 9/2	3/7	2	8-13	69	WON 7/2 Champagne Stk Donc 7f	2nd Dewhurst Stks Newm 7f	*16th 2,000 Guineas Newm 1m	*4th Hungerford Stks Newb 1m
97 Curr 7f 2nd EBF Stks One month	**Saratoga Springs** A O'Brien 9/1	8/9	2	8-10	70	3rd Champagne Stk Donc 7f	WON 7/4F Beresford Stks Curr 1m	WON 9/2 R Post Trophy Donc 1m	*WON 4/1 Dante Stks York 1m2f
96 Ascot 6f 1st Maiden One month	**Revoque** P Chapple-Hyam 5/2	7/7	2	9-00	67	WON 21/10 Pr' Salamandre Long 7f	WON 4/5F Gr'nd Criterium Long 1m	*2nd Greenham Stks Newb 7f	*2nd 2,000 Guineas Newm 1m

12-year median performance rating of the winner: **66** (out of 100)   *next year*

WINNER'S PROFILE Every winner arrived with a **top-three finish last time out** and nine won – only Comfy took this as a maiden – while three took a maiden over the track and trip, which included Bourbonnais, who was the only winner from a maiden held the edge, as did those with winning form over the trip, despite two of the last three having missed out in that sphere.
Middle to high drawn numbers came out best in recent years, as a trend to race down the middle in the straight developed, while it paid to stick with the **first three in the betting**.
On the training front, **Aidan O'Brien** struck twice from only six runners, and **Sir Michael Stoute** won it twice from seven runners – also won it in 1989 and 1987 – while Mark Johnston has a lower strike-rate with two from 10.

FUTURE POINTERS The Acomb has very much proven a hot and cold event, transformed from just a conditions race in 1997 to Listed status through to 2006, when it finally matured into a Group Three.
However, subsequent results were better pre-Millennium when a host of decent individuals went on to land Group One events, including the 1999 winner, King's Best, who marched on to 2,000 Guineas glory the following year. Both the 1997 and 1996 winners became top-class juveniles that won Group One events later in the season, while the 1995 winner, Bijou D'Inde took the Group One St James's Palace Stakes at Royal Ascot the following year.
The only winner to have gained Classic success since 2000 was Rule Of Law five years ago in the St Leger, while Palace Episode secured Group One honours in the Racing Post Trophy – emulating Saratoga Springs – a route that has surprisingly only been trodden on three occasions.

Were Acomb winners profitable to follow on their subsequent three runs?
Yes – 8 wins from 30 returned a **profit of +£21.15** to a £1 level stake.

Placed runners' subsequent record (three runs):
Runners-up: 5 wins from 33 runs returned a loss of -£20.01 to a £1 level stake.

Thirds: 3 wins from 6 runs returned a **profit of +£1.23** to a £1 level stake.

FUTURE SUCCESS RATING: ★ ★ ★ ☆ ☆

GIMCRACK STAKES
August 19-22, York – (Group 2, Class 1, 2yo Colts & Geldings) 6f

Last run	Winner/Trainer & SP	Draw/Ran	Age	Wght	PR	Next four runs			
07 Newm 6f 4th / Conds Stks / One month	Sir Gerry / J Fanshawe 4/1	5/8	2	8-12	68	8th Middle Park Newm 6f	-	-	-
06 Nott 5f 1st / Maiden / Two months	Conquest / W Haggas 9/2	3/6	2	8-12	71	6th Middle Park Newm 6f	*17th Duke of York York 6f	*5th Group 2 Chan 5f	*15th King's Stand Ascot 5f
05 Ches 5f 2nd / Conds Stks / Two months	Amadeus Wolf / K Ryan 7/1	9/13	2	8-11	75	WON 4/1 Middle Park Newm 6f	*7th 2,000 Guineas Newm 1m	*5th Golden Jubilee Ascot 6f	*4th July Cup Newm 6f
04 Newm 6f 5th / July Stks / Two months	Tony James / C Brittain 16/1	2/11	2	8-11	66	6th J-Luc Lagardere Long 7f	9th Group 2 Mais 6f	*16th UAE 2,000 Guin Nad Al 1m	*13th Stakes Nad Al 1m1f
03 Newm 6f 1st / Novice Stks / One month	Belmont / J Noseda 7/2	9/9	2	8-11	73	WON 8/1 Middle Park Newm 6f	7th Dewhurst Newm 7f	*3rd July Cup Newm 6f	*2nd Conds Stks Newm 5f
02 Newm 6f 1st / Maiden / Three weeks	Country Reel / D Loder 3/1F	2/11	2	8-11	67	4th Middle Park Newm 6f	*2nd Chipchase Stks Newc 6f	*8th Hackwood Stks Newb 6f	*5th Bentinck Stks Newm 6f
01 Curr 6f 1st / Railway Stks / Two months	Rock Of Gibraltar / A O'Brien 11/4	9/9	2	9-00	77	2nd Champagne Stk Donc 7f	WON 4/5JF Gr'nd Criterium Long 7f	WON 4/6F Dewhurst Newm 7f	*WON 9/1 2,000 Guineas Newm 1m
00 Newm 6f 2nd / Maiden / Three months	Bannister / R Hannon 11/1	2/9	2	8-11	64	9th Middle Park Newm 6f	*5th Heron Stks Kemp 1m	*11th Chipchase Stks Newc 6f	*7th Hackwood Stks Newb 6f
99 Newm 6f 2nd / July Stks / Two months	Mull Of Kintyre / A O'Brien 4/5F	7/10	2	8-11	68	4th Breeders' Cup Gulf 1m1f	**6th Queen Anne Ascot 1m	**2nd Group 3 Curr 7f	**3rd Lennox Stks Good 7f
98 Ascot 6f 3rd / Maiden / One month	Josr Algarhoud / M Channon 6/1	7/8	2	8-11	69	*WON 13/8F Beeswing Stks Newc 7f	*2nd Celebration Mile Good 1m	*3rd Challenge Stks Newm 7f	*WON 27/10 Group 3 Long 7f
97 Wind 6f 4th / Conds Stks / Two weeks	Carrowkeel / B Hills 16/1	1/7	2	8-11	62	4th Champagne Stk Donc 7f	2nd Middle Park Newm 6f	4th Grand Criterium Long 1m	-
96 Kemp 6f 2nd / Conds Stks / Three months	Abou Zouz / D Loder 4/1	7/9	2	8-11	66	4th Tatts Conds Newm 7f	*10th Temple Stks Sand 5f	*6th Group 3 Newm 7f	*WON 5/4F Conds Stks Donc 6f

12-year median performance rating of the winner: **69** (out of 100)   *next year **two years

WINNER'S PROFILE Not the best race in which to highlight an ideal profile, but one starting point was that six of the last nine winners arrived via **Newmarket last time**, two of whom ran in the July Stakes, while four winners since the Millennium ran at the Royal meeting.
Eleven winners **visited the racecourse three times or less** prior to York, while those that started at **7/1 or shorter** edged matters, including trainer **Aidan O'Brien**'s pair. The Irish handler has a sharp record with two winners from only five runners, including the 8/1 runner-up last year, who made his debut in this.

FUTURE POINTERS A juvenile event that has provided more of a springboard for future sprinters rather than Classic pretenders, as only Rock Of Gibraltar – the best winner of this event since 1996 – scored in the 2,000 Guineas the following year, while the 1993 winner, Turtle Island, took the Irish equivalent.
Two of the above-par winners with decent performance ratings (PR) managed to scoop the valuable Middle Park Stakes next time out at Newmarket, however, that event outfoxed five others, including last year's sub-standard winner, Sir Gerry.

Were Gimcrack winners profitable to follow on their subsequent three runs?
No – 5 wins from 34 runs returned a loss of -£13.92 to a £1 level stake.

Placed runners' subsequent record (three runs):
Runners-up: 6 wins from 35 runs returned a loss of -£13.60 to a £1 level stake.
2006 Wi Dud – Flying Childers, 2005 Red Clubs – Greenham Stakes, 1997 Bold Fact – King Charles II Stakes

Thirds: 2 wins from 23 runs returned a loss of -£19.12 to a £1 level stake.

FUTURE SUCCESS RATING: ★ ★ ☆ ☆ ☆

EBOR
August 20, York – (Heritage Handicap, Class 2, 3yo+) 1m6f

Last run	Winner/Trainer & SP	Draw/Ran	Age	Wght	PR	Next four runs			
07 Good 1m4f 1st Glorious Stks *Three weeks*	**Purple Moon** L Cumani 7/2F	14/19	4	9-04	73	6th Caulfield Cup Caul 1m4f	2nd Melbourne Cup Flem 2m	–	–
06 Ascot 2m 9th Brown Jack Hcp *One month*	**Mudawin** J Chapple-Hyam 100/1	14/19	5	8-04	63	3rd Mallard Hcp York 1m6f	3rd Irish Cesarewitch Curr 2m	2nd Listed Kemp 2m	*9th High-Rise Hcp Pont 1m2f
05 Good 1m6f 3rd Summer Hcp *One month*	**Sergeant Cecil** R Millman 11/1	18/20	6	8-12	74	2nd Doncaster Cup Donc 2m2f	**WON 10/1** **Cesarewitch** **Newm 2m2f**	*4th John Porter Newb 1m4f	*2nd Yorkshire Cup York 1m6f
04 Good 1m6f 1st Summer Hcp *One month*	**Mephisto** L Cumani 6/1	3/19	5	9-04	70	*3rd *Grd 2 Nov Hdl* *Chel 2m5f*	*WON 9/4 *Grd 2 Nov Hdl* *Hayd 3m*	*WON 4/5F *Grd 2 Nov Hdl* *Kels 2m2f*	*3rd *Grd 2 Nov Hdl* *Aint 2m4f*
03 Ascot 2m 6th Tote Hcp *Two months*	**Saint Alebe** D Elsworth 20/1	17/22	4	8-08	64	6th Halls Hcp Yarm 1m6f	5th Listed Ascot 2m	13th Cesarewitch Newm 2m2f	*16th Heritage Hcp Newm 1m6f
02 Good 2m5f 1st Marriott Hcp *Three weeks*	**Hugs Dancer** J Given 25/1	20/22	5	8-05	61	5th Cesarewitch Newm 2m2f	*WON 9/1 *Chester Cup* *Ches 2m2f*	*8th Henry II Stks Sand 2m	*8th Northumberland Newc 2m
01 Leop 1m6f 6th Listed *One month*	**Mediterranean** A O'Brien 16/1	20/22	3	8-04	74	PU St Leger Donc 1m6f	–	–	–
00 Good 1m4f 4th Gordon Stks *One month*	**Give The Slip** Mrs A Perrett 8/1	16/22	3	8-08	65	*WON N/O *Group 3* *Nad Al 1m4f*	*5th Sheema Classic Nad Al 1m4f	*4th Tatts Gold Cup Curr 1m3f	*5th Prince of Wales' Ascot 1m2f
99 Ascot 1m2f 2nd Rated Hcp *One month*	**Vicious Circle** L Cumani 11/1	7/21	5	8-04	68	**WON 13/2** **Ritz Club Hcp** **Ascot 1m4f**	*4th Rated Hcp Good 1m4f	*4th Jockey Club Cup Newm 2m	**2nd Handicap Nad Al 2m
98 Deau 1m6f 2nd Group 2 *Three weeks*	**Tuning** H Cecil 9/2F	1/21	3	8-07	67	7th Park Hill Stks Donc 1m7f	–	–	–
97 Hayd 1m6f 2nd Handicap *Two weeks*	**Far Ahead** L Eyre 33/1	10/21	5	8-00	59	*11th Handicap Donc 1m6f	*7th Handicap Donc 1m6f	*13th Q Mother's Cup York 1m4f	***PU *Hcp Hdle* *Donc 2m1f*
96 Sand 1m6f 1st Maiden *Two months*	**Clerkenwell** Sir M Stoute 17/2	2/21	3	7-11	66	7th Group 3 Long 1m7f	*WON 2/1 *Conds Stks* *Sali 1m6f*	*5th Arc Trial Newb 1m3f	**WON 3/1 **Conds Stks **Ches 1m4f

12-year median performance rating of the winner: **67** (out of 100) *Italic = jumps, *next year **two years ***three years*

WINNER'S PROFILE Recent form was vital as 11 winners recorded a **top-two finish on one of their last two starts**, the same number that **scored during the campaign**. Three of the last six winners carried penalties for winning at Glorious Goodwood and eight of the last nine arrived via either that venue or Ascot. Runners at the head of the handicap struggled and those with **9st 4lb or lighter** were best, while **three to five-year-olds** dominated – six-year-olds plus have struck just once from over 50 runners. Purple Moon last year became the first favourite to oblige since 1998, and in the process gave trainer **Luca Cumani** his third win from 10 runners.

FUTURE POINTERS Europe's richest handicap has regularly attracted a big field, although it lacked improvers from the Classic generation of late, which is a shame as they have a tidy record – borne out by a runner-up and two thirds from just five three-year-olds since 2003. However, there have still been some quality older winners, as Luca Cumani's trio did themselves justice post-York. Vicious Circle took a valuable handicap at Ascot next time and Mephisto became a top-class hurdler, while last year's winner, Purple Moon all but eclipsed them when an agonising second in the Melbourne Cup – Sergeant Cecil and Hugs Dancer both also won valuable handicaps. It is worth noting that the fourth-placed runners have done well *(see below),* two recently took the Old Borough Cup.

Were Ebor winners profitable to follow on their subsequent three runs?
Yes – 7 wins from 31 runs returned a **profit of +£6.55** to a £1 level stake.

Placed runners' subsequent record (three runs):
Runners-up: 3 wins from 30 runs returned a loss of -£24.45 to a £1 level stake.
2000 Boreas – Listed Serlby Stakes
Thirds: 7 wins from 31 runs returned a loss of -£0.29 to a £1 level stake.
2006 Young Mick – Cumberland Lodge, 1998 Yavanas Pace – November Handicap,
1997 Puce – Harvest Stakes, 1996 Corradini – Mallard Handicap
Fourths: 7 wins from 34 runs returned a **profit of +£20.00** to a £1 level stake.
2005 Balkan Knight – Old Borough Cup, 2004 Defining – Old Borough Cup, Listed Fenwolf Stakes,
2000 Afterjacko – Autumn Cup

FUTURE SUCCESS RATING: ★ ★ ★ ★ ☆

YORKSHIRE OAKS
August 21, York – (Group 1, Class 1, 3yo+ Fillies & Mares) 1m4f

Last run	Winner/ Trainer & SP	Draw/ Ran	Age	Wght	PR	Next four runs			
07 Good 1m2f 1st Nassau *Three weeks*	**Peeping Fawn** A O'Brien 4/9F	8/7	3	8-11	81	-	-	-	-
06 Curr 1m4f 1st Irish Oaks *Two months*	**Alexandrova** A O'Brien 4/9F	4/6	3	8-11	79	3rd Prix de l'Opera Long 1m2f	-	-	-
05 Newb 1m4f 1st Chalice Stks *Three weeks*	**Punctilious** S Bin Suroor 13/2	5/11	4	9-04	75	4th Park Hill Stks Donc 1m7f	10th Grade 1 Wood 1m2f	-	-
04 Ascot 1m4f 3rd Ribblesdale *Two months*	**Quiff** Sir M Stoute 7/2	3/8	3	8-08	82	2nd St Leger Donc 1m6f	*4th Gordon Richards Sand 1m2f	-	-
03 Sand 1m2f 6th Eclipse *Two months*	**Islington** Sir M Stoute 8/11F	5/8	4	9-04	84	3rd Irish Champion Leop 1m2f	**WON 10/3F Breeders' Cup Sant 1m2f**	*9th Japan Cup Toky 1m4f	-
02 Good 1m2f 1st Nassau *Three weeks*	**Islington** Sir M Stoute 2/1	9/11	3	8-08	81	5th Arc de Triomphe Long 1m4f	3rd Breeders' Cup Arli 1m2f	*3rd Prince of Wales' Ascot 1m2f	*6th Eclipse Sand 1m2f
01 Deau 1m6f 3rd Group 2 *Three weeks*	**Super Tassa** V Valiani 25/1	7/9	5	9-04	73	-	-	-	-
00 Curr 1m4f 1st Irish Oaks *Two months*	**Petrushka** Sir M Stoute 5/4F	1/6	3	8-08	83	**WON 9/10F Prix de l'Opera Long 1m2f**	5th Breeders' Cup Chur 1m3f	*5th Coronation Cup Epsom 1m4f	-
99 Curr 1m4f 1st Irish Oaks *Two months*	**Ramruma** H Cecil 5/6F	9/11	3	8-08	76	2nd St Leger Donc 1m6f	*11th Jockey Club Stks Newm 1m4f	*3rd Yorkshire Oaks York 1m4f	*3rd Harvest Stks Ascot 1m4f
98 Newm 1m4f 1st Aphrodite Stks *Two months*	**Catchascatchan** H Cecil 2/1F	7/6	3	8-08	72	-	-	-	-
97 Mais 1m5f 3rd Group 2 *One month*	**My Emma** R Guest 7/1	7/8	4	9-04	70	11th Arc de Triomphe Long 1m4f	-	-	-
96 Curr 1m4f 3rd Irish Oaks *Two months*	**Key Change** J Oxx 7/1	1/9	3	8-08	71	2nd St Leger Donc 1m6f	*5th Group 2 Sain 1m4f	-	-

12-year median performance rating of the winner: **77** (out of 100) **next year*

WINNER'S PROFILE Every winner lined up having **run within the past two months**, 10 had won earlier in the season, with **Irish Oaks** winners highly respected – Peeping Fawn last year became the third winner from as many qualifiers – while **Nassau winners** provided two winners from only three runners. Winners of the Ribblesdale from Royal Ascot are worth swerving, though, with Silkwood the latest to flop last year since the early-nineties.
Winning form over the distance can be a bonus, but not vital, although what has been important was a place near the head of the market as 11 winners went off at **7/1 or shorter**.
Three-year-olds held sway numerically, but older horses boast a better strike-rate, including the four-year-old, Islington, who was one of **Sir Michael Stoute**'s four winners from 13 runners – nine losers were 11/2 or bigger.

FUTURE POINTERS Not many of the Yorkshire Oaks' winners had a prolonged career as the majority were carted off to the paddocks at the end of term, but it has been a disappointment that only one winner since 1996 managed to follow up. That honour fell to Petrushka who triumphed in the Prix de l'Opera in France, an event that halted Alexandrova's winning run, however, Sir Michael Stoute's filly was unable to win the Breeder's Cup Filly & Mare, unlike Islington, who went one better in 2003 after failing the year before.
One event that narrowly foiled Yorkshire winners was the St Leger, as the three winners that attempted the Doncaster Classic all finished second.

Were Yorkshire Oaks winners profitable to follow on their subsequent three runs?
No – 2 wins from 20 runs returned a loss of -£13.77 to a £1 level stake.

Placed runners' subsequent record (three runs):
Runners-up: 4 wins from 22 runs returned a loss of -£0.53 to a £1 level stake.
Short Skirt – St Simon Stakes

Thirds: 0 win from 18 runs returned a loss of -£18.00 to a £1 level stake.

FUTURE SUCCESS RATING: ★ ☆ ☆ ☆ ☆

LOWTHER STAKES
August 19-22, York – (Group 2, Class 1, 2yo Fillies) 6f

Last run	Winner/ Trainer & SP	Draw/ Ran	Age	Wght	PR	Next four runs			
07 Ascot 6f 3rd Maiden *One month*	**Nahoodh** M Channon 15/2	4/10	2	8-12	64	-	-	-	-
06 Newm 6f 6th Cherry Hinton *Two months*	**Silk Blossom** B Hills 3/1	4/7	2	8-12	71	WON 9/4F **Goffs Fillies** Curr 7f	*12th Fred Darling Newb 7f	*13th Coronation Stks Ascot 1m	-
05 York 5f 1st Queen Mary *Three months*	**Flasy Wings** M Channon 10/11F	2/6	2	9-02	68	2nd Watership Sales Newb 7f	3rd Cheveley Park Newm 6f	*11th 1,000 Guineas Newm 1m	*2nd Coronation Stks Ascot 1m
04 Ascot 6f 1st Princess Margaret *One month*	**Soar** J Fanshawe 2/1F	8/8	2	9-00	66	6th Cheveley Park Newm 6f	*6th Conds Stks Leic 5f	-	-
03 Ascot 6f 1st Maiden *One month*	**Carry On Katie** J Noseda 3/1	9/9	2	8-11	72	WON 13/8F **Cheveley Park** Newm 6f	*6th 1,000 Guineas Newm 1m	*9th Poule 'Pouliches Long 1m	-
02 Ascot 6f 1st Princess Margaret *One month*	**Russian Rhythm** Sir M Stoute 8/13F	4/5	2	9-00	76	2nd Cheveley Park Newm 6f	*WON 12/1 **1,000 Guineas** Newm 1m	*WON 4/7F Coronation Stks Ascot 1m	*WON 4/5F Nassau Good 1m2f
01 Ascot 5f 1st Queen Mary *Three months*	**Queen's Logic** M Channon 7/1	4/8	2	9-00	74	WON 10/11F **Cheveley Park** Newm 6f	*WON 1/3F **Fred Darling** Newb 7f	-	-
00 Ascot 6f 1st Princess Margaret *One month*	**Enthused** Sir M Stoute 9/4	6/7	2	9-00	68	6th Cheveley Park Newm 6f	*5th 1,000 Guineas Newm 1m	*8th Coronation Stks Ascot 1m	*18th July Cup Newm 6f
99 Ripon 6f 1st Novice Stks *Three weeks*	**Jemima** T Easterby 12/1	6/9	2	8-11	60	8th Yearling Stks Donc 6f	5th Cheveley Park Newm 6f	*9th Nell Gwyn Stks Newm 7f	*19th Coral Sprint Hcp Newm 6f
98 Ascot 5f 1st Queen Mary *Three months*	**Bint Allayl** M Channon 15/8F	1/10	2	9-00	75	-	-	-	-
97 Ascot 7f 2nd Chesham Stks *Three months*	**Cape Verdi** P Chapple-Hyam 7/4F	10/9	2	8-11	76	4th Cheveley Park Newm 6f	*WON 10/3JF **1,000 Guineas** Newm 1m	*9th Derby Epsom 1m4f	**3rd Falmouth Stks Newm 1m
96 Beve 5f 1st Maiden *One week*	**Bianca Nera** D Loder 6/1	6/9	2	8-11	68	WON 3/1 **Moyglare Stud** Curr 7f	4th Prix M Boussac Long 1m	*6th Fred Darling Newb 7f	*11th 1,000 Guineas Newm 1m

12-year median performance rating of the winner: **70** (out of 100)   **next year **two years*

WINNER'S PROFILE More winners of the Lowther had a longer prep than the majority in this book, having **not raced for at least around a month to three months**, while those that ran at Ascot last time stood out. All eight **finished in the top-three at Ascot** – nine if you include Silk Blossom's second in the Albany prior to Newmarket – but winners of the Queen Mary and Princess Margaret have really shined, while two ran in a maiden over this trip at the King George meeting. Cherry Hinton winners should be avoided – You're thrilling the latest flop last year – although other runners from that contest have taken this. A prior victory over the trip wasn't essential, although **no maiden triumphed**, while those at **double-figure odds can be ignored**. Trainer **Mick Channon** has impressed with four wins from only eight runners, while **Sir Michael Stoute** sent out two from five.

FUTURE POINTERS A quality juvenile event for fillies – attracted the Cherry Hinton, Molecomb and Princess Margaret winners last year – which has proven a good guide to the Cheveley Park Stakes and 1,000 Guineas, and above par winners performed creditably in both events.
Ratings are a powerful future pointer and it was no coincidence that both Russian Rhythm and Cape Verdi achieved high performance ratings (PR) here before going on the Classic glory – Harayir also managed the feat in 1994/95 – while two others to score high lifted the Cheveley Park in 2003 and 2001 respectively. Interestingly, the only two Lowther winners not to have trodden the Cheveley route both successfully scored over a furlong further in Ireland.

Were Lowther Stakes winners profitable to follow on their subsequent three runs?
Yes – 8 wins from 28 runs returned a **profit of +£4.00** to a £1 level stake.

Placed runners' subsequent record (three runs):
Runners-up: 7 wins from 30 runs returned a loss of -£4.00 to a £1 level stake.
2006 Indian Ink – Watership Down Sales, Cheveley Park, 2005 La Chunga – Summer Stakes,
2003 Badminton – October Stakes, 1998 Wannabe Grand – Cheveley Park, 1997 Embassy – Cheveley Park,
1996 Arethusa – Fortune Stakes

Thirds: 2 wins from 17 runs returned a loss of -£12.00 to a £1 level stake.

FUTURE SUCCESS RATING: ★ ★ ★ ★ ☆

NUNTHORPE STAKES
August 22, York – (Group 1, Class 1, 3yo+) 5f

Last run	Winner/ Trainer & SP	Draw/ Ran	Age	Wght	PR	Next four runs			
07 Good 5f 2nd Molecomb Stks One month	**Kingsgate Native** J Best 12/1	13/16	2	8-01	75	2nd Prix de l' Abbaye Long 5f	-	-	-
06 Sand 5f 5th Champagne Stk Two months	**Reverence** E Alston 5/1	6/14	5	9-11	85	**WON 11/4F** **Sprint Cup** **Hayd 6f**	2nd Prix de l' Abbaye Long 5f	*5th Champagne Stk Sand 5f	*6th Hackwood Stks Ascot 6f
05 York 6f 1st Heritage Hcp One month	**La Cucaracha** B Hills 7/1	8/16	4	9-08	77	2nd Sprint Cup Hayd 6f	*9th King's Stand Ascot 5f	*11th July Cup Newm 6f	***WON 7/2F** **King George** **Good 5f**
04 Good 5f 6th King George Three weeks	**Bahamian Pirate** D Nicholls 16/1	5/12	9	9-11	75	12th Sprint Cup Hayd 6f	9th Prix de l' Abbaye Long 5f	*6th Chipchase Stks Newc 6f	*5th Champagne Stk Sand 5f
03 Newm 6f 1st July Cup Two months	**Oasis Dream** J Gosden 4/9F	2/8	3	9-09	88	2nd Sprint Cup Hayd 6f	10th Breeders' Cup Sant 1m	-	-
02 Ascot 5f 3rd King's Stand Three months	**Kyllachy** H Candy 3/1F	15/17	4	9-11	78	-	-	-	-
01 Newm 6f 1st July Cup Two months	**Mozart** A O'Brien 4/9F	4/10	3	9-07	88	11th Breeders' Cup Belm 6f	-	-	-
00 Ascot 5f 1st King's Stand Three months	**Nuclear Debate** J Hammond 5/2F	1/13	5	9-09	85	9th H Kong Sprint Sha 5f	*2nd Stakes Nad Al 6f	*4th Group 3 Nad Al 6f	*3rd Temple Stks Sand 5f
99 Newm 6f 1st July Cup Two months	**Stravinsky** A O'Brien EvensF	13/16	3	9-07	86	6th Breeders' Cup Gulf 6f	-	-	-
98 Good 5f 3rd King George One month	**Lochangel** I Balding 6/1	2/17	4	9-06	80	6th Sprint Cup Hayd 6f	6th Prix de l' Abbaye Long 5f	*2nd Temple Stks Sand 5f	*4th King's Stand Ascot 5f
97= Good 6f 11th Stewards' Cup Three weeks	**Coastal Bluff** D Barron 6/1	6/15	5	9-09	74	8th Sprint Cup Hayd 6f	*10th Palace House Newm 5f	*11th King's Stand Ascot 5f	**9th Conds Stks Kemp 6f
97= Good 5f 11th King George One month	**Ya Malak** D Nicholls 11/1	4/15	6	9-09	74	*8th Palace House Newm 5f	*5th Conds Stks Beve 5f	*12th King's Stand Ascot 5f	*7th City Wall Stks Ches 5f
96 Newm 6f 6th July Cup Two months	**Pivotal** Sir M Prescott 10/3	5/8	3	9-07	76	-	-	-	-

12-year median performance rating of the winner: **80** (out of 100)   **next year*

WINNER'S PROFILE No surprise to note that every winning sprinter had been **on the go within the past two months** and 11 winners came via either **Glorious Goodwood, Royal Ascot or the Newmarket July meeting**. The latter has proven a solid guide, as six July Cup winners lined up here, and of the four three-year-old Nunthorpe winners, three won at Newmarket, while more two-year-olds may be seen here after Kingsgate Native's exploits last year – the first juvenile winner since Lyric Fantasy in 1992. A **victory earlier in the campaign** has been key, despite last year's maiden winner, while eight of the last nine winners **scored in Group class** including those with an **official rating of 109 or more**.

FUTURE POINTERS The Nunthorpe is Britain's leading sprint over the minimum trip and one graced by some fine sprinters since 1996, however, it has been a disappointment that only one followed up next time, with Reverence in the Haydock Sprint Cup two years ago – the first to record such a double since Dayjur in 1990, who also recorded the fastest time at York. It can be pointed out that some winners didn't have a long career post-York, but even so, the majority came unstuck in the Sprint Cup, Prix de l'Abbaye and Breeders' Cup, and punters should be on their guard.

Were Nunthorpe winners profitable to follow on their subsequent three runs?
No – 1 win from 26 runs returned a loss of -£22.25 to a £1 level stake.

Placed runners' subsequent record (three runs):
Runners-up: 6 wins from 32 runs returned a loss of -£8.00 to a £1 level stake.
2006 Amadeus Wolf – Duke of York, 2005 & 2004 The Tatling – Dubai World Trophy, 2001 Nuclear Debate – Haydock Sprint Cup, 1996 Eveningperformance – Flying Five

Thirds: 5 wins from 30 runs returned a loss of -£9.43 to a £1 level stake.
2003 Acclamation – Diadem Stakes, 2000 Pipalong – Haydock Sprint Cup

FUTURE SUCCESS RATING: ★ ☆ ☆ ☆ ☆

PRESTIGE STAKES

August 23, Goodwood – (Group 3, Class 1, 2yo Fillies) 7f

Last run	Winner/ Trainer & SP	Draw/ Ran	Age	Wght	PR	Next four runs			
07 Newm 7f 1st Maiden *Three weeks*	**Sense Of Joy** J Gosden 4/7F	6/7	2	9-00	62	-	-	-	-
06 Nott 1m 1st Novice Stks *Two weeks*	**Sesmen** M Botti 9/1	4/10	2	9-00	60	6th Meon Filles' Mile Ascot 1m	*6th Fred Darling Newb 7f	*6th Poule 'Pouliches Long 1m	*7th Summer Stks Newm 6f
05 Newb 6f 3rd Princess Margaret *Two months*	**Nannina** J Gosden 11/4	10/9	2	8-09	68	**WON 5/1** **Meon Filles Mile Newm 1m**	*12th 1,000 Guineas Newm 1m	*WON 6/1JF **Coronation Stks Ascot 1m**	*2nd Falmouth Stks Newm 1m
04 Redc 7f 1st Maiden *One month*	**Dubai Surprise** D Loder 16/1	10/12	2	8-09	62	8th Meon Filles' Mile Ascot 1m	2nd Criterium Int Sain 1m	*WON 11/8F **Conds Stks Leic 1m**	*WON 18/10F **Premio Tesio Capa 1m2f**
03 Sali 6f 1st Maiden *Two months*	**Gracefully** S Kirk 7/1	6/6	2	8-09	54	4th Rockfel Stks Newm 7f	-	-	-
02 Good 7f 1st Maiden *One month*	**Geminiani** B Hills 3/1F	2/8	2	8-09	60	*2nd Musidora Stks York 1m2f	*9th Oaks Epsom 1m4f	*8th Nassau Stks Good 1m2f	-
01 Newm 6f 1st Maiden *Two months*	**Gossamer** L Cumani 5/4F	3/6	2	8-09	71	**WON 4/5F** **Meon Filles Mile Ascot 1m**	*8th 1,000 Guineas Newm 1m	*WON 4/1 **Irish 1,000 Guin Curr 1m**	*11th Coronation Stks Ascot 1m
00 Newm 6f 8th Cherry Hinton *Two months*	**Freefourracing** B Meehan 8/1	3/6	2	8-09	66	**WON 11/4** **Fillies Stks Keen 6f**	*3rd Grade 3 Belm 1m1f	*5th Grade 1 Holl 1m1f	*6th Grade 1 Sant 7f
99 Hayd 6f 2nd Conds Stks *One month*	**Icicle** J Fanshawe 10/1	9/9	2	8-09	60	4th Rockfel Stks Newm 7f	*10th 1,000 Guineas Newm 1m	*3rd Vodafone Stks Epsom 1½m	*5th Criterion Stks Newm 7f
98 Newb 6f 1st Maiden *Two months*	**Circle Of Gold** P Chapple-Hyam 8/13F	1/9	2	8-09	65	6th Cheveley Park Newm 6f	*3rd Nell Gwyn Stks Newm 7f	*14th 1,000 Guineas Newm 1m	*3rd Grade 2 Chur 1m1f
97 Good 7f 1st Maiden *One month*	**Midnight Lane** H Cecil 11/2	2/6	2	8-09	70	**WON 3/1F** **May Hill Stks Donc 1m**	5th Meon Fillies Mile Ascot 1m	*WON 5/2F **Pretty Polly Stk Newm 1m2f**	*2nd Musidora Stks York 1m2f
96 Sand 7f 1st Star Stks *One month*	**Red Camellia** Sir M Prescott 10/11F	1/5	2	8-12	69	4th Fillies' Mile Ascot 1m	*3rd Poule 'Pouliches Long 1m	*4th Supreme Stks Good 7f	-

12-year median performance rating of the winner: **64** (out of 100)   *next year*

WINNER'S PROFILE Profile pointers are thin on the ground, but those that **raced within the past two months** put their fitness to good use, with **last time out maiden winners** worthy of respect.
Two of the three not to have won last time out raced in Group events, though all three got off the mark earlier in the year. Nursery participants have flopped, while the score remains level between seven-furlong winners and those debuting over the distance.
Trainer **John Gosden** last year took his patient tally to two winners and a runner-up from three runners.

FUTURE POINTERS A quality Group Three event for fillies but one in which ante-post bets should be avoided as no winner went on to scoop the 1,000 Guineas during the last 20 years, although Gossamer took the Irish equivalent. Despite that Classic blip, the Prestige Stakes has thrown up several future Group One performers, as two above par winners triumphed in the Meon Valley Fillies' Mile at Ascot next time out, while Dubai Surprise scored at the highest level in Italy. Two sub-standard winners both came up short in the Rockfel Stakes next time out.

Were Prestige Stakes winners profitable to follow on their subsequent three runs?
Yes – 8 wins from 31 runs returned a **profit of +£1.05** to a £1 level stake.

Are placed runners profitable to follow on their subsequent three runs?
Runners-up: 4 wins from 34 runs returned a loss of -£20.42 to a £1 level stake.
2002 Mail The Desert – Moyglare Stud Stakes

Thirds: 0 win from 16 runs returned a loss of -£16.00 to a £1 level stake.

FUTURE SUCCESS RATING: ★ ★ ★ ☆ ☆

CELEBRATION MILE
August 23, Goodwood – (Group 2, Class 1, 3yo+) 1m

Last run	Winner/ Trainer & SP	Draw/ Ran	Age	Wght	PR	Next four runs			
07 Curr 1m2f 6th Pretty Polly Two months	Echelon Sir M Stoute 7/1	3/8	5	8-12	78	WON 9/4F Matron Stks Leop 1m	3rd Sun Chariot Newm 1m	-	-
06 Newb 7f 3rd Hungerford Stks Two weeks	Caradak S Bin Suroor 6/1	5/6	5	9-01	77	WON 4/1 Prix de la Foret Long 7f	3rd Group 1 Siro 1m	*10th Hungerford Stks Newb 7f	-
05 Good 1m 12th Sussex Two months	Chic Sir M Stoute 8/1	7/8	5	8-12	76	2nd Matron Stks Leop 1m	5th Sun Chariot Newm 1m	7th Champion Stks Newm 1m2f	-
04 Newb 7f 1st Hungerford Stks Two weeks	Chic Sir M Stoute 4/1	5/7	4	8-12	78	2nd Sun Chariot Newm 1m	*6th Silver Trophy Ling 1m	*12th Sussex Good 1m	*WON 8/1 Celebration Mile Good 1m
03 Sali 1m 2nd Sovereign Stks Two weeks	Priors Lodge M Tregoning 10/1	6/6	5	9-01	74	4th Select Stks Good 1m2f	-	-	-
02 Ascot 7f 15th International Hcp One month	Tillerman Mrs A Perrett 5/1	2/7	6	9-01	73	3rd Q Elizabeth II Ascot 1m	10th Hong Kong Mile Sha 1m	*WON 10/3 Leicest'shre St Leic 7f	*6th Lockinge Newm 1m
01 Good 1m 2nd Sussex One month	No Excuse Needed Sir M Stoute 8/11F	3/6	3	8-09	78	12th Champion Stks Newm 1m2f	*15th Dubai Duty Free Nad Al 1m2f	*4th Lockinge Newb 1m	*WON 13/2 Queen Anne Ascot 1m
00 Good 1m 3rd Sussex One month	Medicean Sir M Stoute 5/2	4/6	3	8-09	82	4th Q Elizabeth II Ascot 1m	*WON 3/1 Lockinge Newb 1m	*WON 11/2 Queen Anne Ascot 1m	*WON 7/2 Eclipse Sand 1m2f
99 Ascot 1m 1st Queen Anne Three months	Cape Cross S Bin Suroor 5/2	4/5	5	9-07	86	6th Grade 1 Wood 1m	-	-	-
98 Newb 7f 1st Hungerford Stks Three weeks	Muhtahir J Gosden 11/4F	7/9	3	8-09	75	7th Q Elizabeth II Ascot 1m	9th Prix de la Foret Long 7f	*2nd Listed Nad Al 1m	*5th Group 1 Toky 1m
97 Good 1m 4th Sussex One month	Among Men Sir M Stoute 8/11F	2/4	3	8-09	79	*6th Lockinge Newm 1m	*2nd Queen Anne Ascot 1m	*WON 2/7F Conds Stks Yarm 7f	*WON 4/1 Sussex Good 1m
96 Ascot 1m 8th St James Palace Three months	Mark Of Esteem S Bin Suroor 11/4F	7/7	3	9-01	85	WON 10/3 Q Elizabeth II Ascot 1m	7th Breeders' Cup Wood 1m	-	-

12-year median performance rating of the winner: **78** (out of 100)   *next year*

WINNER'S PROFILE Eleven of the last 12 winners **raced within the past two months** and 10 came via the Sussex, Hungerford or Ascot last time out – Echelon last year raced at Royal Ascot before The Curragh.
A **distance victory** was common with the majority, while an **official rating of 109** has been a must, along with **proven form at Group level**. Steer clear of outsiders and stick with the **first three or four in the betting**, as they came out on top most years, while a **high to middle draw** helped – stall one has a bad record.
Fillies and mares held their own having won three of the last four, all three emerged from **Sir Michael Stoute**'s yard, who won it six times from just 10 runners.

FUTURE POINTERS The Celebration Mile has attracted those who fell just short at Group One level in races like the Sussex, but has produced its share of top-class winners over the years with Cape Cross and Mark Of Esteem already proven at the highest level, and several went on to score in that company.
As with all races, the event witnessed some below par winners who never kicked on post-Goodwood, but as a whole, quality winners can be viewed positively especially as the last two both followed up next time out in Group Ones.
Only one of the best winners, Mark Of Esteem, however, managed to land the Queen Elizabeth II, a race that foiled three others, while those with patience may want to wait for the Queen Anne at Royal Ascot the following year, as four took that route, which resulted in two triumphs and two seconds.

Were Celebration Mile winners profitable to follow on their subsequent three runs?
No – 7 wins from 30 runs returned a loss of -£1.31 to a £1 level stake.

Placed runners' subsequent record (three runs):
Runners-up: 6 wins from 30 runs returned a loss of -£0.72 to a £1 level stake.
2000 Observatory – Queen Elizabeth II, Prix d'Ispahan, 1996 Bishop Of Cashel – Park Stakes

Thirds: 1 win from 8 runs returned a **profit of +£1.00** to a £1 level stake.
2005 Court Masterpiece – Prix de la Foret

FUTURE SUCCESS RATING: ★ ★ ★ ☆ ☆

WINTER HILL STAKES
August 23, Windsor – (Group 3, Class 1, 3yo+) 1m2f

Last run	Winner/ Trainer & SP	Draw/ Ran	Age	Wght	PR	Next four runs			
07 Newb 1m4 1st Chalice Stks Three weeks	Queen's Best Sir M Stoute 8/1	1/9	4	8-11	75	2nd Blandford Stks Curr 1m2f	2nd Princess Royal Ascot 1m4f	-	-
06 Newb 1m2f 1st Steventon Stks Two months	Tam Lin Sir M Stoute 5/2F	1/11	3	8-06	74	2nd Dubai Arc Trial Newb 1m3f	*6th Brigadier Gerard Sand 1m2f	*2nd Gala Stks Sand 1m2f	*3rd Pomfret Stks Pont 1m
05 Hayd 1m3f 2nd Totesport Hcp Three weeks	Eccentric A Reid 7/1	8/9	4	9-00	69	8th J Smith's Hcp Newb 1m2f	8th Darley Stks Newm 1m1f	*16th Japan Cup Toky 1m3f	*3rd Group 3 Nad Al 1m1f
04 Sali 1m 8th Sovereign Stks Three weeks	Ancient World S Bin Suroor 5/1	1/8	4	9-00	78	WON 6/4F Premio 'Capua Siro 1m	5th Hong Kong Cup Sha 1m2f	*3rd Conds Stks Newb 1m1f	*2nd Joel Stks Newm 1m
03 Hayd 1m3f 1st Totesport Hcp Two weeks	Leporello P Harris 5/2	3/6	3	8-06	76	WON 15/8 Select Stks Good 1m2f	*3rd Huxley Stks Ches 1m2f	*7th Diomed Stks Epsom 1½m	*5th Gala Stks Sand 1m2f
02 Epso 1m4f 7th Derby Three months	Naheef S Bin Suroor 6/4F	3/5	3	8-07	75	6th September Stks Kemp 1m4f	*WON N/O Listed Nad Al 1m2f	**7th Group 3 Nad Al 1m1f	**7th Duby Duty Free Nad 1m1f
01 Curr 1m2f 4th Group 3 One month	Adilabad Sir M Stoute 9/2	5/6	4	9-04	76	-	-	-	-
00 Good 1m 1st Th'rghbred Stk Three weeks	Adilabad Sir M Stoute 6/4F	5/9	3	8-06	77	3rd Group 2 Long 1m2f	*5th Gordon Richards Sand 1m2f	*WON 4/5F Huxley Stks Ches 1m2f	*3rd Brigadier Gerard Sand 1m2f
99 Ascot 1m2f 1st Diamond Hcp Two months	Zindabad B Hanbury 7/4F	8/8	3	8-06	71	5th Select Stks Good 1m2f	*3rd Mercury Listed Leic 1m4f	*3rd Gala Stks Kemp 1m2f	**WON 15/8F Conds Stks Newm 1m2f
98 Hans 1m2f 3rd Group 2 Three months	Annus Mirabilis S Bin Suroor 5/4F	9/9	6	9-04	73	4th Group 1 Flem 1m2f	*10th Shergar Cup Good 1m2f	-	-
97 Newm 1m2f 1st Conds Stks Three weeks	Annus Mirabilis S Bin Suroor 11/8F	3/4	5	9-08	74	5th Man O'War Belm 1m3f	7th H Kong Int Cup Sha 1m1f	*2nd Stakes Nad Al 1m1f	*2nd Stakes Nad Al 1m1f
96 Ascot 1m4f 5th King George VI One month	Annus Mirabilis S Bin Suroor 85/40	3/5	4	9-00	72	WON N/O Group 2 Toky 1m1f	*3rd QE II Cup Sha 1m2f	*WON 8/11F Conds Stks Newm 1m2f	*WON 11/8F Winter Hill Stks Wind 1m2f

12-year median performance rating of the winner: **74** (out of 100)   *next year **two years*

WINNER'S PROFILE Winners came from various routes, although four of the last five appeared in either a Listed event at Newbury or in a valuable handicap at Haydock. Ten already **scored between nine and 12 furlongs** and only Leporello stepped out of handicaps for the first time, while six finished in the **first two of a Listed event** (five scored), and five recorded a similar feat at Group level (four **took a Group Three**).
Two of the last three winning four-year-olds were officially rated 93 and 94, unlike the remainder that were **109 and above**, and it paid to follow with the younger **three and four-year-olds**, as only the three-times winner, Annus Mirabilis won beyond those age groups. Trainer **Saeed Bin Suroor**'s treble winner was part of their haul of five from only nine runners, a total almost matched by **Sir Michael Stoute**, whose strike-rate reads better at four from just six runners. Both trainers fought out the finish during the last two years, where advantage went to Stoute.

FUTURE POINTERS Windsor's main event of the season was elevated to Group Three status in 1995 and though the Hall of Fame features several household names, none were superstars, as only Ancient World achieved Group One glory in the near future. Those to win again did so mainly in Listed or Group Three company at around this trip, and overall, it's proven difficult to pin down a regular post-route owing to the number of middle-distance opportunities worldwide. Of the 11 to have run again, only three scored next time out – two abroad – so it may prove best to swerve Winter Hill victors on these shores until at least the following term.

Were Winter Hill winners profitable to follow on their subsequent three runs?
No – 6 wins from 31 runs returned a loss of -£20.10 to a £1 level stake.

Placed runners' subsequent record (three runs):
Runners-up: 5 wins from 28 runs returned a loss of -£9.85 to a £1 level stake.
2000 Albarahin – Foundation Stakes, Darley Stakes, 1996 Salmon Ladder – St Simon Stakes

Thirds: 6 wins from 20 runs returned a **profit of +£9.08** to a £1 level stake.
2006 Kandidate – September Stakes, 2005 Fruhlingssturm – Doonside Cup, 1998 Crimson Tide – September Stakes

FUTURE SUCCESS RATING: ★★ ☆ ☆ ☆

SOLARIO STAKES
August 30, Sandown – (Group 3, Class 1, 2yo) 7f

Last run	Winner/ Trainer & SP	Draw/ Ran	Age	Wght	PR	Next four runs			
07 Ascot 7f 1st Winkfield Listed Two months	Raven's Pass J Gosden 11/8F	1/9	2	9-00	70	3rd Dewhurst Stks Newm 7f	-	-	-
06 Newb 7f 2nd Conds Stks Two months	Drumfire M Johnston 6/4F	2/8	2	9-00	64	3rd Goffs Million Curr 7f	11th R Post Trophy Newb 1m	*2nd Conds Stks Newm 1m	*Fell Totesport Mile Hcp Good 1m
05 Good 7f 1st Maiden Three weeks	Opera Cape S Kirk 15/2	6/7	2	8-11	63	2nd Grand Criterium Long 7f	3rd Dewhurst Stks Newm 7f	*14th 2,000 Guineas Newm 1m	*5th Conds Stks Ches 7f
04 Newm 7f 1st Maiden Three weeks	Windsor Knot J Gosden 9/2	2/8	2	8-11	66	*3rd Doonside Cup Ayr 1m2f	**2nd Gala Stks Sand 1m2f	**2nd Steventon Stks Newb 1m2f	**WON 4/5F Conds Stks Newm 1m4f
03 Newm 7f 5th Superlative Stks Two months	Barbajuan N Callaghan 12/1	6/8	2	8-11	67	4th National Stks Curr 7f	3rd Gran Criterium Siro 1m	*5th Easter Stks Kemp 1m	*12th 2,000 Guineas Newm 1m
02 Good 6f 1st Maiden Two months	Foss Way J Gosden 11/2	8/11	2	8-11	63	5th Grand Criterium Long 7f	-	-	-
01 Good 7f 7th Vintage Stks One month	Redback R Hannon 14/1	9/10	2	9-00	70	4th Tattersall Stks Newm 7f	3rd R Post Trophy Donc 1m	*3rd Easter Stks Kemp 1m	*WON 5/1 Greenham Stks Newb 7f
00 Newm 7f 5th Superlative Stks Two months	King's Ironbridge R Hannon 10/1	7/7	2	8-11	68	8th Dewhurst Stks Newm 7f	*WON 12/1 Craven Stks Newm 1m	*10th 2,000 Guineas Newm 1m	*6th Lennox Stks Good 7f
99 Donc 7f 3rd Maiden One month	Best Of The Bests C Brittain 20/1	1/7	2	8-11	69	2nd Royal Lodge Stk Ascot 1m	*3rd Dante York 1m2f	*4th Epsom Epsom 1m4f	*4th G Prix de Paris Long 1m2f
98 Good 7f 2nd Vintage Stks One month	Raise A Grand P Payne 10/3	8/7	2	8-11	64	5th Dewhurst Stks Newm 7f	*8th Easter Stks Kemp 1m	*5th St James Palace Ascot 1m	*2nd Criterion Stks Newm 7f
97 Good 7f 3rd Vintage Stks One month	Little Indian S Woods 12/1	3/5	2	8-11	62	7th R Post Trophy Donc 1m	*6th Craven Stks Newm 1m	*15th 2,000 Guineas Newm 1m	*6th Predominate Stk Good 1m2f
96 Donc 7f 2nd Conds Stks One month	Brave Act Sir M Prescott 9/2	1/7	2	8-11	67	*8th Grade 2 Oakl 1m1f	*WON N/O Handicap Holl 1m	*4th Grade 2 Arli 1m2f	*2nd Grade 2 Del 1m1f

12-year median performance rating of the winner: **66** (out of 100)   *next year **two years*

WINNER'S PROFILE It paid to keep busy prior to Sandown as every winner **raced within the past two months at a Grade One venue** and those who came here via the **Superlative and Vintage Stakes** boast an impressive record – none, however, scored in those Pattern events.

Eleven winners **already found success previously** – those yet to have got off the mark have a bad long-term record – while the same number **raced over seven furlongs last time**.

Trainer **John Gosden** took his tally to three winners from four runners last year, while **Richard Hannon** struck twice from eight runners.

FUTURE POINTERS The Solario hasn't exactly proven a solid breeding ground for 2,000 Guineas winners, as the 2001 victor, Redback, was the only one to be placed when third the following year. In fact, winners from this Group Three event have an abysmal record next time out and even last year's quality winner, Raven's Pass, was unable to follow up when third in the Dewhurst, an event that also halted three others, while the Racing Post Trophy stopped the same number. The Grand Criterium also proved beyond several Solario winners and they are best-avoided or layed next time out, although runners-up have a surprisingly good record, boosted further by City Leader at Ascot last year *(see below)*.

Were Solario winners profitable to follow on their subsequent three runs?
No – 2 wins from 32 runs returned a loss of -£18.00 to a £1 level stake.

Placed runners' subsequent record (three runs):
Runners-up: 12 wins from 35 runs returned a **profit of +£74.67** to a £1 level stake.
2007 City Leader – Royal Lodge Stakes, 2006 Caldra – Stardom Stakes, Autumn Stakes,
2003 Milk It Mick – Tattersall Stakes, Dewhurst Stakes, 2002 Sweet Return – Hollywood Derby,
1999 Sarafan – Stardom Stakes, 1998 Compton Admiral – Craven Stakes, 1996 Falkenham – Stardom Stakes

Thirds: 0 win from 14 runs returned a loss of -£14.00 to a £1 level stake.

FUTURE SUCCESS RATING: ★ ★ ☆ ☆ ☆

FUTURITY STAKES
August 30, Curragh – (Group 2, Class 1, 2yo) 7f

Last run	Winner/ Trainer & SP	Draw/ Ran	Age	Wght	PR	Next four runs			
07 Leop 7f 1st Tyros Stks *One month*	New Approach J Bolger 8/11F	3/5	2	9-01	76	WON 9/4F National Stks Curr 7f	WON 6/4F Dewhurst Stks Newm 7f	-	-
06 Leop 7f 1st Tyros Stks *One month*	Teofilo J Bolger 6/4F	3/7	2	9-01	75	WON 2/1 National Stks Curr 7f	WON 11/8F Dewhurst Stks Newm 7f	-	-
05 Newm 7f 1st Superlative Stks *Two months*	Horatio Nelson A O'Brien 2/7F	4/5	2	9-00	73	WON 4/7F Grand Criterium Long 7f	2nd Dewhurst Stks Newm 7f	*8th 2,000 Guineas Newm 1m	*PU Derby Epsom 1m4f
04 Curr 6f 2nd Phoenix Stks *Two weeks*	Oratorio A O'Brien 5/4F	2/5	2	9-00	74	WON 5/2 Prix Lagardere Long 7f	2nd Dewhurst Stks Newm 7f	*4th 2,000 Guineas Newm 1m	*2nd Irish 2,000 Guin Curr 1m
03 Ascot 7f 1st Chesham Stks *Three months*	Pearl Of Love M Johnston 5/4F	3/8	2	9-00	72	3rd National Stks Curr 7f	WON 4/5F Gran Criterium Siro 1m	*7th Jean Prat Chan 1m1f	*10th St James Palace Ascot 1m
02 Curr 7f 1st Tyros Stks *One month*	Van Nistelrooy A O'Brien EvensF	6/8	2	8-12	68	2nd National Stks Curr 7f	3rd Royal Lodge Ascot 1m	*5th Breeders' Cup Arli 1m1f	-
01 Curr 6f 2nd Railway Stks *Two months*	Hawk Wing A O'Brien 7/4F	3/6	2	8-12	75	WON 8/15F National Stks Curr 7f	*2nd 2,000 Guineas Newm 1m	*2nd Derby Epsom 1m4f	*WON 8/15F Eclipse Sand 1m2f
00 Newm 7f 4th Sweet Solera *Two weeks*	Lady Lahar M Channon 5/1	7/7	2	8-09	65	10th Cheveley Park Newm 6f	4th Group 3 Deau 1m	*4th Fillies Stks Nad Al 1m	*WON 2/9F Conds Stks Hami 1m
99 Naas 6f 1st Maiden *Two months*	Giant's Causeway A O'Brien 2/9F	4/4	2	8-12	72	WON 3/5F Pr' Salamandre Long 7f	*WON 8/11F Gladness Stks Curr 7f	*2nd 2,000 Guineas Newm 1m	*2nd Irish 2,000 Guin Curr 1m
98 Tipp 7f 1st Maiden *Two weeks*	St Clair Ridge J Bolger 2/1F	7/9	2	8-09	62	2nd Grade 2 Chur 1m1f	-	-	-
97 Cork 7f 1st Maiden *Three months*	Impressionist A O'Brien 5/2	8/8	2	8-10	64	3rd Dewhurst Stks Newm 7f	*2nd International Stks Curr 1m	**9th H Kong Derby Sha 1m1f	-
96 Good 7f 3rd Vintage Stks *One month*	Equal Rights P Chapple-Hyam 10/3	7/7	2	8-10	63	4th Royal Lodge Stk Ascot 1m	-	-	-

12-year median performance rating of the winner: **70** (out of 100)   **next year **two years*

WINNER'S PROFILE The standard has increased each year as the last six winners **all scored previously in a Group Three or Listed race** – three in the Tyros Stakes – in comparison to the 2001 to 1996 winners, that could muster only three placed efforts in Group company between them. A top-three performance last time out was also vital, while every winner **scored over six or seven furlongs**.
The market proved accurate as all 12 winners were **shorter than 5/1** – favourites took nine of the last 10 renewals – and six came via trainer **Aidan O'Brien** from 28 runners, while **Jim Bolger** triumphed three times from 13 runners.

FUTURE POINTERS Although no Futurity winner progressed enough to land a Classic since the 1991 winner St Jovite – took the Irish Derby the following year – plenty stepped up to secure Group One glory in recent times since it matured into a Group Two in 2001. Bar three forgettable winners prior to 1999, the majority were high-calibre juveniles that achieved good performance ratings (PR) on the day before further success in top two-year-old races. The last two winners trained by Jim Bolger both took the National and Dewhurst Stakes, while three of Aidan O'Brien's were sent abroad for Group One pickings, and it can only be a matter of time before this event produces a Classic winner to propel its profile even higher.

Were Futurity winners profitable to follow on their subsequent three runs?
No – 10 wins from 30 runs returned a loss of -£7.16 to a £1 level stake, although following the last nine winners next time out returned a **profit of +£5.45.**

Placed runners' subsequent record (three runs):
Runners-up: 5 wins from 32 runs returned a loss of -£0.83 to a £1 level stake.
2004 Democratic Deficit – Craven Stakes, 2001 Sholokhov – Gran Criterium, 1998 Mus-If – National Stakes

Thirds: 0 win from 7 runs returned a loss of -£7.00 to a £1 level stake.

FUTURE SUCCESS RATING: ★ ★ ★ ★ ☆

MOYGLARE STUD STAKES
August 31, Curragh – (Group 1, Class 1, 2yo Fillies) 7f

Last run	Winner/ Trainer & SP	Draw/ Ran	Age	Wght	PR	Next four runs			
07 Curr 6f 1st Phoenix Stks Three weeks	Saoirse Abu J Bolger 13/2	3/9	2	8-12	66	3rd Meon Fillies' Mile Ascot 1m	-	-	-
06 Curr 6f 3rd Phoenix Stks Two weeks	Miss Beatrix K Prendergast 14/1	6/12	2	8-12	68	WON 6/1 Goffs Million Curr 7f	*18th 1,000 Guineas Newm 1m	-	-
05 Curr 7f 1st Debutante Stks One month	Rumplestiltskin A O'Brien 2/7F	8/9	2	8-11	71	WON 2/1F Marcel Boussac Long 1m	*7th 1,000 Guineas Newm 1m	-	-
04 Curr 7f 3rd Debutante Stks One month	Chelsea Rose C Collins 9/1	4/12	2	8-11	65	*WON 4/1 Silver Listed Stk Leop 1m2f	*9th Pretty Polly Curr 1m2f	*9th Irish Oaks Curr 1m4f	*WON 10/1 Ballyroan Stks Leop 1m4f
03 Curr 7f 1st Debutante Stks Three weeks	Necklace A O'Brien 5/4F	9/11	2	8-11	66	10th Marcel Boussac Long 1m	*12th 1,000 Guineas Newm 1m	*6th Irish 1,000 Guin Curr 1m	*4th Oaks Epsom 1m4f
02 Good 7f 2nd Prestige Stks One week	Mail The Desert M Channon 8/1	9/9	2	8-11	64	*3rd Coronation Stks Ascot 1m	*2nd Group 2 Hopp 1m	*10th Maurice 'Gheest Deau 7f	-
01 Curr 7f 2nd Debutante Stks Two weeks	Quarter Moon A O'Brien 7/2F	3/17	2	8-11	69	*5th 1,000 Guineas Newm 1m	*2nd Irish 1,000 Guin Curr 1m	*2nd Oaks Epsom 1m4f	*2nd Irish Oaks Curr 1m4f
00 Curr 7f 2nd Debutante Stks Two weeks	Sequoyah A O'Brien 9/4F	8/10	2	8-11	69	5th Cheveley Park Newm 6f	*4th Irish 1,000 Guin Curr 1m	*10th Coronation Stks Ascot 1m	*4th Irish Oaks Curr 1m4f
99 Leop 7f 1st Debutante Stks Three weeks	Preseli M Grassick 9/1	10/12	2	8-11	68	*WON 7/4F 1,000 Guin Trial Leop 1m	*12th Irish 1,000 Guin Curr 1m	*2nd Pretty Polly Curr 1m2f	*9th Irish Oaks Curr 1m4f
98 Leop 7f 1st Debutante Stks Two weeks	Edabiya J Oxx 9/4F	10/13	2	8-11	67	3rd Meon Fillies' Mile Ascot 1m	*8th Irish 1,000 Guin Curr 1m	*5th Prix Vermeille Long 1m4f	*4th Group 2 Long 1m7f
97 Leop 6f 5th Phoenix Stks One month	Tarascon T Stack 7/1	1/12	2	8-11	69	*16th 1,000 Guineas Newm 1m	*WON 12/1 Irish 1,000 Guin Curr 1m	*6th Oaks Epsom 1m4f	*7th Sussex Good 1m
96 York 6f 1st Lowther Stks Three weeks	Bianca Nera D Loder 3/1	7/10	2	8-11	64	4th Marcel Boussac Long 1m	*6th Fred Darling Newb 7f	*11th 1,000 Guineas Newm 1m	-

12-year median performance rating of the winner: **67** (out of 100)   *next year

WINNER'S PROFILE A recent appearance proved vital as all 12 **raced within the past month**, while 10 of the last 11 winners came **via the Debutante and Phoenix Stakes** – only one failed to make the first three. The last 11 winners also made the **first three over this seven furlong trip** – eight of whom won – while Quarter Moon was the only maiden to get off the mark here. The market spoke volumes as 11 winners went off **single-figure odds**, including all four of trainer Aidan O'Brien's winners from a whopping 31 runners.

FUTURE POINTERS 1992 was the last time a filly won the Moyglare before 1,000 Guineas success the following season, and the juvenile in question was Sayyedati. Since then, six failed so any temptation to snap up a fancy price can be forgotten post-race, although during this period a winner of the Irish equivalent emerged in Tarascon back in 1997. That year turned out to be a vintage renewal as the third-placed, Shahtoush, went on to land the English Oaks – three Moyglare winners failed at Epsom – while in 2000, the sixth-placed, Imagine, also tasted Oaks glory. The Moyglare had its share of average winners too, but several up to scratch winners emerged in recent times that scored at decent odds next time out.

Were Moyglare Stud winners profitable to follow on their subsequent three runs?
No – 5 wins from 32 runs returned a loss of -£1.25 to a £1 level stake.

Placed runners' subsequent record (three runs):
Runners-up: 7 wins from 34 runs returned a loss of -£13.56 to a £1 level stake.
2005 Ugo Fire – Group Three Weld Park Stakes, 2001 Dress To Thrill – Desmond Stakes, Matron Stakes, 1996 Ryafan – Prix Marcel Boussac

Thirds: 5 wins from 34 runs returned a loss of -£14.41 to a £1 level stake.
2004 Saoire – Irish 1,000 Guineas, 2001 Sophisticat – Group Three Prix de la Grotte

FUTURE SUCCESS RATING: ★ ★ ☆ ☆ ☆

SUPREME STAKES
September 2, Goodwood – (Group 3, Class 1, 3yo+) 7f

Last run	Winner/ Trainer & SP	Draw/ Ran	Age	Wght	PR	Next four runs			
07 Newb 7f 1st Handicap *Three weeks*	**Lovelace** M Johnston 5/1	3/10	3	8-09	71	7th Tote Hcp Ascot 7f	11th Challenge Stks Newm 7f	–	–
06 Ling 1m 4th Summer Mile *Three months*	**Stronghold** J Gosden 2/1F	8/8	4	8-12	75	14th Challenge Stks Newm 7f	*3rd Hungerford Stks Newb 7f		
05 Donc 7f 4th Park Stks *Three weeks*	**Arakan** Sir M Stoute 5/1	1/8	5	8-12	80	3rd Challenge Stks Newm 7f	–		
04 Ascot 6f 9th Diadem Stks *One week*	**Mac Love** J Akehurst 14/1	7/11	3	8-09	72	*4th Paradise Stks Ling 1m	*2nd Lockinge Newb 1m	*5th Diomed Stks Epsom 1½m	*4th Queen Anne York 1m
03 Donc 7f 2nd Park Stks *Two weeks*	**With Reason** D Loder 9/2	7/7	5	9-02	74	*13th Lockinge Newb 1m	**WON 11/2** **Superior Mile** **Hayd 1m**	**2nd Superior Mile	**6th Park Stks Donc 7f
02 Good 1m 4th Celebration Mile *Two months*	**Firebreak** S Bin Suroor 5/4F	4/10	3	8-09	76	2nd Challenge Stks Newm 7f	*2nd Listed Sprint Nad Al 6f	*WON 4/1F **Group 2 Mile** **Nad Al 1m**	*11th Golden Jubilee Ascot 6f
01 Donc 1m 3rd Park Stks *Two weeks*	**Late Night Out** W Jarvis EvensF	3/4	6	8-12	69	4th Challenge Stks Newm 7f	*3rd Spring Trophy Hayd 7f	*5th Diomed Stks Epsom 1½m	*6th Listed Stks Good 1m
00 Deau 6f 3rd Group 3 *One month*	**Mount Abu** J Gosden 2/1F	5/8	3	8-09	68	7th Challenge Stks Newm 7f	*3rd Leicestershire St Newm 7f	*WON 5/2F **John of Gaunt** **Hayd 7f**	*6th July Cup Newm 6f
98 Good 1m 4th Celebration Mile *One month*	**Decorated Hero** J Gosden 2/1JF	8/8	6	9-05	79	3rd Group 2 Long 1m	**WON 11/2** **Challenge Stks** **Newm 7f**	3rd Hong Kong Int Sha 7f	–
97 Donc 1m 2nd Park Stks *Two weeks*	**Decorated Hero** J Gosden 6/4F	6/6	5	9-02	78	**WON 6/5** **Group 2** **Long 1m**	5th Challenge Stks Newm 7f	3rd Breeders' Cup Holl 1m	6th Hong Kong Int Sha 7f
96 Curr 1m 5th Irish 2,000 Guin *Four months*	**Tagula** I Balding 4/1	7/9	3	8-09	73	5th Prix de la Foret Long 7f	4th Hong Kong Int Sha 7f	–	–

12-year median performance rating of the winner: **68** (out of 100)   *(1999 abandoned), *next year **two years*

WINNER'S PROFILE The only winner that lined up having scored last time out was Lovelace last year, who was also the lone winner to have run in handicap company beforehand – six ran in either the Park Stakes or Celebration Mile. Every winner **scored at Pattern level** – apart from Lovelace – four in a Listed race, six in Group events, while having only won a handicap, Lovelace was rated low in comparison to the majority **officially rated from 106 to 118**. A distance win wasn't essential, although seven already won over it – three others only scored at six furlongs – however, a place near the head of the betting at **5/1 or shorter** was important.
A **middle to high draw** on the inside helps, as all four of **John Gosden**'s winners, from only six runners, proved.

FUTURE POINTERS Winners of this midweek event have scored again in Pattern company, a few at Group Two level, but not many used it as a stepping stone for greater achievements at the highest level, as only Firebreak since 1996 scored in the Group One Hong Kong Mile a few years later, while the 1992 winner, Soviet Line, also had to wait a few seasons before he lifted the Lockinge Stakes.
The most popular, but not successful route post-Goodwood was the Challenge Stakes – Lovelace last year became the sixth to fail – and only Decorated Hero scored in that event second time around.
Winners have a poor record overall next time out, while two picked up Listed races at Haydock the following season.

Were Supreme winners profitable to follow on their subsequent three runs?
No – 5 wins from 28 runs returned loss of -£4.30 to a £1 level stake.

Placed runners' subsequent record (three runs):
Runners-up: 6 wins from 22 runs returned a loss of -£0.37 to a £1 level stake.
2003 Monsieur Bond – Gladness Stakes, 1996 Wizard King – Concorde Stakes

Thirds: 4 wins from 20 runs returned a **profit of +£6.50** to a £1 level stake.
2000 Last Resort – Challenge Stakes

FUTURE SUCCESS RATING: ★ ★ ☆ ☆ ☆

SPRINT CUP
September 6, Haydock – (Group 1, Class 1, 3yo+) 6f

Last run	Winner/ Trainer & SP	Draw/ Ran	Age	Wght	PR	Next four runs			
07 York 5f 4th Nunthorpe *Three weeks*	**Red Clubs** B Hills 9/1	6/14	4	9-03	80	13th Prix de la Foret Long 7f	-	-	-
06 York 5f 1st Nunthorpe *Two weeks*	**Reverence** E Alston 11/4F	10/11	5	9-03	82	2nd Prix de l'Abbaye Long 5f	*5th Champagne Stk Sand 5f	*6th Hackwood Stks Ascot 6f	-
05 Deau 7f 2nd Maurice 'Gheest *One month*	**Goodricke** D Loder 14/1	4/17	3	8-12	77	*4th Conds Stks Yarm 6f	*9th Guisborough Stk Redc 7f	-	-
04 York 6f 1st Summer Stks *One month*	**Tante Rose** R Charlton 10/1	14/19	4	8-11	80	-	-	-	-
03 Newm 6f 2nd Hopeful Stks *Three weeks*	**Somnus** T Easterby 12/1	7/10	3	8-12	81	7th Prix de l'Abbaye Long 5f	*7th Duke of York York 6f	*2nd Chipchase Stks Newc 6f	*5th July Cup Newm 6f
02 Ascot 6f 6th Golden Jubilee *Three months*	**Invincible Spirit** J Dunlop 25/1	10/14	5	9-00	78	-	-	-	-
01 York 6f 2nd Nunthorpe *Three weeks*	**Nuclear Debate** J Hammond 11/2	9/12	6	9-00	86	8th Prix de l'Abbaye Long 5f	5th Grade 3 Holl 6f	9th H Kong Sprint Sha 5f	*WON 47/20F Grade 2 Wood 6f
00 York 6f 3rd Nunthorpe *Two weeks*	**Pipalong** T Easterby 3/1	7/13	4	8-11	78	3rd Prix de l'Abbaye Long 5f	*10th Grade 3 Nad Al 6f	*13th Palace House Newm 5f	*WON 14/1 Duke of York York 6f
99 Deau 7f 1st Maurice 'Gheest *One month*	**Diktat** S Bin Suroor 13/8F	16/16	4	9-00	85	5th Prix de la Foret Long 7f	*6th Group 2 Toky 7f	*2nd Group 1 Toky 1m	*3rd Prix du Moulin Long 1m
98 Newm 6f 2nd July Cup *Two weeks*	**Tamarisk** R Charlton 13/2	5/13	3	8-12	79	7th Stakes Keen 7f	**5th Stakes Arli 1m1f	**10th Handicap Kent 1m	**7th Stakes Keen 6f
97 Newm 6f 2nd July Cup *Two months*	**Royal Applause** B Hills 15/8F	9/9	4	9-00	82	3rd Prix de l'Abbaye Long 5f	14th Breeders' Cup Holl 6f	-	-
96 Deau 7f 4th Maurice 'Gheest *One month*	**Iktamal** E Dunlop 10/1	9/11	4	9-00	77	6th Breeders' Cup Wood 6f	-	-	-

12-year median performance rating of the winner: **80** (out of 100)   *next year **two years*

WINNER'S PROFILE As to be expected with a sprint, the majority of winners were **on the boil during the past few months** – only Invincible Spirit had a longer prep – although all of them **raced at a Grade One venue last time**, nine in either the **Nunthorpe, Maurice de Gheest or July Cup** where they finished in the first four. Sakhee's Secret last year became the tenth horse to fall short in the July Cup/Sprint Cup double since Ajdal succeeded in 1987. **Distance winning form** was vital, along with an **official rating between 111 to 119**, while 11 winners scored in Listed company at least – nine in Group class.

Age can be a useful pointer as 11 emerged from the **three to five-year-old** bracket – six-year-olds plus scored only once from over 30 runners. Trainers to have triumphed twice in the event since 1996 were **Roger Charlton** (from seven runners), **Tim Easterby** (10) and **Barry Hills** (six).

FUTURE POINTERS Possibly not the strongest Group One sprint as winners failed to shine post-Haydock, and while options are limited during the autumn – a drop in trip for the Abbaye or a trip to the Breeders' Cup both tough assignments – only a few regained the winning thread the following season.

Red Clubs last year was the latest to flop next time out, over in France in the Prix de la Foret, however, three placed runners from here managed to land that event *(see below)* and recent runners-up in the Sprint Cup have proven more profitable to follow than the winners.

Were Sprint Cup winners profitable to follow on their subsequent three runs?
No – 0 win from 24 runs returned a loss of -£24.00 to a £1 level stake.

Placed runners' subsequent record (three runs):
Runners-up: 5 wins from 28 runs returned a **profit of +£2.92** to a £1 level stake.
2006 Quito – Fortune Stakes, 2005 La Cucaracha – King George Stakes, 2004 Somnus – Prix de la Foret, 2001 Mount Abu – Prix de la Foret, 2000 Sampower Star – Diadem Stakes

Thirds: 5 wins from 34 runs returned a loss of -£11.52 to a £1 level stake.
2006 Amadeus Wolf – Duke of York Stakes, 2005 Ashdown Express – Starlit Stakes, 1998 Tomba – Prix de la Foret

FUTURE SUCCESS RATING: ★ ★ ★ ★ ★

SEPTEMBER STAKES

September 6, Kempton (AW) – (Group 3, Class 1, 3yo+) 1m4f

Last run	Winner/ Trainer & SP	Draw/ Ran	Age	Wght	PR	Next four runs			
07 Newm 1m4f 7th *Two months*	**Steppe Dancer** Princess of Wales D Coakley 8/1	6/7	4	9-04	70	7th Irish St Leger Curr 1m6f	-	-	-
06 Wind 1m2f 3rd *One week*	**Kandidate** Winter Hill Stks C Brittain 3/1	3/6	4	9-04	72	6th Cumb'lnd Lodge **Group 3** Ascot 1m4f	***WON 14/1** Group 3 **Nad Al 1m1f**	*6th Dubai World Cup Nad Al 1m2f	*3rd G Richards Sand 1m2f
05 Ayr 1m2f 1st *Two months*	**Imperial Stride** Scottish Derby Sir M Stoute 11/8F	4/6	4	9-08	81	**WON 10/11F** Foundation Stk Group 1 **Good 1m2f**	8th Group 1 Flem 1m2f	*10th Group 3 Nad Al 1m4f	-
04 Deau 1m2f 3rd *Three weeks*	**Mamool** Group 3 S Bin Suroor 3/1	5/4	5	9-03	81	15th Arc de Triomphe Long 1m4f	7th Melbourne Cup Flem 2m	***WON 9/4F** **Glorious Stks** **Good 1m4f**	*4th Geoffrey Freer Newb 1m5f
03 Newb 1m5f 1st *Three weeks*	**Mubtaker** Geoffrey Freer M Tregoning 8/13F	1/5	6	9-08	85	2nd Arc de Triomphe Long 1m4f	***WON 3/10F** **Geoffrey Freer** **Newb 1m5f**	*7th Grosser 'Baden Bade 1m4f	*4th Canadian Int Wood 1m4f
02 Wind 1m4f 1st *Four months*	**Asian Heights** Gala Stks G Wragg 5/4F	1/6	4	9-03	76	14th Arc de Triomphe Long 1m4f	*2nd John Porter Stks Newb 1m4f	***WON EvsF** **Ormonde Stks** **Ches 1m5f**	**7th St Simon Stks Newb 1m4f
01 Ascot 1m4f 9th *Two months*	**Mutamam** King George VI A Stewart 4/6F	2/4	6	9-08	84	**WON 17/4** **Canadian Int** **Wood 1m4f**	11th Breeders' Cup Belm 1m4f	-	-
00 Ascot 1m4f 4th *Three months*	**Mutamam** Hardwicke Stks A Stewart 5/2F	3/7	5	9-00	85	**WON 4/6F** **Cumb'd Lodge** **Ascot 1m4f**	4th Breeders' Cup Chur 1m4f	***WON 11/2** **Princess' Wales** **Newm 1m4f**	*9th King George VI Ascot 1m4f
99 Ascot 1m6f 1st *One week*	**Yavana's Pace** March Stks M Johnston 11/4	3/5	7	9-00	70	2nd Irish St Leger Curr 1m6f	12th Melbourne Cup Flem 2m	6th Group 2 Sand 1m4f	*15th Sheema Classic Nad Al 1m4f
98 Wind 1m2f 3rd *One week*	**Crimson Tide** Winter Hill Stks J Hills 11/4	2/5	4	9-05	68	5th Cumb'lnd Lodge Ascot 1m4f	7th Canadian Int Wood 1m4f	**3rd Sovereign Stks Sali 1m	**5th Winter Hill Stks Wind 1m2f
97 Good 1m4f 1st *Two months*	**Maylane** Gold Trophy A Stewart 3/1	2/6	3	8-05	69	UR Cumb'lnd Lodge Ascot 1m4f	*8th Turf Classic Nad Al 1m4f	*7th Gold Cup Ascot 2m4f	*7th Glorious Hcp Good 1m4f
96 Deau 1m5f 1st *Four months*	**Sacrament** Group 2 Sir M Stoute 11/2	5/7	5	9-05	74	3rd Irish St Leger Curr 1m6f	2nd Pr' Jockey-Club Siro 1m4f	8th Hong Kong Vase Sha 1m4f	*7th John Porter Stks Newb 1m4f

12-year median performance rating of the winner: **76** (out of 100)   *(1997-99 Epsom, 2005 Newmarket)*
*next year **two years

WINNER'S PROFILE No traditional path led to Kempton, although three winners finished in the top-three in the **Winter Hill Stakes last time**, while others took in races like the Fred Archer or the handicap route. Every winner bar Maylane **won a Listed event at least**, while 10 **scored over the trip**, including Steppe Dancer, who broke the run of winners **officially rated 100 or higher**.
Penalties didn't prevent several winners, although being aged three did – only Maylane struck from 16 runners – as **four to six-year-olds** held the edge. The market informs us to stick with the **first three in the betting**, even in such small fields, as both Sir Michael Stoute's winners – from nine runners – emerged from that end of the scale.

FUTURE POINTERS The September Stakes experienced some changes over the years having been run over 11 furlongs on Kempton's turf track back in 1996, before a switch to Epsom for three years, and then to Newmarket in 2005. The last two renewals have been run on Kempton's Polytrack.
What remained consistent since the Millennium, though, was the steady flow of subsequent winners as a couple of stars turned up here in Mubtaker and Mutamam, who both went on to better things – the former almost took the Arc de Triomphe next time out. The Arc also foiled two other September winners, while the Cumberland Lodge halted three, apart from Mutamam, who not only won that event, but also took the Canadian International after his defence the next year. Four winners since 2000 scored at a similar lower level after folding in Group One events, but overall, it proved worthwhile sticking with winners in recent years, even though we may never see a subsequent Melbourne Cup winner again such as Jeune who lifted this in 1992.

Were September Stakes winners profitable to follow on their subsequent three runs?
Yes – 8 wins from 33 runs returned a **profit of +£3.89** to a £1 level stake.

Placed runners' subsequent record (three runs):
Runners-up: 5 wins from 21 runs returned a **profit of +£6.50** to a £1 level stake.
2002 First Charter – Fred Archer, 1999 Blueprint – Jockey Club Stakes, 1996 Salmon Ladder – St Simon Stakes
Thirds: No qualifiers owing to fields of seven runners or below.

FUTURE SUCCESS RATING: ★★★ ☆ ☆

SIRENIA STAKES

September 6, Kempton (AW) – (Group 3, Class 1, 2yo) 6f

Last run	Winner/ Trainer & SP	Draw/ Ran	Age	Wght	PR	Next four runs			
07 York 6f 12th / St Leger Sales / *Three weeks*	**Philario** / K Burke 16/1	4/12	2	9-00	60	4th Mill Reef Stks Newb 6f	-	-	-
06 York 6f 5th / St Leger Sales / *Two weeks*	**Dhanyata** / B Meehan 6/1	7/9	2	8-11	62	2nd Cheveley Park Newm 6f	6th Rockfel Stks Newm 7f	-	-
05 York 6f 1st / Nursery / *Three weeks*	**Prince Of Light** / M Johnston 10/11F	10/9	2	8-11	63	5th Middle Park Stks Newm 6f	*2nd Midsummer Stks Wind 1m	*WON 11/8F Conds Stks Ches 7f	*9th Lennox Stks Good 7f
04 Newm 7f 1st / Nursery / *Two months*	**Satchem** / C Brittain 3/1	5/8	2	8-11	67	4th Middle Park Stks Newm 6f	*9th 2,000 Guineas Newm 1m	**WON 10/3 Listed Good 1m	**2nd Summer Mile Ling 1m
03 Wind 6f 1st / Conds Stks / *One month*	**Pastoral Pursuits** / H Morrison 11/10F	3/8	2	8-11	65	*2nd Surrey Stks Sand 7f	*WON 15/8F Hackwood Stks Newb 6f	*WON 5/1 Park Stks Donc 7f	5th Prix de la Foret Long 7f
02 York 5f 5th / Roses Stks / *Three weeks*	**Sir Edward Landseer** / P Cole 6/1	1/8	2	8-11	61	*4th Euro Free Hcp Newm 7f	*7th Carnarvon Stks Newb 6f	*3rd Conds Stks Ches 7f	*5th Conds Stks Newb 7f
01 Bath 5f 1st / Maiden / *Two weeks*	**Lipstick** / M Channon 2/1F	6/9	2	8-06	57	2nd Watership Sales Ascot 7f	*12th Poule 'Pouliches Long 1m	*2nd Summer Stks York 6f	*4th Oak Tree Stks Good 7f
00 Ascot 6f 4th / Princess Margaret / *Two months*	**Santolina** / J Gosden 9/2	10/9	2	8-06	61	7th Cheveley Park Newm 6f	*8th 1,000 Guineas Newm 1m	-	-
99 Good 6f 1st / Novice Stks / *Two months*	**Primo Valentino** / P Harris 15/8F	6/6	2	8-11	68	WON 6/5F Mill Reef Stks Newb 6f	WON 10/3 Middle Park Newm 6f	*7th 2,000 Guineas Newm 1m	*6th Group 3 Bade 6f
98 Sand 5f 3rd / Dragon Trophy / *Two months*	**Atlantic Destiny** / M Johnston 13/2	6/6	2	8-06	64	5th Cheveley Park Newm 6f	4th Rockfel Stks Newm 7f	*5th Nell Gwyn Stks Newm 7f	*11th 1,000 Guineas Newm 1m
97 Ripo 6f 3rd / 2yo Trophy / *Three weeks*	**Mijana** / J Gosden 7/2	3/9	2	8-11	65	4th Mill Reef Stks Newb 6f	2nd 2yo Trophy Redcar 6f	-	-
96 York 6f 2nd / Lowther Stks / *Three weeks*	**Arethusa** / R Hannon 11/4	5/7	2	8-06	59	5th Cheveley Park Newm 6f	*8th Fred Darling Newb 7f	*2nd Somerset Stks Bath 6f	*5th Fillies' Listed Newm 6f

12-year median performance rating of the winner: **63** (out of 100) *(2005 Newmarket) *next year*

WINNER'S PROFILE Every winner lined up having **raced within the past two months**, five of whom raced at York, including the last three, while no maiden triumphed either – eight already won over the distance, four over the minimum trip. Since this became a Group Three five years ago, no winner experienced Pattern class previously – three had before this period – while the ideal **official rating shaped between 95 to 100**.
With regard to the betting, those around **6/1 or shorter** in the market emerged best – last year's was the biggest outsider at 16/1 – with trainer **John Gosden** responsible for two fancied winners from only three runners.

FUTURE POINTERS The quality of this event has naturally improved since earning Group Three status in 2003, as winners proved more successful subsequently, even if those victories were gained the following season.
Only the best winner of this event with an above par performance rating (PR) – Primo Valentino in 1999 – managed to score again as a juvenile when he took the prestigious Mill Reef and Middle Park Stakes, but those events along with the Cheveley Park, proved too much for seven others. It was a similar story with the runners-up *(see below)* whose most significant winners all scored in the Classic season.

Were Sirenia winners profitable to follow on their subsequent three runs?
No – 6 wins from 31 runs returned a loss of -£8.89 to a £1 level stake.

Placed runners' subsequent record (three runs):
Runners-up: 7 wins from 27 runs returned a **profit of +£26.00** to a £1 level stake.
2004 Council Member – King Charles II, 2002 Hurricane Alan – Craven Stakes,
2001 Twilight Blues – European Free Handicap, 1997 Tadwiga – Masaka Stakes

Thirds: 4 wins from 24 runs returned a loss of -£9.70 to a £1 level stake.
2002 Membership – Listed Spring Cup

FUTURE SUCCESS RATING: ★ ★ ☆ ☆ ☆

MATRON STAKES
September 6, Leopardstown – (Group 1, 3yo+ Fillies & Mares) 1m

Last run	Winner/ Trainer & SP	Draw/ Ran	Age	Wght	PR	Next four runs			
07 Good 1m 1st Celebration Mile *Two weeks*	**Echelon** Sir M Stoute 9/4F	2/9	5	9-03	75	3rd Sun Chariot Newm 1m	-	-	-
06 Good 7f 1st Oak Tree Stks *Two months*	**Red Evie** M Bell 6/1	8/8	3	8-12	78	5th Sun Chariot Newm 1m	*WON 8/1 Lockinge Newb 1m	*7th Queen Anne Ascot 1m	*7th Falmouth Stks Newm 1m
05 Newb 7f 4th Hungerford *One month*	**Attraction** M Johnston 10/3	3/9	4	9-02	75	-	-	-	-
04 Good 1m 1st Sussex *Two months*	**Soviet Song** J Fanshawe 8/13F	7/6	4	9-02	80	6th Q Elizabeth II Ascot 1m	*3rd Windsor Forest Ascot 1m	*WON 7/4F Falmouth Stks Newm 1m	*2nd Sussex Good 1m
03 Chep 1m2f 2nd Daffodil Stks *Two months*	**Favourable Terms** Sir M Stoute 11/10F	5/9	3	8-11	73	5th Sun Chariot Newm 1m	*WON 13/2 Windsor Forest Ascot 1m	*6th Falmouth Stks Newm 1m	*WON 11/2 Nassau Good 1m2f
02 Leop 1m 1st Desmond Stks *Three weeks*	**Dress To Thrill** D Weld 2/1F	4/9	3	8-13	79	WON 8/1 Sun Chariot Newm 1m	8th Breeders' Mile Arli 1m	WON 73/10 Grade 1 Holl 1m1f	*5th Grade 1 Holl 1m1f
01 Good 7f 3rd Oak Tree Stks *One month*	**Independence** E Dunlop 6/1	11/11	3	8-10	77	WON 5/2F Sun Chariot Newm 1m	-	-	-
00 Deau 1m 3rd Prix d'Astarte *Two months*	**Iftiraas** J Dunlop 11/2	7/11	3	9-00	69	11th Group 2 Capa 1m	-	-	-
99 Cork 1m1f 1st Bluebird Listed *Two months*	**Dazzling Park** J Bolger 4/5F	1/6	3	8-10	72	2nd Champion Stks Leop 1m2f	6th Prix de l'Opera Long 1m1f	11th Hong Kong Cup Sha 1m2f	-
98 Ascot 1m 5th Conds Stks *One month*	**Tadwiga** R Hannon 9/2	6/7	3	8-10	68	8th October Stks Ascot 1m	-	-	-
97 Mars 1m2f 1st Listed *Three months*	**Clerico** H-A Pantall 6/1	3/10	3	8-09	67	11th Prix de l'Opera Long 1m1f	9th Group 3 Bord 1m2f	-	-
96 Newm 1m 3rd Falmouth Stks *Two months*	**Donna Viola** C Wall 5/2	3/6	4	9-00	74	WON 137/10 Prix de l'Opera Long 1m1f	WON N/O Grade 1 Sant 1m2f	*WON 17/10 Handicap Holl 1m1f	*3rd Grade 1 Holl 1m2f

12-year median performance rating of the winner: **74** (out of 100)   *(1996-2001 Curragh) *next year*

WINNER'S PROFILE **Winning form earlier in the season** was important and only Attraction, who was lightly raced in 2005 missed out, though like the remainder of winners she **already scored in Pattern company** – all were Group winners since 2004 when it became a Group One event. Eleven winners were **proven over the mile trip** – the exception Iftiraas over a furlong shorter – while six of the nine **British-trained** winners appeared at Royal Ascot that summer. The Brits also landed seven of the last eight renewals, two of whom came from **Sir Michael Stoute**'s yard and were fancied in the market, which proved a worthy guide as every victor since 1996 returned at **6/1 or shorter**.

FUTURE POINTERS Following the subsequent victories of the 2002 and 2001 winners in the Group Two Sun Chariot Stakes at Newmarket, and then the 2003 winner's triumph in the Group One Nassau Stakes the following season, this event rightly acquired Group One status itself in 2004.
That elevation was more than justified, as it attracted the best winner in the event's history during the same year, Soviet Song, who went on to take another Group One the following term, before Red Evie, in 2006, also progressed to scoop another big one in the Lockinge Stakes. All this evidence informs us that the Matron Stakes is very much a race on the up and winners have shown a handsome profit subsequently to boot.

Were Matron winners profitable to follow on their subsequent three runs?
Yes – 9 wins from 24 runs returned a **profit of +£34.45** to a £1 level stake.

Placed runners' subsequent record (three runs):
Runners-up: 5 wins from 28 runs returned a loss of -£6.25 to a £1 level stake.
2004 Attraction – Sun Chariot Stakes, 2002 Marionnaud – Group Three Concorde Stakes, Sun Chariot Stakes

Thirds: 1 win from 14 runs returned a loss of -£10.50 to a £1 level stake.
2007 Eastern Appeal - Group Three Concorde Stakes

FUTURE SUCCESS RATING: ★ ★ ★ ★ ☆

IRISH CHAMPION STAKES
September 6, Leopardstown – (Group 1, 3yo+) 1m2f

Last run	Winner/Trainer & SP	Draw/Ran	Age	Wght	PR	Next four runs			
07 York 1m2f 2nd Juddmonte Int *Three weeks*	**Dylan Thomas** A O'Brien 8/15F	5/6	4	9-07	88	**WON 11/2** Arc de Triomphe Long 1m4f	5th Breeders' Cup Monm 1m4f	-	-
06 York 1m2f 4th Juddmonte Int *Three weeks*	**Dylan Thomas** A O'Brien 13/8F	2/5	3	9-00	87	4th Grade 1 Belm 1m2f	*WON 8/15F Alleged Stks Curr 1m2f	*WON 4/9F Prix Ganay Long 1m3f	*2nd Tatts Gold Cup Curr 1m3f
05 Sand 1m2f 1st Eclipse *Three months*	**Oratorio** A O'Brien 7/1	8/10	3	8-11	83	4th Champion Stks Newm 1m2f	*11th Breeders' Cup Belm 1m2f	-	-
04 Ascot 1m 1st St James' Palace *Three months*	**Azamour** J Oxx 8/1	8/8	3	8-11	89	3rd Champion Stks Newm 1m2f	*4th Tatts Gold Cup Curr 1m3f	*WON 8/15F Prince Of Wales' York 1m2f	*WON 5/2F King George VI Newb 1m4f
03 Curr 1m2f 1st Royal Whip Stks *One month*	**High Chaparral** A O'Brien 4/1	6/7	4	9-04	90	3rd Arc de Triomphe Long 1m4f	WON 11/2 Breeders' Cup Sant 1m4f	-	-
02 Ascot 1m4f 5th King George VI *Two months*	**Grandera** S Bin Suroor 5/2	7/7	4	9-04	83	3rd Cox Plate Moon 1m2f	7th Hong Kong Cup Sha 1m2f	*WON N/O Group 2 Nad Al 1m2f	*4th Dubai World Cup Nad Al 1m2f
01 Ascot 1m4f 2nd King George VI *Two months*	**Fantastic Light** S Bin Suroor 9/4	2/7	5	9-04	95	WON 7/5F Breeders' Cup Belm 1m4f	-	-	-
00 York 1m2f 1st Juddmonte Int *Three weeks*	**Giant's Causeway** A O'Brien 8/11F	7/7	3	8-11	86	2nd Q Elizabeth II Ascot 1m	2nd Breeders' Cup Chur 1m2f	-	-
99 Ascot 1m4f 1st King George VI *Two months*	**Daylami** S Bin Suroor 6/4	4/7	5	9-04	94	9th Arc de Triomphe Long 1m4f	WON 16/10F Breeders' Cup Gulf 1m4f	-	-
98 Ascot 1m4f 1st King George VI *Two months*	**Swain** S Bin Suroor 6/4F	2/8	6	9-04	87	3rd Breeders' Cup Chur 1m2f	-	-	-
97 Ascot 1m4f 2nd King George VI *Two months*	**Pilsudksi** Sir M Stoute 5/4F	1/7	5	9-04	91	2nd Arc de Triomphe Long 1m4f	WON EvsF Champion Stks Newm 1m2f	WON 36/10 Japan Cup Toky 1m4f	-
96 Arli 1m2f 1st Grade 1 *Three weeks*	**Timarida** J Oxx 3/1	6/6	4	9-01	82	3rd Champion Stks Newm 1m2f	-	-	-

12-year median performance rating of the winner: **88** (out of 100)   *next year*

WINNER'S PROFILE Every winner raced at a **Grade One venue last time**, nine came via either Ascot or York, while each victor since 1996 **scored in a Group event during their last two races**, and all were **victorious in Group One company** at some point in their career. The **King George VI** proved a solid guide, Dylan Thomas the latest to emerge from that event last year, and he, along with eight other individuals were **proven over this intermediate trip** – Azamour and Swain the exceptions. Outsiders can be ignored – as can fillies – as it pays to stick with the **first four in the betting**, while **Aidan O'Brien** has won it five times from almost 30 runners.

FUTURE POINTERS A superb Group One event that boasts a gleaming long-term roll call featuring top-class individuals, along with the likes of Dr Devious, Suave Dancer, Indian Skimmer and Sadler's Wells, who all graced Leopardstown prior to 1996. Since then, a further treat of subsequent Group One winners emerged and those that headed to the Breeder's Cup have a tidy record. Not many races supplied three Breeders' Cup winners, and though Dylan Thomas flopped last year on sloppy ground, High Chaparral, Fantastic Light and Daylami all conquered the US, along with the 2006 runner-up from here, Ouija Board.

Dylan Thomas may have lost in States, but he did land the biggest race in Europe beforehand, the Prix de l'Arc de Triomphe, the first to do so since Suave Dancer in 1991. However, the only black mark against Irish Champion winners is their poor record next time out – 10 sunk since 1996 – as events such as the English equivalent at Newmarket proved tricky, and only Pilsudski managed the feat after a near miss in the 1997 Arc.

Were Irish Champion winners profitable to follow on their subsequent three runs?
Yes – 10 wins from 25 runs returned a **profit of +£5.10** to a £1 level stake.

Placed runners' subsequent record (three runs):
Runners-up: 10 wins from 24 runs returned a **profit of +£10.32** to a £1 level stake.
2006 Ouija Board – Breeders' Cup, 2003 Falbrav – QE II Stakes, Hong Kong Cup, 2002 Hawk Wing – Lockinge, 1998 Alborada – Champion Stakes, 1996 Dance Design – Tattersalls Gold Cup, Pretty Polly Stakes

Thirds: 0 win from 8 runs returned a loss of -£8.00 to a £1 level stake.

FUTURE SUCCESS RATING: ★ ★ ★ ★

PARK HILL STAKES
September 11, Doncaster – (Group 2, Class 1, 3yo+ Fillies & Mares) 1m6f

Last run	Winner/ Trainer & SP	Draw/ Ran	Age	Wght	PR	Next four runs			
07 Good 1m6f 1st Lillie Langtry Stk Two months	Hi Calypso Sir M Stoute 9/2	1/14	3	8-07	70	-	-	-	-
06 Arli 1m2f 10th Grade 1 One month	Rising Cross J Best 16/1	4/7	3	8-07	65	5th Group 2 Long 1m5f	5th Prix Royal-Oak Long 2m	*7th Yorkshire Cup York 1m6f	*4th Coronation Cup Epsom 1m4f
05 Deau 1m2f 1st Group 3 One month	Sweet Stream J Hammond 7/2CF	4/11	5	9-03	69	8th Hong Kong Vase Sha 1m4f	*2nd Group 2 Deau 1m2f	*5th Premio Jockey Siro 1m4f	-
04 Good 1m2f 5th Nassau Two months	Echoes In Eternity S Bin Suroor 5/1	3/10	4	9-03	67	11th Group 2 Long 1m5f	-	-	-
03 Good 1m6f 2nd Gladness Stks Two months	Discreet Brief J Dunlop 8/1	6/8	3	8-05	69	4th Group 2 Dort 1m6f	-	-	-
02 York 1m4f 1st Galtres Stks Three weeks	Alexander Three D B Hills 7/4F	3/9	3	8-05	60	-	-	-	-
01 York 1m4f 4th Galtres Stks Three weeks	Ranin E Dunlop 5/1	9/13	3	8-05	69	2nd Group 2 Long 1m5f	9th Princess Royal Ascot 1m4f	-	-
00 York 1m4f 4th Yorkshire Oaks Two weeks	Miletrian M Channon 10/1	3/11	3	8-10	71	*2nd Group 3 Nad Al 1m4f	*14th Sheema Classic Nad Al 1m4f	*8th Yorkshire Cup York 1m6f	*10th Henry II Sand 2m
99 Ripo 1m4f 1st Maiden Two weeks	Mistle Song C Brittain 8/1	3/10	3	8-05	63	6th Princess Royal Ascot 1m4f	-	-	-
98 Ches 1m5f 2nd Rated Hcp Three weeks	Delilah Sir M Stoute 9/1	2/9	4	9-06	70	3rd Irish St Leger Curr 1m6f	2nd Princess Royal Ascot 1m4f	2nd St Simon Stks Newm 1m4f	-
97 Good 1m6f 3rd March Stks Three weeks	Book At Bedtime C Cyzer 11/1	1/7	3	8-05	62	4th St Leger Donc 1m6f	*7th Jockey Club Stks Newm 1m4f	*4th Group 2 Long 2m	*12th Gold Cup Ascot 2m4f
96 York 1m4f 1st Galtres Stks Three weeks	Eva Luna H Cecil 2/1F	5/6	4	9-03	64	4th Jockey Club Cup Newm 2m	3rd St Simon Stks Newb 1m4f	2nd Serlby Stks Donc 1m4f	*5th Ormonde Stks Ches 1m5f

12-year median performance rating of the winner: **67** (out of 100)   *next year*

WINNER'S PROFILE Every Park Hill winner **saw the racecourse within the past two months**, eight came **via Goodwood or York**, while all 12 **scored in Listed company at least**.
However, those that attempted to carry Group One or Two penalties found it tough, as Turbo Linn and Punctilious found out to their cost in two of the last three years. Three-year-olds yet to have won at Group level boast a good record, as do those **drawn in the low to middle stalls**, however, distance-winning fillies were rarely successful here.

FUTURE POINTERS This staying event for fillies and mares was granted Group Two status in 2004, but the majority of past winners hardly trickle off the tongue and subsequent results fail to support the upgrade, despite the fact that several had their career cut short owing to breeding engagements.
The fact remains that none of the nine winners who raced again that term won, as races like the Prix de Royallieu at Longchamp and the Princess Royal proved too strong. A better option, therefore, may be to follow the runners-up from here, as two managed to land the latter race at Ascot *(see below)*.

Were Park Hill winners profitable to follow on their subsequent three runs?
No – 0 win from 23 runs returned a loss of -£23.00 to a £1 level stake.

Placed runners' subsequent record (three runs):
Runners-up: 8 wins from 32 runs returned a **profit of +£10.21** to a £1 level stake.
2006 Anna Pavlova – Harvest Stakes, Salsabil Stakes, 2004 Mazuna – Princess Royal,
2002 Treble Heights – Aphrodite Stakes, 1996 Time Allowed – Princess Royal, Jockey Club Stakes

Thirds: 2 wins from 18 runs returned a loss of -£7.00 to a £1 level stake.
2001 Jalousie – Middleton Stakes

FUTURE SUCCESS RATING: ★ ☆ ☆ ☆ ☆

MAY HILL STAKES

September 11, Doncaster – (Group 2, Class 1, 2yo Fillies) 1m

Last run	Winner/ Trainer & SP	Draw/ Ran	Age	Wght	PR	Next four runs			
07 Leic 7f 1st Maiden *One month*	Spacious J Fanshawe 9/4F	5/12	2	8-12	68	-	-	-	-
06 Curr 7f 7th Moyglare Stud *Two weeks*	Simply Perfect J Noseda 4/1	1/9	2	8-12	72	WON 11/4 Meon Fill' Mile Ascot 1m	*3rd 1,000 Guineas Newm 1m	*6th Oaks Epsom 1m4f	*WON 6/1 Falmouth Stks Newm 1m
05 Newm 7f 1st Sweet Solera *Two months*	Nasheej R Hannon 4/1	2/8	2	8-13	69	3rd Meon Fill' Mile Ascot 1m	*WON 6/4F Fred Darling Newb 7f	*3rd 1,000 Guineas Newm 1m	*14th Irish 1,000 Guin Curr 1m
04 Newm 7f 1st Maiden *Two weeks*	Playful Act J Gosden 8/1	7/8	2	8-10	73	WON 11/4 Meon Fill' Mile Ascot 1m	*WON 11/4 Lanc'shire Oaks Hayd 1m4f	*2nd Irish Oaks Curr 1m4f	*10th Yorkshire Oaks York 1m4f
03 Ascot 7f 1st Shergar Cup *Two months*	Kinnaird P Haslam 9/1	1/10	2	8-10	63	*4th Irish 1,000 Guin Curr 1m	*5th Coronation Stks Ascot 1m	*2nd Daffodil Stks Chep 1m2f	*2nd Group 3 Deau 1m2f
02 Newm 7f 2nd Sweet Solera *Two months*	Summitville J Given 11/2	1/9	2	8-09	62	8th Meon Fill' Mile Ascot 1m	*7th Newm 1m	*8th Prix Saint-Alary Long 1m2f	*3rd Oaks Epsom 1m4f
01 Newm 7f 1st Maiden *Two months*	Half Glance H Cecil 5/2	4/10	2	8-09	65	4th Meon Fill' Mile Ascot 1m	*5th Nell Gwyn Newm 7f	*3rd Pretty Polly Stks Newm 1m2f	*5th Musidora Stks York 1m2f
00 Newm 7f 1st Maiden *Two weeks*	Karasta Sir M Stoute 5/4F	11/12	2	8-09	63	2nd Marcel Boussac Long 1m	*13th 1,000 Guineas Newm 1m	*6th Irish 1,000 Guin Curr 1m	*14th Jersey Stks Ascot 7f
99 Newb 6f 1st Maiden *One month*	Teggiano C Brittain 13/2	5/12	2	8-09	69	WON 11/8F Meon Fill' Mile Ascot 1m	*2nd Ribblesdale Ascot 1m	*10th Irish Oaks Curr 1m4f	-
98 Folk 7f 1st Maiden *Two months*	Calando D Loder 5/2F	2/10	2	8-09	68	2nd Meon Fill' Mile Ascot 1m	*3rd Poule 'Pouliches Long 1m	*8th Prix' Hermes Chan 1m3f	*3rd Pretty Polly Stk Curr 1m2f
97 Good 7f 1st Prestige Stks *Three weeks*	Midnight Line H Cecil 3/1F	9/9	2	9-00	64	5th Meon Fill' Mile Ascot 1m	*WON 5/2F Pretty Polly St Newm 1m2f	*2nd Musidora Stks York 1m2f	*3rd Oaks Epsom 1m4f
96 Newm 7f 1st Maiden *Three weeks*	Reams Of Verse H Cecil 2/1F	11/11	2	8-09	70	WON 5/1 Meon Fill' Mile Ascot 1m	*6th 1,000 Guineas Newm 1m	*WON 11/10F Musidora Stks York 1m2f	*WON 5/6F Oaks Epsom 1m4f

12-year median performance rating of the winner: **67** (out of 100)   *next year*

WINNER'S PROFILE Every winner lined up having **raced within the past two months**, 10 of whom **scored last time out** – the two beaten ran in Pattern company – while seven won maidens, five at Newmarket.
All 12 **scored at either six or seven furlongs**, although none over this mile trip, and you have to go back 18 years since the last maiden opened her account here. Those in the **first four of the betting** came out on top, including trainer **Henry Cecil**'s three winners from only four runners – he also won it five times between 1995 and 1987.

FUTURE POINTERS The main event for juvenile fillies at the St Leger meeting with Classic aspirations, and though Reams Of Verse (1996) was the last winner to land a British Classic, there has been strength in depth involving the placed runners. Both the 2005 third, Speciosa, and 2000 runner-up, Ameerat, both went on to lift the 1,000 Guineas.
The natural path for May Hill winners was to the Meon Valley Fillies' Mile at Ascot later in the month, and a record of four winners from nine runners reads impressive – all four achieved above par performance ratings (PR).
Although the event suffered a dry run from 2003 to 2000, overall, the May Hill should be viewed in a positive light, especially with a good recent record since it gained Group Two status in 2003.

Were May Hill winners profitable to follow on their subsequent three runs?
No – 8 wins from 33 runs returned a loss of -£5.27 to a £1 level stake. However, a small **profit of +£3.62** was returned on the winner's next two runs only.

Placed runners' subsequent record (three runs):
Runners-up: 5 wins from 29 runs returned a loss of -£7.93 to a £1 level stake.
2003 Hathrah – Masaka Stakes, 2000 Ameerat – 1,000 Guineas

Thirds: 10 wins from 35 runs returned a **profit of +£32.94** to a £1 level stake.
2005 Speciosa – Rockfel (20/1), Nell Gwyn (9/1), 1,000 Guineas (10/1), 2004 Maids Causeway – Rockfel, 2002 Nasij – Masaka Stakes, 1997 Glorosia – Meon Fillies' Mile

FUTURE SUCCESS RATING: ★ ★ ★ ★ ☆

DONCASTER CUP
September 12, Doncaster – (Group 2, Class 1, 3yo+) 2m2f

Last run	Winner/ Trainer & SP	Draw/ Ran	Age	Wght	PR	Next four runs			
07 York 2m 1st Lonsdale Cup One month	Septimus A O'Brien 11/10F	8/8	4	9-04	80	-	-	-	-
06 York 2m 1st Lonsdale Cup Three weeks	Sergeant Cecil R Millman EvensF	4/8	7	9-04	81	WON 2/1F Prix du Cadran Long 2m4f	3rd Prix Royal-Oak Long 2m	*4th John Porter Newb 1m4f	*WON 10/3F Yorkshire Cup York 1m6f
05 York 2m 1st Lonsdale Cup One month	Millenary J Dunlop 11/4	7/7	8	9-04	77	3rd Jockey Club Cup Newm 2m	-	-	-
04 York 2m 3rd = Lonsdale Cup One month	Millenary J Dunlop 7/1	4/8	7	9-04	77	WON 7/2JF Jock' Club Cup Newm 2m	*9th Yorkshire Cup York 1m6f	*4th Princess of Wales' Newm 1m4f	*3rd Goodwood Cup Good 2m
04 Weth 2m5f 6th = Hcp Hdle Five months	Kashtari J Howard Johnson 14/1	8/8	5	9-01	70	11th Jockey Club Cup Newm 2m	3rd Hcp Hdle Muss 2m4f	*WON 11/4F Hcp Hdle Donc 2m4f	*PU Coral Cup Chel 2m5f
03 York 2m 4th Lonsdale Stks One month	Persian Punch D Elsworth 3/1	6/6	10	9-04	79	8th Prix du Cadran Long 2m4f	WON 5/2 Jock' Club Cup Newm 2m	*PU Sagaro Stks Ascot 2m	-
02 York 2m 1st Lonsdale Stks One month	Boreas L Cumani 7/2	7/8	7	9-01	75	2nd Jockey Club Cup Newm 2m	*5th Jockey Club Stk Newm 1m4f	*5th Henry II Sand 2m	*4th Goodwood Cup Good 2m
01 Thir 2m 1st Handicap Three weeks	Alleluia Sir M Prescott 14/1	11/11	3	7-11	75	6th Cesarewitch Newm 2m2f	-	-	-
00 Asco 2m4f 8th Gold Cup Three months	Enzeli J Oxx 15/2	7/9	5	9-07	80	5th Prix du Cadran Long 2m4f	15th Melbourne Cup Flem 2m	*14th Grade 1 Caul 7f	-
99 Newc 2m 1st Northumberland Three months	Far Cry M Pipe 6/1	6/6	4	9-00	74	5th Cesarewitch Newm 2m2f	WON 4/5F Nov Hdle Newb 2m1f	2nd Bula Hdle Chel 2m1f	*4th Champ Hdle Trial Hayd 2m
98 Good 2m 1st Goodwood Cup Two months	Double Trigger M Johnston 9/4JF	4/6	7	9-05	79	-	-	-	-
97 Good 2m 7th Goodwood Cup Two months	Canon Can H Cecil 6/1	3/5	4	9-00	72	4th Cesarewitch Newm 2m2f	*9th Henry II Sand 2m	*5th Gold Cup Ascot 2m4f	*2nd Goodwood Cup Good 2m
96 Asco 2m4f 2nd Gold Cup Three months	Double Trigger M Johnston EvensF	5/6	5	9-07	80	5th Prix du Cadran Long 2m4f	*8th Sagaro Stks Ascot 2m	*8th Gold Cup Ascot 2m4f	*WON 16/1 Goodwood Cup Good 2m

12-year median performance rating of the winner: **77** (out of 100)   *next year*

WINNER'S PROFILE The **Lonsdale Cup at York** has been a major pointer for this in recent times as four triumphed here having won at the Knavesmire, while the Goodwood Cup and Ascot Gold Cup provided four winners. All bar one **already scored over two miles**, with a **win earlier in the campaign** a bonus – only two failed in this area – while penalties were shouldered on numerous occasions. Despite the two 14/1 shots that came via handicaps, the rest emerged from the **first four in the betting**,
Ages were spread evenly, although rare three-year-olds are respected having occupied two of the first three in 2001.

FUTURE POINTERS One of the final staying events in the calendar that has attracted some of the season's 'Cup' winners and was elevated to Group Two status in 2003, since when, three winners managed to score again before the end of term. Three subsequent opportunities traditionally remain for Doncaster Cup winners, the Prix du Cadran, Cesarewitch and Jockey Club Cup, and the latter proved the most successful option – only the below par Kashtari failed to figure in recent times – while the record-breaking Sergeant Cecil managed to land the other two events. Sergeant Cecil took the Cesarewitch after a second here in 2005, but overall, winners of the Doncaster Cup found life tough in both that event and the Prix du Cadran.

Were Doncaster Cup winners profitable to follow on their subsequent three runs?
No – 5 wins from 29 runs returned a loss of -£12.45 to a £1 level stake.

Placed runners' subsequent record (three runs):
Runners-up: 7 wins from 30 runs returned a **profit of +£7.25** to a £1 level stake.
2005 Sergeant Cecil – Cesarewitch, 2002 Persian Punch – Jockey Club Cup,
1997 Persian Punch – Sagaro Stakes, 1996 Celeric – Jockey Club Cup, Yorkshire Cup
Thirds: 2 wins from 16 runs returned a loss of -£1.80 to a £1 level stake.
2007 Allegretto – Prix Royal-Oak, 2000 Persian Punch – Jockey Club Cup

FUTURE SUCCESS RATING: ★ ★ ★ ☆ ☆

FLYING CHILDERS STAKES
September 12, Doncaster – (Group 2, Class 1, 2yo) 5f

Last run	Winner/Trainer & SP	Draw/Ran	Age	Wght	PR	Next four runs			
07 York 6f 3rd Lowther Stks *One month*	Fleeting Spirit J Noseda 5/4F	4/8	2	8-11	73	2nd Cheveley Park Newm 6f	-	-	-
06 York 6f 2nd Gimcrack Stks *Three weeks*	Wi Dud K Ryan 11/4F	2/9	2	9-00	66	2nd Middle Park Newm 6f	5th Temple Stks Sand 5f	13th Golden Jubilee Ascot 6f	2nd Champagne Stks Sand 5f
05 Donc 6f 5th St Leger Yearling *One week*	Godfrey Street R Hannon 8/1	6/9	2	8-12	65	7th Cornwallis Stks Sali 5f	*12th Temple Stks Sand 5f	*23rd King's Stand Ascot 5f	*12th Heritage Hcp Newm 6f
04 Newm 6f 7th July Stks *Three months*	Chateau King Prawn N Littmoden 11/1	7/11	2	8-12	65	9th Middle Park Newm 6f	*9th Group 2 Sha 5f	-	-
03 York 5f 1st Roses Stks *One month*	Howick Falls D Loder 7/4F	6/13	2	8-12	68	***11th Handicap Nad Al 6f	***3rd Group 3 Nad Al 6f	***13th Group 1 Nad Al 6f	-
02 York 6f 5th Lowther Stks *One month*	Wunders Dream J Given 9/2	8/14	2	8-12	73	16th Prix de l'Abbaye Long 5f	*9th Palace House Newm 5f	*9th Kilvington Stks Nott 6f	*17th King's Stand Ascot 5f
01 York 6f 5th Gimcrack Stks *One month*	Saddad Sir M Stoute 4/1	13/13	2	8-12	69	*3rd Scarbrough Stks Donc 5f	**4th Temple Stks Sand 5f	**12th King's Stand Ascot 5f	**5th Chipchase Stks Newc 6f
00 Leop 6f 2nd Phoenix Stks *One month*	Superstar Leo W Haggas 2/1F	3/11	2	8-12	74	2nd Prix de l'Abbaye Long 5f	*6th Temple Stks Sand 5f	*14th King's Stand Ascot 5f	*2nd City Wall Stks Ches 5f
99 Beve 6f 2nd Nursery *Two weeks*	Mrs P Mrs L Stubbs 33/1	13/14	2	8-07	64	*16th Palace House Newm 5f	*9th Ballyogan Stks Leop 5f	*18th Rous Stks Newm 5f	-
98 York 6f 2nd Gimcrack Stks *One month*	Sheer Viking B Hills 9/1	2/13	2	8-12	66	7th Middle Park Newm 6f	*2nd Shergar Cup Good 6f	*10th King's Stand Ascot 5f	*17th July Cup Newm 6f
97 Ripon 6f 2nd 2yo Trophy *Three weeks*	Land Of Dreams M Johnston 15/8F	5/7	2	8-07	71	4th Cornwallis Stks Ascot 5f	*4th Palace House Newm 5f	*14th King's Stand Ascot 5f	*WON 5/1 King George Good 5f
96 York 6f 2nd Gimcrack Stks *One month*	Easycall B Meehan 5/1	1/7	2	9-03	72	6th Middle Park Newm 6f	WON 11/2 Cornwallis Stks Ascot 5f	*8th Temple Stks Sand 5f	*5th King's Stand Ascot 5f

12-year median performance rating of the winner: **69** (out of 100)   **next year **two years ***three years*

WINNER'S PROFILE It's no surprise to see that 11 winners of this sprint were **on the boil during the past month**, the same number that had a **previous victory over this minimum trip**, although 10 reverted back in trip from six furlongs. Those that **raced in the north last time** fared well – the Gimcrack and Lowther provided half of the winners – while those that made the first two in either the Molecomb at Goodwood or the Roses Stakes at York are respected. Strangely, **avoiding the winner's enclosure last time** has been a good omen, though it pays to follow the market as 11 winners emerged in the **first five in the betting**, including Fleeting Spirit last year, who became the fifth filly to score since 1996.

FUTURE POINTERS You have to go back to the early nineties to find the last winner of any real subsequent achievement, which came in the form of the 1991 winner, Paris House, who won Group sprints the following year, as did another of Jack Berry's, Mind Games, the 1994 runner-up here.
Recent results post-Doncaster were poor and the race could do with a superstar to emerge in order of justifying its long-term Group Two status. Fleeting Spirit went on to be a gallant runner-up in the Cheveley Park last year, but not since 1996 has the winner scored again in the near future and very few trained on, including Superstar Leo, who at the time looked to have a bright future.

Were Flying Childers winners profitable to follow on their subsequent three runs?
No – 1 win from 33 runs returned a loss of -£26.50 to a £1 level stake.

Placed runners' subsequent record (three runs):
Runners-up: 5 wins from 29 runs returned a **profit of +£37.28** to a £1 level stake (owing to a 50/1 shot)
2005 Hunter Street – Cornwallis Stakes, 2001 Swiss Lake – Lansdown Stakes, 1996 Compton Place – July Cup

Thirds: 5 wins from 28 runs returned a loss of -£10.37 to a £1 level stake.
2006 Hoh Mike – Pavilion Stakes

FUTURE SUCCESS RATING: ★ ☆ ☆ ☆ ☆

BLANDFORD STAKES
September 12, Curragh – (Group 2, 3yo+) 1m2f

Last run	Winner/Trainer & SP	Draw/Ran	Age	Wght	PR	Next four runs			
07 Curr 1m4f 7th / Irish Oaks / *Two months*	**Four Sins** / J Oxx 9/4JF	8/10	3	8-12	68	8th Grade 1 Wood 1m2f	-	-	-
06 Deau 1m2f 3rd / Prix 'Romanet / *One month*	**Red Bloom** / Sir M Stoute 11/8F	2/11	5	9-04	73	6th Grade 1 Wood 1m2f	-	-	-
05 Deau 1m2f 2nd / Prix 'Romanet / *One month*	**Red Bloom** / Sir M Stoute 15/8F	10/11	4	9-03	74	6th Prix de l'Opera Long 1m2f	*4th Middleton Stks York 1m2f	*3rd Pretty Polly Curr 1m2f	*3rd Prix 'Romanet Deau 1m2f
04 Deau 1m2f 2nd / Prix 'Romanet / *One month*	**Monturani** / G Wragg 12/1	13/13	5	9-03	65	11th Premio Tesio Capa 1m2f	-	-	-
03 York 1m4f 8th / Yorkshire Oaks / *One month*	**Chorist** / W Haggas 11/8F	3/6	4	9-06	72	3rd Princess Royal Ascot 1m4f	*WON 4/7F Pipalong Stks Pont 1m	*WON 7/4 Pretty Polly Curr 1m2f	*3rd Nassau Good 1m2f
02 York 1m4f 5th / Yorkshire Oaks / *One month*	**Irrestible Jewel** / D Weld 7/4F	6/8	3	8-13	70	2nd Prix de l'Opera Long 1m2f	11th Japan Cup Naka 1m3f	-	-
01 Curr 1m2f 12th / Pretty Polly / *Three months*	**Dearly** / J Oxx 12/1	1/12	3	8-08	66	-	-	-	-
00 Curr 1m 8th / Irish 1,000 Guin / *Four months*	**Chiang Mai** / A O'Brien 13/8F	2/6	3	8-07	62	6th Group 2 Long 1m3f	4th Prix Royal-Oak Long 2m	*2nd Group 2 Sain 1m4f	*4th Group 2 Chan 1m4f
99 Sand 1m2f 6th / Eclipse / *Three months*	**Insatiable** / Sir M Stoute 2/7F	5/5	6	9-03	74	-	-	-	-
98 Curr 1m4f 4th / Handicap / *One month*	**Lisieux Rose** / D Weld 7/1	4/7	3	8-06	64	*3rd Glencairn Stks Leop 1m1f	*3rd Group 3 Siro 1m4f	*4th Listed Hcp Down 1m4f	*6th Park Hill Stks Donc 1m7f
97 Curr 1m1f 1st / Solonaway Listed / *One month*	**Quws** / K Prendergast 5/2	3/6	3	8-08	65	*2nd Lincolnshire Curr 1m	*3rd Tatts Gold Cup Curr 1m2f	*WON 8/1 Gallinule Stks Curr 1m2f	*5th Prince of Wales Ascot 1m2f
96 Galw 1m4f 1st / Oyster Listed / *Two months*	**Predappio** / J Oxx 9/2	7/7	3	8-07	70	*2nd Brigadier Gerard Sand 1m2f	*WON 6/1 Hardwicke Stks Ascot 1m4f	*7th King George VI Ascot 1m4f	*7th Grosser 'Baden Bade 1m4f

12-year median performance rating of the winner: **69** (out of 100)   *(2000-1996 1m3f) *next year*

WINNER'S PROFILE The last 11 winners **raced at a Grace One racecourse last time out**, six since 2002 came via an Oaks or the Prix Jean Romanet, while five last stopped at The Curragh.
Every winner **scored over at least nine furlongs** – five of the last six were distance winners – and only Lisieux Rose failed to **win in Pattern company beforehand**. The ages were spread evenly, while the market was informative as 10 winners were **7/1 or shorter**, the biggest-priced victor trained by **John Oxx** who leads the way with three wins from 18 runners. Other trainers of note include **Sir Michael Stoute** with three wins and two runners-up from only six runners, while **Dermot Weld** sent out a couple from seven runners.
Aidan O'Brien is one to be wary of with just the single winner from numerous entries in recent years.

FUTURE POINTERS An event that returned to it's Group Two status after being dropped to a Group Three from 1999 to 2003, although it is hard to judge the true merit of the event as several fillies were understandably packed off to the paddocks in the near future clouding subsequent results a touch.
Winners next time out have a poor record, while of those that remained in training, both Red Bloom and Predappio – two of the best winners since 1996 – did themselves justice the following season in landing the Group One Pretty Polly Stakes, and the Group Two Hardwicke Stakes respectively.

Were Blandford winners profitable to follow on their subsequent three runs?
No – 4 wins from 23 runs returned a loss of -£2.67 to a £1 level stake.

Placed runners' subsequent record (three runs):
Runners-up: 6 wins from 31 runs returned a loss of -£12.70 to a £1 level stake.

Thirds: 5 wins from 15 runs returned a **profit of +£40.00** to a £1 level stake
2005 Kinnaird – Prix de l'Opera, 2004 All Too Beautiful – Middleton Stakes

FUTURE SUCCESS RATING: ★ ★ ★ ★ ★

CHAMPAGNE STAKES
September 13, Doncaster – (Group 2, Class 1, 2yo Colts & Geldings) 7f

Last run	Winner/ Trainer & SP	Draw/ Ran	Age	Wght	PR	Next four runs			
07 Sali 1m 1st Stonehenge Stk Three weeks	McCartney M Johnston 8/1	9/10	2	8-12	72	7th Dewhurst Stks Newm 7f	-	-	-
06 Yarm 6f 1st Maiden Three months	Vital Equine E O'Neill 16/1	7/8	2	8-12	70	3rd Prix Lagardere Long 7f	5th Dewhurst Stks Newm 7f	8th Grade 1 Sain 1m	*2nd 2,000 Guineas Newm 1m
05 Sand 7f 6th = Solario Stks Three weeks	Close To You T Mills 8/1	8/7	2	8-10	71	7th Dewhurst Stks Newm 7f	WON EvsF Listed Trial Ling 1m	*10th 2,000 Guineas Newm 1m	-
05 Curr 7f 3rd = Futurity Stks Three weeks	Silent Times E O'Neill 6/1	6/7	2	8-10	67	*11th Grade 2 Turf 1m1f	*8th Tetrarch Stks Curr 7f	-	-
04 Newb 7f 1st Maiden One month	Etlaala B Hills 6/1	3/10	2	8-10	74	8th Dewhurst Stks Newm 7f	*8th Craven Newm 1m	*7th Temple Stks Sand 5f	*7th Golden Jubilee Ascot 6f
03 Good 7f 1st Vintage Stks Two weeks	Lucky Story M Johnston 2/1	2/6	2	9-00	75	*2nd Sovereign Stks Sali 1m	*7th Prix du Moulin Long 1m	*2nd Q Elizabeth II Ascot 1m	*9th Champion Stks Newm 1m2f
02 Newm 7f 1st Maiden Three weeks	Almushahar D Loder 8/11F	8/11	2	8-10	71	-	-	-	-
01 Newm 7f 1st Maiden Three months	Dubai Destination D Loder 3/1	1/8	2	8-10	77	*2nd Predominate Stk Good 1m3f	**WON 2/5F Conds Stks Nott 1m	**WON 9/2 Queen Anne Ascot 1m	***5th Jacques 'Marois Deau 1m
00 Deau 6f 2nd Prix Morny Three weeks	Noverre D Loder 7/2	4/8	2	9-00	71	2nd Dewhurst Stks Newm 7f	11th Breeders' Cup Chur 1m1f	*2nd UAE Guineas Nad Al 1m	*Disq Poule 'Poulains Long 1m
99 Donc 7f 1st Maiden Two months	Distant Music B Hills 13/8F	1/6	2	8-10	78	WON 4/6F Dewhurst Stks Newm 7f	*2nd Greenham Newm 7f	*8th 2,000 Guineas Newm 1m	*WON 4/1 Park Stks Donc 1m
98 York 7f 1st Acomb Stks One month	Auction House B Hills 7/2	8/8	2	8-10	70	2nd Dewhurst Stks Newm 7f	*16th 2,000 Guineas Newm 1m	*4th Hungerford Stks Newb 7f	*8th Park Stks Donc 1m
97 Good 6f 1st Richmond Stks Two months	Daggers Drawn H Cecil 4/6F	4/5	2	9-00	69	6th Dewhurst Stks Newm 7f	*5th Craven Newm 1m	*18th 2,000 Guineas Newm 1m	-
96 Newm 7f 1st Conds Stks Two months	Bahhare J Dunlop 4/6F	3/4	2	8-10	72	*2nd Conds Stks Donc 1m	*4th Q Elizabeth II Ascot 1m	*3rd Champion Stks Newm 1m2f	-

12-year median performance rating of the winner: **72** (out of 100)   *next year **two years*

WINNER'S PROFILE If we ignore the dead-heat in 2005 – a strange renewal – 10 of the remainder all **scored last time out**, the exception, Noverre, was the only one to have tackled Group One company. Noverre also carried a Group penalty here, along with two others that picked up theirs at Goodwood, including Lucky Story from the Mark Johnston yard that won it twice. However, Barry Hills went one better and scored three times from numerous runners, while Eoghan O'Neill won it twice during the last three years.

FUTURE POINTERS Rodrigo De Triano, in 1991, was the last to have taken this before scooping Classic honours the following year, although a couple of placed runners also found 2,000 Guineas success *(see below)*. Last year's winner, McCartney, was the latest to be found out in the Dewhurst, and only Distant Music followed up in that event nine years ago. In fact, both he and Dubai Destination were the best winners of this event – recorded above par performance ratings (PR) – and were the only ones who scored in Group company during their next four runs, while Noverre took the French 2,000 Guineas (disqualified), before compensation in the Sussex two runs later.

Were Champagne winners profitable to follow on their subsequent three runs?
No – 4 wins from 33 runs returned a loss of -£22.43 to a £1 level stake.

Placed runners' subsequent record (three runs):
Runners-up: 5 wins from 27 runs returned a loss of -£8.97 to a £1 level stake.
2006 Eagle Mountain – Beresford Stakes, 2001 Rock Of Gibraltar – Grand Criterium, Dewhurst, 2,000 Guineas, 1998 Commander Collins – Racing Post Trophy

Thirds: 3 wins from 20 runs returned a **profit of +£14.00** to a £1 level stake.
2006 Cockney Rebel – 2,000 Guineas, Irish 2,000 Guineas, 2005 Killybegs – Craven Stakes

FUTURE SUCCESS RATING: ★ ★ ☆ ☆ ☆

PORTLAND HERITAGE HANDICAP
September 13, Doncaster – (Class 2, 3yo+) 5f 140yds

Last run	Winner/ Trainer & SP	Draw/ Ran	Age	Wght	PR	Next four runs			
07 Ripon 6f 10th Great St Wilfrid One month	Fullandby T Etherington 20/1	21/21	5	9-02	70	15th Ayr Gold Cup Ayr 6f	15th Bentinck Stks Newm 6f	-	-
06 Good 6f 1st Handicap Two weeks	Fantasy Believer J Quinn 20/1	5/19	8	8-13	68	14th Ayr Gold Cup Ayr 6f	WON 12/1 Rous Stks Newm 5f	8th Bentinck Stks Newm 6f	*11th Abernant Stks Newm 6f
05 Sand 5f 2nd Totesport Hcp Three weeks	Out After Dark C Cox 14/1	5/21	4	8-12	74	14th Ayr Gold Cup Ayr 6f	*12th Abernant Stks Newm 6f	*3rd Conds Stks Beve 5f	*7th Temple Stks Sand 5f
04 Ripon 6f 9th Great St Wilfrid One month	Halmahera K Ryan 11/1	13/22	9	9-10	65	9th Rous Stks Newm 5f	7th Bentinck Stks Newm 6f	9th Wentworth Stks Donc 6f	7th Littlewoods Hcp Wolv 6f
03 Ripon 6f 6th Great St Wilfrid One month	Halmahera K Ryan 11/1	15/22	8	9-04	64	7th World Trophy Newb 5f	8th Rous Stks Newm 5f	WON 16/1 Ladbrokes Hcp Ascot 5f	12th Bentinck Stks Newm 6f
02 Good 6f 3rd Ladbrokes Hcp Three weeks	Halmahera K Ryan 6/1F	20/22	7	8-13	61	23rd Ayr Gold Cup Ayr 6f	15th Prix de l'Abbaye Long 5f	5th Coral Sprint York 6f	*3rd Conds Stks
01 Sand 5f 2nd Rated Hcp Two weeks	Smokin Beau J Cullinan 14/1	9/22	4	9-04	67	3rd Ayr Gold Cup Ayr 6f	2nd Rous Stks Newm 5f	*WON 7/4 Conds Stks Nott 5f	*2nd Palace House Newm 5f
00 York 5f 4th Falmouth Hcp Two weeks	Compton Banker G Butler 7/2F	8/22	3	8-08	70	12th Rous Stks Newm 5f	*10th Showcase Hcp Donc 5f	*22nd Abernant Stks Newm 6f	*6th Rated Hcp Newm 6f
99 Deau 6f 1st Stakes Two months	Astonished J Hammond 11/2F	16/21	3	9-06	73	13th Ayr Gold Cup Ayr 6f	*WON 2/5F Listed Colo 5f	*WON 11/4F Dash Hcp Epsom 5f	*4th Porcelanosa Stk Sand 5f
98 York 6f 14th Rated Hcp One week	Cadeaux Cher B Hills 20/1	10/21	4	8-07	64	28th Ayr Gold Cup Ayr 6f	20th Coral Sprint York 6f	17th Rated Hcp Newm 5f	*10th Rated Hcp Newm 6f
97 Ling 5f 3rd Conds Stks Two weeks	Dashing Blue I Balding 10/1	6/21	4	9-12	72	2nd World Trophy Newb 5f	WON 2/1F Rous Stks Newm 5f	*5th Abernant Stks Newm 6th	*9th Palace House Newm 5f
96 York 6f 5th Rated Hcp Three months	Musical Season D Barron 33/1	16/21	4	8-05	61	7th Ayr Gold Cup Ayr 6f	7th W Dixon Hcp Ascot 5f	2nd Rated Hcp Newb 6f	-

12-year median performance rating of the winner: **67** (out of 100)   *next year*

WINNER'S PROFILE A **recent spin** went down well, and 10 of the last 12 winners **arrived from either Goodwood, Ripon, Sandown or York**. A nod was also given to those that ran in the **Stewards' Cup or Great St Wilfrid** – nine since 1997 – while every winner since that year, bar Halmahera who peaked here each year, was **victorious during their previous five outings**.
Weights and official ratings haven't thrown up any clues and with the ratings shooting up each year – six ran with a mark of 100 or more last year – they will become even less important, however, of relevance was a position in the first-half of the betting at **20/1 or shorter**, which knocked out 20 runners in the last two years.
Although well respected in these sprints, trainer David Nicholls has yet to strike gold from well over 20 runners.

FUTURE POINTERS The message is clear if contemplating backing the winner of the Portland next time out – leave well alone and consider laying it instead. The natural route post-Doncaster is the following week's Ayr Gold Cup under a penalty, but not since 1992 was the winner, Lochsong, followed up. Interestingly, Sarcita achieved that same double the previous year, and it may not be a coincidence that both were massively improved fillies – none have tried since. Two also-rans improved upon their position from the Portland to triumph at Ayr in recent times, however, with Funfair Wane (12th) and Quito (4th) in 2004 and 2003 respectively.
The Rous Stakes at Newmarket proved a wiser path for Doncaster winners, as two succeeded from six runners, while the Bentinck Stakes at the same venue has been less kind in recent years.

Were Portland winners profitable to follow on their subsequent three runs?
Yes – 6 wins from 35 runs returned a **profit of +£5.90** to a £1 level stake.

Placed runners' subsequent record (three runs):
Runners-up: 2 wins from 34 runs returned a loss of -£23.00 to a £1 level stake.

Thirds: 3 wins from 33 runs returned level to a £1 level stake. *1997 My Best Valentine – Bentinck Stakes*

Fourths: 2 wins from 32 runs returned a loss of -£5.50 to a £1 level stake. *2003 Quito – Ayr Gold Cup*

FUTURE SUCCESS RATING: ★ ★ ☆ ☆ ☆

ST LEGER STAKES
September 13, Doncaster – (Class 1, Group 1, 3yo) 1m6f 132yds

Last run	Winner/ Trainer & SP	Draw/ Ran	Age	Wght	PR	Next four runs			
07 York 1m4f 1st One month	**Lucarno** J Gosden 7/2 Great Voltigeur	8/10	3	9-00	81	-	-	-	-
06 Good 1m4f 1st Two months	**Sixties Icon** J Noseda 11/8F Gordon Stks	11/11	3	9-00	83	6th Arc de Triomphe Long 1m4f	***WON 5/2 Jockey Club Stk Newm 1m4f**	*7th Coronation Cup Epsom 1m4f	*10th Prince of Wales' Newm 1m4f
05 Long 1m4f 1st Two months	**Scorpion** A O'Brien 10/11F G Prix de Paris	2/6	3	9-00	79	10th Arc de Triomphe Long 1m4f	*2nd Listed Curr 1m4f	*5th Breeders' Cup Chur 1m4f	*7th Hong Kong Vase Sha 1m4f
04 York 1m4f 1st One month	**Rule Of Law** S Bin Suroor 3/1JF Great Voltigeur	9/9	3	9-00	80	-	-	-	-
03 York 1m4f 2nd One month	**Brian Boru** A O'Brien 5/4F Great Voltigeur	9/12	3	9-00	76	3rd Canadian Int Wood 1m4f	***WON 1/2F Alleged Stks Leop 1m2f**	*5th Mooresbridge St Curr 1m2f	*5th Coronation Cup Epsom 1m4f
02 York 1m4f 3rd One month	**Bollin Eric** T Easterby 7/1 Great Voltigeur	3/8	3	9-00	75	*4th John Porter Stks Newb 1m4f	*3rd Yorkshire Cup York 1m6f	*2nd Hardwicke Ascot 1m4f	*4th Princess' Wales Newm 1m4f
01 York 1m4f 1st One month	**Milan** A O'Brien 13/8F Great Voltigeur	7/10	3	9-00	82	5th Arc de Triomphe Long 1m4f	2nd Breeders' Cup Belm 1m4f	*PU Mooresbridge St Curr 1m2f	-
00 Good 1m4f 1st Two months	**Millenary** J Dunlop 11/4F Gordon Stks	5/11	3	9-00	83	***WON 11/4 Jockey Club St Newm 1m4f**	*3rd Coronation Cup Epsom 1m4f	*5th King George VI Ascot 1m4f	*2nd Geoffrey Freer Newb 1m5f
99 York 1m4f 4th One month	**Mutafaweq** S Bin Suroor 11/2 Great Voltigeur	6/9	3	9-00	84	*3rd Tatts Gold Cup Curr 1m3f	*7th Hardwicke Ascot 1m4f	***WON 6/4F Group 1 Duss 1m4f**	*8th Grosser 'Baden Bade 1m4f
98 Good 1m4f 1st Two months	**Nedawi** S Bin Suroor 5/2F Gordon Stks	1/9	3	9-00	75	*2nd Dubai Classic Nad Al 1m4f	*5th Gold Cup Ascot 2m4f	*2nd King George VI Ascot 1m4f	-
97 York 1m4f 2nd One month	**Silver Patriarch** J Dunlop 5/4F Great Voltigeur	9/10	3	9-00	78	*2nd Jockey Club St Newm 1m4f	***WON 7/2 Coronation Cup Epsom 1m4f**	*4th G Prix St-Cloud Sain 1m4f	*6th King George VI Ascot 1m4f
96 Wind 1m4f 1st Three weeks	**Shantou** J Gosden 8/1 Conds Stks	10/11	3	9-00	81	WON 14/10F Prem'Jock-Club Siro 1m4f	4th Breeders' Cup Wood 1m4f	***WON N/O Premio 'Milano Siro 1m4f**	***WON 11/4 Princess' Wales Newm 1m4f**

12-year median performance rating of the winner: **80** (out of 100)   *(2006 York), *next year*

WINNER'S PROFILE No winner had been off the track for longer than two months and those that took in the **Great Voltigeur** and **Gordon Stakes** last time have a terrific record. The only two who took separate routes both finished in the top-two of a Derby earlier in the campaign, while winners of the Oaks have a superb long-term record. Another successful stepping stone to Doncaster was the King Edward VII where four figured.
A combination of the **first three in the betting** along with the right trainer pointed the way – **Aidan O'Brien**'s runners below 10/1, **Saeed Bin Suroor** and **John Gosden** – although Sir Michael Stoute's have disappointed.

FUTURE POINTERS The final Classic of the year has been criticised owing to the lack of European Derby winners of late, and the overall dip in quality this century was reflected by the fact that no winner scored again in Group One company – only Scorpion took the Coronation Cup two years later.
In this period, both Sixties Icon and Millenary won the Jockey Club Stakes when dropped in class, whereas pre-Millennium, three of the four winners subsequently secured Group One honours.
It is interesting to note that every St Leger winner to have remained in training since 1996 dropped back in trip next time out – only Nedawi stepped up in trip at all in the near future.
Last year's winning trainer, John Gosden, took this with the classy Shantou back in 1996, and it is hoped Lucarno will have a similar career in order to lift the profile of this historic event.

Were St Leger winners profitable to follow on their subsequent three runs?
No – 7 wins from 30 runs returned a loss of -£10.85 to a £1 level stake.

Placed runners' subsequent record (three runs):
Runners-up: 3 wins from 26 runs returned a loss of -£16.25 to a £1 level stake.
2003 High Accolade – Cumberland Lodge

Thirds: 3 wins from 27 runs returned a loss of -£7.85 to a £1 level stake.
2006 Red Rocks – Breeders' Cup, Gordon Richards, 2003 Phoenix Reach – Canadian International

FUTURE SUCCESS RATING: ★ ★ ☆ ☆ ☆

PARK STAKES
September 13, Doncaster – (Group 2, Class 1, 3yo+) 7f

Last run	Winner/ Trainer & SP	Draw/ Ran	Age	Wght	PR	Next four runs			
07 Good 7f 5th Lennox Stks Two months	Arabian Gleam J Noseda 5/2	1/6	3	8-12	72	6th Challenge Stks Newm 7f	-	-	-
06 Good 7f 1st Lennox Stks Two months	Iffraaj S Bin Suroor 4/6F	1/9	5	9-06	81	-	-	-	-
05 Newm 6f 14th July Cup Three months	Iffraaj M Jarvis 7/1	2/11	4	9-00	80	7th Prix de la Foret Long 7f	*7th Golden Jubilee Ascot 6f	*2nd July Cup Newm 6f	*WON 6/4F Lennox Stks Good 7f
04 Newb 6f 1st Hackwood Stks Two months	Pastoral Pursuits H Morrison 5/1	7/8	3	8-10	79	5th Prix de la Foret Long 7f	*7th Queen Anne York 1m	*WON 22/1 July Cup Newm 6f	-
03 Newm 1m 3rd Conds Stks Two months	Polar Ben J Fanshawe 5/1	9/9	4	9-00	72	8th Prix de la Foret Long 7f	9th Ben Marshall Newm 1m	*2nd Leicestershire St Leic 7f	*2nd Spring Trophy Hayd 7f
02 Leop 1m 2nd Desmond Stks One month	Duck Row J Toller 8/1	7/6	7	9-00	73	*4th Silver Trophy Ascot 1m	*WON 5/1 Conds Stks Newm 1m	*4th Hungerford Stks Newb 7f	*4th Strensall Stks York 1m1f
01 York 1m 1st Brad & Bing Hcp Three weeks	Tough Speed S Bin Suroor 6/1	4/11	4	9-00	77	12th Challenge Stks Newm 7f	11th Hong Kong Mile Sha 1m	*3rd Huxley Stks Ches 1m2f	*3rd Queen Anne Ascot 1m
00 Newm 1m 8th 2,000 Guineas Four months	Distant Music B Hills 4/1	2/5	3	8-09	80	3rd Champion Stks Newm 1m2f	10th Breeders' Cup Chur 1m	*4th Earl of Sefton Newm 1m1f	*WON 5/4F Goffs Int Curr 1m1f
99 York 1m 2nd Brad & Bing Hcp Three weeks	Sugarfoot N Tinkler 15/2	3/10	5	9-00	75	2nd Group 2 Long 1m	5th Challenge Stks Newm 7f	*WON 4/1 Leicest'shre St Donc 7f	*5th Lockinge Newb 1m
98 Newb 1m2f 4th Steventon Stks Two months	Handsome Ridge J Gosden 3/1JF	5/6	4	9-04	78	2nd Group 2 Long 1m2f	WON 26/10 Group 3 Sain 1m	14th H Kong Int Cup Sha 1m1f	*6th Earl of Sefton Newm 1m1f
97 Epso 1m1f 2nd Fortune Stks One week	Almushtarak K Mahdi 25/1	4/8	4	9-00	73	7th Group 3 Curr 7f	9th Challenge Stks Newm 7f	*2nd Earl of Sefton Newm 1m1f	*WON 4/1 Anniversary Mile Sand 1m
96 Good 1m 2nd Celebration Mile Three weeks	Bishop Of Cashel J Fanshawe 4/1	5/8	4	9-04	74	4th Group 2 Long 1m	2nd Challenge Stks Newm 7f	-	-

12-year median performance rating of the winner: **76** (out of 100)   *next year*

WINNER'S PROFILE Every winner raced at a **Grade One racecourse last time out**, 10 came via either Goodwood, Newbury, Newmarket or York. Shocks were rare as 11 winners started at **8/1 or shorter** and the best horses came out on top with **official ratings of 107 or more**, while every victor already acquired a **top-three effort in Pattern company**, bar Iffraaj first time round in 2005.
Saeed Bin Suroor trained Iffraaj when he defended the crown in 2006, which was also the handler's second winner from seven runners, but one with a better record was **James Fanshawe**, who struck twice from as many runners.

FUTURE POINTERS Reduced from a mile to seven furlongs in 2003, before an upgrade to Group Two status a year later, the Park Stakes has provided a stage for those who found competition at the highest level too much, along with those that progressed out of handicap company.
The Hall of Fame doesn't exactly smack of individuals that went on to greater achievements, but Pastoral Pursuits gave the event a boost when he took the July Cup in 2005. Winners also struggled next time out and were best swerved – or layed – in events like the Prix de la Foret, however, runners-up from here have a superior subsequent record and advertise themselves as ones to follow *(see below)*.

Were Park Stakes winners profitable to follow on their subsequent three runs?
No – 3 wins from 30 runs returned a loss of -£15.40 to a £1 level stake.

Placed runners' subsequent record (three runs):
Runners-up: 11 wins from 31 runs returned a **profit of +£15.59** to a £1 level stake.
2005 Sleeping Indian – Duty Free Cup, 2004 Firebreak – Challenge Stakes, Hong Kong Mile,
2003 With Reason – Supreme Stakes, 2002 Desert Deer – Joel Stakes, 2001 China Visit – Prix du Rond-Point,
1997 Decorated Hero – Supreme Stakes, Prix du Rond-Point

Thirds: 3 wins from 20 runs returned a loss of -£6.37 to a £1 level stake.
2005 Court Masterpiece – Prix de la Foret, 1997 Samara – Ben Marshall Stakes

FUTURE SUCCESS RATING: ★ ★ ☆ ☆ ☆

IRISH ST LEGER
September 13, Curragh – (Group 1, 3yo+) 1m6f

Last run	Winner/Trainer & SP	Draw/Ran	Age	Wght	PR	Next four runs			
07 Ascot 2m4f 1st Gold Cup *Three months*	**Yeats** A O'Brien 4/7F	4/9	6	9-11	78	3rd Prix du Cadran Long 2m4f	-	-	-
06 Leop 1m4f 1st Ballyroan Stks *One month*	**Kastoria** J Oxx 6/1	8/8	5	9-07	75	8th Canadian Int' Wood 1m4f	2nd Hong Kong Vase Sha 1m4f		
05 Duss 1m4f 2nd Group 1 *Two months*	**Collier Hill** A Swinbank 10/1	5/9	7	9-08	80	*6th Group 3 Nad Al 1m4f	*2nd Sheema Classic Nad Al 1m4f	*7th Hardwicke Stks Ascot 1m4f	*2nd Curagh Cup Curr 1m6f
04 Leop 1m4f 2nd Ballyroan Stks *Two months*	**Vinnie Roe** D Weld 7/2JF	5/13	6	9-08	82	2nd Melbourne Cup Flem 2m	*WON 8/11F Saval Beg Stks Leop 1m6f	*3rd Gold Cup York 2m4f	*3rd Ballyroan Stks Leop 1m4f
03 Leop 1m4f 1st Ballyroan Stks *One month*	**Vinnie Roe** D Weld 2/1	4/6	5	9-09	82	5th Arc de Triomphe Long 1m4f	4th Prix Royal-Oak Long 2m	*2nd Saval Beg Stks Leop 1m6f	*2nd Ballyroan Stks Leop 1m4f
02 Leop 1m4f 1st Ballyroan Stks *One month*	**Vinnie Roe** D Weld 4/7F	7/8	4	9-09	83	4th Melbourne Cup Flem 2m	*WON 4/5F Ballyroan Stks Leop 1m4f	*WON 2/1 Irish St Leger Curr 1m6f	*5th Arc de Triomphe Long 1m4f
01 Curr 1m6f 1st Ballycullen Stks *Three weeks*	**Vinnie Roe** D Weld 5/1	1/8	3	8-12	80	WON 37/10 Prix Royal-Oak Long 2m	*WON 2/1 Saval Beg Stks Leop 1m6f	*2nd Gold Cup Ascot 2m4f	*WON 9/10F Ballyroan Stks Leop 1m4f
00 Ascot 1m4f 1st Shergar Cup *Two months*	**Arctic Owl** J Fanshawe 7/2	8/8	6	9-08	77	5th Melbourne Cup Flem 2m	**4th Nov Hdle Donc 2m1f	**3rd Ashton Park Newb 1m5f	**WON 13/2 Conds Stks Wind 1m4f
99 Deau 1m7f 1st Group 2 *One month*	**Kayf Tara** S Bin Suroor 1/2F	1/5	5	9-08	85	*WON 15/8F Yorkshire Cup York 1m6f	*WON 11/8F Gold Cup Ascot 2m4f	-	-
98 Deau 1m7f 2nd Group 2 *One month*	**Kayf Tara** S Bin Suroor 4/1	7/7	4	9-08	84	*WON 36/10 Group 2 Long 2m	*3rd Gold Cup Ascot 2m4f	*WON 9/4JF Goodwood Cup Good 2m	*WON 4/5F Group 2 Deau 1m7f
97 Curr 1m2f 3rd Royal Whip Stks *Two months*	**Oscar Schindler** K Prendergast 2/1JF	5/7	5	9-08	76	4th Arc de Triomphe Long 1m4f	3rd Prix Royal-Oak Long 1m7f	8th Japan Cup Toky 1m4f	-
96 Ascot 1m4f 4th King George VI *Two months*	**Oscar Schindler** K Prendergast 4/1	7/9	4	9-08	75	3rd Arc de Triomphe Long 1m4f	15th Melbourne Cup Flem 2m	*2nd Tatts Gold Cup Curr 1m2f	*5th Coronation Cup Epsom 1m4f

12-year median performance rating of the winner: **80** (out of 100)   *next year **two years*

WINNER'S PROFILE There were several simple, but strong clues to finding the winner, the first involved **winning form earlier in the campaign** as 10 boasted such a credential – two exceptions finished runner-up. Winning form beyond 12 furlongs also stood out, as all 12 since 1996 **scored over at least 13 furlongs** beforehand, while a place in the **top four of the betting** showed the way – first and second favourites did well. **Four-year-olds and above** held sway with only the remarkable four-times winner, Vinnie Roe, triumphing for the Classic generation during his first year – over 20 three-year-olds flopped since 1996.

FUTURE POINTERS Unlike the English equivalent, the Irish St Leger is open to all age-groups and has attracted the 'real stayers', as a glance at the subsequent results shows that 11 of the last 12 winners from here ran again over this trip or further, in comparison to the Doncaster version, in which only two ventured as far.
In fact, every winner of the English St Leger stepped back to 12 furlongs in the near future, unlike at The Curragh, from where a future Ascot Gold Cup winner emerged. Three Irish St Leger winners came back to defend their title, and Vintage Crop joined the above list by scoring twice before subsequently going on to land the Melbourne Cup after his first victory in 1993. Further strength in depth comes from the placed runners that provided a wealth of future winners, including a few thirds that went on to Canadian International glory *(see below)*.

Were Irish Leger winners profitable to follow on their subsequent three runs?
No – 9 wins from 32 runs returned a loss of -£4.69 to a £1 level stake.

Placed runners' subsequent record (three runs):
Runners-up: 8 wins from 30 runs returned a loss of -£4.57 to a £1 level stake.
2005 The Whistling Teal – Ormonde Stakes, 2003 Gamut – Jockey Club Stakes,
2001 Millenary – Princess of Wales's, 1998 Silver Patriarch – Group One Gran Premio del Jockey-Club,
Jockey Club Stakes, 1997 Persian Punch – Sagaro Stakes
Thirds: 4 wins from 17 runs returned a **profit of +£9.60** to a £1 level stake.
2002 Ballingarry – Canadian International, 2001 Marienbard - Jockey Club Stakes,
2000 Mutafaweq – Canadian International

FUTURE SUCCESS RATING: ★ ★ ★ ★ ☆

SELECT STAKES
September 13-14, Goodwood – (Group 3, Class 1, 3yo+) 1m2f

Last run	Winner/ Trainer & SP	Draw/ Ran	Age	Wght	PR	Next four runs			
07 Good 1m4f 3rd Glorious Stks Two months	Stotsfold W Swinburn 7/1	3/6	4	9-00	71	-	-	-	-
06 Sali 1m2f 1st Upavon Stks One month	Pictavia S Bin Suroor EvensF	7/6	4	8-11	76	5th Group 1 Capa 1m2f	*3rd Grade 3 Sara 1m3f	-	-
05 Hayd 1m3f 2nd Rose' Lancaster Two months	David Junior B Meehan 15/8F	6/8	3	8-07	81	WON 25/1 Champion Stks Newm 1m2f	*WON 9/2F Dubai Duty Free Nad Al 1m1f	*4th Prince of Wales' Ascot 1m2f	*WON 9/4 Eclipse Sand 1m2f
04 Good 1m4f 3rd Glorious Stks Two months	Alkaadhem M Tregoning 11/2	8/7	4	9-00	76	WON 6/4F Foundation Stk Good 1m2f	*WON 11/4F Group 2 Nad Al 1m1f	*4th Dubai Duty Free Nad Al 1m1f	*6th Earl of Sefton Newm 1m1f
03 Wind 1m2f 1st Winter Hill Stks Three weeks	Leporello P Harris 15/8	3/5	3	8-10	72	*3rd Huxley Stks Ches 1m2f	*7th Diomed Stks Epsom 1½m	**5th Gala Stks Sand 1m2f	**7th Steventon Stks Newb 1m2f
02 Epso 1m4f 3rd Derby Four months	Moon Ballad S Bin Suroor 4/6F	4/6	3	8-12	80	2nd Champion Stks Newm 1m2f	*WON N/O Maktoum Stks Nad Al 1m1f	*WON 11/4 Dubai World Cup Nad Al 1m2f	*9th Prince of Wales' Ascot 1m2f
01 Hayd 1m3f 1st Rose' Lancaster Two months	Nayef M Tregoning 8/13F	2/3	3	8-10	83	WON 8/13F Cumb'ld Lodge Ascot 1m4f	WON 3/1F Champion Stks Newm 1m2f	*WON 9/4F Sheema Classic Nad Al 1m4f	*3rd Tatts Gold Cup Curr 1m3f
00 Hayd 1m3f 1st Rose' Lancaster One month	Ekraar M Tregoning 10/11F	3/5	3	8-10	80	*4th Maktoum Stks Nad Al 1m2f	*7th Dubai World Cup Nad Al 1m2f	*3rd Prix d'Ispahan Long 1m1f	*4th Coronation Cup Epsom 1m4f
99 Sand 1m2f 8th Eclipse Three months	Lear Spear D Elsworth 9/2	4/7	4	9-05	74	9th Champion Stks Newm 1m2f	3rd Hong Kong Cup Sha 1m2f	*2nd Maktoum Stks Nad Al 1m2f	*9th Dubai World Cup Nad Al 1m2f
98 Hayd 1m3f 1st Rose' Lancaster Two months	Mutamam A Stewart 11/8F	4/4	3	8-10	79	4th Champion Stks Newm 1m2f	*8th Turf Classic Nad Al 1m2f	**2nd Conds Stks Newm 1m2f	**WON 4/9F Conds Stks Good 1m4f
97 Wind 1m2f 3rd Winter Hill Stks Three weeks	Fahris B Hanbury 10/3	2/5	3	8-07	72	4th Cumb'lnd Lodge Ascot 1m4f	WON 11/10F Darley Stks Newm 1m1f	*8th Brigadier Gerard Sand 1m2f	**6th Turf Classic Nad Al 1m2f
96 Newm 1m4f 2nd Princess' Wales Three months	Singspiel Sir M Stoute 11/10F	2/4	4	9-03	84	WON 19/10F Canadian Int Wood 1m4f	2nd Breeders' Cup Wood 1m4f	WON 66/10 Japan Cup Toky 1m4f	*WON N/O Dubai World Cup Nad Al 1m2f

12-year median performance rating of the winner: **77** (out of 100)   *next year **two years

WINNER'S PROFILE Eleven **three and four-year-olds** lined up having recorded a **top-three finish in Pattern company**, while all bar last year's winner **visited the winner's enclosure earlier in the campaign**. Winning form **over this intermediate trip** was also vital as 10 boasted such credentials – the other two won over nine and 11 furlongs – and shocks were rare, as the **first three in the betting** dominated.
An **official rating of 104 or more** was a must – the majority were 110 or higher – including trainer **Marcus Tregoning**'s three winners from seven runners, while **Saeed Bin Suroor** sent out two from the same number.

FUTURE POINTERS It can only be a matter of time before this historic event for middle-distance performers is upgraded to Group Two status as it boasts an impressive Hall of Fame that has featured a host of subsequent globetrotting Group One performers stretching back to Dancing Brave in 1986.
Amongst the last 12 victors were two subsequent World Cup and Champion Stakes winners, while the likes of Mutamam and Ekraar eventually took honours at the highest level in the Canadian International and Gran Premio Del Jockey Club respectively. The last four winners that raced in Dubai the following spring all succeeded, three of whom collected big prizes at the World Cup meeting.

Were Select winners profitable to follow on their subsequent three runs?
Yes – 12 wins from 32 runs returned a **profit of +£31.96** to a £1 level stake.

Placed runners' subsequent record (three runs):
Runners-up: 0 win from 18 runs returned a loss of -£18.00 to a £1 level stake.

Thirds: There was only one qualifier that never raced again.

FUTURE SUCCESS RATING: ★ ★ ★ ★ ☆

NATIONAL STAKES
September 14, Curragh – (Group 1, Class 1, 2yo Colts & Fillies) 7f

Last run	Winner/ Trainer & SP	Draw/ Ran	Age	Wght	PR	Next four runs			
07 Curr 7f 1st Futurity Stks One month	New Approach J Bolger 9/4F	7/9	2	9-01	81	WON 6/4F Dewhurst Stks Newm 7f	- U ?ER3~/	-	-
06 Curr 7f 1st Futurity Stks One month	Teofilo J Bolger 2/1	5/6	2	9-01	80	WON 11/8F Dewhurst Stks Newm 7f	-	-	-
05 Curr 6f 1st Phoenix Stks Two months	George Washington A O'Brien 2/11F	2/7	2	9-00	78	*WON 6/4F 2,000 Guineas Newm 1m	*2nd Irish 2,000 Guin Curr 1m	*3rd Celebration Mile Good 1m	*WON 13/8F Q Elizabeth II Ascot 1m
04 Newm 7f 1st Superlative Stks Three months	Dubawi S Bin Suroor 8/13F	2/7	2	9-00	80	*5th 2,000 Guineas Newm 1m	*WON 7/4JF Irish 2,000 Guin Curr 1m	*3rd Derby Epsom 1m4f	*WON 10/3 Jacques 'Marois Deau 1m
03 Curr 6f 1st Phoenix Stks Two months	One Cool Cat A O'Brien 4/6F	2/8	2	9-00	76	*13th 2,000 Guineas Newm 1m	*5th International Stks Curr 1m	*WON 3/1 Phoenix Sprint Curr 6f	*3rd Nunthorpe Stks York 5f
02 Gowr 7f 1st Maiden Two months	Refuse To Bend D Weld 7/1	3/7	2	9-00	74	*WON 4/7F 2,000 Guin Trial Leop 1m	*WON 9/2 2,000 Guineas Newm 1m	*13th Derby Epsom 1m4f	*WON 8/11F Desmond Stks Leop 1m
01 Curr 7f 1st Futurity Stks One month	Hawk Wing A O'Brien 8/15F	5/7	2	9-00	82	*2nd 2,000 Guineas Newm 1m	*2nd Derby Epsom 1m4f	*WON 8/15F Eclipse Sand 1m2f	2nd Irish Champion Leop 1m2f
00 Curr 7f 3rd Futurity Stks One month	Beckett A O'Brien 10/1	10/9	2	9-00	72	*2nd Solonaway Stks Curr 1m	*WON 3/1F Joel Stks Newm 1m	*10th Champion Stks Newm 1m2f	
99 Curr 1m 1st Maiden Two weeks	Sinndar J Oxx 7/1	9/8	2	9-00	75	*2nd Ballysax Stks Leop 1m2f	*WON 7/4F Derby Trial Leop 1m2f	*WON 7/1 Derby Epsom 1m4f	*WON 11/10F Irish Derby Curr 1m4f
98 Curr 7f 2nd Futurity Stks One month	Mus-If D Weld 8/1	6/9	2	9-00	68	*2nd 2,000 Guin Trial Leop 1m	*4th Irish 2,000 Guin Curr 1m	*5th International Stk Curr 1m 1f	*4th Group 2 Colo 1m
97 Curr 7f 1st Listed Stks Two months	King Of Kings A O'Brien 4/9F	4/9	2	9-00	72	*WON 7/2 2,000 Guineas Newm 1m	*15th Derby Epsom 1m4f	-	-
96 Tral 1m 1st Maiden One month	Desert King A O'Brien 11/1	2/10	2	9-00	74	6th Dewhurst Stks Newm 7f	*2nd Gladness Stks Curr 7f	*WON 2/1F Tetrarch Stks Curr 7f	*WON 3/1 Irish 2,000 Guin Curr 1m

12-year median performance rating of the winner: **76** (out of 100) *next year*

Eleven winners arrived following a **top-three position in the Futurity or Phoenix Stakes last time out**, or **off the back of a maiden victory**. Nine winners in total were Group winners beforehand, while eight already proved themselves at The Curragh. The market was a valuable guide as the last 11 winners all emerged from the **first-three in the betting**, including five of **Aidan O'Brien's** six winners from over 30 runners since 1996. **Jim Bolger** and **Dermot Weld** also got on the scoresheet twice each from nine and 10 runners respectively.

The National Stakes has grown so quickly in stature over the past 12 years that it is now arguably the leading juvenile contest in Britain and Ireland, such is the strength of the winner's subsequent results. Quite simply, nine winners since 1996 all went on to score again in Group One company, including three winners of the 2,000 Guineas, two in the Irish equivalent, and a dual winner of the English and Irish Derby – a mouth-watering record. Throw in a handful more subsequent Group Ones such as the QEII, Jacques le Marois and the Eclipse, and it is clear to see why bookmakers now react sharply towards the winner's ante-post Classic odds after the race. The increasing strength in depth of the National Stakes was also highlighted by the last two runners-up, both of whom took Group One events next time out *(see below)*.

Were National Stakes winners profitable to follow on their subsequent three runs?
Yes – 13 wins from 31 runs returned a **profit of +£13.97** to a £1 level stake.

Placed runners' subsequent record (three runs):
Runners-up: 6 wins from 26 runs returned a loss of -£14.44 to a £1 level stake.
2007 Rio De La Plata – Group One Prix Jean-Luc Lagardere,
2006 Holy Roman Emperor – Group One Prix Jean-Luc Lagardere, 2001 Naheef – Winter Hill Stakes

Thirds: 3 wins from 18 runs returned a loss of -£3.91 to a £1 level stake.
2003 Pearl Of Love – Gran Criterium, 1998 Festival Hall – Beresford Stakes

FUTURE SUCCESS RATING: ★ ★ ★ ★ ★

DUBAI DUTY FREE ARC TRIAL
September 19, Newbury – (Group 3, Class 1, 3yo+) 1m3f

Last run	Winner/Trainer & SP	Draw/Ran	Age	Wght	PR	Next four runs			
07 Good 1m2f 5th Select Stks *One week*	**Halicarnassus** M Channon 9/1	5/6	3	8-13	75	17th Japan Cup Toky 1m4f	-	-	-
06 York 1m2f 3rd Juddmonte Int *One month*	**Blue Monday** R Charlton 2/1F	2/9	5	9-06	76	4th Canadian Int Wood 1m4f	*5th Group 2 Caul 7f	-	-
05 Newm 1m4f 4th Fred Archer Stks *Three months*	**Compton Bolter** G Butler 25/1	4/6	8	9-02	75	3rd Cumb'lnd Lodge Newm 1m4f	3rd Churchill Stks Ling 1m2f	2nd Handicap Wolv 1m4f	*5th Tolworth Hdle Sand 2m1f
04 Epso 1m2f 1st Conds Stks *Three weeks*	**Sights On Gold** S Bin Suroor 3/1F	3/8	5	9-02	74	7th Group 2 Long 1m2f	2nd Darley Stks Newm 1m1f	2nd Hong Kong Vase Sha 1m4f	*14th Dubai Duty Free Nad Al 1m1f
03 Ches 1m5f 1st Rated Hcp *Three weeks*	**Compton Bolter** G Butler 9/2	3/6	6	9-02	75	2nd Cumb'lnd Lodge Ascot 1m4f	2nd Godolphin Stks Newm 1m4f	7th St Simon Stks Newb 1m4f	**WON 7/2JF** **Churchill Stks** Ling 1m2f
02 Wind 1m4f 3rd Conds Stks *One month*	**Legal Approach** M Johnston 4/1	3/6	3	8-09	65	**4th Conds Stks Ripo 1m4f	**10th Listed Hcp Hami 1m4f	***10th Handicap Nad Al 1m	***8th Handicap Nad Al 1m
01 York 1m2f 2nd Juddmonte Int *Two months*	**Grandera** J Fanshawe 5/6F	4/5	3	8-09	80	*2nd Group 3 Nad Al 1m4f	*5th QE II Cup Sha 1m2f	**WON N/O** Intern'tnl Cup Kran 1m2f	**WON 4/1** **Prince of Wales** Ascot 1m2f
00 Kemp 1m4f 3rd September Stks *Two weeks*	**Pawn Broker** D Elsworth 6/4F	7/7	3	8-08	75	2nd Godolphin Stks Newm 1m4f	*2nd Magnolia Stks Kemp 1m2f	*3rd Gordon Richards Sand 1m2f	*3rd Festival Stks Good 1m2f
99 York 1m4f 1st Great Voltigeur *Two months*	**Fantastic Light** Sir M Stoute 9/4	6/6	3	9-00	80	11th Arc de Triomphe Long 1m4f	**WON N/O** **Sheema Classic** Nad Al 1m4f	*2nd Coronation Cup Epsom 1m4f	*5th Eclipse Sand 1m2f
98 Bade 1m3f 2nd Group 3 *Three weeks*	**Scorned** I Balding 7/1	1/7	3	8-09	73	7th Cumb'lnd Lodge Ascot 1m4f	***6th Conds Stks Sali 1m6f	***15th Handicap Donc 1m4f	***2nd Rated Hcp Ayr 1m5f
97 Epso 1m4f 3rd September Stks *Two weeks*	**Posidonas** P Cole 8/1	5/5	5	9-02	68	9th Arc de Triomphe Long 1m4f	2nd H Kong Int Vase Sha 1m4f	**WON 5/1** **John Porter** Newb 1m4f	*6th Coronation Cup Epsom 1m4f

11-year median performance rating of the winner: **74** (out of 100)   **next year **two years ***three years*

WINNER'S PROFILE There wasn't an ideal prep for Newbury as winners came from all different directions and races, however, five finished in the top-three at either Epsom or York last time. Nine winners already **scored between 10 and 12 furlongs**, the other two were second over the former trip, while eight **won in Pattern company** – two of the exceptions finished second in Group One and Two events. The last two winners carried a Group penalty and were **officially rated of 105 or more** which has been important – seven of the last nine were at least 111. **Three-year-olds** won over half the renewals and struck six times from 30 runners, however, their presence was less scattergun of late, only five ran in the last three years that resulted in a winner and runner-up.

FUTURE POINTERS An event in which the race title somewhat camouflages the fact that it has proven a quality Group Three within it's own right, despite having had little impact on proceedings over in Longchamp the next month. Although only two winners went on to contest the Arc, plenty of decent performers lined up here, including the three-year-olds Fantastic Light and Grandera, who both went on to record multiple Group/Grade One honours. Only Compton Bolter, however, managed to get back on the scoresheet later that year, as every winner flopped next time out in events like the Cumberland Lodge Stakes.

Were Arc Trial winners profitable to follow on their subsequent three runs?
No – 3 wins from 30 runs returned a loss of -£22.00 to a £1 level stake.

Placed runners' subsequent record (three runs):
Runners-up: 3 wins from 24 runs returned a loss of -£19.12 to a £1 level stake.
2001 Mubtaker – Godolphin Stakes

Thirds: 1 win from 6 runs returned a loss of -£3.37 to a £1 level stake.

FUTURE SUCCESS RATING: ★ ★ ★ ★ ★

FIRTH OF CLYDE STAKES

September 20, Ayr – (Group 3, Class 1, 2yo Fillies) 6f

Last run	Winner/ Trainer & SP	Draw/ Ran	Age	Wght	PR	Next four runs			
07 York 6f 4th Lowther Stks One month	Unilateral B Smart 5/1	10/11	2	8-12	60	9th Cheveley Park Newm 6f	-	-	-
06 Good 7f 6th Prestige Stks Three weeks	Princess Iris E O'Neill 11/1	6/7	2	8-12	58	*10th Grade 3 Sant 1m	*6th Handicap Holl 7f	-	-
05 Donc 7f 1st Nursery Two weeks	Violette Sir M Prescott 9/4F	9/12	2	8-08	64	2nd 2yo Trophy Redc 6f	2nd Rockfel Stks Newm 7f	3rd Group 3 Mais 7f	*6th Germ 1,000 Guin Duss 1m
04 Ches 6f 3rd Conds Stks One month	Golden Legacy R Fahey 7/1	1/9	2	8-08	60	4th Cheveley Park Newm 6f	*6th Spring Cup Ling 7f	*6th Nell Gwyn Newm 7f	*11th 1,000 Guineas Newm 1m
03 Sali 6f 3rd Dick Poole Stks Three weeks	Ruby Rocket H Morrison 7/2	4/6	2	8-08	59	4th Cheveley Park Newm 6f	*5th Fred Darling Newb 7f	*2nd Cecil Frail Stks Hayd 6f	*3rd Chipchase Stks Newc 6f
02 Donc 6f 4th Yearling Sales Two weeks	Airwave H Candy 2/1F	7/10	2	8-08	64	WON 11/2 Cheveley Park Newm 6f	*WON 5/2JF Temple Stks Sand 5f	*2nd Golden Jubilee Ascot 6f	*3rd July Cup Newm 6f
01 Sali 6f 2nd Dick Poole Stks Three weeks	Misterah M Tregoning 2/1F	1/8	2	8-08	61	3rd Rockfel Stks Newm 7f	*WON 9/2 Nell Gwyn Newm 7f	*6th 1,000 Guineas Newm 1m	*4th Coronation Stks Ascot 1m
00 Sali 6f 3rd Dick Poole Stks Three weeks	Alshadiyah J Dunlop 4/1CF	9/9	2	8-08	55	5th Cornwallis Stks Newb 5f	*3rd Fred Darling Newb 7f	*2nd Class Stks Yarm 6f	*4th Rated Hcp Newm 6f
99 Ripo 6f 3rd 2yo Trophy Three weeks	Femme Fatale W Jarvis 3/1	3/6	2	8-08	59	*4th Conds Stks Newm 6f	*WON 7/2 Conds Stks Yarm 6f	*16th Rous Stks Newm 5f	-
98 Donc 6f 4th Conds Stks One week	Evening Promise B McMahon 16/1	5/10	2	8-08	57	*9th Fred Darling Newb 7f	*16th 1,000 Guineas Newm 1m	*3rd Fillies' Listed Newm 6f	*17th Silver Bowl Hcp Hayd 1m
97 Sali 6f 1st Dick Poole Stks Three weeks	Regal Revolution P Walwyn 16/1	10/14	2	8-13	58	*13th 1,000 Guineas Newm 1m	*6th Surrey Stks Epsom 7f	*7th Chipchase Stks Newc 6f	*4th Conds Stks Newm 6f
96 Good 7f 4th Prestige Stks One month	Queen Sceptre B Hills 8/1	1/6	2	8-11	60	6th Cheveley Park Newm 6f	-	-	-

12-year median performance rating of the winner: **59** (out of 100)   *next year*

WINNER'S PROFILE Every filly entered the stalls fit having **raced within the past month**, while the same number raced at either Chester, Doncaster, Goodwood, Ripon or Salisbury earlier in the campaign, four of whom ran in the Dick Poole Fillies' Stakes at the latter venue last time.
Only Femme Fatale took this as a maiden, the remainder **already scored over a sprint trip** – eight over six furlongs – while the **last five winners all experienced Pattern class.**

FUTURE POINTERS Despite being granted Group Three status in 2004, the standard of this fillies' juvenile event has failed to progress from Listed level, as only five of the 39 participants in the last four years were officially rated above 100. Winners' subsequent efforts following the Western meeting have hardly set the pulse racing, with more forgettable names than distinguished ones, and Group One Cheveley Park scorer Airwave stood out from the crowd. Unilateral last year became the fourth filly to be turned over in that race at Newmarket, while those to have taken the Fred Darling/Guineas route were also outclassed.

Were Firth of Clyde winners profitable to follow on their subsequent three runs?
No – 4 wins from 31 runs returned a loss of -£11.00 to a £1 level stake.

Placed runners' subsequent record (three runs):
Runners-up: 2 wins from 29 runs returned a loss of -£9.50 to a £1 level stake.
2004 Castelletto – Cornwallis, 2002 Irrestible – Kilvington Stakes

Thirds: 2 wins from 17 runs returned a loss of -£13.50 to a £1 level stake.

FUTURE SUCCESS RATING: ★ ☆ ☆ ☆

AYR GOLD CUP

September 20, Ayr – (Heritage Handicap, 3yo+) 6f

Last run	Winner/ Trainer & SP	Draw/ Ran	Age	Wght	PR	Next four runs			
07 Hayd 6f 10th Sprint Cup *Two weeks*	**Advanced** K Ryan 20/1	22/28	4	9-09	72	4th Guisborough Stk Redc 7f	5th Bentinck Stks Newm 6f	2nd Group 3 Mais 6f	9th Wentworth Stks Donc 6f
06 Hayd 5f 9th Be Friendly Hcp *Two weeks*	**Fonthill Road** R Fahey 16/1	6/23	6	9-02	67	2nd Conds Stks Hami 6f	5th Handicap Newm 5f	*3rd Conds Stks Hayd 6f	*7th Duke of York York 6f
05 Good 6f 1st Totesport Hcp *Three weeks*	**Presto Shinko** R Hannon 12/1	2/27	4	9-02	71	**WON 5/1 Wentworth Stks Donc 6f**	*2nd Conds Stks Kemp 6f	*10th Abernant Stks Newm 6f	*2nd Leisure Stks Wind 6f
04 Donc 5½f 12th Portland Hcp *Two weeks*	**Funfair Wane** D Nicholls 33/1	8/24	5	8-06	63	6th Conds Stks Hami 6f	*9th Handicap Donc 6f	*2nd Conds Stks Beve 5f	*18th Handicap York 6f
03 Donc 5½f 4th Portland Hcp *Two weeks*	**Quito** D Chapman 20/1	10/26	6	8-06	65	16th Tote Hcp Ascot 7f	12th Coral Sprint York 6f	5th Conds Stks Donc 7f	2nd Rated Hcp Sout 5f
02 Donc 1m 3rd Conds Stks *Two weeks*	**Funfair Wane** D Nicholls 16/1	16/28	3	9-03	70	*12th Cammidge Tr'py Donc 6f	*8th Conds Stks Thir 6f	**WON 11/2 Conds Stks Beve 5f**	*8th Achilles Stks Kemp 5f
01 Good 6f 12th Stewards' Cup *Two months*	**Continent** D Nicholls 10/1	22/28	4	8-10	69	3rd Tote Hcp Ascot 7f	*11th Showcase Hcp Donc 5f	*2nd Conds Stks Kemp 6f	*2nd Abernant Stks Newm 6f
00 Kemp 6f 13th Handicap *Two weeks*	**Bahamian Pirate** D Nicholls 33/1	7/28	5	8-03	65	5th Rated Hcp Newm 7f	**WON 9/1 Bentinck Stks Newm 6f**	*9th Cammidge Tr'py Donc 6f	*6th Abernant Stks Newm 6f
99 Newm 6f 3rd Hopeful Stks *One month*	**Grangeville** I Balding 11/1	17/28	4	9-00	70	**2nd Listed Keen 6f	***3rd Stakes Keen 6f	-	-
98 Hayd 7f 4th Handicap *Two weeks*	**Always Alight** K Burke 16/1	8/29	4	8-07	63	5th Coral Sprint York 6f	7th Bentinck Stks Newm 6f	3rd Rated Hcp Newb 6f	10th Wentworth Stks Donc 6f
97 Good 6f 1st Sprint Cup *One week*	**Wildwood Flower** R Hannon 14/1	24/29	4	9-03	62	5th Rated Hcp Newm 6f	9th Bentinck Stks Newm 6f		
96 Good 6f 1st Stewards' Cup *Two months*	**Coastal Bluff** D Barron 3/1F	28/28	4	9-10	73	*5th July Cup Newm 6f	**WON 8/11F Conds Stks Newm 5f**	*11th Stewards' Cup Good 6f	**WON 6/1 Nunthorpe York 5f**

12-year median performance rating of the winner: **68** (out of 100)   *next year **two year ***three years*

WINNER'S PROFILE The majority were **on the boil within the past month** – two exceptions came straight from the Stewards' Cup – while 11 were **proven over the trip**, the same number that started at double-figure odds. Since Coastal Bluff followed up from the Stewards' Cup in 1996, six Ayr winners were unplaced at Goodwood, while two carried penalties here after landing a sprint handicap there earlier in the month. In fact, 10 had their **prep at Goodwood, Doncaster or Haydock**. **Four to six-year-olds** dominated, while **David Nicholls**, **Richard Hannon** and **Karl Burke** all have good pedigrees. As with the Wokingham, the official ratings and weights have changed massively allowing those at the top a chance, Advanced was a leading example last year.

FUTURE POINTERS A talented bunch amongst the Hall of Fame that did themselves proud during long careers following Ayr, however, from a potential point of view, only three went on to lift Group One honours going back to 1987 – Continent, Coastal Bluff and Lochsong. The problem winners face from these type of events is that they are forced into better company as their handicap mark becomes uncompetitive, which is represented by their subsequent results, although two handled Listed company later that term. Overall, Ayr Gold Cup winners have been a shade disappointing in the near future and punters may want to think twice about backing them next time out.

Were Ayr Gold Cup winners profitable to follow on their subsequent three runs?
No – 4 wins from 34 runs returned a loss of -£9.77 to a £1 level stake.

Placed runners' subsequent record (three runs):
Runners-up: 2 wins from 31 runs returned a loss of -£13.50 to a £1 level stake (*2002 The Tatling – Coral Sprint Trophy*)
Thirds: 3 wins from 36 runs returned a loss of -£26.00 to a £1 level stake.
Fourths: 5 wins from 34 runs returned a loss of -£0.53 to a £1 level stake (*White Heart – Festival Hcp, Doncaster Mile*)

Were badly drawn horses worth following?
Concentrating purely on the years when there was a clear bias, six qualifiers emerged since 1996, and although they all lost next time out, two scored in Listed company a run later – Majestic Times and Pipalong – while the future winners of the Stewards' Cup and Ayr Gold Cup were pointed up in Guinea Hunter and Wildwood Flower.

FUTURE SUCCESS RATING: ★★☆☆☆

MILL REEF STAKES
September 20, Newbury – (Group 2, Class 1, 2yo) 6f

Last run	Winner/Trainer & SP	Draw/Ran	Age	Wght	PR	Next four runs			
07 Donc 5f 7th Flying Childers *Two weeks*	**Dark Angel** B Hills 9/4F	1/6	2	9-01	72	**WON 8/1** **Middle Park Stk** **Newm 6f**	9th Dewhurst Stks Newm 7f	-	-
06 Deau 6f 3rd Prix Morny *One month*	**Excellent Art** N Callaghan 15/8	4/6	2	9-01	75	*4th Poule 'Poulains Long 1m	*WON 8/1 **St James Palace** **Ascot 1m**	*2nd Sussex Good 1m	-
05 Donc 7f 4th Champagne Stk *Two weeks*	**Cool Creek** R Hannon 5/1F	4/13	2	8-12	65	*12th Futurity Stks Keen 1m1f	-	-	-
04 Donc 6f 1st Conds Stks *One week*	**Galeota** R Hannon 7/1	6/9	2	8-12	69	*3rd Greenham Newb 7f	*WON 10/3F **Surrey Stks** **Epsom 7f**	*2nd Golden Jubilee York 6f	*18th July Cup Newm 6f
03 York 6f 4th Gimcrack Stks *One month*	**Byron** D Loder 9/1	1/10	2	8-12	69	*3rd Poule 'Poulains Long 1m	*8th St James Palace Ascot 1m	*WON 16/1 **Lennox Stks** **Good 7f**	*9th Jacques 'Marois Deau 1m
02 Deau 6f 2nd Prix Morny *One month*	**Zafeen** M Channon 8/11F	5/8	2	8-12	68	5th Middle Park Stks Newm 6f	4th Dewhurst Stks Newm 7f	*2nd Greenham Newb 7f	*2nd 2,000 Guineas Newm 1m
01 Deau 6f 4th Prix Morny *One month*	**Firebreak** I Balding 10/3	8/10	2	9-01	71	*2nd UAE 2,000 Guin Nad Al 1m	*10th UAE Derby Nad Al 1m2f	*6th Poule 'Poulains Long 1m	*5th Celebration Mile Good 1m
00 York 6f 1st Roses Stks *One month*	**Bouncing Bowdler** M Johnston 10/1	4/7	2	8-12	65	*21st Cork & Orrery Ascot 6f	*12th Chipchase Stks Newc 6f	*3rd Hackwood Stks Newb 6f	*8th Shergar Cup Ascot 6f
99 Kemp 6f 1st Sirenia Stks *Two weeks*	**Primo Valentino** P Harris 6/5F	2/4	2	8-12	68	**WON 10/3** **Middle Park Stk** **Newm 6f**	*7th 2,000 Guineas Newm 1m	*6th Group 3 Bade 6f	*4th July Cup Newm 6f
98 Bade 6f 1st Group 2 *Three weeks*	**Golden Silca** M Channon 7/2	6/5	2	8-12	62	8th Cheveley Park Newm 6f	*2nd Fred Darling Newb 7f	*7th 1,000 Guineas Newm 1m	*2nd Irish 1,000 Guin Curr 1m
97 Ripon 6f 1st 2yo Trophy *One month*	**Arkadian Hero** L Cumani 4/9F	5/7	2	8-12	69	4th Middle Park Stks Newm 6f	*4th Euro Free Hcp Newm 7f	*10th 2,000 Guineas Newm 1m	*2nd Leisure Stks Ling 6f
96 Ripon 6f 1st 2yo Trophy *One month*	**Indian Rocket** J Dunlop 10/3	1/10	2	8-12	67	10th Middle Park Stks Newm 6f	*5th Cork & Orrery Ascot 6f	*3rd July Cup Newm 6f	*3rd King George Good 5f

12-year median performance rating of the winner: **68** (out of 100)   **next year*

WINNER'S PROFILE A **recent run within the past month** was important, along with experience, as every winner since 1996 **appeared at least three times** at the racecourse, the same number that **performed in Pattern company**. A recent victory or second in the form-line was common and 10 winners already **scored over six furlongs** – two exceptions over the minimum – while the **first three or four in the betting** boast a tremendous record.
Two trainers with a couple of victories by their name include **Mick Channon** and **Richard Hannon**, from 10 and 12 runners respectively, while Brian Meehan has yet to strike from nine attempts.

FUTURE POINTERS Not an event that has provided a solid breeding ground for Classic winners, in fact you have to go back around 35 years when Mon Fils went on to lift the 2,000 Guineas. However, the Mill Reef has produced some decent performers since 1999 as the likes of Firebreak and Zafeen won Group Ones in the long-term, the latter took the St James's Palace at Royal Ascot, a feat matched by the 2006 winner Excellent Art. Winners haven't exactly covered themselves in glory next time out, although last year's winner, Dark Angel, joined Primo Valentino in Middle Park Stakes glory, while the six Mill Reef victors that waited until next term before their next appearance were all beaten.

Were Mill Reef winners profitable to follow on their subsequent three runs?
Yes – 5 wins from 33 runs returned a **profit of +£10.66** to a £1 level stake.

Placed runners' subsequent record (three runs):
Runners-up: 2 wins from 29 runs returned a loss of -£18.87 to a £1 level stake.
1996 Proud Native – Redcar 2yo Trophy

Thirds: 3 wins from 14 runs returned a **profit of +£14.50** to a £1 level stake.
2005 Nantyglo – Conqueror Stakes, 2002 Cassis – Musidora, 2001 Twilight Blues – European Free Handicap

FUTURE SUCCESS RATING: ★ ★ ★ ☆ ☆

JOHN SMITH'S STAKES
September 20, Newbury – (Heritage Handicap, Class 2, 3yo+) 1m2f

Last run	Winner/ Trainer & SP	Draw/ Ran	Age	Wght	PR	Next four runs			
07 Beve 1m2f 2nd Totesport Hcp *One month*	**Monte Alto** L Cumani 9/2	19/15	3	8-10	73	6th Cambridgeshire Newm 1m1f	-	-	-
06 Ascot 1m 6th Royal Hunt Cup *Three months*	**Pinpoint** W Swinburn 7/1	16/20	4	9-03	68	3rd Cambridgeshire Newm 1m1f	8th Tote Hcp Wind 1m2f	***WON 8/1** **Spring Cup** **Newb 1m**	*2nd Suffolk Stks Hcp Newm 1m1f
05 York 1m2f 2nd Motability Hcp *One month*	**Star Of Light** B Meehan 16/1	20/19	4	8-13	71	16th Cambridgeshire Newm 1m1f	***WON 9/1** **Suffolk Hcp** **Newm 1m1f**	*3rd Rose Bowl Hcp Epsom 1m2f	*5th Wolferton Hcp Ascot 1m2f
04 Ascot 1m2f 6th Diamond Hcp *Two months*	**Spuradich** L Cumani 14/1	7/18	4	8-09	65	**2nd Maiden Hdle Cart 2m2f*	**3rd Nov Hdle Sout 2m1f*	**2nd Maiden Hdle Worc 2m*	***3rd Hcp Hdle Towc 2m*
03 York 1m4f 18th Knavesmire Hcp *One month*	**Navado** Sir M Stoute 25/1	9/19	4	9-09	64	2nd Rated Hcp Ascot 1m2f	**11th Nov Hdle Hayd 2m4f*	**10th Nov Hdle Hayd 2m4f*	**WON 11/2 Nov Hdle Mark 2m2f*
02 Donc 1m4f 2nd Handicap *One week*	**Solo Flight** B Hills 20/1	10/18	5	8-13	62	10th Tote Hcp Ascot 1m4f	6th Rated Hcp Newm 1m4f	11th Handicap Newb 1m2f	*9th Rosebery Hcp Kemp 1m2f
01 York 1m1f 4th Strensall Stks *Three weeks*	**Albuhera** M Johnston 7/1	7/16	3	9-10	68	23rd Cambridgeshire Newm 1m1f	7th Darley Stks Newm 1m1f	*23rd Lincoln Hcp Donc 1m	*4th Conds Stks Ascot 1m2f
00 Pont 1m4f 3rd Handicap *Two months*	**Komistar** P Harris 16/1	9/17	5	8-06	62	9th Handicap Newb 1m2f	-	-	-
99 Leic 1m2f 6th Handicap *One month*	**Komistar** P Harris 16/1	4/16	4	8-06	63	7th Rated Hcp Newb 1m1f	*12th City & Sub Hcp Epsom 1m2f	*2nd Class Stks Chep 1m2f	*8th Ladbroke Hcp Ascot 1m2f
98 Newm 1m2f 2nd Rated Hcp *Three months*	**Brilliant Red** P Hedger 12/1	11/18	5	9-01	61	24th Cambridgeshire Newm 1m1f	9th Autumn Hcp Newm 1m	*8th Handicap Good 1m	*2nd Doubleprint Hcp Sand 1m
97 Chep 1m2f 5th Handicap *Two months*	**Sharp Consul** H Candy 9/1	5/15	5	8-07	57	3rd Handicap Newb 1m2f	**3rd Maiden Hdle Down 2m2f*	**6th Maiden Hdle Tram 2m*	**Fell Maiden Hdle Down 2m*
96 Chep 1m2f 2nd Handicap *Two weeks*	**Game Ploy** D Haydn Jones 5/1	12/17	4	8-05	55	19th Cambridgeshire Newm 1m1f	9th Handicap Newb 1m2f	12th November Hcp Donc 1m4f	*5th Walker Hcp Ches 1m2f

12-year median performance rating of the winner: **64** (out of 100)   *italic = jumps, *next year*

WINNER'S PROFILE Eleven winners ran in **handicap company last time out**, while 10 were **proven over this intermediate distance** of 10 furlongs, the two exceptions, Pinpoint and Navado were the only pair that ran just twice that season. Not many emerged from the top of the official ratings band for this handicap as 11 were **rated 94 or lower**, while **three to five-year-olds** dominated, and though the Classic generation only struck twice since 1996, they won it four times from 1990 to 1995. Those aged six and above are without a win from over 40 runners, while favourites also have a poor record. Trainer **Luca Cumani** won it twice in recent years, while the retired Peter Harris's protégé, **Walter Swinburn**, may look for a second victory like his mentor.

FUTURE POINTERS Formerly known as the Courage Handicap, this valuable event has become an informative stepping stone towards the Cambridgeshire a fortnight later. However, as the table above highlights, winners of this event may have peaked too early as they struggled at Newmarket under a penalty, where as those in behind did better, such as Formal Decree (third), Blue Monday (second) and Spanish Don (ninth) in three of the last four years. Winners overall have a horrid record next time out and could be ones to avoid or lay, and none went on to greater achievements – three went hurdling – although two recent victors took valuable handicaps early the following term.

Were winners of this handicap profitable to follow on their subsequent three runs?
No – 2 wins from 32 runs returned a loss of -£13.00 to a £1 level stake.

Placed runners' subsequent record (three runs):
Runners-up: 6 wins from 28 runs returned a **profit of +£5.33** to a £1 level stake.
2005 Blue Monday – Cambridgeshire, Goodwood Festival Stakes, 2002 Far Lane – John Smith's Cup, 2001 Kirovski – City & Suburban Handicap
Thirds: 8 wins from 31 runs returned a **profit of +£12.35** to a £1 level stake.
2006 Formal Decree – Cambridgeshire, 2005 Crosspeace – Serlby Stakes
Fourths: 5 wins from 33 runs returned a **profit of +£22.83** to a £1 level stake.
2001 Scotty's Future – Victoria Cup

FUTURE SUCCESS RATING: ★ ★ ★ ☆ ☆

DUBAI WORLD TROPHY
September 20, Newbury – (Group 3, Class 1, 3yo+) 5f

Last run	Winner/ Trainer & SP	Draw/ Ran	Age	Wght	PR	Next four runs			
07 Sand 5f 3rd Handicap Three weeks	Rowe Park Mrs L Jewell 25/1	7/8	4	9-00	80	2nd Rous Stks Newm 5f	-	-	-
06 Leic 5f 2nd Conds Stks Two weeks	Dixie Belle M Quinlan 50/1	7/10	3	8-10	68	-	-	-	-
05 Curr 5f 2nd Flying Five Two weeks	The Tatling M Bradley 5/2	10/13	8	8-13	79	6th Prix de l'Abbaye Long 5f	5th Bentinck Stks Newm 5f	*13th Abernant Stks Newm 5f	*5th Palace House Newm 5f
04 Long 5f 2nd Group 3 Two weeks	The Tatling M Bradley 5/1	6/11	7	9-04	81	3rd Diadem Stks Ascot 6f	2nd Prix de l'Abbaye Long 5f	12th H Kong Sprint Sha 5f	*7th Group 3 Long 5f
03 Ascot 7f 15th International Hp Two months	Ratio J Hammond 9/2	8/9	5	8-13	75	14th Diadem Stks Ascot 6f	*WON 124/10 Listed Deau 5f	*10th Sprint Cup Hayd 6f	*11th Diadem Stks Ascot 6f
02 Curr 5f 2nd Flying Five Three weeks	Lady Dominatrix Mrs N Dutfield 9/1	13/12	3	9-09	70	*8th Palace House Newm 5f	*12th Duke of York York 6f	*5th Group 2 Chan 5f	*20th King's Stand Ascot 5f
01 Donc 5f 6th Scarbrough Stks Two weeks	The Trader M Blanshard 9/1	7/11	3	8-12	78	3rd Rous Stks Newm 5f	5th H Kong Sprint Sha 5f	*8th Palace House Newm 5f	*WON 5/1 Achilles Stks Kemp 5f
00 Epsom 5f 2nd Showcase Hcp Three weeks	Ivory's Joy K Ivory 16/1	6/11	5	8-08	73	9th Rous Stks Newm 5f	*16th Rated Hcp Newb 5f	*2nd Lansdown Stks Bath 5f	*7th Palace House Newm 5f
99 Hayd 6f 8th Sprint Cup Three weeks	Imperial Beauty P Makin 6/1	9/13	3	8-07	75	2nd Prix de l'Abbaye Long 5f	*4th Temple Stks Sand 5f	*4th King's Stand Ascot 5f	**4th Group 3 Long 5f
98 Donc 5½f 8th Portland Hcp Two weeks	Cathedral B Meehan 14/1	9/12	4	8-13	72	-	-	-	-
97 York 5f 5th Nunthorpe One month	Eveningperformance H Candy 9/1	5/16	6	8-08	74	11th Prix de l'Abbaye Long 5f	-	-	-

11-year median performance rating of the winner: **75** (out of 100)   **next year **two years*

WINNER'S PROFILE Nine winners arrived having **raced within the past three weeks** – 10 at a **Grade One venue** – while just one dropped into this sprint from seven furlongs. Only proven speedsters need apply as all 11 had **scored over a sprint trip** – eight over the minimum – while all bar one had secured a **top-four finish in Pattern class** already. Favourites have a woeful record as plenty of big priced-winners popped up, including the last two who emerged from the favoured **three to five-year-old band** – ignoring dual winner The Tatling.
It may only be a coincidence, but stalls one to four have struggled, so side with a **high to middle draw**.

FUTURE POINTERS Still in it's infancy, this sprint doesn't draw much attention on the racing calendar despite acquiring Group Three status in 2002, but winners haven't really moved onwards following here although a couple ran well in the Prix de l'Abbaye at Longchamp. In fact, the first two home here in 2004 went on to reverse roles in finishing first and second in the Abbaye that year, while Imperial Beauty also finished runner-up in 1999. Three winners were held in the Rous Stakes next time out, however, as a trio of third-placed runners from here succeeded in that event *(see below)* – including Judd Street last year – and it is that group who have proven the more worthy of following.

Were World Trophy winners profitable to follow on their subsequent three runs?
No – 1 win from 23 runs returned a loss of -£9.60 to a £1 level stake.

Placed runners' subsequent record (three runs):
Runners-up: 4 wins from 30 runs returned a loss of -£1.50 to a £1 level stake.
2007 Judd St – Rous Stakes, 2004 Var – Prix de l'Abbaye

Thirds: 8 wins from 30 runs returned a **profit of +£0.80** to a £1 level stake.
2005 Boogie Street – Rous Stakes, 2004 Airwave – Ridgewood Peal Stakes, 2000 Andreyev – Wentworth Stakes, 1998 Bishops Court – Rous Stakes, 1997 Bollin Joanne – Duke of York

FUTURE SUCCESS RATING: ★ ★ ★ ★ ★

ROYAL LODGE STAKES
September 27, Ascot – (Group 2, Class 1, 2yo Colts & Geldings) 1m

Last run	Winner/Trainer & SP	Draw/Ran	Age	Wght	PR	Next four runs			
07 Sand 7f 2nd Solario Stks One month	City Leader B Meehan 9/1	7/11	2	8-12	74	2nd R Post Trophy Donc 1m	-	-	
06 Newm 7f 3rd Superlative Stk Three months	Admiralofthefleet A O'Brien 11/2	7/7	2	8-12	72	*7th Leop 1m	*WON 7/2 Dee Stks Ches 1m2f	*10th Derby Epsom 1m4f	*5th Eclipse Sand 1m2f
05 Good 1m 2nd Stardom Stks Three weeks	Leo J Gosden 8/1	2/8	2	8-11	66	9th Breeder's Cup Belm 1m1f	-	-	
04 Sali 1m 1st Listed Stks Two months	Perfectperformance S Bin Suroor 4/6F	1/8	2	8-11	70	7th Dewhurst Stks Newm 7f	*5th Rose' Lancaster Hayd 1m3f	**WON 7/4 Conds Stks Newm 1m4f	***WON 4/5F Conds Stks Nott 1m2f
03 Kemp 7f 1st Conds Stks Three weeks	Snow Ridge M Tregoning 15/8F	6/10	2	8-11	69	9th Dewhurst Stks Newm 7f	*2nd 2,000 Guineas Newm 1m	*7th Derby Epsom 1m4f	
02 Sand 7f 1st Novice Stks Two weeks	Al Jadeed J Gosden 3/1	8/9	2	8-11	70	10th Dewhurst Stks Newm 7f	*3rd Conds Stks Donc 1m	*2nd Conds Stks Kemp 1m	*9th Darley Stks Newm 1m1f
01 Gowr 1m 1st Maiden Two months	Mutinyonthebounty A O'Brien 16/1	7/9	2	8-11	67	4th Criterium Int Sain 1m	-	-	
00 Good 1m 1st Stardom Stks Three weeks	Atlantis Prince S Woods 11/2	1/8	2	8-11	69	*11th UAE Derby Nad Al 1m1f	*5th Prix Lupin Long 1m3f	*16th Derby Italiano Capa 1m4f	**6th Listed Nad Al 1m
99 Curr 7f 1st Listed Two months	Royal Kingdom A O'Brien 10/11F	5/6	2	8-11	68	5th Criterium St-Cloud Sain 1m2f	Group 3 Long 1m	*5th Dante York 1m2f	-
98 Good 1m 1st Stardom Stks Three weeks	Mutaahab E Dunlop 5/1	6/6	2	8-11	71	*4th Greenham Newb 7f	*4th Dante York 1m2f	*5th Conds Stks Epsom 1m2f	***6th Stakes Fair 1m2f
97 Donc 7f 1st Conds Stks Three weeks	Teapot Row J Toller 9/1	4/8	2	8-11	65	*6th Dante York 1m2f	*2nd Conds Stks Donc 1m	*2nd Rose' Lancaster Hayd 1m3f	*8th Celebration Mile Good 1m
96 Newm 7f 1st Maiden Three months	Benny The Dip J Gosden 9/4F	3/8	2	8-11	73	3rd R Post Trophy Donc 1m	*2nd Classic Trial Sand 1m2f	*WON 10/3F Dante York 1m2f	*WON 11/1 Derby Epsom 1m4f

12-year median performance rating of the winner: **70** (out of 100)   **next year **two years *** three years*

(2005 Newmarket)

WINNER'S PROFILE Trends remain thin on the ground, although until recently, it appeared rude not to arrive at Ascot without a victory last time out, but that trend shifted in the last three years as winners finished placed. Only Leo had yet to **score over seven furlongs or a mile** – no maidens won this – while only four tackled Group rivals prior and were all placed, however, nursery participants should be ignored. Not many big-priced winners emerged as those that **started at single-figure odds** came out best on 11 occasions.
Trainers **Aidan O'Brien** and **John Gosden** won it three times each from 13 and nine runners respectively.

FUTURE POINTERS St Paddy took this back in 1959 before Derby and St Leger glory the following year and though Mister Baileys (1993) and Benny The Dip (1996) also went on to Classic success, the Royal Lodge hasn't a great recent history for providing top-notch performers. In fact, none since Benny The Dip kicked on in Group One company, and overall, winners from here should be swerved – or layed – especially next time out, although a couple of recent third-placed horses did land major events subsequently at big odds *(see below)*.

Were Royal Lodge winners profitable to follow on their subsequent three runs?
No – 3 wins from 30 runs returned a loss of -£18.42 to a £1 level stake.

Placed runners' subsequent record (three runs):
Runners-up: 7 wins from 32 runs returned a loss of -£12.83 to a £1 level stake.
2000 Turnberry Isle – Blandford Stakes,1997 Prolix – Dee Stakes, 1996 Desert Story – Horris Hill, Craven Stakes

Thirds: 4 wins from 23 runs returned a **profit of +£29.04** to a £1 level stake.
2007 Scintillo – Gran Criterium, 2005 Palace Episode – Racing Post Trophy (20/1),
2004 Wilko – Breeders' Cup (20/1)

FUTURE SUCCESS RATING: ★ ★ ☆ ☆ ☆

MEON VALLEY STUD FILLIES' MILE
September 27, Ascot – (Group 1, Class 1, 2yo Fillies) 1m

Last run	Winner/ Trainer & SP	Draw/ Ran	Age	Wght	PR	Next four runs			
07 Curr 7f 2nd Moyglare Stud *One month*	**Listen** A O'Brien 10/3	6/7	2	8-12	72	-	-	-	-
06 York 1m 1st May Hill Stks *Two weeks*	**Simply Perfect** J Noseda 11/4	5/8	2	8-12	75	*3rd 1,000 Guineas Newm 1m	*6th Oaks Epsom 1m4f	**WON 6/1** **Falmouth** **Newm 1m**	*3rd Prix d'Astarte Deau 1m
05 Good 7f 1st Prestige Stks *One month*	**Nannina** J Gosden 5/1	2/6	2	8-10	76	*12th 1,000 Guineas Newm 1m	**WON 6/1JF** **Coronation Stk** **Ascot 1m**	*2nd Falmouth Newm 1m	*3rd Nassau Good 1m2f
04 Donc 1m 1st May Hill Stks *Three weeks*	**Playful Act** J Gosden 11/4	2/9	2	8-10	72	**WON 11/4** **Lanc'shire Oaks** **Hayd 1m4f**	*2nd Irish Oaks Curr 1m4f	*10th Yorkshire Oaks York 1m4f	*8th Prix de l'Opera Long 1m2f
03 Newm 7f 1st Maiden *Two months*	**Red Bloom** Sir M Stoute 3/1	3/7	2	8-10	70	*4th 1,000 Guineas Newm 1m	*3rd Coronation Stks Ascot 1m	**WON EvsF** **Strensall Stks** **York 1m1f**	*4th Blandford Stks Curr 1m2f
02 Newm 7f 1st Sweet Solera *Two months*	**Soviet Song** J Fanshawe 11/10F	10/10	2	8-10	71	*4th 1,000 Guineas Newm 1m	*2nd Coronation Stks Ascot 1m	*4th Prix du Moulin Long 1m	*5th Q Elizabeth II Ascot 1m
01 Good 7f 1st Prestige Stks *Two months*	**Gossamer** L Cumani 4/5F	8/7	2	8-10	76	*8th 1,000 Guineas Newm 1m	**WON 4/1F** **Irish 1,000 Guin** **Curr 1m**	*11th Coronation Stks Ascot 1m	*3rd Prix du Moulin Long 1m
00 Sand 1m 1st Conds Stks *Two months*	**Crystal Music** J Gosden 4/1	8/9	2	8-10	68	*4th 1,000 Guineas Newm 1m	*2nd Irish 1,000 Guin Curr 1m	*3rd Coronation Stks Ascot 1m	*6th Prix de l'Opera Long 1m2f
99 Donc 1m 1st May Hill Stks *Three weeks*	**Teggiano** C Brittain 11/8F	1/6	2	8-10	64	*2nd Ribblesdale Ascot 1m4f	*10th Irish Oaks Curr 1m4f	-	-
98 Curr 7f 5th Moyglare Stud *Three weeks*	**Sunspangled** A O'Brien 9/1	6/8	2	8-10	69	*15th 1,000 Guineas Newm 1m	*7th Irish 1,000 Guin Curr 1m	*6th Oaks Epsom 1m4f	*2nd Irish Oaks Curr 1m4f
97 Donc 1m 3rd May Hill Stks *Three weeks*	**Glorosia** L Cumani 10/1	4/8	2	8-10	70	*3rd Group 2 Long 1m4f	*5th Irish Oaks Curr 1m4f	*2nd Conds Stks Chep 1m2f	**4th Vodafone Listed Epsom 1m1f
96 Donc 1m 1st May Hill Stks *Three weeks*	**Reams Of Verse** H Cecil 5/1	2/8	2	8-10	67	*6th 1,000 Guineas Newm 1m	**WON 11/10F** **Musidora Stks** **York 1m2f**	**WON 5/6F** **Oaks** **Epsom 1m4f**	*4th Yorkshire Oaks York 1m4f

12-year median performance rating of the winner: **71** (out of 100)   *(2005 Newmarket) *next year **two years*

WINNER'S PROFILE Every winner **raced within the past two months at a Grade One racecourse**, with winners of the **May Hill** (4) and **Prestige Stakes** (2) providing six winners, while two more scored at Newmarket last time out. Listen last year became a rare victor not to have **already scored over at least seven furlongs** – was a narrow runner-up over that trip – while it paid to stick with the **first three in the betting** during the last nine years. Trainer **Aidan O'Brien** recorded his second victory from eight runners in 2007, however, two handlers with better strike-rates were **John Gosden** with three from six runners – two of his outsiders at 16/1 & 20/1 were well beaten – and **Luca Cumani** struck twice with just four fillies.

FUTURE POINTERS Those with 1,000 Guineas aspirations were put to the test in this strong fillies' event, and though several Group One performers emerged in recent years, you have to go back to 1995 for the last subsequent winner at Newmarket in Bosra Sham – the 1996 third-placed here, Sleepytime, also triumphed.
Eight have failed since, including Reams Of Verse, who gained compensation in the Oaks, an event two runners-up since 1990 went on to win. Overall, winners of the Fillies' Mile have been worthwhile following of late and returned a profit in the near future since 2001, however, it could prove wise to avoid them in the 1,000 Guineas.

Were Meon Fillies' Mile winners profitable to follow on their subsequent three runs?
No – 7 wins from 32 runs returned a loss of -£3.31 to a £1 level stake.

Placed runners' subsequent record (three runs):
Runners-up: 7 wins from 29 runs returned a loss of -£4.17 to a £1 level stake.
2005 Alexandrova – Oaks, Irish Oaks, 2003 Sundrop – Severals Stakes, 2002 Casual Look – Oaks

Thirds: 3 wins from 16 runs returned a loss of -£0.25 to a £1 level stake.
1997 Exclusive – Coronation Stakes, 1996 Sleepytime – 1,000 Guineas

FUTURE SUCCESS RATING: ★ ★ ★ ☆ ☆

TOTESPORT HERITAGE HANDICAP
September 27, Ascot – (Class 2, 3yo+) 7f

Last run	Winner/Trainer & SP	Draw/Ran	Age	Wght	PR	Next four runs			
07 Warw 7f 2nd Conds Stks Two months	Candidato Roy W Haggas 50/1	1/23	6	9-07	68	7th Challenge Stks Newm 7f	-	-	-
06 Ling 7f 14th Totesport Hcp Four months	All Ivory R Charlton 16/1	14/18	4	8-10	70	8th Handicap York 1m	*7th Handicap Nad Al 1m	*10th Handicap Nad Al 1m	-
05 Sand 1m 2nd Handicap Three weeks	All Ivory R Charlton 13/2F	1/18	3	8-08	68	*5th Handicap Newm 7f	*14th Totesport Hcp Ling 7f	*WON 16/1 Totesport Hcp Ascot 7f	*8th Handicap York 1m
04 Good 7f 11th Class Stks Two months	Kehaar M Magnusson 13/2	12/15	3	8-06	67	-	-	-	-
03 Newb 7f 8th Handicap Two weeks	Master Robbie M Channon 20/1	30/25	4	8-02	63	2nd Handicap Newm 7f	WON 9/2 Rated Hcp York 7f	6th Showcase Hcp Newm 7f	14th Handicap Muss 7f
02 Good 7f 3rd Rated Hcp Two weeks	Millennium Force M Channon 14/1	17/23	4	8-07	61	2nd Handicap Newm 7f	WON 3/1F Conds Stks Donc 7f	6th Wentworth Stks Donc 6f	*WON 5/1 Gladness Stks Curr 7f
01 Hayd 7f 8th Handicap One month	Downland D Barron 40/1	8/24	5	7-10	60	21st Handicap Newm 6f	18th Handicap York 7f	WON 10/1 Showcase Hcp Newc 6f	12th Handicap Wolv 7f
00 Newb 7f 6th Rated Hcp Two months	Duke Of Modena T Balding 9/1	1/26	3	8-09	68	4th Showcase Hcp Newb 6f	*6th Handicap Ling 7f	*2nd Doubleprint Hcp Sand 1m	*29th Royal Hunt Cup Ascot 1m
98 Ayr 6f 4th Ayr Gold Cup One week	White Heart M Johnston 10/1	11/25	3	8-09	74	*WON 9/4 Doncaster Mile Donc 1m	*8th Earl of Sefton Newm 1m1f	*4th Leic'strshre Stk Leic 7f	*6th Shergar Cup Good 7f
97 Donc 1m 6th Porcelanosa Hcp Two weeks	Jo Mell T Easterby 14/1	2/25	4	9-00	66	WON 11/8F Conds Stks Donc 7f	*15th Rated Hcp Newm 7f	*4th Spring Trophy Hayd 7f	*8th Hambleton Hcp York 1m
96 Donc 1m 1st Porcelanosa Hcp Two weeks	Decorated Hero J Gosden 7/1	22/26	4	9-13	73	WON N/O Listed Long 1m	WON N/O Listed Evry 1m	2nd Listed Sain 1m	2nd Wulfrun Stks 1m1½f

12-year median performance rating of the winner: 67 (out of 100)*(1999 abandoned, 2005 Newmarket) *next year*

WINNER'S PROFILE There were no obvious stepping stones to Ascot – not many ran in the International here or the Bunbury Cup – although several took part in the Porcelanosa at Doncaster, while four arrived via efforts over this trip at Goodwood and Newbury. Last year's winner defied a weight trend but it may help to ignore that gelding – raced alone on better ground – and stick with those on the **light side of 9st**. Candidato Bay was also the first six-year-old scorer which indicates he may have been a red herring and **three to four-year-olds** were the ones to side with long-term, more so the Classic generation who won it six times from 1988 to 1995. Ten of the last 11 winners boasted a **prior victory over seven furlongs**, while an **official rating from 85 to 95** proved ideal.

FUTURE POINTERS Run for the first time as the Challenge Cup last year, this is the final instalment of three distinguished seven-furlong handicaps here after the Victoria Cup and International Handicap.
Although field sizes dropped slightly in recent times, it still attracted a host of improving three-year-olds, including the Ayr Silver Cup winner, Utmost Respect and third-placed, Docofthebay, who went on to finish a close second in the Cambridgeshire last year. Winners of this have tended not to head for that Newmarket race, although the 2001 Ascot runner-up, Icriedforyou, was successful.
Overall, winners of this Handicap were worth monitoring and while none followed up since 1998, three won again before the end of term, although last year's questionable winner was asked a lot in Group company next time.

Were winners of this handicap profitable to follow on their subsequent three runs?
Yes – 8 wins from 28 runs returned a **profit of +£17.12** to a £1 level stake.

Placed runners' subsequent record (three runs):
Runners-up: 4 wins from 28 runs returned a **profit of +£23.75** to a £1 level stake.
2001 I Cried For You – Cambridgeshire, 2000 Nice One Clare – Wokingham, 1998 Sugarfoot – Listed Hambleton

Thirds: 3 wins from 32 runs returned a loss of -£7.00 to a £1 level stake.

Fourths: 2 wins from 26 runs returned a loss of -£16.00 to a £1 level stake

FUTURE SUCCESS RATING: ★ ★ ★ ★ ☆

QUEEN ELIZABETH II STAKES
September 27, Ascot – (Group 1, Class 1, 3yo+) 1m

Last run	Winner/ Trainer & SP	Draw/ Ran	Age	Wght	PR	Next four runs			
07 Long 1m 2nd Prix du Moulin *Three weeks*	**Ramonti** S Bin Suroor 5/1	8/7	5	9-03	90	-	-	-	-
06 Good 1m 3rd Celebration Mile *One month*	**George Washington** A O'Brien 13/8F	7/8	3	8-13	92	6th Breeders' Cup Chur 1m2f	*4th Queen Anne Ascot 1m	*3rd Eclipse Sand 1m2f	-
05 Long 1m 1st Prix du Moulin *Three weeks*	**Starcraft** L Cumani 7/2	2/6	5	9-01	84	7th Breeders' Cup Belm 1m2f	-	-	-
04 Leop 1m2f 5th Irish Champion *Two weeks*	**Rakti** M Jarvis 9/2	13/11	5	9-01	89	14th Grade 1 Kyot 1m	7th Hong Kong Cup Sha 1m2f	***WON 7/4F Lockinge Newb 1m**	*2nd Queen Anne Ascot 1m
03 Leop 1m2f 2nd Irish Champion *Three weeks*	**Falbrav** L Cumani 6/4F	4/8	5 .	9-01	90	3rd Breeders' Cup Sant 1m4f	**WON 5/4F Hong Kong Cup Sha 1m2f**	-	-
02 Good 1m 4th Celebration Mile *Two months*	**Where Or When** T Mills 7/1	3/5	3	8-11	82	*2nd Lockinge Newb 1m	*3rd Queen Anne Ascot 1m	*4th Celebration Mile Good 1m	*6th Prix du Moulin Long 1m
01 York 1m1f 2nd Strensall Stks *One month*	**Summoner** S Bin Suroor 33/1	7/8	4	9-01	80	*6th Group 3 Nad Al 1m1f	*9th Dubai Duty Free Nad Al 1m1f	*10th Lockinge Newb 1m	***7th Stakes Abu 1m
00 Good 1m 2nd Celebration Mile *One month*	**Observatory** J Gosden 14/1	6/12	3	8-11	87	***WON 11/10F Prix d'Ispahan Long 1m1f**	*4th Prince of Wales' Ascot 1m2f	-	-
99 Deau 1m 1st Jacques 'Marois *Two months*	**Dubai Millennium** S Bin Suroor 4/9F	3/4	3	8-11	91	***WON N/O Listed Nad Al 1m2f**	***WON N/O Dub' World Cup Nad Al 1m2f**	***WON 5/4 Prince of Wales' Ascot 1m2f**	-
98 Long 1m 1st Prix du Moulin *Three weeks*	**Desert Prince** D Loder 10/3F	1/7	3	8-11	86	14th Breeders' Cup Chur 1m	-	-	-
97 Good 1m 7th Sussex *Two months*	**Air Express** C Brittain 9/1	7/9	3	8-11	83	*7th Lockinge Newb 1m	*4th Group 3 Long 7f	-	-
96 Good 1m 1st Celebration Mile *Two months*	**Mark Of Esteem** S Bin Suroor 10/3	5/7	3	8-11	90	7th Breeders' Cup Wood 1m	-	-	-

12-year median performance rating of the winner: **87** *(out of 100)* *(2005 Newmarket) *next year, ***three years*

WINNER'S PROFILE Nine of the 12 winners raced in either the Celebration Mile, Irish Champion Stakes or the Prix du Moulin last time, the same number that took in Royal Ascot, leaving Dubai Millennium – who ran in the Derby – and pacemaker Summoner as the only two not to have sampled a traditional build-up.
Every winner **scored earlier in the campaign**, while a previous victory **either at Ascot or over the distance of a mile** was a common link shared by all 12, with a Group Two win at least a bonus.
Three-year-olds held sway for a long time until 2003, since when four **five-year-olds** scored, although four-year-olds disappointed and are best swerved. One long-term record to be wary of was the poor record of fillies, Darjina the latest flop last year at 11/4, while trainers to note include **Saeed Bin Suroor**, with four wins from 20 runners, and **Luca Cumani**, with two from as many runners.

FUTURE POINTERS The QEII is often viewed as the event that decides the best miler around, and although many top-class horses have graced this Hall of Fame, from a punting angle it may prove best to appreciate them on the day rather than support any in the future. Several were packed off to stud soon after Ascot, and while four did go on to lift Group/Grade One honours again, a loss was shown to level stakes on their next few runs – only two followed up next time – five met with defeat in the Breeders' Cup. Of those who stayed in training the following year, only one of four succeeded in the Lockinge, a race that was kinder to runners-up from here *(see below)*.

Were QEII winners profitable to follow on their subsequent three runs?
No – 6 wins from 24 runs returned a loss of -£13.90 to a £1 level stake.

Placed runners' subsequent record (three runs):
Runners-up: 5 wins from 19 runs returned a loss of -£6.18 to a £1 level stake.
2003 Russian Rhythm – Lockinge, 2002 Hawk Wing – Lockinge,
1996 Bosra Sham – Champion Stakes, Brigadier Gerard, Prince of Wales's Stakes

Thirds: 3 wins from 16 runs returned a loss of -£6.83 to a £1 level stake.

FUTURE SUCCESS RATING: ★ ★ ☆ ☆ ☆

MARCHPOLE

TOTESPORT HANDICAP
September 28, Ascot – (Class 2, Handicap, 3yo+) 1m4f

Last run	Winner/ Trainer & SP	Draw/ Ran	Age	Wght	PR	Next four runs			
07 Donc 1m2f 4th Handicap Three weeks	All The Good G Butler 8/1	10/13	4	9-04	64	-	-	-	-
06 Yarm 1m2f 4th Handicap Two weeks	Pevensey M Buckley 16/1	4/13	4	8-08	60	6th Ladbrokes Hcp Ascot 1m4f	5th Handicap Ling 1m4f	2nd Maiden Hdle Sout 2m	WON 6/5F Maiden Hdle Catt 2m
05 Newm 1m4f 1st Handicap One month	Ouninpohja A Swinbank 7/2JF	11/12	4	9-04	67	*2nd Braveheart Stks Hami 1m4f	*2nd Listed Cup Muss 1m6f	*2nd Fred Archer Stks Newm 1m4f	*2nd Old Newton Cup Hayd 1m4f
04 Donc 1m2f 5th Class Stks Three weeks	Fort M Johnston 16/1	9/14	3	8-02	61	6th Handicap Newm 1m4f	**3rd Group 2 Jana 1m4f	***2nd Conds Stks Jana 1m4f	-
03 York 1m6f 1st Melrose Hcp Two months	Jagger G Butler 8/1	2/11	3	8-02	60	*13th Northumberland Newc 2m	*3rd Summer Hcp Good 1m6f	*8th Ebor York 1m6f	*4th Hopeful Stks Kemp 1m4f
02 York 1m4f 1st Rated Hcp One month	Scott's View M Johnston 11/2	13/15	3	9-03	65	4th St Simon Stks Newb 1m4f	*4th Conds Stks Newm 1m4f	*2nd March Stks Good 1m6f	*2nd Conds Stks Sali 1m6f
01 Donc 1m4f 16th Handicap Three weeks	Hannibal Lad M Brisbourne 20/1	1/12	5	8-05	60	*9th Handicap Ling 1m2f	*2nd Handicap Ling 1m4f	*5th Handicap Wolv 1m4f	*2nd Doncaster Shield Donc 1m4f
00 Good 1m2f 5th Select Stks Three weeks	Kind Regards M Johnston 15/2	9/11	3	8-04	71	4th Group 2 Long 1m4f	-	-	-
99 York 1m6f 1st Ebor Two months	Vicious Circle L Cumani 13/2	1/16	5	9-09	73	*4th Glorious Hcp Good 1m4f	*4th Jockey Club Cup Newm 2m	**2nd Handicap Nad Al 2m	**PU Gold Cup Ascot 2m4f
98 Ayr 1m5f 1st Rated Hcp Two weeks	Raise A Prince S Woods 8/1	5/16	5	8-13	69	3rd Conds Stks Hayd 1m4f	4th Serlby Stks Donc 1m4f	*2nd Conds Stks Hayd 2m	*WON 15/8 Conds Stks Nott 1m6f
97 Long 1m4f 6th Prix Vermeille Two weeks	Ridaiyma L Cumani 9/2F	12/14	3	8-04	68	9th November Hcp Donc 1m4f	*2nd Group 3 Siro 1m4f	*4th Silver Cup Hcp York 1m6f	*3rd Glorious Hcp Good 1m4f
96 York 1m6f 7th Ebor Two months	Better Offer G Harwood 9/1	14/20	4	9-06	65	14th Cesarewitch Newm 2m2f	18th November Hcp Donc 1m4f	*13th Bessborough Hcp Ascot 1m4f	*6th Silver Cup Hcp York 1m6f

12-year median performance rating of the winner: **60** (out of 100)   *(2005 Newmarket) *next year **two years*

italic=jumps

WINNER'S PROFILE Nine winners **raced within the last month** – three exceptions arrived via the Ebor meeting at York – while **winning form in handicaps earlier in the campaign** was vital as 11 obliged. Those with **winning form between 12 to 14 furlongs** scored 10 times, apart from two trainer **Mark Johnston**'s winners that rose in trip. The Middleham handler won this three times with the Classic generation – two carried penalties – while those carrying big weights of around 9st 7lb or more are to be avoided – four lost last year.
Three to five-year-olds are the ages to stick with as those six and above failed on over 30 occasions, while another trainer to note is **Luca Cumani**, who struck twice in the nineties.

FUTURE POINTERS A handicap stripped of it's 'Heritage' title last year and one that has deteriorated since the Millennium when it regularly attracted 16 runners or more. The subsequent results of winners back up this theory as they have a woeful record post-Ascot – none scored again during their next three runs – and only a few boasted any sort of notable long-term victory in Listed events, while Pevensey won last year's Duke of Edinburgh Stakes at the Royal meeting. However, it could pay to keep an eye on placed runners from here, especially the runners-up *(see below)*, as two went on to scoop the November Handicap later that term.

Were winners of this handicap profitable to follow on their subsequent three runs?
No – 0 win from 31 runs returned a loss of -£31.00 to a £1 level stake.

Placed runners' subsequent record (three runs):
Runners-up: 6 wins from 33 runs returned a loss of -£0.50 to a £1 level stake.
2006 Group Captain – November Handicap, 2000 Romantic Affair – Listed Handicap, 1998 Yavana's Pace – November Handicap, 1997 Taufan's Melody – Serlby Stakes.

Thirds: 5 wins from 31 runs returned a loss of -£0.50 to a £1 level stake.

Fourths: 2 wins from 9 runs returned a loss of -£4.00 to a £1 level stake.
1998 Alcazar – Serlby Stakes

FUTURE SUCCESS RATING: ★ ★ ★ ★ ★

CUMBERLAND LODGE STAKES
September 28, Ascot – (Group 3, Class 1, 3yo+) 1m4f

Last run	Winner/Trainer & SP	Draw/Ran	Age	Wght	PR	Next four runs			
07 Ches 1m5f 1st Ormonde Stks *Five months*	**Ask** Sir M Stoute 11/4	1/8	4	9-03	81	2nd Canadian Int Wood 1m4f	-	-	-
06 York 1m6f 3rd Ebor *Two months*	**Young Mick** G Margarson 7/2	3/8	4	9-00	72	*8th Cumb'lnd Lodge Ascot 1m4	8th Godolphin Stk Newm 1m4f	2nd Conds Stks Leic 1m4f	5th Listed Stks Kemp 1m4f
05 Donc 1m4f 1st Troy Stks *Three weeks*	**Mubtaker** M Tregoning 5/6F	7/6	8	9-00	80	4th St Simon Stks Newb 1m4f	***WON 9/1** John Porter Stk Newb 1m4f	*5th Ormonde Stks Ches 1m5f	*6th Henry II Stks Sand 2m
04 Donc 2m2f 4th Doncaster Cup *Three weeks*	**High Accolade** M Tregoning 3/1	8/9	4	9-00	75	*3rd Aston Park Stks Newb 1m5f	-	-	-
03 Donc 1m6f 2nd St Leger *Three weeks*	**High Accolade** M Tregoning 9/4F	3/5	3	8-11	74	2nd St Simon Stks Newb 1m4f	*4th Coronation Cup Epsom 1m4f	*2nd Hardwicke Stks Ascot 1m4f	*3rd Princess' Wales Newm 1m4f
02 Donc 1m4f 1st Troy Stks *Three weeks*	**Systematic** M Johnston 1/2F	2/5	3	8-06	76	*2nd Geoffrey Freer Newb 1m5f	*5th Grosser 'Baden Bade 1m4f	*5th Dubai Arc Trial Newb 1m3f	*3rd Doncaster Shield Donc 1m4f
01 Good 1m2f 1st Select Stks *Three weeks*	**Nayef** M Tregoning 8/13F	6/7	3	8-09	82	**WON 3/1F** Champion Stks Newm 1m2f	***WON 9/4F** Sheema Classic Nad Al 1m4f	*3rd Tatts Gold Cup Curr 1m3f	*4th Prince of Wales' Ascot 1m2f
00 Kemp 1m4f 1st September Stks *Three weeks*	**Mutamam** A Stewart 4/6F	6/6	5	9-03	80	4th Breeders' Cup Chur 1m4f	***WON 11/2** Princess' Wales Newm 1m4f	*9th King George VI Ascot 1m4f	***WON 4/6F** September Stks Kemp 1m4f
98 Newm 1m7f 2nd Bahrain Trophy *Three months*	**Capri** H Cecil 9/2	5/9	3	8-07	79	*7th John Porter Stk Newb 1m4f	**Group 2** Chan 1m4f	*7th Princess' Wales Newm 1m4f	**2nd John Porter Stk Newb 1m4f
97 York 1m4f 3rd Great Voltigeur *Two months*	**Kingfisher Mill** Mrs J Cecil 7/2	2/8	3	8-11	75	*4th Jockey Club Stk Newm 1m4f	*9th Brigadier Gerard Sand 1m2f	*5th Troy Stks Donc 1m4f	*9th Cumb'lnd Lodge Ascot 1m4f
96 Good 1m2f 2nd Select Stks *Two weeks*	**Wall Street** S Bin Suroor 2/1F	7/7	3	8-06	74	8th Breeders' Cup Wood 1m4f	-	-	-

12-year median performance rating of the winner: **77** (out of 100)   *(1999 abandoned, 2005 Newmarket)*
*next year **two years

WINNER'S PROFILE Ten of the 11 winners **already tasted victory that season**, while all 11 recorded a **top-four finish last time out**, eight came via either the Ebor meeting, Select Stakes at Goodwood, or the St Leger meeting, which included two victors of the Troy Stakes. All bar one **had experience in Group company**, and eight won at that level – numerous winners shouldered penalties here – while the biggest clue was found in the market, as every winner emerged from **the first two in the betting**.
The ages were spread around during recent years, however, the **Classic generation** boast by far the best strike-rate with six winners from just over 25 runners, including Nayef, who came from the **Marcus Tregoning** yard that scored four times from as many runners.

FUTURE POINTERS A Group Three event that has drawn those middle-distance performers deemed not good enough for the Arc a week later, although it was won by some decent performers including Nayef, who subsequently proved himself at Group One level. Nayef was also the only Cumberland Lodge winner to score again next time out, possibly not a surprise as he recorded the best performance rating (PR) during the last 12 years.
There wasn't an obvious route following Ascot and those looking to profit from winners may have to wait until the following season before cashing in, as three victors scored on one of their first two runs the next term.

Were Cumberland Lodge winners profitable to follow on their subsequent three runs?
Yes – 5 wins from 27 runs returned a **profit of +£0.65** to a £1 level stake.

Placed runners' subsequent record (three runs):
Runners-up: 6 wins from 30 runs returned a **profit of +£7.00** to a £1 level stake.
2002 Warrsan – John Porter Stakes, Jockey Club Stakes, 1997 Romanov – Jockey Club Stakes, 1996 Salmon Ladder – St Simon Stakes

Thirds: 0 win from 10 runs returned a loss of -£10.00 to a £1 level stake.

FUTURE SUCCESS RATING: ★ ★ ★ ☆ ☆

DIADEM STAKES
September 28, Ascot – (Group 2, Class 1, 3yo+) 6f

Last run	Winner/ Trainer & SP	Draw/ Ran	Age	Wght	PR	Next four runs			
07 Leop 1m 3rd Desmond Stks Two months	Haatef K Prendergast 8/1	11/17	3	8-12	74	-	-	-	-
06 Hayd 6f 5th Sprint Cup One month	Red Clubs B Hills 6/1	17/10	3	8-12	81	9th Prix de l'Abbaye Long 5f	*2nd Duke of York York 6f	*8th Temple Stks Sand 5f	*4th Golden Jubilee Ascot 6f
05 Good 6f 5th Starlit Stks Three weeks	Baron's Pit Mrs A Perrett 20/1	2/13	5	9-00	72	10th Challenge Stls Newm 7f	**5th Handicap Newb 5f	**7th Conds Stks Hayd 6f	**2nd Conds Stks Beve 5f
04 Newb 5f 5th Int World Trophy One week	Pivotal Point P Makin 11/2	6/12	4	9-00	77	13th H Kong Sprint Sha 5f	*9th Chipchase Stks Newc 6f	*19th July Cup Newm 6f	**8th Palace House Newm 5f
03 Good 6f 1st Starlit Stks Two weeks	Acclamation L Cottrell 9/1	2/14	4	9-00	74	4th Prix de l'Abbaye Long 5f	5th H Kong Sprint Sha 5f	-	-
02 Deau 6f 1st Group 3 One month	Crystal Castle J Hammond 3/1F	7/11	4	9-00	81	*4th Group 3 Nad Al 6f	*7th Golden Shaheen Nad Al 6f	*3rd Group 3 Deau 6f	*10th Diadem Ascot 6f
01 Donc 7f 1st Sceptre Stks Three weeks	Nice One Clare P Payne 6/1	7/15	5	8-11	77	5th Challenge Stks Newm 7f	6th H Kong Sprint Sha 5f	-	-
00 Hayd 6f 2nd Sprint Cup One month	Sampower Star S Bin Suroor 7/4F	4/11	4	9-00	74	-	-	-	-
99 Hayd 6f 4th Sprint Cup One month	Bold Edge R Hannon 12/1	7/11	4	9-04	80	*13th Golden Shaheen Nad Al 6f	*3rd Duke of York York 6f	*4th Cork & Orrery Ascot 6f	*WON 91/10 Maurice 'Gheest Deau 7f
98 Leop 6f 2nd Phoenix Stks Two months	Bianconi A O'Brien 7/1	5/9	3	8-12	78	12th Prix de l'Abbaye Long 5f	*4th Greenlands Stks Curr 6f	*11th Cork & Orrery Ascot 6f	*9th July Cup Newm 6f
97 Newm 6f 1st Hopeful Stks Two months	Elnadim J Dunlop 4/1	11/14	3	8-12	85	4th Challenge Stks Newm 7f	*2nd Duke of York York 6f	*3rd Temple Stks Sand 5f	*WON 3/1F July Cup Newm 6f
96 Newm 7f 9th Criterion Stks Two months	Diffident S Bin Suroor 12/1	10/12	4	9-00	75	WON 12/1 Conds Stks Donc 7f	2nd Wentworth Stks Donc 6f	*5th Duke of York York 6f	*5th Group 3 Bade 6f

12-year median performance rating of the winner: **77** (out of 100) *(2005 Newmarket) *next year*

WINNER'S PROFILE Every winner **arrived via a Grade One racecourse**, although a number of various routes were taken earlier that season, with a mix of handicaps and Pattern sprints. However, one interesting angle was that none were overraced during the current campaign – **a maximum of six races** – while every winner **already scored over the six furlong trip**. Ten were **previous Pattern winners**, while three to five-year-olds dominated – six-year-olds and above have yet to score in the last 12 years from almost 40 runners.
Trainer **Saeed Bin Suroor** was careful with his entries, resulting in two winners from only four runners.

FUTURE POINTERS This should be one of the best sprints during the autumn but it hasn't attracted the big winners from top sprint events like the July Cup, Nunthorpe and Haydock Sprint Cup, as many were kept fresh for the Abbaye at Longchamp a week later. As a result, the strength of the Diadem has weakened over the years judged on subsequent results as only Red Clubs and Elnadim went on to win major sprints since 1996, when it became a Group Two event, in comparison to it's phase as a Group Three, when it produced three-year-old winners like Lake Coniston, Wolfhound, Cadeaux Genereux and Dowsing, all of whom went on to land Group One sprints.
From a punting angle, winners of the Diadem may be swerved – or layed – in the near future, unless an above par winner comes along and clocks a time like Elnadim's at 1:12.56s (old course) then we could have one to follow!

Were Diadem winners profitable to follow on their subsequent three runs?
No – 1 win from 28 runs returned a loss of -£15.00 to a £1 level stake.

Placed runners' subsequent record (three runs):
Runners-up: 4 wins from 30 runs returned a loss of -£20.73 to a £1 level stake.
2004 Airwave – Ridgewood Pearl Stakes, 1997 Monaasib – Cammidge Trophy

Thirds: 2 wins from 32 runs returned a loss of -£20.00 to a £1 level stake.
2005 Avonbridge – Prix de l'Abbaye

FUTURE SUCCESS RATING: ★ ☆ ☆ ☆ ☆

BERESFORD STAKES
September 28, Curragh – (Group 2, Class 1, 2yo) 1m

Last run	Winner/ Trainer & SP	Draw/ Ran	Age	Wght	PR	Next four runs			
07 Curr 7f 2nd Futurity Stks *Two months*	**Curtain Call** Mrs J Harrington 9/2	10/9	2	9-01	70	5th R Post Trophy Donc 1m	-	-	-
06 York 7f 2nd Champagne Stk *One month*	**Eagle Mountain** A O'Brien 4/7F	3/7	2	9-01	74	4th R Post Trophy Newb 1m	*5th 2,000 Guineas Newm 1m	*2nd Derby Epsom 1m4f	*3rd Irish Derby Curr 1m4f
05 Leop 7f 1st Maiden *One month*	**Septimus** A O'Brien 4/6F	4/6	2	9-00	73	3rd R Post Trophy Donc 1m	*7th Group 3 Long 1m2f	*WON 13/8F Dante Stks York 1m2f	*12th Derby Epsom 1m4f
04 Curr 7f 2nd Maiden *Three weeks*	**Albert Hall** A O'Brien 4/5F	2/5	2	9-00	70	2nd R Post Trophy Donc 1m	*5th Dante Stks York 1m2f	*5th Irish 2,000 Guin Curr 1m	
03 Curr 7f 1st Maiden *One month*	**Azamour** J Oxx 6/4F	7/6	2	9-00	73	*3rd 2,000 Guineas Newm 1m	*2nd Irish 2,000 Guin Curr 1m	*WON 9/2 St James Pal' Ascot 1m	*WON 8/1 Irish Champion Leop 1m2f
02 List 1m 1st Maiden *Three weeks*	**Alamshar** J Oxx 7/1	8/10	2	9-00	72	*2nd Ballysax Stks Leop 1m2f	*WON 8/15F Derby Trial Leop 1m2f	*3rd Derby Epsom 1m4f	*WON 4/1 Irish Derby Curr 1m4f
01 Cork 6f 1st Maiden *Six months*	**Castle Gandolfo** A O'Brien EvensF	6/7	2	9-00	65	2nd R Post Trophy Donc 1m	2nd Crit' St-Cloud Sain 1m2f	*WON 2/5F Intern'tnl Stk Ling 1m	*12th Kentucky Derby Chur 1m2f
00 Ascot 1m 2nd Royal Lodge *Three weeks*	**Turnberry Isle** A O'Brien 4/11F	3/6	2	9-00	70	6th Breeders' Cup Chur 1m1f	*10th Grade 1 Gulf 1m1f	-	-
99 Gowr 7f 1st Maiden *Five months*	**Lermontov** A O'Brien 4/1	7/6	2	9-00	72	2nd R Post Trophy Donc 1m	*4th Foxrock Listed Leop 1m2f	*8th Irish St Leger Curr 1m6f	*11th Q Elizabeth II Ascot 1m
98 Cork1m1f 3rd Maiden *One week*	**Festival Hall** A O'Brien 10/1	5/9	2	9-00	67	*5th Classic Trial Sand 1m2f	*10th Irish Derby Curr 1m4f	-	-
97 Donc 7f 3rd Champagne Stk *Two months*	**Saratoga Springs** A O'Brien 7/4F	4/7	2	8-11	75	WON 9/2 R Post Trophy Donc 1m	*WON 4/1 Dante Stks York 1m2f	*4th Prix 'Jock-Club Chan 1m4f	*10th Derby Epsom 1m4f
96 Curr 7f 5th National Stks *One month*	**Johan Cruyff** A O'Brien 1/2F	3/5	2	8-11	67	*WON 8/1 Gallinule Stks Curr 1m2f	*4th Irish Derby Curr 1m4f	*12th Hong Kong Int Sha 1m1f	**3rd QE II Cup Sha 1m2f

12-year median performance rating of the winner: **71** (out of 100)   *next year **two years*

WINNER'S PROFILE Eleven winners finished in the **first three over seven furlongs or a mile** – bar Castle Gandolfo – the same number that filled a **top-three slot last time out**, including five maiden winners.
Seven winners in total ran in a maiden last time out, while the remaining five performed in Group company, two of whom had yet to get off the mark. It may be a coincidence, but stall 1 has a poor record – runner-up three times – but one with better luck was trainer **Aidan O'Brien**, who boasts a super record with nine winners – including seven favourites – from almost 30 runners. **John Oxx** also won it more than once, striking twice from just five runners.

FUTURE POINTERS Although not an event to have unearthed many Classic winners, the Beresford Stakes did produce several Group One winners. Not many did a great deal in their remaining months as juveniles, with Curtain Call the latest to flop in the Racing Post Trophy next time out, and only Saratoga Springs managed that feat in 1997 – 2002 runner-up Brian Boru also scored at Doncaster.
It should be noted that despite trainer Aidan O'Brien's reign in the event, the most distinguished subsequent winners came via John Oxx, with Azamour and Alamshar going on to notable Group One victories, both of whom landed the King George VI Stakes. In fact, apart from Septimus's Group Cup victories last year, the majority of O'Brien's winners never really hit the top, including several red herrings that failed to win again.

Were Beresford winners profitable to follow on their subsequent three runs?
No – 7 wins from 32 runs returned a loss of -£1.45 to a £1 level stake.

Placed runners' subsequent record (three runs):
Runners-up: 4 wins from 28 runs returned a loss of -£15.51 to a £1 level stake.
2002 Brian Boru – Racing Post Trophy

Thirds: 1 win from 6 runs returned a profit of +£5.00 to a £1 level stake.

FUTURE SUCCESS RATING: ★ ★ ★ ★ ★

TATTERSALL STAKES
October 3, Newmarket – (Group 3, Class 1, 2yo Colts & Geldings) 7f

Last run	Winner/ Trainer & SP	Draw/ Ran	Age	Wght	PR	Next four runs			
07 Donc 7f 8th Champagne Stk Three weeks	**River Proud** P Cole 11/4	4/8	2	8-12	65	7th R Post Trophy Newb 1m	-	-	-
06 York 7f 6th Champagne Stk Three weeks	**Thousand Words** B Hills 15/2	12/10	2	8-12	68	5th R Post Trophy Newb 1m	*3rd Craven Stks Newm 1m	*5th Poule 'Poulains Long 1m	*8th Jersey Stks Ascot 7f
05 Curr 6f 2nd Group 3 One month	**Aussie Rules** A O'Brien 3/1JF	4/9	2	8-09	73	*5th Group 3 Long 1m	**WON 4/1** Poule 'Poulains Long 1m	*7th Prix' Jock-Club Chan 1m3f	*4th Eclipse Sand 1m2f
04 Sand 7f 1st Maiden Two months	**Diktatorial** A Balding 3/1	9/9	2	8-09	66	*15th 2,000 Guineas Newm 1m	*9th Superior Mile Hayd 1m	*8th Supreme Stks Good 7f	*4th Conds Stks Donc 7f
03 Donc 7f 5th Champagne Stk Three weeks	**Milk It Mick** J Osborne 12/1	6/8	2	8-09	70	WON 33/1 Dewhurst Stks Newm 7f	*2nd International Trial Ling 1m	*5th Greenham Stks Newb 7f	*8th 2,000 Guineas Newm 1m
02 York 7f 1st Maiden One month	**Governor Brown** P Cole 6/1	1/5	2	8-09	62	14th Dewhurst Stks Newm 7f	3rd Criterium Int Sain 1m	-	-
01 Sand 7f 4th Solario Stks Two months	**Where Or When** T Mills 6/1	9/9	2	8-09	63	4th Dewhurst Stks Newm 7f	*11th 2,000 Guineas Newm 1m	*4th Dante Stks York 1m2f	*6th Derby Epsom 1m4f
00 Leop 6f 1st Maiden Three weeks	**King Charlemagne** A O'Brien 11/2	6/13	2	8-09	72	**WON 3/1** Ballycorus Stks Leop 7f	**WON 8/11F** Minstrel Stks Curr 7f	**WON 4/5JF** Maurice 'Gheest Deau 7f	-
99 Newb 7f 1st Maiden Two weeks	**Best Light** D Elsworth 9/2	3/5	2	8-09	64	7th R Post Trophy Donc 1m	*4th Greenham Stks Newb 7f	*19th 2,000 Guineas Newm 1m	*5th Irish 2,000 Guin Curr 1m
98 Good 7f 1st Maiden Three months	**Enrique** H Cecil 4/6F	1/5	2	8-09	71	4th Dewhurst Stks Newm 7f	**WON 5/4F** Greenham Stks Newb 7f	*2nd 2,000 Guineas Newm 1m	*2nd Irish 2,000 Guin Curr 1m
97 Sand 7f 3rd Solario Stks Two months	**Haami** J Dunlop 5/1	2/8	2	8-09	65	*5th 2,000 Guineas Newm 1m	*14th Derby Epsom 1m4f	*2nd Conds Stks Sand 1m	*2nd Conds Stks Newb 1m1f
96 Good 7f 2nd Vintage Stks Three months	**Grapeshot** L Cumani 5/4F	5/8	2	8-09	69	*2nd Craven Stks Newm 1m	**WON 2/1F** Predominate Stks Good 1m2f	-	-

12-year median performance rating of the winner: **67** (out of 100) *(1999 July Course) *next year*

WINNER'S PROFILE A Grade One venue was visited by every winner last time out, five came via the Champagne or Solario Stakes, while the only winners not to have contested a Group event were last time out maiden scorers. Those yet to have tasted victory need not apply as every winner **previously triumphed over six or seven furlongs**, and it also helped to concentrate on horses in the **first-half of the betting** – only Milk It Mick won at double-figure odds.

Two trainers not to have wasted many entries were **Paul Cole**, with two winners and a runner-up from as many runners, almost matched by **Aidan O'Brien**, who had just two more unplaced runners.

FUTURE POINTERS A decent juveniles event rightly upgraded to Group Three status in 2000 having had such a superb long-term roll of honour, with the likes of Salse (Prix de la Foret), Opening Verse (Breeders' Cup) and Grand Lodge (St James's Palace) all going on to land victory at the highest level in the last 20 years.

That trend continued as the 2005, 2003, 2001 and 2000 winners emulated their predecessors in Group One races, however, this event hasn't provided British Classic winners, as six failed in the 2,000 Guineas, although Aussie Rules took the French equivalent.

As with all races in this book, it experienced several sub-standard renewals in which the winner achieved a low performance rating (PR) before disappointing in the future, so make sure to use them before considering backing the winner next time out (see website).

Were Tattersall winners profitable to follow on their subsequent three runs?
Yes – 7 wins from 32 runs returned a **profit of +£19.77** to a £1 level stake.

Placed runners' subsequent record (three runs):
Runners-up: 3 wins from 34 runs returned a loss of -£17.00 to a £1 level stake.
2006 Dijeerr – Horris Hill, 2005 Killybegs – Craven, 2002 Muqbil – Greenham Stakes

Thirds: 4 wins from 24 runs returned a **profit of +£1.61** to a £1 level stake.
2003 Bachelor Duke – Irish 2,000 Guineas

FUTURE SUCCESS RATING: ★ ★ ★ ☆ ☆

CHEVELEY PARK STAKES
October 3, Newmarket – (Group 1, Class 1, 2yo Fillies) 6f

Last run	Winner/ Trainer & SP	Draw/ Ran	Age	Wght	PR	Next four runs			
07 Deau 6f 2nd Prix Morny *Two months*	**Natagora** P Bary 7/2	11/14	2	8-12	75	-	-	-	-
06 Ascot 7f 1st Watership Sales *One week*	**Indian Ink** R Hannon 3/1JF	7/11	2	8-12	72	*2nd **Fred Darling** Newb 7f	*5th 1,000 Guineas Newm 1m	***WON 8/1 Coronation Stks Ascot 1m**	-
05 Newm 6f 1st Cherry Hinton *Three months*	**Donna Blini** B Meehan 12/1	5/10	2	8-11	67	*13th 1,000 Guineas Newm 1m	*13th Coronation Stks Ascot 1m	*2nd Summer Stks York 6f	***WON 11/4 Conds Stks Newm 5f**
04 Leic 6f 1st Nursery *Two weeks*	**Magical Romance** B Meehan 40/1	4/7	2	8-11	64	*6th Poule 'Pouliches Long 1m	*6th Oaks Epsom 1m4f	*11th Nassau Good 1m2f	*7th Fortune Stks Epsom 7f
03 York 6f 1st Lowther Stks *Two months*	**Carry On Katie** J Noseda 13/8F	4/10	2	8-11	68	*6th 1,000 Guineas Newm 1m	*9th Poule 'Pouliches Long 1m		
02 Ayr 6f 1st Firth of Clyde *Two weeks*	**Airwave** H Candy 11/2	2/6	2	8-11	71	***WON 5/2JF Temple Stks Sand 5f**	*2nd Golden Jubilee Ascot 6f	*3rd July Cup Newm 6f	*3rd Sprint Cup Hayd 6f
01 York 6f 1st Lowther Stks *Two months*	**Queen's Logic** M Channon 10/11F	3/8	2	8-11	79	***WON 1/3JF Fred Darling Newb 7f**	-	-	-
00 Ascot 6f 1st Maiden *Two months*	**Regal Rose** Sir M Stoute 11/2	2/13	2	8-11	65	-	-	-	-
99 Kemp 6f 1st Sirenia Stks *Three weeks*	**Seazun** M Channon 10/1	8/14	2	8-11	66	2nd Nell Gwyn Newm 7f	*4th 1,000 Guineas Newm 1m	*4th Irish 1,000 Guin Curr 1m	*8th Coronation Stks Ascot 1m
98 Curr 7f 4th Moyglare Stud *One month*	**Wannabe Grand** J Noseda 3/1F	7/9	2	8-11	69	*2nd 1,000 Guineas Newm 1m	*3rd Coronation Stks Ascot 1m	*7th July Cup Newm 6f	*2nd Oak Tree Stks Good 7f
97 York 6f 2nd Lowther Stks *Two months*	**Embassy** D Loder 5/2	3/8	2	8-11	70	-	-	-	-
96 Evry 6f 1st Group 3 *Three weeks*	**Pas De Response** Mme C Head 7/1	3/8	2	8-11	76	***WON N/O Listed Mais 7f**	*4th 1,000 Guineas Newm 1m	***WON 7/10F Group 3 Deau 6f**	*2nd Prix de l'Abbaye Long 5f

12-year median performance rating of the winner: **70** (out of 100)   *(1999 July Course) *next year*

WINNER'S PROFILE The last eight winners came into this event off the back of a **victory last time** and two landed the **Lowther Stakes** – Embassy was runner-up in 1997 – while every winner already **scored over the distance**. It may be a coincidence, but those drawn in the highest stalls struggled, while on the training front, **British trainers** dominated since 1997 – **Brian Meehan** and **Mick Channon** had two apiece – while Irish and French raiders fell short until last year. Vincent O'Brien was the last Irish handler to succeed in 1990.

FUTURE POINTERS Although viewed as a guide for the following year's Classics, 16 years have passed since the winner of the Cheveley Park lifted the 1,000 Guineas, that honour went to Sayyedati in 1992, while Ravinella achieved the same feat five years earlier.
Since then, eight Cheveley Park winners failed with Wannabe Grand going closest in second to Wince in 1999, while the only Guineas winner to emerge from this event was the 2002 runner-up Russian Rhythm.
Following the winner from here proved costly – runners-up have a better record – although the 2006 winner, Indian Ink, gave the Cheveley Park a lift when she took the Coronation Stakes at Royal Ascot last year.

Were Cheveley Park winners profitable to follow on their subsequent three runs?
No – 5 wins from 24 runs returned a loss of –£7.47 to a £1 level stake.

Placed runners' subsequent record (three runs):
Runners-up: 8 wins from 26 runs returned a **profit of +£4.87** to a £1 level stake.
2003 Majestic Desert – Fred Darling, 2002 Russian Rhythm – 1,000 Guineas, Coronation, Nassau, 1996 Moonlight Paradise – Rockfel

Thirds: 1 win from 23 runs returned a loss of – £19.25 to a £1 level stake.
2003 Badminton – October Stakes

FUTURE SUCCESS RATING: ★★☆☆☆

MIDDLE PARK STAKES
October 3, Newmarket – (Group 1, Class 1, 2yo Colts) 6f

Last run	Winner/ Trainer & SP	Draw/ Ran	Age	Wght	PR	Next four runs			
07 Newb 6f 1st Mill Reef Stks Two weeks	**Dark Angel** B Hills 8/1	1/9	2	8-12	72	9th Dewhurst Newm 7f	-	-	-
06 Deau 6f 1st Prix Morny Two months	**Dutch Art** P Chapple-Hyam 6/5F	2/6	2	8-12	79	*2nd Greenham Newb 7f	*3rd 2,000 Guineas Newm 1m	*4th St James Palace Ascot 1m	*2nd July Cup Newm 6f
05 York 6f 1st Gimcrack Stks Two months	**Amadeus Wolf** K Ryan 4/1	4/6	2	8-11	76	*7th 2,000 Guineas Newm 1m	*5th Golden Jubilee Ascot 6f	*4th July Cup Newm 6f	*3rd Maurice 'Gheest Deau 7f
04 Curr 6f 1st Blenheim Stks Two weeks	**Ad Valorem** A O'Brien 9/2	4/9	2	8-11	81	*2nd St James Palace Ascot 1m	*5th Jean Prat Chan 1m	*3rd Sussex Good 1m	*6th Grade 1 Keen 1m
03 Curr 6f 3rd Phoenix Stks Two months	**Three Valleys** R Charlton 2/1F	10/11	2	8-11	77	2nd Dewhurst Newm 7f	*2nd Craven Stks Newm 1m	*11th 2,000 Guineas Newm 1m	*3rd Grade 1 Holl 1m1f
02 Nott 6f 1st Maiden Two weeks	**Oasis Dream** J Gosden 6/1	9/10	2	8-11	82	*3rd King's Stand Ascot 5f	**WON 9/2** July Cup Newm 6f	**WON 4/9F** Nunthorpe York 5f	*2nd Sprint Cup Hayd 6f
01 Deau 6f 1st Prix Morny Two months	**Johannesburg** A O'Brien 3/10F	4/7	2	8-11	86	**WON 72/10** Breeders' Cup Belm 1m	*2nd Gladness Stks Curr 7f	*8th Kentucky Derby Chur 1m2f	*9th Golden Jubilee Ascot 6f
00 Leop 6f 1st Phoenix Stks Two months	**Minardi** A O'Brien 5/6F	3/9	2	8-11	79	*4th 2,000 Guineas Newm 1m	*3rd Irish 2,000 Guin Curr 1m	*8th St James Palace Ascot 1m	*6th Maurice 'Gheest Deau 7f
99 Newb 6f 1st Mill Reef Stks Two weeks	**Primo Valentino** P Harris 10/3	1/6	2	8-11	74	*7th 2,000 Guineas Newm 1m	*6th Group 3 Bade 6f	*4th July Cup Newm 6f	*9th Prix de l'Abbaye Long 5f
98 York 6f 1st Novice Stks One month	**Lujain** D Loder 8/11F	2/7	2	8-11	75	6th Dewhurst Stks Newm 7f	*5th Duke of York York 6f	*12th King's Stand Ascot 5f	-
97 Donc 6f 3rd Conds Stks Three months	**Hayil** D Morley 14/1	4/8	2	8-11	71	*5th Listed Mais 7f	*3rd Group 3 Long 7f	*8th Group 3 Deau 1m	*10th Maurice 'Gheest Deau 7f
96 Deau 6f 1st Prix Morny Two months	**Bahamian Bounty** D Loder 7/4F	2/11	2	8-11	74	4th Dewhurst Stks Newm 7f	*6th Poule 'Poulains Long 1m	*4th July Cup Newm 6f	

12-year median performance rating of the winner: **77** (out of 100) *(2003 Three Valleys disqualified) *next year*
(1999 July Course)

WINNER'S PROFILE Maidens need not apply as every winner had **already got off the mark**, 10 scored last time out – three in the Group One Prix Morny – while all 12 since 1996 **won over this trip**.
Nine victors were **proven in Pattern company** – two of other three had no more than three runs – including trainer Aidan O'Brien's three winners from 19 runners. The Irish handler hasn't a great record in recent times, however, with only one winner from 13 since 2002, including flops at 7/1, 9/2, 2/1, 4/1 and 5/1.
It paid to stick with the **first three or four in the betting** – a double-figure outsider only struck once – while a draw in **stalls one to four** along the stands' side can be a bonus.

FUTURE POINTERS It has been 17 years since the Middle Park winner took the 2,000 Guineas the following season and the majority of these precocious juveniles took a while to get back to winning ways later in their career. The two exceptions were the best winners of this event – recording high performance ratings (PR) – and both managed to secure Group/Grade One honours in the near future, with Oasis Dream stuck to sprint trips with victories in the July Cup and Nunthorpe. The clock gave an indication of what was in store with Oasis Dream, as he smashed the course record in this event with a time of 1:09.61 – average Middle Park time 1:11 to 11:12 – so any future winner who gets within that figure could be one to note.

Were Middle Park winners profitable to follow on their subsequent three runs?
No – 3 wins from 34 runs returned a loss of -£18.85 to a £1 level stake.

Placed runners' subsequent record (three runs):
Runners-up: 5 wins from 30 runs returned a loss of -£16.30 to a £1 level stake.
2005 Red Clubs – Greenham Stakes, 1998 Bertolini – European Free Handicap

Thirds: 2 wins from 18 runs returned a loss of -£5.38 to a £1 level stake.
1996 In Command – Dewhurst Stakes

FUTURE SUCCESS RATING: ★ ★ ★ ★ ★

JOEL STAKES

October 4, Newmarket – (Group 3, Class 1, 3yo+) 1m

Last run	Winner/Trainer & SP	Draw/Ran	Age	Wght	PR	Next four runs			
07 Ascot 1m 6th St James Palace *Four months*	**Creachadoir** S Bin Suroor 11/4JF	2/10	3	9-00	80	4th Champion Stks Newm 1m2f	-	-	-
06 Newb 7f 3rd Duty Free Cup *Three weeks*	**Satchem** S Bin Suroor 10/3	6/8	4	9-00	78	3rd Challenge Stks Newm 7f	-	-	-
05 Donc 1m 3rd Conds Stks *Three weeks*	**Rob Roy** Sir M Stoute 17/2	9/10	3	8-10	82	14th Champion Stks Newm 1m2f	*WON 6/4F Betfred Mile Sand 1m	*6th Lockinge Newb 1m	*3rd Sussex Good 1m
04 Newm 7f 8th Criterion Stks *Four months*	**Polar Ben** J Fanshawe 16/1	2/13	5	9-00	72	9th Challenge Stks Newm 7f	*8th Betfred Mile Sand 1m	*4th Spring Trophy Hayd 7f	*4th Conds Stks Ches 7f
03 Donc 1m2f 3rd Conds Stks *Five months*	**Splendid Era** B Hills 25/1	1/4	3	8-11	70	-	-	-	-
02 Newb 1m1f 1st Conds Stks *Two weeks*	**Desert Deer** M Johnston 15/8F	6/8	4	9-00	76	2nd Earl of Sefton Newm 1m1f	*WON 11/10F Sandown Mile Sand 1m	*9th Queen Anne Ascot 1m	**14th Lockinge Newb 1m
01 Curr 1m 2nd Listed *Three weeks*	**Beckett** A O'Brien 3/1F	11/11	3	8-11	71	10th Champion Stks Newm 1m2f	-	-	-
00 York 1m1f 4th Strensall Stks *One month*	**Hopeful Light** J Gosden 20/1	9/12	3	9-00	70	-	-	-	-
99 Donc 1m 2nd Porcelanosa *Three weeks*	**Indian Lodge** Mrs A Perrett 7/1	7/13	3	8-10	78	WON 9/2 Darley Stks Newm 1m1f	*WON 10/1 Earl of Sefton Newm 1m1f	*WON 9/4F Sandown Mile Sand 1m	*3rd Lockinge Newb 1m
98 Sand 1m 1st Conds Stks *Six months*	**Im Proposin** J Dunlop 8/1	3/6	3	8-11	71	5th Troy Stks Donc 1m4f	-	-	-
97 Epso 1m1f 1st Fortune Stks *One month*	**Intikhab** D Morley 11/4	5/6	3	9-01	77	*WON N/O Stakes Nad Al 1m1f	*2nd Dubai Duty Free Nad Al 1m1f	*WON 2/1F Diomed Stks Epsom 1½m	*WON 9/4F Queen Anne Ascot 1m
96 Bade 1m 8th Group 3 *Two months*	**Yeast** W Haggas 11/2	8/9	4	9-00	70	34th Cambridgeshire Newm 1m1f	*2nd Doncaster Mile Donc 1m	*25th Victoria Cup Ascot 7f	*11th Porcelanosa Hcp Donc 1m

12-year median performance rating of the winner: **75** (out of 100)   *(1999 July Course) *next year **two years*

WINNER'S PROFILE A number of different routes and preparations were used leading to Newmarket, although one common link amongst the past eight winners was a **previous top-three position in Pattern company**, which became more important as the standard of this event improved.

An **official rating of 102 or higher** was also vital, along with **winning form over seven furlongs or a mile**, while **three and four-year-olds** dominated – only one older horse triumphed from almost 20 runners.

On the training front, only **Saeed Bin Suroor** won it twice – both in the last two years – and he has an accurate record with a further three runners-up from just seven runners.

FUTURE POINTERS Not many winners of the Joel Stakes progressed to the highest level, although plenty went on to land Group Two events, including the 2002, 1999 and 1997 winners, which eventually prompted the upgrade of this event from Listed to Group Three status in 2003.

Since then, Rob Roy also graduated to take the Group Two Sandown Mile the following season, along with Desert Deer and Indian Lodge, a route that proved the most effective post-Newmarket, as only one of the nine that attempted to follow up later that backend succeeded.

Were Joel winners profitable to follow on their subsequent three runs?
Yes – 7 wins from 22 runs returned a **profit of +£6.35** to a £1 level stake.

Placed runners' subsequent record (three runs):
Runners-up: 2 wins from 24 runs returned a loss of -£17.76 to a £1 level stake.
1998 Generous Rosi – Magnolia Stakes, Gordon Richards

Thirds: 6 wins from 16 runs returned a **profit of +£6.35** to a £1 level stake.

FUTURE SUCCESS RATING: ★ ★ ★ ☆ ☆

SUN CHARIOT STAKES
October 4, Newmarket – (Group 1, Class 1, 3yo+ Fillies & Mares) 1m

Last run	Winner/ Trainer & SP	Draw/ Ran	Age	Wght	PR	Next four runs			
07 Donc 7f 1st Sceptre Stks One month	Majestic Roi M Channon 16/1	7/9	3	8-13	71	-	-	-	-
06 Newb 7f 2nd Duty Free Cup Three weeks	Spinning Queen B Hills 12/1	9/5	3	8-12	75	-	-	-	-
05 Newm 1m 3rd Falmouth Three months	Peeress Sir M Stoute 7/1	10/10	4	9-00	80	4th Challenge Stks Newm 7f	*WON 4/1 Lockinge Newb 1m	*4th Queen Anne Ascot 1m	*4th Falmouth Newm 1m
04 Leop 1m 1st Matron Stks One month	Attraction M Johnston 11/4	3/5	3	8-11	83	*11th Champions Mile Sha 1m	*4th Hungerford Stks Newb 7f	*WON 10/3 Matron Stks Leop 1m	-
03 Yarm 1m2f 1st Fillies' Listed Three weeks	Echoes In Eternity S Bin Suroor 9/1	4/10	3	8-10	74	*4th Dahlia Stks Newm 1m1f	*4th Ridgewood Pearl Curr 1m	*5th Nassau Good 1m2f	*WON 5/1 Park Hill Stks Donc 1m7f
02 Leop 1m 1st Matron Stks One month	Dress To Thrill D Weld 11/8F	5/10	3	8-10	78	8th Breeders' Cup Arli 1m	WON 73/10 Grade 1 Holl 1m1f	*5th Grade 1 Holl 1m1f	*6th Grade 1 Arli 1m2f
01 Curr 1m 1st Matron Stks Two months	Independence E Dunlop 5/2F	7/16	3	8-10	73	-	-	-	-
00 Curr 1m 2nd Matron Stks One month	Danceabout G Wragg 9/2	1/9	3	8-09	70	*4th Lockinge Newb 1m	*4th Falmouth Newm 1m	*6th Nassau Good 1m2f	*3rd Matron Stks Curr 1m
99 York 1m4f 11th Yorkshire Oaks Two months	Lady In Waiting P Cole 5/1	4/8	4	8-13	69	5th Grade 1 Wood 1m2f	*5th Brigadier Gerard Sand 1m2f	*5th Pretty Polly Curr 1m2f	-
98 Sand 1m 1st Atalanta Stks Two months	Kissogram L Cumani 5/4F	3/5	3	8-08	74	*4th Brigadier Gerard Sand 1m2f	*4th Nassau Good 1m2f	*9th Juddmonte Int York 1m2f	-
97 Sand 1m 1st Atalanta Stks Two months	One So Wonderful L Cumani 5/2	6/8	3	8-08	73	*7th Brigadier Gerard Sand 1m2f	*WON 11/8F Daffodil Stks Chep 1m2f	*WON 6/1 Juddmonte Int York 1m2f	*4th Irish Champion Leop 1m2f
96 Good 1m2f 1st Nassau Three months	Last Second Sir M Prescott 9/4F	8/9	3	8-11	72	*7th Prix Ganay Long 1m3f	*5th Nassau Good 1m2f		

12-year median performance rating of the winner: **74** (out of 100) *(1996-99 1m2f, 1999 July Course) *next year*

WINNER'S PROFILE Recent solid form helped, with a **top-three finish last time out** vital. Four emerged from a top-two slot in the Matron Stakes, while those that figured in the Falmouth Stakes on the July Course also did well. Proven ability at this level put past winners in good stead – the majority scored in **Pattern company earlier in the campaign** – while it was an advantage to stay on the right side of **three-year-olds.** The Classic generation regularly outgun their rivals, including during the last two years when outnumbered by six runners to eight elders collectively.

FUTURE POINTERS The Sun Chariot has gone through a period of change in the last eight years, reduced to a mile from 10 furlongs in 2000, before being allocated Group One status in 2004, but as several winners went off to the paddocks soon after Newmarket, subsequent results were clouded somewhat.
Some shocks have been witnessed of late, possibly due to several of the best fillies having gone over the top at the end of a tough season, but the winners on the day have produced some decent results post-Newmarket – although none followed up next time out – as three since 2002 took Group/Grade One events.

Were Sun Chariot winners profitable to follow on their subsequent three runs?
Yes – 5 wins from 26 runs returned a **profit of +£1.00** to a £1 level stake.

Placed runners' subsequent record (three runs):
Runners-up: 2 wins from 11 runs returned a loss of -£1.00 to a £1 level stake.
2004 Chic – Celebration Mile

Thirds: 1 win from 13 runs returned a loss of -£9.75 to a £1 level stake.
2001 Riberac – Ben Marshall Stakes

FUTURE SUCCESS RATING: ★ ★ ★ ★ ★

CAMBRIDGESHIRE
October 4, Newmarket – (Class 2, Heritage Handicap, 3yo+) 1m1f

Last run	Winner/Trainer & SP	Draw/Ran	Age	Wght	PR	Next four runs			
07 Good 1m2f 1st / Heritage Hcp / *Three months*	**Pipedreamer** J Gosden 5/1F	11/34	3	8-12	76	-	-	-	-
06 Newb 1m2f 3rd / J Smith's Hcp / *Two weeks*	**Formal Decree** A Swinbank 9/1	17/33	3	8-09	74	*WON 11/4F Handicap Nad Al 1m1f	*WON 11/10F Group 3 Nad Al 1m1f	*2nd Group 2 Nad Al 1m1f	*7th Dubai Duty Free Nad Al 1m1f
05 Newb 1m2f 2nd / J Smith's Hcp / *Two weeks*	**Blue Monday** R Charlton 5/1F	28/30	4	9-03	77	*2nd Conds Stks Ripon 1m2f	*WON 10/3F Festival Stks Good 1m2f	*WON 24/10 Group 3 Long 1m2f	*4th Wolferton Hcp Ascot 1m2f
04 Newb 1m2f 9th / J Smith's Hcp / *Two weeks*	**Spanish Don** D Elsworth 100/1	3/32	6	8-10	72	WON 4/1 J Seymour Stks Newm 1m2f	11th Churchill Stks Ling 1m2f	*2nd Suffolk Hcp Newm 1m1f	*10th Rose Bowl Hcp Epsom 1m2f
03 Newb 1m2f 4th / Handicap / *One year*	**Chivalry** Sir M Prescott 14/1	17/34	4	8-01	64	WON EvensF Nov Hdle Ayr 2m	*WON 6/4F Hcp Hdle Kels 2m1f	*4th Kelso Hdle Kels 2m2f	*18th Lincoln Hdle Donc 1m
02 Ascot 1m 4th / Shergar Cup / *Two months*	**Beauchamp Pilot** G Butler 9/1	26/30	4	9-05	71	3rd Darley Stks Newm 1m1f	3rd Ben Marshall Stk Newm 1m	WON 2/1F Churchill Stks Ling 1m2f	*3rd Group 2 Nad Al 1m2f
01 Ascot 7f 2nd / Tote Hcp / *One week*	**I Cried For You** J Given 33/1	11/35	6	8-06	64	5th Mile Hcp Newm 1m	*3rd Wint Derby Trial Ling 1m2f	*2nd Winter Derby Ling 1m2f	*3rd Lincoln Hcp Donc 1m
00 Donc 1m 1st / Spring Mile Hcp / *Six months*	**Katy Nowaitee** P Harris 6/1	34/34	4	8-08	69	WON 11/8F Severals Stks Newm 1m2f	*6th Earl of Sefton Newm 1m1f	*2nd Dahlia Stks Newm 1m1f	*2nd Upavon Stks Sali 1m2f
99 Curr 1m 1st / Handicap / *Two weeks*	**She's Our Mare** T Martin 11/1	14/33	6	7-12	63	2nd Hcp Hdle Chel 2m1f	*3rd Hcp Hdle Leop 2m	*2nd Fillies' Stks Curr 1m	*7th Irish Champ Hdle Punc 2m
98 Donc 1m 3rd / Conds Stks / *One month*	**Lear Spear** D Elsworth 20/1	33/35	3	8-04	66	4th Darley Stks Newm 1m1f	*5th Earl of Sefton Newm 1m1f	*4th Mile Stks Sand 1m	*6th Shergar Cup Good 1m2f
97 York 1m2f 1st / Magnet Cup / *Three months*	**Pasternak** Sir M Prescott 4/1F	17/35	4	9-01	69	*2nd J Smith's Hcp York 1m2f	*2nd Handicap Leop 1m1f	*21st W Hill Mile Hcp Good 1m	*10th Cambridgeshire Newm 1m1f
96 Donc 1m2f 1st / Ladbroke Hcp / *One month*	**Clifton Fox** J Glover 14/1	17/38	4	8-02	65	3rd J Seymour Stks Newm 1m2f	WON 9/1 November Hcp Donc 1m4f	*WON 9/2 Nov Hdle Newc 2m	*2nd Nov Hdle Newc 2m

12-year median performance rating of the winner: **69** (out of 100) *Italic = jumps (1999 July Course), *next year*

WINNER'S PROFILE Plenty of strong clues to work with, the first involves crisp recent form as 11 winners finished in the **first four last time out**, the exception was one of three that arrived via the John Smith's Handicap at Newbury, however, winners from that event have a poor long-term record here. Eleven winners also **scored between a mile and ten furlongs**, the same number that **won during their last four runs**, while it paid to follow those **below 9st 5lb** – over 10 perished with more weight in the last three years. The market proved correct as 10 winners were **20/1 or shorter**, which helped eliminate plenty and David Elsworth was responsible for two big-prices from nine runners. The draw was also important as those **drawn in double-figures** held an edge, and only nine of the 33 placed fell to single-figure stalls on the Rowley Course since 1996, including 2004 when it came up low.

FUTURE POINTERS One of the most prestigious handicaps of the season, the Cambridgeshire has pointed up many a Pattern performer, although it must be noted that the last subsequent scorer at the highest level was the 1994 winner Halling, who went on to land several Group Ones. That said, above par winners have moved up the ladder, as four of the last five winners – excluding Pipedreamer – proved themselves in Pattern company in the near future, while the likes of Lear Spear, eventually won the then Group Two Prince of Wales's Stakes.
There was also strength in depth behind the Cambridgeshire winner, enhancing it's reliability, with placed runners profitable to follow collectively – two recent thirds took the Spring Cup the following year (see below).

Were winners of the Cambridgeshire profitable to follow on their subsequent three runs?
Yes – 11 wins from 33 runs returned a **profit of +£10.95** to a £1 level stake.

Placed runners' subsequent record (three runs):
Runners-up: 3 wins from 29 runs returned a loss of -£13.79 to a £1 level stake.
2002 Far Lane – John Smith's Cup, 1999 Bomb Alaska – Ben Marshall Stakes
Thirds: 6 wins from 31 runs returned a **profit of +£20.00** to a £1 level stake.
2006 Pinpoint – Spring Cup, 2004 Fine Silver – Spring Cup, 1997 Hunters Of Brora – Lincoln
Fourths: 6 wins from 30 runs returned a **profit of +£7.43** to a £1 level stake. *2005 Crosspeace – Serlby Stakes*

FUTURE SUCCESS RATING: ★ ★ ★ ★ ★

TWO-YEAR-OLD TROPHY
October 4, Redcar – (Listed, Class 1, 2yo) 6f

Last run	Winner/ Trainer & SP	Draw/ Ran	Age	Wght	PR	Next four runs			
07 Donc 7f 1st Nursery *One month*	**Dubai Dynamo** J S Moore 40/1	14/23	2	9-02	57	6th **Horris Hill Stks** **Newb 7f**	-	-	-
06 York 5f 8th Flying Childers *One month*	**Danum Dancer** N Bycroft 16/1	17/24	2	8-03	54	6th **Rockingham Stk** **York 6f**	*8th **Cammidge Tr'py** **Newc 6f**	*5th **Handicap** **Newm 6f**	*22nd **2,000 Guineas** **Newm 1m**
05 Newb 6f 11th Mill Reef Stks *Two weeks*	**Misu Bond** B Smart 28/1	1/24	2	9-00	61	*WON 5/2F **Euro Free Hcp** **Newm 7f**	*5th **2,000 Guineas** **Newm 1m**	*3rd **Ballycorus Stks** **Leop 7f**	**6th **Chipchase Stks** **Newc 6f**
04 Newm 6f 1st Nursery *One week*	**Obe Gold** M Channon 15/2	24/24	2	8-03	55	2nd **Tatts Autumn Stk** **Newm 6f**	5th **Group 2** **Mais 6f**	*WON 4/1 **Conds Stks** **Kemp 6f**	*2nd **Euro Free Hcp** **Newm 7f**
03 Yarm 6f 1st Conds Stks *Three weeks*	**Peak To Creek** J Noseda 13/2	20/23	2	9-00	62	WON 7/2 **Rockingham St** **York 6f**	WON 5/1 **Horris Hill Stk** **Newb 7f**	*3rd **Craven Stks** **Newm 1m**	*2nd **King Charles II** **Newm 7f**
02 Donc 6f 1st St Leger Yearling *One month*	**Somnus** T Easterby 11/2	1/18	2	8-12	64	*5th **Pavilion Stks** **Ascot 6f**	*8th **Jersey Stks** **Ascot 7f**	*WON 6/1 **Conds Stks** **Hayd 6f**	*WON 5/1 **Hackwood Stks** **Newb 6f**
01 Ayr 5f 3rd Harry Rosebery *Three weeks*	**Captain Rio** R Whitaker 16/1	8/25	2	8-10	65	WON 5/2 **Group 2** **Mais 6f**	*4th **Listed** **Nad Al 6f**	*7th **Group 1** **Nad Al 6f**	*11th **Poule 'Poulains** **Long 1m**
00 Newm 6f 1st Nursery *Two months*	**Dim Sums** D Barron 6/4F	6/23	2	8-04	59	-	-	-	-
99 Ayr 5f 1st Harry Rosebery *Three weeks*	**Khasayl** P Walwyn 9/4F	2/26	2	8-08	65	*WON 2/1 **Listed** **Chan 5f**	*7th **Group 3** **Deau 6f**	*2nd **Group 3** **Chan 6f**	*8th **Abbaye** **Long 5f**
98 Newm 7f 4th Oh So Sharp Stk *Two weeks*	**Pipalong** T Easterby 5/2F	8/22	2	7-13	62	*4th **Conds Stks** **Thir 1m**	*5th **Shergar Cup** **Good 6f**	*5th **Listed** **Newm 6f**	*2nd **Cecil Frail Stks** **Hayd 6f**
97 Newm 6f 2nd Maiden *Two weeks*	**Grazia** Sir M Prescott 7/2F	3/26	2	8-02	63	*WON 5/2 **Hackwood Stks** **Newb 6f**	*9th **Maurice 'Gheest** **Deau 7f**	**6th **Leic'strshre Stk** **Leic 7f**	**3rd **Champagne Stk** **Newb 6f**
96 Newb 6f 2nd Mill Reef Stks *One month*	**Proud Native** A Jarvis 13/2	5/25	2	8-07	58	5th **Group 2** **Evry 7f**	*8th **Euro Free Hcp** **Newm 7f**	*4th **Sprint Stks** **Sand 5f**	*11th **Hackwood Stks** **Newb 6f**

12-year median performance rating of the winner: **60** (out of 100)   *next year **two years*

WINNER'S PROFILE Eleven of the last 12 lined up fit having **raced within the past month**, while 10 finished in the **first four last time out** – two exceptions ran in Group events. Those with **experience in Pattern company** are respected, as are last time out nursery winners, however, horses that scored in maiden company last time should be ignored. Only the Sir Mark Prescott-trained Grazia had yet to get off the mark, while the remaining 11 all **won one of their previous four outings**. Fillies have held their own, three of whom went off favourite, and that end of the market dominated until recently, when a shift in the trends threw up three big-priced winners.
One trainer of note was **Tim Easterby**, having sent out two winners from eight runners.

FUTURE POINTERS Following the subsequent glowing achievements of the 2003, 2002 and 2001 winners, this juvenile event – based approximately on sales prices – was rightly granted Listed status in 2004.
Although winners since proved a shade disappointing – three in the last four years earned sub-standard PR's – it has been a wise move to follow above par winners, as several scored in Pattern events next time out, while Somnus and Pipalong had successful long-term careers. In fact, both of trainer Tim Easterby's winners eventually went on to land the Group One Haydock Sprint Cup, while two victors found success in the Hackwood Stakes at Newbury the following season.
Overall, an event to view in a positive light as the runners-up offered strength in depth, and fingers crossed a vintage renewal like 2002 – Somnus beat Tout Seul – may be only around the corner.

Were Two-Year-Old Trophy winners profitable to follow on their subsequent three runs?
Yes – 8 wins from 31 runs returned a **profit of +£5.00** to a £1 level stake.

Placed runners' subsequent record (three runs):
Runners-up: 5 wins from 32 runs returned a **profit of +£14.54** to a £1 level stake.
2002 Tout Seul – Dewhurst Stakes

Thirds: 0 win from 28 runs returned a loss of -£28.00 to a £1 level stake.

FUTURE SUCCESS RATING: ★★★★ ★

BENGOUGH STAKES
October 11, Ascot – (Group 3, Class 1, 3yo+) 6f

Last run	Winner/ Trainer & SP	Draw/ Ran	Age	Wght	PR	Next four runs			
07 Yarm 6f 1st Conds Stks *Two months*	Greek Renaissance S Bin Suroor 12/1	11/17	4	9-01	75	5th Wentworth Stks Donc 6f	-	-	-
06 Hami 6f 1st Conds Stks *Three weeks*	Bygone Days S Bin Suroor 7/2F	6/14	5	9-01	81	*4th Leisure Stks Wind 6f	*6th Golden Jubilee Ascot 6f	*13th Maurice 'Gheest Deau 7f	*3rd Supreme Stks Good 7f
05 Ches 6f 8th Queensferry Stks *Three months*	Welsh Emperor T Tate 16/1	14/12	6	8-12	78	2nd Group 3 Mais 6f	*WON 6/1 Conds Stks Thir 6f	*14th Duke of York York 6f	*WON 13/2 Hungerford Stk Newb 7f
04 Long 5f 3rd Prix de l'Abbaye *Two weeks*	Royal Millennium M Channon 7/2F	4/14	6	9-02	75	4th H Kong Sprint Sha 5f	*4th Cammidge Tr'py Donc 6f	*10th Duke of York York 6f	*4th Golden Jubilee
03 Ascot 6f 4th Diadem Stks *Three weeks*	Ashdown Express C Wall 13/2	6/14	4	8-12	73	8th Wentworth Stks Donc 6f	*3rd Abernant Stks Newm 6f	*12th Duke of York York 6f	*2nd Leisure Stks
02 Newb 5f 4th World Trophy *One month*	Needwood Blade B McMahon 7/1	13/14	4	8-12	78	*4th Cammidge Tr'py Donc 6f	*WON 11/4 Abernant Stks Newm 6f	*WON 9/4F Palace House Newm 5f	*13th Duke of York
01 Long 5f 11th Prix de l'Abbaye *Two weeks*	Danehurst Sir M Prescott 9/1	1/17	3	8-06	80	WON 11/10F Wentworth Stks Donc 6f	*2nd Golden Jubilee Ascot 6f	*3rd July Cup Newm 6f	*14th Nunthorpe York 5f
00 Newm 7f 5th Rated Hcp *Two weeks*	Bahamian Pirate D Nicholls 9/1	14/15	5	8-12	72	*9th Cammidge Tr'py Donc 6f	*6th Abernant Stks Newm 6f	*6th Palace House Newm 5f	*8th Duke of York York 6f
99 Ayr 6f 8th Ayr Gold Cup *One month*	Gaelic Storm M Johnston 14/1	9/20	5	8-12	70	2nd Rated Hcp Newb 6f	6th Wentworth Stks Donc 6f	*9th Leisure Stks Ling 6f	*6th Conds Stks Yarm 6f
98 Ascot 6f 5th Diadem Stks *Three weeks*	Bold Edge R Hannon 7/1	7/16	3	8-11	79	*WON 9/1 Abernant Stks Newm 6f	*14th Duke of York York 6f	*WON 16/1 Cork & Orrery Ascot 6f	*2nd July Cup Newm 6f
97 Ascot 6f 12th Diadem Stks *Three weeks*	My Best Valentine V Soane 14/1	3/16	7	8-12	69	WON 10/1 Rated Hcp Newb 6f	2nd Wentworth Stks Donc 6f	*8th Abernant Stks Newm 6f	*2nd Palace House Newm 5f
96 Yarm 6f 1st Conds Stks *One month*	Russian Revival S Bin Suroor 20/1	3/15	3	8-11	77	2nd Conds Stks Donc 7f	3rd Wentworth Stks Donc 6f	*3rd Leisure Stks Ling 6f	*WON 8/1 Duty Free Cup Newb 7f

12-year median performance rating of the winner: **76** (out of 100)   *next year*

WINNER'S PROFILE **A victory earlier in the season** was key as all 12 winners boasted such form, and the three that scored last time out were the only ones to have arrived via a conditions event – two of them at Yarmouth. Ten winners had a **victory over this distance** to their name, the same number with **experience in Group company** – only two won at that level – while four took Listed events. An **official rating of 106 or more** helped, and only Bahamian Pirate since the Millennium was lower than 100, while those that looked for **value** were rewarded in the long-term – two decent priced winners came via **Saeed Bin Suroor** who sent out three winners in total.

FUTURE POINTERS Transferred to Ascot this year, the Bengough Stakes received Group status in 2003 although the standard hasn't changed significantly from when it was a Listed event as there isn't much between top handicap/Listed and Group Three performers in the sprint division. Sensibly, the majority of Bengough winners stuck to similar company in the future and several scored again at Listed/Group Three level – only Bold Edge went further in the Group Two Cork & Orrery (now Golden Jubilee). Those that reappeared before the end of term did well with two winners and a few runners-up, including in the Wentworth Stakes at Doncaster on the final day, although placed runners from here have a better record in that race *(see below)*. Two winners also won the Abernant back here the following year – from five runners – however six that attempted the Duke of York at the Dante meeting failed.

Were Bengough winners profitable to follow on their subsequent three runs?
Yes – 7 wins from 34 runs returned a **profit of +£20.10** to a £1 level stake.

Placed runners' subsequent record (three runs):
Runners-up: 5 wins from 33 runs returned a loss of -£8.00 to a £1 level stake.
2000 Andreyev – Wentworth Stakes, 1999 Pipalong – Wentworth Stakes, 1998 Tedburrow – Cammidge Trophy, 1997 Bollin Joanne – Duke of York

Thirds: 6 wins from 29 runs returned a **profit of +£19.75** to a £1 level stake.
2005 Moss Vale – Group Three Greenlands Stakes, 2004 Quito – Wentworth Stakes, 2000 Rushcutter Bay – Palace House Stakes, 1997 Snow Kid – Wentworth Stakes

FUTURE SUCCESS RATING: ★★★☆☆

CORNWALLIS STAKES
October 11, Ascot – (Group 3, Class 1, 2yo) 5f

Last run	Winner/ Trainer & SP	Draw/ Ran	Age	Wght	PR	Next four runs			
07 Ayr 5f 1st Harry Rosebery One month	**Captain Gerrard** B Smart 9/4F	12/12	2	9-00	75	-	-	-	-
06 Ayr 5f 1st Harry Rosebery One month	**Alzerra** M Channon 4/1F	9/10	2	8-11	67	*6th Conds Stks Nad Al 7f	-	-	-
05 Donc 5f 2nd Flying Childers One month	**Hunter Street** P Chapple-Hyam 4/1	5/12	2	8-12	67	-	-	-	-
04 Ayr 6f 3rd Firth of Clyde One month	**Castelletto** B McMahon 15/2	6/11	2	8-09	62	*9th Fillies Stks Nad Al 7f	*9th Scurry Stks Sand 5f	*9th Summer Stks York 6f	*4th King George Stk Good 5f
03 York 6f 6th Gimcrack Stks Two months	**Majestic Missile** W Haggas 11/4	3/11	2	9-01	73	*5th King's Stand Ascot 5f	*8th King George Stk Good 5f	*6th World Trophy Newb 5f	**4th Group 3 Long 5f
02 Sand 5f 1st Maiden One month	**Peace Offering** T Mills 8/1	5/11	2	8-12	68	*7th Greenham Stks Newb 7f	*5th Palace House Newm 5f	*7th Temple Stks Sand 5f	*13th King's Stand Ascot 5f
01 Muss 5f 1st Maiden Two weeks	**Dominica** M Tregoning 12/1	7/11	2	8-07	71	**WON 16/1 King's Stand Ascot 5f**	*5th Nunthorpe York 5f	**4th King's Stand Ascot 5f	*4th Nunthorpe York 5f
00 Wolv 5f 1st Novice Stks Three weeks	**Danehurst** Sir M Prescott 7/2F	2/17	2	8-07	73	*9th King's Stand Ascot 5f	*11th Memorial Stks Curr 5f	**WON 7/2JF City Wall Stks Ches 5f**	*11th Prix de l'Abbaye Long 5f
99 Ling 5f 1st Maiden Two weeks	**Kier Park** M Jarvis 4/1	11/13	2	8-12	65	*2nd Palace House Newm 5f	**15th Conds Stks Nott 5f	**8th Palace House Newm 5f	**2nd Conds Stks Good 5f
98 Curr 6f 1st Listed Stks Two months	**Show Me The Money** N Meade 3/1	6/12	2	8-08	63	**WON 7/2 1,000 Guin Trial Leop 7f**	*15th Irish 1,000 Guin Curr 1m	*10th Flying Five Leop 5f	*3rd Boland Stks Curr 7f
97 Ayr 5f 1st Harry Rosebery One month	**Halmahera** I Balding 8/1	4/13	2	8-12	65	*5th Field Marshal Stk Newm 5f	*7th Group 2 Chan 5f	*4th Chipchase Stks Newc 6f	*4th Porcelanosa Stks Sand 5f
96 Newm 6f 6th Middle Park Stk Two weeks	**Easycall** B Meehan 11/2	12/11	2	9-04	69	*8th Temple Stks Sand 5f	*5th King's Stand Ascot 5f	*6th July Cup Newm 6f	*2nd Conds Stks Newm 5f

12-year median performance rating of the winner: **68** (out of 100)   (2005 Salisbury, 2004 Newmarket, 2000 Newbury)

*next year **two years*

WINNER'S PROFILE Unusually for an Ascot event, the majority had their **prep outside of the south**, as four came via Ayr, three of whom won the Listed Harry Rosebery Stakes. All bar one winner already **scored over this minimum distance**, while three of the four not to have tackled Pattern company beforehand were all maiden winners last time out – exception took a novice stakes.

Fillies held their own on more than one occasion, two of whom were winning favourites and it paid to stick with those that **started at 8/1 or shorter**, as not many triumphed at a double-figure price.

FUTURE POINTERS This juvenile sprint hasn't the strongest roll call over the past 20 years, as the majority failed to have any sort of notable career and only a handful managed to score again in Group company.

No winner reappeared again during the backend that year, and Listed/Group Three sprints featured heavily on next season's schedule, although only Dominica scored in the Group Two King's Stand Stakes at Royal Ascot, an event where three others failed.

Overall, Cornwallis victors could prove best left alone, as not even some of the above par winners were able to find the winner's enclosure again in the near future.

Were Cornwallis winners profitable to follow on their subsequent three runs?
No – 3 wins from 28 runs returned a loss of -£2.00 to a £1 level stake.

Placed runners' subsequent record (three runs):
Runners-up: 3 wins from 32 runs returned a loss of -£23.25 to a £1 level stake.
2006 Hoh Mike – Pavilion Stakes, Scurry Stakes

Thirds: 4 wins from 30 runs returned a loss of -£8.91 to a £1 level stake.
2006 Enticing – Lansdown Fillies' Stakes, 2000 Red Millennium – Lansdown Fillies' Stakes, 1999 Watching – Field Marshall

FUTURE SUCCESS RATING: ★ ★ ☆ ☆ ☆

AUTUMN STAKES
October 11, Ascot – (Group 3, Class 1, 2yo) 1m

Last run	Winner/ Trainer & SP	Draw/ Ran	Age	Wght	PR	Next four runs			
07 Ascot 7f 1st Nursery *Two weeks*	**Ibn Khaldun** S Bin Suroor 4/7F	4/8	2	9-00	74	WON 11/4F R Post Trophy Donc 1m	-	-	-
06 Newm 6f 1st Tatts Auction Stk *Two weeks*	**Caldra** S Kirk 6/4F	1/8	2	9-00	65	*4th Sovereign Stks Sali 1m	*3rd Superior Mile Hayd 1m	-	-
05 Sand 7f 2nd Novice Stks *One month*	**Blitzkrieg** V Smith 20/1	2/12	2	8-11	62	-	-	-	-
03 Good 1m 1st Stardom Stks *One month*	**Fantastic View** R Hannon 13/8F	3/5	2	9-00	64	2nd R Post Trophy Donc 1m	*5th Craven Stks Newm 1m	*4th Conds Stks Donc 1m	****9th Royal Hunt Cup Ascot 1m
02 Ascot 1m 1st Conds Stks *Three weeks*	**Big Bad Bob** J Dunlop 3/1	4/6	2	8-11	70	*2nd Dee Stks Ches 1m2f	*8th King Edward VII Ascot 1m4f	**WON 5/6F** Conds Stks Hayd 1m3f	**WON N/O** Conds Stks Deau 1m2f
01 Newb 1m 1st Conds Stks *One month*	**Fight Your Corner** M Johnston 11/2	4/8	2	8-11	73	*7th Feilden Stks Newm 1m1f	**WON 9/2** Chester Vase Ches 1m4f	*5th Derby Epsom 1m4f	**5th Group 3 Nad Al 1m4f
00 Newb 1m 1st Conds Stks *One month*	**Nayef** M Tregoning 7/4F	4/6	2	8-11	75	*3rd Craven Stks Newm 1m	*8th 2,000 Guineas Newm 1m	*3rd Gordon Stks Good 1m4f	**WON 5/4F** Rose' Lancaster Hayd 1m3f
99 Donc 1m 1st Nursery *One month*	**Epic Express** T Easterby 5/2F	5/11	2	8-11	65	*2nd Classic Trial Thir 1m	*17th 2,000 Guineas Newm 1m	**WON 8/15F** Conds Stks Donc 1m	*3rd Rose' Lancaster Hayd 1m3f
98 Newb 1m 3rd Conds Stks *One month*	**Daliapour** L Cumani 2/1	3/7	2	8-11	75	**WON 8/13F** Blue Rib' Trial Epsom 1m2f	*2nd Derby Trial Ling 1m3f	*2nd Derby Epsom 1m4f	*2nd Irish Derby Curr 1m4f
97 Newm 7f 1st Maiden *One month*	**Dr Fong** H Cecil 9/4	1/4	2	8-11	67	**WON 11/4F** Newmarket Stk Newm 1m2f	*4th Dante Stks York 1m2f	*3rd Prix Jean Prat Chan 1m1f	**WON 4/1** St James Palace Ascot 1m
96 Yarm 1m 1st Maiden	**High Roller** H Cecil 2/5F	1/5	2	8-11	64	-	-	-	-

12-year median performance rating of the winner: **64** (out of 100) (2005 Salisbury, 2004 abandoned)

*next year**two years****four years*

WINNER'S PROFILE A **recent run within the past month** formed part of every winner's preparation – nine scored – the majority outside of Pattern company. Two of the last four took Listed events beforehand suggesting the trends may have changed, but last year's winner stuck to tradition as he won a nursery.
Every winner **already scored over seven furlongs or a mile**, while they were all officially rated from 85 (last year) to 107 – the majority were in the 100s – and none **had yet to race more than six times**.
Trainer **Henry Cecil** is the one name to appear more than once, with two victories from three runners.

FUTURE POINTERS Twenty years have passed since a British Classic winner landed the Autumn Stakes, that honour fell to Nashwan in 1988, and the only contestant to have emerged that went on to Classic success in recent times was the 2005 runner-up, Dylan Thomas, who took the Irish Derby. However, several notable winners found Group One glory in Nayef, Daliapour and Dr Fong – the former pair recorded the best performance ratings since 1996 – while last year's winner, Ibn Khaldun, gave this event a needed boost in the Group One Racing Post Trophy next time out.
In terms of profiting by following the winner, perhaps the best policy may be to wait for a step up to at least 10 furlongs the following spring.

Were Autumn winners profitable to follow on their subsequent three runs?
No – 6 wins from 24 runs returned a loss of -£6.03 to a £1 level stake.

Placed runners' subsequent record (three runs):
Runners-up: 3 wins from 20 runs returned a loss of -£3.17 to a £1 level stake.
2001 Coshocton – Predominate Stakes

Thirds: 0 win from 6 runs returned a loss of -£6.00 to a £1 level stake.

FUTURE SUCCESS RATING: ★ ★ ★ ☆ ☆

PRINCESS ROYAL STAKES* (new title to be named)
October 17-18, Newmarket – (Group 2, Class 1, 3yo+ Fillies & Mares) 1m4f

Last run	Winner/ Trainer & SP	Draw/ Ran	Age	Wght	PR	Next four runs			
07 Donc 1m7f 7th Park Hill Stks *One month*	**Trick Or Treat** J Given 14/1	3/12	4	9-00	68	-	-	-	-
06 Chan 1m4f 1st Listed *One month*	**Acts Of Grace** J Dunlop 14/1	1/13	3	8-06	65	6th Premio Tesio Capa 1m2f	-	-	-
05 York 1m2f 7th Prince of Wales' *Four months*	**Ouija Board** E Dunlop 11/8F	4/13	4	9-00	73	2nd Breeders' Cup Belm 1m2f	5th Japan Cup Toky 1m4f	**WON 5/2 Hong Kong Vase Sha 1m4f**	*4th Sheema Classic Nad Al 1m4f
04 Donc 1m7f 2nd Park Hill Stks *Three weeks*	**Mazuna** C Brittain 14/1	3/8	3	8-06	65	6th Premio Tesio Capa 1m2f	*6th Handicap Nad Al 1m4f	*6th Handicap Nad Al 1m4f	*8th Handicap Nad Al 1m4f
03 Ascot 1m2f 1st Diamond Hcp *Three months*	**Itnab** B Hanbury 9/2	3/9	3	8-07	69	-	-	-	-
02 Ascot 1m4f 1st Harvest Stks *Three weeks*	**Love Everlasting** M Johnston 8/11F	3/4	4	9-00	70	-	-	-	-
01 York 1m4f 9th Yorkshire Oaks *Two months*	**Head In The Clouds** J Dunlop 7/1	4/11	3	8-07	69	2nd St Simon Stks Newm 1m4f	-	-	-
00 Yarm 1m2f 2nd Fillies' Listed *One month*	**Sacred Song** H Cecil 12/1	5/15	3	8-07	71	*3rd Aston Park Stk Newb 1m5f	*3rd Mercury Listed Leic 1m4f	**WON 7/4F Lanc'shre Oaks Hayd 1m4f**	*2nd Yorkshire Oaks York 1m4f
99 Ascot 1m4f 1st Harvest Stks *Two weeks*	**Signorina Cattiva** J Dunlop 7/1	7/12	3	8-07	70	**WON 13/8F St Simon Stks Newb 1m4f**	3rd Premio Roma Capa 1m2f	-	-
98 Hayd 1m4f 3rd Lancashire Oaks *Four months*	**Silver Rhapsody** H Cecil 3/1	6/7	3	8-07	67	5th St Simon Stks Newm 1m4f	*2nd Jock' Club Stks Newm 1m4f	*4th Group 2 Sain 1m4f	*3rd Princess' Wales Newm 1m4f
97 Ascot 1m4f 4th Harvest Stks *Two weeks*	**Delilah** Sir M Stoute 4/1	2/7	3	8-07	65	5th Premio Roma Capa 1m2f	*6th John Porter Stk Newb 1m4f	*2nd Rated Hcp Ches 1m5f	**WON 9/1 Park Hill Stks Donc 1m7f**
96 Ascot 1m4f 2nd Harvest Stks *Two weeks*	**Time Allowed** Sir M Stoute 15/2	4/11	3	8-07	68	**WON 13/2 Jockey Club Stks Newm 1m4f**	-	-	-

12-year median performance rating of the winner: **68** (out of 100) *(2005 & 2000 Newmarket) *next year*

WINNER'S PROFILE Eleven winners **raced at a Grade One venue last time out**, where eight ran in either the Harvest Stakes at Ascot, Park Hill at Doncaster, or an Oaks. A **previous victory that season** was also vital – only Ouija Board who had been injured arrived without a recent win – while every winner **experienced Pattern company** and 10 made the top-three. It's worth looking for a decent priced winner as favourites have a poor record, the only two market leaders to succeed were Ouija Board and Love Everlasting – in the smallest field of just four.
Two of the last four winners had official ratings in the 90's, while the majority were 100 plus, including trainer **Henry Cecil**'s pair from seven runners. Others to note include **John Dunlop** with three from 13 runners, and **Sir Michael Stoute** with two from 12 – last 10 have all lost – while **Mark Johnston** has a careful record with one victory and two seconds from just the three runners.

FUTURE POINTERS The roll of honour for this recently upgraded Group Two event doesn't feature many superstar fillies, as only Ouija Board stood out in recent times, while Snow Bride back in 1989, won that year's Oaks through the disqualification of Aliysa. It's hard to make a case for following winners as the majority went off to the paddocks at the end of the season, while three had their final runs of the campaign in Italy. The only three who raced again that season in Britain headed to Newbury for the St Simon Stakes where one triumphed, while of those to have remained in training leading up to the Millennium, three took notable events as four-year-olds.

Were Princess Royal* winners profitable to follow on their subsequent three runs?
No – 4 wins from 20 runs returned a loss of -£3.62 to a £1 level stake.

Placed runners' subsequent record (three runs):
Runners-up: 1 win from 12 runs returned a loss of -£5.50 to a £1 level stake.

Thirds: 3 wins from 9 runs returned a loss of -£3.67 to a £1 level stake.
2003 Chorist – Pretty Polly Stakes

FUTURE SUCCESS RATING: ★ ★ ☆ ☆ ☆

DARLEY STAKES
October 17, Newmarket – (Group 3, Class 1, 3yo+) 1m1f

Last run	Winner/ Trainer & SP	Draw/ Ran	Age	Wght	PR	Next four runs			
07 Good 1m2f 3rd Foundation Stks One month	Windsor Knot S Bin Suroor 7/1	6/13	5	9-03	74	-	-	-	-
06 York 1m1f 2nd Strensall Stks Two months	Stage Gift Sir M Stoute 11/4	5/12	3	8-13	77	*14th Group 3 Nad Al 1m1f	*8th Group 2 Nad Al 1m1f	*WON 18/10 Group 3 Long 1m2f	*WON 8/1 York Stks York 1m2f
05 Long 1m2f 2nd Foundation Stks One month	Enforcer W Muir 12/1	2/12	3	8-10	70	*6th Group 2 Long 1m2f	*4th Gordon Richards Sain 1m2f	*5th Jockey Club Stk Newm 1m4f	*3rd Coronation Cup Epsom 1m4f
04 Long 7f 5th Group 3 One month	Autumn Glory G Wragg 9/2JF	7/16	4	9-04	76	*WON 15/8JF Donc'str Shield Donc 1m	*2nd Group 2 Sain 1m	*3rd Group 3 Long 1m2f	*WON 9/1 Silver Trophy Ling 1m
03 Newm 1m1f 5th Cambridgeshire Two weeks	Far Lane B Hills 9/2	1/11	4	9-00	78	WON 6/1 J Seymour Stk Newm 1m2f	*16th Group 1 Caul 1m1f	**10th Group 1 Morp 2m	-
02 Long 1m2f 5th Prix de l'Opera Two weeks	Golden Silca M Channon 16/1	13/12	6	8-09	73	12th Group 2 Capa 1m2f	9th Group 2 Capa 1m	*3rd Dahlia Stks Newm 1m1f	*5th Middleton Stks York 1m2f
01 Ayr 1m2f 4th Scottish Classic Four months	Right Wing J Dunlop 5/1	9/8	7	9-07	71	6th B Marshall Stks Newm 1m	-	-	-
00 Long 1m2f 2nd Group 2 Two weeks	Albarahin M Tregoning 6/4F	5/11	5	9-04	77	WON 8/11F B Marshall Stks Newm 1m	*2nd Doncaster Mile Donc 1m	*2nd Earl of Sefton Newm 1m1f	*4th Masai Mile Sand 1m
99 Newm 1m 1st Joel Stks Three weeks	Indian Lodge Mrs A Perrett 9/2	9/9	3	9-00	80	*WON 10/1 Earl of Sefton Newm 1m1f	*WON 9/4F UK Mile Sand 1m	*3rd Lockinge Newb 1m	*7th Queen Anne Ascot 1m
98 Newb 1m1f 2nd Conds Stks One month	Haami J Dunlop 10/1	3/13	3	8-10	72	*2nd Earl of Sefton Newm 1m1f	*7th Credit Mile Stks Sand 1m	*4th Festival Stks Good 1m2f	*2nd Int Silver Trophy Ascot 1m
97 Ascot 1m4f 4th Cumberland Lodge Three weeks	Fahris B Hanbury 11/10F	1/7	3	9-03	75	*8th Brigadier Gerard Sand 1m2f	*6th Turf Classic Nad Al 1m4f	**8th Grade 1 Belm 1m4f	*3rd Grade 2 Belm 1m3f
96 Newm 1m1f 7th Cambridgeshire Two weeks	Tarawa N Callaghan 9/2	5/10	4	9-00	70				

12-year median performance rating of the winner: **74** (out of 100) *(1999 July Course) *next **two years*

WINNER'S PROFILE The majority arrived having **run within the past month**, and two recent winners came via the Foundation Stakes at Goodwood, while 11 raced over a **minimum of a mile last time out**.
Eleven winners **already scored between a mile and 10 furlongs**, the same number that **recorded a top-two spot in Pattern company**. The classier individuals came out on top with an **official rating between 106 to 116**, two of whom were trained by John Dunlop from 16 runners – last eight were all unplaced.

FUTURE POINTERS As you'd expect from an end of season Group Three, the Darley Stakes has regularly attracted a combination of those dropped in class that failed to cut the mustard against the big boys, along with improving handicappers on the prowl for Group scalps. However, not many went to the top post-Newmarket, as only Indian Lodge managed to land a couple of Group Ones in France including the Prix du Moulin, while a few Darley winners went on to score in Group Two company, including Stage Gift in the York Stakes last year.
Those that reappeared quickly before the end of term performed well, as two returned to HQ to land Listed events, including the Ben Marshall Stakes, an event in which two third-placed Darley runners also triumphed in *(see below)*.

Were Darley winners profitable to follow on their subsequent three runs?
Yes – 6 wins from 28 runs returned a **profit of +£0.64** to a £1 level stake.

Placed runners' subsequent record (three runs):
Runners-up: 5 wins from 32 runs returned a loss of -£17.73 to a £1 level stake.
2007 Mashaahed – Listed James Seymour Stakes, 2006 Windsor Knot – Darley Stakes

Thirds: 3 wins from 27 runs returned a loss of -£16.25 to a £1 level stake.
2005 St Andrews – Ben Marshall Stakes, 2002 Beauchamp Pilot – Ben Marshall Stakes, 2001 Lagudin – James Seymour Stakes

FUTURE SUCCESS RATING: ★★★☆☆

CHALLENGE STAKES
October 18, Newmarket – (Group 2, Class 1, 3yo+) 7f

Last run	Winner/ Trainer & SP	Draw/ Ran	Age	Wght	PR	Next four runs			
07 Ascot 7f 1st October Stks One month	**Miss Lucifer** B Hills 20/1	4/15	3	8-12	76	-	-	-	-
06 Long 7f 11th Prix de la Foret Two weeks	**Sleeping Indian** J Gosden 9/2F	11/16	5	9-03	78	4th Breeders' Cup Chur 1m	-	-	-
05 Good 1m 5th Celebration Mile Two months	**Le Vie Dei Colori** L Cumani 20/1	6/15	5	9-00	80	-	-	-	-
04 Donc 7f 2nd Park Stks Two months	**Firebreak** S Bin Suroor 11/2	9/12	5	9-04	83	WON 10/1 Hong Kong Mile Sha 1m	-	-	-
03 Newm 6f 12th July Cup Four months	**Just James** J Noseda 16/1	10/11	4	9-00	77	*15th Duke of York York 6f	*13th Queen Anne Ascot 1m	*11th Hungerford Stks Newb 7f	**8th Criterion Stks Newm 7f
02 Hayd 6f 10th Sprint Cup Two months	**Nayyir** G Butler 7/1	3/17	4	9-00	82	*6th Chipchase Stks Newc 6f	*WON 6/1 Lennox Stks Good 7f	*8th Maurice 'Gheest Deau 7f	*2nd Challenge Stks Newm 7f
01 Good 7f 4th Supreme Stks One month	**Munir** B Hills 20/1	10/14	3	8-12	75	-	-	-	-
00 Good 7f 4th Supreme Stks One month	**Last Resort** B Hills 20/1	7/9	3	8-09	75	14th Hong Kong Mile Sha 1m	-	-	-
99 Donc 7f 1st Sceptre Stks Two months	**Susu** Sir M Stoute 8/1	10/10	6	8-11	78	12th Breeders' Cup Gulf 1m	-	-	-
98 Long 1m 3rd Group 2 Two weeks	**Decorated Hero** J Gosden 11/2	4/10	6	9-04	75	3rd Group 2 Sha 1m	-	-	-
97 Good 7f 1st Conds Stks Two months	**Kahal** S Bin Suroor 9/2	4/12	3	8-12	71	*4th Lockinge Newb 1m	*7th Cork & Orrery Ascot 6f	*11th July Cup Newm 6f	*6th Maurice 'Gheest Deau 7f
96 Ascot 1m 4th QE II Stks Three weeks	**Charnwood Forest** S Bin Suroor 15/8F	8/8	4	9-04	80	9th Breeders' Cup Wood 1m	-	-	-

12-year median performance rating of the winner: **78** (out of 100) *next year **two years*

WINNER'S PROFILE Every winner **arrived via a Grade One racecourse** last time out – 10 came from either Ascot, Doncaster, Goodwood or Longchamp – while all 12 **experienced Pattern company along the way**, 10 of whom scored. Another vital component shared by all 12 victors was **winning form over seven furlongs** – every winner also **scored during the campaign** – while the best horses with an **official rating of 113 or higher** came out on top, though two of **Barry Hills**'s three winners were rated in the 90s. All three of the Newmarket handler's winners went off at 20/1 and it **paid to look for value** as only two favourites obliged, while two other trainers to note were **John Gosden** and **Saeed Bin Suroor** with a pair each – Newmarket trainers in general fared well.

FUTURE POINTERS It is difficult to draw conclusions regarding the subsequent results of Challenge Stakes winners as the majority were packed off to stud soon after. Of the limited information available, it's encouraging to see that one of the best recent winners, Firebreak, went and scored in Group One company next time out, however, the three who took the Breeders' Cup route were all soundly beaten.
Of those to have remained in training, only Nayyir scored again in Pattern company, while the other two failed to build on this victory.

Were Challenge Stakes winners profitable to follow on their subsequent three runs?
Yes – 2 wins from 15 runs returned a **profit of +£3.00** to a £1 level stake.

Placed runners' subsequent record (three runs):
Runners-up: 4 wins from 22 runs returned a loss of -£8.50 to a £1 level stake.
2005 Sleeping Indian – Duty Free Cup, 2002 Firebreak – Group Two Godolphin Mile,
1999 Lend A Hand – Duke of York

Thirds: 10 wins from 28 runs returned a **profit of +£7.68** to a £1 level stake.
2006 Satchem – Joel Stakes, 2003 Arakan – Abernant,
2001 Warningford – Leicestershire Stakes, John of Gaunt Stakes, 1997 Muchea – Gladness Stakes

FUTURE SUCCESS RATING: ★ ★ ☆ ☆ ☆

DEWHURST STAKES
October 18, Newmarket – (Group 1, Class 1, 2yo) 7f

Last run	Winner/Trainer & SP	Draw/Ran	Age	Wght	PR	Next four runs			
07 Curr 7f 1st National Stks One month	New Approach J Bolger 6/4F	5/10	2	9-01	81	-	-	-	-
06 Curr 7f 1st National Stks One month	Teofilo J Bolger 11/8F	4/15	2	9-01	86	-	-	-	-
05 Good 7f 1st Vintage Stks Three months	Sir Percy M Tregoning 9/2	8/8	2	9-00	82	*2nd 2,000 Guineas Newm 1m	*WON 6/1 Derby Epsom 1m4f	*7th Champion Stks Newm 1m2f	*4th Sheema Classic Nad Al 1m4f
04 Good 7f 1st Vintage Stks Three months	Shamardal M Johnston 9/2	4/9	2	9-00	83	*9th UAE Derby Nad Al 1m1f	*WON 4/1 Poule 'Poulains Long 1m	*WON 4/1 Prix Jock' Club Chan 1m3f	*WON 7/4F St James Pal' York 1m
03 Newm 7f 1st Tattersall Stks Three weeks	Milk It Mick J Osborne 33/1	11/12	2	9-00	75	*2nd Shadwell Stks Ling 1m	*5th Greenham Newb 7f	*8th 2,000 Guineas Newm 1m	*3rd Conds Stks Donc 6f
02 Redc 6f 2nd 2yo Trophy Two weeks	Tout Seul F Johnson Houghton 25/1	2/16	2	9-00	76	*4th 2,000 Guineas Newm 1m	*3rd Irish 2,000 Guin Curr 1m	*7th St James Palace Long 1m	*6th Group 2 Long 1m
01 Long 7f 1st Grand Criterium Two weeks	Rock Of Gibraltar A O'Brien 4/6F	3/8	2	9-00	82	*WON 9/1 2,000 Guineas Newm 1m	*WON 4/7F Irish 2,000 Guin Curr 1m	*WON 4/5F St James Pal' Ascot 1m	*WON 8/13F Sussex Good 1m
00 Long 7f 1st Prix 'Salamandre One month	Tobougg M Channon 7/4F	6/10	2	9-00	79	*9th 2,000 Guineas Newm 1m	*3rd Derby Epsom 1m4f	*4th Eclipse Sand 1m2f	*2nd Champion Stks Newm 1m2f
99 Donc 7f 1st Champagne Stk One month	Distant Music B Hills 4/6F	2/5	2	9-00	81	*2nd Greenham Newb 7f	*8th 2,000 Guineas Newm 1m	*WON 4/1 Park Stks Donc 1m	*3rd Champion Stks Newm 1m2f
98 York 6f 5th Gimcrack Stks Two months	Mujahid J Dunlop 25/1	3/7	2	9-00	76	*5th Craven Stks Newm 1m	*3rd 2,000 Guineas Newm 1m	*5th Poule 'Poulains Long 1m	*7th St James' Palace Ascot 1m
97 Long 7f 1st Prix 'Salamandre One month	Xaar A Fabre 11/8F	1/7	2	9-00	85	*WON 8/11F Craven Stks Newm 1m	*4th 2,000 Guineas Newm 1m	*2nd Prix d'Ornano Deau 1m2f	*3rd Irish Champion Leop 1m2f
96 Newm 6f 3rd Middle Park Three weeks	In Command B Hills 10/1	2/8	2	9-00	74	*4th Greenham Newb 7f	*6th St James' Palace Ascot 1m	*7th Park Stks Donc 1m	**8th Doncaster Mile Donc 1m

12-year median performance rating of the winner: **80** (out of 100)   *next year*

WINNER'S PROFILE Clues aren't easy to find, although small stepping stones have paved the way. Winning form was a must, as the last 11 winners **struck within their last two runs**, the last four took either the National or Vintage Stakes last time out. Two more victors won the Prix de la Salamandre directly before Newmarket, however, ones to avoid came via the Champagne Stakes at Doncaster and the Middle Park Stakes here.

Ten of the last 11 winners **proved themselves over this intermediate trip of seven furlongs**, while nine since 1997 were Group winners, one of the exceptions took a valuable sales race.

Not many trainer patterns to follow, although **Jim Bolger** obviously stands out of late with a 100% record, and **Barry Hills** won it twice from eight runners. However, Aidan O'Brien only hit the goal once from almost 25 runners.

FUTURE POINTERS Unlike the Middle Park Stakes run here a fortnight earlier, the Dewhurst has very much become a juvenile event to note with a view to the Classics, as the likes of Sir Percy, Shamardal and Rock Of Gibraltar all went on to land big ones the following year, while three placed runners since the Millennium also found Guineas success *(see below)*. Such recent subsequent winners helped put the Dewhurst firmly back on the map after a drought between 1996 to 2000, which came immediately after a golden era when the race produced Pennekamp (1994), Zafonic (1992), Dr Devious (1991) and Generous (1990), all of whom took Classics.

Were Dewhurst winners profitable to follow on their subsequent three runs?
Yes – 8 wins from 30 runs returned a **profit of +£7.09** to a £1 level stake.

Placed runners' subsequent record (three runs):
Runners-up: 6 wins from 29 runs returned a loss of -£0.25 to a £1 level stake.
2001 Landseer – Poule d'Essai des Poulains (French 2,000 Guineas),
2000 Noverre (disqualified) – Poule d'Essai des Poulains (French 2,000 Guineas)

Thirds: 6 wins from 21 runs returned a loss of -£4.01 to a £1 level stake.
2003 Haafhd – Craven Stakes, 2,000 Guineas, 2002 Trade Fair – King Charles II Stakes, Criterion

FUTURE SUCCESS RATING: ★ ★ ★ ★ ☆

CHAMPION STAKES
October 18, Newmarket – (Group 1, Class 1, 3yo+) 1m2f

Last run	Winner/ Trainer & SP	Draw/ Ran	Age	Wght	PR	Next four runs			
07 Long 1m2f 1st Prix du 'Orange One month	Literato J-C Rouget 7/2	5/12	3	8-12	86	-	-	-	-
06 Long 1m4f 2nd Arc de Triomphe Two weeks	Pride A Royer-Dupre 7/2	2/8	6	9-00	85	WON 51/20 Hong Kong Cup Sha 1m2f	-	-	-
05 Good 1m4f 1st Select Stks One month	David Junior B Meehan 25/1	13/15	3	8-11	89	*WON 9/2F Dubai Duty Free Nad Al 1m1f	*4th Prince of Wales Ascot 1m2f	*WON 9/4 Eclipse Sand 1m2f	*13th Breeders' Cup Chur 1m2f
04 Good 1m 9th Sussex Three months	Haafhd B Hills 12/1	9/11	3	8-11	84	-	-	-	-
03 Ascot 1m2f 2nd Prince of Wales' Four months	Rakti M Jarvis 11/1	3/11	4	9-02	87	2nd Hong Kong Cup Sha 1m2f	*WON 3/1 Prince of Wales Ascot 1m2f	*8th Eclipse Sand 1m2f	*5th Irish Champion Leop 1m2f
02 Newm 1m4f 1st Godolphin Stks Three weeks	Storming Home B Hills 8/1	4/11	4	9-02	82	15th Japan Cup Naka 1m3f	*WON 28/10 Handicap Holl 1m4f	*WON 3/10F Grade 1 Holl 1m2f	*4th Arlington Million Arli 1m2f
01 Ascot 1m4f 1st Cumb'lnd Lodge Three weeks	Nayef M Tregoning 3/1F	1/12	3	8-11	84	*WON 9/4F Sheema Classic Nad Al 1m4f	*3rd Tatts Gold Cup Curr 1m3f	*4th Prince of Wales' Ascot 1m2f	*2nd King George VI Ascot 1m4f
00 York 1m2f 2nd Juddmonte Int Two months	Kalanisi Sir M Stoute 5/1	3/15	4	9-02	90	WON 46/10 Breeders' Cup Chur 1m4f	*3rd Tatts Gold Cup Curr 1m3f	*2nd Prince of Wales' Ascot 1m2f	-
99 Good 1m2f 5th Nassau Three months	Alborada Sir M Prescott 5/1	10/13	4	8-13	83	-	-	-	-
98 Leop 1m2f 2nd Irish Champion Two months	Alborada Sir M Prescott 6/1	5/10	3	8-08	82	*5th Nassau Good 1m2f	*WON 5/1 Champion Stks Newm 1m2f	-	-
97 Long 1m4f 2nd Arc de Triomphe Two weeks	Pilsudski Sir M Stoute EvensF	1/7	5	9-02	90	WON 36/10 Japan Cup Toky 1m4f	-	-	-
96 Ascot 1m 2nd Q Elizabeth II Three weeks	Bosra Sham H Cecil 9/4	4/6	3	8-08	87	*WON 1/5F Brig' Gerard Sand 1m2f	*WON 4/11F Prince of Wales Ascot 1m2f	*3rd Eclipse Sand 1m2f	*4th Juddmonte Int York 1m2f

12-year median performance rating of the winner: **86** (out of 100) *next year*

WINNER'S PROFILE An array of events provided the final prep for Newmarket – two runners-up of the Arc gained compensation here – while the only two not to have finished in the first-two last time out arrived after a break from Glorious Goodwood. Only those proven at this level need apply as every winner had **faced Group One company previously**, 10 of whom **finished in the top-three**, although none scored at that level last time out – three winners prior to Newmarket all scored in Listed/Group Three company. **Three to four-year-olds** held the call – five-year-olds and above struck just once from over 30 runners – while a win over this intermediate distance was a bonus. **French-trained runners** have a good long-term record as they took it six times from 1984 to 1995, while **Barry Hills** and **Sir Michael Stoute** won it twice each from 10 and 18 runners respectively. Two yards to be wary of, however, are Aidan O'Brien's with nine losers and Saeed Bin Suroor's, who shot 19 blanks since 1996.

FUTURE POINTERS The Champion Stakes has seen it's share of sub-standard and vintage renewals, and last year's was of the former category as it featured only two runners that won a Group/Grade One event earlier in the year. However, winners have done themselves proud long-term post-Newmarket, in fact, of the nine who remained in training, all won again during their next two outings – eight of whom scored at the top level – while five took Group Ones next time out in major international events. Both of Sir Michael Stoute's older winners were worth following later that term, while two others returned the following year to land the Prince of Wales's Stakes.

Were Champion Stakes winners profitable to follow on their subsequent three runs?
Yes – 12 wins from 22 runs returned a **profit of +21.44** to a £1 level stake.

Placed runners' subsequent record (three runs):
Runners-up: 5 wins from 22 runs returned a loss of -£10.15 to a £1 level stake.
2005 Pride – Group Two Prix Corrida, 2002 Moon Ballad – Dubai World Cup, 1999 Shiva – Brigadier Gerard

Thirds: 5 wins from 20 runs returned a **profit of +£5.62** to a £1 level stake.
2004 Azamour – Prince of Wales's, King George VI, 2001 Indian Creek – Earl of Sefton,
2000 Distant Music – Goffs International Stakes, 1998 Daylami – Coronation Cup

FUTURE SUCCESS RATING: ★ ★ ★ ★

CESAREWITCH
October 18, Newmarket – (Heritage Handicap, Class 2, 3yo+) 2m2f

Last run	Winner/Trainer & SP	Draw/Ran	Age	Wght	PR	Next four runs			
07 *List 2m 7th* *Hurdle* *One month*	**Leg Spinner** T Martin 14/1	23/33	6	8-11	68	-	-	-	-
06 *Aint 2m1f 1st* *Nov Hdle* *Five months*	**Detroit City** P Hobbs 9/2F	29/31	4	9-01	71	WON 6/5F *Greatwood Hdle* *Chel 2m1f*	WON 4/6F *Intern'tnl Hdle* *Chel 2m1f*	*WON 1/3F *Agfa Hdle* *Sand 2m1f*	*6th *Champion Hdle* *Chel 2m1f*
05 *Donc 2m2f 2nd* *Doncaster Cup* *Two months*	**Sergeant Cecil** R Millman 10/1	28/34	6	9-08	74	*4th John Porter Newb 1m4f	*2nd Yorkshire Cup York 1m6f	*5th Gold Cup Ascot 2m4f	*2nd Esher Stks Sand 2m
04 *Ches 2m 4th* *Handicap* *Two months*	**Contact Dancer** M Johnston 16/1	18/34	5	8-02	60	3rd Handicap Donc 2m1f	*3rd Chester Cup Ches 2m2f	*3rd Handicap Hayd 2m	*10th Ascot Stks Ascot 2m4f
03 *Newc 2m 10th* *Northumberland* *Four months*	**Landing Light** N Henderson 12/1	36/36	8	9-04	70				
02 *Ascot 2m 3rd* *G Carter Hcp* *Three weeks*	**Miss Fara** M Pipe 12/1	36/36	7	8-05	62	PU *Hcp Hdle* *Mark 2m6f*	*20th *Pertemps Final* *Chel 3m2f*	*12th *Hcp Hdle* *Aint 3m1f*	*12th *Rated Hcp* *Good 1m6f*
01 *Newm 1m6f 5th* *Rated Hcp* *One month*	**Distant Prospect** I Balding 14/1	32/31	4	8-08	60	4th Rated Hcp Newm 2m	*11th Chester Cup Ches 2m2f	*2nd Showcase Hcp Hayd 2m	*8th Ascot Stks Ascot 2m4f
00 *Newc 2m 13th* *Northumberland* *Four months*	**Heros Fatal** M Pipe 11/1	18/33	6	8-01	63	*Fell *Nov Chase* *Taun 3m*	*3rd Northumberland Newc 2m	*4th Shergar Cup Ascot 2m	*14th Cesarewitch Newm 2m2f
99 *Ayr 1m5f 1st* *Rated Hcp* *One month*	**Top Cees** I Balding 7/1	17/32	9	8-10	67	*PU *Chester Cup* *Ches 2m2f*	-	-	-
98 *Hayd 1m6f 3rd* *Conds Stks* *One month*	**Spirit Of Love** M Johnston 11/1	19/29	3	8-08	72	*4th Sagaro Stks Ascot 2m	*8th Henry II Sand 2m	*8th Gold Cup Ascot 2m4f	*14th Cesarewitch Newm 2m2f
97 *Ches 2m 2nd* *Handicap* *One month*	**Turnpole** Mrs M Reveley 16/1	6/31	6	7-10	59	3rd *Hcp Hdle* *Chel 2m1f*	*3rd *Hdle* *Chel 3m*	*WON 13/2 **Handicap** *Donc 2m2f*	*2nd Chester Cup Ches 2m2f
96 *Warw 2m 1st* *Handicap* *Two weeks*	**Inchcailloch** J King 20/1	15/26	7	7-10	57	WON 2/1F *Hcp Chase* *Sand 3m1f*	WON EvsJF *Hcp Chse* *Ascot 3m1f*	WON 4/6F *Hcp Chse* *Sand 3m6f*	6th *Hcp Chse* *Ascot 3m1f*

12-year median performance rating of the winner: **65** (out of 100)   *italic=jumps, *next year*

WINNER'S PROFILE Some had lengthy absences, others success-free light campaigns, while several showed good recent form in the previous month. Three racecourses linked every winner bar the late Detroit City, however, as they **all ran at Ascot, Chester or Newcastle** – in the Northumberland – during the same year.
Dual-purpose horses are respected, as are the first six or seven in the betting at around **16/1 or shorter**, which eliminated quite a few over the years. The draw also knocked out several as **stalls 15 and above** dominated – including the places – while nine of the last 10 winners had an **official rating from 83 to 98**.
Those **aged four and above** sparkled, while three year-olds struck just once from around 30 runners.

FUTURE POINTERS The penultimate major handicap of the season and one whose roll call has several distinguished names, although only a few recent winners went on to better things. Detroit City became a top-class hurdler, while Sergeant Cecil lifted Group honours in Cup races, before the Group One Prix du Cadran at the end of the following season. No obvious path was trodden by Cesarewitch winners post-Newmarket – two of the five that went jumping succeeded – while four failed in the Chester Cup seven months later.
Overall, winners proved hard to profit from, and it has paid to follow placed runners from here instead, several gained compensation back here over two miles at the final fixture of the season – two in Listed Handicaps.

Were Cesarewitch winners profitable to follow on their subsequent three runs?
No – 7 wins from 28 runs returned a loss of -£9.97 to a £1 level stake.

Placed runners' subsequent record (three runs):
Runners-up: 6 wins from 31 runs returned a **profit of +£8.75** to a £1 level stake.
1999 Dominant Duchess – Queen Alexandra, Shergar Cup

Thirds: 9 wins from 34 runs returned a profit of **+£14.03** to a £1 level stake.
2001 Give Notice – Sagaro Stakes, 1999 Heros Fatal – Ladbrokes Casino Handicap Hurdle, 1996 Canon Can – Queen Alexandra
Fourths: 3 wins from 29 runs returned a loss of -£16.75 to a £1 level stake.

FUTURE SUCCESS RATING: ★ ★ ★ ★ ☆

ROCKFEL STAKES
October 18, Newmarket – (Group 2, Class 1, 2yo) 7f

Last run	Winner/ Trainer & SP	Draw/ Ran	Age	Wght	PR	Next four runs			
07 Naas 6f 1st Maiden One week	Kitty Matcham A O'Brien 10/1	5/10	2	8-12	73	-	-	-	-
06 Long 1m 1st Marcel Boussac Two weeks	Finsceal Beo J Bolger 9/4F	1/14	2	9-02	75	*WON 5/4F 1,000 Guineas Newm 1m	2nd Poule 'Pouliches Long 1m	*WON 9/10F Irish 1,000 Guin Curr 1m	*8th Coronation Stks Ascot 1m
05 Donc 1m 3rd May Hill Stks Two months	Speciosa Mrs P Sly 20/1	5/14	2	8-09	71	*WON 9/1 Nell Gwyn Stks Newm 7f	*WON 10/1 1,000 Guineas Newm 1m	*4th Oaks Epsom 1m4f	*9th Coronation Stks Ascot 1m
04 Ascot 1m 2nd Meon Valley Mile Three weeks	Maids Causeway B Hills 3/1F	1/8	2	8-12	70	*2nd 1,000 Guineas Newm 1m	*5th Irish 1,000 Guin Curr 1m	*WON 9/2 Coronation Stk York 1m	*7th Sun Chariot Newm 1m
03 Sali 6f 1st Maiden Two months	Cairns M Channon 12/1	2/10	2	8-09	65	*10th 1,000 Guineas Newm 1m	*6th Poule 'Pouliches Long 1m	*9th Coronation Stks Ascot 1m	*5th Conds Stks Donc 7f
02 Ascot 6f 2nd Princess Margaret Three months	Luvah Girl R Charlton 13/2	5/11	2	8-09	70	*WON 9/10F Stakes Sant 7f	-	-	-
01 Newb 7f 2nd Conds Stks One month	Distant Valley R Hannon 8/1	1/10	2	8-09	66	*14th American Oaks Holl 1m2f	*7th QE II Cup Keen 1m1f	-	-
00 Newb 7f 2nd Conds Stks One month	Sayedah M Tregoning 25/1	16/16	2	8-09	69	*12th 1,000 Guineas Newm 1m	*4th Chalice Stks Newb 1m4f	*2nd Atlanta Stks Sand 1m	*3rd Listed Long 1m2f
99 Redc 7f 1st Maiden Two weeks	Lahan J Gosden 7/2JF	1/12	2	8-09	71	*4th Fred Darling Newb 7f	*WON 14/1 1,000 Guineas Newm 1m	-	-
98 Newm 7f 3rd Oh So Sharp Two weeks	Hula Angel B Hills 10/1	5/14	2	8-09	69	*6th 1,000 Guineas Newm 1m	*WON 16/1 Irish 1,000 Guin Curr 1m	*8th Coronation Stks Ascot 1m	*7th Falmouth Stks Newm 1m
97 Newm 7f 1st Oh So Sharp Two weeks	Name Of Love D Loder 9/4F	1/12	2	8-12	61	-	-	-	-
96 Newm 6f 2nd Cheveley Park Three weeks	Moonlight Paradise S Bin Suroor 11/8F	3/6	2	8-12	67	*10th 1,000 Guineas Newm 1m	*6th Coronation Stks Ascot 1m	*5th Conds stks Yarm 6f	-

12-year median performance rating of the winner: **69** (out of 100)   *next year*

WINNER'S PROFILE Sayedah was the only winner in 2000 not to have **already got off the mark**, as 10 **scored over six or seven furlongs**. Every winner finished in the **top-three last time out**, including three maiden winners, while eight finished in the first three in Pattern company at some point – five carried penalties.
The draw had an impact and helped those in the **bottom-half of the stalls** on 11 occasions since 1996, while the only trainer to appear twice was **Barry Hills** from 15 runners.

FUTURE POINTERS A superb juvenile event for fillies that has proven a sound springboard towards the following year's Classics and provided seven winners since 1998, in comparison to only one subsequent 1,000 Guineas winner during the previous 10 years, which was Musical Bliss, stretching back to 1988.
After last year's 1,000 Guineas, the Rockfel again put itself in the window as a leading Classic pointer during the past decade, with the best winner for many a year, Finsceal Beo recording a very smart performance rating (PR) here, before achieving the British/Irish Guineas double – only just failed to land a record treble in the French version.
Three winners went on to lift the 1,000 Guineas during the last 10 years – Ameerat (2000) and Wince (1998) also took that event after finishing unplaced here – while two runners-up, Casual Look (2002) and Imagine (2000) both landed the Oaks. There was also further strength in depth as several of the placed runners took Classic honours in Ireland and France *(see below)*.

Were Rockfel winners profitable to follow on their subsequent three runs?
Yes – 8 wins from 26 runs returned a **profit of +£38.55** to a £1 level stake.

Placed runners' subsequent record (three runs):
Runners-up: 9 wins from 34 runs returned a **profit of +£2.70** to a £1 level stake.
2004 Penkenna Princess – Fred Darling, 2002 Casual Look – Oaks, 2000 Imagine – Irish 1,000 Guineas
1998 Valentine Waltz – Nell Gwyn, Poule d'Essai des Pouliches (French 1,000 Guineas)

Thirds: 4 wins from 27 runs returned a loss of -£5.50 to a £1 level stake.
2002 Yesterday – Irish 1,000 Guineas, 2001 Misterah – Nell Gwyn

FUTURE SUCCESS RATING: ★ ★ ★ ★ ★

JOCKEY CLUB CUP
October 18, Newmarket – (Group 3, Class 1, 3yo+) 2m

Last run	Winner/ Trainer & SP	Draw/ Ran	Age	Wght	PR	Next four runs			
07 Long 1m7f 3rd Prix Chaudenay *Two weeks*	**Royal And Regal** A Fabre 2/1F	10/8	3	8-04	72	-	-	-	-
06 Ascot 2m 1st Fenwolf Listed *Three weeks*	**Hawridge Prince** B Millman 6/5F	3/7	6	9-00	73	*4th Listed Nott 1m6f	*4th Sagaro Stks Ascot 2m	*4th August Stks Wind 1m4f	-
05 Donc 2m2f 7th Doncaster Cup *Two months*	**Cover Up** Sir M Stoute 20/1	8/10	8	9-00	77	*WON 4/1 Sagaro Stks Ling 2m	*7th Henry II Stks Sand 2m	*2nd Queen Alexandra Ascot 2m6f	*10th Goodwood Cup Good 2m
04 Donc 2m2f 1st Doncaster Cup *Two months*	**Millenary** J Dunlop 7/2F	6/11	7	9-05	80	*9th Yorkshire Cup York 1m6f	*4th Princess' Wales Newm 1m4f	*3rd Goodwood Cup Good 2m	*WON 12/1 Lonsdale Cup York 2m
03 Long 2m4f 8th Prix du Cadran *Two weeks*	**Persian Punch** D Elsworth 5/2	6/6	10	9-05	81	*PU Sagaro Stks Ascot 2m	-	-	-
02 Long 2m4f Disq Prix du Cadran *Two weeks*	**Persian Punch** D Elsworth 9/2	2/8	9	9-00	80	*4th Ashton Park Stks Newb 1m5f	*4th Henry II Stks Sand 2m	*2nd Gold Cup Ascot 2m4f	*WON 6/4F Esher Stks Sand 2m
01 Long 1m7f 2nd Prix Chaudenay *Two weeks*	**Capal Garmon** J Gosden 9/1	5/7	3	8-04	74	*10th John Porter Stks Newb 1m4f	*6th Mercury Listed Leic 1m4f	*4th Conds Stks Newm 1m4f	**9th Conds Stks Newm 1m2f
00 Long 2m4f 2nd Prix du Cadran *Two weeks*	**Persian Punch** D Elsworth 7/1	3/9	7	9-05	80	*4th Sagaro Stks Newm 2m	*3rd Henry II Stks Sand 2m	*2nd Gold Cup Ascot 2m4f	*WON 6/1 Goodwood Cup Good 2m
99 Donc 2m2f 2nd Doncaster Cup *Two months*	**Rainbow High** B Hills 11/4	1/3	4	9-00	73	*5th Chester Cup Ches 2m2f	*4th Goodwood Cup Godd 2m	*2nd Lonsdale Stks York 2m	*4th Doncaster Cup Donc 2m2f
98 Deau 1m7f 1st Prix Kergorlay *Two months*	**Arctic Owl** J Fanshawe 7/2	2/7	4	9-05	84	*3rd Yorkshire Cup York 1m6f	*WON 5/1 Henry II Stks Sand 2m	*2nd Princess' Wales Newm 1m4f	*2nd Lonsdale Stks York 2m
97 Newb 2m 2nd Handicap *Three weeks*	**Grey Shot** I Balding 10/1	1/7	5	9-05	71	10th Prix Royal-Oak Long 1m7f	WON 1/3F Nov Hdle Taun 2m1f	*2nd Tolworth Hdle Sand 2m1f	*WON 8/11F Nov Hdle Ascot 2m1f
96 Donc 2m2f 2nd Doncaster Cup *One month*	**Celeric** D Morley 11/4	4/8	4	9-00	75	*4th Jockey Club Stk Newm 2m	*WON 7/2 Yorkshire Cup York 1m6f	*2nd Henry II Stks Sand 2m	*WON 11/2 Gold Cup Ascot 2m4f

12-year median performance rating of the winner: **77** (out of 100)   *next year **two years*

WINNER'S PROFILE Ten winners arrived via either **Doncaster or France last time out**, but all 12 finished in the **first-three of a Pattern event earlier in their career** – nine won.
The only two winners not to have **won over at least 15 furlongs** were both three-year-olds who were placed over that trip in a Group Two at Longchamp last time out. Winning form earlier in the year can be a bonus but not essential, although the market was a solid guide and favoured those in the **top-half of the betting**.

FUTURE POINTERS An event dominated by Further Flight for five years prior to 1996, a feat almost matched by Persian Punch in recent times with three victories, but it may be a while before we see the likes of such likeable stayers, although the likes of Celeric and Millenary have been worthy title-holders.
From a punting perspective, it proved difficult to profit from Jockey Club Cup winners, as the majority never appeared until the following season. Only Cover Up took the Sagaro Stakes at the next time of asking, although it might be interesting to see if any future winners take a leaf out of Further Flight's book, who struck twice while the iron was hot during the backend in 1994 and 1991 – won the St Simon Stakes on the first occasion.

Were Jockey Club Cup winners profitable to follow on their subsequent three runs?
No – 4 wins from 31 runs returned a loss of -£14.17 to a £1 level stake.

Placed runners' subsequent record (three runs):
Runners-up: 7 wins from 29 runs returned a **profit of +£3.26** to a £1 level stake.
2005 Tungsten Strike – Henry II Stakes, 2004 Franklins Gardens – Yorkshire Cup,
2003 Millenary – Yorkshire Cup, 1998 Celeric – Sagaro Stakes, 1996 Sanmartino – Grade Two Novices' Hurdle

Thirds: 3 wins from 12 runs returned a **profit of +£2.50** to a £1 level stake.
2000 Rainbow High – Chester Cup, 1996 Persian Punch – Ashton Park Stakes, Henry II Stakes

FUTURE SUCCESS RATING: ★ ★ ★ ☆ ☆

RACING POST TROPHY

October 25, Doncaster – (Group 1, Class 1, 2yo) 1m

Last run	Winner/ Trainer & SP	Draw/ Ran	Age	Wght	PR	Next four runs			
07 Ascot 1m 1st Autumn Stks Two weeks	Ibn Khaldun Saeed Bin Suroor 11/4F	6/12	2	9-00	77	-	-	-	-
06 Newb 1m 3rd Conds Stks Two months	Authorized P Chapple-Hyam 25/1	8/14	2	9-00	80	*WON 10/11F Dante Stks York 1m2f	*WON 5/4F Derby Epsom 1m4f	*2nd Eclipse Sand 1m2f	*WON 6/4F Juddmonte Int York 1m2f
05 Newm 7f 5th Dewhurst One week	Palace Episode K Ryan 20/1	1/7	2	9-00	72	*6th Dante Stks York 1m2f	-	-	-
04 Newm 1m 1st Maiden Three months	Motivator M Bell 6/4F	5/8	2	9-00	77	*WON EvsF Dante Stks York 1m2f	*WON 3/1F Derby Epsom 1m4f	*2nd Eclipse Sand 1m2f	*2nd Irish Champion Leop 1m2f
03 Long 7f 1st Grand Criterium Three weeks	American Post Mme C Head 5/6F	4/4	2	9-00	74	*WON 3/10F Listed Sain 1m	*WON 1/2F Group 3 Long 1m	*WON 4/11F Poule 'Poulains Long 1m	*6th Derby Epsom 1m4f
02 Curr 1m 2nd Beresford Stks Two weeks	Brian Boru A O'Brien 11/8F	2/9	2	9-00	76	*3rd Derby Trial Leop 1m2f	*4th Irish Derby Curr 1m4f	*2nd Great Voltigeur York 1m4f	*WON 5/4F St Leger Donc 1m6f
01 Tipp 7f 1st Maiden Three weeks	High Chaparral A O'Brien 9/2	3/6	2	9-00	80	*WON 4/6F Ballysax Stks Leop 1m2f	*WON 1/5F Derby Trial Leop 1m2f	*WON 7/2 Derby Epsom 1m4f	*WON 1/3F Irish Derby Curr 1m4f
00 Sand 7f 2nd Novice Stks Two months	Dilshaan Sir M Stoute 14/1	9/10	2	9-00	81	*WON 9/4F Dante Stks York 1m2f	*7th Derby Epsom 1m4f	-	-
99 Galw 7f 1st Maiden Three months	Our Aristotle A O'Brien 10/1	8/9	2	9-00	73	*3rd Group 2 Long 1m3f	*10th Derby Epsom 1m4f	**WON EvsF Stakes Kran 1m2f	**5th Stakes Kran 1m1f
98 Donc 7f 2nd Champagne Stk Two months	Commander Collins P Chapple-Hyam 2/1F	4/6	2	9-00	72	*11th 2,000 Guineas Newm 1m	*4th Prix d'Ornano Deau 1m2f	**4th Gordon Richards Sand 1m2f	**3rd Princess' Wales Newm 1m4f
97 Curr 1m 1st Beresford Stks One week	Saratoga Springs A O'Brien 9/2	4/8	2	9-00	77	*WON 4/1 Dante Stks York 1m2f	*4th Prix Jockey Club Chan 1m4f	*10th Derby Epsom 1m4f	*6th Irish Derby Curr 1m4f
96 Ascot 1m 5th Royal Lodge One month	Medaaly S Bin Suroor 14/1	6/9	2	9-00	70	*8th Dante Stks York 1m2f	-	-	-

12-year median performance rating of the winner: **76** (out of 100)   *next year **two years*

WINNER'S PROFILE A combination of those proven in Pattern company, maiden winners and individuals yet to have scored formed mixed backgrounds of winners, although traditional stepping stones were the Beresford Stakes, Royal Lodge Stakes (beaten runners), Champagne Stakes and the Autumn Stakes (Ibn Khaldun last year emulated Beauchamp King in 1995).

A **last time out victory or second** was popular, along with a **top-three slot over seven furlongs or a mile** – 10 won – while from a training angle, **Aidan O'Brien** scored four times from 25 runners. Two that boasted better strike-rates were dual winners **Peter Chapple-Hyam**, from four runners, and **Saeed Bin Suroor**, from five.

FUTURE POINTERS A superb juvenile guide for the following year's Classics and one that has supplied three of the last six Derby winners, a record rivalled only by the Derrinstown Derby Trial earlier this decade.

The same rules applied here as for any other in the book, with preference given to those recording above par performance ratings (PR) on the day, as several red herrings lurked pre-Millennium. Sub-standard winners aside – three of whom raced more than three times prior to Doncaster – five of the other six went on to take a European Classic; American Post landed the French Guineas and Brian Boru scooped the St Leger. Following those behind the winner has proven less profitable long-term, especially in the English Classics, as only Benny The Dip scored in either the 2,000 Guineas or Derby from 35 placed/unplaced Racing Post Trophy runners going back to 1990.

Were Racing Post Trophy winners profitable to follow on their subsequent three runs?
Yes – 13 wins from 28 runs returned a **profit of +£3.92** to a £1 level stake.

Placed runners' subsequent record (three runs):
Runners-up: 5 wins from 25 runs returned a loss of -£11.94 to a £1 level stake.
2002 Powerscourt – Great Voltigeur

Thirds: 5 wins from 18 runs returned a **profit of +£5.85** to a £1 level stake.
1996 Benny The Dip – Dante Stakes, Derby

FUTURE SUCCESS RATING: ★ ★ ★ ★ ★

HORRIS HILL STAKES
October 25, Newbury – (Group 3, Class 1, 2yo Colts & Geldings) 7f

Last run	Winner/ Trainer & SP	Draw/ Ran	Age	Wght	PR	Next four runs			
07 Newb 7f 1st / Maiden / *Three weeks*	**Beacon Lodge** C Cox 14/1	4/11	2	8-12	63	-	-	-	-
06 Newm 7f 2nd / Tattarsall Stks / *One month*	**Dijeerr** M Jarvis 9/2	9/10	2	8-12	64	*11th Poule' Poulains Long 1m	-	-	-
05 Cork 7f 1st / Maiden / *One week*	**Hurricane Cat** A O'Brien 6/1	9/13	2	8-09	70	*3rd Tetrarch Stks Curr 7f	*7th Irish 2,000 Guin Curr 1m	*15th Prix 'Jock-Club Chan 1m3f	*5th International Stk Curr 1m
04 Curr 6f 3rd / Blenheim Stks / *Two months*	**Cupid's Glory** Sir M Prescott 2/1F	8/13	2	8-09	65	4th Criterium Int Sain 1m	*7th Thoroughbred St Good 1m	*WON 13/8F Conds Stks Ches 1m	*2nd Group 3 Deau 1m
03 York 6f 1st / Rockingham Stk / *Two weeks*	**Peak To Creek** J Noseda 5/1	6/9	2	8-09	70	*3rd Craven Stks Newm 1m	*2nd King Charles II Newm 7f	*3rd Surrey Stks Sand 7f	-
02 Good 1m 3rd / Stardom Stks / *Two months*	**Makhlab** B Hills 5/1	8/10	2	8-09	69	*8th Greenham Stks Newb 7f	*8th Irish 2,000 Guin Curr 1m	*WON 2/1F Conds Stks Ayr 1m	**5th Doncaster Mile Donc 1m
01 Ascot 7f 1st / Conds Stks / *Two weeks*	**Rapscallion** J Eustace 7/2	9/10	2	8-09	67	*21st 2,000 Guineas Newm 1m	*6th Dubai Arc Trial Newb 1m3f	*4th Ben Marshall Stk Newm 1m	**9th Hambleton Hcp York 1m
00 Ches 7f 1st / Maiden / *One month*	**Clearing** J Gosden 9/2	6/9	2	8-09	71	*WON 7/4F Euro Free Hcp Newm 7f	*2nd Poule' Poulains Long 1m	-	-
99 Ascot 7f 5th / Conds Stks / *Two weeks*	**Umistim** R Hannon 20/1	8/9	2	8-09	70	*WON 8/1 Craven Stks Newm 1m	*6th 2,000 Guineas Newm 1m	*5th Heron Stks Kemp 1m	*2nd Jersey Stks Ascot 7f
98 Hayd 7f 1st / Maiden / *One month*	**Brancaster** P Chapple-Hyam 7/2CF	5/6	2	8-09	66	*2nd Craven Stks Newm 1m	*4th 2,000 Guineas Newm 1m	*10th Derby Epsom 1m4f	*8th G Prix de Paris Long 1m2f
97 Ascot 7f 1st / Conds Stks / *Two weeks*	**La-Faah** B Hills 9/1	3/8	2	8-09	65	*2nd Greenham Stks Newb 7f	*4th Poule' Poulains Long 1m	*5th Surrey Stks Epsom 7f	*11th Jersey Stks Ascot 7f
96 Ascot 1m 2nd / Royal Lodge / *One month*	**Desert Story** Sir M Stoute 6/4F	1/8	2	8-09	70	*WON 5/2F Craven Stks Newm 1m	*6th 2,000 Guineas Newm 1m	*2nd Dante Stks York 1m2f	*2nd Select Stks Good 1m2f

12-year median performance rating of the winner: **68** (out of 100)   **next year **two years*

WINNER'S PROFILE Winning form was an advantage as the last 11 winners **won one of their last two races**, 10 of whom **already won over the distance**. A good effort last time out also pointed the way, as four scored in maidens, the same number beaten in a Pattern event, while three came via a conditions event at Ascot.
Peak To Creek took a separate route having raced more than 10 times that year and landed the Redcar 2yo Trophy before Listed success.
Those drawn one to three only made the frame twice since the Millennium, as **stalls four and above** took the last 10 renewals, which included the second of trainer **Barry Hills**'s winning pair from 10 runners, however, two handlers to be wary of include Mick Channon and Brain Meehan, who sent out almost 15 losers between them.

FUTURE POINTERS With Tirol the last to go on and secure Classic success in the 1990 2,000 Guineas, the Horris Hill doesn't smack as one of the strongest guides for the following season's big events and could do with a quality winner to give it a much needed lift. In fact, winning this has proven to be more of a jinx than an achievement as only three victors went on to win Guineas' trials at Newmarket before flopping in the Classics, and that may prove to be the best way of profiting from a punting angle, as two others who took a similar route also finished runner-up and third at HQ in the spring.

Were Horris Hill winners profitable to follow on their subsequent three runs?
No – 5 wins from 30 runs returned a loss of -£9.12 to a £1 level stake.

Placed runners' subsequent record (three runs)
Runners-up: 5 wins from 30 runs returned a loss of -£15.75 to a £1 level stake.
1999 Cape Town – European Free Handicap, 1997 Victory Note – Greenham, Poule des Poulains

Thirds: 8 wins from 30 runs returned a **profit of +£33.73** to a £1 level stake.
2005 Araafa – Irish 2,000 Guineas, St James's Palace, 2003 Millbag – Pavilion Stakes, 1996 Hidden Meadow – European Free Handicap

FUTURE SUCCESS RATING: ★ ★ ★ ★ ★

ST SIMON STAKES
October 25, Newbury – (Group 3, Class 1, 3yo+) 1m4f

Last run	Winner/Trainer & SP	Draw/Ran	Age	Wght	PR	Next four runs			
07 Newm 1m4f 4th Godolphin Stks One month	Crime Scene S Bin Suroor 8/1	6/6	4	9-03	73	-	-	-	-
06 Long 1m5f 6th Group 2 Three weeks	Short Skirt Sir M Stoute 13/2	6/11	3	8-10	80	*WON 11/8F Severals Stks Newm 1m2f	*7th Premio Tesio Capa 1m2f	-	-
05 Newm 1m4f 2nd Princess of Wales' Four months	Day Flight J Gosden 3/1JF	3/8	4	9-03	81	2nd Serlby Stks Donc 1m4f	*WON 10/3 G Richards Stk Sand 1m2f	*2nd Group 2 Bade 1m3f	*4th Hardwicke Stks Ascot 1m4f
04 Newm 1m1f 5th Darley Stks One month	Orcadian J Eustace 33/1	8/8	3	8-07	70	*10th John Porter Stks Newb 1m4f	*6th Hardwicke Stks York 1m4f	*3rd Conds Stks Newm 1m4f	*6th Conds Stks Newm 1m2f
03 Newm 1m2f 4th Champion Stks One week	Imperial Dancer M Channon 4/1	6/9	5	9-00	77	WON 4/1 Premio Roma Capa 1m2f	7th Hong Kong Vase Sha 1m4f	*3rd John Porter Stks Newb 1m4f	*6th International Cup Kran 1m2f
02 Donc 1m4f 2nd Troy Stks Two months	The Whistling Teal G Wragg 13/2	4/13	6	9-00	75	*4th September Stks Kemp 1m4f	*4th Godolphin Stks Newm 1m4f	*5th St Simon Stks Newb 1m4f	*2nd Serlby Stks Donc 1m4f
01 Newm 1m4f 1st Rated Hcp One month	High Pitched H Cecil 9/2	3/5	3	8-07	79	*7th Jockey Club Stk Newm 1m4f	*WON 4/1 Aston Park St Newb 1m5f	*4th Hardwicke Stks Ascot 1m4f	*2nd Geoffrey Freer Newb 1m5f
00 Newm 1m4f 1st Godolphin Stks One month	Wellbeing H Cecil 4/7F	5/7	3	8-07	80	*4th Jockey Club Stk Newm 1m4f	*2nd Coronation Cup Epsom 1m4f	*4th Hardwicke Stks Ascot 1m4f	**8th Group 3 Long 1m4f
99 Ascot 1m4f 1st Princess Royal Two weeks	Signorina Cattiva J Dunlop 13/8F	2/10	3	8-07	76	3rd Premio Roma Capa 1m2f	-	-	-
98 Donc 1m7f 6th St Leger Two months	Dark Moondancer P Chapple-Hyam 6/1	1/5	3	8-07	79	*4th Group 3 Sain 1m2f	*WON 36/10 Group 2 Long 1m2f	*WON 43/10 Prix Ganay Long 1m3f	*WON 2/5F Premio di Milano Siro 1m4f
97 Long 1m4f 5th Prix Vermeille Two months	Kaliana L Cumani 7/2	6/10	3	8-04	76	*4th Mercury Listed Leic 1m4f	-	-	-
96 Ascot 1m4f 2nd Cumberland Lodge One month	Salmon Ladder P Cole 11/2	12/12	4	9-00	74	*4th John Porter Stks Newb 1m4f	*7th Ormonde Stks Ches 1m5f	*WON 10/11F Conds Stks Wind 1m2f	*2nd Group 3 Siro 1m3f

12-year median performance rating of the winner: **77** (out of 100) *(1998, 2001 Newmarket) *next year **two years*

WINNER'S PROFILE A **Grade One venue** provided a stepping stone to Newbury on each occasion since 1996, with Ascot, Doncaster, Longchamp and Newmarket the courses to note, especially the latter as six of the last eight emerged from Suffolk. A **victory earlier in the campaign** was vital, as only the 33/1 shot Orcadian missed out, who was also the only double-figure priced winner, highlighting the importance of those in the **first-half of the betting**. One of trainer **Henry Cecil**'s two winners, High Pitched, was the only one not to have **competed in Pattern company**, and both of his victors were also **three-year-olds**, who boast the best strike-rate. Neither of Cecil's were fillies, although they held their own, as did those that carried penalties.

FUTURE POINTERS Not one of the strongest middle-distance Group events on the calendar and one whose roll call contains mainly forgettable winners, with Further Flight, one of the more distinguished names back in 1991. Only two since 1996 raised their game at Group One level, as Imperial Dancer and Dark Moondancer both scored abroad, and along with three other St Simon winners, they all benefited from the step back to 10 furlongs, while those that stuck to this distance in Britain came unstuck in events like the Hardwicke, John Porter and Jockey Club Stakes. As with other races in this book, rewards came via the quality winners, and five of the six that recorded above par performance ratings (PR) scored again during their next two runs.

Were St Simon winners profitable to follow on their subsequent three runs?
Yes – 7 wins from 28 runs returned a **profit of +£0.50** to a £1 level stake.

Placed runners' subsequent record (three runs):
Runners-up: 4 wins from 23 runs returned a **profit of +£3.83** to a £1 level stake.
2002 Warrsan – John Porter Stakes, Jockey Club Stakes, 2000 Marienbard – Yorkshire Cup

Thirds: 3 wins from 24 runs returned a loss of -£8.38 to a £1 level stake.
2003 Dubai Success – John Porter Stakes, 1997 Busy Flight – Yorkshire Cup

FUTURE SUCCESS RATING: ★ ★ ★ ☆ ☆

NOVEMBER HANDICAP
November 8, Doncaster – (Heritage Handicap, Class 2, 3yo+) 1m4f

Last run	Winner/Trainer & SP	Draw/Ran	Age	Wght	PR	Next four runs			
07 Newm 1m4f 1st / Handicap / Two months	Malt Or Mash R Hannon 5/1	13/21	3	8-10	71	-	-	-	-
06 Ascot 1m4f 2nd / Totesport Hcp / Two months	Group Captain R Charlton 10/1	20/20	4	9-05	66	7th Churchill Stks Ling 1m2f	*7th Listed Nott 1m6f	*3rd Group 3 Long 1m4f	*3rd Aston Park Newb 1m5f
05 Newm 1m4f 9th / Handicap / Two months	Come on Jonny R Beckett 14/1	18/21	3	8-03	65	*12th Ladbrokes Hcp Ascot 1m4f	*11th Novemebr Hcp Wind 1m4f	*PU Maiden Hdle Utt 2m	
04 Leic 1m4f 3rd / Tote Hcp / One month	Carte Diamond B Ellison 12/1	3/24	3	9-06	70	WON 5/4JF Nov Hdle Newc 2m	3rd Grade 2 Hdle Ling 2m1f	*WON 1/3F Nov Hdle Muss 2m	*PU Triumph Hdle Chel 2m1f
03 Newb 1m2f 2nd / Rated Hcp / Two weeks	Turbo G Balding 25/1	14/24	4	9-02	63	10th Hcp Hdle Newb 2m1f	*14th Handicap Ling 1m2f	*10th Rosebery Hcp Kemp 1m2f	*4th Handicap Newb 1m4f
02 Donc 1m2f 1st / GNER Hcp / Two weeks	Red Wine J Osborne 16/1	20/23	3	8-01	64	*3rd Juv Nov Hdle Leic 2m	*WON 9/2 Juv Nov Hdle Newb 2m1f	*9th Triumph Hdle Chel 2m1f	*5th Listed Hcp Hami 1m4f
01 Newm 1m 4th / Mile Hcp / One week	Royal Cavalier R Hollinshead 50/1	5/24	4	7-13	55	11th Handicap Sout 1m4f	*WON 16/1 Showcase Hcp Hayd 1m4f	*2nd Walker Hcp Ches 1m2f	*8th Handicap York 1m4f
00 Kels 2m1f 2nd / Hcp Hdle / Two months	Batswing B Ellison 14/1	14/20	5	8-08	59	*WON 2/1F Hcp Hdle Donc 2m1f	*BD Imperial Cup Sand 2m1f	*3rd Hcp Hdle Aint 2m1f	*11th Handicap York 1m4f
99 Newb 1m2f 2nd / Handicap / Three weeks	Flossy C Thornton 5/1	10/16	3	7-12	57	*14th Rated Hcp Newm 1m2f	*4th Class Stks Newm 1m4f	*4th Rated Hcp York 1m4f	*WON 2/1F Handicap Ches 1m4f
98 Ascot 1m4f 2nd / Showcase Hcp / Two months	Yavana's Pace M Johnston 8/1	12/23	6	9-10	73	*4th Yorkshire Cup York 1m6f	*WON 9/4 Mercury Listed Leic 1m4f	*2nd Fred Archer Newm 1m4f	*2nd Listed Cope 1m4f
97 Hayd 1m2f 1st / Maiden / One month	Sabadilla J Gosden 10/1	22/24	3	7-11	70	*2nd Rated Hcp Epsom 1m4f	*2nd Bessborough Hcp Ascot 1m4f	*5th Princess' Wales Newm 1m4f	*WON 7/2 Glorious Stks Good 1m4f
96 Newm 1m2f 3rd / James Seymour / Two weeks	Clifton Fox J Glover 9/1	14/22	4	8-10	69	***WON 9/2 Nov Hdle Newc 2m	***2nd Nov Hdle Newc 2m	***16th Hcp Hdle Kemp 2m	***2nd Hcp Hdle Chep 2m4f

12-year median performance rating of the winner: **65** (out of 100)   *(2006 Windsor) italic = jumps*
*next year ***three years or longer

WINNER'S PROFILE A **top-three outing last time out** was relevant – exceptions were in the first two penultimately – while a **victory during their previous five** runs was a factor shared by 11 winners since 1996. **Three to four-year-olds** held sway as those aged five and above won just twice from around 100 runners. Favourites have a shocking record – 1995 was the last jolly – and it pays to search for value as seven of the last eight returned at double-figure odds, while those drawn in **double-figure stalls** came out on top.
The only trainer to have struck more than once was **Brian Ellison** with two winners from six runners.

FUTURE POINTERS The final handicap of the Flat season has at times taken place on bad ground and featured runners that may have had enough for the season, which tempers enthusiasm regarding the future, however, the odd high-quality renewal emerged like last year when it was run on decent ground and attracted improving sorts. Several winners went on to score in Listed company the following year, while others took a career switch and were sent over the sticks, but there has yet to be a future Group One winner over the past few decades with probably the most distinguished winner, Quick Ransom in 1993 – won the Ebor in 1992 – who went on to land the Northumberland the following season.

Were November winners profitable to follow on their subsequent three runs?
Yes – 7 wins from 33 runs returned a **profit of +£4.83** to a £1 level stake.

Placed runners' subsequent record (three runs):
Runners-up: 3 wins from 27 runs returned a loss of -£5.00 to a £1 level stake.
2004 Distant Prospect – Listed Gerry Feilden Handicap Hurdle
Thirds: 7 wins from 29 runs returned a loss of -£6.51 to a £1 level stake.
Fourths: 5 wins from 33 runs returned a loss of -£1.83 to a £1 level stake.
1996 Dato Star – Grade Two Hurdle

FUTURE SUCCESS RATING: ★ ★ ★ ☆ ☆